Lecture Notes in Computer Science   1254

Edited by G. Goos, J. Hartmanis and J. van Leeuwen

Advisory Board: W. Brauer   D. Gries   J. Stoer

Springer
Berlin
Heidelberg
New York
Barcelona
Budapest
Hong Kong
London
Milan
Paris
Santa Clara
Singapore
Tokyo

Orna Grumberg (Ed.)

Computer Aided Verification

9th International Conference, CAV'97
Haifa, Israel, June 22-25, 1997
Proceedings

 Springer

Series Editors

Gerhard Goos, Karlsruhe University, Germany

Juris Hartmanis, Cornell University, NY, USA

Jan van Leeuwen, Utrecht University, The Netherlands

Volume Editor

Orna Grumberg
The Technion, Department of Computer Science
Haifa 32000, Israel
E-mail: orna@cs.technion.ac.il

Cataloging-in-Publication data applied for

Die Deutsche Bibliothek - CIP-Einheitsaufnahme

Computer aided verification : 9th international conference ; proceedings / CAV
'97, Haifa, Israel, June 22 - 25, 1997. Orna Grumberg (ed.). - Berlin ;
Heidelberg ; New York ; Barcelona ; Budapest ; Hong Kong ; London ; Milan ;
Paris ; Santa Clara ; Singapore ; Tokyo : Springer, 1997
  (Lecture notes in computer science ; Vol. 1254)
  ISBN 3-540-63166-6

CR Subject Classification (1991): F.3, D.2.4, D.2.2, F.4.1, B.7.2, C.3, I.2.3

ISSN 0302-9743
ISBN 3-540-63166-6 Springer-Verlag Berlin Heidelberg New York

Typesetting: Camera-ready by author
SPIN 10550007   06/3142 – 5 4 3 2 1 0   Printed on acid-free paper

Preface

This volume contains the proceedings of the Ninth International Conference on Computer-Aided Verification (CAV'97), held in Haifa, Israel, June 22-25, 1997.

The CAV conferences are dedicated to the advancement of theory and practice of computer-aided formal methods for software and hardware verification. The conference covers the spectrum from theoretical results to concrete applications, with an emphasis on verification tools and the algorithms and techniques that are needed for their implementation.

Of the 84 regular papers submitted this year, 34 were accepted for presentation at the conference. In addition, 12 short papers on tool descriptions were accepted.

The conference will include three invited lectures, given by Gary J. Powers (Carnegie Mellon University, USA) on *Formal Verification of a Thermal Oxidation Pollution Control System*, by David Harel (Weizmann Institute, Israel) on *Some Thoughts on Statecharts, 13 Years Later*, and by Gerard Berry (Ecole des Mines de Paris, France) on *Boolean and 2-adic Numbers Based Techniques for Verifying Synchronous Designs*.

A morning session will be dedicated to invited talks by representatives from industry. The talks will be given by F. Erich Marschner (COMPASS Design Automation) on *Practical Challenges for Industrial Formal Verification Tools*, by Roger B. Hughes (Abstract Hardware) on *Formal Verification of Digital Systems, from ASICs to HW/SW Codesign – a Pragmatic Approach*, by Arne Borälv (Logikkonsult NP) on *The Industrial Success of Verification Tools Based on Staalmarck's Method*, and by Martin Rowe (Chrysalis Symbolic Design) on *Formal Verification – Applications and Case Studies*. The industrial session will be concluded with a panel on *Future Trends in Industrial Computer-Aided Verification* with the following participants: Bob Brennan (Intel, USA), E. Allen Emerson (Moderator; The University of Texas at Austin, USA), Thomas A. Henzinger (UC Berkeley, USA), Robert P. Kurshan (Bell Labs, USA), Carol Logan (IBM, USA), Natarajan Shankar (SRI International, USA), and Yaron Wolfstal (IBM, Israel).

It is our pleasure to congratulate Amir Pnueli for receipt of the Turing Award. The dinner speech in honor of this occasion will be given by David Harel (Weizmann Institute, Israel) on *Amir Pnueli: A Man for all (the Right) Reasons*.

The program of CAV'97 has been selected by the program committee consisting of Rajeev Alur (Bell Labs and UC Berkeley, USA), Edmund Clarke (Carnegie Mellon University, USA), Rance Cleaveland (North Carolina State University, USA), Werner Damm (Oldenburg University, Germany), E. Allen Emerson (The University of Texas at Austin, USA), Limor Fix (Intel, Israel), Susanne Graf (VERIMAG, France), Orna Grumberg (Chair; the Technion, Israel), Nicolas Halbwachs (VERIMAG, France), Thomas A. Henzinger (UC Berkeley, USA), Bengt Jonsson (Uppsala University, Sweden), Robert Kurshan (Bell Labs, USA), Kim Larsen (Aalborg University, Denmark), Ken McMillan (Cadence Berkeley Labs, USA), Carl Pixley (Motorola, USA), Mandayam Srivas (SRI International, USA), Frits Vaandrager (University of Nijmegen, The Netherlands), Antti Valmari (Tampere University of Technology, Finland), Moshe Vardi (Rice University, USA), and Pierre Wolper (University of Liège, Belgium).

The program committee chair and the general chair of the conference is Orna Grumberg of the Technion–Israel Institute of Technology, Haifa. The steering committee consists of the conference founders Edmund Clarke (Carnegie Mellon University, USA), Robert Kurshan (Bell Labs, USA), Amir Pnueli (Weizmann Institute, Israel), and Joseph Sifakis (VERIMAG, France).

CAV'97 is financially supported by DSP Group Inc., Galileo Technology, Intel Israel, the Haifa Tourist Board, Israel, the Ministry of Science, Israel, the Ministry of Tourism, Israel, and the Technion–Israel Institute of Technology. The workstations and the communication equipment at the conference site are donated by E & M Computing and by ADANET-IIS Communications Ltd. We thank all sponsors for their generosity.

Last year's chairs, Rajeev Alur and Thomas A. Henzinger, are thanked for valuable advice on the organization of the conference. E. Allen Emerson is thanked for his assistance in organizing the panel, and Robert P. Kurshan for his help in establishing the connection with the industrial speakers.

Special thanks go to Yvonne Sagi, who helped with the secretarial work involved in the submission, selection and publication of the scientific program. We are grateful to Yael Dubinski for organizing the hardware and software needed for the demonstrations. Anat Reshef of Unitours is thanked for her assistance with the local organization.

Finally, the following people helped in the evaluation of the submissions and we are grateful for their efforts: P. Abdulla, L. Aceto, J. Adair, N. Amla, H. R. Andersen, J. H. Andersen, A. Aziz, I. Beer, S. Ben-david, S. Bensalem, S. Berezin, Z. Binyanimi, R. Bol, A. Bouajjani, D. Cyrluk, D. Dams, E. Dantsin, G. Doehmen, C. Eisner, A. Ermedahl, J.-C. Fernandez, J. Geldenhuys, D. Giest, E. Gukovsky, P. Habermehl, V. Hartonas-Garmhausen, K. Havelund, H. Hungar, H. Huttel, A. Ingolfsdottir, A. Iron, A. Isles, S.P. Iyer, B. Josko, R. Kaivola, T. Kam, G. Kamhi, K. Karsisto, T. Karvi, S. Katz, O. Kedem, P. Kellomäki, A. Kerbrat, M. Kindah, I. Kokkarinen, S. Krishnamurthi, L. M. Kristensen, K. K. Kristoffersen, O. Kupferman, Y. Lakhnech, K. Laster, D. Lesens, Y. Levy, J. Lilius, S. Ma, O. Maler, P. Manolios, H. Miller, M. Minea, L. Mounier, K. Namjoshi, M. Nielsen, I. Niemelä, J. Nyström, D. Peled, P. Pettersson, A. Pnueli, A. Puri, S. Qadeer, S. Rajamani, A. Rauzy, Y. Rodeh, R. Rosner, J. Rushby, H. Saidi, D. Sangiorgi, R. Schloer, T. Shiple, I. Shitsevalov, Z. Shtadler, S. Shukla, A. Skou, F. Somenzi, J. Springintveld, S. Tasiran, A. Tiemeyer, M. Tienari, M. Tiusanen, R. Trefler, Y.-K. Tsay, K. Varpaaniemi, B. Victor, A. Voronkov, P. Weidmann, W. Yi, J. Yuan, L. Yuan.

Haifa, April 1997   Orna Grumberg

Table of Contents

Tool Papers

Practical Challenges for Industrial Formal Verification Tools

F. Erich Marschner
COMPASS Design Automation
5457 Twin Knolls Road, Suite 100
Columbia MD 21045, U.S.A.
Email: erich@compass-da.com

Formal verification of hardware design is rapidly becoming accepted as an alternative to the traditional strategy of verification via simulation. However, there are still major barriers to widespread acceptance of formal verification tools and methodologies. These barriers generally have very little to do with the robustness of the theory underlying formal verification; instead they are much more a function of the degree to which the formalism has been adapted to address practical concerns.

First of all, formal verification tools must be applicable to typical design styles. Altough simplifying assumptions may make a tool easier to build or give it better performance, they may also restrict a tool to the point where it is not useful enough to justify its expense. Even though synchronous design is often the rule, asynchronicity is nonetheless a universal exception. Similarly, while single-clock systems exist, multiple-clock systems are more and more common, especially in certain industry segments. A successful formal verification tool must be flexible enough to support the exceptional cases as well as the typical cases, otherwise it will not find a place in the mainstream design flow.

Equally important is the requirement to support standard interfaces, to fit into existing design flows. In the hardware design world today, this usually means support for the two IEEE standard hardware description languages, VHDL and Verilog - but it may also involve support for related standards, such as IEEE Std 1164 (standard multi-valued logic for VHDL), and IEEE Stds 1076.3 (Synthesis packages) and 1076.4 (VITAL packages for timing-accurate modeling of primitives). Support for pseudo-standards is also an issue, such as the de-facto standards created by the dominant vendors in the Electronic Design Automation (EDA) industry, or the library formats of the major semiconductor manufacturers. This is complicated by the fact that such languages and formats are not always well-defined - even those that are IEEE standards! Even so, a usable formal verification tool must be able to work with them.

Capacity and performance are always major issues in the EDA industry. The fact that formal verification technology provides a more robust verification strategy than simulation does not matter to a design manager if his designs regularly exceed the size or complexity that such tools can handle. And the technical challenges of handling various kinds of circuits are no excuse; the designer needs results no matter what the situation. Multiplication may be difficult to verify formally, but this just reinforces the need for a better solution. Use of hierarchy may be recommended for a formal verification methodology, but it may not be possible in a given environment. A good formal verification tool must adapt to the designer's requirements as much as possible, and impose as few constraints as possible on the design process.

The biggest challenge for formal verification tools is providing good diagnostic information when problems are detected. Few hardware designers want to become experts in formal verification; they typically want to focus on solving the design problems instead. As a result, it is imperative that formal verification tools require the minimum possible input other than the design itself, and generate the most insightful reports possible to highlight potential errors. The fact that a formal verification tool cannot read the designer's mind does not lessen the demand for such a tool, or the expectations of evaluators of such tools.

Even the best formal verification tool cannot be successful until it has been adopted by a user community, and that involves a major barrier: fitting into an existing "design flow", or network of inter-operating design tools that has been shown to support the design process at least moderately well. The bulk of EDA tool sales involve replacement of tools already in the customer's design flow with ostensibly better tools that perform the same functions. But formal verification tools are not already present in most design flows, so adoption of a formal verification tool requires a much more ambitious change, a change to the design flow itself. While swapping individual tools within a flow involves nearly zero risk - one can always revert to the old tool, after all - adopting a new design flow can be much more dangerous, and design managers tend to avoid such risks for as long as possible.

Ultimately, the major barrier to the adoption of formal verification technology for hardware design is the difficulty of conveying to potential users the concept of formal verification as it applies to their particular needs. Every design team has different requirements, and every team uses somewhat different terminology to describe what they do. While formal verification tools are inherently general purpose, and thus can be adapted to meet various requirements, this in itself can make them difficult to grasp; design managers seem to feel more comfortable with focused tools tuned to specific applications. At the same time, it is economically infeasible to develop different tools for each application, because every design team has a unique application in mind.

Formal verification of hardware design has become a reality and will become a more and more essential part of the design process as advancing technology continues to enable more and more complex designs. It is certainly true that there are still open problems to address in the fundamental theory underlying formal verification methods. At the same time, there is just as much work or more to be done in the practical application of formal techniques. And unlike the theory, which has been under development for decades, this work is only just beginning.

Formal Verification of Digital Systems, from ASICs to HW/SW Codesign - a Pragmatic Approach

Roger B. Hughes

VP Marketing & Technical Support,
Abstract Hardware,
47211 Lakeview Boulevard,
Fremont, CA 94538-6530
rhughes@wcdf.viewlogic.com
WWW. http://www.ahl.co.uk VP

In order to verify digital systems one has to consider the particular verification approach to be adopted and what is meant to be achieved by the application of the method chosen. Over the past few years thee has been increasing use of formal verification both from a specification standpoint and from an equivalency-checking standpoint. Basically these techniques amount to "a priori" and "a posteriori" verification. In hte "a priori" class there are very few tools, LAMBDA being one of these. The LAMBDA system is based on a theorem-prover core and is interesting owing to its ability to transform an initial specification into a lower-level (typically RTL) description of a design. The design partitioning is such that at each stage the partial implementation is formally proven to meet its specification as an *integral* part of the design process, i.e. verification takes place "in situ". The assumption that is made being that the specification is what the engineer actually wants to build. Such a technique allows the engineer to reason about hardware and software as equal entities in the design process, only thinking of partitioning functionality until the functions have been broken down to the stage where they may eeither be implemented in hardware (as RTL for a synthesis process) or software (for a compilation process). It is possible in both cases to go down to either gate-level or assembly code but it is recommended that the LAMBDA approach only be used to get to synthesisable RTL and or readily compilable software.

One of the difficulties of theorem proving is that one needs a language with a formal semantics, not just a formal grammar in which to specify the system which you wish to build. The L2 (Lambda Logic) description language, based on the functional programming language ML with some additional mathematical constructs derived fom HOL (Higher Order Logic) is one of very few such languages. It is clearly a succinct way to abstractly specify digital systems' functionality but most engineers are still reluctant to learn a new language. In fact, it is more than that, it requires a paradigm shift in that a new methodology must be adopted. One cannot "reverse engineer" specifications from quickly "hacked" implementations. As a way to assist the engineering community to bridge this mathematical void, a tool called TimeWarp was developed, based on the theorem proving core of LAMBDA, to totally automatically transform a graphical (or textual) specification of data-flow functionality into a synthesisable piece of RTL Verilog or VHDL. All the complexities of partial and full loop-pipelining are automatically handled and the engineer gets a graphical display of resource allocation and scheduling information. The hraphical display is interactive allowing the engineer to *alter* the automatically generated result, thereby allowing his/her design expertise to optimise the design further. Naturally, to assist in this process the engineer is provided with information such as throughput, maximum estimated frequency, latency etc. of the design. Whilst TomeWarp does not have the same capability or generality as LAMBDA, it is very easy to use (unlike LAMBDA) and is an important step on the learning curve which all engineers must emabark on now in order to cope with the complexity of designs tomorrow.

At the other end of the verification spectrum lies equivalence-checking. The idea here being to show if two existing designs are equivalent. Equivalence here means functional equivalence, i.e. are the output functions the same in both designs. Theorem provers can also be used here but it is both awkward to enter the design descriptions into rules representing the design state and awkward to use the theorem prover to show equivalence. Quite often, experienced mathematical skill is essential in doing even the most trivial of equivalence proofs. Thus an alternative technique is used. One technique is to represent the output functions as boolean equations (this assumes that the state mappings in both designs, viz. number of registers, is the same). By reducing the boolean equations to a simpler form, they can be compared to see if they are the same. Various comparison methods are used. Another technique is to use Binary Decision Diagrams (BDDs), preferably Reduced Ordered Binary Decision Diagrams (ROBDDs). There are advantages to both of these techniques.

In the equational approach, the advantage is one of speed. This is because it is fairly straightforward to show if two boolean equations are equivalent or not. Basically, there is a choice between reducing the equations to a canonical form, thereby permitting an extremely rapid test of equivalence or a partial reduction, making the comparison process a little more arduous. It is the reduction process that is often the most time-consuming aspect of such equational equivalence checking. As such, the majority of practical tools do not usually seek to reduce down to a canonical form but just a simple set of reductions to minimise the time taken. Of course, this approach can only be simple (and in practice only works for) designs which have the same number of state-bits and identical state-encodings. That is, the state information in the design is effectively ignored, only the combinational logic between register stages is checked for equivalence. Clearly, this demands that the registers in both designs are used to store the same information. Not all designs are of this type, but a large subset of desgns are. For example, a gate-level design compared with a design with a few hand tweaks is typically of this class. An RTL design fed through a non-optimising (i.e. states are not optimised) synthesiser and compared with its gate-level will also fall into this class. Designs that can be handled by equational equivalence checking are typically large, e.g. 500,000 gates is quite achievable in one go. The CheckOff-S product from Abstract achieves this in a matter of 2 minutes. Clearly such a technique is fast, much faster than simulation, yet exhaustive, which simulation typically isn't.

The ROBDD approach also has advantages in that it can compare designs very quickly once the BDD model (actually an FSM (Finite State Machine) view of the design built using BDDs) of the designs have been built, or "compiled". Abstract Hardware's equivalence checker is called CheckOff-E and is based on the same ROBDD technology as used in CheckOff-M, the model checking product. In the case, as in equational equivalence checking, where designs have the same number of states, the comparison process is exceedingly quick owing to the fact that time was taken compiling the design respresentation down to a canonical form. A comparison of such canonical forms is very fast, requiring just a reordering of the nodes followed by a simple graph isomorphism check. Computers are very efficient at such checks, e.g. a 50,000 gate circuit may be fully checked in just 50 seconds. However, one must add that the compilation process for each of the designs can easily take 10 minutes. However, BDD technology has one other major advantage over equational equivalence checking. It is possible to check the equivalence of designs that are not structurally equivalent, but behaviourally equivalent in a sequential sense, i.e. the outputs on a clock-by-clock basis correspond in both designs, regardless of the number of internal states, or state-mappings in each of the designs. This type of equivalence checking is extremely important when an engineer recodes a piece of RTL or if optimising compilers are used to remove state-bits or if the engineer uses one-hot encoding. There are many such cases. Only ROBDD based technology can allow such equivalencies to be shown, equational equiovalence checking will simply state that the two design are not equivalent, despite the fact that they are. Another advantage of compiling down to an intermediate form is that it facilitates the easy comparison of designs written in any level of language and also between different languages, e.g. RTL VHDL vs. GTL Verilog or RTL Verilog vs. EDIF netlist. All combinations of language and level of language used in comaprison being equally possible. What happens if the two designs are not equivalent? In this case, a complete simulation test bench is written, in either VHDL or Verilog, to illustrate the shortest path to find a difference between the two designs. The engineer can feed this test-bench into his favorite simulator to further narrow down the cause of the problem.

Another approach used quite recently is that of model-checking or property-checking. Here a design, quite often the RTL that is supposed to be the golden model, is taken and essential properties that it is supposed to satisfy are proven about it, e.g. absence of deadlock, a bus arbiter responding within a certain time, a traffic light controller satsfying a safety property that both lights are not green at the same time. etc. Model checking can also be used as a wekaer form of equivalence checking, nameely algorithmic equivalence checking. For example, consider two RTL Verilog descriptions of a design for a multiplier. The first multiplier is a booth implementation, the second is a shift & add implementation. Clearly, both multipliers are doing the same thing but: they are not structurally equivalent, owing to the different numbers of state bits and state encodings; they are not sequentially equivalent, owing to the fact that the outputs do not correspond on a clock-by-clock basis, the time taken being data-dependent and not a simple fixed offset from one design to the other. Yet both are doing the same basic computation, are they not? How do we show this? If we use model-checking, we can define a property which compares the outputs of both designs, independent of time taken, when the "done" flag in both designs is raised. The model-checker can thus show that for all combinations of inputs over all time that the designs are equivalent. Abstract Hardware's model-checking technology is called CheckOff-M.

It is envisaged that the ideal technique is to marry the technologies of theorem-proving and BDD based model-checking. The ability to handle design complexity of the former is well known, yet the automation provided by the latter is regarded as essential. Such a marriage can work in two ways: firstly, to use theorem-proving technology to keep an eye on system obligations that have to be proven during the model-checking process and secondly, to use model-checking to prove awkward lemmas suggested by a theorem based view of design. The difficulty is toi arrange the external appearance of such tools such that it does not appear totally alien to the practising engineer. The author believes that education is still going to be required, but new engineers with these skills are now beginning to be produced by many academic institutions. Senior management need to make themselves aware of the capabilities of these new technologies.

During the talk various slides will be shown to illustrate what can be done with each of the technologies and how best to position them into an existing commercial design-flow. With a suitable use of these technologies it has already been shown that the time-to-market can be reduced by a factor of two to five fold. This is a significant reduction in overall cost as well as ensuring a market window. As more companies adopt this type of technology, the others will be forced to follow suite if they are to meet their return-on-investment in new product development, or their competitors will fill the market gap before them. Formal verification can give the designer the freedom to explore the design space, to find better, more efficient designs in complete safety. Formal verification of properties or equivalence does give exhaustive coverage in far less time than non-exhaustive simulation. This does not mean an end to simulation, but a large reduction in what is required. e.g. it is easier to take a 128-bit adder and give it the numbers 4 and 5 and see if the answer is 9. If the answer is 10, there is clearly no need to formally verify the operation of the adder! Thus simulation will still be used as a fast "sanity-check" on designs and will be used to illustrate when two designs are not equivalent.

The Industrial Success of Verification Tools Based on Stålmarck's Method

Arne Borälv
arne@lk.se

Logikkonsult NP AB,
Swedenborgsgatan 2,
S-118 48 Stockholm, Sweden,
http://www.lk.se

Abstract. Stålmarck's Method is a patented natural deduction proof method with a novel proof-theoretic notion of *proof depth*, defined as the largest number of nested assumptions in the proof. An implementation of the method, called Prover, has been used as proof engine in various commercial tools since 1990, and is now integrated in a formal verification framework called NP-Tools. Prover searches for shallow sub-formula proofs, which has proven to be an efficient strategy for solving many industrial problems, the largest of which today consists of several 100,000's of sub-formulas. Stålmarck's method is in industrial use, for instance in the areas of telecom service specification analysis, analysis of railway interlocking software, analysis of programmable controllers and analysis of aircraft systems. The method seems suitable also for hardware verification.

1 Railway Interlocking Software: First Tool

In 1989, ADtranz Signal had problems with system availability due to run-time errors ("double values") in their computerized interlockings, which caused their interlocking to enter a safe state at times. This problem made extensive testing necessary, but since computerized interlocking is a complex task, even a very long test phase could not give enough coverage. The runtime errors remained.

Logikkonsult found that a sufficient condition for ensuring that this type of error could not occur was that certain boolean formulas representing the generic interlocking software program were unsatisfiable. Proving this seemed to work in practise, so the tool CVT [SS90] was developed. Proving this property for a complete program is done automatically by a simple pressing of a button; the proof takes roughly about one minute CPU time on a Sparc 10. The tool was released in 1990 and has been part of ADtranz' development environment since. CVT is also regularly used by the Swedish National Railroad Administration for comparing different revisions of interlocking software (a compare fuctionality of interlocking software programs is built-in in CVT). The reported benefits from ADtranz are a 90% reduction of the test phase time, and an overall development cost reduction of more than 15%. Furthermore, since the introduction of the tool, no run-time errrors due to double values have occured.

2   Railway Interlocking Software: Second Tool

Inspired by the success of the CVT tool for proving properties of generic software, an attempt to analyse complete railyard interlockings was made [BÅ95]. Replacing parts of the rigourous system-level test phase with formal proofs can potentially save a lot of time, and also improve quality as given by rigorous formal proofs. A new tool SVT was developed, which is a translator for complete (or partial) railyard interlockings into the general-purpose formal verification framework NP-Tools (see Section 3). Using SVT and NP-Tools, a logic model of any of ADtranz' interlockings can be produced automatically, and safety requirements on the system level can be proved. The approach has already proved its usefulness and errors have been found in interlockings, even after the standard test phase [Bor97][1]. A medium-sized railyard model consists of some 100,000 sub-formulas; the largest system analyzed (in which both proofs and counter-models for properties have been found) consists of 350,000 sub-formulas. In the latter case, the proof times were about 20 seconds after an initial 1-saturation [Wid96] of the system (done only once per system) which took 100 minutes CPU time on an HP 9000/715 work-station. A commercial release of SVT is planned in 1997.

2.1   Proof Logging and Proof Checking

In order to replace (parts of) ADtranz' extensive system-level test phase with formal proofs, ADtranz requires that Prover generated proofs must be possible to check separately. Therefore, the Prover implementation (and thereby also NP-Tools) is augmented with the possibility of logging proofs, which thereafter can be checked by a (relatively simple) proof checker program. This strenghtens the confidence in the proofs generated, especially since the proof checker can be written using a rigorous formal approach, for instance the well-known B-Method.

3   NP-Tools

The foremost usage of Prover today is in the general-purpose formal verification framework NP-Tools [E+96], developed by Logikkonsult. NP-Tools offers a set of automatic translators, a graphical user interface for construction of designs and integration of automatically imported systems and a system analysis facility. Figure 1 illustrates a system analysis where a set of requirements have been proved for an interlocking software system.

3.1   NP-Tools Applications

NP-Tools is currently evaluated and used by Saab AB (formerly Saab Military Aircraft) and the Swedish Defence Material Adminstration for verification

---

[1] The case study consisted of about 35,000 sub-formulas, and the proof time for some 50 requirements was about 15 CPU seconds on an HP 9000/715 work-station.

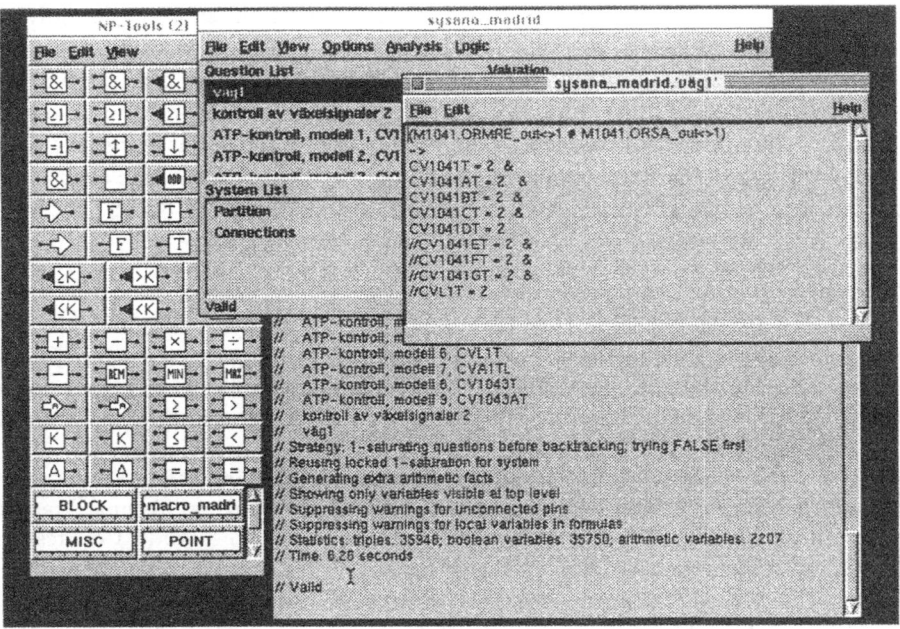

Fig. 1. An NP-Tools System Analysis with proven requirements

of safety properties, e.g., in CASE tool designs. In this context, an automatic NP-Tools translator from Verilog's ASA tool has been developed [Bol96] and a Statecharts translator is under development [Mei97a]. Saab are also currently exploring NP-Tools for FMEA and FTA. The Swedish avionics consultant firm LUTAB are regularly using NP-Tools for assessing safety properties in electronic designs and airborne software.

ABB Network Partner are currently using NP-Tools for verification of PLC programs, based on the IEC standard 1131-3. An NP-Tools translator is under development.

Volvo Bus uses NP-Tools for verifying and analysing formal specifications, for instance proving that the specifications are unambigous, handles all input combinations and that safety requirements hold [Mei97b]. Also Volvo Car Corporation have used NP-Tools for developing formal specifications.

Recently, NP-Tools has been used to verify VHDL designs, with promising results compared to commercial VHDL verification tools.

4 Stålmarck's Method

The patented [Stå92] Stålmarck Method [Stå94] is a natural deduction proof system with a novel proof-theoretic notion of *proof depth* [Wid96, Har96]. The depth of a proof is the largest number of nested assumptions in the proof. Searching for shallow sub-formula proofs has proven to be an efficient strategy for solving many industrial problems, as reported for a few applications here. The decision procedure was originally defined for boolean formulas only, but has in a natural way been extended to finite domain integer arithmetic. In 1994 a former version of Prover, the (resolution based) Otter prover and a BDD based prover were used for verifying industrial problems in the railway field. Prover was clearly the only one that managed to prove all properties automatically [GKvV94].

References

[BÅ95]   Arne Borälv and Herman Ågren. Feasibility Study SVT. Technical Report U-95002, Logikkonsult NP AB, 1995. Internally published at Logikkonsult.

[Bol96] Hans Bolinder. LSA 1.0. Technical Report NPT-01-07-0-3, Issue 2 Rev 1, Logikkonsult NP AB, 1996.

[Bor97] Arne Borälv. A Fully Automated Approach for Proving Safety Properties in Interlocking Software Using Automatic Theorem-Proving. Technical report, Logikkonsult NP AB, March 1997. Submitted to the World Congress on Railway Research 1997 (WCRR'97).

[E⁺96]   Love Ekenberg et al. *Reference Manual, NP-Tools 2.2.* Logikkonsult NP AB, October 1996. NPT-01-07-02 2.0.

[GKvV94] J.F. Groote, J.W.C. Koorn, and S.F.M. van Vlijmen. The safety guaranteeing system at station Hoorn-Kersenboogerd. Technical report, Department of Philosophy – Utrecht University, 1994.

[Har96] John Harrison. The Stålmarck Method as a HOL Derived Rule. In *Theorem Proving in Higher Order Logics*, pages 221–234. TPHOLs'96, Springer Verlag, 1996.

[Mei97a] Karl Meinke. Axiomatic Semantics and Automatic Verification of Statecharts. Technical report, Logikkonsult NP AB, April 1997.

[Mei97b] Karl Meinke. Industrial Formal Methods: A Case Study in Public Transport Vehicles, February 1997. In Formal Methods Europe Tour 2, 1997. http://www.ifad.dk/projects/tour2.html.

[SS90]   Mårten Säflund and Gunnar Stålmarck. Modelling and Verifying Systems and Software in Propositional Logic. In *Proceedings of IFAC/EWICS/SARS Symposium SAFECOMP '90*, pages 31–36. Pergamon Press, 1990.

[Stå92] Gunnar Stålmarck. A System for Determining Propositional Logic Theorems by Applying Values and Rules to Triplets that are Generated from a Formula, 1992. Swedish Patent No. 467 076 (approved 1992), U.S. Patent No. 5 276 897 (1994), European Patent No. 0403 454 (1995).

[Stå94] Gunnar Stålmarck. A Proof Theoretic Concept of Tautological Hardness. Unpublished manuscript, 1994.

[Wid96] Filip Widebäck. Stålmarck's Notion of n-saturation. Technical Report NP-K-FW-200, Logikkonsult NP AB, January 1996.

Formal Verification - Applications & Case Studies

Martin Rowe
Chrysalis Symbolic Design Europe
Bix Manor
Broadplat Lane
Bix, Henley on Thames RG9 4RS United Kingdom

Chrysalis is delivering formal verification products and support to over sixty customer sites world-wide. Design VERIFYer(r) software is an equivalence checking tool that proves the functional equivalence of two design descriptions. It is being applied to a variety of steps in the design process. This paper will include example applications that include RTL to gate, gate to gate, gate to switch, and RTL to switch comparisons. A case study that demonstrates the success of Design VERIFYer for a customer's verification requirements throughout the design process will be presented. Included in the case study are examples of applications stated above. This paper will also describe our recently introduced Design INSIGHT(r) formal RTL design tools for model checking and symbolic simulation which enable customers to complete correct RTL designs faster than with simulation alone.

Automatic Abstraction Techniques for Propositional μ-calculus Model Checking*

Abelardo Pardo and Gary D. Hachtel

University of Colorado
ECEN Campus Box 425, Boulder, CO, 80309, USA
{abel,hachtel}@vlsi.colorado.edu

Abstract. An abstraction/refinement paradigm for the full propositional μ-calculus is presented. No distinction is made between universal or existential fragments. Necessary conditions for conservative verification are provided, along with a fully automatic symbolic model checking abstraction algorithm. The algorithm begins with conservative verification of an initial abstraction. If the conclusion is negative, it derives a "goal set" of states which require further resolution. It then successively refines, with respect to this goal set, the approximations made in the subformulas, until the given formula is verified or computational resources are exhausted.

1 Introduction

The success of formal verification in detecting incorrect designs has been proven over the last decade. However, limitations on the size of verifiable problems continue to be a serious drawback. Typically, a sequential system is modeled as a collection of interacting subsystems. As new subsystems are added the number of states may grow exponentially. This is known as the *state explosion* problem. This problem has become the focus of intense research in the last few years. Symbolic techniques based on BDDs (Reduced Ordered Binary Decision Diagrams [3]), such as symbolic model checking [5, 16] have significantly increased the size of the systems which can be verified. However, there are numerous examples for which additional techniques are required.

Abstract interpretation [7] is one approach to alleviate the state explosion problem. An *abstracted* system is obtained from a given *concrete* system by modeling groups of states as a single state. In contrast, BDD-based techniques tend to stay in the given state space, while providing a more compact representation. In [15] Long proposed a conservative abstraction paradigm that preserved the validity of the logic ∀CTL. This method was one-sided, in that it considered only upper bound approximations of the underlying Kripke structure. In [6], a procedure for approximate traversal of large systems was presented, based on automatic state space decomposition. This technique was similarly one-sided, and applied only to reachability analysis. Neither of these methods provided a procedure for automatically refining the approximation until verification was conclusive.

In [13], Kurshan described an abstraction paradigm called "localization reduction" in the context of ω-regular language containment based on reducing the parts of a system that are *irrelevant* with respect to the task being verified. A systematic procedure

---

* Work supported by NSF/DARPA grant MIP-94–22268 and SRC contract 95-DJ-560.

was sketched which refined the approximations based on error trace analysis. A related iterative approach to abstraction in language containment verification was presented in [1]. In contrast to Kurshan's method, this was BDD-based, and the refinement considered sets of error traces. However, the details of iterating their method to a definite conclusion were omitted. These methods used only upper bound approximations of the underlying Kripke structure.

In [14], a method was given for conservative CTL model checking. Although this approach used both upper and lower bounds, and included a complete procedure for refining the initial approximation, it was limited to ∀CTL. In [11] Kelb *et al.* proposed an abstraction mechanism for μ-calculus model checking based on two novel approximations, which were called universal and existential. The process required the intervention of the user. Although this approach applied to the full μ-calculus, and used both upper and lower bounds, only one (very interesting) type of approximation was used, and no automatic refinement procedure was given.

In this paper, novel techniques are presented for generic, BDD-based, fully automated abstraction for μ-calculus model checking. A complete procedure for automatically refining the approximations is included. This procedure is "lazy", in the sense, that it refines approximations in sub-formulas only where necessary. The "goal set" refinement method differs from the error trace refinement methods of [13] and [1] in that it is uniformly applicable to upper and lower bounds and to all μ-calculus formulas, whereas error traces are available only for upper bounds applied to universal CTL formulas or language containment. However, a superficial resemblance between the two can be discerned for some sub-formulas.

The plan of the paper is as follows. In Section 2 an overview of the propositional μ-calculus is given, and a labeled operational graph is defined. Section 3 lays the foundation for conservative μ-calculus symbolic model checking. A condition is given, in terms of the operational graph labels, to determine whether an over-approximation or under-approximation is required at the level of any sub-formula. In Section 4, a fully automatic BDD based model checking procedure is presented. The algorithm has two phases. First, it is shown how the given formula is tentatively verified with an initial abstraction. Then, it is shown how the algorithm recursively traverses every sub-formula and checks if the current approximation can be refined to achieve exact verification.

2 Propositional μ-calculus and Symbolic Model Checking

The propositional μ-calculus was introduced in [12]. It consists of propositional modal logic with a least fixed point operator. This calculus has been shown to be strictly more expressive than conventional temporal logics such as CTL, LTL and CTL* [8,9]. Also, it can express the language containment relation between two deterministic ω-automata.

2.1 Syntax and Semantics of the Propositional μ-calculus

Let us denote by A a set of atomic propositions with $p \in A$ and let X denote a set of variables with $x \in X$. The syntax of a formula ϕ is defined by

$$\phi ::= \phi_1 \wedge \phi_2 \mid \neg\phi \mid \mathbf{EX}\phi \mid \mu x.\phi \mid p \mid x. \tag{1}$$

In order to insure well-definedness of the semantics, each occurrence of the variable x in the formula $\mu x.\phi$ must be within the scope of an even number of negations. This restriction ensures monotonicity and therefore existence of the fixed point.

A state satisfies the formula $\mathbf{EX}\phi$ if ϕ is satisfied in one of its immediate successors. We will denote by $L\mu$ the set of closed formulas obtained with the sets A and X and the grammar in Equation 1.

Definition 1. A Kripke structure is a tuple $M = (S, R, A, \lambda)$ in which S is a set of states, $R \subseteq S \times S$ is a transition relation, A is a set of atomic propositions, and $\lambda : A \to 2^S$ is a labeling function that returns the set of states in S labeled with a given atomic proposition.

Definition 2. Given a Kripke structure $M = (S, R, A, \lambda)$ and a set of states $S_1 \subseteq S$, we define the image function $Img(R, S_2)$ as the set of states S_1 such that $\forall s \in S_1, \exists s' \in S_2 \ni (s', s) \in R$. We also define the reverse image function $Pre(R, S_1)$ as the set of states S_2 such that $\forall s \in S_2, \exists s' \in S_1 \ni (s, s') \in R$.

Note that both Img and Pre are monotonic functions, that is, if we replace either operand by a subset or a superset, we obtain a subset or a superset of the exact result.

Given the set of variables X and a state space S, we define an *environment* as a function $e : X \to 2^S$. Given a Kripke structure M the semantics of $\phi \in L$ are defined as the function Sat that given a formula and an environment, it returns the set of states satisfying the formula. When necessary, we will write Sat_M to make the intended Kripke structure explicit. Figure 1 shows the algorithm to compute this function. Emerson *et al.* proved that model checking problem for this calculus is exponential in the alternation depth of the formula [9]. However, the depth of most useful temporal formulas is two or less.

```
funct Sat(v, e) ≡                              funct EvalNot(v₁, e) ≡
  case TypeOf(v) do                              return ‾Sat(v₁,e);
    and(v₁, v₂): return EvalAnd(v₁, v₂, e);    end
    not(v₁): return EvalNot(v₁, e);            funct EvalEX(v₁, e) ≡
    EX(v₁): return EvalEX(v₁, e);                return Pre(R, Sat(v₁, e));
    μx.v₁: return Evalμx(v₁, e);               end
    Atom(p): return λ(p);                      funct Evalμx(v, e) ≡
    Variable(x): return e(x);                    x := ReadVariable(v);
  end case                                       result := ∅;
end                                              do
funct EvalAnd(v₁, v₂, e) ≡                         e(x) := result;
  return Sat(v₁, e) ∩ Sat(v₂, e);                  result := Sat(v₁, e);
end                                              while (result ≠ e(x)) od;
                                                 return result;
                                               end
```

Fig. 1. μ-Calculus Model Checking Algorithm.

Given a Kripke structure M, a state s satisfies the formula ϕ, denoted by $(M, s) \models \phi$, if and only if $s \in Sat(\phi, e_\perp)$, where $e_\perp$ is the environment that maps every variable to the empty set.

2.2 Graph Representation of a Formula

The verification algorithm of Figure 1 uses a graph representation based on the parse graph.

Definition 3. We define the *labeled operational graph* of the formula $\phi \in L\mu$ as $G = (V, E, P)$. V is a set of vertices. Each vertex is of the type $\{\textbf{and}, \textbf{not}, \textbf{EX}, \mu x\} \cup \{\textbf{Atom}(p) \ni p \in A\} \cup \{\textbf{Variable}(x) \ni x \in X\}$ and represents a sub-formula of ϕ. We will refer to a vertex or the sub-formula it represents interchangeably. $(v_1, v_2) \in E$ if v_2 is a direct sub-formula of v_1. We will denote by $top_\phi \in V$ the vertex representing ϕ. Every vertex v is labeled with a *polarity* which is the number of vertices of type **not** that are traversed in the path from v to top_ϕ excluding v itself. P is a function $P : V \rightarrow \{+, -\}$ such that $P(v) = +$ if v has odd polarity and $P(v) = -$ if v has even polarity.

Identical sub-graphs with identical polarity labeling represent common sub-formulas and therefore are shared.

2.3 BDDs and Symbolic Model Checking

BDDs [3] provide a canonical and efficient representation of boolean functions. Furthermore, although BDD size is exponential in its worse case, practical cases have been shown to present very compact representations. By a *symbolic model checking* algorithm we refer to an algorithm in which boolean functions are represented by BDDs [5].

In order to manipulate BDDs it is necessary to encode the state space with boolean variables. Let us denote by **u** the array of boolean variables required to encode the state space S of a given Kripke structure. Following this notation, we will represent a set in the state space S as a boolean function $S(\mathbf{u})$ such that, if $s \in S$ then $S(\beta(s)) = 1$ where $\beta(s)$ is the binary encoding of s. Analogously, a relation R will be represented as a boolean function $R(\mathbf{u}, \mathbf{w})$. Henceforth, whenever a set or a relation is mentioned we will be referring to its symbolic representation.

3 Conservative Abstraction

Abstract interpretation is a paradigm first introduced by Cousot *et al.* [7] in the context of static analysis of programs. The main idea is to interpret the behavior of a system in a different *abstracted* (and therefore simplified) system with fewer states. In the context of symbolic model checking, the complexity of the algorithms depends no longer on the number of states but on its representation as BDDs. An abstracted system therefore must be simplified so as to provide more compact BDD representations of the sets appearing in the verification algorithm.

The abstraction techniques presented in this paper assume that the state space in the concrete and abstract systems are the same. The simplification is based on taking supersets and subsets of a given set with a more compact representation.

3.1 Conservative μ-calculus Model Checking

In our abstraction, the concrete and abstract system share the same state space. Thus, we state the conservativeness property in terms of an approximation $\widehat{Sat}$ of the function Sat.

Definition 4. Given a Kripke structure M, we say the function $\widehat{Sat}$ provides a conservative interpretation if and only if $\forall \phi \in L\mu$, $\widehat{Sat}(\phi, e_{\perp}) \subseteq Sat(\phi, e_{\perp})$.

If the conservative verification algorithm proves the formula true, we can conclude that the formula is true in the concrete system. However, if the formula is proved false, no conclusion can be drawn in the concrete system. This definition can be reversed to provide conclusive verification when a formula is false, providing a reliable false result. "Reliable positive" conservativeness is assumed in the sequel. However, the techniques presented apply dually for both cases.

Let us denote by I the set of initial states of the system represented by the Kripke structure M. The system satisfies the formula ϕ if and only if $I \subseteq Sat(\phi, e_{\perp})$. Due to the conservativeness property $I \subseteq \widehat{Sat}(\phi, e_{\perp}) \Rightarrow I \subseteq Sat(\phi, e_{\perp})$.

Lemma 5. *Let us consider an operational graph $G = (V, E, P)$ and two vertices v_1, v_2 such that $(v_1, v_2) \in E$. Let us assume that in the computation of $Sat(v_1, e)$ the evaluation of v_2 has been approximated by $\widehat{Sat}(v_2, e)$. If v_1 is of type **not** and $\widehat{Sat}(v_2, e)$ is a superset (subset), then the computed $Sat(v_1, e)$ is a subset (superset) of the exact result. If v_1 is of type **and**, **EX**, or μx and $\widehat{Sat}(v_2, e)$ is a superset (subset), then $Sat(v_1, e)$ also is a superset (subset) of the exact result.*

Proof. The first part of the lemma is trivial by set complementation. If v_1 is of type **and** the lemma is true by monotonicity of boolean conjunction. If v_1 is of type **EX** then by monotonicity of the *Pre* function the lemma holds. If v_1 is of type μx the lemma is proved by induction over the number of symbols in the formula represented by v_2. If the length is 1 the lemma is trivially true. Let us assume the lemma is true for formulas of length up to n. The approximation is reflected in the value of the variable x. By definition this variable must be within the scope of an even number of negations. By the induction hypothesis, approximation of the vertex v_2 is consistently of the same type throughout the fixed point iteration, thus the lemma holds. $\square$

Theorem 6. *Let us consider a Kripke structure M, a formula $\phi \in L\mu$, and its labeled operational graph $G = (V, E, P)$. Any function $\widehat{Sat}$ such that for every vertex $v \in V$*

$$Sat(v, e) \subseteq \widehat{Sat}(v, e) \quad \text{if } P(v) = + \tag{2}$$
$$Sat(v, e) \supseteq \widehat{Sat}(v, e) \quad \text{if } P(v) = -$$

provides a conservative interpretation of ϕ in M.

Proof. By Lemma 5, all the vertices propagate the direction of the approximation except those of type **not** which switch the direction. By Definition 4, the set $Sat(top_{\phi}, e)$ must be under-approximated. The approximation taken at any sub-formula must be such that when propagated to the top vertex it translates into a subset of $Sat(top_{\phi}, e)$. This condition is guaranteed by the function P. $\square$

This result is advantageous in the verification process. For example, there is no need to distinguish between universal and existential sub-formulas. Also, the approximations can be produced at the level of any sub-formula.

An approximation may be created not only on the transition relation of the system inside the function *EvalEX* but on any type of vertex. For example, in a vertex v of type **and** such that $P(v) = +$, we may evaluate only one of the operands and return it as the result since it is a valid superset of the exact *Sat* function. Further, this paradigm allows for an incremental approach to verification. First, an initial approximation of all the vertices is obtained. Second, a set of vertices is chosen in which the approximations are to be refined. This is the essence of the algorithm presented in Section 4.

Theorem 6 also provides a condition that is local for every vertex. Two vertices of the same type representing different sub-formulas need not have the same kind of approximation. For example, we may provide different estimations of the transition relation R in the evaluation of different **EX** vertices. This property may be considered an advantage if we have a local measure of how the approximation must be refined locally to increase its exactness globally.

4 An Automatic Abstraction and Refinement Algorithm

In this section a novel verification algorithm is presented that exploits the advantages of the above paradigm. The conservativeness property is preserved by the local approximations made at relevant vertices. The automatic procedure successively refines these approximations until the formula is decided or resources are exhausted.

The proposed algorithm has as one of its parameters, a limit on the size of the BDD representation of the intermediate results. At the end of the computation either the formula is proved true, the formula is proved false or the memory limit is reached and therefore no conclusion can be drawn.

The algorithm has two phases: Creation of the initial approximation, and successive refinement. In the first step, the algorithm traverses the labeled operational graph and obtains an approximation for every evaluation of the function *Sat* at every vertex. To guarantee conservativeness, the type of approximation is determined by the condition in Theorem 6. Once the first abstraction is obtained, if the formula is proved false, the graph is traversed by depth first search to detect vertices whose approximation can be refined. At a given vertex, the algorithm attempts to improve the approximation with respect to a given "goal set". This set is obtained by propagating to other vertices in the graph the condition to achieve verification in the top vertex.

4.1 Incremental Approximations

The elementary units of the algorithm are the evaluation functions shown in Figure 1. If they satisfy the following two properties, we will call them *incremental approximations*. First, they must return a superset or subset of the exact result according to the polarity. Second, note that the BDD size limit may be reached at any point in the computation. Thus, we require that all partial results constitute valid approximations.

The generality of this paradigm leaves the choice of the type of approximation techniques open. A candidate set of techniques are provided which meet the requirements of our paradigm. In principle, any other technique that complies with the above conditions can be used.

We now show how to generate the two types of approximations. Since the negation of a function represented by a BDD is a constant time operation that has no effect on its size, the function *EvalNot* is computed exactly.

Conjunction Operation: The function *EvalAnd* takes the conjunction of the result of evaluating its two sub-formulas. We rely on the monotonicity property of this function to provide the required approximations. A superset is obtained by over-approximating either of its operands. A BDD representing the characteristic function of a set may be reduced in size by either adding or subtracting elements to that set. In the case of an over-approximation the operands are simplified by adding elements to the sets. In a vertex of type **and** the algorithm checks if the size of either of the operands exceeds its limit. If so, the operand(s) are simplified before the conjunction is taken.

If an under-approximation is required we rely on the following decomposition

$$a(\mathbf{u}) \wedge b(\mathbf{u}) = (u_i \wedge (a(\mathbf{u}) \wedge b(\mathbf{u}))_{u_i}) \vee (\neg u_i \wedge (a(\mathbf{u}) \wedge b(\mathbf{u}))_{\neg u_i}) \tag{3}$$

where the subscript symbolizes the cofactor operation with respect to a variable. This decomposition is applied recursively. At each recursive step, both operands are cofactored with respect to a variable, thus reducing the size of the candidate conjunction. When enough reduction has been achieved, the conjunction is returned as a valid subset of the exact result.

Fixed Point Computation: The partial results μ_i obtained while iterating the least fixed point satisfy $\emptyset = \mu_0 \subseteq \ldots \subseteq \mu_\infty$. If an under-approximation is required, any set μ_i constitutes a valid result. In this case, the algorithm iterates for an arbitrary number of steps and returns the result without reaching convergence. This scheme also provides a natural way to refine the approximation. If the approximation previously computed needs to be refined, it is enough to apply several additional iterations, since each of them creates a superset of the previous result.

The other possible scenario is that the fixed point vertex has $P(v) = +$ and therefore an over-approximation is required. In this case the fixed point iteration has to reach convergence before returning a correct approximation. At each iteration of the fixed point, the algorithm monitors the size of the representation of μ_i. Whenever this size reaches a certain limit, it applies a BDD simplification procedure that reduces its size while creating a superset. When convergence is reached, the result is guaranteed to be an over-approximation of the real result.

***Pre* Computation:** The *Pre* operation is often responsible for the increase in size during the verification process. Even though both the operands and the final result may have a compact representation, the intermediate results may go beyond the computational limit. One method that significantly minimizes this effect is to manipulate the transition relation as a conjunction of relational blocks [4]. The reverse image is now obtained by successive steps of conjunction and variable existential abstraction. Several heuristics have been develop to compute the way the relation is broken into blocks and the order of the blocks so to minimize the size of the intermediate results (i.e. [10]).

The proposed *EvalEX* function modifies such reverse image computation in two different ways. The first method takes the conjunction and existential abstraction of the relational blocks until a certain limit in the size of the intermediate result is reached. At that point, no more conjunctions are taken and all the remaining variables are quantified, yielding a superset. The second method amounts to sub-setting or super-setting C in $Pre(R, C)$.

If a vertex of type **EX** has $P(v) = -$ then the algorithm must provide an under-estimation. The algorithm builds its result incrementally, and it is a modification of the one proposed in [17]. With this scheme, the algorithm builds the reverse image by recursive cofactoring the set C. If at any point during this recursion, the intermediate results grow too large, the algorithm returns the current partial result.

4.2 Refining the Abstraction

We assume that for every vertex v an initial approximation denoted by Sat_v has been obtained, and the verification of the formula is false. We describe the approximation of a vertex with respect to a set f_v. If the vertex has been over-approximated, the refinement amounts to producing a new result such that f_v is not included in it. If the vertex has been under-approximated, the refinement amounts to computing a new set which includes f_v.

Figure 2 shows the pseudo code for the generic procedure to refine the approximation in a given vertex. The specifics depend on the type of vertex and are explained subsequently. This procedure is preliminary and may be substantially improved, so only the main ideas behind it are presented.

```
funct RefineVertex(v, fᵥ):boolean ≡
    if (fᵥ = ∅) then return TRUE;
    if (Satᵥ is an approximation) then
        (Sat'ᵥ, f'ᵥ) := RefineApproximation(Satᵥ, fᵥ);
        if (f'ᵥ = ∅) return TRUE;
        fᵥ := f'ᵥ;
    endif
    Sort Sub-formulas;
    foreach (Sub-formula vᵢ) do
        f_{vᵢ} := PropagateGoalSet(v, vᵢ);
        resultᵢ = RefineVertex(vᵢ, f_{vᵢ});
    od
    if (RefinementInSubFormulas(result)) then
        Sat'ᵥ := ReEvaluate(v);
        if ((P(v) = +) ∧ (fᵥ ∩ Sat'ᵥ = ∅)) return TRUE;
        if ((P(v) = -) ∧ (fᵥ ⊆ Sat'ᵥ)) return TRUE;
    endif
    return FALSE;
end
```

Fig. 2. Algorithm to Refine the Approximation in a Vertex.

Definition 7. Let us assume that an evaluation of the function Sat at a vertex v has been approximated. For a given set of states f_v the refinement of Sat_v with respect to f_v computed in the procedure of Figure 2 is successful if the new approximation Sat'_v satisfies

$$Sat'_v \subseteq Sat_v \setminus f_v \quad \text{if } P(v) = + \qquad (4)$$
$$Sat_v \cup f_v \subseteq Sat'_v \quad \text{if } P(v) = -.$$

In other words, if Sat_v has been over-approximated, the refinement attempts to exclude the elements of f_v from the approximation. Conversely, if Sat_v has been under-approximated, the refinement attempts to increase the set to include the elements in f_v. Note that since the algorithm works with memory limits, it is possible that in the attempt to refine the approximation, a limit is reached and the refinement fails. The procedure in Figure 2 returns TRUE if the new refinement satisfies Equation 4 and FALSE otherwise.

When the procedure is applied to a generic vertex v, there are two possible scenarios. The initial approximation Sat_v has been either computed in the vertex itself, or it has been propagated from the approximation of any of its sub-formulas.

If the approximation has been produced in the vertex itself, the proper incremental approximation procedure described in Section 4.1 is re-executed. However, this time the approximation process is modified so as to include or exclude the set f_v from the result. For example, in a vertex of type EX the initial result has been over-approximated by considering a subset of relational blocks. The refinement algorithm computes a new approximation but this time considering the relational blocks that exclude the set f_v from the result.

If the new approximation succeeds with respect to the whole set f_v, the procedure returns TRUE. If not, the set f'_v contains the elements of f_v that were not refined from Sat_v. If no further approximation has been produced in v the whole set f_v is recursively propagated to the sub-formulas.

The sub-formulas of v are scheduled for refinement with criteria based on the size of the BDDs and the depth. The depth of a formula is defined as the length of the longest path to a leaf vertex. The propagation of the set f_v to the sub-formulas is different depending on the type of v.

- **Negation Vertex:** The vertex of type **not** has a single sub-formula v_1 and the set f_v is propagated such that $f_{v_1} = f_v$.
- **Conjunction Vertex:** Let us assume that v has sub-formulas v_1 and v_2 already sorted by increasing depth. If $P(v) = +$ then $f_{v_1} = f_v$ and $f_{v_2} = Sat'_{v_1} \cap f_v$. If $P(v) = -$ then $f_{v_1} = f_v$ and $f_{v_2} = f_v$.
- **EX Vertex:** In this vertex, $Sat_v = Pre(R, Sat_{v_1})$. The set f_{v_1} is propagated such that $f_{v_1} = Img(R, f_v)$.
- **Fixed Point Vertex:** For this type of vertex the algorithm has stored the sequence of intermediate results $\mu_1, \ldots, \mu_m$. The refinement process is applied at first to the set μ_m. If the approximations cannot be improved, the refinement keeps propagating to the sub-formula and eventually the refinement is applied to the set μ_{m-1}. The propagation of the set f_v is $f_{v_1} = f_v$.
- **Variable(x) Vertex:** Although this vertex does not have any sub-formulas, the refinement process may be propagated through it. Intuitively, if a vertex of this type needs to be refined, that refinement refers in fact to the temporary result produced by the fixed point that binds the variable x. Therefore, the refinement

process is propagated to the vertex representing the fixed point sub-formula. The refinement of the fixed point vertex refers now to the set μ_{i-1} where μ_i is the set that has been considered for refinement the last. Independently of the value of $P(v)$, the propagation is such that $f_{v_1} = f_v$.

The vertex of type **Atom**(p) constitutes the trivial case of the recursive procedure, and since no approximations are computed, the procedure returns FALSE with no further computation.

After the algorithm recursively refined the approximations in the sub-formulas, it checks if v needs to be re-evaluated again. For example, in a vertex of type μx with $P(v) = +$ if the last set computed in the fixed point has been refined, the fixed point has to be iterated until it reaches convergence again. In the case of a vertex of type **and** it simply re-computes the conjunction.

To guarantee the correctness of the procedure in Figure 2 we need to prove that the refinement process succeeds in v if the propagated refinement succeeds in the sub-formulas.

Proposition 8. *Given a vertex v with sub-formulas v_1 (and v_2 when applicable), for every sub-formula v_i, $RefineVertex(v_i, f_{v_i}) = TRUE \Rightarrow RefineVertex(v, f_v) = TRUE$.*

Proof. If v is of type **not**, since no approximation is made, $Sat_v = \neg Sat_{v_1}$ and $Sat'_v = \neg Sat'_{v_1}$. For $P(v) = +$, the polarity of v_1 is $P(v_1) = -$ and therefore $Sat_{v_1} \cup f_{v_1} \subseteq Sat'_{v_1} \Rightarrow Sat'_v \subseteq Sat_v \setminus f_v$. If $P(v_1) = -$ then $P(v_1) = +$ and since $Sat'_{v_1} \subseteq Sat_{v_1} \setminus f_v$ then $Sat_v \cup f_v \subseteq Sat'_v$.

If v is of type **and** and $P(v) = -$, then the proposition holds because if the refinement process succeeds in both sub-formulas, then $f_v \subseteq Sat'_{v_1}$ and $f_v \subseteq Sat'_{v_2}$. Since $Sat'_v = Sat'_{v_1} \cap Sat'_{v_2}$ then $f_v \subseteq Sat'_v$. If $P(v) = +$ the refinement of f_v propagates to both formulas. If the process succeeds in both sub-formulas then $f_v \nsubseteq Sat'_{v_1}$ and $f_v \nsubseteq Sat'_{v_2}$ and therefore $f_v \nsubseteq Sat'_v$.

If v is of type **EX** then $Sat_v = Pre(R, Sat_{v_1})$. If $P(v) = +$ the success of the refinement at the sub-formula v_1 implies $Sat'_{v_1} \subseteq Sat_{v_1} \setminus f_{v_1}$. Since $f_{v_1} = Img(R, f_v)$ there is no pair of states s_1, s_2 such that $s_1 \in f_v$, $s_2 \in Sat'_{v_1}$ and $(s_1, s_2) \in R$. Therefore $Pre(R, Sat'_{v_1}) \subseteq Sat_v \setminus f_v$. The proof when $P(v) = -$ is analogous.

When v is of type μx the theorem holds independently of the polarity. The fixed point does not perform any type of computation over the result obtained from its sub-formula. Thus the refinement of v_1 propagates to v.

If v is of type **Variable**(x) it is true that $Sat_v = Sat_{v_1}$ then $Sat'_v = Sat'_{v_1}$. Therefore if the refinement succeeds in v_1 it also succeeds in v. □

Theorem 9. *For a given vertex v, an approximation Sat_v, and a set f_v, the algorithm of Figure 2 returns TRUE if Equation 4 is satisfied and FALSE otherwise.*

Proof. If the approximation Sat_v has been computed locally in v (independently of the result of its sub-formulas) the first part of the algorithm guarantees that the elements of f_v are included or excluded from Sat_v depending on $P(v)$. Those elements that could not be refined from f_v are propagated to the sub-formulas of v following the rules discussed above and the theorem holds because of Proposition 8. □

The initial refinement set f_v is obtained from the top vertex in the graph. Since we assumed that our verification procedure is conservative and the initial approximation proved the formula false, then $I \nsubseteq Sat(top_\phi, e_\perp)$. Since $P(top_\phi) = -$, if the set $Sat(top_\phi, e_\perp)$ is increased by $I \setminus Sat(top_\phi, e_\perp)$ the verification is successful. Therefore the refinement process starts with the function call $RefineVertex(top_\phi, I \setminus Sat(top_\phi, e_\perp))$.

5 Conclusions and Future Work

We have presented a general abstraction/refinement paradigm for propositional μ-calculus. It provides general conditions to obtain conservative abstract interpretations of a system. These conditions are local to the verification process in each sub-formula of the given formula. Also, a fully automatic symbolic model checking abstraction algorithm was presented. The algorithm includes a set of techniques for providing incremental approximations for every type of sub-formula. Also included is a procedure for gradually refining these approximations, until the formula is verified or resources are exhausted.

The algorithm and techniques described above are being implemented inside the framework provided by VIS [2]. The first prototype of the algorithm correctly verified small examples, but after finishing its implementation, we plan to apply it to examples that are known to be hard to verify with conventional techniques.

In the future, we plan to enrich the set of approximation techniques provided in the algorithm. In particular, generic BDD sub-setting and super-setting may be enhanced by adapting them to the context of refining a previous approximation. We are also working on efficient techniques for computing Pre and Img when domain and codomain constraint sets are given.

References

1. F. Balarin and A. L. Sangiovanni-Vincentelli. An iterative approach to language containment. In C. Courcoubetis, editor, *Fifth Conference on Computer Aided Verification (CAV '93)*. Springer-Verlag, Berlin, 1993. LNCS 697.
2. R. K. Brayton et al. VIS: A system for verification and synthesis. In T. Henzinger and R. Alur, editors, *Eigth Conference on Computer Aided Verification (CAV'96)*, pages 428–432. Springer-Verlag, Rutgers University, 1996. LNCS 1102.
3. R. E. Bryant. Graph-based algorithms for boolean function manipulation. *IEEE Transactions on Computers*, C-35(8):677–691, Aug. 1986.
4. J. R. Burch, E. M. Clarke, and D. E. Long. Representing circuits more efficiently in symbolic model checking. In *Proceedings of the Design Automation Conference*, pages 403–407, San Francisco, CA, June 1991.
5. J. R. Burch, E. M. Clarke, K. L. McMillan, and D. L. Dill. Sequential circuit verification using symbolic model checking. In *Proceedings of the Design Automation Conference*, pages 46–51, June 1990.
6. H. Cho, G. D. Hachtel, E. Macii, B. Plessier, and F. Somenzi. Algorithms for approximate FSM traversal based on state space decomposition. In *Proceedings of the Design Automation Conference*, pages 25–30, Dallas, TX, June 1993.
7. P. Cousot and R. Cousot. Abstract interpretation: A unified lattice model for static analysis of programs by constructions or approximation of fixpoints. In *Proceedings of the ACM Symposium on the Principles of Programming Languages*, pages 238–250, 1977.
8. M. Dam. CTL* and ECTL* as fragments of the modal μ-calculus. *Theoretical Computer Science*, 126:77–97, 1994.
9. E. A. Emerson and C.-L. Lei. Efficient model checking in fragments of the propositional mu-calculus. In *Proceedings of the First Annual Symposium of Logic in Computer Science*, pages 267–278, June 1986.

10. D. Geist and I. Beer. Efficient model checking by automated ordering of transition relation parititons. In D. L. Dill, editor, *Sixth Conference on Computer Aided Verification (CAV'94)*, pages 299–310, Berlin, 1994. Springer-Verlag. LNCS 818.

11. P. Kelb, D. Dams, and R. Gerth. Practical symbolic model checking of the full μ-calculus using compositional abstractions. Technical Report 95-31, Department of Computing Science, Eindhoven University of Technology, 1995.

12. D. Kozen. Results on the propositional μ-calculus. *Theoretical Computer Science*, 27:333–354, 1983.

13. R. P. Kurshan. *Computer-Aided Verification of Coordinating Processes*. Princeton University Press, Princeton, NJ, 1994.

14. W. Lee, A. Pardo, J. Jang, G. Hachtel, and F. Somenzi. Tearing based abstraction for CTL model checking. In *Proceedings of the IEEE International Conference on Computer Aided Design*, pages 76–81, 1996.

15. D. E. Long. *Model Checking, Abstraction, and Compositional Verification*. PhD thesis, Carnegie-Mellon University, July 1993.

16. K. L. McMillan. *Symbolic Model Checking*. Kluwer Academic Publishers, Boston, MA, 1994.

17. C. Pixley, S.-W. Jeong, and G. D. Hachtel. Exact calculation of synchronization sequences based on binary decision diagrams. In *Proceedings of the Design Automation Conference*, pages 620–623, Anaheim, CA, June 1992.

A Compositional Rule for Hardware Design Refinement

K. L. McMillan

Cadence Berkeley Labs
1919 Addison St., suite 303
Berkeley, CA 94704-1144
mcmillan@cadence.com

Abstract. We present an approach to designing verified digital systems by a sequence of small local refinements. Refinements in this approach are not limited to a library of predefined transformations for which theorems have been previously established. Rather, the approach relies on localizing the refinement steps in such a way that they can be verified efficiently by model checking. Toward this end, a compositional rule is proposed by which each design refinement may be verified independently, in an abstract environment. This rule supports the use of downward refinement maps, which translate abstract behavior detailed behavior. These maps may involve temporal transformations, including delay. The approach is supported by a verification tool based on symbolic model checking.

1 Introduction

Although significant progress has been made in automated verification of digital systems, most designs are still far too large and complex to be verified in a fully automatic way. The classical solution proposed to this problem is compositional reasoning. This means that properties of individual modules or components of a large system are verified in isolation, and these properties are then combined to prove properties of the system as a whole. One commonly proposed specification language for these properties is temporal logic [Pnu85], and systems of compositional inference rules have been developed to support "assume-guarantee" style proofs [Lam83] using various temporal logics (*e.g.*, [GL94]). In a compositional proof, one reasons thus:

$$\frac{P, \phi \models \psi \qquad Q \models \phi}{P \parallel Q \models \psi}$$

Here, P and Q are processes, and ϕ is an environment assumption, necessary to prove that P satisfies specification ψ. Typically, however, the environment assumptions needed to verify interacting processes are interdependent. For example, process P may guarantee to satisfy an invariant ψ up to time $t+1$ only if Q satisies ψ up to time t, and *vice versa*. Such an inductive argument cannot be expressed in the above rule. If one attempts it, the result is a circular argument. One way to break the circularity is to model the environment as an abstract process. Kurshan [Kur87, Kur94] introduced the following style of reasoning for Moore machines:

$$P \parallel Q' \Rightarrow P'$$
$$\frac{P' \parallel Q \Rightarrow Q'}{P \parallel Q \Rightarrow P' \parallel Q'}$$

where $\Rightarrow$ can be replaced by any suitable process preorder. Here, the abstract process Q' takes the role of environment assumption when verifying P, and P' does the same when verifying Q. The circularity is broken inductively, as a result of the delay of one time unit from input to output of the Moore machines. Alur and Henzinger [AH96] extended this to the case of Mealy machines where there are no combinational cycles.

A limitation of this kind of proof rule is that the abstract processes P' and Q' do not typically have the same inputs and outputs as the detailed processes P and Q. In order for P' and Q' to be simple, they necessarily communicate at a more abstract level. In Kurshan's methology, this problem is approached by using process homomorphisms. This means that the user provides a function ϕ that maps detailed signals to abstract signals. One can thus reason compositionally as follows:

$$\phi(P) \Rightarrow P'$$
$$\frac{\phi(Q) \Rightarrow Q'}{\phi(P \parallel Q) \Rightarrow P' \parallel Q'}$$

Note, however, that we cannot use Q' as an environment assumption unless we are able to effectively invert the function ϕ. This is necessary to translate outputs of the abstract process Q' into inputs of the detailed process P. On the other hand, *downward* maps can be used effectively to provide the both the inputs of P (*i.e.*, its environment) and also the correctness conditions for its outputs, as a function of the abstract behavior of P' and Q'. This effectively puts the verification of P in an abstract context, an observation has been made in the context of symbolic simulation by Bryant and Beatty [BB94] and in the context of theorem provers by Cyrluk [Cyr96].

Note also that upward maps can be very complex. In the case of pipelines, for example, the upward abstraction map involves flushing the entire state of the pipeline, which may contain many instructions. Although in some cases this complexity can be dealt with, using BDD's [BF89] or sophisticated decision procedures [BD94, JDB95], we would prefer a methodology that decomposes the verification problem into small subproblems. In the case of pipelines, for example, downward refinement maps involving delay can yield separate verification subproblems for each stage of the pipeline.

To support such a compositional methodology in a model checking context, we present a system based on a generalized compositional rule for Mealy machines. It allows both upward and downward refinement maps, which are represented as arbitrary processes. Hence, maps may involve state and delay, if necessary. Further, the system is flexible enough to allow non-hierarchical abstractions. That is, an abstract specification may have a different structural decomposition from the low level implementation, and many abstract-level components may be multiplexed onto the same collection of low-level components. This flexibility to choose an arbitrary decomposition of the specification can be used to simplify the resulting verification subproblems. The system is implemented on top of the SMV symbolic model checker [McM93].

2   A compositional rule for Mealy machines

We begin by introducing a compositional rule for Mealy machines. For the present purposes, a Mealy machine will be defined as a collection of recurrence equations involving either zero delay or unit delay. For flexibility in specification, we allow machines to be underspecified, in the sense that there may be many solutions of the equations for any given input sequence. This does not however, imply nondeterminism in the automata theoretic sense, since our "machines" have no notion of internal state.

To be more specific, let S be a finite collection of signals, and let V be a finite universe of values. We interpret a signal as a sequence of values, or a function $\mathbb{N} \to V$. Let a *model* be any function $\pi : S \to \mathbb{N} \to V$. A *machine* is a predicate M of the form:

$$\bigwedge_{\sigma \in S} M_\sigma$$

The assertions M_σ, called components, may be in one of two forms, representing generalized *gates* and *latches*. A gate is of the form:

$$\bigvee_j \sigma(t) = f(\gamma_1(t) \ldots \gamma_k(t))$$

where the signals $\gamma_1 \ldots \gamma_k$ are the inputs of the gate, and f is a function $V^k \to V$. The finite disjunction allows the output of the gate to be incompletely specified as a function of its inputs. A latch is similar to a gate, but involves one time unit of delay, and a set of possible initial values. It is a component M_σ of the form:

$$\bigvee_j \sigma(t+1) = f(\gamma_1(t) \ldots \gamma_k(t))$$

$$\wedge$$

$$\bigvee_j \sigma(0) = init_j$$

This specifies the possible values of σ at time $t + 1$ as of function of the inputs at time t, and also specifies the possible values $init_j$ at time $t = 0$.

We will tacitly identify a machine with the set of models that satisfy it. We will say that machine Q implements machine P when $Q \Rightarrow P$, which is the same as saying that the set of models of Q is contained in the set of models of P.

Now, suppose we wish to prove that $Q \Rightarrow P$. Since P is a conjunction of assertions P_σ, expressible in temporal logic, we could simply use model checking to verify $Q \models P_\sigma$ for each σ. However, this would be unlikely to be effective in practice, since the state space of Q would be too large. To simplify the model checking problem, we could take only a subset of the components of Q as the "environment" when checking P_σ (a technique called localization), but it still might require a large number of components. Instead, assuming that P is simple and abstract, while Q is complex, we might like to take some other components of P as environment assumptions while proving P_σ. Intuitively, this would put the verification of P_σ in a more "abstract" context. Thus, for example, we might assume $P_{\sigma'}$ is correctly implemented when checking P_σ and vice versa. We can show that this reasoning is sound, provided there are no cycles of "gates".

To be more precise, let $<_M$, the dependency relation of machine M, be the set of pairs (γ, σ) such that M_σ is a gate (has zero delay) and γ is and input of M_σ. Now suppose there are no cycles in the joint dependency relations of machines Q and P. To verify $Q \Rightarrow P_\sigma$, we may instead verify $\mathcal{E}^\sigma \Rightarrow P_\sigma$, where $\mathcal{E}^\sigma$ is an "environment" machine, made up of arbitarily chosen components of P and Q, provided of course we do not chose P_σ itself.

Theorem 1. *Let P and Q be machines. For all $\sigma \in \mathcal{S}$, let $\mathcal{E}^\sigma$ be a machine such that:*

- *for all $\sigma' \in$ signals: $\mathcal{E}^\sigma_{\sigma'} = P_{\sigma'}$ or $\mathcal{E}^\sigma_{\sigma'} = Q_{\sigma'}$, and*
- *$\mathcal{E}^\sigma_\sigma = Q_\sigma$.*

Let $<^*$ be the relation $(<_P \cup <_Q)^*$. If $<^*$ is irreflexive then the following inference rule is sound:

$$\frac{\text{for all } \sigma : \mathcal{E}^\sigma \Rightarrow P_\sigma}{Q \Rightarrow P}$$

Proof. Define a lexical order $<$ over $\mathbb{N} \times \mathcal{S}$ where $(\tau', \sigma') < (\tau, \sigma)$ iff $\tau' < \tau$, or $\tau' = \tau$ and $\sigma' <^* \sigma$. Further, let $P_\sigma(\tau)$ denote P_σ for $t = \tau$. Now, consider a model π. Assume $\pi \models Q$ and assume by inductive hypothesis that $\pi \models \mathcal{E}^\sigma_{\sigma'}(\tau')$ for all $(\sigma', \tau') < (\tau, \sigma)$. Note that by definition, $\pi \models \mathcal{E}^\sigma_\sigma(\tau)$, since $\mathcal{E}^\sigma_\sigma = Q_\sigma$.

Now construct a model π' from π by changing only the values $\sigma'(\tau')$ for $(\sigma, \tau) < (\sigma', \tau')$, such that $\pi' \models \mathcal{E}^\sigma$. This can be done because $<^*$ containts $<_{\mathcal{E}^\sigma}$, hence each $\sigma'(\tau')$ can be chosen only as a function of previous values w.r.t. $<$. Since $\mathcal{E}^\sigma \Rightarrow P_\sigma$ it follows in particular that $\pi' \models P_\sigma(\tau)$, and hence $\pi \models P_\sigma(\tau)$. By induction over $<$, it follows that $\pi \models P$.

We can extend the above result to the case of proving that Q simultaneously implemements a collection of specifications $P_1, \ldots, P_n$. This theorem forms the basis of a system for design refinement, described in the next section. The proof is omitted here, but is along the same lines as the previous theorem.

Theorem 2. *Let Q and $P^1 \ldots P^n$ be machines. For all $i = 1 \ldots n$ and $\sigma \in \mathcal{S}$, let $\mathcal{E}^{i\sigma}$ be a machine such that:*

- *for all $\sigma' \in$ signals: $\mathcal{E}^{i\sigma}_{\sigma'} = Q_{\sigma'}$ or $\mathcal{E}^{i\sigma}_{\sigma'} = P^j_{\sigma'}$ for some j, and*
- *$\mathcal{E}^{i\sigma}_\sigma = Q_\sigma$.*

Let $<^*$ be the relation $[(\bigcup_i <_{P^i}) \cup <_Q]^*$. If $<^*$ is irreflexive then the following inference rule is sound:

$$\frac{\text{for all } i, \sigma : \mathcal{E}^{i\sigma} \Rightarrow P^i_\sigma}{Q \Rightarrow \bigwedge_i P_i}$$

3 Partial machines and refinement

We now introduce a *refinement* framework, that makes it possible to define a design by a collection of incremental changes to a specification machine, and to verify that the resulting machine (called the implementation machine) implies the orignal abstract machine. Each incremental change will be referred to as a *layer*, and is essentially a partially defined machine.

Let a *layer* M be an assertion of the form $\bigwedge_{\sigma \in \mathcal{S}(M)} M_\sigma$ where $\mathcal{S}(M) \subseteq \mathcal{S}$ and the assertions M_σ are either gates or latches, as before. A *design* is a partial order

$\mathcal{D} = (\mathcal{M}, <_\mathcal{D})$, where $\mathcal{M}$ is a set of layers. The intuition behind $<_\mathcal{D}$ is that $Q<_\mathcal{D}P$ when Q is intended as an incremental modification of P, in which case we say Q *refines* P. In order for an implementation to be uniquely defined, we require that for any signal σ, there is a unique least layer $\mathcal{I}^\sigma$ w.r.t. $<_\mathcal{D}$ such that $\sigma \in \mathcal{S}(\mathcal{I}^\sigma)$. The conjunction of these minimal definitions $\mathcal{I}^\sigma$ is termed the *implementation machine* of $\mathcal{D}$ and is denoted $\mathcal{I}^\mathcal{D}$. In the simplest case $<_\mathcal{D}$ will be a linear order over machines $\mathcal{M}_1, \dots, \mathcal{M}_n$. In this case, the implementation machine is the result obtained by starting with $\mathcal{M}_1$ (the specification) and substituting components of $\mathcal{M}_2, \dots, \mathcal{M}_n$ in sequence.

A design $\mathcal{D}$ will be said to be *correct* when

$$\mathcal{I}^\mathcal{D} \Rightarrow \bigwedge \mathcal{M}_\mathcal{D}$$

that is, when the implementation machine implies every layer of $\mathcal{D}$. In the linear order case, this implies in particular that it implements the original specification $\mathcal{M}_1$.

Note that we can verify correctness of a design compositionally using the inference rule of theorem 2. This requires us to choose an environment machine $\mathcal{E}^{M\sigma}$ to verify each component M_σ of each layer M in the design, excepting the implementation components. While the environments may be chosen manually, the following two heuristics can be applied automatically:

- For each σ, choose $\mathcal{E}^\sigma = M_\sigma$, where M is the maximal layer under $<_\mathcal{D}$ that defines σ.
- Drop any signal definitions that topologically cannot influence σ.

If we use these rules when verifying a sequence of local modifications, the verification of any given modification does not see the other modifications, since the environment is selected from the earliest, most abstract definitions.

3.1 Implementation in SMV

The verification framework described in the previous two sections has been implemented on top of the SMV model checker. The system has a simple language for describing Mealy machines. In this language, a gate is described by a statement of the form:

```
<σ> := <f(γ₁,...,γₖ)>;
```

while a latch is specified in the following way:

```
init(<σ>) := <initσ>;
next(<σ>) := <f(γ₁,...,γₖ)>;
```

In either case, we can leave a signal underspecified by indicating a choice of values in set brackets. For example,

```
x := y + {0,1};
```

stands for

$$x(t) = y + 0$$
$$\vee$$
$$x(t) = y + 1$$

The language also includes some "syntactic sugar" over the basic gates and latches, including nested conditional statements, and a method of specifying default values when one branch of a conditional is unspecified.

Each layer of the design is given a name, and is introduced by the keyword "layer". The partial order $<_{\mathcal{D}}$ is specified by statements of the form:

$<Q>$ refines $<P>$;

which denotes $Q<_{\mathcal{D}}P$. The SMV system verifies that the design thus specified is correct, according to the definition of the previous section. It does this by translating each non-implementation component of M_σ of each layer M into temporal logic.[1] For each such component an evironmeont $\mathcal{E}^{M\sigma}$ is selected, using user input and the above described heuristics. This environment is used as a model for model checking the temporal formula. The system also verifies the side condition of the compositional rule, requiring that the joint dependency relation be acyclic.

3.2   Example

As an example of compositional verification using the system, consider a "resource manager" circuit, which is used to allocate and free a collection of resources (say a collection of packet buffers). The module maintains a vector of status bits that indicate, for each resource, whether it is currently allocated or not. When an "allocate" request is received, the module may output the index of some free resource (changing the status of this resource to "allocated") or it may output a negative acknowledgement (NACK). When a "free" request is received, the module inputs a resource index and changes the status of that resource to "free". Allocation requests have either high or low priority. A low priority request must result in a NACK if fewer than k buffers are currently free (where k is a fixed constant).

A naïve and somewhat underspecified original specification of the resource manager is shown in figure 1. When an allocate request is received, it chooses a resource arbitrarily. If that resource is currently allocated, it produces a NACK. To check whether a low priority request is allowed, it simply sums up the vector of "allocated" bits and compares the result to k. Notice the "dafault" construct in the definition of "allocated". The meaning of this construct is that the first statement provides the default value for any given element of the vector when the second statement does not define it. For a latch, the default in case neither statement defines it is to keep the old value.

There are two refinements we would like to make to this specification. First, it is too time consuming to sum up the vector of "allocated" bits on every cycle. We would prefer to use an up/down counter to maintain a running total the number of "allocated" bits that are set. This refinement is shown in figure 2. Second, we need to choose a policy for selecting a resource to allocate. To do this, we will use a priority encoder to choose the unallocated resource of lowest index. To compute the NACK signal more quickly, we simply test the "sum"

---

[1] Note, this requires a minor extension to CTL that allows the "next" value of a variable to be expressed. This does not increase the complexity of the model checking problem over ordinary CTL.

```
layer toplevel : {
  init(allocated) := 0;
  index_out := 0 ..(n - 1);
  NACK := alloc_req & (allocated[index_out]
                      | ~high_priority & (n - sum) < k);
  default
    if(free_req)next(allocated[index_in]) := 0;
  in
    if(alloc_req & ~NACK)next(allocated[index_out]) := 1;
  sum := sigma(i = 0; i < n; i = i + 1)allocated[i];
}
```

Fig. 1. Original specification of resource manager.

value to see if there are any available resources. This refinement is shown in figure 2.

```
layer refinement1 : {
  init(sum) := 0;
  next(sum) := sum + (alloc_req & ~NACK)
            - (free_req & allocated[index_in]);
}
refinement1 refines toplevel;

layer refinement2 : {
  index_out := priority_encode(~allocated);
  NACK := alloc_req & (high_priority ? sum = n : (n - sum) < k);
}
refinement2 refines toplevel;
```

Fig. 2. Two refinements of the resource manager.

Note that these two refinements are mutually dependent. That is, if the refined "sum" logic computes its value incorrectly, then the NACK signal we produce may be incorrect. On the other hand, if the refined "NACK" logic is incorrect, causing an already allocated buffer to be allocated, then the "sum" counter will be corrupted. These two parts of the circuit are, in effect, engaged in a protocol, where each part guarantees to produce a correct output only if all its previous inputs have been correct. Despite this circularity, we can use the compositional rule to verify the two refinements separately, where each refinement uses the original specification as its environment. This simplifies the verification process, since the original specification has fewer latches than the refined version. Note also, that if the resource manager is used as part of the system, we can use the simple original specification as part of the enviroment when verifying other parts of the system, and need not take into account the refinements.

4 Hiding internal state of specifications

Typically, a specification contains some intermediate signals that are not intended to be part of the implementation *per se*, but are used only for specification purposes. For example, we might want to specify that a machine counts, producing a one at its output for every n ones occurring at the input. To do this, we could introduce a signal representing, for example, a binary modulo-n counter:

```
init(count) := 0;
next(count) := count + inp mod n;
out := inp & (count = n - 1);
```

There is, however, no reason why "count" should appear in the implementation, as it would be perfectly valid for the implementation to use, for example, a "one hot" encoded counter. What we would actually like to specify is that, for any implementation behavior, *there exists* a valuation for the signal "count" that makes it a legal behavior of the specification. In other words, we would like to be able to hide certain signals in the specification, in order to specify only externally visible behavior. Toward this end, we define a notion of "projected design" that makes it possible to write specifications with hidden internal state.

Let a *projected design* be a structure $\mathcal{P} = (\mathcal{D}, A_\mathcal{P})$, where $\mathcal{D} = (\mathcal{M}, <_\mathcal{D})$ is a design, and $A_\mathcal{P} \subseteq S$ is the set of internal, or unobservable signals. The implementation of a projected design is

$$\mathcal{I}^\mathcal{P} = \bigwedge_{\sigma \notin A_\mathcal{P}} \mathcal{I}_\sigma^\mathcal{D}$$

That is, in the projected design, the implementation includes only those implementation components of $\mathcal{D}$ that are *not* considered internal to the specification. A projected design $\mathcal{P}$ is said to be *correct* when

$$\mathcal{I}^\mathcal{P} \Rightarrow \exists A_\mathcal{P}. \bigwedge \mathcal{M}_\mathcal{D}$$

That is, for every behavior of the implementation, there must exist a valuation of the internal signals such that every layer in $\mathcal{D}$ is satisfied. This is in fact guaranteed to hold provided $\mathcal{D}$ is correct, and the unprojected implementation machine $\mathcal{I}^\mathcal{D}$ satisfies a simple condition: no signal not in $A_\mathcal{P}$ may depend on a signal in $A_\mathcal{P}$, via a gate or a latch. Put another way, the signals that remain in the projected implementation must be closed under the dependency relation. If this is the case, then for every model of the projected implementation, we can construct a valuation for the internal signals to create a model of the unprojected implementation. Thus, if the unprojected design is correct, then the projected design must also be correct.

Note that in the unprojected implementation, we do allow a dependency of internal signals on "visible" signals. These functions play the role of witness functions for the hidden signals, as we see in the proof of the following theorem:

Theorem 3. *Let $\mathcal{P} = (\mathcal{D}, A_\mathcal{P})$ be a projected design, such that for all $\sigma \notin A_\mathcal{P}$, for all inputs γ of $\mathcal{I}_\sigma^\mathcal{D}$, $\gamma \notin A_\mathcal{P}$. If*

$$\mathcal{I}^\mathcal{D} \Rightarrow \bigwedge \mathcal{M}_\mathcal{D}$$

then

$$\mathcal{I}^\mathcal{P} \Rightarrow \exists A_\mathcal{P}. \bigwedge \mathcal{M}_\mathcal{D}$$

Proof. Let π be a model of $\mathcal{I}^P$ and let $<$ be the same lexical order used in the proof of theorem 1. By modifying only the values of signals in A_P, we can construct a model π' of $\mathcal{I}^D$, the unprojected design. This is because the values of these signals depend functionally on only previous values w.r.t $<$, and no signals not in A_P depend on values that are modified. It follows that $\pi' \models \bigwedge \mathcal{M}_D$ and hence $\pi \models \exists A_P. \bigwedge \mathcal{M}_D$.

4.1 Refining internal signals – witness functions

An internal signal that is underspecified may be thought of as representing a nondeterministic choice. By refining this signal, we can in effect provide a "witness" that shows why any given execution of the implementation satisfies the specification. Note that neither the original specification nor the refinement of an internal signal is part of the implementation. The witness function merely serves as part of the proof of correctness of the design.

As an example, figure 3 shows an abstract specification for a two-way synchronous arbiter. An underspecified signal called "choice" determines which of the two requesters will be acknowledged. This is an internal signal, declared elsewhere using the keyword "abstract". Note that "choice" is nondeterministic when both request simultaneously. Figure 3 also shows a refinement of this specification, in which a latched signal called "turn" is used to break ties in a fair manner. The signal "choice" is redefined to be a function of "turn". This definition is not part of the implementation, but is simply used to prove that there exists a valuation of "choice" that makes the specification true in all cases.

```
layer toplevel : {
    choice := (req[0] & ~req[1]) ? 0 : (req[1] & ~req[0]) ? 1 : {0,1};
    ack[0] := req[0] & (choice = 0);
    ack[1] := req[1] & (choice = 1);
}

layer refinement : {
    init(turn) := 0;
    if(ack[turn]) next(turn) := ~turn;
    ack[0] := req[0] & (~req[1] | turn = 0);
    ack[1] := req[1] & (~req[0] | turn = 1);
    choice := (req[0] & ~req[1]) ? 0 : (req[1] & ~req[0]) ? 1 : turn;
}
refinement refines toplevel;
```

Fig. 3. Using a witness function for a nondeterministic choice.

5 Refinement maps

One important use of refinements is in specifying the downward refinement maps that give the detailed signals in terms of abstract signals. In the present framework, a refinement map is simply an itermediate layer in the design. To use a refinement map, one creates a sequence of two layers. The first defines the refinement maps, giving some implementation signals as a function of specification signals. Each component of the refinement map must be verified. When verifying one component, we can we can choose to use any other refinement map components in the environment. Thus, when verifying that the outputs of a given module are correct, we can use the refinement maps to generate the inputs to that module as a function of the abstract specification. In fact, the signal "sum" in the example of figure 1 can be viewed as playing the role of a refinement map. Notice how it divides the refinement verification problem into two parts, where each can be verified in the environment of the abstract specification. Note also that when we specify refinement maps, we can use any function that can be defined by a Mealy machine. In particular, this allows us to use refinement maps that involve delay. This is useful for hardware structures that have "latency", such as pipelines. The refinement maps may also include arbitrary finite state machines.

5.1 Example

As an example, suppose we would like to design a tranmitter/receiver pair that sends n-bit bytes (for fixed n) serially over a single wire. The original specification might look something like the code of figure 4. A "send" signal indicates that input data are ready to be sent, "NACK" indicates that the transmitter is busy, "DAV" indicates that data are available at the receiving end, and "received" indicates the the receiving end is ready for new data. Notice that "DAV" is underspecified, in the sense that when data are available, it may be either true or false. This is intended to allow for arbitrary delay in the actual transmission of the data. Notice also the conditional in the definition of "output_data". Because this is a gate, the default in case the condition is false is that the signal is unspecified. This means the implementation may output any data value in the case when "DAV" is false.

```
layer toplevel :  {
  init(full) := 0;
  next(full) := received ? 0 : send ? 1 : full;
  NACK := send & full;
  if(send & ~full) next(data) := input_data;
  DAV := full ? {0,1} : 0;
  if(DAV) output_data := data;
  received := DAV ? {0,1} : 0;
}
```

Fig. 4. Specification of transmitter/receiver.

The next step in the design is to formulate a refinement map that defines the sequence of bits seen on the serial line as a function of the abstract specification signals. To do this, we need to introduce some state, in the form of a counter that keeps track of the bit number being transmitted. The refinement map is shown in figure 5.

Given this refinement map, we can now design and verify the receiver and transmitter separately. The actual implementation of these components might use shift registers, as shown in figure 6. The enviromnent for verifying each of

```
layer refinement_map :  {
  init(transmitting) := 0;
  if(send & ~NACK) next(transmitting) := 1;
  else if(count = (n - 1)) next(transmitting) := 0;
  init(count) := 0;
  if(transmitting){
    next(count) := count + 1 mod n;
    serial_line := data[count];
  }
}
refinement_map refines toplevel;
```

Fig. 5. Refinement map definining serial line behavior

these two component refinements includes the refinement map and the abstract specification, but not the other component. The purpose of the refinement map is to define the interface between two components, and thus allow separate design and verification of the two components. In general, refinement maps can provide a way of managing the complexity of interfaces between modules, by defining interface signals, which may be encoded in fairly complex ways, in terms of simpler, more abstract data streams.

```
layer tx_refinement :  {
  if(send & ~NACK) next(tx_shifter) := input_data;
  else next(tx_shifter) := tx_shifter >> 1;
  serial_line := tx_shifter[0];
}
tx_refinement refines refinement_map;

layer rx_refinement :  {
  if(transmitting){
    next(rx_shifter[n-1]) := serial_line;
    next(rx_shifter[(n-2)..0]) := rx_shifter >> 1;
  }
  DAV := full & ~transmitting;
  output_data := rx_shifter;
}
rx_refinement refines refinement_map;
```

Fig. 6. Separate refinements of transmitter and receiver.

6 Conclusions

We have described a compositional framework for the verification of hardware designs. It is designed to allow the expression of downward refinement masps as Mealy machines, and to support design by a sequence of incremental modifications that may be verified independently. The framework has been implemented on top of the SMV symbolic model checking system. Although it is not discussed here, the system also supports assume-guarantee style reasoning using linear time temporal logic. This is intended mainly for reasoning about eventualities.

One extension to the system that is planned is to support a notion of streams (such as streams of intructions of memory transactions) that are ordered, but are not assigned specific times in the implementation. Each element of such a stream could be defined as a finite state machine representing the different stages of execution of the given operation in the machine. By making each abstract operation a distinct "layer" of the specification, one could verify in a modular way that a single operation is processed through the system correctly, and then deal separately with other issues such as ordering guarantees and liveness. Finally, it is also possible that a hybrid approach could be taken, where some refinement obligations are handled by a model checker and others by a general-purpose proof assistant, or a collection of predefined transformations. This might be particularly useful for handling large, regular structures such as memories, and hardware that manipulates large data items, such as packets. A compositional framework of this sort could provide a practical way of integrating model checking and theorem proving.

References

[AH96]   R. Alur and T. A. Henzinger. Reactive modules. In *11th annual IEEE symp. Logic in Computer Science (LICS '96)*, 1996.

[BB94]   D. L. Beatty and R. E. Bryant. Formally verifying a microprocessor using a simulation methodology. In *31st Design Automation Conference*, pages 596–602, 1994.

[BD94]   J. R. Burch and D. L. Dill. Automatic verification of pipelined microprocessor control. In D. L. Dill, editor, *Conf. Computer-Aided Verification (CAV '94)*, volume 818 of *LNCS*. Springer-Verlag, 1994.

[BF89]   S. Bose and A. Fisher. Verifying pipelined hardware using symbolic logic simulation. In *IEEE International Conference on Computer Design*, 1989.

[Cyr96]   D. Cyrluk. Inverting the abstraction mapping: a methodology for hardware verification. In M. Srivas and A. Camilleri, editors, *Formal Methods in Computer-Aided Design (FMCAD '96)*, volume 1166 of *LNCS*. Springer-Verlag, 1996.

[GL94]   O. Grümberg and D. E. Long. Model checking and modular verification. *ACM Trans. Programming Languages and Systems*, 16(3):843–871, 1994.

[JDB95]   R. B. Jones, D. L. Dill, and J. R. Burch. Efficient validity checking for processor verification. In *IEEE/ACM Int. Conf. on Computer Aided Design (ICCAD '95)*, 1995.

[Kur87]   R. P. Kurshan. Reducibility in analysis of coordination. In *LNCS*, volume 103, pages 19–39. Springer-Verlag, 1987.

[Kur94]   R. P. Kurshan. *Computer-Aided Verification of Coordinating Processes*. Princeton, 1994.

[Lam83]   L. Lamport. Specifying concurrent program modules. *ACM Trans. Programming Languages and Systems*, 5:190–222, 1983.

[McM93]   K. L. McMillan. *Symbolic Model Checking*. Kluwer, 1993.

[Pnu85]   A. Pnueli. In transition from global to modular temporal reasoning about programs. In K. Apt, editor, *Logics and Models of Concurrent Systems*, pages 123–144. Springer-Verlag, 1985.

[Wol83]   P. Wolper. Temporal logic can be more expressive. *Information and Control*, 56:72–99, 1983.

Module Checking Revisited*

Orna Kupferman[1]** and Moshe Y. Vardi[2]***

[1] EECS Department, UC Berkeley, Berkeley CA 94720-1770, U.S.A.
Email: orna@eecs.berkeley.edu
[2] Rice University, Department of Computer Science, Houston, TX 77251-1892, U.S.A.
Email: vardi@cs.rice.edu, URL: http://www.cs.rice.edu/~vardi

Abstract. When we verify the correctness of an open system with respect to a desired requirement, we should take into consideration the different environments with which the system may interact. Each environment induces a different behavior of the system, and we want all these behaviors to satisfy the requirement. *Module checking* is an algorithmic method that checks, given an open system (modeled as a finite structure) and a desired requirement (specified by a temporal-logic formula), whether the open system satisfies the requirement with respect to all environments. In this paper we extend the module-checking method with respect to two orthogonal issues. Both issues concern the fact that often we are not interested in satisfaction of the requirement with respect to all environments, but only with respect to these that meet some restriction. We consider the case where the environment has *incomplete information* about the system; i.e., when the system has internal variables, which are not readable by its environment, and the case where some *assumptions* are known about environment; i.e., when the system is guaranteed to satisfy the requirement only when its environment satisfies certain assumptions. We study the complexities of the extended module-checking problems. In particular, we show that for universal temporal logics (e.g., LTL, ∀CTL, and ∀CTL*), module checking with incomplete information coincides with module checking, which by itself coincides with model checking. On the other hand, for non-universal temporal logics (e.g., CTL and CTL*), module checking with incomplete information is harder than module checking, which is by itself harder than model checking.

1 Introduction

Temporal logics, which are modal logics geared towards the description of the temporal ordering of events, have been adopted as a powerful tool for specifying and verifying reactive systems [Pnu81]. One of the most significant developments in this area is the discovery of algorithmic methods for verifying temporal-logic properties of *finite-state* systems [CE81, QS81, LP85, CES86]. This derives its significance both from the fact that many synchronization and communication protocols can be modeled as finite-state systems, as well as from the great ease of use of fully algorithmic methods.

We distinguish between two types of temporal logics: *universal* and *non-universal*. Both logics describe the computation tree induced by the system. Formulas of universal temporal logics describe requirements that should hold in all the branches of the tree [GL94]. These requirements may be either linear (e.g., in all computations, only finitely many requests are sent) or branching (e.g., in all computations we eventually reach a state from which, no matter how

---

* Part of this work was done in Bell Laboratories during the DIMACS special year on Logic and Algorithms.
** Supported in part by the ONR YIP award N00014-95-1-0520, by the NSF CAREER award CCR-9501708, by the NSF grant CCR-9504469, by the AFOSR contract F49620-93-1-0056, by the ARO MURI grant DAAH-04-96-1-0341, by the ARPA grant NAG2-892, and by the SRC contract 95-DC-324.036.
*** Supported in part by the NSF grant CCR-9628400.

we continue, no requests are sent). In both cases, the more behaviors the system has, the harder it is for the system to satisfy the requirements. Indeed, universal temporal logics induce the *simulation* order between systems [Mil71, CGB86]. That is, a system M simulates a system M' if and only if all universal temporal logic formulas that are satisfied in M' are satisfied in M as well. On the other hand, formulas of non-universal temporal logics may also impose possibility requirements on the system (e.g., there exists a computation in which only finitely many requests are sent). Here, it is no longer true that simulation between systems corresponds to agreement on satisfaction of requirements. Indeed, it might be that adding behaviors to the system helps it to satisfy a possibility requirement or, equivalently, that disabling some of its behaviors causes the requirement not to be satisfied.

We also distinguish between two types of systems: *closed* and *open* [HP85]. A closed system is a system whose behavior is completely determined by the state of the system. An open system is a system that interacts with its environment and whose behavior depends on this interaction. Thus, while in a closed system all the nondeterministic choices are internal, and resolved by the system, in an open system there are also external nondeterministic choices, which are resolved by the environment [Hoa85]. In order to check whether a closed system satisfies a required property, we translate the system into some formal model, specify the property with a temporal-logic formula, and check formally that the model satisfies the formula. Hence the name *model checking* for the verification methods derived from this viewpoint. In order to check whether an open system satisfies a required property, we should check the behavior of the system with respect to any environment, and often there is much uncertainty regarding the environment [FZ88]. In particular, it might be that the environment does not enable all the external nondeterministic choices. To see this, consider a sandwich-dispensing machine that serves, upon request, sandwiches with either ham or cheese. The machine is an open system and an environment for the system is an infinite line of hungry people. Since each person in the line can like either both ham and cheese, or only ham, or only cheese, each person suggests a different disabling of the external nondeterministic choices. Accordingly, there are many different possible environments to consider.

It turned out that model-checking methods are applicable also for verification of open systems with respect to universal temporal-logic formulas [MP92, KV96]. To see this, consider a composition of an open system with a maximal environment; i.e., an environment that enables all the external nondeterministic choices. This composition is a closed system, and it is simulated by any other composition of the system with some environment. Therefore, one can check satisfaction of universal requirements in an open system by model checking the composition of the system with this maximal environment. As discussed in [KV96], this approach can not be adapted when verifying an open system with respect to non-universal requirements. Here, satisfaction of the requirements with respect to the maximal environment does not imply their satisfaction with respect to all environments. Hence, we should explicitly make sure that all possibility requirements are satisfied, no matter how the environment restricts the system. For example, verifying that the sandwich-dispensing machine described above can always eventually serve ham, we want to make sure that this can happen no matter what the eating habits of the people in line are. Note that while this requirement holds with respect to the maximal environment, it does not hold, for instance, in an environment in which all the people in line do not like ham.

In [KV96], we suggested *module checking* as a general method for verification of open systems. Given an open system M and a temporal-logic formula ψ, the module-checking problem asks whether for all possible environments $\mathcal{E}$, the composition of M with $\mathcal{E}$ satisfies ψ. In this paper we extend the module-checking method with respect to two orthogonal issues. Both issues concern the fact that often we are not interested in satisfaction of ψ with respect to all environments, but only with respect to those that meet some restriction. In particular, we consider the case where $\mathcal{E}$ has *incomplete information* about M; i.e., not all the variables of M are readable by $\mathcal{E}$, and the case where some *assumptions* are known about $\mathcal{E}$. We now describe these extensions in more detail.

An interaction between a system and its environment proceeds through a designated set of input and output variables. In addition, the system often has internal variables, which the environment cannot read. If two states of the system differ only in the values of unreadable variables, then the environment cannot distinguish between them. Similarly, if two computations of the system differ only in the values of unreadable variables along them, then the environment cannot distinguish between them either and thus, its behaviors along these computations are the same. More formally, when we compose a system M with an environment $\mathcal{E}$, and several states in the composition look the same and have the same history according to $\mathcal{E}$'s incomplete information, then the nondeterministic choices done by $\mathcal{E}$ in each of these states coincide. In the sandwich-dispensing machine example, the people in line cannot see whether the ham and the cheese are fresh. Therefore, their choices are independent of this missing information. Given an open system M with a partition of M's variables into readable and unreadable, and a temporal-logic formula ψ, the module-checking problem with incomplete information asks whether the composition of M with $\mathcal{E}$ satisfies ψ, for all environments $\mathcal{E}$ whose nondeterministic choices are independent of the unreadable variables (that is, $\mathcal{E}$ behaves the same in indistinguishable states).

Often, the environment is known to satisfy some assumptions. In the sandwich-dispensing machine example, it may be useful to know that the machine is located in a vegetarian village. In the *assume-guarantee* paradigm [Jon83, Lam83], the specification of an open system consists of two parts. One part describes the guaranteed behavior of the system. The other part describes the assumed behavior of the environment with which the module is interacting. A system M then satisfies a specification with assumption φ and guarantee ψ if and only if in all compositions of M with $\mathcal{E}$, if the composition satisfies φ, then it satisfies ψ as well. Checking assume-guarantee specifications is helpful in modular verification [GL94]. For universal temporal logics, automatic methods for this check are suggested in [Pnu85, Var95, KV95]. These methods depend on the fact that the simulation order captures agreement on universal temporal-logic formulas, and they cannot be extended to handle non-universal formulas. Module checking can be viewed as a special case of the assume-guarantee paradigm, where the guarantee may be any formula, not necessarily a universal one, and the assumption is **true**. We extend here module checking to handle arbitrary assumptions. This suggests a complete and uniform assume-guarantee paradigm, for both the universal and non-universal settings, with both complete and incomplete information.

We solve the problems of module checking with assume-guarantee specifications and with incomplete information and consider their complexities. It turns out that while checking assume-guarantee specifications is not harder than module checking, the presence of incomplete information makes module checking more complex. To see why, consider an environment of a system with unreadable variables. Recall that several states in the composition of the system and the environment may be different and still be indistinguishable by the environment. Accordingly, the environment should behave the same in these states. Such a condition on the behavior of the environment relates remote nodes in the computation tree of the system, and there is no regular condition that relates these nodes (i.e., one cannot define an automaton that accepts all trees in which nodes that are indistinguishable by the environment have the same label). This need to relate indistinguishable nodes makes incomplete information very challenging.

We claim that *alternation* is a suitable and helpful mechanism for coping with incomplete information. Using *alternating tree automata*, we show that the problem of module checking with incomplete information is decidable. In particular, it is EXPTIME-complete and 2EXPTIME-complete for CTL and CTL*, respectively. As the module-checking problem for CTL is hard for

EXPTIME already for environments with complete information, it might seem as if incomplete information can be handled at no cost. This is, however, not true. While both problems can be solved in time that is exponential in the size of the formula, only the one with complete information can be solved in time that is polynomial in the size of the system [KV96]. On the other hand, module checking with incomplete information requires time that is exponential in both the formula and the system. Keeping in mind that the system to be checked is typically a parallel composition of several components, which by itself hides an exponential blow-up, this implies that checking non-universal properties of open systems with internal variables is rather intractable.

2 Preliminaries

2.1 Trees and Labeled Trees

Given a finite set Υ, an Υ-*tree* is a nonempty set $T \subseteq \Upsilon^*$ such that if $s \cdot v \in T$, where $s \in \Upsilon^*$ and $v \in \Upsilon$, then also $s \in T$. When Υ is not important or clear from the context, we call T a tree. The elements of T are called *nodes*, and the empty word ϵ is the *root* of T. For every $s \in T$, the nodes $s \cdot v \in T$ where $v \in \Upsilon$ are the *children* of s. An Υ-tree T is a *full infinite tree* if $T = \Upsilon^*$. Each node s of T has a *direction* in Υ. The direction of the root is some designated $v_0 \in \Upsilon$. The direction of a node $s \cdot v$ is v. An *infinite path* π of T is a set $\pi \subseteq T$ such that $\epsilon \in \pi$ and for every $s \in \pi$ there exists a unique $v \in \Upsilon$ such that $s \cdot v \in \pi$. Given two finite sets Υ and Σ, a Σ-*labeled* Υ-*tree* is a pair $\langle T, V \rangle$ where T is an Υ-tree and $V : T \rightarrow \Sigma$ maps each node of T to a letter in Σ. When Υ and Σ are not important or clear from the context, we call $\langle T, V \rangle$ a labeled tree.

For finite sets X and Y, and a node $s \in (X \times Y)^*$, let $hide_Y(s)$ be the node in X^* obtained from s by replacing each letter $(x \cdot y)$ by the letter x. For example (see figure), when $X = Y = \{0, 1\}$, the node 0010 of the $(X \times Y)$-tree on the right corresponds, by $hide_Y$, to the node 01 of the X-tree on the left. Note that the nodes 0011, 0110, and 0111 of the $(X \times Y)$-tree also correspond to the node 01 of the X-tree.

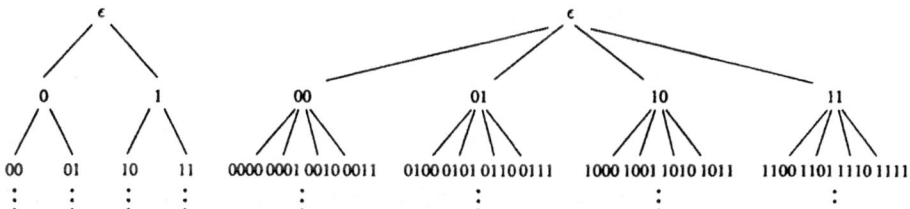

Let Z be a finite set. For a Z-labeled X-tree $\langle T, V \rangle$, we define the Y-*widening* of $\langle T, V \rangle$, denoted $wide_Y(\langle T, V \rangle)$, as the Z-labeled $(X \times Y)$-tree $\langle T', V' \rangle$ where for every $s \in T$, we have $hide_Y^{-1}(s) \subseteq T'$ and for every $t \in T'$, we have $V'(t) = V(hide_Y(t))$. Note that for every node $t \in T'$, and $x \in X$, the children $t \cdot (x \cdot y)$ of t, for all y, agree on their label in $\langle T', V' \rangle$. Indeed, they are all labeled with $V(hide_Y(t) \cdot x)$.

2.2 Modules and Composition of Modules

We describe a system by a *module* $M = \langle I, O, H, W, w_0, R, L \rangle$, where

- I, O, and H are sets of input, readable output, and hidden (internal) variables, respectively. We assume that I, O, and H are pairwise disjoint, we use K to denote the variables known to the environment; thus $K = I \cup O$, and we use P to denote all variables; thus $P = K \cup H$.
- W is a set of states, and $w_0 \in W$ is an initial state.

- $R \subseteq W \times W$ is a total transition relation. For $\langle w, w' \rangle \in R$, we say that w' is a successor of w. Requiring R to be total means that every state w has at least one successor.
- $L : W \to 2^P$ maps each state to the set of variables that hold in this state. The intuition is that in every state w, the module reads $L(w) \cap I$ and writes $L(w) \cap (O \cup H)$.

Note that M has no fairness condition. The difficulties caused by adding such a condition are orthogonal to the problems considered in this work. As we shall further discuss in Section 3.2, our framework can be easily adjusted to handle modules with fairness conditions. A *computation* of M is a sequence $w_0, w_1, \ldots$ of states, such that for all $i \geq 0$ we have $\langle w_i, w_{i+1} \rangle \in R$. We define the *size* $|M|$ of M as $(|W| * |P|) + |R|$. We assume, without loss of generality, that all the states of M are labeled differently; i.e., there exist no w_1 and w_2 in W for which $L(w_1) = L(w_2)$ (otherwise, we can add variables in H that differentiate states with identical labeling). With each module M we can associate a computation tree $\langle T_M, V_M \rangle$ obtained by pruning M from the initial state. More formally, $\langle T_M, V_M \rangle$ is a 2^P-labeled 2^P-tree (not necessarily with a fixed branching degree). Each node of $\langle T_M, V_M \rangle$ corresponds to a state of M, with the root corresponding to the initial state. A node corresponding to a state w is labeled by $L(w)$ and its children correspond to the successors of w in M. The assumption that the nodes are labeled differently enable us to embody $\langle T_M, V_M \rangle$ in a $(2^P)^*$-tree, with a node with direction v labeled v.

A module M is *closed* iff $I = \emptyset$. Otherwise, it is *open*. Consider an open module M. The module interacts with some environment $\mathcal{E}$ that supplies its inputs. When M is in state w, its ability to move to a certain successor w' of w is conditioned by the behavior of its environment. If, for example, $L(w') \cap I = \sigma$ and the environment does not supply σ to M, then M cannot move to w'. Thus, the environment may disable some of M's transitions. We can think of an environment to M as a *strategy* $\mathcal{E} : (2^K)^* \to \{\top, \bot\}$ that maps a finite history s of a computation (as seen by the environment) to either $\top$, meaning that the environment enables M to trace s, or $\bot$, meaning that the environment does not enable M to trace s. In other words, if M reaches a state w by tracing some $s \in (2^K)^*$, and a successor w' of w has $L(w) \cap K = \sigma$, then an interaction of M with $\mathcal{E}$ can proceed from w to w' iff $\mathcal{E}(s \cdot \sigma) = \top$. We say that the tree $\langle (2^K)^*, \mathcal{E} \rangle$ *maintains* the strategy applied by $\mathcal{E}$. We denote by $M \lhd \mathcal{E}$ the composition of M with $\mathcal{E}$; that is, the tree obtained by pruning from the computation tree $\langle T_M, V_M \rangle$ subtrees according to $\mathcal{E}$. Note that $\mathcal{E}$ may disable all the successors of w. We say that a composition $M \lhd \mathcal{E}$ is *deadlock free* iff for every state w, at least one successor of w is enabled. Given M, we can define the *maximal environment* $\mathcal{E}_{max}$ for M. The maximal environment has $\mathcal{E}_{max}(x) = \top$ for all $x \in (2^K)^*$; thus it enables all the transitions of M.

The hiding and widening operators (see Section 2.1) enable us to refer to the interaction of M with $\mathcal{E}$ as seen by both M and $\mathcal{E}$. As we shall see below, this interaction looks different from the two points of views. First, clearly, the labels of the computation tree of M, as seen by $\mathcal{E}$, do not contain variables in H. Consequently, $\mathcal{E}$ thinks that $\langle T_M, V_M \rangle$ is a 2^K-tree, rather than a 2^P-tree. Indeed, $\mathcal{E}$ cannot distinguish between two nodes that differ only in the values of variables in H in their labels. Accordingly, a branch of $\langle T_M, V_M \rangle$ into two such nodes is viewed by $\mathcal{E}$ as a single transition. This incomplete information of $\mathcal{E}$ is reflected in its strategy, which is independent of H. Thus, successors of a state that agree on the labeling of the readable variables are either all enabled or all disabled. Formally, if $\langle (2^K)^*, \mathcal{E} \rangle$ is the $\{\top, \bot\}$-labeled 2^K-tree that maintains the strategy applied by $\mathcal{E}$, then the $\{\top, \bot\}$-labeled 2^P-tree $wide_{(2^H)}(\langle (2^K)^*, \mathcal{E} \rangle)$ maintains the "full" strategy for $\mathcal{E}$, as seen by someone that sees both K and H.

Another way to see the effect of incomplete information is to associate with each environment $\mathcal{E}$ a tree obtained from $\langle T_M, V_M \rangle$ by pruning some of its subtrees. A subtree with root $s \in T_M$ is pruned iff $K'(hide_{(2^H)}(s)) = \bot$. Every two nodes s_1 and s_2 that are indistinguishable according to $\mathcal{E}$'s incomplete information have $hide_{(2^H)}(s_1) = hide_{(2^H)}(s_2)$. Hence, either both subtrees with roots s_1 and s_2 are pruned or both are not pruned. Note that once $\mathcal{E}(x) = \perp$ for some $s \in (2^K)^*$, we can assume that $\mathcal{E}(s \cdot t)$ for all $t \in (2^K)^*$ is also $\perp$. Indeed, once the environment disables the transition to a certain node s, it actually disables the transitions to all the nodes in the subtree with root s. Note also that $M \lhd \mathcal{E}$ is deadlock free iff for every $s \in T_M$ with $\mathcal{E}(hide_{(2^H)}(s)) = \top$, at least one direction $v \in 2^P$ has $s \cdot v \in T_M$ and $\mathcal{E}(hide_{(2^H)}(s \cdot v)) = \top$.

3 Module Checking

The *module-checking* problem (with complete information) is defined as follows. Let M be a module with $H = \emptyset$, and let ψ be a temporal-logic formula over the set P of M's variables. Does $M \lhd \mathcal{E}$ satisfy ψ for every environment $\mathcal{E}$ for which $M \lhd \mathcal{E}$ is deadlock free? When the answer to the module-checking question is positive, we say that M *reactively satisfies* ψ, denoted $M \models_r \psi$. The module-checking problem is introduced and solved in [KV96][3]. We define two orthogonal extensions of the module-checking problem:

- *Module Checking with Incomplete Information*: Let M be a module and let ψ be a temporal-logic formula over P. Does $M \lhd \mathcal{E}$ satisfy ψ for every environment $\mathcal{E}$ for which $M \lhd \mathcal{E}$ is deadlock free?
- *Assume-Guarantee Module Checking*: Let M be a module with $H = \emptyset$ and let φ and ψ be temporal-logic formulas over P. Does $M \lhd \mathcal{E}$ satisfy ψ for every environment $\mathcal{E}$ for which $M \lhd \mathcal{E}$ is deadlock free and satisfies φ? When the answer to the assume-guarantee module-checking question is positive, we say that M reactively satisfies ψ with assumption φ, denoted $\langle \varphi \rangle M \langle \psi \rangle$.

In this section we solve the two extended problems, as well as the problem of assume-guarantee module checking with incomplete information, which subsumes them. We consider temporal-logic formulas in LTL, CTL, and CTL*. We first handle the case where ψ and φ are universal temporal-logic formulas. As shown in [KV96], checking whether M reactively satisfies a universal formula ψ can be reduced to checking whether $M \lhd \mathcal{E}_{max}$ satisfies ψ. Since $M \lhd \mathcal{E}_{max}$ is simulated by any composition $M \lhd \mathcal{E}$ irrespective of the variables readable by $\mathcal{E}$, this remains valid in the presence of incomplete information. In addition, the assume-guarantee problem for LTL, $\forall$CTL, and $\forall$CTL* (the universal fragments of CTL and CTL*, in which only universal path quantification is allowed) has been studied in the literature. Hence the following theorem.

Theorem 1.

(1) [KV96] *The module-checking problem with incomplete information is PTIME-complete (and solvable in linear time) for $\forall$CTL and is PSPACE-complete for LTL and $\forall$CTL*.*

(2) [Pnu85, KV95] *The assume-guarantee module-checking problem is PSPACE-complete for LTL and $\forall$CTL and is EXPSPACE-complete for $\forall$CTL*.*

As with module checking, things become more challenging when we turn to solve the problems for the case ψ and φ are not necessarily universal temporal-logic formulas. We first show that assume-guarantee module checking can be easily reduced to module checking.

Lemma 2. *For every module M and formulas φ and ψ, we have $\langle \varphi \rangle M \langle \psi \rangle$ iff $M \models_r \varphi \to \psi$.*

---

[3] In [KV96], we define a module using system and environment states, and only transitions from environment states may be disabled. Here, the interaction of the system with its environment is more explicit, and transitions are disabled by the environment assigning values to the system's input variables.

Lemma 2 follows immediately from the definition of assume-guarantee module checking. As the reduction to module checking is so simple, one may wonder why the original assume-guarantee problem, with φ and ψ in universal logics could not be simply reduced to model checking. The reason lies in the fact that universal temporal logics are not closed under negation. Thus, the formula $\varphi \to \psi$ is no longer a universal temporal-logic formula, and checking it with respect to any environment cannot be done easily. The reduction above implies that assume-guarantee module checking is not harder than module checking. As assume-guarantee module checking is also at least as hard as module checking, the theorem below follows from the known complexity bounds for the module-checking problem [KV96].

Theorem 3. *The assume-guarantee module-checking problem is EXPTIME-complete for CTL and is 2EXPTIME-complete for CTL*.*

While handling of assumptions about the environment is easy, handling incomplete information is complicated. The solution we suggest is based on alternating tree automata and is outlined below. In Sections 3.1 and 3.2, we define alternating tree automata and describe the solutions in detail. We start by recalling the solution to the module-checking problem. Given M and ψ, we proceed as follows.

A1. Define a nondeterministic tree automaton $\mathcal{A}_M$ that accepts all the 2^P-labeled trees that correspond to compositions of M with some $\mathcal{E}$ for which $M \lhd \mathcal{E}$ is deadlock free. Thus, each tree accepted by $\mathcal{A}_M$ is obtained from $\langle T_M, V_M \rangle$ by pruning some of its subtrees.

A2. Define a nondeterministic tree automaton $\mathcal{A}_{\neg\psi}$ that accepts all the 2^P-labeled trees that do not satisfy ψ.

A3. $M \models_r \psi$ iff no composition $M \lhd \mathcal{E}$ satisfies $\neg\psi$, thus iff the intersection of $\mathcal{A}_M$ and $\mathcal{A}_{\neg\psi}$ is empty.

The reduction of the module-checking problem to the emptiness problem for tree automata implies, by the finite-model property of tree automata [Eme85], that defining reactive satisfaction with respect to only *finite-state* environments is equivalent to the current definition.

In the presence of incomplete information, not all possible pruning of $\langle T_M, V_M \rangle$ correspond to compositions of M with some $\mathcal{E}$. In order to correspond to such a composition, a tree should be *consistent in its pruning*. A tree is consistent in its pruning iff for every two nodes that the paths leading to them differ only in values of variables in H (i.e., every two nodes that have the same history according to $\mathcal{E}$'s incomplete information), either both nodes are pruned or both nodes are not pruned. Intuitively, hiding variables from the environment makes it easier for M to reactively satisfy a requirement: out of all the pruning of $\langle T_M, V_M \rangle$ that should satisfy the requirement in the case of complete information, only these that are consistent should satisfy the requirement in the presence of incomplete information. Unfortunately, the consistency condition is non-regular, and cannot be checked by an automaton. In order to circumvent this difficulty, we employ alternating tree automata. We solve the module-checking problem with incomplete information as follows.

B1. Define an alternating tree automaton $\mathcal{A}_{M,\neg\psi}$ that accepts a $\{\top, \bot\}$-labeled 2^K-tree iff it corresponds to a strategy $\langle (2^K)^*, \mathcal{E} \rangle$ such that $M \lhd \mathcal{E}$ is deadlock free and does not satisfy ψ.

B2. $M \models_r \psi$ iff all deadlock free compositions of M with $\mathcal{E}$ that is independent of H satisfy ψ, thus iff no strategy induces a computation tree that does not satisfy ψ, thus iff $\mathcal{A}_{M,\neg\psi}$ is empty.

We now turn to a detailed description of the solution of the module-checking problem with incomplete information, and the complexity results it entails. For that, we first define formally alternating tree automata.

3.1 Alternating Tree Automata

Alternating tree automata generalize nondeterministic tree automata and were first introduced in [MS87]. An alternating tree automaton $\mathcal{A} = \langle \Sigma, Q, q_0, \delta, \alpha \rangle$ runs on full Σ-labeled Υ-trees (for an agreed set Υ of directions). It consists of a finite set Q of states, an initial state $q_0 \in Q$, a transition function δ, and an acceptance condition α (a condition that defines a subset of Q^ω).

For a set Υ of directions, let $\mathcal{B}^+(\Upsilon \times Q)$ be the set of positive Boolean formulas over $\Upsilon \times Q$; i.e., Boolean formulas built from elements in $\Upsilon \times Q$ using $\wedge$ and $\vee$, where we also allow the formulas **true** and **false** and, as usual, $\wedge$ has precedence over $\vee$. The transition function $\delta : Q \times \Sigma \to \mathcal{B}^+(\Upsilon \times Q)$ maps a state and an input letter to a formula that suggests a new configuration for the automaton. For example, when $\Upsilon = \{0, 1\}$, having

$$\delta(q, \sigma) = (0, q_1) \wedge (0, q_2) \vee (0, q_2) \wedge (1, q_2) \wedge (1, q_3)$$

means that when the automaton is in state q and reads the letter σ, it can either send two copies, in states q_1 and q_2, to direction 0 of the tree, or send a copy in state q_2 to direction 0 and two copies, in states q_2 and q_3, to direction 1. Thus, unlike nondeterministic tree automata, here the transition function may require the automaton to send several copies to the same direction or allow it not to send copies to all directions.

A *run of an alternating automaton* $\mathcal{A}$ on an input Σ-labeled Υ-tree $\langle T, V \rangle$ is a tree $\langle T_r, r \rangle$ in which the root is labeled by q_0 and every other node is labeled by an element of $\Upsilon^* \times Q$. Each node of T_r corresponds to a node of T. A node in T_r, labeled by (x, q), describes a copy of the automaton that reads the node x of T and visits the state q. Note that many nodes of T_r can correspond to the same node of T; in contrast, in a run of a nondeterministic automaton on $\langle T, V \rangle$ there is a one-to-one correspondence between the nodes of the run and the nodes of the tree. The labels of a node and its children have to satisfy the transition function. For example, if $\langle T, V \rangle$ is a $\{0, 1\}$-tree with $V(\epsilon) = a$ and $\delta(q_0, a) = ((0, q_1) \vee (0, q_2)) \wedge ((0, q_3) \vee (1, q_2))$, then the nodes of $\langle T_r, r \rangle$ at level 1 include the label $(0, q_1)$ or $(0, q_2)$, and include the label $(0, q_3)$ or $(1, q_2)$. Each infinite path ρ in $\langle T_r, r \rangle$ is labeled by a word $r(\rho)$ in Q^ω. Let $inf(\rho)$ denote the set of states in Q that appear in $r(\rho)$ infinitely often. A run $\langle T_r, r \rangle$ is accepting iff all its infinite paths satisfy the acceptance condition. In *Büchi* alternating tree automata, $\alpha \subseteq Q$, and an infinite path ρ satisfies α iff $inf(\rho) \cap \alpha \neq \emptyset$. As with nondeterministic automata, an automaton accepts a tree iff there exists an accepting run on it. We denote by $\mathcal{L}(\mathcal{A})$ the language of the automaton $\mathcal{A}$; i.e., the set of all labeled trees that $\mathcal{A}$ accepts. We say that an automaton is *nonempty* iff $\mathcal{L}(\mathcal{A}) \neq \emptyset$.

We define the *size* $|\mathcal{A}|$ of an alternating automaton $\mathcal{A} = \langle \Sigma, Q, q_0, \delta, \alpha \rangle$ as $|Q| + |\alpha| + |\delta|$, where $|Q|$ and $|\alpha|$ are the respective cardinalities of the sets Q and α, and where $|\delta|$ is the sum of the lengths of the satisfiable (i.e., not **false**) formulas that appear as $\delta(q, \sigma)$ for some q and σ.

3.2 Solving the Problem of Module-Checking with Incomplete Information

Theorem 4. *Given a module M and a CTL formula ψ over the sets I, O, and H, of M's variables, there exists an alternating Büchi tree automaton $A_{M,\psi}$ over $\{\top, \bot\}$-labeled $2^{I \cup O}$-trees, of size $O(|M| * |\psi|)$, such that $\mathcal{L}(A_{M,\psi})$ is exactly the set of strategies $\mathcal{E}$ such that $M \lhd \mathcal{E}$ is deadlock free and satisfies ψ.*

Proof (sketch): Let $M = \langle I, O, H, W, w_0, R, L \rangle$, and let $K = I \cup O$. For $w \in W$ and $v \in 2^K$, we define $s(w, v) = \{w' \mid \langle w, w' \rangle \in R$ and $L(w') \cap K = v\}$ and $d(w) = \{v \mid s(w, v) \neq \emptyset\}$. That is, $s(w, v)$ contains all the successors of w that agree in their readable variables with v. Each such successor corresponds to a node in $\langle T_M, V_M \rangle$ with a direction in $hide_{(2^H)}^{-1}(v)$. Accordingly,

$d(w)$ contains all directions v for which nodes corresponding to w in $\langle T_M, V_M \rangle$ have at least one successor with a direction in $hide^{-1}_{(2^H)}(v)$.

Essentially, the automaton $\mathcal{A}_{M,\psi}$ is similar to the product alternating tree automaton obtained in the alternating-automata theoretic framework for CTL model checking [BVW94]. There, as there is a single computation tree with respect to which the formula is checked, the automaton obtained is a 1-letter automaton. Here, as there are many computation trees to check, we get a 2-letter automaton: each $\{\top, \bot\}$-labeled tree induces a different computation tree, and $\mathcal{A}_{M,\psi}$ considers them all. In addition, it checks that the composition of the strategy in the input with M is deadlock free. We assume that ψ is given in a positive normal form, thus negations are applied only to atomic propositions. We define $\mathcal{A}_{M,\psi} = \langle \{\top, \bot\}, Q, q_0, \delta, \alpha \rangle$, where

- $Q = (W \times (cl(\psi) \cup \{p_\top\}) \times \{\forall, \exists\}) \cup \{q_0\}$, where $cl(\psi)$ denotes the set of ψ's subformulas. Intuitively, when the automaton is in state $\langle w, \varphi, \forall \rangle$, it accepts all strategies for which w is either pruned or satisfies φ, where $\varphi = p_\top$ is satisfied iff the root of the strategy is labeled $\top$. When the automaton is in state $\langle w, \varphi, \exists \rangle$, it accepts all strategies for which w is not pruned and it satisfies φ. We call $\forall$ and $\exists$ the *mode* of the state. While the states in $W \times \{p_\top\} \times \{\forall, \exists\}$ check that the composition of M with the strategy in the input is deadlock free, the states in $W \times cl(\psi) \times \{\forall, \exists\}$ check that this composition satisfies ψ. The initial state q_0 sends copies to check both the deadlock freeness of the composition and the satisfaction of ψ.

- The transition function $\delta : Q \times \Sigma \to \mathcal{B}^+(2^K \times Q)$ is defined as follows (with $m \in \{\exists, \forall\}$).
  - $\delta(q_0, \bot) = \textbf{false}$, and $\delta(q_0, \top) = \delta(\langle w_0, p_\top, \exists \rangle, \top) \wedge \delta(\langle w_0, \psi, \exists \rangle, \top)$.
  - For all w and φ, we have $\delta(\langle w, \varphi, \forall \rangle, \bot) = \textbf{true}$ and $\delta(\langle w, \varphi, \exists \rangle, \bot) = \textbf{false}$.
  - $\delta(\langle w, p_\top, m \rangle, \top) =$
    $$(\bigvee_{v \in 2^K} \bigvee_{w' \in s(w,v)} (v, \langle w', p_\top, \exists \rangle)) \wedge (\bigwedge_{v \in 2^K} \bigwedge_{w' \in s(w,v)} (v, \langle w', p_\top, \forall \rangle)).$$
  - $\delta(\langle w, p, m \rangle, \top) = \textbf{true}$ if $p \in L(w)$, and $\delta(\langle w, p, m \rangle, \top) = \textbf{false}$ if $p \notin L(w)$.
  - $\delta(\langle w, \neg p, m \rangle, \top) = \textbf{true}$ if $p \notin L(w)$, and $\delta(\langle w, \neg p, m \rangle, \top) = \textbf{false}$ if $p \in L(w)$.
  - $\delta(\langle w, \varphi_1 \wedge \varphi_2, m \rangle, \top) = \delta(\langle w, \varphi_1, m \rangle, \top) \wedge \delta(\langle w, \varphi_2, m \rangle, \top)$.
  - $\delta(\langle w, \varphi_1 \vee \varphi_2, m \rangle, \top) = \delta(\langle w, \varphi_1, m \rangle, \top) \vee \delta(\langle w, \varphi_2, m \rangle, \top)$.
  - $\delta(\langle w, AX\varphi, m \rangle, \top) = \bigwedge_{v \in 2^K} \bigwedge_{w' \in s(w,v)} (v, \langle w', \varphi, \forall \rangle)$.
  - $\delta(\langle w, EX\varphi, m \rangle, \top) = \bigvee_{v \in 2^K} \bigvee_{w' \in s(w,v)} (v, \langle w', \varphi, \exists \rangle)$.
  - $\delta(\langle w, A\varphi_1 U \varphi_2, m \rangle, \top) =$
    $$\delta(\langle w, \varphi_2, m \rangle, \top) \vee (\delta(\langle w, \varphi_1, m \rangle, \top) \wedge \bigwedge_{v \in 2^K} \bigwedge_{w' \in s(w,v)} (v, \langle w', A\varphi_1 U \varphi_2, \forall \rangle)).$$
  - $\delta(\langle w, E\varphi_1 U \varphi_2, m \rangle, \top) =$
    $$\delta(\langle w, \varphi_2, m \rangle, \top) \vee (\delta(\langle w, \varphi_1, m \rangle, \top) \wedge \bigvee_{v \in 2^K} \bigvee_{w' \in s(w,v)} (v, \langle w', E\varphi_1 U \varphi_2, \exists \rangle)).$$
  - $\delta(\langle w, AG\varphi, m \rangle, \top) = \delta(\langle w, \varphi, m \rangle, \top) \wedge \bigwedge_{v \in 2^K} \bigwedge_{w' \in s(w,v)} (v, \langle w', AG\varphi, \forall \rangle)$.
  - $\delta(\langle w, EG\varphi, m \rangle, \top) = \delta(\langle w, \varphi, m \rangle, \top) \wedge \bigvee_{v \in 2^K} \bigvee_{w' \in s(w,v)} (v, \langle w', EG\varphi, \exists \rangle)$.

Consider, for example, a transition from the state $\langle w, AX\varphi, \exists \rangle$. First, if the transition to w is disabled (that is, the automaton reads $\bot$), then, as the current mode is existential, the run is rejecting. If the transition to w is enabled, then w's successors that are enabled should satisfy φ. The state w may have several successors that agree on some labeling $v \in 2^K$ and differ only on the labeling of variables in H. These successors are indistinguishable by the environment, and the automaton sends them all to the same direction v. This guarantees that either all these successors are enabled by the strategy (in case the letter to be read in direction v is $\top$) or all are disabled (in case the letter in direction v is $\bot$). In addition, since the requirement to satisfy φ concerns only successors of w that are enabled, the mode of the new states is universal. The copies of $\mathcal{A}_{M,\psi}$ that check the composition with the strategy to be deadlock free guarantee that at least one successor of w is enabled. Note that as the transition relation R is total, the conjunctions and disjunctions in δ cannot be empty.

- $\alpha = W \times G(\psi) \times \{\exists, \forall\}$, where $G(\psi)$ is the set of all formulas of the form $AG\varphi$ or $EG\varphi$ in $cl(\psi)$. Thus, while the automaton cannot get trapped in states associated with "Until-formulas" (then, the eventuality of the until is not satisfied), it may get trapped in states associated with "Always-formulas" (then, the safety requirement is never violated).

We now consider the size of $\mathcal{A}_{M,\neg\psi}$. Clearly, $|Q| = O(|W| * |\psi|)$. Also, as the transition associated with a state $\langle w, \varphi, m \rangle$ depends on the successors of w, we have that $|\delta| = O(|R| * |\psi|)$. Finally, $|\alpha| \leq |Q|$, and we are done. $\qquad\qquad\qquad\qquad\qquad\qquad\qquad\qquad\qquad\qquad\qquad\square$

Extending the alternating automata described in [BVW94] to handle incomplete information is possible thanks to the special structure of the automata, which alternate between universal and existential modes. This structure (the "hesitation condition", as called in [BVW94]) exists also in automata associated with CTL* formulas, and imply the following analogous theorem.

Theorem 5. *Given a module M and a CTL* formula ψ over the sets $I, O,$ and $H,$ of M's variables, there exists an alternating Rabin tree automaton $\mathcal{A}_{M,\psi}$ over $\{\top, \bot\}$-labeled $2^{I\cup O}$-trees, with $|W| * 2^{O(|\psi|)}$ states and two pairs, such that $\mathcal{L}(\mathcal{A}_{M,\psi})$ is exactly the set of strategies $\mathcal{E}$ such that $M \lhd \mathcal{E}$ is deadlock free and satisfies ψ.*

The alternating-automata-theoretic approach to CTL and CTL* model checking is extended in [KV95] to handle Fair-CTL and Fair-CTL*[EL85]. Using the same extension, we can handle here modules augmented with fairness conditions.

We now consider the complexity bounds that follow from our algorithm.

Theorem 6. *The module-checking problem with incomplete information is EXPTIME-complete for CTL and is 2EXPTIME-complete for CTL*.*

Proof (sketch): The lower bounds follows from the known bounds for module checking with complete information [KV96]. For the upper bounds, in Theorems 4 and 5 we reduced the problem $M \models_r \psi$ to the problem of checking the nonemptiness of the automaton $\mathcal{A}_{M,\neg\psi}$. When ψ is a CTL formula, $\mathcal{A}_{M,\neg\psi}$ is an alternating Büchi automaton of size $O(|M| * |\psi|)$. By [VW86, MS95], checking the nonemptiness of $\mathcal{A}_{M,\neg\psi}$ is then exponential in the sizes of M and ψ. When ψ is a CTL* formula, the automaton $\mathcal{A}_{M,\neg\psi}$ is an alternating Rabin automaton, with $|W| * 2^{O(|\psi|)}$ states and two pairs. Accordingly, by [EJ88, MS95], checking the nonemptiness of $\mathcal{A}_{M,\neg\psi}$ is exponential in $|W|$ and double exponential in $|\psi|$. $\qquad\qquad\square$

By Lemma 2, the bounds above hold also for the problem of assume-guarantee module checking with incomplete information. As the module-checking problem for CTL is already EXPTIME-hard for environments with complete information, it might seem as if incomplete information can be handled at no cost. This is, however, not true. Let us define the *program complexity* of module checking as the complexity of the problem in terms of the size of the system, assuming that the specification is fixed [VW86]. Since the system is typically much bigger than the specification, this complexity is of particular interest [LP85]. By [KV96], the program complexity of CTL module checking with complete information is PTIME-complete. On the other hand, the time complexity of the algorithm we present here is exponential in the size of the both the formula and the system. Can we do better? In Theorem 7 below, we answer this question negatively. To see why, consider a module M with hidden variables. When M interacts with an environment $\mathcal{E}$, the module seen by $\mathcal{E}$ is different from M. Indeed, every state of the module seen by $\mathcal{E}$ corresponds to a set of states of M. Therefore, coping with incomplete information involves some subset construction, which blows-up the state space exponentially. In our algorithm, the subset construction hides in the emptiness test of $\mathcal{A}_{M,\neg\psi}$.

Theorem 7. *The program complexity of CTL module checking with incomplete information is EXPTIME-complete.*

Proof (sketch): The upper bound follows from Theorem 6. For the lower bound, we do a reduction from the outcome problem for two-players games with incomplete information, proved to be EXPTIME-hard in [Rei84]. A two-player game with incomplete information consists of an AND-OR graph with an initial state and a set of designated states. Each of the states in the graph is labeled by readable and unreadable observations. The game is played between two players, called the OR-player and the AND-player. The two players generate together a path in the graph. The path starts at the initial state. Whenever the game is at an OR-state, the OR-player determines the next state. Whenever the game is at an AND-state, the AND-player determines the next state. The outcome problem is to determine whether the OR-player has a strategy that depends only on the readable observations (that is, a strategy that maps finite sequences of sets of readable observations to a set of known observations) such that following this strategy guarantees that, no matter how the AND-player plays, the path eventually visits one of the designated states.

Given an AND-OR graph G as above, we define a module M_G such that M_G reactively satisfies a fixed CTL formula φ iff the OR-player has no strategy as above. The environments of M_G correspond to strategies for the OR-player. Each environment suggests a pruning of $\langle T_{M_G}, V_{M_G} \rangle$ such that the set of paths in the pruned tree corresponds to a set of paths that the OR-player can force the game into, no matter how the AND-player plays. The module M_G is very similar to G, and the formula φ requires the existence of a computation that never visits a designated state. The formal definition of M_G and φ involves some technical complications required in order to make sure that the environment disables only transitions from OR-states. $\square$

4 Discussion

Module checking considers the verification of open systems. In [KV96], we claim that the complexity of the module-checking problem, which is EXPTIME for specifications in CTL and only PSPACE for specifications in LTL, questions the traditional belief of the computational superiority of the branching-time paradigm. In this paper we considered open systems that have internal variables. In this common case, the environment has incomplete information about the system, and the module-checking problem should be revised accordingly. We showed that incomplete information makes CTL module checking even harder, while it comes at no cost for linear (and universal) logics. Hence, it provides an additional evidence that checking CTL properties is actually harder than checking LTL properties.

The setting we consider here is more general than the one in [KV96], but can still be generalized further. In both [KV96] and here, we assume that an environment may disable some of the system's transition. More general settings allow more dominant environments. For example, if we consider environments that are modules, then a composition of a system with an environment may not only disable some of the system's transitions, but also add new transitions (e.g., the environment may cause a certain transition of the system to branch into two transitions, each leading to a state with different assignments to the environment's variables). As in module checking, while verification of universal properties in these settings can be done using closed-system verification methods, there is a need to revise verification methods in order to handle non-universal properties.

Acknowledgment We thank Rajeev Alur for referring us to [Rei84] and pointing its relevance to the lower bound in Theorem 7.

References

[BVW94] O. Bernholtz, M.Y. Vardi, and P. Wolper. An automata-theoretic approach to branching-time model checking. In *Proc. 6th CAV*, LNCS 818, pp. 142–155, June 1994.

[CE81] E.M. Clarke and E.A. Emerson. Design and synthesis of synchronization skeletons using branching time temporal logic. In *Proc. LP*, LNCS 131, pp. 52–71, 1981.

[CGB86] E.M. Clarke, O. Grumberg, and M.C. Browne. Reasoning about networks with many identical finite-state processes. In *Proc. 5th PODC*, pp. 240–248, August 1986.

[CES86] E.M. Clarke, E.A. Emerson, and A.P. Sistla. Automatic verification of finite-state concurrent systems using temporal logic specifications. *ACM TPLS*, 8(2):244–263, 1986.

[EJ88] E.A. Emerson and C. Jutla. The complexity of tree automata and logics of programs. In *Proc. 29th FOCS*, pp. 368–377, October 1988.

[EL85] E.A. Emerson and C.-L. Lei. Temporal model checking under generalized fairness constraints. In *Proc. 18th Hawaii International Conference on System Sciences*, Hawaii, 1985.

[Eme85] E.A. Emerson. Automata, tableaux, and temporal logics. In *Proc. LP*, LNCS 193, pp. 79–87, 1985.

[FZ88] M.J. Fischer and L.D. Zuck. Reasoning about uncertainty in fault-tolerant distributed systems. In *Proc. Formal Techniques in Real-Time and Fault-Tolerant Sys.*, LNCS 331, pp. 142–158, 1988.

[GL94] O. Grumberg and D.E. Long. Model checking and modular verification. *ACM Trans. on Programming Languages and Systems*, 16(3):843–871, 1994.

[Hoa85] C.A.R. Hoare. *Communicating Sequential Processes*. Prentice-Hall, 1985.

[HP85] D. Harel and A. Pnueli. On the development of reactive systems. In *Logics and Models of Concurrent Systems*, volume F-13 of *NATO Advanced Summer Institutes*, pp. 477–498, 1985.

[Jon83] C.B. Jones. Specification and design of (parallel) programs. In *Proc. 9th IFIP*, pp. 321–332, North-Holland, 1983.

[KV95] O. Kupferman and M.Y. Vardi. On the complexity of branching modular model checking. In *Proc. 6th CONCUR*, LNCS 962, pp. 408–422, August 1995.

[KV96] O. Kupferman and M.Y. Vardi. Module checking. In *Proc. 8th CAV*, LNCS 1102, pp. 75–86, August 1996.

[Lam83] L. Lamport. Specifying concurrent program modules. *ACM Trans. on Programming Languages and Systenms*, 5:190–222, 1983.

[LP85] O. Lichtenstein and A. Pnueli. Checking that finite state concurrent programs satisfy their linear specification. In *Proc. 12th POPL*, pp. 97–107, January 1985.

[Mil71] R. Milner. An algebraic definition of simulation between programs. In *Proc. 2nd IJCAI*, British Computer Society, pp. 481–489, September 1971.

[MP92] Z. Manna and A. Pnueli. Temporal specification and verification of reactive modules. 1992.

[MS87] D.E. Muller and P.E. Schupp. Alternating automata on infinite trees. *Theoretical Computer Science*, 54,:267–276, 1987.

[MS95] D.E. Muller and P.E. Schupp. Simulating aternating tree automata by nondeterministic automata: New results and new proofs of theorems of Rabin, McNaughton and Safra. *Theoretical Computer Science*, 141:69–107, 1995.

[Pnu81] A. Pnueli. The temporal semantics of concurrent programs. *Theoretical Computer Science*, 13:45–60, 1981.

[Pnu85] A. Pnueli. Applications of temporal logic to the specification and verification of reactive systems: A survey of current trends. In *Proc. Advanced School on Current Trends in Concurrency*, LNCS 224, pp. 510–584, 1985.

[QS81] J.P. Queille and J. Sifakis. Specification and verification of concurrent systems in Cesar. In *Proc. 5th International Symp. on Programming*, LNCS 137, pp. 337–351, 1981.

[Rei84] J.H. Reif. The complexity of two-player games of incomplete information. *J. on Computer and System Sciences*, 29:274–301, 1984.

[Var95] M.Y. Vardi. On the complexity of modular model checking. In *Proc. 10th LICS*, June 1995.

[VW86] M.Y. Vardi and P. Wolper. Automata-theoretic techniques for modal logics of programs. *Journal of Computer and System Science*, 32(2):182–221, April 1986.

Using Compositional Preorders in the Verification of Sliding Window Protocol

Roope Kaivola*

Department of Computer Science
PO Box 26 (Teollisuuskatu 23)
FIN-00014 University of Helsinki, Finland

Abstract The main obstacle to automatic verification of temporal logic properties of finite-state systems is the state explosion problem. One way to alleviate this is to replace components of a system with smaller ones and verify the required properties from the smaller system. This approach leads to notions of compositional property-preserving equivalences and preorders. Previously we have shown that the NDFD preorder is the weakest preorder which is compositional w.r.t. standard operators and preserves nexttime-less linear temporal logic properties. In this paper we describe a case study where NDFD preorder was used to verify semi-automatically both safety and liveness properties of the Sliding Window protocol for arbitrary channel lengths and realistic parameter values. In this process we located a previously undiscovered fault leading to lack of liveness in a version of the protocol.

1 Introduction

A promising approach to verification of finite-state concurrent systems is the use of propositional temporal logic as a specification language and the application of model-checking algorithms for the verification task (for an overview, see [4, 14]). In practice the main obstacle to this approach is that the execution graphs of realistic systems are too large for feasible model-checking, as in the general case the size of an execution graph is exponential in the number of concurrent processes. Several techniques have been proposed for alleviating this *state explosion* problem. Most of these are based on the fact that the components of a system are often reasonably small, even though the total system may be large [2, 10].

One particular technique is *compositional reduction*. Here the idea is to replace the individual components of a system by smaller ones before building the model of the whole system, and to do this in such a way that if the reduced model fulfils the required properties, then the full system does so as well. This approach leads to notions of compositional property-preserving equivalences and preorders between modules. Assuming that we have a preorder for which the required properties that hold of a model also hold of all models which are lower in the preorder, and which is congruent with respect to the composition operators

---

* e-mail: Roope.Kaivola@helsinki.fi

used in building the system, we can replace a module of a system with any module which is smaller in size but lies higher in the preorder, and if the required properties hold of the resulting system then they also hold of the original one.

In this paper we describe a case study where compositional preorders were used to verify safety and liveness properties of the Sliding Window or SW communication protocol [13]. The SW protocol forms the basis of the data transfer function of the HDLC protocol [6], and an extreme simplification of it is the Alternating Bit protocol, a stock example in the literature on formal verification. Although almost any method seems to cope with the AB protocol, analysis of the more general SW protocol is harder; even with small window sizes and channel lengths the state space becomes far too large for direct model-checking.

In the case study the components of the protocol were modelled by ordinary labelled transition systems, and the complete protocol was built from these by Basic LOTOS [1] operators. The properties that were required of the protocol were expressed using a transition-oriented variant of the propositional nexttime-less linear temporal logic. To express the requirements in a propositional language and to model the system in a finitary way, we used the technique of *data independence* [17, 12], which allows us to deduce that the system works correctly for all sequences of data, if it works correctly for data sequences of certain forms.

The notion of preorder used in the verification was the so-called *non-divergent failures divergences* or *NDFD* preorder. In [8, 9] it was shown that the related NDFD equivalence preserves all nexttime-less linear temporal logic properties, and in [16] that it is a congruence with respect to all Basic LOTOS operators. Moreover, in [9] it was shown that NDFD equivalence is the weakest or loosest possible criterion of equivalence which has these properties. These results can be generalised to the NDFD preorder in a natural way [7].

In practive the main task in the verification was the construction of an *abstraction* of the sender part of the protocol. This was done manually, guided by intuitions about the protocol. Next, it was verified that this abstraction is higher in the NDFD preorder than the sender combined with a channel of arbitrary length. This was done automatically, using the ARA toolset [15]. Finally, the abstraction was combined with the receiver end of the protocol, and it was verified that the resulting system fulfils the required properties of the protocol. In this extended abstract, only the main steps are presented. For a full analysis, see [7].

In the case study we succesfully verified that the SW-protocol meets its safety and liveness requirements for a variety of realistic window sizes and *arbitrary* channel lengths. A more surprising observation was that a variant of the protocol *fails* to fulfil usual liveness requirements. This variant arises from a modification which seems harmless enough that it has sometimes appeared in the literature. In our opinion this result illustrates well the advantages of rigorous verification.

The verification of the SW protocol has been studied extensively (see [7, Sect. 7.3] for a survey). Like the original proof [13], most work has been manual or concentrated on safety properties, often both. Closest to the current work is [11], where safety properties of the protocol are expressed in temporal logic and verified by direct model-checking, with limits set by the state-explosion problem.

2 Background

Definition 1. For any set A, 2^A denotes the powerset of A, A^* the set of finite strings of elements of A and A^ω the set of infinite strings of elements of A. Define $A^\infty = A^* \cup A^\omega$. If $\sigma = a_0 a_1 \ldots \in A^\infty$, $\sigma(n)$ denotes the element a_n and $\sigma[n \ldots]$ the string $a_n a_{n+1} \ldots$ We use $\cdot$ to denote catenation and $|\sigma|$ the length of σ.

Definition 2. Fix an infinite *transition alphabet* Σ, which does not contain the *empty transition label* τ. Define $\Sigma_\tau = \Sigma \cup \{\tau\}$. A *labelled transition system (lts)* is a triple $L = (S, s, \Delta)$, where S is a finite set of states, $s \in S$ a unique initial state, and $\Delta \subseteq S \times \Sigma_\tau \times S$ a finite transition relation. If $\rho \in \Sigma_\tau^*$, we write $s_0 \xrightarrow{\rho} s_n$ iff there are $s_1, \ldots, s_{n-1}$ such that for all $0 \le i < n$, $(s_i, \rho(i), s_{i+1}) \in \Delta$, and $s_0 \xrightarrow{\rho}$ iff there is an s_n such that $s_0 \xrightarrow{\rho} s_n$. If $\rho \in \Sigma_\tau^\infty$, we write $s_0 \xrightarrow{\rho}$ iff there are $s_1, s_2, \ldots$ such that for all $i \ge 0$, $(s_i, \rho(i), s_{i+1}) \in \Delta$. If $\sigma \in (\Sigma^* \cup \Sigma^\infty)$, we write $s_0 \xRightarrow{\sigma} s_n$ ($s_0 \xRightarrow{\sigma}$) iff there is some $\rho \in (\Sigma_\tau^* \cup \Sigma_\tau^\infty)$ such that $s_0 \xrightarrow{\rho} s_n$ ($s_0 \xrightarrow{\rho}$) and σ is the string obtained from ρ by removing all τ symbols.

We use parallel composition, hiding and renaming operators to combine ltss. We abuse notation slightly in the following, and write for example **hide** $sc*$ **in** L to mean that all labels beginning with sc are hidden, and $L[sc*/cr*]$ to mean that each label of the form $scxx$ is renamed to $crxx$.

Definition 3. Let $L_1 = (S_1, s_1, \Delta_1)$, $L_2 = (S_2, s_2, \Delta_2)$ be ltss and G, H sets $G = \{g_1, \ldots, g_n\} \subset \Sigma$ and $H = \{h_1, \ldots, h_n\} \subset \Sigma$. Then
- $L_1 \|[g_1, \ldots, g_n]\| L_2$ is the lts $(S_1 \times S_2, (s_1, s_2), \Delta)$, where $((t, u), l, (t', u')) \in \Delta$ iff either $l \in G$, $(t, l, t') \in \Delta_1$ and $(u, l, u') \in \Delta_2$, or $l \notin G$, $(t, l, t') \in \Delta_1$ and $u = u'$, or $l \notin G$, $(u, l, u') \in \Delta_2$ and $t = t'$,
- **hide** $g_1, \ldots, g_n$ **in** L_1 is the lts (S_1, s_1, Δ), where $(t, l, t') \in \Delta$, iff either $l \notin G$ and $(t, l, t') \in \Delta_1$ or $l = \tau$ and there is a $g_i \in G$ such that $(t, g_i, t') \in \Delta_1$,
- $L_1[h_1/g_1, \ldots, h_n/g_n]$ is the lts (S_1, s_1, Δ), where $(t, l, t') \in \Delta$, iff either $l \notin G$ and $(t, l, t') \in \Delta_1$ or $l = h_i$ and $(t, g_i, t') \in \Delta_1$.

Definition 4. Let $L = (S, \Delta, s)$ be a labelled transition system. We say that
- $\rho \in \Sigma_\tau^\infty$ is a *maximal behaviour* of L iff either ρ is infinite and $s \xrightarrow{\rho}$, or ρ is finite and there is some s' such that $s \xrightarrow{\rho} s'$ and $s' \xrightarrow{a}$ for no $a \in \Sigma_\tau$,
- $\sigma \in \Sigma^\omega$ is an *infinite trace* of L iff $s \xRightarrow{\sigma}$,
- $\sigma \in \Sigma^*$ is a *divergence trace* of L iff there is some s' such that $s \xRightarrow{\sigma} s' \xrightarrow{\tau^\omega}$,
- $(\sigma, A) \in \Sigma^* \times 2^\Sigma$ is a *nondivergent failure* of L iff σ is not a divergence trace of L, and there is some s' such that $s \xRightarrow{\sigma} s'$ and $s' \xRightarrow{a}$ for no $a \in A$,

We use $maxbeh(L)$ to denote the set of maximal behaviours of L, $inftr(L)$ the set of infinite traces of L, $divtr(L)$ the set of divergence traces of L, and $ndfail(L)$ the set of nondivergent failures of L.

Definition 5. Let L and L' be ltss. We say that L is lower than L' in the *nondivergent failures divergences preorder* or *NDFD preorder* and write $L \overset{\text{ndfd}}{\preceq} L'$ iff
- $inftr(L) \subseteq inftr(L')$,

- $divtr(L) \subseteq divtr(L')$, and
- $ndfail(L) \subseteq ndfail(L') \cup (divtr(L') \times 2^{\Sigma})$.

For a full analysis of the NDFD preorder and its relation to other related failure-based preorders, see [16]. As far as the current paper is concerned, its two important properties are that and it preserves all maximal finite and infinite traces, and thereby also all nexttime-less linear temporal logic properties, and it is congruent with respect to the composition operators above,

Proposition 6 [16]. *If* $L_1 \overset{ndfd}{\prec} L_1'$ *and* $L_2 \overset{ndfd}{\prec} L_2'$, *then*

- $L_1[[g_1, \ldots, g_n]]L_2 \overset{ndfd}{\prec} L_1'[[g_1 \ldots, g_n]]L_2'$,
- **hide** $g_1, \ldots, g_n$ **in** $L_1 \overset{ndfd}{\prec}$ **hide** $g_1, \ldots, g_n$ **in** L_1' *and*
- $L_1[h_1/g_1, \ldots, h_n/g_n] \overset{ndfd}{\prec} L_1'[h_1/g_1, \ldots, h_n/g_n]$.

Most temporal logics used in program specification are essentially state-based, describing properties of execution states and sequences of them. However, here we would like to make reference to transitions and their labels directly. To this purpose we define a variant of the usual nexttime-less linear temporal logic LTL'. Similar extensions from state-based to transition-based logics are discussed in [3]. In [7] we describe a general model where both states and transitions of a transition system carry labels and both of these can be referred to in the logic. However, in the current case study ordinary ltss suffice.

Definition 7. The formulae of the logic $tLTL'$ are defined by the abstract syntax: $\phi ::= \top \mid \neg\phi \mid \phi \vee \phi' \mid \phi\mathcal{U}\phi' \mid \phi\mathcal{U}^a\phi'$, where a varies over Σ. We use $\bot, \wedge, \Rightarrow$ and $\Leftrightarrow$ as derived operators in the usual way, and define $\Diamond\phi = \top\mathcal{U}\phi$, $\Box\phi = \neg\Diamond\neg\phi$, $\boxed{a}\phi = \top\mathcal{U}^a\phi$ and $\boxed{a} = \top\mathcal{U}^a\top$. If ϕ is a formula, we use $\Sigma(\phi)$ to denote the set of labels $a \in \Sigma$ occurring in operators $\mathcal{U}^a$ in ϕ.

We say that ϕ *is true of* a sequence $\sigma \in \Sigma_\tau^\infty$, denoted by $\sigma \models \phi$, according to the following inductive rules: $\sigma \models \top$ always, $\sigma \models \neg\phi$ iff not $\sigma \models \phi$, $\sigma \models \phi \vee \psi$ iff $\sigma \models \phi$ or $\sigma \models \psi$, $\sigma \models \phi\mathcal{U}\psi$ iff there is some $0 \leq i \leq |\sigma|$ such that $\sigma[i\ldots] \models \psi$ and $\sigma[j\ldots] \models \phi$ for all $0 \leq j < i$, and finally, $\sigma \models \phi\mathcal{U}^a\psi$ iff there is some $0 \leq i < |\sigma|$ such that $\sigma(i) = a$, $\sigma[i+1\ldots] \models \psi$, and for all $0 \leq j < i$, $\sigma(j) \neq a$ and $\sigma[j\ldots] \models \phi$. We say that ϕ is true of an lts L and write $L \models \phi$ iff $\sigma \models \phi$ for all $\sigma \in maxbeh(L)$.

Here, $\mathcal{U}$ is the standard *until* operator. The less familiar $\phi\mathcal{U}^a\psi$ operator says that ψ holds immediately after the next transition labelled with a, such a transition exists, and until that moment ϕ holds. The derived operator $\boxed{a}\phi$ says that ϕ holds after the next transition labelled with a, and there is such a transition, and $\boxed{a}$ that some future transition is labelled with a.

Proposition 8 [8, 7]. *If* ϕ *is a* $tLTL'$*-formula,* $L' \models \phi$ *and* $L \overset{ndfd}{\prec} L'$, *then* $L \models \phi$.

We use to following simple result to ignore uninteresting labels in a model.

Proposition 9 [7]. *If* ϕ *is a* $tLTL'$*-formula and* $\Pi \subseteq \Sigma$ *a set of labels such that* $\Sigma(\phi) \cap \Pi = \emptyset$, *then* $L \models \phi$ *iff* **hide** Π **in** $L \models \phi$.

SENDER
Variables
    $d[0\ldots(tw-1)]$: table of data items; i, j, k : int /* x, a: temporary variables */
Initially $i = 0, j = 0, k = 0$
loop infinitely
    choose nondeterministically
          $i < tw$ $\longrightarrow$ receive(data source, $d[i]$); $i := i + 1$;
    [] $j < i$ $\longrightarrow$ send(channel, $(j \oplus k, d[j])$); $j := j + 1$;
    [] $j = i \wedge i > 0 \longrightarrow$ receive(timeout); $j := 0$;
    [] $\top$ $\longrightarrow$ receive(ack channel, x); $a := (x \ominus k) + 1$;
                        if $(a \leq tw)$ then
                            $d[0\ldots(tw-1-a)] := d[a\ldots(tw-1)]$;
                            $i := \max(0, i - a)$; $j := \max(0, j - a)$; $k := x \oplus 1$
                        end if;
    end choose;
end loop;

RECEIVER
Variables
    $t[0\ldots(rw-1)]$: table of data items; $r[0\ldots(rw-1)]$: table of booleans
    e : int;   /* x, y, s: temporary variables */
Initially $e = 0, r[0\ldots(rw-1)] = (\bot, \ldots, \bot)$
loop infinitely
    receive(channel, (x, y)); $s := x \ominus e$;
    if $(s < rw)$ then $r[s] := \top$; $t[s] := y$; end if;
    while $(r[0] \neq \bot)$ do
        send(data target, $t[0]$);
        $t[0\ldots(rw-2)] := t[1\ldots(rw-1)]$; $r[0\ldots(rw-2)] := r[1\ldots(rw-1)]$;
        $r[rw-1] := \bot$; $e := e \oplus 1$;
    end while;
    send(ack channel, $(e \ominus 1)$);
end loop;

Notation: $x \oplus y = (x + y) \bmod (w + 1)$ and $x \ominus y = (x - y) \bmod (w + 1)$

Figure1. Sender and receiver

3 Sliding Window protocol

The object of the case study is a unidirectional version of the Sliding Window protocol [13], which tries to provide reliable transmission of data over an unreliable communication medium. The system consists of six components. The *sender* receives data items from an external *data source*, sends messages consisting of a sequence number and a data item to the *channel*, receives acknowledgement messages from the *acknowledgement channel*, and receives timeout signals from an unspecified external source. The *receiver* reads messages from the channel, forwards correctly received data items to an external *data target*, and sends acknowledgement messages consisting of a sequence number to the acknowledge-ment channel. The channel and acknowledgement channel may distort or lose messages but may not change their order. Three parameters to the protocol are the *transmission window* size tw the *reception window* size rw, and the maximum value w for the sequence numbers. These must fulfil the constraint $tw+rw \leq w+1$ [13]. The sender and receiver processes are described in Figure 1.

We have specified only a very simple timeout mechanism for the protocol: instead of presenting explicitly the setting and cancelling of timers, we have specified that the sender may receive a timeout signal in situations where it cannot send any new data items to the channel. We make the assumption that timeouts should not occur prematurely, i.e. when some acknowledgement is still on its way to the sender. This is not reflected in the description so far, but will be taken into account when modelling the protocol. In reality this could be achieved by setting the timeout delay to be longer than the maximum message transit time from the sender to the receiver and back. The assumptions regarding timeouts are only needed for liveness properties of the protocol, not for safety.

The aim of the protocol is to transmit a sequence of data items from the data source to the target in the correct order. Reflecting this, the requirements to the protocol which we tried to verify were:

SAFE The data delivered to the target should be correct, i.e. the data sequence transmitted to the target before any given moment should be a prefix of the data sequence received from the source before that moment.

LIVE1 If n data items are read from the source along an execution sequence, and the execution sequence is complete under the assumption that no more data is available for reading from the source, then n data items should be delivered to the target along the execution sequence.

LIVE2 If infinitely many data items are read from the data source along an execution sequence, then infinitely many data items should be delivered to the target along that execution sequence.

LIVE3 The sender should accept data from the source, i.e. for any moment in a maximal execution sequence there should be a future moment when the sender reads a data item from the source, unless no more data is available.

The liveness properties are expected to hold under the fairness condition:

FAIR Let $i \in \{0, \ldots, w\}$ be any sequence number. If messages with sequence number i are sent to the channel infinitely often, then messages with that sequence number will also be transmitted successfully to the receiver infinitely often. The same holds for the acknowledgement channel.

4 Modelling the protocol

As the first step in the verification of the protocol, we appeal to a syntactic property of the system called *data-independence* [17, 12], which allows us to verify the requirements to the system just for certain representative data sequences or certain data sources and conclude that the system works correctly with all possible sequences of data items. We shall omit the details here and just state:

Figure2. Data source ltss D_{safe} (left) and D_{live} (right)

- The protocol satisfies the requirement SAFE iff on any maximal execution of the protocol connected to the data source D_{safe} in Fig. 2, the sequence of data items delivered to the target belongs to the language $0^\infty \cdot (1 \cdot 2^\infty \cup \epsilon)$.
- Assuming that the protocol satisfies the safety requirement, it satisfies the requirements LIVE1-3 iff on any maximal execution of the protocol connected to the data source D_{live} in Fig. 2, either the data item 1 or infinitely many 0:s are delivered to the target.

The analysis showing that it is enough to consider these data sources and sequences [7, App. A and Sect. 3.3] is similar to that of [17, 12]. However, for safety properties they consider the data sequences $0^* \cdot 1 \cdot 0^* \cdot 2 \cdot 0^\omega$, whereas here we found it more convenient to use the data sequences $0^\infty \cdot (1 \cdot 2^\infty \cup \epsilon)$. For liveness properties, we use sequences $0^\infty \cdot 1$ instead of 0^ω of [17, 12] to cover also finite sequences of data.

To model the protocol by labelled transition systems, we fix the set of data items as $\{0, 1, 2\}$ and set some upper bounds n_c and n_a for the capacity of the channel and the acknowledgement channel. Having decided the values of w, tw, rw, n_c and n_a, we build a model of the system from six basic ltss: **S** modelling the sender process, **R** modelling the receiver process, **C** modelling a channel with the capacity of one message, **A** modelling an acknowledgement channel with the capacity of one message, **C_F** modelling a faulty channel with the capacity of one message, and **A_F** modelling a faulty acknowledgement channel with the capacity of one message.

The ltss S and R can be constructed straightforwardly from the descriptions in Fig. 1. The lts C is just a one-place buffer and easy to construct. To represent the unreliability of the channel, we use the lts C_F, a one-place buffer which may lose the message it has received. Distorted messages are assumed to be detected by some checksum mechanism and discarded, to be treated as lost.

The lts modelling the whole protocol is constructed from the basic ltss as described in Figure 3. We use synchronisation labels **dsy** to correspond to transmission of data item y from data source to sender, **scxy** to messages from sender to channel, **crxy** to messages from channel to receiver, **rax** to acknowledgement messages from receiver to ack. channel, **asx** to ack. messages from ack. channel to sender, **rty** to transmission of data items from receiver to target, and **tim** to the timeout signal. Here x ranges over $\{0, \ldots, w\}$ and y over $\{0, 1, 2\}$.

The lts P modelling the whole protocol can be formally defined as follows:

$$SC_0 = S$$
$$SC_{i+1} = \textbf{hide } sc* \textbf{ in } (SC_i[sc*/cr*]\,|[sc*, tim]|\,C)$$

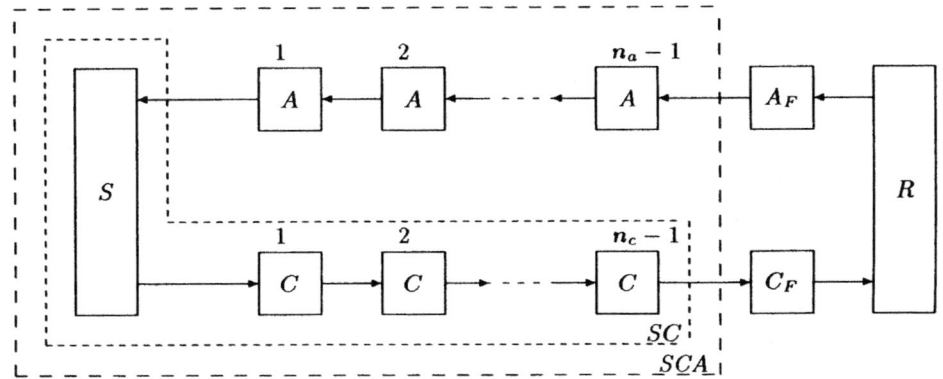

Figure3. Structure of the model

$$SCA_0 = SC = SC_{n_c-1}$$
$$SCA_{i+1} = \textbf{hide } as* \textbf{ in } (SCA_i[as*/ra*] \,|[as*, tim]|\, A)$$
$$SCA = SCA_{n_a-1}$$
$$SC_F A = SCA[sc*/cr*] \,|[sc*, tim]|\, C_F$$
$$SC_F A_F = SC_F A[as*/ra*] \,|[as*, tim]|\, A_F$$
$$P = SC_F A_F \,|[cr*, ra*, tim]|\, R$$

To capture the assumption that timeouts do not occur prematurely, we synchronised all components of the system with respect to the *tim* action so that a timeout could occur only if all components agree on that. A *tim* transition is allowed in C, C_F, A and A_F only when the corresponding buffer is empty, and in R only when the receiver cannot send any acknowledgements.

To verify that the protocol satisfies the safety requirement, we express the property *the sequence of data items delivered to the target belongs to the language* $0^\infty \cdot (1 \cdot 2^\infty \cup \epsilon)$ by the following formula ϕ_{safe}

$$(\widehat{rt1} \Rightarrow \widehat{rt1}(\neg\widehat{rt0} \wedge \neg\widehat{rt1})) \wedge (\widehat{rt2} \Rightarrow \widehat{rt2}(\neg\widehat{rt0} \wedge \neg\widehat{rt1})) \wedge (\widehat{rt2} \Rightarrow \widehat{rt1})$$

and verify that $D_{safe} \,|[ds*]|\, P \models \phi_{safe}$. Similarly, to verify the liveness requirements, we try to verify that $D_{live} \,|[ds*]|\, P \models \phi_{live}$, where ϕ_{live} is the formula

$$\phi_{fair} \Rightarrow (\Box\Diamond\widehat{rt0} \vee \Diamond\widehat{rt1})$$

and the fairness constraint is expressed by the following formula ϕ_{fair}

$$\bigwedge_{0 \le i \le w} (\Box\Diamond(\bigvee_{0 \le j \le 2} \widehat{sc_{ij}}) \Rightarrow \Box\Diamond(\bigvee_{0 \le j \le 2} \widehat{cr_{ij}})) \wedge \bigwedge_{0 \le i \le w} (\Box\Diamond\widehat{ra_i} \Rightarrow \Box\Diamond\widehat{as_i})$$

5   Verification

For verifying both safety and liveness properties of the SW-protocol, we used the general approach of constructing an abstraction $\overline{S}$ on the basis of the sender lts S. The particular abstractions used for safety and liveness properties are different, but the techniques and reasoning are very similar. Because of this, we shall just discuss liveness properties here. Full details are in [7].

Before constructing the abstraction for liveness, we can ease the verification by a couple of simple techniques. First of all, the fixed data source D_{live} produces only a fraction of all the potential data sequences, which means that a large part of the state space of P will not be reachable in $D_{live}\,||[ds*]||\,P$. Therefore, rather than build P first and then compose it with D_{live}, it is better to start by composing the sender S with D_{live} and then build the other ltss on that basis; the resulting ltss will be the same up to isomorphism. Secondly, when trying to determine the validity of ϕ_{live} over a model, by Prop. 9 we are allowed to hide labels $ds*$ and tim which do not appear in ϕ_{live}. What is more, as **hide** distributes over parallel composition as long as the hidden labels are not used for synchronisation, we can hide $ds*$ immediately after the data source is combined with the sender.

Let $\overline{S}$ denote the abstraction, and define $\overline{DS} = $ **hide** $ds*$ **in** $(D_{live}||[ds*]||\overline{S})$. Furthermore, let $\overline{DP}$ denote the system built by combining $\overline{DS}$ with the faulty elements C_F and A_F and the receiver R, in the same way as P was built on the basis of SCA. The essential properties of the abstraction are

A: (**hide** $ds*$ **in** $D_{live}||[ds*]||S) \overset{\text{ndfd}}{\prec} \overline{DS}$

B: **hide** $sc*$ **in** $(\overline{DS}[sc*/cr*]||[sc*,tim]|C) \overset{\text{ndfd}}{\prec} \overline{DS}$

C: **hide** $as*$ **in** $(\overline{DS}[as*/ra*]||[as*,tim]||A) \overset{\text{ndfd}}{\prec} \overline{DS}$

D: $\overline{DP} \models \phi_{live}$

Here A states that the abstraction is higher in the NDFD-preorder than the sender combined with D_{live}, and B and C that the abstraction alone is higher in the preorder than when combined with a one-place channel or acknowledge-ment channel. On the basis of compositionality of $\overset{\text{ndfd}}{\prec}$, it is easy to see from claims A-C that (**hide** $ds*$ **in** $(D_{live}||[ds*]||SCA)) \overset{\text{ndfd}}{\prec} \overline{DS}$, no matter what the channel capacities n_c and n_a are. From claim D and Prop. 8 it follows then that $D_{live}||[ds*]||P \models \phi_{live}$, as required. This approach to dealing with channels of arbitrary length has appeared previously in [18].

The abstraction $\overline{S}$ for liveness properties is described in Fig. 4. The two basic intuitions behind it are the following. First, it mimics the behaviour of the sender with channels of unspecified length. What this means is that sent messages do not necessarily appear or acknowledgements cause effect immediately. Secondly, in the context of the complete system often only a subset of all possible acknow-ledgement messages can actually occur. In the abstraction it is specified that after the reception of an unexpected acknowledgement message, the abstraction becomes 'chaotic', capable of performing any action (same idea appears in [5]).

The abstraction was formulated manually, aided by intuitions on which char-acteristics of the protocol were relevant for liveness properties. Once the ab-straction was constructed, claims A-C were checked by the ARA toolset [15].

SENDER ABSTRACTION
Variables
$d[(-tw)\ldots(tw-1)]$: table of data items; i,j,k : int; ch : bool;
Initially $i=0, j=0, k=0, ch=\bot$
loop infinitely
    choose nondeterministically
        ch $\longrightarrow$ perform any action; /* (also τ possible) */
        [] $\neg ch \wedge i < tw$ $\longrightarrow$ receive(data source, $d[i]$); $i := i+1$;
        [] $\neg ch \wedge j < i$ $\longrightarrow$ send(channel, $(j \oplus k, d[j])$); $j := j+1$;
                                                if $j < 0$ then $j := rnd(j,\ldots,0)$ end if;
        [] $\neg ch \wedge j = i \wedge i > 0$ $\longrightarrow$ receive(timeout); $j := 0$;
        [] $\neg ch$ $\longrightarrow$ receive(ack channel, x); $a := (x \ominus k) + 1$;
                                                if $((a - \min(j,0)) \le tw)$ then
                                                    $d[(-tw)\ldots(tw-1-a)] := d[(-tw+a)\ldots(tw-1)]$;
                                                    $i := \max(-tw, i-a)$; $j := j - a$;
                                                    if $j < 0$ then $j := rnd(j,\ldots,0)$ end if
                                                    $k := x \oplus 1$
                                                else if $a \ne w + 1$ then $ch := \top$ end if;
    end choose;
end loop;

Notation: $rnd(x,\ldots,y)$ returns a random element from $\{x,\ldots,y\}$

Figure4. Abstraction for liveness properties

Although originally designed for a slightly different semantic model, with added pre-processing steps it could deal with the NDFD preorder. Since no temporal logic model checker was available, claim D was also verified using the ARA toolset, by combining $\overline{DP}$ with tester processes trying to find a path violating ϕ_{live} [7, App. B]. The table below lists sizes of some ltss involved in the verification:

Parameters			Reachable nodes				
w	tw	rw	DS	$D_{live} \parallel S$	$DS \parallel C$	$DS \parallel A$	DP
1	1	1	22	12	56	95	61
3	2	2	98	48	280	723	915
5	3	3	266	120	838	2851	5179
6	3	3	310	140	977	3791	6018
7	4	4	562	240	1940	8117	21379

6   Faulty variant of the protocol

In the sender process of the SW protocol an acknowledgement is treated as valid, if it contains a sequence number anywhere in the current transmission window. In another variant of the protocol, occasionally found in the literature [11], an acknowledgement is treated as valid, if it contains a sequence number between the beginning of the transmission window and the sequence number to be sent

Step	Action	Explanation
1	$ds0$	sender receives data item 0 from source
2	$ds0$	sender receives data item 0 from source
3	$sc00$	sender sends first data item to channel
4	$cr00$	channel forwards it to receiver
5	$rt0$	receiver forwards it to target
6	$ra0$	receiver sends an ack to first data item to ack channel
7	τ	ack channel loses it
8	$sc10$	sender sends second data item to channel
9	$cr10$	channel forwards it to receiver
10	$rt0$	receiver forwards it to target
11	$ra1$	receiver sends an ack to second data item to ack channel
12	τ	ack channel loses it
13	tim	timeout: sender starts sending data items again
14	$sc00$	sender sends first data item to channel
15	$cr00$	channel forwards it to receiver
16	$ra1$	receiver sends an ack to **second** data item to ack channel
17	$as1$	ack channel forwards it to sender, **sender ignores it as invalid**
18	$sc10$	sender sends second data item to channel
19	$cr10$	channel forwards it to receiver
20	$ra1$	receiver sends an ack to second data item to ack channel
21	τ	ack channel loses it
22 –		repeating from 13 –

Parameters: $w = 2$ (or any $w \geq 2$), $tw = 2$, $rw = 1$, $n_c = n_a = 1$.

Figure5. Failure of liveness

next. In the sender process this corresponds to changing the last if-statement from 'if $(a \leq tw)$' to 'if $(a \leq j)$'. This change to the protocol seems innocent enough: How could there be an acknowledgement to any of the data items in the remaining part of the transmission window, anyway? After all, these data items are only just to be sent.

The safety properties of the variant can be verified as with the original protocol. However, when trying to verify the liveness properties, we were unable to produce an abstraction fulfilling the claims A-D above. After analysing the reasons behind this, it emerged that the variant actually *fails* to fulfil the liveness requirements. Fig. 5 describes one execution sequence of the variant where this failure appears. Although the sequence is fair, it fails to fulfil property LIVE3, requiring the system to accept data from the source; after the first two data items, no more data is accepted. Intuitively, although $as1$ is delivered to the sender infinitely often, it always arrives at a time when the sender regards it as invalid.

In our opinion this failure illustrates two issues. First, the change causing the protocol to fail liveness is natural and seems unimportant enough that, for example, [11] used the faulty variant when verifying safety properties of the protocol. We feel that this is a good example of the benefits of the rigorousness induced by a formal verification method. Secondly, the example reminds of the fact that liveness properties cannot be reliably verified unless divergences and fairness conditions are properly kept track of. For example, if channel events were hidden and the services provided by the protocols compared with respect to observation equivalence, ignoring divergences, both versions would be considered equivalent. In effect, divergences corresponding to fair executions would be confused with ones corresponding to unfair executions, and ignored.

References

1. Bolognesi, T. & Brinksma, E.: Introduction to the ISO specification language LOTOS, in *The Formal Descr. Technique LOTOS*, North-Holland, 1989, pp. 23-73
2. Clarke, E. M. & Long, D. E. & McMillan, K. L.: Compositional model checking, in *Proceedings of the Fourth IEEE LICS*, 1989, pp. 353-362
3. De Nicola, R. & Vaandrager, F.: Action vs. state based logics for transition systems, in *Semantics of Sys. of Conc. Proc.*, LNCS vol. 469, Springer, 1990, pp. 407- 419
4. Emerson, E. A.: Temporal and modal logic, in van Leeuwen, J. (ed.): *Handbook of Theoretical Computer Science*, Elsevier/North-Holland, 1990, pp. 997-1072
5. Graf, S. & Steffen, B. & Lüttgen, G.: Compositional Minimisation of Finite State Systems Using Interface Spec., in *Formal Asp. of Comp.*, vol. 8, 1996, pp. 607-616
6. International Standards Organisation: *Data Communications – HDLC Unbalanced Class of Procedures*, Ref. No. ISO 6159, ISO, Geneva, 1980
7. Kaivola, R.: *Equivalences, Preorders and Compositional Verification for Linear Time Temp. Logic and Conc. Sys.*, A-1996-1, Univ. of Helsinki, Dept. of Comp. Sci., 1996, 176+9 p., also in http://www.cs.Helsinki.FI/~rkaivola/research/ft.ps
8. Kaivola, R. & Valmari, A.: Using truth-preserving reductions to improve the clarity of Kripke-models, in *CONCUR'91*, LNCS vol. 527, Springer, 1991, pp. 361-375
9. Kaivola, R. & Valmari, A.: The weakest compositional semantic equivalence preserving nexttime-less linear temporal logic, *CONCUR'92*, LNCS vol. 630, Springer, 1992, pp. 207-221
10. Manna, Z. & Pnueli, A.: *The Temporal Logic of Reactive and Concurrent Systems, vol. 1, Specification*, Springer, 1991
11. Richier, J. L. & Rodriguez, C. & Sifakis, J. & Voiron, J.: Verification in Xesar of the sliding window protocol, in *PSTV VII*, North-Holland, 1987, pp. 235-248
12. Sabnani, K.: An algorithmic technique for protocol verification, in *IEEE Transactions on Communications*, vol. 36, no. 8, 1988, pp. 924-931
13. Stenning, N. V.: A data transfer protocol, in *Computer Networks*, vol. 11, 1976, pp. 99-110
14. Stirling, C.: Modal and temporal logics, in Abramsky, S. & al. (eds.): *Handbook of Logic in Computer Science*, Oxford University Press, 1992, pp. 477-563
15. Valmari, A. & Kemppainen, J. & Clegg, M. & Levanto, M.: Putting advanced reachability analysis techniques together: the "ARA" tool, in *FME'93: Industrial-Strength Formal Methods*, LNCS vol. 670, Springer, 1993, pp. 597-616
16. Valmari, A. & Tienari, M.: Compositional failure-based semantic models for Basic LOTOS, in *Formal Aspects of Computing*, vol. 7, 1995, pp. 440-468
17. Wolper, P.: Expressing interesting properties of programs in propositional temporal logic, in *Proceedings of the 13th ACM POPL*, 1986, pp. 184-193
18. Wolper, P. & Lovinfosse, V.: Verifying Properties of Large Sets of Processes with Network Invariants, in *Proc. of International Workshop on Automatic Verification Methods for Finite State Systems*, LNCS vol. 407, Springer, 1990, pp. 68-80

An Efficient Decision Procedure
for the Theory of Fixed-Sized Bit-Vectors

David Cyrluk*, Oliver Möller**, Harald Rueß**

* Computer Science Laboratory ** Fakultät für Informatik
SRI International   Universität Ulm
Menlo Park, CA 94025, USA   D-89069 Ulm, Germany
cyrluk@csl.sri.com   {moeller,ruess}@ki.informatik.uni-ulm.de

Abstract. In this paper we describe a decision procedure for the core theory of fixed-sized bit-vectors with extraction and composition that can readily be integrated into Shostak's procedure for deciding combinations of theories. Inputs to the solver are unquantified bit-vector equations $t = u$ and the algorithm returns *true* if $t = u$ is valid in the bit-vector theory, *false* if $t = u$ is unsatisfiable, and a system of solved equations otherwise. The time complexity of the solver is $\mathcal{O}(|t| \cdot log\, n + n^2)$, where t is the length of the bit-vector term t and n denotes the number of bits on either side of the equation. Then, the solver for the core bit-vector theory is extended to handle other bit-vector operations like bitwise logical operations, shifting, and arithmetic interpretations of bit-vectors. We develop a BDD-like data-structure called bit-vector BDDs to represent bit-vectors, various operations on bit-vectors, and a solver on bit-vector BDDs.

1 Introduction

The advantage of using a theorem prover to verify the correctness of large hardware circuits such as microprocessors is that the user can intelligently decompose and guide the high-level verification task. However, in order to be effective, low-level verification needs to be as automatic as possible. In the PVS verification system this is accomplished through the use of a method due to Shostak [3,7] for combining decision procedures. Currently any proof goal that can be proven by reasoning about equality, arrays, tuples, and linear arithmetic in PVS is proven automatically.

Experience with the verification of a commercial microprocessor [8], and the verification of multipliers [6] has shown that the lack of specialized decision procedures for notions related to bit-vectors is the main impediment to effective automation in theorem proving systems like PVS or SVC [2]. This insight forms the starting point of this paper, and we develop an efficient decision procedure for a theory of fixed-sized bit-vectors. Moreover, this decision procedure can readily be incorporated into Shostak's procedure for combinations of theories [7], since our algorithm fulfills the requirements for component theories as stated in [3].

By way of introduction, consider the following true statement in the combined theory of equality and bit-vectors: $(u_{[m]} \otimes v_{[n]})XOR(x_{[m]} \otimes y_{[n]}) = 0_{[m+n]} \supset f(x_{[m]}, y_{[n]}) = f(u_{[m]}, v_{[n]})$, where $\otimes$ denotes compostion of bit-vectors. To prove this by hand we would have to state and introduce several lemmas. One of which is that when the XOR of two bit-vectors is 0 then the two bit-vectors are identical. The user would have to manually apply these lemmas to the hypothesis in our example to conclude that $u_{[m]} = x_{[m]}$ and $v_{[n]} = y_{[n]}$. Once this has been established equality reasoning shows that $f(x_{[m]}, y_{[n]}) = f(u_{[m]}, v_{[n]})$

This example is illustrative of the type of unnecessary reasoning that took place in [8]. The algorithm that we present below takes equations such as the one that appears in the hypothesis in the above example and *solves* for some of the variables in that equation in terms of the remaining variables. In this case the solver would return $u_{[m]} = x_{[m]}$ and $v_{[n]} = y_{[n]}$. The rest of Shostak's algorithm works roughly by using this *solution* to replace the solved variables with their solved form. We have successfully applied this solver to eliminate manual reasoning about bit-vectors in some of the microprocessor correctness proofs in [8].

The paper is organized as follows. In Section 2 we present the theory of fixed-sized bit-vectors with composition and extraction as a many-sorted conditional equational theory. Section 3 contains a description of a canonizer and a solver [7] for this bit-vector together with an analysis of their time complexities. For lack of space we are not able to include the complete algorithm; an in-depth description of this decision procedure can be found in [4]. In Section 4 we describe how to add boolean bitwise operations to the core solver by a special data-structure called bit-vector BDDs, and in Section 5 we report on some preliminary experiment with an implementation of the bit-vector solver within the PVS system. The paper closes with some final remarks in Section 6.

2   Core Theory of Bit-Vectors

In this section we describe the core equational theory of fixed-sized bit-vectors of length n with composition and extraction of one or several consecutive bits. The length n of bit-vectors is constrained to be a positive natural number, since bit-vectors of length 0 are not permitted, and the bits of a bit-vector of length n are indexed, from left to right, from $n-1$ down to 0. In the following, $n, m, k, \ldots$ denote valid lengths of bit-vectors. The bit-vector theory contains constant bit-vectors $0_{[n]}$ and $1_{[n]}$ of length n, *composition* $t \otimes u$ of bit-vectors t and u, and *extraction* $t^{\wedge}(i,j)$, where $i, j \in \mathbb{N}$, of $i - j + 1$ many bits i through j from bit-vector t. These considerations lead to a many-sorted signature with infinitely many sort symbols $bvec_n$, $n \in \mathbb{N}^+$.

Definition 1. Let Σ be the signature

$$\langle \{ bvec_n \mid n \in \mathbb{N}^+ \},$$
$$\{ 0_{[n]} \mid n \in \mathbb{N}^+ \} \cup \{ 1_{[n]} \mid n \in \mathbb{N}^+ \} \cup$$
$$\{ . \otimes_{n,m} . \mid n, m \in \mathbb{N}^+ \} \cup \{ .^{\wedge}_n(i,j) \mid n \in \mathbb{N}^+ \wedge i, j \in \mathbb{N} \wedge n > i \geq j \geq 0 \} \rangle$$

$$
\begin{array}{lll}
1) & (t_{[n]} \otimes u_{[m]})^{\wedge}(i,j) = u_{[m]}^{\wedge}(i,j) & \text{IF } m > i \geq j \geq 0 \\
2) & (t_{[n]} \otimes u_{[m]})^{\wedge}(i,j) = t_{[n]}^{\wedge}(i-m, j-m) & \text{IF } m+n > i \geq j \geq m \\
3) & (t_{[n]} \otimes u_{[m]})^{\wedge}(i,j) = t_{[n]}^{\wedge}(i-m,0) \otimes u_{[m]}^{\wedge}(m-1,j) & \text{IF } m+n > i \geq m > j \\
4) & t_{[n]}^{\wedge}(n-1,0) = t_{[n]} \\
5) & t_{[n]}^{\wedge}(i,j) \otimes t_{[n]}^{\wedge}(j-1,k) = t_{[n]}^{\wedge}(i,k) \\
6) & (t_{[n]} \otimes u_{[m]}) \otimes v_{[p]} = t_{[n]} \otimes (u_{[m]} \otimes v_{[p]}) \\
7) & t_{[n]}^{\wedge}(i,j)^{\wedge}(k,l) = t_{[n]}^{\wedge}(k+j, l+j)
\end{array}
$$

Fig. 1. Bit-Vector Equations

such that for appropriate n, i, and j: $0_{[n]} :\rightarrow bvec_n$, $1_{[n]} :\rightarrow bvec_n$, . $\otimes _{n,m}$. : $bvec_n \times bvec_m \rightarrow bvec_{n+m}$, and . $^{\wedge}{}_n(i,j) : bvec_n \rightarrow bvec_{i-j+1}$

The dots to the left and to the right of function symbols indicate the use of infix notation, and extraction $^{\wedge}{}_n(i,j)$ is assumed to bind stronger than composition $\otimes _{n,m}$. In the following, $x_{[n]}, y_{[m]}, z_{[k]}, \ldots$ denote variables of sort $bvec_n$, $bvec_m$, and $bvec_k$ respectively. The set of well-formed terms is defined in the usual way and $t_{[n]}, u_{[m]}, v_{[k]}, \ldots$ denote bit-vector terms of respective lengths. Subscripts are omitted whenever possible and can be inferred from the context. Moreover, $t \equiv u$ denotes syntactic equality of bit-vectors t and u, $vars(t)$ denotes the set of variables in t.

A bit-vector term t is called *atomic* if it is a variable or a constant $0_{[n]}$ or $1_{[n]}$, and *simple terms* are either atomic or of the form $x_{[n]}^{\wedge}(i,j)$ where $x_{[n]}$ is a variable, and $i \neq n-1$ or $j \neq 0$. Moreover, terms of the form $t_1 \otimes t_2 \otimes \ldots \otimes t_k$ (modulo associativity), where t_i are all *simple*, are referred to as being in *composition normal form*. If, in addition, none of the neighboring simple terms denote the same constant (modulo length) and a simple term of the form $t^{\wedge}(i,j)$ is not followed by a simple term of the form $t^{\wedge}(j-1,k)$, then a term in composition normal form is called *maximally connected*.

Definition 2. Let Σ be the bit-vector signature defined in Definition 1; the core theory of bit-vectors is defined by the (conditional) Σ-equalities in Figure 1, and semantic entailment $\models$ in this theory is defined in the usual way.

Well-formedness of the bit-vector terms in Figure 1 implies that $n > i \geq j > k \geq 0$ in equation *5)* and $n > i \geq j \geq 0 \wedge i - j \geq k \geq l \geq 0$ in equation *7)* above. Obviously, the bit-vector theory in Definition 2 is consistent, and a possible interpretation of fixed-sized bit-vectors of length n are finite functions with domain $[0..n)$ and codomain $\{0,1\}$.

3 Solving Bit-Vector Equations

Now, we describe a decision procedure for the bit-vector theory as introduced above. This decision procedure can readily be integrated with Shostak's framework for deciding combinations of theories, since it is subdivided into a *canonizer* and a *solver* [7] which satisfy the requirements stated in [3].

$$\alpha(s) \ ::= \ \text{CASES } s \text{ OF}$$

$$t \otimes u \to \alpha(t) \otimes \alpha(u),$$

$$t_{[n]}{}^\wedge(n-1,0) \to \alpha(t_{[n]}),$$

$$t^\wedge(i,j)^\wedge(k,l) \to \alpha(t^\wedge(k+j,l+j)),$$

$$(t_{[n]} \otimes u_{[m]})^\wedge(i,j) \to \ \text{IF } m > i \text{ THEN } \alpha(u_{[n]}{}^\wedge(i,j))$$

$$\text{ELSEIF } j \geq m \text{ THEN } \alpha(t_{[n]}{}^\wedge(i-m,j-m))$$

$$\text{ELSE } \alpha(t_{[n]}{}^\wedge(i-m,0)) \otimes \alpha(u_{[m]}{}^\wedge(m-1,j))$$

$$\text{ENDIF },$$

$$\text{OTHERWISE } \quad s$$

$$\text{ENDCASES}$$

$$\beta(s) \ ::= \ \text{CASES } s \text{ OF} \quad c_{[n]} \otimes c_{[m]} \otimes u \to \beta(c_{[n+m]} \otimes u),$$

$$x_{[n]}{}^\wedge(i,j) \otimes x_{[n]}{}^\wedge(j-1,k) \otimes u \to \beta(x_{[n]}{}^\wedge(i,k) \otimes u),$$

$$x_{[n]}{}^\wedge(i,j) \otimes u \to x_{[n]}{}^\wedge(i,j) \otimes \beta(u),$$

$$\text{OTHERWISE} \quad s$$

$$\text{ENDCASES}$$

$$\sigma(t) \ ::= \ \beta(\alpha(t))$$

Fig. 2. Canonizer

3.1 Canonizer

The canonizer $\sigma(t)$ in Figure 2 computes the maximally connected composition normal form of t and is a straightforward transliteration of the equalities in Figure 1. In the first phase $\alpha(t)$ this canonizer normalizes a bit-vector term t to an equivalent term in composition normal form (see Section 2). The resulting composition normal form may still contain sub-terms such as $c_{[n]} \otimes c_{[m]}$ or $x_{[2]}{}^\wedge(1,1) \otimes x_{[2]}{}^\wedge(0,0)$, which can be further normalized to $c_{[n+m]}$ and $x_{[2]}$ respectively. These kinds of merging are accomplished in the second phase of canonization by the function β (see Figure 2). Altogether, $\sigma(t) \ ::= \ \beta(\alpha(t))$ computes the maximally connected composition normal form for a bit-vector term t.

Using this result one can prove that σ fulfills the requirements given in [3] for a canonizer in Shostak's framework.

Theorem 3.

1) *An equation $t = u$ in the theory is valid if and only if $\sigma(t) \equiv \sigma(u)$.*
2) *If t is a term not in the theory, then $\sigma(t) \equiv t$*
3) *$\sigma(\sigma(t)) \equiv \sigma(t)$*
4) *If $\sigma(t) \equiv f(t_1, ..., t_n)$ for a term t in the theory then $\sigma(t_i) \equiv t_i$ for $1 \leq i \leq n$.*
5) *$vars(\sigma(t)) \subseteq vars(t)$.*

```
solve(t = u)  ::=
    t ← σ(t)
    u ← σ(u)
    IF t ≡ u THEN RETURN true ENDIF
    IF vars(t) = ø THEN swap(t, u) ENDIF
    IF vars(t) = ø THEN RETURN false ENDIF
    {t₁ = u₁, t₂ = u₂, ..., tₘ = uₘ} ← slice({t, u})
    E ← ⋃ᵢ₌₁ᵐ csolve(tᵢ = uᵢ)
    IF false ∈ E THEN RETURN false ENDIF
    E_{x₁} ⊎ E_{x₂} ⊎ ... ⊎ E_{xₚ} ← E
    /* t.i. {E_{xᵢ}} is a partition of E where E_{xᵢ} contains all equations xᵢ = . */
    FOREACH i ∈ {1, ..., p} DO E_{xᵢ} ← slice(E_{xᵢ}) OD
    FOREACH i ∈ {1, ..., p} DO lazy_constant_propagation(E_{xᵢ}) OD
    {E_{x₁}, E_{x₂}, ..., E_{xₚ}} ← coarsest_slicing({E_{x₁}, E_{x₂}, ..., E_{xₚ}})
    FOREACH i ∈ {1, ..., p} DO equality_propagation(E_{xᵢ}) OD
    RETURN ⋀ᵢ₌₁ᵖ (xᵢ = β(find(E_{xᵢ})) )
    /* 'find' meaning a composition of representants of each column in E_{xᵢ} */
```

Fig. 3. Pseudo-Code for Bit-Vector Solver

The only non-trivial part of the proof is to show that $t = u$ implies $\sigma(t) \equiv \sigma(u)$; this is proved by contradiction (we refer to [4]).

Given a proper data-structure, say abstract syntax trees of bit-vector terms, the function α (Figure 2) visits each subterm a constant number of times, since the topmost bit-vector operator is eliminated in each step. The case analysis takes at most $\mathcal{O}(\log n)$ time, since it involves only comparison of integers which can be coded with $\log n$ bits. Thus, α is called at most $\mathcal{O}(|t|)$ times, and each call takes $\mathcal{O}(\log n)$ time. In phase β the number of steps equals the number of simple terms; an upper bound of this number is $\mathcal{O}(|t|)$, and, as above, each test is performed in $\mathcal{O}(\log n)$ time. Altogether, this gives the following worst-case complexity for the canonizer in Figure 2.

Theorem 4. *The time complexity of canonization $\sigma(t_{[n]})$ is $\mathcal{O}(|t| \cdot \log n)$, where $|t|$ is the length of the bit-vector t.*

3.2 Solver

A *solver* rewrites any unquantified equality $t = u$ in an equivalent *solved* form $\bigwedge_i x_i = s_i$, where each x_i occurs in none of the s_i. A particular simple approach for solving equations $t = u$ over fixed-sized bit-vectors proceeds by (see [4] for details)

1. replacing any bit-vector variable $x_{[n]}$ with $x_{n-1} \otimes \ldots \otimes x_0$, where x_i are (fresh) variables of sort $bvec_1$,

2. computing the composition normal form of each side,
3. bitwise comparing the corresponding left-hand and right-hand sides of the equations,
4. propagating the resulting equalities by processing the bitwise equalities one-by-one and building up a union-find structure,
5. and finally, replacing the bit-variables with their canonical representatives.

This simple solver, however, can be improved considerably, since, in most cases, it is not necessary to reduce the problem to a bitwise comparison of t and u. In the sequel, we describe the basic ideas of a refined version of the brute force algorithm above by means of an example; pseudocode for the crucial parts of the algorithm can be found in Figure 3.

Example 1.

$$\underbrace{x_{[3]} \otimes (y_{[4]} \otimes z_{[5]})^{\wedge}(5,4) \otimes 0_{[4]}}_{t} = \underbrace{((y_{[4]}{}^{\wedge}(2,1) \otimes x_{[3]})^{\wedge}(4,0) \otimes z_{[5]} \otimes x_{[3]})^{\wedge}(10,2)}_{u}$$

Given an equation $t = u$, the bit-vector solver in Figure 3 first canonizes both sides of the equation to obtain the equation $\sigma(t) = \sigma(u)$ over the maximally connected composition normal forms $\sigma(t)$ and $\sigma(u)$. Thus the equation in Example 1 canonizes to

$$\underbrace{x_{[3]} \otimes y_{[4]}{}^{\wedge}(0,0) \otimes z_{[5]}{}^{\wedge}(4,4) \otimes 0_{[4]}}_{\sigma(t)} = \underbrace{x_{[3]} \otimes z_{[5]} \otimes x_{[3]}{}^{\wedge}(2,2)}_{\sigma(u)}$$

The next step of the algorithm, called *slicing*, computes composition normal forms $t_1 \otimes \ldots \otimes t_m$ and $u_1 \otimes \ldots \otimes u_m$ of $\sigma(u)$ and $\sigma(t)$ respectively, such that each t_i and u_i are of the same length; moreover, it does so by minimizing the number m, called *granulation*, of simple terms on each side. Slicing of the canonized equation above, for example, leads to the following equation.

$$\begin{array}{ccccccccc}
\underbrace{x_{[3]}}_{t_1} & \otimes & \underbrace{y_{[4]}{}^{\wedge}(0,0)}_{t_2} & \otimes & \underbrace{z_{[5]}{}^{\wedge}(4,4)}_{t_3} & \otimes & \underbrace{0_{[3]}}_{t_4} & \otimes & \underbrace{0_{[1]}}_{t_5} \\
= \underbrace{x_{[3]}}_{u_1} & \otimes & \underbrace{z_{[5]}{}^{\wedge}(4,4)}_{u_2} & \otimes & \underbrace{z_{[5]}{}^{\wedge}(3,3)}_{u_3} & \otimes & \underbrace{z_{[5]}{}^{\wedge}(2,0)}_{u_4} & \otimes & \underbrace{x_{[3]}{}^{\wedge}(2,2)}_{u_5}
\end{array}$$

Obviously, this equation holds if and only if the conjunction of the equations in the set E holds.

$$E ::= \{ \ x_{[3]} = x_{[3]}, \ y_{[4]}{}^{\wedge}(0,0) = z_{[5]}{}^{\wedge}(4,4), \ z_{[5]}{}^{\wedge}(4,4) = z_{[5]}{}^{\wedge}(3,3),$$
$$0_{[3]} = z_{[5]}{}^{\wedge}(2,0), \ 0_{[1]} = x_{[3]}{}^{\wedge}(2,2)\}$$

Since E contains only equations over simple terms, the problem of solving an equation over arbitrary terms is reduced to solving equations over simple terms by means of a function *csolve* (see [4] for details). A call *csolve*($t = u$) results in a set of equations which

- is empty, if $t \equiv u$,
- contains **false** , if and only if t and u are different constants,
- contains exactly one solved equation of the form $x = s$, with $x \in vars(t = u)$ and s is a simple term (this case occurs whenever x is the only variable in $t = u$), or
- contains exactly two solved equations of the form $x = s_1$, $y = s_2$, with $x, y \in vars(t = u)$ and s_1, s_2.

Note that *csolve* introduces fresh variables with the convention that a-variables are known to occur only once in the system of solved equations, b-variables occur at least twice in a single right-hand side, and c-variables occur in exactly two different right-hand sides. This information is used to perform the following steps more efficiently.

In our running example, solving equations over simple terms yields the following new equations (possibly containing fresh variables).

$$csolve(x_{[3]} = x_{[3]}) = \varnothing$$
$$csolve(y_{[4]}{}^{\wedge}(0,0) = z_{[5]}(4,4)) = \{y = a^{(1)}{}_{[3]} \otimes c^{(1)}{}_{[1]}, z = c^{(1)}{}_{[1]} \otimes a^{(2)}{}_{[4]}\}$$
$$csolve(z_{[5]}{}^{\wedge}(4,4) = z_{[5]}(3,3)) = \{z = b^{(1)}{}_{[1]} \otimes b^{(1)}{}_{[1]} \otimes a^{(3)}{}_{[3]}\}$$
$$csolve(0_{[3]} = z_{[5]}{}^{\wedge}(2,0)) = \{z = a^{(4)}{}_{[2]} \otimes 0_{[3]}\}$$
$$csolve(0_{[1]} = x_{[3]}{}^{\wedge}(2,2)) = \{x = 0_{[1]} \otimes a^{(5)}{}_{[2]}\}$$

In order to perform the next steps it is convenient to rearrange the sets of equations obtained by *csolve* and group together the solved equations for variable x in a so-called *block* E_x. In our running example we get the following three blocks.

$$E_x = |\, 0_{[1]} \,|\, a^{(5)}{}_{[2]} \,|; \qquad E_y = |\, a^{(1)}{}_{[3]} \,|\, c^{(1)}{}_{[1]} \,|; \qquad E_z = \begin{vmatrix} c^{(1)}{}_{[1]} & a^{(2)'}{}_{[1]} & a^{(2)''}{}_{[3]} \\ b^{(1)}{}_{[1]} & b^{(1)}{}_{[1]} & a^{(3)}{}_{[3]} \\ a^{(4)'}{}_{[1]} & a^{(4)''}{}_{[1]} & 0_{[3]} \end{vmatrix}$$

In this example, the constant $0_{[3]}$ in the last column of E_z may be propagated by equating both $a^{(4)'}{}_{[1]}$ and $a^{(4)''}{}_{[1]}$ with $0_{[3]}$. No further propagation is necessary, since both variables are of kind-a variables. In the general case, however, propagation of constants in one column may trigger further propagations in other columns. Moreover, propagation of constants may result in additional slicings, since block entries may well be compositions. While propagation of constants is an optional step in our algorithm it may be used to detect inconsistencies — i.e. different constants in one column — at the earliest possible stage.

A *coarsest slicing* is a transformation of a set of equations of the form $x = t$, where t is in composition normal form, such that the cross-references between the terms in composition normal form on the right hand sides are resolved. More precisely, if a fresh variable c of kind C is split up into several parts $c', c'', \dots$ in one equation (and possibly into parts $\hat{c}, \hat{\hat{c}}, \dots$ in another one) these split-ups are sliced with each other, thus increasing the number of splinters of

c, but computing what is the coarsest granulation possible at this point of the propagation.

In our example, this operation leaves the blocks untouched; given the blocks $E_v = |\ c'\ |\ c''\ |\ a\ |$ and $E_w = |\ c\ |$, however, E_w gets updated to $|\ c'\ |\ c''\ |$.

Finally, the *propagation of equalities* step transforms all blocks to the coarsest slicing, so all references between them can be made explicit. The principle thereto is very much the same as in the brute force solver above. However, it is applied on (hopefully) vast parts of the variables instead of tiny bits. Note also that it is not necessary to check the consistency with the constants, since any such conflict has already been detected in the *propagation of constants* step.

Applying *propagation of constants*, *coarsest slicing*, and *propagation of equalities* to the equalities of our running examples we obtain the following solved form for the equation in Example 1 :

$$
\begin{aligned}
solve(E) \quad = \quad \{ \ x_{[3]} \ &= \ 0_{[1]} \ \otimes \ a^{(5)}{}_{[2]}, \\
y_{[4]} \ &= \ a^{(1)}{}_{[3]} \ \otimes \ c^{(1)}{}_{[1]}, \\
z_{[5]} \ &= \ c^{(1)}{}_{[1]} \ \otimes \ c^{(1)}{}_{[1]} \ \otimes \ 0_{[3]} \ \}
\end{aligned}
$$

Altogether, it can be shown that *solve* in Figure 3 is indeed a correct and complete solver for the given bit-vector theory.

Theorem 5. $\vdash t = u$ *if and only if* $solve(t = u) = $ **true**.

Moreover, the bit-vector decision procedure *solve* can be readily used in Shostak's framework for deciding combinations of theories, since it fulfills, besides Theorem 5, Shostak's requirements for individual solvers as stated in [3].

Theorem 6. *Let* $E ::= solve(e)$; *then:*

a) $E \in \{$ **true** , **false** $\}$ *or* $E \equiv \bigwedge_i (x_i = t_i)$.
b) *If* $vars(e) = \varnothing$ *then* $E \in \{$ **true** , **false** $\}$.
c) *If* $E \equiv \bigwedge_i (x_i = t_i)$ *then the following holds:*
    1. $x_i \in vars(e)$
    2. *for all* i, j: $\ x_i \notin vars(t_j)$
    3. *for all* $i \neq j$: $\ x_i \neq x_j$
    4. *for all* i: $\ \sigma(t_i) = t_i$.

Finally, we analyze the time complexity of the solver in Figure 3 in terms of the maximum $|t|$ of the lengths of t and u, and the number n of bits of the bit-vectors on either side of the equation $t = u$. Obviously, *slicing* can be computed in linear time and each call to *csolve* takes at most logarithmic time. It is a bit tricky, however, to determine the complexity of the propagations; but in a worst-case estimation one can say that: First, *lazy_constant_propagation* results either in a speed-up or "wastes" only linear time by unsuccessfully searching for constants to propagate. Second, slicing can be done in linear time by introducing, for example, a boolean vector of length n for each variable to denote the positions where splits have been introduced while processing the *coarsest slicing* routine. Third, propagation of equalities between the simple terms takes at most $\mathcal{O}(n^2)$

time, since there are at most $\mathcal{O}(n)$ such simple terms and equality within columns is propagated by browsing each column and computing canonical representatives for each entry; using specialized *union-find* structures this takes linear time. This analysis, together with the complexity of the canonizer (see Theorem 4) yields the following result.

Theorem 7. *The time complexity of* $solve(t_{[n]} = u_{[n]})$ *is* $\mathcal{O}(|\, t\, |\cdot \log n + n^2)$.

4 Bit-Vector BDDs

To this point we have described a solver for the *core* theory of bit-vectors with only the operations of composition and extraction. We now describe how to add the boolean bitwise operations, and call this new theory the *extended* theory of bit-vectors.

The two basic requirements that we must satisfy when adding the boolean operations is canonicity and solvability. As will be seen *binary decision diagrams* (BDDs) [1] over bit-vectors satisfy both these criteria.

A bit-vector BDD of size n is a BDD with bit-vector variables of size n as the internal nodes and the constant bit-vectors $1_{[n]}$ and $0_{[n]}$ as the terminals. The intended meaning of such a bit-vector BDD is the conjunction of the constraints that the n BDDs impose on the n individual bits of the bit-vector variables. The meaning, for example, of the bit-vector BDD,

$$\textbf{ite}(x_{[3]}, \textbf{ite}(y_{[3]}, 1_{[3]}, 0_{[3]}), 0_{[3]}) \tag{1}$$

where $\textbf{ite}(.,.,.)$ is the common *if-then-else* conditional, is given by:

$$\textbf{ite}(x_{[3]}{}^\wedge(2,2), \textbf{ite}(y_{[3]}{}^\wedge(2,2), 1_{[1]}, 0_{[1]}), 0_{[1]})\ \wedge$$
$$\textbf{ite}(x_{[3]}{}^\wedge(1,1), \textbf{ite}(y_{[3]}{}^\wedge(1,1), 1_{[1]}, 0_{[1]}), 0_{[1]})\ \wedge$$
$$\textbf{ite}(x_{[3]}{}^\wedge(0,0), \textbf{ite}(y_{[3]}{}^\wedge(0,0), 1_{[1]}, 0_{[1]}), 0_{[1]})$$

Now, consider the additional constraint $x_{[3]}{}^\wedge(0,0) = 1_{[1]}$. In this case, the example bit-vector BDD in (1) specializes to

$$\textbf{ite}(x_{[3]}{}^\wedge(2,1), \textbf{ite}(y_{[3]}{}^\wedge(2,1), 1_{[2]}, 0_{[2]}), 0_{[2]}) \otimes \textbf{ite}(y_{[3]}{}^\wedge(0,0), 1_{[1]}, 0_{[1]})$$

Thus, the use of bit-vector-BDDs permits maintaining the paradigm of largest chunks possible that has already guided the development of the efficient solver for the core theory.

The canonicity of BDDs immediately provides a canonical form for bit-vector BDDs. Both extraction and composition distribute over bit-vector BDDs so the normal form for the core theory can still be used for extended bit-vectors. Thus, the new normal form is composition of bit-vector BDDs whose variables are either bit-vector variables or extractions of bit-vector variables; in the following we assume a function γ that computes this new normal form.

Bit-wise operations over bit-vectors are represented by canonical bit-vector BDDs. For example, bit-wise conjunction "*AND*" and right-shift "*RSH*" are represented in this extended theory using the following correspondences.

$$BDD^1{}_{[n]} \; AND \; BDD^2{}_{[n]} = \gamma(\mathbf{ite}(BDD^1{}_{[n]}, \mathbf{ite}(BDD^2{}_{[n]}, 1_{[n]}, 0_{[n]}), 0_{[n]}))$$
$$RSH(BDD_{[n]}) = \gamma(BDD_{[n]}{}^{\wedge}(0,0)) \otimes \gamma(BDD_{[n]}{}^{\wedge}(n-1,1))$$

Now we have collected all the ingredients to describe a solver on bit-vector BDDs. Consider the BDD B:

$$\mathbf{ite}(P, B_P, B_{\bar{P}}). \tag{2}$$

where B_P and $B_{\bar{P}}$ respectively are the positive and negative cofactors of B with respect to variable P. We now describe a procedure for solving Equation 2 for the propositional variable P in terms of the variables in the rest of the BDD. The procedure will if necessary successively solve for the remaining variables lower in the BDD variable ordering. Equation 2 can be rewritten as follows:

$$(\neg(P \wedge \neg B_P) \wedge \neg(\neg P \wedge \neg B_{\bar{P}})) \wedge (B_P \vee B_{\bar{P}}). \tag{3}$$

This is equivalent to:

$$\bigl(P = \mathbf{ite}(B_P, \mathbf{ite}(B_{\bar{P}}, \delta, \mathbf{true}), \mathbf{false})\bigr)\wedge \tag{4}$$

$$(B_P \vee B_{\bar{P}}), \tag{5}$$

where δ is a newly generated variable that indicates that, when both B_P and $B_{\bar{P}}$ are true, BDD 2 imposes no constraint on the truth value of P. Equation 4 gives a solution for P in terms of variables lower in the BDD variable ordering. Equation 5 does not contain P and can be recursively solved for variables lower in the ordering than P. By successively solving the Equations 5 that are generated, a triangular system of equations is produced. By back substitution we then generate a completely solved system.

Consider, for example, solving the BDD $\mathbf{ite}(p, \mathbf{ite}(q, \mathbf{false}, \mathbf{true}), \mathbf{false})$ first for p and then for q. Our procedure yields

$$p = \mathbf{ite}(\mathbf{ite}(q, \mathbf{false}, \mathbf{true}), \mathbf{ite}(\mathbf{false}, \delta, \mathbf{true}), \mathbf{false}) \tag{6}$$

which simplifies to $p = \mathbf{ite}(q, \mathbf{false}, \mathbf{true})$. The procedure also generates the constraint $\mathbf{ite}(q, \mathbf{false}, \mathbf{true}) \vee \mathbf{false}$ which simplifies to $\mathbf{ite}(q, \mathbf{false}, \mathbf{true})$. This BDD is then recursively solved to yield $q = \mathbf{false}$ with a trivial constraint. Back substituting this solution for q produces $p = \mathbf{true}$ and the procedure terminates.

Given this solver on bit-vector BDDs, the core solver developed in Section 3 can easily be extended by, first, enabling the function *csolve* to accept bit-vector BDD arguments and, second, modifying the propagation of equalities step. While the complexity of solving the core theory of bit-vectors was analyzed above to be polynomial, the bit-vector theories containing bit-wise operations are *NP*- and *coNP*-hard, and, therefore, are not expected to be solvable in polynomial time. However, in the processor verification examples that we have looked at, the amount of bit-wise manipulations are quite limited and we do not expect the manipulations described in this section to dominate the complete solver.

#	Lemma	Time[$msec$]
1.	$fill_{[32]}(0) \; XOR \; x_{[32]} \; = \; x_{[32]}$	7
2.	$(NOT(x_{[32]}))^{\wedge}(15,0) \; = \; NOT(x_{[32]}{}^{\wedge}(15,0))$	14
3.	$(x_{[32]} \; XOR \; y_{[32]})^{\wedge}(15,0) \; = \; x_{[32]}{}^{\wedge}(15,0) \; XOR \; y_{[32]}{}^{\wedge}(15,0)$	26
4.	$(fill_{[12]}{}^{\wedge}(0) \otimes nat2bv_{[4]}(1)) \; = \; nat2bv_{[16]}(1)$	1
5.	$(x_{[32]}{}^{\wedge}(31,16)^{\wedge}(7,0) \otimes x_{[32]}{}^{\wedge}(15,0)) \; = \; x_{[32]}{}^{\wedge}(23,0)$	2
6.	$fill_{[16]}(nat2bv_{[10]}(511)^{\wedge}(9)) \otimes fill_{[8]}(nat2bv_{[10]}(511)^{\wedge}(8)) \otimes$ $\otimes nat2bv_{[10]}(511)^{\wedge}(7,0) \; = \; (fill_{[16]}(0) \otimes fill_{[16]}(1))$	22
7.	$(bv2nat(fill_{[16]}(x_{[16]}{}^{\wedge}(15)) \otimes x_{[16]}) \; = \; 0) \Leftrightarrow (bv2nat(x_{[16]}) = 0)$	3500

Fig. 4. Bit-Vector Lemmas

5   Experiments

The bit-vector decision procedures described above have been implemented and integrated with the decision procedures of the PVS [5] proof system. Most of the examples we have dealt with so far have been extracted from the verification of the AAMP5 [8], an industrial-strength microprocessor. Figure 4 lists a collection of representative lemmas automatically proven using our bit-vector decision procedures together with the run-times (in milli-seconds) of the bit-vector decision procedures. Note that these timings do not include the preprocessing step of PVS formulas and the run-time of the other decision procedures.

In addition to the above lemmas we redid some proofs that had previously required manual reasoning. In these proofs we were able to eliminate the manual proof steps. We were also able to turn off much of the bit-vector rewriting that took place as that was replaced with our decision procedure.

In order to apply our decision procedures to a larger number of lemmas from the AAMP5 verification, we had to make some extensions to support further bit-vector operations. The operation $nat2bv_{[n]}(m)$ is used in the lemmas in Figure 4 to generate a bit-vector of length n with unsigned interpretation m, $bv2nat$ is an interpreted function that computes the unsigned interpretation for bit-vectors, $fill_{[n]}(b)$ is a bit-vector of length n containing the bit b at every position, and $t^{\wedge}(i)$ extracts the i-th bit from bit-vector t. The extensions of the solver to support these bit-vector operations are mostly straightforward. Equations of the form $bv2nat(x_{[n]}) \; = \; bv2nat(y_{[m]})$, for example, can be solved by padding 0's to the left of the shorter bit-vector argument until the lengths of x and y are equal and by solving the bit-vector equation over the resulting arguments.

Most of the examples we have tried so far have been proven automatically in a fraction of a second by the bit-vector decision procedures. Even more interestingly, the run-time performance of the decision procedures is in many cases *independent* of the width of the data-paths. The processing of Lemma 3 in Figure 4, for example, results in bit-vector BDDs with variables of the form $z_{[32]}{}^{\wedge}(15,0)$ and no further splits are necessary.

6 Conclusions

The main achievement of this paper is the development of an efficient decision procedure for a fundamental theory of fixed-sized bit-vectors. We have successfully applied this procedure to proofs and lemmas that arise in the verification of a commercial microprocessor. The decision procedure obviated manual proof effort that was previously necessary.

To the best of our knowledge this is the first time that a specialized, efficient decision procedure for this bit-vector theory has been developed. Clearly, more experiments are needed to demonstrate the practical gain over the simple approach – that is reduction to bit-wise comparisons. Further work includes extensions of the bit-vector decision procedures to deal with arbitrary-sized bit-vectors and extraction positions possibly containing variables. However, we can not expect to have a polynomial solver for this theory, since, using a reduction from 3SAT, it can be shown that solvability is NP-complete in this case.

Acknowledgments: Thanks to J. Skakkebaek and Clark Barrett for many useful comments, M.K. Srivas for supplying interesting test examples, and the second author expresses his gratitude to F.W. von Henke and J. Rushby for supporting a fruitful visit at SRI International, Menlo Park.

References

1. R.E. Bryant. Symbolic Boolean Manipulation with Ordered Binary Decision Diagrams. *ACM Computing Surveys*, 24(3):293–318, September 1992.
2. D. Dill C. Barrett and J. Levitt. Validity Checking for Combinations of Theories with Equality. In M. Srivas, editor, *FMCAD '96*, volume 1166 of *Lecture Notes in Computer Science*, pages 187–201, Palo Alto, CA, November 1996. Springer-Verlag.
3. D. Cyrluk, P. Lincoln, and N. Shankar. On Shostak's Decision Procedure for Combination of Theories. In M. A. McRobbie and J. K. Slaney, editors, *Proc. of CADE'96*, volume 1104 of *Lecture Notes in Artificial Intelligence*, pages 463–477, New Brunswick, NJ, July/August 1996. Springer-Verlag.
4. D. Cyrluk, O. Möller, and H. Rueß. An Efficient Decision Procedure for a Theory of Fixed-Sized Bitvectors with Composition and Extraction. Technical report, Universität Ulm, D-89069 Ulm, Oberer Eselsberg, December 1996.
5. S. Owre, J. Rushby, N. Shankar, and F. von Henke. Formal Verification for Fault-Tolerant Architectures: Prolegomena to the Design of PVS. *IEEE Transactions on Software Engineering*, 21(2):107–125, February 1995.
6. H. Rueß. Hierarchical Verification of Two-Dimensional High-Speed Multiplication in PVS: A Case Study. In M.K. Srivas and A. Camilleri, editors, *Formal Methods in Computer-Aided Design*, volume 1166 of *Lecture Notes in Computer Science*. Springer-Verlag, November 1996.
7. R.E. Shostak. Deciding Combinations of Theories. *Journal of the ACM*, 31(1):1–12, January 1984.
8. M.K. Srivas and S.P. Miller. Formal Verification of the AAMP5 Microprocessor. In M.G. Hinchey and J.P. Bowen, editors, *Applications of Formal Methods*, International Series in Computer Science, chapter 7, pages 125–180. Prentice Hall, Hemel Hempstead, UK, 1995.

Construction of Abstract State Graphs with PVS

Susanne Graf and Hassen Saidi
VERIMAG[1]
{graf,saidi}@imag.fr

Abstract. In this paper, we propose a method for the automatic construction of an abstract state graph of an arbitrary system using the PVS theorem prover.
Given a parallel composition of sequential processes and a partition of the state space induced by predicates $\varphi_1, ..., \varphi_\ell$ on the program variables which defines an abstract state space, we construct an abstract state graph, starting in the abstract initial state. The possible successors of a state are computed using the PVS theorem prover by verifying for each index i if φ_i or $\neg\varphi_i$ is a postcondition of it. This allows an abstract state space exploration for arbitrary programs.

keywords: *abstract interpretation, state graph exploration, theorem proving*

1 Introduction

It is now widely accepted that abstraction techniques are useful, and even necessary for a successful verification [Kur94,CGL94,GL93,LGS$^+$95,Gra95,Dam96] [DF95]. However, in case that the system has an infinite state space, it is difficult to mechanize the construction of an abstract system or state graph. In [GL93,KDG95] tools are described which, given a system (with variables on finite domains), a set of abstract (boolean) variables, and an abstraction relation relating the concrete and the abstract variables, construct automatically a corresponding abstract system, which then may be analyzed by any model-checker. For the analysis of real-time and particular hybrid systems, there exist tools for the abstract analysis by means of abstract interpretation methods based on the use of polyhedra [HH95,DOTY96,HPR94] but they are restricted to systems with linear assignments. In [Gra95,DF95], methods for the construction of abstract state graphs of more general infinite state systems are proposed, but they require an important amount of user intervention, as it is necessary to give for any atomic operation of the system a corresponding abstract operation which must be proven to be correct. The definition of abstract operations and the corresponding correctness proofs are in general rather time consuming, and in case of modification of the system or non satisfaction of the desired properties on the abstract system, some of them need to be modified.

We describe a method based on abstract interpretation which, from a theoretical point of view, is similar to the splitting method proposed in [DGG93,Dam96] but the weaker abstract transition relation we use, allows us to construct automatically abstract state graphs paying a reasonable price.

We consider a particular set of abstract states: the set of the monomials on a set of state predicates $\varphi_1, ..., \varphi_\ell$. The successor of an abstract state $\widehat{m}$ for a

---

[1] Centre Equation, 2, Avenue de la Vignate, 38610 Grenoble-Gières

transition τ of the program is the *least* monomial satisfied by all successors via τ of concrete states satisfying $\hat{m}$. This successor can be determined exactly if for each predicate φ_i it can be determined if φ_i or $\neg\varphi_i$ is a postcondition of $\hat{m}$ for τ. In order to do this, we use the PVS theorem prover [SOR93] and our PVS-interface defined in [GS96]. If the tactic used for the proof of the verification conditions is not powerful enough, an upper approximation of the abstract successor is constructed.

This allows us to compute upper approximations of the set of reachable states which is sufficient for the verification of invariants. Also, for almost the same price, an abstract *state graph* can be constructed: the expensive part of the algorithm is the computation of an abstract successor as it requires several validity checks. Therefore, only relatively small state graphs can be constructed and the additional cost for the storage of the transition relation is almost negligible. An abstract state graph can be used for the verification of any property expressible as a temporal logic formula without existential quantification over paths, due to the results on property preservation [CGL94,LGS+95] using a model checker.

An abstract state graph represents also a relatively precise global control graph of the system (the guards of the system are used for the construction of the abstract state graph) which can be used for a backwards verification of invariants as described in [GS96]. A global control graph allows us to obtain much stronger structural invariants using the tool described in [BLS96,BBC+96] than the initial presentation as a parallel composition of processes.

We have implemented a particular case of this method in our tool [GS96] where only successors of canonical monomials are constructed: if a successor is not a canonical monomial (that is some non-determinism is introduced by the abstraction), it is split into its canonical monomials. We have also interfaced the tool with the state space analysis tool ALDÉBARAN [FGK+96].

We have verified a bounded retransmission protocol developed by Philips which has already been proven correct before using theorem provers [GvdP93] [HSV94,HS96]. But for all these proofs powerful auxiliary invariants had to be given by the user. Using our tool, this protocol can be verified without user intervention.

2 Construction of abstract state graphs

2.1 Preliminary definitions

We consider systems which are parallel compositions of processes of the following form, where we consider parallel composition by interleaving and synchronization by shared variables as in Unity [CM88]:

Definition 1 (Processes).
Name : P
Declarations : $x_1 : T_1, ..., x_n : T_n$
Transitions : $\tau_1, ..., \tau_p$
Initial States : *init*

where P is a name, x_i are variables of type T_i (which may be any type definable in PVS). The list of variables declared in one process indicates which variables are (intended to be) used in this process, but in fact all variable declarations are *global*. Each transition τ_i is a guarded assignment of the form

$$g_i(\overline{x}) \longmapsto \quad \overline{x} := ass_i(\overline{x}) \tag{1}$$

where $g_i(\overline{x})$ is a boolean PVS-expression and $ass_i(\overline{x})$ a tuple of PVS-expressions ass_{i_j} of type T_j.

Semantics: As parallel composition is as in Unity, the state graph associated with a parallel composition of processes is the state graph associated with a *single* process having, as variables the union of the variables of all processes, as transitions the union of the transitions of all processes, and as initial predicate the intersection of the initial predicates of all processes. That means, parallel composition is only useful for better readability and for the generation of structural invariants [BLS96]. Therefore, we consider here only systems with a single process P. P defines a state graph $\mathcal{S}_P = (Q_P, R_P, I_P)$, where

- $Q_P = T_1 \times ... \times T_n$
- $R_P = \bigcup_{i=1}^p \tau_i$, where $\tau_i(q) = \begin{cases} \bot & \text{if } g_i(q) \equiv \textit{false} \\ ass_i(q) & \textit{otherwise} \end{cases}$

  denotes also the (partial) transition function associated with transition τ_i.
- $I_P = \{q \mid init(q) \equiv \textit{true}\}$ is the set of initial states.

Predicate transformers: Let us first recall briefly the notion of predicate transformers associated with relations and their well-known characterization for guarded command programs. In the sequel, we always consider sets of (concrete) states to be represented by predicates φ on the program variables (hence the name predicate transformer).

Definition 2 (predicate transformers). Let R be a binary relation on a set Q and $\varphi \in \mathcal{P}(Q)$ represent a subset of Q. Then,

- $\textbf{post}[R](\varphi) = \exists q' . R(q', q) \wedge \varphi(q')$
- $\widetilde{\textbf{pre}}[R](\varphi) = \forall q' . (R(q, q') \Rightarrow \varphi(q'))$

$\textbf{post}[R](\varphi)$ defines the set of successors of φ by R (strongest postcondition). $\widetilde{\textbf{pre}}[R](\varphi)$ represents the largest set of states such that all its successors satisfy φ (weakest precondition). Preconditions for guarded commands τ_i of the form (1) can be expressed without quantifiers:

$$\widetilde{\textbf{pre}}[\tau_i](\varphi) \equiv (g_i(\overline{x}) \Rightarrow \varphi[ass_i(\overline{x})/\overline{x}]) \tag{2.1}$$

These predicate transformers have many interesting properties (see for example [Sif82]), but here we need only the following:

$$\textbf{post}[R](\varphi) \Rightarrow \varphi' \quad \text{iff} \quad \varphi \Rightarrow \widetilde{\textbf{pre}}[R](\varphi')^2 \tag{2.2}$$

Abstract semantics of programs: All the results presented in this section are an application of abstract interpretation [CC77].

---

[2] this property is due to the fact that $(\widetilde{\textbf{pre}}[R](), \textbf{post}[R]())$ forms a Galois connection

Definition 3 (abstract state graphs). Let $\mathcal{S} = (Q, \cup \tau_i, I)$ be the state graph of a program, $\mathbf{Q}^A$ a lattice of abstract states and $(\alpha : \mathcal{P}(Q) \mapsto \mathbf{Q}^A, \gamma : \mathbf{Q}^A \mapsto \mathcal{P}(Q))$ a Galois connection[3]. $\mathcal{S}^A = (\mathbf{Q}^A, \cup \tau_i^A, I^A)$ is an *abstraction* of $\mathcal{S}$ iff

- $I \subseteq \gamma(I^A)$
- $\forall i \ \forall \mathbf{Q}^A \in \mathbf{Q}^A \ . \ \mathbf{post}[\tau_i](\gamma(\mathbf{Q}^A)) \subseteq \gamma(\tau_i^A(\mathbf{Q}^A))$

The *abstraction function* α associates with any set of concrete states a corresponding abstract state (the abstract state space is a lattice where larger abstract states represent larger sets of concrete states). The *concretisation function* γ associates with every abstract state the set of concrete state that it represents. The above definition simply expresses that the abstract initial state represents (at least) all concrete initial states, and the successor of any abstract state $\mathbf{Q}^A$ by some abstract transition represents all successors of the set of concrete states represented by $\mathbf{Q}^A$ by the corresponding concrete transition. Thus, every concrete execution sequence is represented by at least one abstract one. Intuitively, the smaller the represented superset of execution paths is, the more properties are satisfied on the abstract system.

2.2 A particular abstraction scheme

Choice of an abstract state lattice: We consider an abstract state lattice $\mathbf{Q}^A$ induced by a set of *predicates* $\varphi_1, ..., \varphi_\ell$ on the variables of P^4. We choose as abstract state space the lattice $\widehat{\mathcal{M}}$ of the $3^\ell + 1$ monomials on abstract *boolean variables* $\widehat{\varphi}_1, ..., \widehat{\varphi}_\ell$[5]. Notice that,

- $\widehat{\mathcal{M}}$ forms a complete lattice with order relation $\Rightarrow$ (implication), *glb* operator $\wedge$ (conjunction,), *lub* operator $\sqcup$ which is weaker than $\vee$ (e.g. $\widehat{\varphi}_1 \wedge \widehat{\varphi}_2 \sqcup \widehat{\varphi}_2 \wedge \neg \widehat{\varphi}_3 = \widehat{\varphi}_2$). The set of atoms of the lattice is the set $\widehat{\mathcal{M}}^c$ of the 2^ℓ *canonical* monomials.
- Each abstract state $\widehat{m} \in \widehat{\mathcal{M}}$ represents a set of concrete states defined by the predicate on concrete program variables obtained by substituting every abstract variable $\widehat{\varphi}_i$ by the concrete predicate φ_i, that is

$$\gamma(\widehat{m}) = \widehat{m}[\varphi_i / \widehat{\varphi}_i]$$

- Sets of abstract states can be represented by arbitrary boolean expressions on $\widehat{\varphi}_1, ..., \widehat{\varphi}_\ell$.

Abstract transitions: For each concrete transition τ_i of the program, we define an abstract transition function τ_i^A associating with any abstract state $\widehat{m}$ the least abstract state representing all successors of the concrete states represented by $\widehat{m}$. The fact that the abstract successor $\widehat{m}'$ is a monomial, allows to determine it as follows: it is *"false"* ($\widehat{m}$ has no successor) if in all concrete states satisfying

---

[3] a Galois connection is a pair of functions (α, γ) satisfying $\alpha(\gamma(\mathbf{Q}^A)) = \mathbf{Q}^A$ and $\varphi \Rightarrow \gamma(\alpha(\varphi))$. Given γ, α is implicitly defined by $\alpha(\varphi) = \sqcap\{\mathbf{Q}^A \in \mathbf{Q}^A | \varphi \Rightarrow \gamma(\mathbf{Q}^A)\}$.

[4] predicates $\varphi_1, ..., \varphi_\ell$ define a partition of Q_P, even if they are not independent

[5] a monomial is a conjunction of $\widehat{\varphi}_i$'s and $\neg \widehat{\varphi}_i$'s containing each $\widehat{\varphi}_i$ at most once. Furthermore, we consider the predicate *false* as a monomial.

$\gamma(\widehat{m})$, τ_i is not enabled; $\widehat{m}'$ has a conjunct $\widehat{\varphi}_j$ (resp. $\neg\widehat{\varphi}_j$) if all successors of states satisfying $\gamma(\widehat{m})$ satisfy φ_j (resp. $\neg\varphi_j$); otherwise, $\widehat{m}'$ depends not on $\widehat{\varphi}_j$:

$$\tau_i^A(\widehat{m}) = \begin{cases} false & \text{if } \gamma(\widehat{m}) \Rightarrow \neg g_i \quad (3.0) \\ \bigwedge \widehat{m}'_j, \widehat{m}'_j = \begin{cases} \widehat{\varphi}_j & \text{if } \mathbf{post}[\tau_i](\gamma(\widehat{m})) \Rightarrow \varphi_j \quad (3.1) \\ \neg\widehat{\varphi}_j & \text{if } \mathbf{post}[\tau_i](\gamma(\widehat{m})) \Rightarrow \neg\varphi_j \quad (3.2) \\ true & \text{otherwise} \quad (3.3) \end{cases} & \text{otherwise} \end{cases} \quad (3)$$

The properties (2.1) and (2.2) allow to recognize easily that the involved implications can be expressed without introducing existential quantifiers. E.g. (3.1) is equivalent to

$$\gamma(\widehat{m}) \wedge g_i \Rightarrow \varphi_j[ass_i(\overline{x})/\overline{x}] \qquad (3.1)$$

That means that the successor of a given abstract state can be "computed" if it is possible to check the validity of the implications in (3). In order to prove these implications, one can use a theorem prover. In this case, we are sure to compute the "exact" result defined by (3) if for all indices i either (3.0), (3.1) or (3.2) can be proved. Otherwise, the negative results can either be due to the fact that $\mathbf{post}[\tau_i](\widehat{m})$ has a non-empty intersection with both φ_i and with $\neg\varphi_i$ or simply to the fact that the applied proof strategy is not powerful enough. This allows us to do a state space exploration, starting in the abstract initial state which can be computed analogously.

2.3 Abstract state space exploration methods

Using the above defined abstract transition functions τ_i^A, different upper approximations of the set of reachable states (invariants) can be defined.

First approximation: $\mathcal{I}_1$ is obtained by identifying the abstract state and property lattices:

$$\mathcal{I}_1 = \bigsqcup_{j=0}^{\infty} X_j \quad \text{where} \quad \begin{aligned} X_0 &= I^A \\ X_{j+1} &= \bigsqcup_{i=1}^{p} \tau_i^A(X_j) \end{aligned}$$

All approximations X_j are abstract states (elements of $\widehat{\mathcal{M}}$). Thus, $\mathcal{I}_1$ can be computed in at most ℓ iterations, as the longest chains in $\widehat{\mathcal{M}}$ are of length ℓ.

Second approximation: The strongest invariant that can be obtained using τ_i^A, is obtained by allowing abstract properties to be arbitrary disjunctions of abstract states (the abstract property lattice is the lattice of boolean expressions on $\widehat{\varphi}_1, ..., \widehat{\varphi}_\ell$) and by applying τ_i^A only on canonical monomials $\widehat{m}^c \in \widehat{\mathcal{M}}^c$:

$$\mathcal{I}_2 = \bigvee_{j=0}^{\infty} X_j \quad \text{where} \quad \begin{aligned} X_0 &= I^A \\ X_{j+1} &= \bigvee\{\tau_i^A(\widehat{m}^c) \mid \widehat{m}^c \in \widehat{\mathcal{M}}^c \wedge \widehat{m}^c \Rightarrow X_j, \ i = 1..p\} \end{aligned}$$

$\mathcal{I}_2$ can be obtained by a state space exploration, where only canonical monomials are treated as "states", and each constructed abstract successor is split into its set of canonical monomials.

Complexity issues: It is reasonable to express the complexity of the computation of the above invariants by means of the number of necessary proofs. In order to compute the successor of an arbitrary abstract state $\widehat{m}$, at most $K = 2*p*\ell+1$ proofs (1 proof for the enabledness and 2 proofs for each predicate φ_i and each transition τ_j) are needed. The computation of the invariant $\mathcal{I}_1$ needs therefore maximally $\ell * K$ proofs, but it is in general too weak. For the second invariant, in the worst case, the successors of (almost) all 2^ℓ minimal abstract states (canonical monomials) have to be computed, leading to maximally $2^\ell * K$ proofs. However, in practice, the number of necessary proofs is much smaller as

1. some transitions τ_j leave some predicates φ_i trivially unchanged or transform φ_i independently of all (or most) other predicates φ_k
2. only a subset of states are reachable
3. we have not required the predicates $\varphi_1, ..., \varphi_\ell$ to be independent. If they are not, not all 2^ℓ canonical monomials are consistent (that is states). In this case, a *dependency predicate* allows us to eliminate inconsistent states.

Improvement of the computed invariants: The invariants $\mathcal{I}_K$ can be improved by using them as the starting point of a backward analysis

$$\mathcal{I}_K^+ = \bigwedge_{j=0}^{\infty} Y_j \quad \text{where} \quad \begin{array}{l} Y_0 = \mathcal{I}_K \\ Y_{j+1} = Y_j \wedge \bigwedge_{i=1}^{p} \widetilde{\mathbf{pre}}[\tau_i](Y_j) \end{array} \tag{4}$$

Improved versions of this backward analysis which use theorem proving to discharge verification conditions are implemented in [BBC$^+$96,GS96]. Notice that the approximations Y_i are arbitrary predicates of the concrete property lattice and not necessarily boolean combinations of $\varphi_1, ..., \varphi_\ell$. In order to do an abstract backward analysis (cf. [CC77]) a *lower* approximation of $\widetilde{\mathbf{pre}}[\tau_i](Y_j)$ is needed, e.g., the weakest monomial completely contained in $\widetilde{\mathbf{pre}}[\tau_i](Y_j)$ which can be obtained with at most $2 * \ell$ proofs.

Construction of state graphs: As the computation of a successor requires several proofs, only relatively small abstract state spaces (a few thousand successor computations) can reasonably be explored. Under these circumstances, the additional cost for the representation of the transition relation is almost negligible. The construction of a complete state graph has at least two advantages:

- any property representable as a temporal logic property without existential quantification over executions can be verified using a model checker.
- It represents a relatively precise global control graph, especially if all abstract states represent a set of concrete states enabling exactly the same transitions. The method and tool described in [BLS96] generate stronger structural invariants for this control graph than for the initial control structure. These invariants can be used to improve the result of the backward analysis defined by (4).

Refinement of an abstract state graph: If the abstract state space exploration by means of τ_i^A does not allow some property to be verified, one can try to construct a more precise abstraction by adding more predicates to $\varphi_1, ..., \varphi_\ell$, that is, to consider a finer partition of the concrete state space. For the computation of a successor of $\widehat{m} \wedge \widehat{m}_{new}$ by the refined transition relation, not all implications of Definition (3) — already checked during the construction of the successor of $\widehat{m}$ — have to be checked, but only those which could *not* be proved valid in the previous check (and this information can be deduced from the so far constructed transition relation; it is not necessary to keep a list of valid assertions). That means the construction of a sufficiently precise state graph can be obtained in an incremental manner.

3   An implementation

In [GS96] and [Sa97], we presented a tool implementing the backward computation of inductive invariants (4) and also the methods described in [BLS96]and [BBC+96] for the generation of structural invariants. We have also implemented an abstract state graph generation corresponding to the second approximation. We have achieved an integration with the Pvs theorem prover, where all the implications necessary to compute the successors of an already reached state are submitted to the Pvs prover. A proof strategy combining decision procedures, rewriting and boolean simplification using BDDs, is systematically applied. This proof strategy is often sufficient to prove all valid implications that are generated.

As our tool also deals with explicit control, an abstract state $\widehat{m}$ consists of the concrete control configuration c and a valuation of a set of boolean variables $\widehat{\varphi}_1, ..., \widehat{\varphi}_\ell$ as defined in the preceding section.

1. Given a set of predicates $\varphi_1, ..., \varphi_\ell$, an upper approximation of a dependency predicate is computed and used in order to generate only consistent successors.
2. Auxiliary invariants described in [BLS96] are generated using the initial control structure where all control configurations of a system consisting of several parallel components are considered reachable.
3. A state graph is generated. The conjunction $\mathcal{I}$ of already known invariants of the system is used to construct smaller successors for each abstract state by replacing the implications of (3) by weaker ones. For example the implication (3.1) becomes:

$$\mathcal{I} \wedge \gamma(\widehat{m}) \wedge g_i \Rightarrow \varphi_j[ass_i(\overline{x})/\overline{x}] \qquad (3.1')$$

Also, not all the implications of (3) are generated, but only those compatible with the generated dependency predicate. (3.1') considers only successors of states in $\mathcal{I}$. Furthermore, only successors having a non-empty intersection with $\mathcal{I}$ should be added to the set of reachable states. If $\mathcal{I}$ is (provably) inductive, only such successors are constructed. Otherwise, for each abstract state $\widehat{m}$ obtained by (4), it should be verified if

$$\gamma(\widehat{m}) \Rightarrow \neg \mathcal{I} \qquad (5)$$

holds. If the proof of (5) succeeds, no state in $\gamma(\widehat{m})$ is reachable, otherwise, we don't know, and $\widehat{m}$ must be considered as reachable. If an abstract state is reached, such that for some enabled transition no (consistent) successor in $\mathcal{I}$ is constructed, this state is itself not in $\mathcal{I}$, and is eliminated.

The generation of the abstract graph is *completely automatic* as we never try to prove interactively a generated implication: if the proof of a valid implication fails, a weaker successor is obtained. The user guides the verification by (re)defining the predicates $\varphi_1, ..., \varphi_\ell$ for the definition of the abstract state graph and by defining the automatic proof strategy. The constructed abstract state graph is generated in the format of the ALDÉBARAN tool [FGK$^+$96], and can therefore be analyzed by all the techniques available in ALDÉBARAN, such as minimization, model-checking and automatic display of graphs. In a near future it is foreseen to represent abstract state sets and transition relation by BDDs, which is convenient for an incremental construction of the abstract state graph.

Choice of the predicates φ_i**:** In order to prove that ψ is an invariant of the system (or any other property involving ψ), we can try to use ψ for the definition of the abstract state space. But it is essential to use the *guards* appearing in the transitions of the system. This allows us to construct successors only via transitions enabled in all represented concrete states and replaces the enabledness check (3.0) by a boolean test. Furthermore, each predicate is split into its literals. E.g., for the verification of the invariant (6) below we take $\varphi_1 = (OUT = IN)$ and $\varphi_2 = (OUT = tail(IN))$ instead of the disjunction $\varphi_1 \vee \varphi_2$; otherwise, in most cases, too much information is lost.

Example: We have applied this method for the verification of an alternating bit protocol. The protocol is correct if the list of already received messages OUT is a prefix of the list of so far sent messages IN such that OUT has at most one element less than IN. This can be expressed by

$$\Box(OUT = IN \vee OUT = tail(IN)) \qquad (6)$$

Using only the already implemented backward method to prove (6), the computation of the appropriate inductive invariant[6] does not terminate (also using the generated structural invariants).

Using the predicates appearing in the guards, the abstract state graph of Figure 1 is constructed. These two predicates express the fact that the bit joint with the message (respectively the bit representing the acknowledgment) is of the expected value. 34 implications are submitted to the prover, 5 abstract states are created, and the construction takes 68 seconds.

Using the literals φ_1 and φ_2 of (6) for the construction of the abstract state graph does not result in more precision. We have used two methods to obtain a better approximation:

1. We have refined the so far obtained state graph by using also the internal predicate $message(message\_channel) = head(IN)$ — expressing that the last sent message is the head of IN. The constructed state graph is again the one of Figure 1, but all its states satisfy either $IN = OUT$ or $OUT = tail(IN)$.
2. We have used the state graph of Figure 1 as a control graph which allows to generate more structural invariants using the methods of [BLS96,BBC$^+$96]. Then, we apply the suggested backward analysis to strengthen the already obtained invariant. The Property (6) can be proved with a single iteration.

In this simple protocol, the control depends only on finite domain variables, and it would be much faster to construct the control graph using the expansion

---

[6] The weakest inductive invariant implying $IN = OUT \vee OUT = tail(IN)$

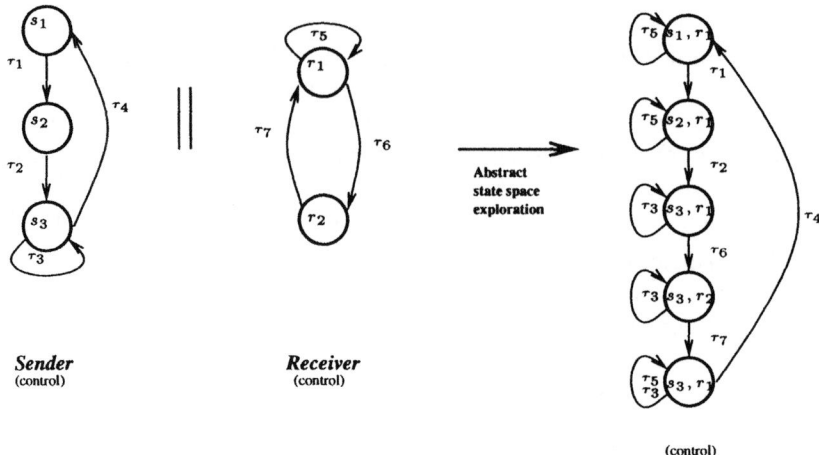

Fig. 1. Abstract control graph for the alternating bit protocol

method described in [HGD95]. In the example of the next section however, the control depends partially on infinite domain variables, and the expansion method does not work.

4 Verification of a Bounded Retransmission Protocol

We have used this method to verify a Bounded Retransmission Protocol (BRP) developed by Philips [GvdP93]. The BRP protocol is an extension of the alternating bit protocol, where not single messages, but message packets are transmitted and the number of possible retransmissions per message is bounded by some number *max*. We consider a fully parameterized version of the protocol where the packets can be of any size, and *max* any positive number. The protocol has already been proved using a theorem prover [GvdP93,HSV94,HS96], where a large amount of user interaction has been necessary to provide powerful enough auxiliary invariants.

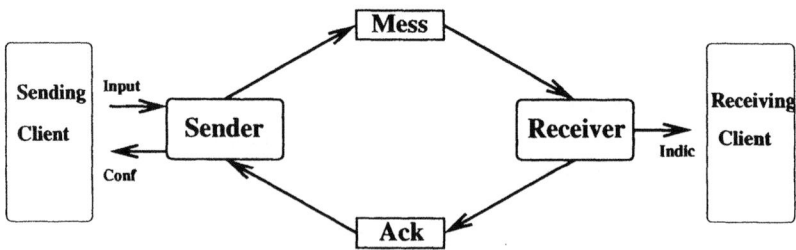

Fig. 2. The architecture of the BRP protocol

Description of the protocol: The sender receives from a sending client a message packet to transmit. The sender delivers a confirmation to its client: OK, if all messages have been transmitted and acknowledged, NOT_OK, if the transmission has been aborted as more than *max* retransmissions would have been necessary to deliver a message, DONT_KNOW, if the last message has not been acknowledged (in this case, it is not possible to know if this message or its acknowledgment has been lost).

The receiver acknowledges each received message, and delivers an indication to the receiving client. The indication is FIRST for the first received message of a packet, INCOMPLETE for any intermediate message, and OK for the last message. If the sender abandons the transmission of a packet after sending successfully at least one message, the receiver delivers a not NOT_OK indication.

Correctness criterion: We have to prove that the sequences of received messages and of sent messages are consistent, that is, Property (6) of Section 3. We have also to prove that for each packet, the indication and the confirmation delivered to the clients are consistent. That means, if the sender delivers a OK confirmation, the receiver delivers an OK indication. If the receiver delivers a NOT_OK indication, the sender delivers the DONT_KNOW or NOT_OK confirmation. These properties can easily be expressed by temporal logic formulas.

Verification of the protocol: To construct the abstract state graph for the BRP, we have used 19 predicates appearing in the guards of the transitions of the system. The constructed abstract graph has 475 states and 685 transitions and has been obtained in five hours on a Sparc 10. Of the 24 possible global control configurations, only 9 are found reachable. On this graph the properties concerning confirmations and indications have been verified using ALDÉBARAN. Property (6) has been verified on a weaker abstraction where only predicates concerning the transmission of a single message are considered relevant. The obtained abstract state graph is similar to the one obtained for the alternating bit protocol (cf Figure 1), except that at any moment the transmission can be abandoned because the maximal number of retransmissions has been reached.

5 Conclusions

We have presented and implemented a method allowing to construct abstract state graphs of arbitrary infinite state systems, where abstract states are valuations of a set of predicates $\varphi_1, ..., \varphi_\ell$ on concrete variables. At a first sight, the method may look rather expensive as the construction of a successor requires several proofs, and the construction of an abstract state graph for the BRP with 500 states takes 5 hours. However, all proofs are done without user interaction using a single tactic, and if this tactic fails to prove some valid statements, a weaker abstraction is obtained. Once the user has provided the predicates $\varphi_1, ..., \varphi_\ell$ (the tool proposes a set consisting of the literals occurring in the guards and properties to be proved), the construction is *completely automatic*. In this case, the execution time is not really a problem. One can always apply this method to get a first approximation of a system which — from the point of view of human effort — is for free. The constructed state graph is always of a reasonable size and can be explored by a model-checker. It can also be used as a finite global control graph which can be used for invariant generation and backward analysis already implemented [BLS96,GS96].

If the initial set of predicates, defining the abstract state space, does not give a satisfactory abstraction, one can try to add new predicates to obtain a more precise abstraction. To provide a new predicate is similar to providing an auxiliary invariant, which is usually necessary to prove program properties. However, it is easier to provide some predicates leading to a sufficiently refined state graph than the corresponding auxiliary invariant (expressing when these predicates hold and when not).

This method is in some sense complementary to the tableau construction implemented in STeP [BBC+96] where the tableau of the property to be proved (or disproved) is taken as the starting point for an abstract state graph construction by expanding it until it fits with the program. Our method takes the control of the program of the program as a starting point and refines it until it satisfies the property to be verified. The particularity of our method is that it integrates a reachability analysis.

It has also some other interesting characteristics:

- it is *incremental*: a refinement generates new implications and strengthens the left hand side of previously generated implications. All implications valid for a given partition, are also valid for a finer partition. Furthermore, in order to use this fact, it is not necessary to store the already proved implications, but only the corresponding abstract transition relation.
- It is *compositional*: for each component a separate abstract state graph can be constructed, where in each component the predicates involving its variables are used. The obtained global abstraction is in general weaker, and for the examples presented in this paper, the compositional approach turned out not to be interesting.
- The abstract state graphs constructed by our method are interesting for debugging. It can be used to guide the search of a concrete execution sequence violating a required property, especially as any transition enabled in some abstract state is enabled in *all* concrete states it represents.

References

[BBC+96] N. Bjorner, A. Browne, E. Chang, M. Colon, A. Kapur, Z. Manna, H. Sipma, and T. Uribe. Step: Deductive-algorithmic verification of reactive and real-time systems. In *CAV'96*. LNCS 1102, 1996.

[BBL97] K. Baukus, S. Bensalem, and Y. Lakhnech. A PVS based tool for the verification of invariants. submitted to CAV'97.

[BLS96] S. Bensalem, Y. Lakhnech, and H. Saidi. Powerful techniques for the automatic generation of invariants. In *CAV'96*, LNCS 1102, 1996.

[CC77] P. Cousot and R. Cousot. Abstract interpretation: a unified lattice model for static analysis of programs by construction or approximation of fixpoints. In *4th POPL*, January 1977.

[CGL94]   E.M. Clarke, O. Grumberg, and D.E. Long. Model checking and abstraction. *ACM Transactions on Programming Languages and Systems*, 16(5), 1994.

[CM88]   K. M. Chandy and J. Misra. *Parallel Program Design*. 1988.

[Dam96]   D. Dams. *Abstract interpretation and partition refinement for model checking*. Phd Thesis, Technical University of Eindhoven, July 1996.

[DF95]   J. Dingel and Th. Filkorn. Model checking for infinite state systems using data abstraction, assumption-commitment style reasoning and theorem proving. In *CAV'95*. LNCS 939, 1995.

[DGG93]   D. Dams, O. Grumberg, and R. Gerth. Generation of reduced models for checking fragments of CTL. In *CAV'93*, LNCS 697, 1993.

[DOTY96] C. Daws, A. Olivero, S. Tripakis, and S. Yovine. The tool KRONOS. In *Hybrid Systems III, Verification and Control*, LNCS 1066, 1996.

[FGK+96] J.-C. Fernandez, H. Garavel, A. Kerbrat, R. Mateescu, L. Mounier and M. Sighireanu. CADP (Cæsar/Aldébaran Development Package): A protocol validation and verification toolbox. In *CAV'96*. LNCS 1102.

[GL93]   S. Graf and C. Loiseaux. A tool for symbolic program verification and abstraction. In *CAV'93*. LNCS 697, 1993.

[Gra95]   S. Graf. Characterization of a sequentially consistent memory and verification of a cache memory by abstraction. *accepted to Distributed Computing*.

[GS96]   S. Graf and H. Saidi. Verifying invariants using theorem proving. In *CAV'96*, LNCS 1102, 1996.

[GvdP93] J.F Groote and J. van de Pol. A bounded retransmission protocol for large data packets. Technical Report Logic Group 100, Utrecht University, 1993.

[HGD95]   H. Hungar, O. Grumberg, and W. Damm. What if model checking must be truly symbolic. In *TACAS'95*. LNCS 1019, 1995.

[HH95]   T. Henzinger and P.H. Ho. Hytech: the Cornell hybrid technology tool. In *Hybrid Systems II*. LNCS 999, 1995.

[HPR94]   N. Halbwachs, Y.-E. Proy, and P. Raymond. Verification of linear hybrid systems by means of convex approximations. In *SAS'94*. LNCS 864.

[HS96]   K. Havelund and N. Shankar. Experiments in theorem proving and model checking for protocol verification. In *Formal Methods in Europe'96*, 1996.

[HSV94]   L. Helmink, M. Sellink, and F. Vaandrager. Proof-checking a data link protocol. Technical report CS-R9420, CWI, 1994.

[KDG95]   P. Kelb, D. Dams, and R. Gerth. Efficient symbolic model-checking for the full μ-calculus using compositional abstractions. Tech Rep 31, TU Eindhoven, 1995.

[Kur94]   R.P. Kurshan. *Computer-Aided Verification of Coordinating processes, the automata theoretic approach*. Princeton Series in Computer Science. 1994.

[LGS+95] C. Loiseaux, S. Graf, J. Sifakis, A. Bouajjani, and S. Bensalem. Property preserving abstractions for the verification of concurrent systems. *Formal Methods in System Design, Vol 6, Iss 1, 1995*

[Sa97]   H. Saïdi. The invariant checker: Automated deductive verification of reactive systems. In *this volume*.

[Sif82]   Joseph Sifakis. A unified approach for studying the properties of transition systems. *TCS* 18, 1982.

[SOR93]   N. Shankar, S. Owre, and J.M. Rushby. *A Tutorial on Specification and Verification using PVS*. SRI International, Menlo Park, CA, 1993.

Verification of a Chemical Process Leak Test Procedure

Adam L. Turk, Scott T. Probst and Gary J. Powers
Department of Chemical Engineering
Carnegie Mellon University

Abstract

A leak test procedure for a combustion system which is used in the chemical industry was verified. This procedure is important since it reduces the probability of explosions. Both government and internal company standards where employed in creating the initial leak test procedure. Several major faults were discovered by the verification of a logic model of the procedure and equipment using SMV. This paper describes the leak test procedure with its corresponding combustion system pipe network, the approach employed in modeling the process, failure modes included in the process model, computational challenges, and verification results. This study indicates that the formal method, SMV, is an appropriate tool for verification of industrial processes of modest complexity

1. Introduction

The synthesis of high integrity industrial processes is becoming a more significant goal of companies. A small industrial process may contain 50 to 100 binary variables in its model. The total combinatorial space of a process model with 50 binary variables has 10^{15} states. Analysis of even a modest size system is difficult with current industrial practices, such as simulation and field testing. Automated formal methods can exhaustively verify large state spaces, typically, on the order of 10^{20} states [2], for a given property of the system.

Originally, formal methods, in particular symbolic model verification (SMV) [11], were developed for the verification of integrated circuits and communication protocols [5,6]. The power of verification using SMV is its ability to find faults in very large, sequential and finite state spaces. This ability comes from symbolically representing the set of states and state transitions. SMV internally converts a process model into a symbolic representation, an ordered binary decision diagram, which implicitly describes the state space. Recently, several industrial processes including a batch reactor, a solids transport system and a furnace standard, have been represented in a logic model and verified by SMV [1. 9, 12, 13, 14, 15, 16, 17]. One problem of verification that has laid dormant is the efficient modeling of a complete and compact representation for an industrial process. This paper describes the modeling and verification of a part of a chemical process that involves a leak test procedure and is intended to test the ability of SMV to effectively verify industrial processes. This example illustrates the importance of selecting an appropriate modeling framework to capture necessary process behavior while controlling computational difficulties.

2. Process Verification

Process flowsheets, operating procedures, control logic, human operators, and failure modes are needed to describe the behavior of a chemical process. The compactness and completeness of a model significantly influences the quality of the analysis and the computational time required for the verification. Excessively complicated models can often described a state space that is too large for efficient verification. For process verification, an appropriate level of complexity and behavior must be captured by the logic model.

The process specifications and key process properties are used as guides in identifying the behavior and complexity necessary to represent the process. These behaviors are appropriately modeled with the aid of several comprehensive strategies. The strategies involve:

- Exclusion of process behavior that does not effect the specifications being verified.
- Discretization of the continuous and dynamic process behavior into a set of finite transition relations.
- Representation of different time domains implicitly in order to reduce model complexity.
- Minimization of the number of state variables required to represent the system.
- Application of symmetry [7] and modularity in order to reduce the model complexity.
- Application of non-determinism selectively in modeling uncertain properties of the process.
- Combination of similar failure events into macro failure modes.

The union of these strategies is an attempt to tame combinatorial explosion by efficiently building logic models while remaining true to the underlying physics, chemistry, control logic, and operating goals of the process. An understanding of the physical phenomena found in the process must be developed in order to identify the behavior that may have been omitted or spuriously included.

3. Leak Test Procedure Description

The correct detection and replacement of leaking valves in a combustion system can lead to the reduction in the number of explosions from methane escaping into a shutdown furnace. The leak test procedure is a series of steps that check for leaks across shut off valves. The valve diagram for a combustion system is shown in figure 1. The original procedure (base case) pressurizes the system by igniting the pilot and main burner. Once the burners have been ignited then the hand valves *bv7* and *bv15* are closed which extinguishes the burners. The blocking valves, *l14*, *b13*, *ls12*, and *bs11* automatically close since they are linked to a safety interlock which is triggered when the burners are extinguished. The closure of these valves creates a series of pressurized pipe segments between the valves. Pressure in each of these segments is assumed by the test procedure to leak down stream to a lower pressure location. The system is allowed to reach equilibrium by waiting 5 minutes before proceeding with testing of the system. The main line is checked first by opening the tap valves *tp3* and then *tp2*. Each section is checked for bubbling, which indicates no leaking downstream, or for bubbling to stop, which indicates no leaking upstream. The pipe segments in-between the locking valves, l14, b13, ls12, and bs11, are tested for both conditions. If at any time, a leak is detected then the apparently leaking valve is replaced and the test procedure is started over. Once the main line has been completed the pilot line is opened allowing this section of the valve train to be re-pressurized before continuing with the procedure. The test steps outlined for the main line are repeated for the pilot line.

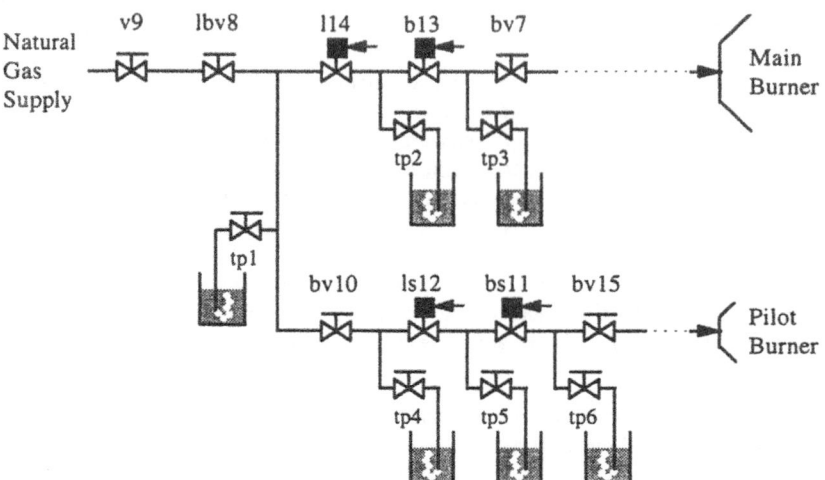

Figure 1: Piping and Valve Diagram for Combustion System

4. Properties

The properties for the process were created from quality, operability, and safety issues that concern process engineers [8,10]. General specifications developed from these issues are given below:

- Are leaking valves detected?
- Are non-leaking valves being replaced needlessly?
- Does the procedure terminate?

Specifications which represent process concerns were used as guides in abstracting and constructing process logic models.

5. Modeling of the Leak Test Procedure

5.1 Modeling Continuous Behavior

In order for the model to be comprehensive, the underlying physical phenomena of a leak must be understood either from experimentation or theory. The theory for the dynamics of a compressible fluid, such as methane gas, is well established and is based upon the following equations of continuity (eqn. 2), motion (eqn. 3), and energy (eqn. 4).

$$\frac{D\rho}{Dt} = -\rho(\nabla \bullet v) \tag{2}$$

$$\rho\frac{Dv}{Dt} = -\nabla p - [\nabla \bullet \tau] + \rho g \tag{3}$$

$$\rho\frac{D}{Dt}(\hat{U} + \frac{1}{2}v^2) = -(\nabla \bullet q) + \rho(v \bullet g) - (\nabla \bullet pv) - (\nabla \bullet [\tau \bullet v]) \tag{4}$$

where ρ is the density,   g is the gravitational constant,

v is the velocity,   q is the heat flux vector,

p is the pressure, $\hat{U}$ is the internal energy, and

τ is the shear forces.

A leak between two pipe sections can be simplified into two pressure vessels connected with a valve or nozzle. The effects of the nozzle on velocity and pressure in the radial direction can be removed by taking a macroscopic view of the system. It can also be assumed that no work is being performed on or by the system. Based upon these assumptions, the partial differential equation for motion can be simplified further by assuming that the variables in the z-axis do not change in the other axis directions.

$$\rho(\frac{\partial v_z}{\partial t} + v_z\frac{\partial v_z}{\partial z}) = -\frac{\partial p}{\partial z} - (\frac{1}{r}\frac{\partial}{\partial r}(r\tau_{rz}) + \frac{1}{r}\frac{\partial \tau_{\theta z}}{\partial \theta} + \frac{\partial \tau_{zz}}{\partial z}) \qquad (5)$$

This system of equations still can not be solved analytically for the leak rate of the methane gas. However, the leak procedure does not examine the leak rate of a valve directly, but checks for bubbling and/or the bubbling to have stopped from the pipe section being tested which in turn confirms the tightness of the valves isolating that pipe segment.. The rate of the gas escaping and therefore the bubbling is continuous in behavior and not discrete as the written procedure perceives it. Based upon the procedure, the system was modeled to reflect this discrete observation of bubbling and bubbling stopped. The model assumes that the operator checks for bubbling almost instantaneously after opening the tap valves and for bubbling to have stopped after a suitable time period which is not explicitly defined by the procedure. Both of these assumptions limit the behavior captured by the logic model and by the procedure. Faults caused by leak rates slower then the time period set for bubbling to stop can not be verified with the base case model. Modifications discovered during SMV verification of the procedure were added to the model which allowed this behavior to be captured.

The leak rate of a valve affects the amount of pressure remaining in a pipe segment. The altered pressure causes the time period necessary for the pipe segment to bleed to atmospheric pressure to be shorter or longer. The model of the process assumes that the leak will not decrease or increase the time needed to normally bleed a pipe segment. However, this assumption raises the questions of how much delay time is required for detecting bubbling to stop and how small of a test time interval is needed to isolate these leaks. Both the temperature of the environment and the current pressure of the methane source will affect the delay time. These interactions makes the selection of an explicit delay time difficult. This problem can be solved by allowing the transitions to the bubbling and bubble stopped states to represent different time periods.

The time period between states was allowed to vary according to the task being performed during the transition. The only time requirements were a five minute delay, the instantaneous checking for bubbles, and the suitable delay for bubbles to stop. The verification of this leak test procedure benefits from the flexible transition time periods since it represents any leak test procedure that specifies the time necessary for an operator to wait before he can assume that the bubbling has not stopped. Time was also implicitly included in the model through the variable step which indicates the current step an operator is performing in the leak test procedure.

5.2 Modeling Pressure

Pressure was declared as a Boolean variable as it is treated in the leak test procedure. This variable as described in the procedure only needed values for atmospheric pressure at which no bubbling would occur, and a higher pressure at which bubbling would occur. A local pressure variable was created for each segment of pipe. These local variables were connected through a series of definition variables. The transition relation of these definition variables would link the pressure in the pipe segments together if they shared a common leaking or open valve. The value of the definition variable for local pressure in a pipe segment would then be mapped into the correct local pressure variable. This modeling strategy assumes the pressure to quickly equalize through the pipe network due to leaks in the connecting valves. These modeling assumptions can be traced back to the defining equations 2, 3, and 4 for validation.

5.3 Modeling the Procedure

The leak test procedure, itself, was modeled using two state variables, *step* and *status*. The variable *step* was declared as an integer range between 0 and 17 while *status* was declared as four discrete values; conducting the leak test (test), repairing a valve (repairing), valve repair done (repair_done), start pilot burner (pilot_start), start main burner (main_start), and combustion system operational (burn).

$$step = \{0..17\} \tag{6}$$

$$status = \{testing, repair, repair\_done, pilot\_start, main\_start, burn\} \tag{7}$$

The transition relation of the variable, *step*, defines the various tasks of the test procedure and their ordering in the model (fig. 2). At each step n, several logic constraints need to be satisfied before *step* can progress to the next interval, $n+1$. Step one allows the pressure in the pipe network to come to equilibrium before the tap valve, *tp3*, is opened at the next step. Step 4 checks for the process condition of bubbling at *tp3*. Step 4 opens *tp2* and checks for bubbling at the next pipe segment. The condition of the bubbles stopping is tested in step 5. The tasks, performed in these steps are repeated for each pipe segment in the network. If no bubbles were seen by the human operator performing the test procedure at step 3, then the variable, *status*, initiates the repair sequence for valve *bv7*.

$$
step' = \begin{cases}
0 & \text{if status} = \text{repair\_done} \\
step & \text{if status} = \text{repair} \\
1 & \text{if step} = 0 \wedge \text{status} = \text{test} \\
2 & \text{if step} = 1 \\
3 & \text{if step} = 2 \\
4 & \text{if step} = 3 \wedge \text{bubbling @ tp3} \\
5 & \text{if step} = 4 \wedge \text{bubbling @ tp4} \\
6 & \text{if step} = 4 \wedge \text{bubbles\_stop @ tp4} \\
7 & \text{if step} = 6 \\
\quad \cdot \\
17 & \text{if step} = 16 \wedge \text{bubbles\_stop @ tp1} \\
0 & \text{if step} = 17 \\
step
\end{cases}
$$

Figure 2: Logical Abstraction of the Transition Relation for Variable *Step*

The *status* variable defines the transition of the process from the test procedure to other conditions such as repairing a valve or igniting the combustion system (fig. 3).

5.4 Modeling Failure Events

Failure Events for leaking valves were included in the logic model. State variables for valve leaks were defined for each valve that could leak. The initial conditions of these variables were made non-deterministic in order to capture the possible random failures of one or more values.

$$leak @ bv7 = \{0,1\} \tag{8}$$

$$leak @ bv7' = \begin{cases} 0 & \text{if } status = \text{repairing} \wedge step = 3 \\ leak @ bv7 \end{cases} \tag{9}$$

Variables retained their selected value until they were repaired at the correct point in the test procedure. Intermittent leaks were not included in these failure modes.

$$status' = \begin{cases} \text{test} & \text{if } status = \text{burn} \vee step = 6 \\ \text{repair} & \text{if } step = 3 \wedge \neg \text{bubbling} @ \text{tp3} \\ \text{repair} & \text{if } step = 4 \wedge \neg \text{bubbling} @ \text{tp4} \\ \text{repair} & \text{if } step = 5 \wedge \neg \text{bubble\_stop} @ \text{tp4} \\ \quad . \\ \text{repair} & \text{if } step = 16 \wedge \neg \text{bubble\_stop} @ \text{tpl} \\ \text{repair\_done} & \text{if } status = \text{repair} \\ \text{pilot\_start} & \text{if } step = 17 \vee (step = 0 \wedge \neg \text{pilot\_flame}) \vee step = 5 \\ \text{main\_start} & \text{if } status = \text{pilot\_start} \wedge \text{pilot\_flame} \\ \text{burn} & \text{if } \neg status = \text{test} \wedge \text{pilot\_flame} \wedge \text{main\_flame} \\ status \end{cases}$$

Figure 3: Logical Abstraction of the Transition Relation for Variable *status*

6. Results

Table 1 gives the number of Boolean variables, reachable states, nodes in the transition relation, and the CPU time for the base case leak test models developed by Probst [16]. The time for verification and counterexamples generation is included in the values reported for the CPU time. These models revealed the general fault that leaks in the tap valves are not accounted for in the procedure and could cause non leaking valves, *bv7* and *b13*, to be replaced needlessly. In order to avoid this error, the tap valves in the pipe network must be tested prior to conducting the leak test procedure. The authors of the procedure modified the leak test method to include this additional test.

6.1 New Failure Modes

The subsequent models of the leak procedure were amended in order to captures both fast and slow valve leaks. The time scale of fast leaks was assumed to be seconds while the scale for slow leaks was assumed to be on the order of several minutes. The logic model does not need modifications in order to verify the procedure for fast leaks since the time

Table 1 Information on Verified Leak Test Procedure Models

Model Name	Boolean Variables	Reachable States	Transition Relations (OBDD Nodes)	CPU Time (sec)[a]
Base Case	24	5,944	11,221	5
Leak_tp1	25	11,859	14,804	2
Leak_tp1,tp2	26	22,263	18,734	4
Leak_tp1,tp2, tp3	27	42,154	22,961	5
Leak_tp1,tp2, tp3,tp4	28	84,313	28,215	26
Leak_tp1,tp2, tp3,tp4,tp5	29	169,049	33,701	39
Leak_tp1,tp2, tp3,tp4,tp5,tp6	30	340,193	39,087	52

[a]Computations were performed on a Hewlett-Packard 715/75 workstation

required for the leak to reduce the pressure in a particular pipe segment to atmospheric is assumed to be fast when compared with the other time constants of the system. The slow leaks are modeled by allowing the transition relation of *step* to skip testing pipe sections and their corresponding valves. It was assumed that the human operator could not observe the slowly leaking valves and this phenomena was treated as if there was no leaking valve (or equivalently that the pipe section was skipped). The pressure in the skipped pipe segment was still affected by the leaking valve and adjusted accordingly.

$$
step' = \begin{cases}
0 & \text{if } status = \text{repair\_done} \\
step & \text{if } status = \text{repair} \\
1 & \text{if } step = 0 \wedge status = \text{test} \\
2 & \text{if } step = 1 \\
\{3,4\} & \text{if } step = 2 \\
\{4,6\} & \text{if } step = 3 \wedge bubbling @ tp3 \\
5 & \text{if } step = 4 \wedge bubbling @ tp4 \\
6 & \text{if } step = 4 \wedge bubbles\_stop @ tp4 \\
7 & \text{if } step = 6 \\
\vdots \\
17 & \text{if } step = 16 \wedge bubbles\_stop @ tp1 \\
0 & \text{if } step = 17 \\
step
\end{cases}
$$

Figure 4: Logical Abstraction of the Transition Relation for Variable *step* with Skipping

Table 2 Information on Verified Leak Test Procedure Models

Model Name	Boolean Variables	Reachable States	Transition Relations (OBDD Nodes)	CPU Time (sec)[a]
Base_Case	24	5,944	11,495	2.80
Press_Skip1	24	14,611	14,205	7.86
Valves_Tap	30	14,611	28,102	25.65
Valves_All	38	14,611	95,100	323.49
Valves_Two	32	14,611	54,064	128.31
Remove_Press	32	14,552	37,632	71.48
Expand_Proc	32	5,153	44,688	6.45
Press_Skip2	32	15,984	49601	18.3

[a]Computations were performed on a Hewlett-Packard 812/70 workstation

Failure events for slowly leaking valves and for the human operator skipping pipe segments and not testing them for leaks were added to the logic model through a macro failure mode Both of these failure events lead to the result of a leaking valve not being detected. This failure mode was included in the model by adding non-determinism to the transition relation of the variable, *step* (fig. 4). Before testing for pressure in each pipe segment, the procedure was allowed either to continue checking the current pipe section or to skip over it.

The *Press_Skip1* model added the step skipping failure mode to the base case model (table 2). The models *Valves_tap* through *Expand_Proc* contain a series of sequential refinements to the base case model which added resolution for capturing the combined failure event. The *Valves_Tap* model redefined the tap valves as state variables instead of definition variables to see if sequential behavior of these variables was important. *Valves_All* includes all the connecting and tap valves as state variables. In table 2, the data indicates that the size, complexity level, and CPU time of the models was increasing in an exponential manner. Strategic reduction in the model was used to control complexity. The *Valve_Two* model kept all connecting valves as definition variables except for *lbv8* and *bv10*, which were changed to state variables. These valves were left as state variables since they are explicitly closed in the test procedure. *Remove_Press* simplified the pressurization and segmenting of the pipe network to one macro step (fig. 5) instead of several complicated steps since the leak test procedure did not check for faults in both the ignition and extinguish sequence of the furnace. The skipping step model uncovered that the original modeling of the leak test procedure added invalid process behavior. The representation was incrementally refined in order to eliminate this added behavior until its size and complexity began to have a negative effect on verification. A series of reductions in the representation of the model were incorporated into the leak test model. These models illustrates the struggle to balance the completeness of the model with its compactness.

Through the expansion and reduction of the original model, it was discovered that some of the procedure steps overlapped and could not be distinguished from each other. The amendments to the representation allowed the user to distinctly perceive the individual steps of the procedure. The *Expand_Proc* model expanded the test procedure so that only one task was performed at every step which increased the number of steps from 17 to 24 (fig. 6). The *Expand_Proc* model increased verification time by a factor of 2 compared to

$$
status' = \begin{cases}
\text{test} & \text{if } status = \text{pressurize} \\
\text{repair\_done} & \text{if } status = \text{repair} \\
\text{repair} & \text{if } step = 3 \land \neg bubbling \ @ \ tp3 \\
\text{repair} & \text{if } step = 4 \land \neg bubble\_stop \ @ \ tp3 \\
\quad . \\
\text{repair} & \text{if } step = 23 \land \neg bubble\_stop \ @ \ tp1 \\
\text{presurize} & \text{if } step = 0 \lor step = 8 \\
status
\end{cases}
$$

Figure 5: Logical Abstraction of the Transition Relation for Variable *status* with a Macro Pressurization step

the base case. However, a factor of 10 increase in the verification time was observed for *Valve_All* model before the model size and complexity was reduced. Overall, the new representation from the one in the base case model increased verification time but not as dramatically as the trend indicated by the *Valve_All* model due to reduction and modeling strategies.

The final model, *Press_Skip2*, added the combined failure mode event to the *Expand_Proc* model. The *Press_Skip2* model revealed that slow leaks in the valves *bv7*, *bv15*, and *lbv8* were neglected by the test procedure. A correction to the base case test procedure ensured that all other connecting valves were double tested by the pipe segment downstream and upstream from them. This double checking by the test procedure detected when these valves had slow leaks. The procedure was revised by explicitly checking for the starting and stopping of bubbling at each tap. These changes effectively detect slowly leaking valves.

$$
step' = \begin{cases}
0 & \text{if } status = \text{repair\_done} \\
step & \text{if } status = \text{repair} \\
1 & \text{if } step = 0 \\
2 & \text{if } step = 1 \\
3 & \text{if } step = 2 \\
4 & \text{if } step = 3 \land bubbling \ @ \ tp3 \\
5 & \text{if } step = 4 \land bubbles\_stop \ @ \ tp3 \\
6 & \text{if } step = 5 \\
7 & \text{if } step = 6 \land bubbling \ @ \ tp4 \\
\quad . \\
24 & \text{if } step = 23 \land bubbles\_stop \ @ \ tp1 \\
0 & \text{if } step = 24 \\
step
\end{cases}
$$

Figure 6: Logical Abstraction of the Transition Relation for Variable *step* with Expanded Pipe Segment Testing

7. Conclusions

The formal verification of the leak test procedure, a modestly complex chemical process, discovered several significant faults that were repaired by revising the procedure. A modeling strategy that controlled the state space size while retaining process physics, procedures, and failure modes was necessary for efficient and reasonably complete verification. The original process model was refined in order to capture appropriate behavior caused by increasingly detailed failure events. Process verification using SMV has demonstrated its potential for aiding in the synthesis of high integrity industrial processes. Modeling time and completeness remain as challenges to wider application.

Model Source

The base case model by Probst is available at:

> http://www.cheme.cmu.edu/who/faculty/powers/probst/html/research.html

References

[1] R. Anderson, P. Beame, S. Burns, W. Chan, F. Modugno, D Notkin, and J. Reese, Model Checking Large Software Specifications. Proceedings of the Fourth ACM Symposium on the Foundation of Software Engineering: 156, 166, October, 1996.

[2] Bryant, R. E., "Graph-Based Algorithms for Boolean Function Manipulation", *IEEE Tans. on Computers*, 35(8), 677-691, 1986.

[3] Bryant, R. E., "Symbolic Boolean Manipulation with Ordered Binary Decision Diagrams", *Computing Surveys*, 24(3), 298-318, 1992.

[4] J. R. Burch, E. M. Clarke, K. L. McMillan, D. L. Dill, and L. J. Hawng, Symbolic Model Checking: 10^{20} states and Beyond. Information and Computation, 98(2): 142-170, June 1992.

[5] J. R. Burch, E. M. Clarke, D. E. Long, K. L. McMillan and D. L. Dill, Symbolic Model Checking for Sequential Circuit Verification. *IEEE Transactions on Computer-Aided Design of Integrated Circuits and Systems*, 13, 401- 424, 1994.

[6] E. M. Clarke, A. Emerson and A. P. Sistla, Automatic Verification of Finite-State Concurrent Systems Using Temporal Logic Specifications. *ACM Transactions on Programming Languages and Systems*, 8 (2), 244-263, 1986.

[7] E. M. Clarke, T. Filkorn, and S. Jha, Exploiting Symmetry in Temporal Logic Model Checking. *Proceedings of the Fifth Workshop on Computer-Aided Verification*, Ed. C. Courcoubetis. June/July 1993.

[8] E. M. Clarke, O. Grumberg, K. L. McMillan, and X. Zhao, Effective Generation of Counterexamples and Witnesses in Symbolic Model Checking. Technical Report No. CMU-CS-94-204, Carnegie Mellon University, PA, 1994.

[9] V. Hartonas-Garmhausen, T. Kurfess, E. M. Clarke, and D. E. Long, Automatic Verification of Industrial Designs. Proceedings of the 1995 IEEE Workshop on Industrial -Strength Formal Specification Techniques. 88-96. IEEE Comput. Soc. Press, April 1995.

94

[10] M. Jackson, *Software Requirements and Specifications*, ACM and Addison-Wesley, New York, 1995.

[11] K. L. McMillan, *Symbolic Model Checking - An Approach to the State Explosion Problem*, Ph.D. Thesis, Carnegie Mellon University, 1992.

[12] I. Moon, *Automatic Verification of Discrete Chemical Process Control Systems*, Ph.D. Thesis, Carnegie Mellon University, 1992.

[13] S. T. Probst, G. J. Powers, D. E. Long, and I. Moon, Verification of a Logically Controlled Solids Transport System using Symbolic Model Checking. Submitted for publication in *Computers and Chemical Engineering*, 1994.

[14] S. T. Probst, and G. J. Powers, Automatic Verification of Control Logic in the Presence of Process Faults. Presented at the Annual AIChE Conference, San Francisco, CA, November 1994.

[15] S. T. Probst, A. L. Turk, and G. J. Powers, Formal Verification of a Furnace System Standard. Presented at the Annual AIChE Conference, Miami Beach, FL, November 1995.

[16] S. T. Probst, *Chemical Process Safety and Operability Analysis using Symbolic Model Checking*, Ph.D. Thesis, Carnegie Mellon University, 1996.

[17] T. Sreemani and J. Atlee, Feasibility of Model Checking Software Requirements: A Case Study. Technical Report CS96-05, Department of Computer Science, University of Waterloo, January, 1996.

Automatic Datapath Extraction for Efficient Usage of HDD

Gila Kamhi, Osnat Weissberg, Limor Fix
Ziv Binyamini, Ze'ev Shtadler
Design Technology
Intel, Haifa, Israel
gkamhi@iil.intel.com

Abstract

Hybrid Decision Diagrams (HDD) have been proven in Intel to be an important enabler for the formal verification of datapath intensive circuits and in particular the verification of arithmetic units. However, extensive user interaction with the formal verification tool was required in order to use the HDD technology efficiently. The user had to analyze the circuit and its specification and manually partition the signals and operations into control and datapath.

In this paper, we will demonstrate how we have made use of the automatic datapath extraction techniques widely used in the synthesis world in order to efficiently integrate HDDs to an SMV-based formal verification system. The intention of this paper is to illustrate how existing technology can help improve the usability and productivity of the formal verification process and enable efficient integration of new technology, in our case HDDs.

The system described in this paper, *Prover*, statically analyzes the model to be verified and partitions the representation of the logic to HDDs and Binary Decision Diagrams (BDDs). Moreover, the partitioning algorithm decides which vector operations will be represented more efficiently as word-level (i.e. using HDD) versus bit-level (i.e using BDD).

The new methodology of integrating HDD into the formal verification process increases the productivity of the verification process. At the same time, experiments with *Prover* show that verification is (both computation and memory usage wise) as efficient as the previously known manual method.

1 Introduction

The Binary Decision Diagram (BDD) technology is a key enabler to several VLSI-CAD solutions. However, since BDDs are inefficient in dealing with datapath intensive circuits, the synthesis and formal verification of these circuits still challenge the VLSI-CAD community.

BDD-based approaches cannot handle, particularly, the verification of arithmetic functions such as multiplication and division, mainly because the BDD representations for these functions grow exponentially relative to the bit size. Bryant and Chen [1] have addressed the limitation of BDDs by introducing Binary Moment Diagrams (BMDs). BMDs and their extensions, e.g.*BMDs, enable compact word-level representation of arithmetic functions including multipliers. Although BMDs can represent datapath portion of the logic efficiently, the control portion of the logic can still be represented more efficiently using BDD or MTBDD (multi-terminal BDD).

Clarke and Zhao [2] have introduced Hybrid Decision Diagrams (HDDs) which represent logic as a combination of MTBDDs and BMDs. Previous applications of

HDDs in Intel's tools [3] required the user to manually provide the information on how to partition HDDs into MTBDDs and BMDs. In most cases, a design and a verification expert had to manually extract the datapath. This approach was time-consuming, unproductive and often involved a third party's understanding of the design. Therefore, we believe that automatic identification and partitioning of datapath and control logic is essential for the efficient embedding of HDDs in the industrial formal verification tools.

State-of-the-art architectural and datapath synthesis systems automatically identify the Hardware Design Language (HDL) statements describing datapath and replace the corresponding logic with optimized predefined macros that fit the description. The encapsulation of datapath functions in the synthesis tools is mainly done to optimize the datapath portion of the logic taking into consideration timing and area constraints. In this paper, we demonstrate how we have made use of the automatic datapath extraction techniques widely used in the synthesis world to efficiently integrate HDDs to an SMV-based [16] formal verification tool. Our intention is to illustrate how existing technology can help improve the usability and productivity of the formal verification process and enable efficient integration of new technology, in our case HDDs.

This paper presents two capabilities of Intel's formal verification tool, *Prover* : the automatic encapsulation of datapath and HDD partitioning. The HDD partitioning algorithm decides which datapath bits will be encoded as BMDs and which as BDDs. This decision is not trivial since some of the datapath bits are still more efficiently represented as BDDs. *Prover* accepts as input a high-level hardware specification language and generates an hierarchical intermediate netlist. The intermediate representation contains an additional layer of hierarchy for datapath operations. The partitioning algorithm of *Prover* when fed the intermediate netlist builds and analyzes a two-level Data Flow Graph (DFG) of the circuit. One level of the DFG represents the bit-level connectivity of the model and the second level represents the word-level connectivity. The algorithm decides which components of the circuit will be more efficiently represented using BMD and which using MTBDDs and BDDS and generates word-level Symbolic Model Language (SML) for both the model and its specification. Using *Prover* we have successfully verified circuits for division and square root computation that are based on SRT algorithm used by Intel's *Pentium®* microprocessor. The novelty of *Prover* is that it reduces the required user expertise and intervention compared to other formal verification systems.

This paper is organized as follows: Section 2 contains a brief overview of Intel's formal verification tool, *Prover*. Section 3 describes how the datapath statements in the model and specification languages are automatically extracted. Section 4 discusses the efficiency and deficiency of HDDs and especially BMDs to represent logic. In Section 5, we describe the partitioning algorithm used to partition the logic into BDDS and HDDs and HDDs into MTBDDs and BMDs. Section 6 presents results obtained using *Prover* to verify complex real-life arithmetic properties including the floating-point division (FDIV) in *Pentium®* processor. We compare our results to the manual datapath extraction experiments.

2 The System

Prover, Intel's formal verification tool, is based on two major components: the formal specification language and the symbolic model checking engine. Our specification language, called Formal Specification Language (FSL), is a linear-time temporal language that allows the specification of a complex behavior as a series of timed expressions. The model building stage of *Prover* synthesizes the register-transfer-level (RTL) model and the specification to a gate-level intermediate format [8]. *Prover* performs property-specific model extraction to prune the parts of the model that are irrelevant to the property and automatically generates extended SML as input to its SMV-based [16] model checking core. The temporal properties expressed in FSL are translated internally to SML checkers and simple CTL formulas.

Prover's model checking core implements the word-level model-checking algorithm of Clarke and Zhou [2]. However, we allow word-level expressions both in the model description and in the specification. As a result, the intermediate functions needed for the construction of the transition relation and the specification are represented using HDD while the final representation of the transition relation and the specification are in BDDs.

Embedding HDDs[1] in *Prover*'s verification engine [3] made it possible to handle circuits containing both control logic and wide datapaths. Recently, we have automated the use of HDDs in *Prover* by integrating an automatic datapath extraction mechanism to the model building stage of the tool. The synthesizer automatically encapsulates arithmetic functions in the model and the specification. A partitioning algorithm decides which signals and which operations will be more efficiently implemented using BDDs and which using HDDs. Moreover, within the HDD representation, the algorithm decides on the partitioning between the MTBDDs and the BMDs.

3 Encapsulation of Datapath Operators

The logic of a hardware system can be classified as (pure) control, (pure) datapath, or (mixed) control/datapath. The control portion of a hardware system consists of a set of interacting FSM's which depending on data values and states, produce a set of control signals for the datapath. The datapath consists of functions and registers which, based on control signals, operate on data. The data often consists of

---

1. The reader is referred to Section 4 and [1, 2, 3, 5, 12] for detailed description of BDDs, MTBDDs, BMDs and HDDs.

integers. The memory acts as a container for values, and communicates with datapath.

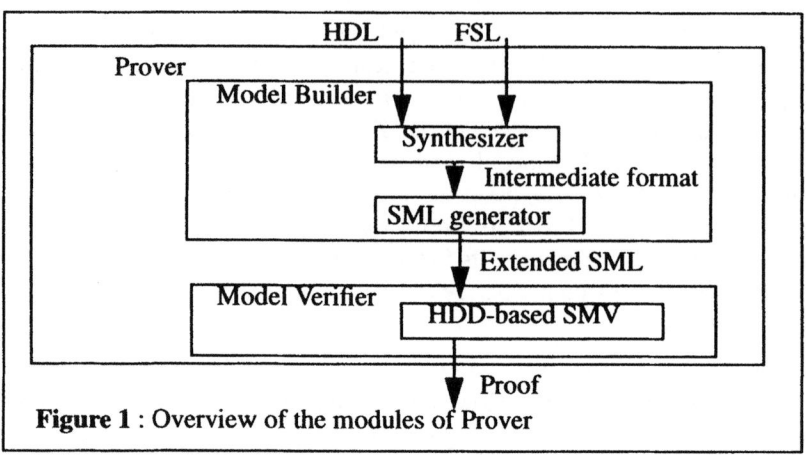

Figure 1 : Overview of the modules of Prover

The BDD-based approaches fail to represent efficiently wide datapath operators. BMDs and extensions to BMDs, e.g. *BMDs, enable very compact word-level representation of arithmetic functions including multipliers. The symbolic model checking engine of *Prover* is HDD-based. The model under test can be represented as a combination of MTBDDs and BMDs. The motivation is to represent control logic as BDD/MTBDDs and datapath logic as BMDs. The automatic extraction of datapath [7] and control logic is essential for the success of the hybrid approach taken in HDD where MTBDDs and BMDs coexist.

In the model-building stage, *Prover* encapsulates the HDL and FSL operators related with datapath and maps the isolated operators to generic predefined subcircuits. The predefined subcircuits are generic in the sense that all the subcircuits that describe a plus operation of any width will have only two inputs and one output. The bit-width of the input and output signals varies depending on the size of the operation. In other words, the generic parameter of the predefined subcircuits is the bit-width of the operation.

Prover, currently automatically encapsulates the arithmetic operations, e.g. multiplication. In addition to the arithmetic operators, the relational operations, i.e. comparison, equality and inequality operations, and other vector operations, e.g. concatenation, are automatically identified. Furthermore, the automatic encapsulation mechanism in *Prover* extracts memories, and control logic, e.g. multiplexers, that controls the datapath. For example, "if", and "case" expressions in HDL and FSL are preserved by mapping them to predefined generic multiplexer templates of the respective width.

The encapsulated operators generate an extra hierarchy in the intermediate netlist generated by the synthesizer of the model builder (See Figure 1). Information on the functionality (e.g. addition, subtraction) of these implicit tool-generated subcircuits is stored as attributes. The SML netlist generator of *Prover*, when fed the intermediate netlist, decides which isolated operators can be more efficiently

99

represented by BMDs and generates an extended SML netlist which is fed to the verification core. The partitioning algorithm used in the SML generator is explained in more detail in Section 5. The SML netlist contains information on which signals are to be represented as BMDs by means of the new constructs that have been added to the language. The verification core of *Prover* identifies the datapath circuitry in the SML netlist and represents the relevant portions of the logic as BMDs.

The benefits of a datapath extraction mechanism are numerous. The idea of automatically extracting the datapath operators and mapping them to predefined generic modules can be extended. For example, it would be quite reasonable to create a library of optimized standard arithmetic functions (addition, multiplication, relational operators) and re-use the size-wise optimized (BDD or extensions to BDD) modules. The portion of the logic (e.g. memory) which cannot be represented efficiently neither by BDDs nor by BMDs can be treated as a black box.

4 Efficiencies and Deficiencies of BMDs versus BDDs

Ordered binary decision diagrams (BDDs) [5, 12] are a canonical efficient representation for Boolean formulas. A BDD representing a formula is a directed acyclic graph (DAG) with a unique order on the occurrence of variables from root to leaf. Multi-terminal BDDs (MTBDDs) have a similar structure; however instead of having boolean leaves they have integer leaves. Both BDD and MTBDD representation of certain arithmetic functions such as multiplier requires exponential resources. Bryant and Chen [1] have shown that BMD can represent compactly certain arithmetic functions which have exponential MTBDD representation.

HDDs (BMDs and MTBDDs) can represent functions that map boolean bit vectors to integers; whereas BDDs can represent only boolean functions. An array or bit vector of state variables represented as a HDD is referred to as a word [1, 2, 3]. The value of the word is the value of the integer represented by the bit vector. BMD representation is more compact for some arithmetic functions which have exponential size if represented as MTBDDs. In general, BMDs and BDDs have comparable size for boolean functions, however, our experience shows that BMDs are less compact in these cases. Similar results were reported for some boolean functions in [15].

The method of building BMD from an arithmetic expression, e.g. multiplication, can blow up exponentially in the building phase of a single bit [6]. Therefore, two verification methods for multipliers based on Multiplicative Binary Moment Diagrams (*BMDs) have been introduced. Bryant has proposed a hierarchical approach in which the building blocks of the multiplier being verified, for instance a carry-save adder, are checked against their *word-level* specification. Once the individual sub-blocks have been verified, they are composed to yield the function of the entire block. The shortcoming of this approach is that it assumes that the specification has the same hierarchy as the implementation, and that the corresponding blocks in the specification and the implementation are equivalent which is not always the case. Hamaguchi [9] proposed a method to overcome this limitation which is a non-hierarchical variation of Bryant's scheme which compute BMD from outputs to inputs instead of inputs to outputs and verify successfully wide-size, e.g. 64-bit, multipliers. However, if there are errors in the circuits, BMD can easily blow up and the verification program may not terminate, since these circuits represent different logic functions from multiplier which can have exponential sizes of BMD. In [10, 11], BDD-based techniques that overcome this limitation of the BMD-based methods are presented.

In *Prover*, the decision on which HDL and FSL operations are to be translated to *word-level* SML operators and consequently to be represented as HDD by the verification core is based on mainly the efficiency of HDD in comparison with BDD to represent these operations. As mentioned above, the BMD representation of single bit/bits of an arithmetic expression may be huge, even when the BMD representation of the whole expression is very compact. Therefore, expressions involving relations among single bits of arithmetic sub-expressions are not good candidates to be represented as BMD.

Moreover, the relational operations, e.g., inequalities, equalities, can be represented more efficiently by BDD than BMD. Clarke and Zhao [2] present an algorithm that can substantially reduce the cost of computing arithmetic relations between *word-level* functions. However, our experience shows that the BDD representation of the relational operations is more efficient than the BMD representation.

In Section 5, we will present the algorithm currently used by *Prover* in order to decide which portion of the logic will be represented as BDD and which portion of the logic will be represented as BMD.

5 Automatic Partitioning

The algorithm for partitioning the logic into BDD (*bit-level*) and BMD (*word-level*) representations within the HDD is mainly based on the efficiency of HDD (BMD/ MTBDD) compared to BDD for representing datapath operations.

The partitioning algorithm in the first stage decides which vectors will be represented as words and which operations will be represented as *word-level* operators. These vectors and operations will be represented as HDD. The rest of the logic will be represented as BDD. The BMD/MTBDD partitioning within HDD is performed by marking the datapath variables in HDD as data variables; thus, causing the datapath operations to be represented as BMD.

Based on the encapsulation of the datapath operators described in Section 3, a two-level Data Flow Graph (DFG) of the model is built. One level of the DFG represents the *bit-level* connectivity of the entire model. That is, given a signal bit *sig* one can extract from the DFG information on the signals in the *fan-in* and *fan-out* of *sig*. The second level of the DFG represents the *word-level* connectivity of the model. That is, given a word (vector) *vec* one can extract from the DFG the *fan-in* and *fan-out* information on *vec*. The *word-level* connectivity graph also contains information on the *fan-in* and *fan-out* of each vector operation: the operands are the *fan-in* and the result is the *fan-out*.

The *bit-level* and *word-level* connectivity graphs are used to detect the case where a single bit is extracted from the result of a vector operation. In other words, if we compute an intermediate *word-level* expression and represent it using BMD it will be inefficient to extract from it the BDD/BMD representation of one of its bits. For example, the intermediate expression *temp* below

```
temp := word1 + word2;
sig := temp[3];
```

will be represented as BDD instead of BMD since we need to extract bit 3 out of *temp*. On the other hand, we may choose to represent an operation using BMD even in the case this operation is more efficiently represented using BDD. The reason for such a decision lays again in the context of the operation.

The BDD representation of some bit vector operations, e.g. concatenation, is more efficient than the BMD representation. Bit vector operators and relational operators, e.g. <=, >=, are mapped to their corresponding *word-level* SML operators if and only if the operators in the *fan-in* cone of these operators are arithmetic operators (+,-,*). For example, the concatenation operation (&) in the assignment below has to be represented at *word-level*, in order to represent the multiplication operation (*) at *word-level*.

```
c[3n+2:0] := (a[n:0] * b[n:0]) & d[n:0];
```

In other words, to represent the multiplication expression (a[n:0] * b[n:0]) as a BMD, we choose to perform the concatenation operation (&) on BMDs even though it is more efficient to perform it on BDDs.

The partitioning algorithm first analyzes the DFG and marks every vector and every datapath operator as either *bit-level* or *word-level*. After the preliminary marking of all vectors and operations as *bit-level* or *word-level*, the DFG is scanned again and a final decision on which vectors to represent as words (HDDs) and which as BDDs is made. The outcome of the algorithm is a list of vectors and operations that need to be represented at *word-level* and a list of signal bits that need to be specified as data variables.

The partitioning algorithm is depicted below. In summary, initially (Step 1) the algorithm marks as many vectors and operators as possible as *word-level*. Then (Step 2), the algorithm reclassifies the word-level vectors and operators by propagating backwards the need to represent some vectors at *bit-level* instead of *word-level* and the need to represent datapath operators at *bit-level* instead of *word-level*. Finally (Step 3), marks all bit-vector and relational operators as *bit-level*, if it is not necessary for them to be *word-level*.

102

The Partitioning Algorithm:

Step 1 (Initial marking):

    Step 1.1 (Mark datapath operators):
    For each datapath operator *op*,
        If no single bit of fan-out vectors of *op* is
        referenced (read) by other expressions, then mark
        op as *bit-level.*
        Otherwise, mark *op* as *bit-level*.

    Step 1.2 (Mark datapath vectors - words):
    For each vector *vec*,
        If the fan-out of every bit of *vec* is equal to the
        fan-out of *vec*, then mark *vec* as *word-level*.
        Otherwise, mark *vec* as *bit-level*.

Step 2 (Propagating backward):

    For each datapath operator *op* marked as *bit-level,*
        For each datapath vector *vec* in the fan-in of *op*,
            Mark *vec* as *bit-level*
            For each datapath operator *op'* in the
            fan-in of *vec*,
                Mark *op'* as *bit-level*

Step 3 (If necessary, mark bit-vector and relational operations as *bit-level* - correction):

    For each *word-level* bit-vector and relational operation *op*
        Recursively mark *op* as bit-level if none of its
        fan-in vectors is *word-level*
        If the fan-out vector *vec* of *op* is *word-level*,
        then mark *vec* as *bit-level* and recursively apply
        step 3 on all operations *op'* which are in the
        fan-out of *vec*

6 Experimental Results

Intel's new generation microprocessors are being massively verified using the automatic datapath extraction algorithm integrated into *Prover*. Below is a simple example that demonstrates *Prover*'s capability to verify complex arithmetic specifications.

The division and square-root algorithms similar to the ones in *Pentium®* processor that we have re-verified are described in several published papers [2, 3, 4, 13]. For the completeness and readability of this paper we include below the description of the division algorithm adopted from [3]. The square-root operation shares common datapath with the division operation; thus, we only illustrate here the capability of our system to verify complex arithmetic algorithms by concentrating mainly on the division algorithm. The number of state variables after the property-specific extraction in *Prover* is in the order of 300-400. During the re-verification process we did not exceed the memory requirements to verify these properties. On a HP or IBM machine with about 100MB, these properties have been verified. The verification of all the properties took less than 30 minutes.

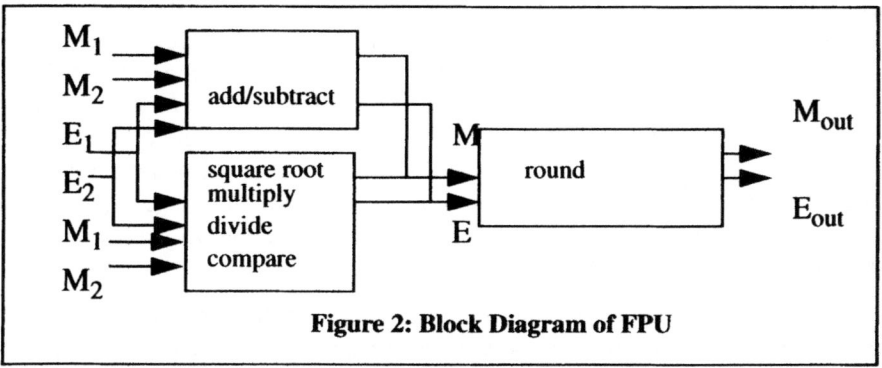

Figure 2: Block Diagram of FPU

The floating-point unit (FPU) of the processor under test uses a radix-4 SRT division algorithm. Since the SRT division algorithm is iterative, the loop invariant verification technique described in [3] is used.[1] Given the mantissa d (from M1 in Figure 2) of the dividend and the mantissa b (from M2 in Figure 2), the radix-4 SRT algorithm iteratively computes a partial remainder r_i and a quotient digit q_i. The partial remainder r_0 is initialized to $d/4$ and the quotient digit q_0 is initialized to zero. Each iteration the algorithm gets the quotient digit from the lookup table and subtracts $q_i \cdot b$ from the partial remainder r_i that has been shifted left by 2 bits. In other words, $r_{i+1} = 4.r_i - q_i.b$. The algorithm terminates when enough quotient bits have been computed. Suppose that the quotient digits are within the range $\{-n, -n+1, \ldots, -1, 0, 1, \ldots, n-1, n\}$ for some positive n. Then a radix-4 SRT division algorithm is guaranteed to be correct if both of the following properties are true in each division loop [14]:

$$r_{i+1} = 4.r_i -q_i.b$$
$$|r_i| <= n.b/3$$

The loop invariant INV_i that we want to verify is the conjunction of the two properties above. We want to verify that the invariant INV_0 is true initially and also $INV_i => INV_{i+1}$.

---

1. The correctness of this property decomposition was only manually proved.

In the previous experiments, the loop invariants INV_i were expressed in extended SML. For example, for any constant n, the second property of INV_i was specified as follows.

```
AG(3.r_i <= n.b) & (0 <= 3r_i + n.b)
```

Additionally, in order to represent the arithmetic expressions (e.g. $3.r_i$) internally as words, the bit-level signals had to be grouped to form an array. The grouping had to be specified explicitly in extended SML. In order to represent the words that will be represented as HDD in the formal verification engine as BMD instead of MTBDD, the state variables in the fan-in cone of the operands of the expression (e.g. r_i) had to be specified as data variables. In the case of the property above, if the state variables in the fan-in cone of r_i are not specified as data variables, the expression $3.r_i$ will be represented as an MTBDD instead of a BMD. Since the MTBDD representation of multiplication operation has exponential size relative to the bit size and the bit size of r_i exceeds 64, this expression is not representable as MTBDD. In short, a failure in the specification of data variables and the grouping of bits to words may cause the system to blow up, and a lot of user expertise, and knowledge on BMD and MTBDD technology were required to manually specify the properties in extended SML.

Prover, in order to prevent the generation of inefficient SML and reduce the work that needs to be performed by the user, automates the process of extended SML generation. The user is required to write the specifications in FSL. In the case of the CTL property specified above, the user instead of writing an extended CTL/SML property writes the semantically equivalent FSL correspondent of the property above. The user will not need to decide which operations and which vectors will be represented at *word-level*. The decision to represent vectors as BMD/MTBDD is done internally in the model builder stage of *Prover* (See Figure 1). The model builder automatically generates for the FSL checkers extended SML checkers.

The experimental results demonstrate that the verification of these properties by *Prover* is as efficient (with respect to the computation time and memory usage) as the method that requires extensive user guidance.

7 Conclusions

In this paper, we have illustrated how automatic datapath extraction techniques can help improve the productivity of the formal verification process by reducing the need for user intervention and expertise required in the current HDD-based applications. Furthermore, in order to prove the efficiency and applicability of this technique to verify arithmetic circuits of industrial size and complexity, we have re-verified some of the selected floating-point operations (e.g. FDIV, FSQRT) in the floating point unit (FPU) of Intel's *Pentium*® microprocessor. The division and square-root algorithms of the FPU have been verified using manual extraction of datapath in [3]. Our system reduces extensively the user intervention and expertise that was needed to verify these operations by integrating an automatic datapath extraction mechanism to Intel's formal verification system, *Prover*. The experimental results demonstrate that the verification of these properties by *Prover* is as efficient (with respect to the computation time and memory usage) as the method that requires extensive user guidance.

By automating the process of extended SML generation, we have broadened the usage of the HDD technology. The manual specification and identification of all the datapath operations in industrial size models is not humanly possible. Therefore, *Prover* automatically detects the datapath operations in the model, in addition to the specification, that can be more efficiently represented by HDD. Additionally, the specification of the properties in a high-level linear-time language, FSL, that is more close to the hardware than CTL, reduces the risk of verifying specifications that do not specify exactly what the user meant to verify. In other words, *Prover* by enabling the user to specify the properties in a high-level specification language ensures that he/she specifies what he/she really meant to verify.

Prover with the new high-level specification entry and automatic datapath extraction mechanism is being successfully used to verify Intel's new generation microprocessors. Lately, complex arithmetic operations in an Intel's next generation micro-processor have been successfully verified using *Prover*. The techniques specified in this paper promote the mass usage of formal verification in Intel's design environment.

8 Acknowledgments

We would like to thank Dany Khabaza, Roni Rosner, and Andreas Tiemeyer for their continuous involvement in the development of *Prover*. Orit Kedem has helped a great deal in the verification of the floating-point operations using *Prover*. We would also like to thank our colleagues at Intel Development Labs for providing us the test cases for the experiments reported in this paper.

9 References

[1] R.E.Bryant and Y.A. Chen.Verification of Arithmetic Functions with Binary Moment Diagrams. In Proceedings of the 32nd ACM/IEEE Design Automation Conference, IEEE Computer Society Press

[2] E.Clarke, X.Zhao. Word Level Symbolic Model Checking, CMU-CS-95-161

[3] Y.Chen, E.Clarke, Pei-Hsin Ho, Y. Hoskote, T. Kam, M. Khaira, J. O'Leary, X. Zhao. Verification of All Circuits in a Floating-Point Unit Using Word-Level Model Checking, In Proceedings of the International Conference on Formal Methods in Computer-Aided Design, November 1996

[4] R.E.Bryant. Bit-level Analysis of an SRT Divider Circuit. Technical Report, Carnegie Mellon University, 1995

[5] R.E.Bryant. Graph-based Algorithms for Boolean Function Manipulation. IEEE Transactions on Computers, c-35(8):677-691, Aug. 1986

[6] Laurent Arditi. *BMDs Can Delay the Use of Theorem Proving for Verifying Arithmetic Assembly Instructions, In Proceedings of the International Conference on Formal Methods in Computer-Aided Design, November 1996

[7] R.Hojati, R.K.Brayton. Automatic Datapath Abstraction In Hardware Systems, In Proceedings of the International Conference on Computer-Aided Verification Conference, 1995

[8] A.Aziz et.al. HSIS: A BDD-Based Environment for Formal Verification, In Proceedings of the 31st Design Automation Conference, IEEE Computer Society Press

[9] K.Hamaguchi, A. Morita, and S.Yajima. Efficient Construction of Binary Moment Diagrams for Verifying Arithmetic Circuits. In Proceedings of the International Conference on Computer-Aided-Design, pages 78-82, San Jose, CA, November 1995.

[10] K.Ravi, A.Pardo, G.Hachtel, F.Somenzi. Modular Verification of Multipliers. In Proceedings of the International Conference on Formal Methods in Computer-Aided Design, Palo Alto, CA, November 1996

[11] M.Fujita. Verification of Arithmetic Circuits by Comparing Two Similiar Circuits. In Proceedings of the International Conference on Computer-Aided Verification, 1996

[12] K.S.Brace, R.L.Rudell, and R.E.Bryant. Efficient Implementation of a BDD Package. In Proceedings of the Design Automation Conference, pages 535-541, San Francisco, CA, June 1995.

[13] E.M.Clarke, M. Khaira, and X.Zhao. Word Level Model Checking - A New Approach for Verifying Arithmetic Circuits. In Proceedings of the 33rd ACM/IEEE Design Automation Conference. IEEE Computer Society Press, June 1996.

[14] D.E.Atkins. Higher-radix Division Using Estimates of the Divisor and Partial remainders. IEEE Transactions on Computers, C-17(10):925-934, October 1968.

[15] R.Enders. Note on the Complexity of Binary Moment Diagram Representations. unpublished paper, Siemens AG, Munich Germany, 1994.

[16] K.L.McMillan. Symbolic Model Checking, Kluwer Academic Publishers.

An $n \log n$ Algorithm for
Online BDD Refinement[*]

Nils Klarlund

AT&T Labs Research
600 Mountain Ave.
Murray Hill, NJ 07974
klarlund@research.att.com

Abstract. Binary Decision Diagrams are in widespread use in verification systems for the canonical representation of finite functions. Here we consider multi-valued BDDs, which represent functions of the form $\varphi : \mathbb{B}^\nu \to \mathcal{L}$, where $\mathcal{L}$ is a finite set of leaves.

We study a rather natural online BDD refinement problem: a partition of the leaves of several shared BDDs is gradually refined, and the equivalence of the BDDs under the current partition must be maintained in a discriminator table. We show that it can be solved in $O(n \log n)$ if n bounds both the size of the BDDs and the total size of update operations. Our algorithm is based on an understanding of BDDs as the fixed points of an operator that in each step splits and gathers nodes.

We apply our algorithm to show that automata with BDD-represented transition functions can be minimized in time $O(n \cdot \log n)$, where n is the total number of BDD nodes representing the automaton. This result is not an instance of Hopcroft's classical algorithm for automaton minimization, which breaks down for BDDs because of their path compression property.

1 Introduction

Binary Decision Diagrams [3] form the backbone of many symbolic methods for verification of hardware and software. BDDs are essentially acyclic automata whose state spaces are shrunk by a technique called *path compression*. More precisely, a BDD is an acyclic, rooted, directed graph that represents a function $\varphi : \mathbb{B}^\nu \to \mathcal{L}$ from ν Boolean variables to a finite codomain $\mathcal{L}$ of leaves. (These BDDs are sometimes called Multi-Terminal BDDs to distinguish them from two-terminal BDDs that denote Boolean functions.)

The Problem

We consider the following problem, which is at the heart of the minimization problem for BDD-represented automata. We are given several functions

---

[*] This work was carried out while the author was with BRICS, Department of Computer Science, Aarhus, Denmark.

$\phi_i : \mathbb{B}^\nu \to \mathcal{L}$. They can be represented by a shared BDD, which is an acyclic, directed graph with a distinguished root for each i, where each root induces a subgraph that constitutes a BDD for ϕ_i. Now given a partition of the leaves (or codomain), we would like to calculate a *function discriminator*, which associates a discriminator value $R(i)$ to each i such that $R(i) = R(j)$ if and only ϕ_i and ϕ_j are equivalent under the leaf partition, i.e., if for all $\mathbf{u} \in \mathbb{B}$, $\phi_i(\mathbf{u})$ is equivalent to $\phi_j(\mathbf{u})$. Note that the leaf partition itself can also be represented by a discriminator D such that v and v' are equivalent if and only if $D(v) = D(v')$.

The online version of this problem is to maintain the function discriminator after an online operation specifies an *update*, which is a further refinement of the current leaf partition. Initially, the leaf partition consists of only one equivalence class, i.e., all functions ϕ_i are equivalent and D and R are a constant functions.

A simple algorithm for the online BDD refinement problem can be based on the linear time reduction of BDDs [12]: after each refinement operation, the whole BDD structure can be reduced to a canonical BDD for the functions that map into equivalence classes. This strategy implies that each node is touched potentially as many times as the number of operations. Thus an $O(n^2)$ algorithm arises, if we assume n online operations.

Our Solution

In this paper, we formulate a more efficient algorithm, which runs in time $O(n \min(k, \log n) + k)$, where n is the number of nodes in the BDDs and k is the total size of all update operations. Thus, if n also bounds k, then the algorithm is $O(n \log n)$.

Unfortunately, no simple solution seems to achieve $O(n \log n)$. Instead, our analysis proceeds roughly as follows.

For BDDs, the *Split* operation of partition refinement algorithms such as [11] does not directly yield a partition refining the current one. Rather, the result of a split operation, which we call a *decision partition* must be followed by a *Grow* operation that gathers all nodes equivalent under path compression. We show that the canonical BDD representation of ϕ can be obtained as the fixed point of *Grow* ∘ *Split* (even though this composed operator is not monotone). This characterization is not surprising, since usual BDD algorithms are also able to calculate a canonical representation in one sweep.

The *Grow* operation cannot be used with Hopcroft's "process the lesser half" strategy [8], since all decision blocks must be grown as opposed to the situation in traditional partition refinement algorithms, where the largest blocks created can be ignored.

Fortunately, the canonical BDD can be calculated under weaker assumptions about the fixed point operator. The *Grow* operation can be weakened to an operation, which we call *CGrow* since it allows certain blocks resulting from the normal *Grow* operation to be coalesced. As a result, information is lost. Curiously, it turns out that if a partition is a fixed point under *Split* and *CGrow*, then it is also a fixed point under *Split* and *Grow*.

We use this property in our online algorithm to discard any large block that arises during the iteration of the fixed point operator. The block is discarded by being coalesced with another, smaller block, while the expense of calculating it can be attributed to a third block known also to be small.

Consequences and Comparison to Previous Work

It has been known for a long time [8] that deterministic finite-state automata can be minimized in time $O(m \cdot n \log n)$, where n is the number of states and m is the size of the input alphabet. A recent variation on the standard method yields a similar bound [2].

BDDs allow automata with n states and 2^n letters—each inducing a different behavior in the automaton—to be represented by graphs of polynomial size in n; see [5, 7], where also $O(n^2)$ minimization algorithms are presented. The automaton representation in [5] allows symbolic calculations involving inductive definitions of sequential circuits, whereas the representation in [7] is the backbone of a practical implementation of Monadic Second-order Logic on Strings. For a comparison of these related representations, see [1].

The $O(n^2)$ minimization algorithms are a potential bottleneck for the use of BDD represented automata. In the Mona project at Aarhus (http://www.brics. dk/~klarlund/MonaFido), we have observed that for big automata (with thousands of states), the time to minimize using the straightforward algorithm is an order of magnitude larger than the time spent in constructing the automata.

In this paper, we show that our online BDD refinement algorithm allows minimization to be carried out in only $O(n \cdot \log n)$ steps, where n is the size of the representation. To our knowledge, the only other algorithm for large alphabets that reach a similar bound is that of [4], where incompletely specified transition functions are considered. The compression possible with the BDD representation is exponentially greater.

It should also be noted that when automata are represented with BDDs that are not path compressed an $O(n \log n)$ algorithm follows easily by considering the automaton as working on words over $\mathbb{B}$. Path compression, however, seems to be of major practical significance although the asymptotic gain is only slight [10].

Finally, we mention that online minimization of automata on large, implicitly represented state spaces (not alphabets) have been considered in [9]. Online minimization here refers to incremental exploration of the state space. This algorithm bears a superficial resemblance to ours in that it also alternates between minimal and maximal fixed point iterations.

Overview

In Section 2, we define the online BDD refinement problem. We develop a theoretical framework for understanding BDDs as fixed points in Section 3. We show that a weak composed operator suffices for generating the minimum fixed point. In Section 4, we provide a description of our online algorithm, which is based on the weak operator. Section 5 discusses the application of our algorithm to automaton minimization.

2   Online BDD Refinement

Notation

Assume we are given a set $x_0, x_1, \ldots, x_{\nu-1}$ of Boolean variables. A *truth assignment* to these variables is a vector $\mathbf{u} \in \mathbb{B}^\nu$. An *assignment prefix* $\mathbf{u}$ up to i is a truth assignment to variables $x_0, \ldots x_i$. A *Binary Decision Diagram* or *BDD* φ is a rooted, directed graph with the following properties. The root is named $^\wedge\varphi$. Each node v in φ is either an *internal node* or a *leaf*. An internal node possesses an *index* denoted $v.i$. Also, it contains edges $v \cdot 0$, which points to a node called the *low successor* of v, and $v \cdot 1$, which points to the *high successor*. The index of a successor of v is always greater than the index of v. A leaf has no successors and no index. Let the set of leaves be $\mathcal{L}$. The graph φ denotes a function, also called φ, from $\mathbb{B}^\nu \to \mathcal{L}$. To calculate $\varphi(\mathbf{x})$, one starts at the root. If the root is a leaf, then the value $\varphi(\mathbf{x})$ is the root; otherwise, let i be the index of the root. If x_i is 1 then go to the high successor, and if x_i is 0 go to the low successor. Continue in this way until a leaf is reached. This leaf is the value of $\varphi(\mathbf{x})$. (Since there may be jumps greater than one in the index of some of the variables, some of the values in the assignment may be irrelevant.) In general, if v is a node of index i and $\mathbf{u}$ is a value assignment to $x_i, \ldots, x_j$, then $v \cdot \mathbf{u}$ denotes the node reached by following $\mathbf{u}$ from v.

The BDD φ defines a partition $\equiv_\varphi$ of assignment prefixes given by $\mathbf{u} \equiv_\varphi \mathbf{u}'$ if $^\wedge\varphi \cdot \mathbf{u} = {}^\wedge\varphi \cdot \mathbf{u}'$.

We shall consider the case where the leaves are used to differentiate between finer and finer partitions of $\mathbb{B}^\nu$. The partition is given by a *leaf discriminator* $D : \mathcal{L} \to \mathbb{N}$. Two assignments $\mathbf{x}$ and $\mathbf{y}$ are then equivalent if $D \circ \varphi(\mathbf{x}) = D \circ \varphi(\mathbf{y})$.

BDDs may also be shared. For example, we use $\varphi = \varphi_0, \cdots, \varphi_{n-1}$ to denote a directed graph with roots $^\wedge\varphi_i$ such that the nodes reachable from each root constitute a BDD. If D is a discriminator for the leaves, then we say that $R : [n] \to \mathbb{N}$ is a *function discriminator* for $D \circ \varphi$ if $D \circ \varphi_i = D \circ \varphi_j$ iff $R(i) = R(j)$.

Note that if D is a constant discriminator (i.e. if D is a constant function), then all $D \circ \varphi_i$ are equivalent.

The Problem

The BDD online refinement problem is to maintain a function discriminator R for $D \circ \varphi$ when D is updated piecemeal. Each update operation specifies a partial mapping $E : \mathcal{L} \to \mathbb{N}$, which defines the change to D. Thus, if

$$D'(v) = \begin{cases} D(v) & \text{if } v \notin \mathbf{domain}(E) \\ E(v) & \text{if } v \in \mathbf{domain}(E) \end{cases}$$

then the new value of D is D'. In order for the new D to specify a partition refining the one given by the current D, we require that the range of E is disjoint from the range of the current D. The time requirements of our algorithm will prevent it from updating all values $R(i)$ with each iteration. Thus, we require as an additional output after each update operation the list of i for which $R(i)$ has changed. The desired functionality can be summarized as follows.

BDD Online Refinement Problem

Input: n shared BDDs φ with leaves $\mathcal{L}$ and discriminator D, which is initially a constant function.

Maintained : A functional discriminator R of length n.

Update: A partial mapping $E : \mathcal{L} \to \mathbb{N}$ such that **range**(E) does not intersect the current leaf discriminator. The leaf discriminator D is updated according to E as explained above. After each update operation, the contents of R discriminates $D \circ \varphi$. The size of operation E is the size of **domain**(E).

Output: A list of numbers i for which $R(i)$ has changed.

In Section 4, we prove:

Theorem 1 Multiple BDD Online Refinement can be solved in time $O(n \min(k, \log n) + k)$, where n is the number of nodes in the BDDs and k is the total size of all operations. Thus, if n also bounds k, then the algorithm is $O(n \log n)$.

3   A Theoretical Framework for BDDs

This section develops a theory of how BDDs arise as fixed points. The main insight is the formulation of composed operators that refine partitions and that carry out path compression. We show that canonical BDDs arise as fixed points of such operators; in particular, a weak operator is exhibited that calculates the proper fixed point even as it seemingly loses information.

The Canonical BDD We define the canonical BDD for function $\psi : \mathbb{B}^\nu \to D$, where D is finite, as follows. A *partial assignment* $\mathbf{u}$ *from i to j* is a truth assignment to variables $x_i, \ldots, x_j$. The partial assignment $\mathbf{u}$ may be narrowed to a partial assignment from i' to j', where $i \leq i' \leq j' \leq j$. It is denoted $\mathbf{u}[i'..j']$. If only a prefix of $\mathbf{u}$ up to $i' - 1$ is cut off, we write $\mathbf{u}[i'..]$. An *extension* $\mathbf{v}$ *of $\mathbf{u}$ up to j* is a partial assignment from $i + 1$ to j. A *full* extension is one that assigns up to $\nu - 1$. For any assignment prefix $\mathbf{u}$ up to i, we may consider the *residue* function $\psi_\mathbf{u} : \mathbf{v}' \mapsto \psi(\mathbf{u}\mathbf{v}')$, where $\mathbf{v}'$ is a full extension. Define $\mathbf{u} \sim_\psi \mathbf{u}'$ if $\psi_\mathbf{u} = \psi_{\mathbf{u}'}$. The equivalence class of $\mathbf{u}$ is denoted $[\mathbf{u}]_\psi$. In particular, if $\mathbf{u} \sim_\psi \mathbf{u}'$ then $\mathbf{u}$ and $\mathbf{u}'$ are assignment prefixes up to some i, which is called the *index* of the equivalence class $[\mathbf{u}]_\psi = [\mathbf{u}']_\psi$.

The equivalence classes of $\sim_\psi$ correspond to the states of a canonical automaton that upon reading a value assignment is in a state designating the value of ψ.

The *path compression* of BDDs can now be understood as a least fixed point calculation that involves coalescing equivalence classes. If $[\mathbf{u}0]_\psi = [\mathbf{u}1]_\psi$, then

$[\mathbf{u}]_\psi$ and $[\mathbf{u}0]_\psi = [\mathbf{u}1]_\psi$ are coalesced. Note that if also $[\mathbf{v}0]_\psi = [\mathbf{v}1_\psi]$ for some $\mathbf{v}$, then this identity still holds after $[\mathbf{u}]_\psi$ and $[\mathbf{u}0]_\psi = [\mathbf{u}1]_\psi$ are coalesced. Thus there is a unique least fixed point reached by repeatedly coalescing $\sim_\psi$ classes. The equivalence classes of the resulting partition $\approx_\psi$ is the *canonical* BDD for ψ. Each such new equivalence class M consists of a number of equivalence classes of $\sim_\psi$. When M contains internal nodes, the index $M.i$ of M is defined as the highest index of an old class. It can be seen that there is at most one old class in M of highest index. The high successor $M.1$, defined if the index is less than ν, is the equivalence class of $\mathbf{u} \cdot 1$, where $\mathbf{u}$ is a prefix of maximal length in M. The low successor is defined similarly.

Lemma 1 Consider i and assignment prefix $\mathbf{u}$ up to $j < i$. The following are equivalent:

1. The residue function $\psi_{\mathbf{u} \cdot \mathbf{v}}$ is the same function for all extensions $\mathbf{v}$ up to i.
2. $u \approx_\psi u \cdot v$ for all extensions v up to i.
3. $u \approx_\psi u \cdot v$ for some extension v up to i.

The equivalence $\equiv_\varphi$, which is derived from the BDD viewed as a graph, refines the equivalence $\approx_\varphi$, which is derived from the function represented by the BDD.

Lemma 2 $\equiv_\varphi$ refines $\approx_\varphi$.

Partitions of BDD Nodes A *partition* $\mathcal{P}$ of a BDD φ is a set of non-empty, disjoint subsets or *blocks* of nodes, whose union is the set of all nodes. Alternatively, $\mathcal{P}$ may be viewed as an equivalence relation $\equiv_\mathcal{P}$ defined by $v \equiv_\mathcal{P} v'$ iff $\exists B \in \mathcal{P} : v, v' \in B$. Since any assignment prefix $\mathbf{u}$ leads to a unique node φ, $\equiv_\mathcal{P}$ induces an equivalence relation on assignment prefixes that is also denoted $\equiv_\mathcal{P}$.

To simplify matters, we assume in the following that *all partitions are over the same BDD φ*. Also for simplicity, we shall often write $\mathcal{P}$ for $\equiv_\mathcal{P}$.

For a partition Q, we may we define a discriminator labeling D of the leaves of φ such that for leaves v and v', $D(v) = D(v')$ iff $v \equiv_Q v'$. The canonical BDD for the function $D \circ \phi$ is denoted $\approx_Q$. Note that this BDD is dependent only on the partition of the leaves defined by Q—not the partition of internal nodes. These distinctions will be further elaborated on in the next section. Note here that the partition of internal nodes may not even induce a BDD on equivalence classes. We usually regard the canonical BDD $\approx_Q$ as a partition of the nodes of φ.

Decision Partitions An important part of our algorithm is to work with partitions that become refinements of canonical partitions only after certain nodes have been moved around.

A node v is a *decision node* if it is a leaf or it has at least one successor outside its own block. Any other node is *redundant*. A *decision partition* $\mathcal{M}$ of a partition Q specifies a partition of the decision nodes of each block B in Q into *decision blocks* such that any decision block M either contains internal nodes of the same index or contains only leaves. If for each block B, all decision nodes of B are gathered in just one decision block, then $\mathcal{M}$ is said to be the *stable decision partition*.

The *Split* Operator We say that the *behavior* of an internal node v with respect to a partition $\mathcal{Q}$ is the pair $([v \cdot 0]_\mathcal{Q}, [v \cdot 1]_\mathcal{Q})$; the behavior of a leaf v is just itself.

Given $\mathcal{Q}$, we can form a decision partition $\mathcal{M} = Split(\mathcal{Q})$ as follows. For every block B, put all decision nodes v with the same index and the same behavior in the same decision block. All leaves in B are also put into a decision block. Formally, $\mathcal{M}$ is defined as

$$\{M \neq \emptyset \mid \exists B, B_0, B_1 \in \mathcal{M} : \exists i :$$
$$M = \{v \mid v \in B \text{ and } v \text{ is a leaf}\} \text{ or}$$
$$M = \{v \mid v.i = i \text{ and } v \in B, \ v0 \in B_0, \text{ and } v1 \in B_1\}\}$$

Partition $\mathcal{Q}$ is *stable* if $Split(\mathcal{Q})$ is the stable decision partition.

Note that if $\mathcal{Q}$ is stable, then both successors of any internal decision node are outside its own block—for if some block B contained a decision node v with only one successor not in B, then by following the other successor, we would reach another node in B (which may be a decision node or a redundant node); by continuing, we would eventually reach a decision node in B that is either a leaf or both of whose successors are outside B and in both cases, this node would have a different behavior than that of v, and that would contradict that $\mathcal{Q}$ is stable.

Note also that $\approx_\mathcal{Q}$ is stable.

The *Grow* Operator Let $\mathcal{M}$ be a decision partition for a partition $\mathcal{Q}$. For any node v in a block B and any extension $\mathbf{u}$, there will be a first decision node w in some decision block M along the path induced by following nodes from v according to u. In this case, we say that extension $\mathbf{u}$ from v *hits* M. In particular, if $v \in M$, then any extension hits M.

If M is a decision block of B, then its *closure*, denoted $Cl(\mathcal{Q}, M)$, is the set of nodes in B all of whose extensions hit M. This set can also be defined inductively by *growing* the decision block: initially, let $Cl(\mathcal{Q}, M)$ be the decision block and add any node both of whose successors are in $Cl(\mathcal{Q}, M)$ until there are no more such nodes. Note that if M and M' are different decision blocks, then $Cl(\mathcal{Q}, M)$ and $Cl(\mathcal{Q}, M')$ are disjoint.

For each block B, let the *remainder*, denoted $Rem(\mathcal{Q}, \mathcal{M}, B)$, be defined as B minus all nodes in $Cl(M)$, where M is contained in B, i.e. $Rem(\mathcal{Q}, \mathcal{M}, B) = B \backslash \bigcup_{M \in \mathcal{M}, M \subseteq B} Cl(\mathcal{Q}, M)$. Then, all sets $Cl(\mathcal{Q}, M), M \in \mathcal{M}$, together with $Rem(\mathcal{Q}, \mathcal{M}, B), B \in \mathcal{Q}$, form a partition, called $Grow(\mathcal{Q}, \mathcal{M})$. Since, $Grow(\mathcal{Q}, \mathcal{M})$ is gotten from $\mathcal{Q}$ by carving out closures of decision blocks, $Grow(\mathcal{Q}, \mathcal{M})$ refines $\mathcal{Q}$. Note that $\mathcal{Q}$ is stable if and only if it is a fixed point under $Grow \circ Split$.

Sometimes it is convenient to assume that $Split(Q)$ really stands for $(Q, Split(Q))$. Then, we refer to the composed operator $Grow \circ Split(Q)$ as an abbreviation of $Grow(Q, Split(Q))$.

It is not necessarily the case that if $\mathcal{P}$ refines Q, then $Grow \circ Split(\mathcal{P})$ refines $Grow \circ Split(Q)$. This non-monotonicity can be illustrated by the following example, where the original partitions are shown in solid lines and the additional subdivisions introduced by the $Grow \circ Split$ operator are shown in dotted lines:

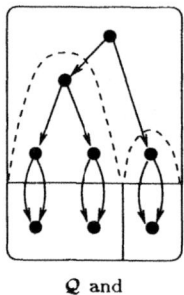
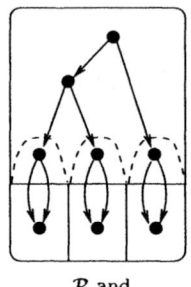

Q and
$Grow \circ Split(Q)$
$\qquad\qquad$
$\mathcal{P}$ and
$Grow \circ Split(\mathcal{P})$

Here, $\mathcal{P}$ refines Q, but the two top-most nodes are equivalent in $Grow \circ Split(\mathcal{P})$, but not in $Grow \circ Split(Q)$.

Lemma 3 Let $\mathcal{P}$ be a stable partition and let $v \equiv_{\mathcal{P}} v'$, where v is of index i and v' of index j with $i \leq j$. Then for any extension $\mathbf{u}$ from v, $v \cdot \mathbf{u} \equiv_{\mathcal{P}} v' \cdot \mathbf{u}[j..]$.

Let $\mathcal{M}$ be a decision partition of Q. We say that $\mathcal{P}$ *refines* $\mathcal{M}$ if whenever v and v' in are different decision blocks of $\mathcal{M}$, they are in different blocks of $\mathcal{P}$.

Lemma 4 Let stable $\mathcal{P}$ refine Q and $\mathcal{M}$, where $\mathcal{M}$ is a decision partition of Q. Then $\mathcal{P}$ refines $Grow(Q, \mathcal{M})$.

Lemma 5 If stable $\mathcal{P}$ refines Q, then $\mathcal{P}$ refines $Split(Q)$.

Proposition 1 If stable $\mathcal{P}$ refines Q, then $\mathcal{P}$ refines $Grow \circ Split(Q)$.

Proposition 2 If $Q = Grow \circ Split(Q)$, then Q refines $\approx_Q$.

Proposition 3 If $\approx_Q$ refines Q and if $Q' = (Grow \circ Split)^i(Q)$ is stable, then Q' is $\approx_Q$.

The $CGrow$ Operator The $CGrow$ operator is defined as $Grow(Q, \mathcal{M})$ except that for each block B of Q, $Rem(Q, \mathcal{M}, B)$ may or may not be coalesced with some designated $Cl(Q, \mathcal{M})$, where $\mathcal{M}$ is a decision block in B. Thus the operation is not fully specified, but whether coalescing takes place or not and with which $Cl(Q, \mathcal{M})$ will be inconsequential for establishing the following general properties. Note that $Grow \circ Split(Q)$ refines $CGrow \circ Split(Q)$. Even though information is dropped by $CGrow$, a fixed point involving $CGrow$ is also a fixed point involving $Grow$:

Proposition 4 If $CGrow \circ Split(Q) = Q$, then $Grow \circ Split(Q) = Q$.

Theorem 2 If $\approx_Q$ refines Q and if $Q' = (CGrow \circ Split)^i(Q)$ is stable, then Q' is $\approx_Q$.

Our concept of leaf partition can then be understood as a decision partition $\mathcal{E}$ of the current canonical partition Q. The only non-trivial decision blocks of a leaf partition are those that contain leaves. A canonical equivalence relation $\approx_{\mathcal{E}}$ is defined as before for $\approx_Q$.

Theorem 2 then can be formulated:

Theorem 2' If $\approx_{\mathcal{E}}$ refines Q and if $Q' = CGrow \circ (Split \circ CGrow)^i(Q, \mathcal{E})$ is stable, then Q' is the canonical partition $\approx_{\mathcal{E}}$.

4 Online Algorithm

The online problem in Section 2 can be solved by maintaining the canonical partition by means of a node discriminator for all nodes, not only the roots. In this way, we may focus on the refinement problem for a single BDD, since multiple BDDs can be embedded within a single one by introducing dummy variables near the root. The modified problem is:

> **Single BDD Online Refinement Problem**
> **Input**: A BDD φ with leaves $\mathcal{L}$ and constant discriminator D.
> **Maintained** : For each node v, the discriminator value $D(v)$ is maintained so that D expresses the canonical partition $\approx_{\mathcal{E}}$.
> **Update**: A partial mapping $E : \mathcal{L} \to \mathbb{N}$ such that **range**$(E) \cap$ **range**$(D) = \{\}$. E and the current partition of leaves determine a leaf partition $\mathcal{E}$.
> **Output**: A list of nodes for which $D(v)$ has changed.

As an example, consider the BDD in Figure 1. The leaf partition at this stage has been refined into two decision blocks. The canonical partition with respect to this decision partition is indicated by dotted lines. An update operation E might split the two leaves in the left most block, and as a result, the four nodes in the left, bottom corner would each become a singleton equivalence class.

The basic problem encountered when trying to construct a fast algorithm is that after nodes have been split, it is necessary to calculate equivalence under path compression—corresponding to our notion of growing decision blocks. There is now evident way of carrying out the grow phase, which must proceed bottom-up, without touching nodes more than $\Theta(\log n)$ times. Our notion of coalesced growth opens an escape hatch that allows the process to be halted at certain critical moments.

Our algorithm works as follows. The canonical partition $\approx_{\mathcal{E}}$ induced by the leaf partition $\mathcal{E}$ refines the current partition Q expressed by D. Therefore, according to Theorem 2', we can apply the combined operator $Split \circ CGrow$ until a new fixed point Q' is reached. Then, Q' is the canonical partition $\approx_{\mathcal{E}}$.

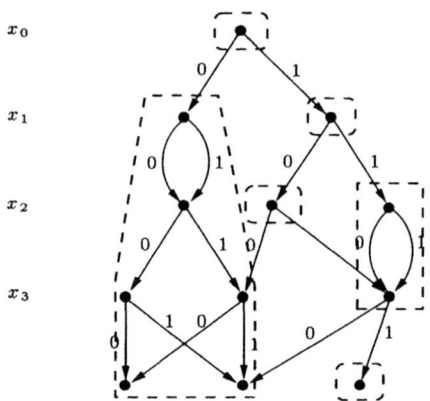

Figure 1. A canonical BDD

To make this abstract description into an algorithm, we must choose data structures and explain how the split and grow operations are implemented. We also must explain how we choose the coalescing of blocks in *CGrow*.

Each discriminator value d represents a block that we denote by d. We maintain a doubly-linked list $L(d)$ of all v in d. A decision partition is specified for a block d_{old} by *explicit* decision blocks and a *implicit* decision block. They are carved out of the block d_{old} as follows. Each explicit decision block is represented by a discriminator value d, and all nodes in the decision block d are placed in the list $L(d)$, which is carved out of $L(d_{old})$. Later, when the decision blocks are grown, these discriminator values will denote their closures. In addition, the implicit decision block consists of all decision nodes in the block not appearing in an explicit decision block. The algorithm will in a gradual fashion convert the implicit decision nodes to explicit ones carrying some distinct discriminator value $d_{implicit}$ reserved for the explicit version of the implicit block.

The algorithm uses a mapping $new(d_{old})$ that records the set of discriminator values for the decision blocks in d_{old}.

Initially, we call the *CGrow* algorithm with decision blocks of leaves and *new* initialized according to E.

The *CGrow* phase is implemented for each decision block $L(d)$ by adding the nodes in $L(d_{old})$ for which both successors are already in $L(d)$; such nodes are removed from $L(d_{old})$. To locate nodes that should be considered for inclusion in a closure, we assume that the BDD is equipped with a backwards pointer structure such that the parents of any node can be sequentially accessed. This process of exploring parents is done in a tightly controlled manner according to the sizes of the lists $L(d)$ for $d \in new(d_{old})$. When a parent has been explored from both the left and right successor, and both are in the same closure, then the parent is moved into this closure as well. The exploration of a closure finishes when all parents of all nodes in the closure have been explored.

The *CGrow* phase returns a list of all nodes possessing a successor whose discriminator has changed. These nodes are the explicit decision nodes of the next iteration.

The *Split* algorithm calculates the new discriminator of the nodes in this list according to their behavior. It also calculates the value of *new*.

Main Idea

The main idea behind the *CGrow* phase is that all unfinished closures are grown in parallel steps, where each step consists of exploring yet another parent of a node in the closure until either (a) a closure becomes too big, say half the size of d_{old}, or (b) until only one closure is unfinished or (c) until all closures are finished. In case (a) and (b), the closure in question is coalesced with the remainder by moving nodes back to d_{old}. (If the conversion of implicit decision nodes is not yet finished, the step for the implicit block is simply to convert another node to $L_{d_{implicit}}$. When all nodes have been converted, this decision block is treated as an ordinary one.) In case (a), all remaining closures are then finished and they will all be small since a big one already was found. In case (b), all closures, possibly except the last one (if it was finished), will by the absence of the condition in case (a) be small.

In case (a), the work involved in building the aborted closure can be charged to a small, finished closure. For this argument to be correct, it is crucial that the work done is the same (to within a constant factor) for all the closures grown in parallel.

In case (b), there may be no small, finished closure to charge the wasted work to. This situation occurs when there is only one decision block to begin with. In this case, the work involved will be proportional to the size of the decision block, and it can be assumed to be part of the work involved in building the decision block. The algorithm makes sure that the original discriminating value d_{old} of the whole block is maintained despite a possible new value assigned to the decision block. In this way, only blocks that are really split may result in further splitting.

In case (c), all blocks will be small. The work done in building a closure is not proportional to the size of the closure, since each parallel step consists of exploring a parent (of which there may be unboundedly many). But each parent has only two successors, and so, the work of visiting the parent can be charged to the closure of the child from which it is explored (unless the work is attributed to another block as a result of the abandonment of a closure calculation). Thus, every time a parent is explored from the same successor, it will be done when the resulting closure the successor resides in is at most half as big as the last time.

In the full paper, we provide a more detailed description, a complexity analysis, and a discussion about how hashing can be avoided.

Theorem 1′ The Single BDD Online Problem can be solved in time $O(n \min(k, \log n) + k)$, where n is the number of nodes in the BDDs and k is the total size of all operations. Thus, if n also bounds k, then the algorithm is $O(n \log n)$. Theorem 1 follows from Theorem 1′.

5 Minimizing BDD Represented Automata

In the full paper, we explain how to obtain:

Corollary 1 Minimization is $O(n \log n)$ for BDD-represented automata, where n bounds the number of states and the number of BDD nodes.

Acknowledgments

Thanks to Robert Paige and Theis Rauhe for their careful reading of an earlier version of this paper, for pointing out errors, and for exploring the possible existence of a simpler $n \log n$ BDD online refinement algorithm. The example of non-monotonicity of the composed operator in Section 3 was suggested by Robert Paige to illustrate an error in the earlier version. Michael Yannakakis kindly pointed out the reference [2].

References

1. D. Basin and N. Klarlund. Beyond the finite in hardware verification. Submitted. Extended version of: "Hardware verification using monadic second-order logic," *CAV '95*, LNCS 939, 1996.
2. Norbert Blum. An $o(n \log n)$ implementation of the standard mothod for minimizing n-state finite automata. *Information Processing Letters*, 1996.
3. R. E. Bryant. Symbolic Boolean manipulation with ordered binary-decision diagrams. *ACM Computing surveys*, 24(3):293–318, September 1992.
4. A. Cardon and M. Crochemore. Partitioning a graph in $O(|A| \log_2 |V|)$. *TCS*, 19:85–98, 1982.
5. Aarti Gupta. *Inductive Boolean function manipulation*. PhD thesis, Carnegie Mellon University, 1994. CMU-CS-94-208.
6. Aarti Gupta and Allan L. Fisher. Representation and symbolic manipulation of linearly inductive boolean functions. In *Proceedings of the IEEE International Conference on Computer-Aided Design*, pages 192–199. IEEE Computer Society Press, 1993.
7. J.G. Henriksen, J. Jensen, M. Jørgensen, N. Klarlund, B. Paige, T. Rauhe, and A. Sandholm. Mona: Monadic second-order logic in practice. In *Tools and Algorithms for the Construction and Analysis of Systems, First International Workshop, TACAS '95, LNCS 1019*, 1996. Also available through http://www.brics.dk/~klarlund/MonaFido/papers.html.
8. J. Hopcroft. An $n \log n$ algorithm for minimizing states in a finite automaton. In Z. Kohavi and Paz A., editors, *Theory of machines and computations*, pages 189–196. Academic Press, 1971.
9. D. Lee and M. Yannakakis. Online minimization of transition systems. In *Proc. STOC*, pages 264–274. ACM, 1992.
10. H-T. Liaw and C-S. Lin. On the OBDD-representation of general Boolean functions. *IEEE Trans. on Computers*, C-41(6):661–664, 1992.
11. R. Paige and R. Tarjan. Three efficient algorithms based on partition refinement. *SIAM Journal of Computing*, 16(6), 1987.
12. D. Sieling and I. Wegener. Reduction of OBDDs in linear time. *IPL*, 48:139–144, 1993.

Weak Bisimulation for Fully Probabilistic Processes

Christel Baier[1] and Holger Hermanns[2]

[1] Fakultät für Mathematik & Informatik, Universität Mannheim, Germany
e-mail: baier@pi1.informatik.uni-mannheim.de
[2] Informatik VII, Universität Erlangen, Germany
e-mail: hrherman@informatik.uni-erlangen.de

Abstract. Bisimulations that abstract from internal computation have proven to be useful for verification of compositionally defined transition system. In the literature of probabilistic extensions of such transition systems, similar bisimulations are rare. In this paper, we introduce weak bisimulation and branching bisimulation for transition systems where nondeterministic branching is replaced by probabilistic branching. In contrast to the nondeterministic case, both relations coincide. We give an algorithm to decide weak bisimulation with a time complexity cubic in the number of states of the transition system. This meets the worst case complexity for deciding branching bisimulation in the nondeterministic case.

1 Introduction

In recent years, the need to formally reason about probabilistic phenomena in software and hardware systems has incented the study of probabilistic models of computation. A variety of models has been proposed in the literature, most of them based on transition systems. These models can be classified with respect to their treatment of nondeterminsm. Several approaches replace the concept of nondeterministic branching by probabilistic branching, e.g. [9, 19, 26, 13, 36], whereas others allow for both, nondeterministic as well as probabilistic branching, e.g. [34, 31, 17, 23, 33]. Following [13], the former model can be subdivided according to the relationship between occurences of actions and transition probabilities. In "reactive" systems, transition probability distributions are dependent on the occurrences of actions. In contrast, in "generative" (also called "fully probabilistic") systems (which can be viewed as discrete Markov chains labelled with actions), these distributions implicitly assign probabilities also to occurrences of actions. "Stratified" systems allow for levelwise probabilistic branching.

Verification techniques for such models have been inspired by succesful experiences in the nonprobabilistic case. This includes probabilistic variants of temporal logics, e.g. [2, 5, 11, 17, 19, 20, 31, 32, 34, 35]. Another research strand focusses on equivalences and preorders used to established that one system "implements" another, according to some notion of implementation, such as strong bisimulation [26], simulation [22, 33], testing preorders [7, 8, 9, 23, 37, 36], trace, failure and ready equivalence [24]. For mechanised verification purposes, the complexity of deciding such equivalences for finite state systems is a crucial aspect. In the nonprobabilistic case, for instance, (strong) bisimulation can be decided in time $\mathcal{O}(m \cdot \log n)$ [30] where n is the number of states and m the number of transitions in the underlying transition system. Most of the coarser equivalences are PSPACE-complete [25]. In the probabilistic framework, the situation is slightly different. Most of the equivalences for probabilistic processes (e.g. strong bisimulation or trace, failure, ready and testing equivalence) can be decided in time polynomial in the size of the probabilistic transition system [8, 21, 3].

Several authors mentioned that the definition of a weak bisimulation that abstracts from internal computation is desirable, but problematic in a probabilistic setting [24, 17]. In the nonprobabilistic case, weak bisimulation [29] is fundamental for compositional verification methods that exploit abstraction from internal computation (see [6] for an impressive example). The time complexity for deciding weak bisimulation is $\mathcal{O}(n^{2.3})$, using the transitive closure operation from [10]. Branching bisimulation [14] is a slightly finer relation for the same purpose, it has time complexity $\mathcal{O}(n \cdot m)$ (but a better space complexity than weak bisimulation) [15]. To the best of our knowledge, [33] is the only paper that introduces notions of weak and branching bisimulation for probabilistic transition systems. Their model can be seen as a generalization of reactive transition systems, since transition probability distributions are dependent on occurences of actions, but nondeterministic choices between different distributions are possible for the same action. The definition of weak and branching bisimulation à la [33] replaces Milner's "double arrow relation" (the transitive, reflexive closure of internal transitions) by assigning a (possibly infinite) set of distributions to each state. For a given state, this set represents the (nondeterministic) alternatives of probability distributions on those states that are reachable by sequences of internal transitions. In contrast to the nonprobabilistic case, the transitions involved form a tree rather than a linear chain. It seems to be hard to adapt this notion to other types of probabilistic transition systems, such as fully probabilistic systems.

In this paper, we propose notions of weak bisimulation and branching bisimulation for fully probabilistic transition systems that appear to be rather natural extensions of the corresponding relations in the nonprobabilistic case. We replace Milner's "double arrow relation" by the probabilities to reach states via sequences of internal transitions. In contrast to the nonprobabilistic case where branching bisimulation is strictly finer than weak bisimulation, these two relations coincide in the fully probabilistic case. We present an algorithm to compute the weak bisimulation equivalence classes in time $\mathcal{O}(n^3)$ where n is the number of states in the underlying probabilistic transition system. It is worth noting that this is the same worst case complexity as computing the branching bisimulation equivalence classes of a nonprobabilistic transition system [15].

The paper is organized as follows. In Section 2 we introduce basic notations and properties of fully probabilistic transition systems. Section 3 introduces weak and branching bisimulation and shows that both coincide. Section 4 is devoted to an algorithm to compute weak bisimulation equivalence classes. Section 5 indicates directions for further work. Due to space constraints we only provide sketches of proofs. The complete proofs are contained in [4].

2 Fully probabilistic transition systems

In this section we introduce fully probabilistic transition systems together with some definitions and notations that will be useful in the sequel.

A *fully probabilistic transition system* is a tuple (S, Act, P) where S is a finite set of states, Act a set of actions that contains the internal action τ (which represents any invisible computation) and $P : S \times Act \times S \to [0, 1]$ a function such that $\sum_{(a,t) \in Act \times S} P(s, a, t) = 1$ for all $s \in S$. In what follows, we use arabic letters $a, b, \ldots$ to denote (internal or non-internal) actions, greek letters $\alpha, \beta, \ldots$ to denote non-internal actions. For $C \subseteq S$, we define $P(s, a, C) = \sum_{t \in C} P(s, a, t)$. An *execution fragment* is a finite "sequence" $\sigma = s_0 \overset{a_1}{\to} s_1 \overset{a_2}{\to} s_2 \overset{a_3}{\to} \ldots \overset{a_k}{\to} s_k$ such that $s_0, s_1, \ldots, s_k \in S$, $a_1, \ldots, a_k \in Act$ and $P(s_{i-1}, a_i, s_i) > 0$, $i = 1, \ldots, k$. We define $last(\sigma) = s_k$, $first(\sigma) = s_0$, $length(\sigma) = k$, $trace(\sigma) = a_1 a_2 \ldots a_k$ and

$$Prob(\sigma) = P(s_0, a_1, s_1) \cdot P(s_1, a_2, s_2) \cdot \ldots \cdot P(s_{k-1}, a_k, s_k).$$

An *execution* in (S, Act, P) is an infinite "sequence" $\pi = s_0 \overset{a_1}{\to} s_1 \overset{a_2}{\to} s_2 \overset{a_3}{\to} \ldots$ where $s_0, s_1, \ldots, \in S$, $a_1, a_2, \ldots \in Act$ and $P(s_{i-1}, a_i, s_i) > 0$, $i = 1, 2, \ldots$. We define $first(\pi) = s_0$, and $\pi(k) = s_k$. $\pi^{(k)} = s_0 \overset{a_1}{\to} s_1 \overset{a_2}{\to} \ldots \overset{a_k}{\to} s_k$ is called the k-th prefix of π. For σ to be an execution fragment with $length(\sigma) = k$, let $\sigma \uparrow$ be the set of executions π with $\pi^{(k)} = \sigma$.

Example 1. A fully probabilistic transition system with 8 states and $Act = \{\alpha, \beta, \tau\}$. If $P(s, a, t)$ is different from zero, its value is annotated to an a-transition joining s and t. To illustrate the above definitions, we calculate $P(s_2, \beta, \{s_3, s_4, s_5\}) = 0.9$. Concerning the execution $\pi = s_0 \overset{\tau}{\to} s_1 \overset{\tau}{\to} s_3 \overset{\alpha}{\to} s_6 \overset{\tau}{\to} s_5 \overset{\tau}{\to} s_5 \overset{\tau}{\to} \ldots$, we have $Prob(\pi^{(3)}) = 0.5 \cdot 0.6 \cdot 0.1 = 0.003$ and $trace(\pi^{(3)}) = \tau\tau\alpha$.

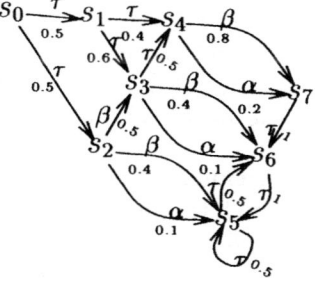

We suppose the reader to be familiar with basic notions of probability theory (see e. g. [16]). For fixed $s \in S$, we define a probability space on the executions starting in s: Let $Exec(s)$ be the set of executions starting in s (i.e. the set of executions π with $first(\pi) = s$), $ExecFrag(s)$ the set of execution fragments σ with $first(\sigma) = s$. Let $\Sigma(s)$ be the smallest sigma field on $Exec(s)$ which contains the basic cylinders $\sigma \uparrow$, $\sigma \in ExecFrag(s)$, and let $\mathcal{P}$ be the unique probability measure on $\Sigma(s)$ with $\mathcal{P}(\sigma \uparrow) = Prob(\sigma)$. For $\Lambda \subseteq Act^*$, $C \subseteq S$, we define $Exec(\Lambda, C)$ to be the set of executions π that lead from $first(\pi)$ to a state in C via a sequence of actions belonging to Λ. Formally, if $\pi = s_0 \overset{a_1}{\to} s_1 \overset{a_2}{\to} \ldots$ is an execution then $\pi \in Exec(\Lambda, C)$ iff there is some $k \geq 0$ with $trace(\pi^{(k)}) \in \Lambda$ and $s_k \in C$. Let $Exec(s, \Lambda, C) = Exec(\Lambda, C) \cap Exec(s)$. Clearly, $Exec(s, \Lambda, C)$ is measurable in $\Sigma(s)$ as $Exec(s, \Lambda, C) = \bigcup_\sigma \sigma \uparrow$ where σ ranges over all execution fragments starting in s such that $trace(\sigma) \in \Lambda$ and $last(\sigma) \in C$. The probabilities $\mathcal{P}(s, \Lambda, C) = P(Exec(s, \Lambda, C))$ solve the equation system:

$$\mathcal{P}(s, \Lambda, C) = 1 \quad \text{if } s \in C \text{ and } \varepsilon \in \Lambda$$

$$\mathcal{P}(s, \Lambda, C) = \sum_{(a,t) \in Act \times S} P(s, a, t) \cdot \mathcal{P}(t, \Lambda/a, C) \quad \text{otherwise}$$

where $\Lambda/a = \{\lambda : a\lambda \in \Lambda\}$. Here, ε denotes the empty word in Act^*. If $t \in S$ then we write $\mathcal{P}(s, \Lambda, t)$ rather than $\mathcal{P}(s, \Lambda, \{t\})$. In what follows, we identify a regular expression (e.g. τ^*, $\tau^* \alpha$ or $\tau^* \alpha \tau^*$) with the corresponding set of traces. For instance, $\mathcal{P}(s, \tau^*, C)$ denotes the probability to reach C from s via internal actions.

Example 2. For the fully probabilistic transition system of Example 1, we calculate $\mathcal{P}(s_1, \tau^* \beta \tau^*, \{s_5, s_6, s_7\}) = 0.4 \cdot 0.8 \cdot 1 + 0.6 \cdot (0.4 \cdot 1 + 0.5 \cdot 0.8 \cdot 1) = 0.8$.

3 Weak and branching bisimulation

In this section we define weak and branching bisimulation for fully probabilistic transition systems. While in the nonprobabilistic case branching bisimulation is strictly finer than weak bisimulation, these two relations coincide in the fully probabilistic case.

For the definition of weak bisimulation, we replace Milner's "double arrow" relation $\Rightarrow$ (the transitive, reflexive closure of $\xrightarrow{\tau}$) by the function $\mathcal{P}(s, \tau^*, t)$, which assigns to each pair (s, t) of states the probability to reach state t from s via internal actions. Similarly, for $\alpha \in Act \setminus \{\tau\}$, we deal with the probabilities $\mathcal{P}(s, \tau^* \alpha \tau^*, t)$ rather than Milners weak transition relations $\Rightarrow \xrightarrow{\alpha} \Rightarrow$. In what follows, we fix a fully probabilistic transition system (S, Act, P).

Definition 1. A *weak bisimulation* on (S, Act, P) is an equivalence relation R on S such that for all $(s, s') \in R$, $\lambda \in (Act \setminus \{\tau\}) \cup \{\varepsilon\}$ and all equivalence classes $C \in S/R$:

$$\mathcal{P}(s, \tau^* \lambda \tau^*, C) = \mathcal{P}(s', \tau^* \lambda \tau^*, C).$$

(Note that ε denotes the empty trace and that $\tau^* \varepsilon \tau^* = \tau^*$.) Two states s, s' are called *weakly bisimulation equivalent* (denoted by $s \approx s'$) iff $(s, s') \in R$ for some weak bisimulation R.

Example 3. For the system of Example 1, the smallest equivalence relation R which identifies the states s_5, s_6, s_7 and s_1, s_3, s_4 is a weak bisimulation. To illustrate this, we compute, for instance, $\mathcal{P}(s_4, \tau^* \alpha \tau^*, C_{567}) = 0.2$, as well as $\mathcal{P}(s_3, \tau^* \alpha \tau^*, C_{567}) = 0.5 \cdot \mathcal{P}(s_4, \tau^* \alpha \tau^*, C_{567}) + 0.1 = 0.2$ and

$\mathcal{P}(s_1, \tau^*\alpha\tau^*, C_{567}) = 0.4 \cdot \mathcal{P}(s_4, \tau^*\alpha\tau^*, C_{567}) + 0.6 \cdot \mathcal{P}(s_3, \tau^*\alpha\tau^*, C_{567}) = 0.2$
where $C_{567} = \{s_5, s_6, s_7\}$. As a whole, we obtain the following values of $\mathcal{P}$ (where $C_{134} = \{s_1, s_3, s_4\}$) indicating that the states s_5, s_6, s_7 and s_1, s_3, s_4 are weakly bisimulation equivalent.

$\mathcal{P}$	$\{s_0\}$	$\{s_2\}$	C_{134}	C_{567}	$\{s_0\}$	$\{s_2\}$	C_{134}	C_{567}	$\{s_0\}$	$\{s_2\}$	C_{134}	C_{567}
			τ^*				$\tau^*\alpha\tau^*$				$\tau^*\beta\tau^*$	
s_5 (also s_6, s_7)	0	0	0	1	0	0	0	0	0	0	0	0
s_1 (also s_3, s_4)	0	0	1	0	0	0	0	0.2	0	0	0	0.8
s_2	0	1	0	0	0	0	0	0.1	0	0	0.5	0.4
s_0	1	0.5	0.5	0	0	0	0	0.15	0	0	0.25	0.6

It can be shown that $\approx$ is a weak bisimulation. In the nonprobabilistic case, it holds for weakly bisimulation equivalent states s, s' that if $s \overset{\alpha_1 \ldots \alpha_k}{\Longrightarrow} t$ then $s' \overset{\alpha_1 \ldots \alpha_k}{\Longrightarrow} t'$ such that t and t' are weakly bisimulation equivalent. Here, $\overset{\alpha_1 \ldots \alpha_k}{\Longrightarrow}$ denotes $\Rightarrow \overset{\alpha_1}{\rightarrow} \Rightarrow \ldots \Rightarrow \overset{\alpha_k}{\rightarrow} \Rightarrow$. This result carries over to the probabilistic case.

Theorem 2. *Let Λ be a regular expression of the form $\tau^*\alpha_1\tau^*\alpha_2\tau^* \ldots \tau^*\alpha_k$ or $\tau^*\alpha_1\tau^*\alpha_2\tau^* \ldots \tau^*\alpha_k\tau^*$. Then:*

$$\text{If } s \approx s' \text{ then } \mathcal{P}(s, \Lambda, C) = \mathcal{P}(s', \Lambda, C) \text{ for all } C \in S/\approx.$$

Proof. by induction on k. The basis of induction $(k = 1)$ follows by the fact that, for each state s, the vector $(\mathcal{P}(s, \tau^*\alpha, C))_{C \in S/\approx}$ is the unique solution of the linear equation system $\mathbf{x} \cdot \mathbf{A} = \mathbf{a}$ where $\mathbf{A} = (\mathcal{P}(C, \tau^*, C'))_{C, C' \in S/\approx}$ and $\mathbf{a} = (\mathcal{P}([s], \tau^*\alpha\tau^*, C'))_{C' \in S/\approx}$. Here, $[s]$ denotes the weak bisimulation equivalence class of s and $\mathcal{P}(C, \tau^*\lambda\tau^*, C') = \mathcal{P}(t, \tau^*\lambda\tau^*, C')$ for some (all) $t \in C$. The induction step follows by the induction hypothesis, the basis of induction and the fact that

$$\mathcal{P}(s, \tau^*\alpha_1\tau^* \ldots \tau^*\alpha_k, C) = \sum_{A \in S/\approx} \mathcal{P}(s, \tau^*\alpha_1, A) \cdot \mathcal{P}(A, \tau^*\alpha_2\tau^* \ldots \tau^*\alpha_k, C)$$

and $\mathcal{P}(s, \tau^*\alpha_1\tau^* \ldots \tau^*\alpha_k\tau^*, C) = \sum_{A \in S/\approx} \mathcal{P}(s, \tau^*\alpha_1\tau^*\alpha_2\tau^* \ldots \tau^*\alpha_k, A) \cdot \mathcal{P}(A, \tau^*, C)$.

$\square$

Van Glabbeek & Weijland [14] introduces branching bisimulation which is strictly finer than weak bisimulation. The basic idea of branching bisimulation is that in order to simulate a step $s \overset{\alpha}{\rightarrow} t$ by an equivalent state s', s' is allowed to perform arbitrary many internal actions leading to a state which is still equivalent to s (i.e. the intermediate states before s' also fall in the equivalence class of s and s') and then to perform α reaching a state t' which is equivalent to t. In the probabilistic case, we require that for equivalent states s, s', the probabilities for s and s' to perform internal actions inside the equivalence class of s and s' and then to perform a visible action α leading to state of a certain equivalence class C are the same.

Definition 3. A *branching bisimulation* on (S, Act, P) is an equivalence relation R on S such that
$$\mathcal{P}_R(s, \tau^*\lambda, C) = \mathcal{P}_R(s', \tau^*\lambda, C)$$
for all $(s, s') \in R$, $C \in S/R$ and $\lambda \in (Act \setminus \{\tau\}) \cup \{\varepsilon\}$. Here, $\mathcal{P}_R(s, \tau^*\lambda, C) = P(Exec_R(s, \tau^*\lambda, C))$ and $Exec_R(s, \tau^*\lambda, C)$ is the set of executions $\pi \in Exec(s)$ such that there is some $k \geq 0$ with $(s, \pi(i)) \in R$, $i = 1, \ldots, k-1$, $trace(\pi^{(k)}) \in \tau^*\lambda$ and $\pi(k) \in C$.

Two states s, s' are called *branching bisimulation equivalent* (denoted $s \approx_{br} s'$) iff $(s, s') \in R$ for some branching bisimulation R.

It can be shown that $\approx_{br}$ is a branching bisimulation. In contrast to the non-probabilistic case, branching and weak bisimulation coincide:

Theorem 4. $s \approx s'$ *iff* $s \approx_{br} s'$.

Proof. It is easy to see that $\approx_{br}$ is a weak bisimulation. Hence, $\approx_{br} \subseteq \approx$. For the converse, we show that $\approx$ is a branching bisimulation where we use the characterization of branching bisimulations that we give in the next section (Lemma 5). Condition (2) is an easy verification. For condition (1), one first shows that, for all $C \in S/\approx$ and $s \in S \setminus C$,
$$\mathcal{P}(s, \tau^*, C) = \sum_{A \in S/\approx} P'(s, \tau, A) \cdot \mathcal{P}(A, \tau^*, C)$$
where $\mathcal{P}(A, \tau^*\lambda\tau^*, C) = \mathcal{P}(t, \tau^*\lambda\tau^*, C)$ for some (all) $t \in A$, $P'(s, a, A) = P(s, a, A)/(1 - P(s, \tau, [s]))$ if $s \notin A$ or $a \neq \tau$ and $P'(s, \tau, [s]) = 0$ (Again, $[s]$ denotes the weak bisimulation equivalence class of s.). Thus, the vector $(P'(s, \tau, A))_{A \in S/\approx}$ is a solution of the linear equation system $x_{[s]} = 0$, $\sum_{A \in S/\approx} x_A \cdot \mathcal{P}(A, \tau^*, C) = \mathcal{P}([s], \tau, C)$. The matrix $(\mathcal{P}(A, \tau^*, C))_{A,C \in S/\approx}$ can be shown to be regular. Hence, the above equation system has a unique solution. This yields $P'(s, \tau, A) = P'(s', \tau, A)$ for all s, $s' \in S$ with $s \approx s'$. For all $\alpha \in Act$, $s \in S$ and $C \in S/\approx$ we have:
$$\mathcal{P}(s, \tau^*\alpha\tau^*, C) = \sum_{A \in S/\approx} P'([s], \tau, A) \cdot \mathcal{P}(A, \tau^*\alpha\tau^*, C) + P'(s, \alpha, C)$$
where $P'([s], \tau, A) = P'(s, \tau, A)$. This yields $P'(s, \alpha, C) = P'(s', \alpha, C)$ for all s, $s' \in S$ with $s \approx s'$. $\qquad\square$

4 Computing weak bisimulation equivalence classes

In this section we develop an algorithm to compute weak (and branching) bisimulation equivalence classes. The general idea is to use a partitioning/splitter-technique similar to the ones proposed by Kanellakis & Smolka [25] resp. Paige & Tarjan [30] for deciding strong bisimulation in the nonprobabilistic case. The algorithm starts with the trivial partition $X = \{S\}$ and then successively refines the given partition X (with the help of a "splitter" of X), eventually resulting in the set of weak bisimulation equivalence classes.

A *partition* of S is a set X containing pairwise disjoint subsets of S such that each element $s \in S$ is contained in some $C \in X$. Let $[s]_X$ refer to the (unique) element of X with $s \in [s]_X$. For a partition X, let $T_X = \{s \in S : P(s, \tau, [s]_X) < 1\}$. T_X contains all states that with nonzero probability can perform something visible or silently step into a different class. If $s \in T_X$ then we define

$$P_X(s, a, C) = \frac{P(s, a, C)}{1 - P(s, \tau, [s]_X)}.$$

A partition X of S is called a branching bisimulation iff the induced equivalence relation $R_X := \bigcup_{C \in X} C \times C$ is a branching bisimulation. A possible candidate for a "splitter" of a partition X is a pair (α, C) (or a pair (τ, C)) that violates the condition for X to be a branching bisimulation, i.e. $\mathcal{P}_{R_X}(s, \tau^* \alpha, C) \neq \mathcal{P}_{R_X}(s', \tau^* \alpha, C)$ $(\mathcal{P}_{R_X}(s, \tau^*, C) \neq \mathcal{P}_{R_X}(s', \tau^*, C)$, respectively) for some $B \in X$ and $s, s' \in B$. The following characterization of branching bisimulations yields a simpler condition for splitters as it does not require the computation of the probabilities $\mathcal{P}_{R_X}$.

Lemma 5. *A partition X is a branching bisimulation iff the following conditions (1) are (2) are satisfied:*

(1) For all $A \in X$, $s, s' \in A \cap T_X$: $P_X(s, \tau, C) = P_X(s', \tau, C)$ for all $C \in X \setminus \{A\}$, and $P_X(s, \alpha, C) = P_X(s', \alpha, C)$ for all $C \in X$, $\alpha \in Act \setminus \{\tau\}$.
(2) For all $A \in X$ either $A \cap T_X = \emptyset$ or for each $s_0 \in A \setminus T_X$ there is an execution fragment $s_0 \xrightarrow{\tau} \dots \xrightarrow{\tau} s_k$ with $s_0, \dots, s_{k-1} \in A \setminus T_X$, $s_k \in A \cap T_X$.

Moreover, if X is a branching bisimulation then $\mathcal{P}_{R_X}(s, \tau^* \lambda, C) = P_X(A, \lambda, C)$ for all $A, C \in X$, $s \in A$. Here, $P_X(A, \lambda, C)$ denotes $P_X(t, \lambda, C)$ for arbitrary $t \in A \cap T_X$ unless $A \cap T_X = \emptyset$. If $A \cap T_X = \emptyset$ then $P_X(A, \tau, A) = 1$ and $P_X(A, a, C) = 0$ if $a \neq \tau$ or $A \neq C$.

Definition 6. A *splitter* of a partition X is a tuple (a, C) consisting of an action $a \in Act$ and some $C \in X$ such that there exists some $B \in X$ (with $B \neq C$ if $a = \tau$) and $P_X(s, a, C) \neq P_X(s', a, C)$ for some states $s, s' \in B \cap T_X$.

The main idea for refining a given partition X via a splitter (a, C) is to isolate in each $B \in X$ (with $B \neq C$ if $a = \tau$) those states $s, s' \in B \cap T_X$ where $P_X(s, a, C) = P_X(s', a, C)$. By condition (2), each such equivalence class A of $B \cap T_X$ has to be enriched with exactly those states $s \in B \setminus T_X$ that can reach A via internal actions and that cannot reach any other equivalence class A' of $B \cap T_X$ without passing A.

Definition 7. For (a, C) to be a splitter of a partition X and $B \in X$ (with $B \neq C$ if $a = \tau$), we define $Split(B, a, C) = (B \cap T_X)/\equiv$ where $s \equiv s'$ iff $P_X(s, a, C) = P_X(s', a, C)$. If $A \in Split(B, a, C)$ then we define the closure $\overline{A}$

of A in X with respect to (a, C) to be the largest set $V \subseteq B$ which contains A and such that for all $s \in V \setminus A$: $P(s, \tau, V) = 1$ and there exists an execution fragment $s = s_0 \xrightarrow{\tau} \ldots \xrightarrow{\tau} s_k$ with $s_0, \ldots, s_{k-1} \in V$ and $s_k \in A$. We define $Refine(B, \tau, B) = \{B\}$ and, if $a \neq \tau$ or $B \neq C$,

$$Refine(B, a, C) = \{\overline{A} : A \in Split(B, a, C)\} \cup Res(B, a, C),$$
$$Refine(X, a, C) = \bigcup_{B \in X} Refine(B, a, C),$$

where $Res(B, a, C) = \{B \setminus \bigcup_{A \in Split(B, a, C)} \overline{A}\} \setminus \{\emptyset\}$.

It is easy to see that for each partition X which is coarser than $S/\approx_{br}$ and each splitter (a, C) of X, the partition $Refine(X, a, C)$ is coarser than $S/\approx_{br}$ and strictly finer than X. If there is no splitter for X and X is coarser than $S/\approx_{br}$ then $X = S/\approx_{br} = S/\approx$.

Algorithm for computing the weak bisimulation equivalence classes

Input: fully probabilistic transition system (S, Act, P)
Output: $S/\approx$
Method: $X := \{S\}$;
        While X contains a splitter (a, C) do $X := Refine(X, a, C)$;
        Return X.

Example 4. Partitioning the transition system from Example 1 proceeds as follows. For the initial partition $\{S\}$, we consider the set $T_{\{S\}} = \{s_2, s_3, s_4\}$. (α, S) and (β, S) are splitters, since, for example, $P_{\{S\}}(s_2, \alpha, S) = 0.1 \neq 0.2 = P_{\{S\}}(s_3, \alpha, S)$. $Split(S, \alpha, S)$ refines $S \cap T_{\{S\}}$ into $\{s_2\}$ and $\{s_3, s_4\}$. The closure in $\{S\}$ yields $\overline{\{s_2\}} = \{s_2\}$ and $\overline{\{s_3, s_4\}} = \{s_1, s_3, s_4\}$, which leads to $Res(S, \alpha, S) = \{\{s_0, s_5, s_6, s_7\}\}$. We have $Refine(\{S\}, \alpha, S) = \{\{s_0, s_5, s_6, s_7\}, \{s_1, s_3, s_4\}, \{s_2\}\}$. This new partition X contains a splitter $(\tau, \{s_2\})$, because $P_X(s_0, \tau, \{s_2\}) = 0.5 \neq 0 = P_X(s_5, \tau, \{s_2\})$. The subsequent refinement step merely seperates s_0 from its former partition, i.e. $Refine(X, \alpha, \{s_2\}) = \{\{s_0\}, \{s_5, s_6, s_7\}, \{s_1, s_3, s_4\}, \{s_2\}\}$. This partition does not contain further splitters, it thus represents the weak bisimulation equivalence classes.

In what follows, $n = |S|$. We suppose that the alphabet Act is fixed.

Theorem 8. *The algorithm above can be implemented in time* $\mathcal{O}(n^3)$ *and space* $\mathcal{O}(n^2)$.

Proof. In order to avoid multiple computations of the values $P(s, a, C)$ where C is a block in X that has not been changed in the last refinement step we replace the assignment $X := Refine(X, a, C)$ by $Y := Refine(X, a, C)$; $X_{new} := Y \setminus X$;

$X := Y$. (I.e. X_{new} contains the set of blocks that have been modified in the last iteration step. Initially, $X_{new} = \{S\}$.) Initially, $X_{new} = \{S\}$.

Initialization of the refine step: Let X be the current partition. We compute the values $P(s, a, C)$ and $P_X(s, a, C)$ for each $s \in S$, $a \in Act$, $C \in X_{new}$. The set T_X can be derived from the probabilities $P(s, \tau, C)$, $s \in C$. For each pair (a, C) (where $a \in Act$, $C \in X_{new}$) and $A \in X$ we compute $min(A, a, C) = min_{s \in A} P_X(s, a, C)$ and $max(A, a, C) = max_{s \in A} P_X(s, a, C)$. Then, (a, C) is a splitter of X iff $min(A, a, C) < max(A, a, C)$ for some A with $a \neq \tau$ if $A = C$. If there is no splitter of X then $X = S/\approx$. Otherwise we choose some splitter (a, C) of X.

Refinement step: For all $B \in X$ with $B \neq C$ if $a = \tau$ we compute the set $Refine(B, a, C)$ as follows. We construct an ordered binary tree $Tree(B)$ by successively inserting the values $P_X(s, a, C)$, $s \in B \cap T_X$. Each node v of $Tree(B)$ is represented as a record with components $v.key$ and $v.states$. $v.key$ is the key value of v (i. e. one of the values $P_X(s, a, C)$, $s \in B \cap T_X$) such that $v.key < w.key$ ($v.key > w.key$) for all nodes w in the right (left) subtree of v. For each state $s \in B \cap T_X$ we traverse the tree $Tree(B)$ starting in the root and search for the value $P_X(s, a, C)$. If we reach a node v with $v.key = P_X(s, a, C)$ then we insert s into $v.states$. Otherwise, $P_X(s, a, C)$ is not yet represented in $Tree(B)$ and we insert a node v with $v.key = P_X(s, a, C)$ and $v.states = \{s\}$. In the final tree, $v.states$ is the set of states $s \in B \cap T_X$ with $P_X(s, a, C) = v.key$. Thus, the nodes of the final tree $Tree(B)$ represent the sets $A \in Split(B, a, C)$. More precisely, $Split(B, a, C)$ consists of the sets $v.states$ where v ranges over all nodes of $Tree(B)$. We derive $Refine(B, a, C)$ as follows. Let G_B be the directed graph (B, E_B) where $(s, t) \in E_B$ iff $P(t, \tau, s) > 0$ and $t \in B \setminus T_X$. We compute the sets $\overline{A}$, $A \in Split(B, a, C)$, by a breadth first search like method: We define $label(s) = A$ for all $s \in A$ and $A \in Split(B, a, C)$ and $label(s) = \perp$ ("undefined" or "not yet visited") for all $s \in B \setminus T_X$. In what follows, we use label $*$ for states that are reachable in G_B from two or more sets $A \in Split(B, a, C)$. Thus, all successors of a $*$-labelled state in G_B are also labelled by $*$. We use a queue Q which initially contains the states $s \in A$, $A \in Split(B, a, C)$. While Q is not empty we take the first element s of Q, remove s from Q and, if $label(s) \neq *$ then for all $t \in B \setminus T_X$ with $(s, t) \in E_B$ we do:

(1) If $label(t) = \perp$ then we add t to Q and set $label(t) = label(s)$.
(2) If $label(t) \in Split(B, a, C)$, $label(t) \neq label(s)$, then we set $label(u) = *$ for $u = t$ and all successors u of t in G_B.

(In step (2), we use a depth first search starting in t to find all successors of t. States that are already labelled by $*$ are ignored.) Then, $\overline{A} = \{s \in B : label(s) = A\}$ and $Res(B, a, C) = \{\{s \in B : label(s) \in \{\perp, *\}\}\} \setminus \{\emptyset\}$.

Complexity: It is clear that the method described above can be implemented in space $\mathcal{O}(n^2)$. We show that the time complexity of our method is $\mathcal{O}(n^3)$. First, we observe that there are at most n iterations of the refinement step. Thus it suffices to show that each refinement step takes time $\mathcal{O}(n^2)$: It is clear that for each refinement step, the initialization requires $\mathcal{O}(n^2)$ time. (For each tuple (s, a, C), one has to calculate the sum $\sum_{t \in C} P(s, a, t)$. Hence, for fixed a and ranging over all $s \in S$ and $C \in X$ we get the time complexity $\mathcal{O}(n^2)$. Since we suppose Act to be fixed, the values $P(s, a, C)$ can be computed in time $\mathcal{O}(n^2)$.) Ranging over all B, the construction of the trees $Tree(B)$ (thus, the computation of the sets $Split(B, A, C)$) takes $\mathcal{O}(n \cdot \log n)$ time if one uses some kind of balanced trees, e.g. AVL-trees [1]. We show that, ranging over all $B \in X$, the sets $\overline{A}$ and $Res(B, a, C)$ can be derived in time $\mathcal{O}(n^2)$: For fixed $B \in X$, the directed graph G_B can be constructed in time $\mathcal{O}(|B|^2)$. Each state $s \in B$ is added to Q at most once. (Note that only states with label $\perp$ can be added to Q.) Each state t which is visited during a depth first search in step (2) is labelled by $*$. Thus, it can never be visited in step (2) once again. As a consequence, each state causes time costs (at most) of order $2n$ in the computation of $Refine(B, a, C)$: as an element of Q and as a state with label $\neq *$ that is visited in step (2). Either case involves $\mathcal{O}(n)$ computations. Summing up over all $s \in B$, the computation of $Refine(B, a, C)$ has time complexity $\mathcal{O}(|B| \cdot n)$. So, we obtain $Refine(X, a, C)$ in time $\mathcal{O}(n^2)$. Thus, we get the overall time complexity $\mathcal{O}(n^3)$.

$\square$

5 Further directions

In this paper we have extended the notions of weak and branching bisimulation equivalence to fully probabilistic transition systems. In contrast to the non-probabilistic case, both relations coincide. We have described an algorithm that computes weak (and branching) bisimulation equivalence classes in time $\mathcal{O}(n^3)$ and space $\mathcal{O}(n^2)$.

Obviously, our notion of equivalence is coarser than strong bisimulation equivalence [26]. In addition, it can be shown that weak bisimulation equivalence is finer than the testing equivalences of [7, 8]. It is also finer than the testing equivalence of [9, 36] that considers τ-free tests only but incomparable with their test equivalence that allows for general tests.

The definition of composition operators for fully probabilistic transition systems is an important subject for further work. In the presence of composition operators, a proper notion of equality should be preserved; that is, it is required that weak bisimulation equivalence is a congruence with respect to the operators. Indeed, prefixing, hiding, restriction and (guarded) probabilistic choice can be easily adopted from the nonprobabilistic to the fully probabilistic setting such that weak bisimulation is a congruence for them, see [4]. Unfortunately it is not straightforward to adapt parallel composition to this framework. Other fully probabilistic calculi like PCCS [12] and similar calculi [18, 27], are based on synchronous CCS [28]. In particular, their parallel composition is synchronous. In the essence, activities (of different components) that may happen with nonzero probability occur synchronously, with a probability given by the product of the individual probabilities. Such synchrony includes internal activities, because they do not play a distinguished role in PCCS. This reflects the lack of a notion of equivalence that abstracts from internal computation. In our framework, it seems promising to allow internal computation to occur asynchronously, similar to the asynchronous product in synchronous CCS. However, the shape of this operator still has to be settled.

We restricted ourselves to fully probabilistic transition systems that are generative in nature. This model is not adequate to represent the truly asynchronous behaviour of concurrent probabilistic processes [34]. For this purpose, some kind of probabilistic transition system is required that allows for nondeterministic branching. As far as the authors know, the question of decidable notions of weak bisimulation is still open in this setting. The weak bisimulation of [33] for such a model is based on a "double arrow relation" that assigns a set of transition probability distributions to each state. In general, this set, representing nondeterministic alternatives, is infinite. This substantially differs from the nonprobabilistic and the fully probabilistic case where weak bisimulation equivalence can be decided using a finitely branching transition system.

References

1. G. Adel'son-Velshii, Y. Landis: An Algorithm for the Organization of Information. Soviet. Math. Dokl. 3, pp 1259-1262, 1962.
2. A. Aziz, V. Singhal, F. Balarin, R. Brayton, A. Sangiovanni-Vincentelli: It usually works: The Temporal Logic of Stochastic Systems. Proc. CAV'95, LNCS 939, pp 155-165, 1995.
3. C. Baier: Polynomial Time Algorithms for Testing probabilistic Bisimulation and Simulation. Proc. CAV'96, LNCS 1102, pp 38-49, 1996.
4. C. Baier, H. Hermanns: Weak Bisimulation for Fully Probabilistic Processes. Techn. Bericht IMMD-VII/1-97, Universität Erlangen.
5. A. Bianco, L. de Alfaro: Model Checking of Probabilistic and Nondeterministic Systems. Proc. Foundations of Software Technology and Theoretical Computer Science, LNCS 1026, pp 499-513, 1995.
6. G. Chehaivbar, H. Garavel, N. Tawbi, F. Zulian: Specification and Verification of the Powerscale Bus Arbitration Protocol: An Industrial Experiment with LOTOS. Formal Description Techniques IX, Chapmann Hall, 1996.
7. I. Christoff: Testing Equivalences and Fully Abstract Models for Probabilistic Processes, Proc. CONCUR'90, LNCS 458, pp 126-140, 1990.
8. L. Christoff, I. Christoff: Efficient Algorithms for Verification of Equivalences for Probabilistic Processes. Proc. CAV'91, LNCS 575, pp 310-321, 1991.
9. R. Cleaveland, S. Smolka, A. Zwarico: Testing Preorders for Probabilistic Processes. Proc. ICALP'92, LNCS 623, pp 708-719, 1992.
10. D. Coppersmith, S. Winograd: Matrix Multiplication via Arithmetic Progressions. Proc. 19th ACM Symposium on Theory of Computing, pp 1-6, 1987.
11. C. Courcoubetis, M. Yannakakis: Verifying Temporal Properties of Finite-State Probabilistic Programs. Proc. FOCS'88, pp 338-345, 1988.
12. A. Giacalone, C. Jou, S. Smolka: Algebraic Reasoning for Probabilistic Concurrent Systems. Proc. IFIP TC2 Working Conf. on Programming Concepts and Methods, 1990.
13. R. van Glabbeek, S.A. Smolka, and B. Steffen: Reactive, generative, and stratified models of probabilistic processes. Information and Computation, Vol 121, pp 59-80, 1995.

14. R. van Glabbeek, W. Weijland: Branching Time and Abstraction in Bisimulation Semantics. Journal of the ACM 43(3), pp. 555-600,1996.
15. J. Groote, F. Vaandrager: An Efficient Algorithm for Branching Bisimulation and Stuttering Equivalence. Proc. ICALP'90, LNCS 443, 1990.
16. P. Halmos: Measure Theory. Springer-Verlag, 1950.
17. H. Hansson: Time and Probability in Formal Design of Distributed Systems. Ph.D.Thesis, Uppsala University, 1994.
18. H. Hansson, B. Jonsson: A Calculus for Communicating Systems with Time and Probabilities. Proc. IEEE Real-Time Systems Symposium, 1990.
19. H. Hansson, B. Jonsson: A Logic for Reasoning about Time and Probability. Formal Aspects of Computing, Vol. 6, pp 512-535, 1994.
20. S. Hart, M. Sharir: Probabilistic Temporal Logic for Finite and Bounded Models. Proc. 16th ACM Symposium on Theory of Computing, 1984.
21. T. Huynh, L. Tian: On some Equivalence Relations for Probabilistic Processes. Fundamenta Informaticae, Vol. 17, pp 211-234, 1992.
22. B. Jonsson, K.G. Larsen: Specification and Refinement of Probabilistic Processes. Proc. LICS'91, pp 266-277,1991.
23. B. Jonsson, W. Yi: Compositional Testing Preorders for Probabilistic Processes. Proc. LICS'95, pp 431-443, 1995.
24. C.C. Jou, S. Smolka: Equivalences, Congruences and Complete Axiomatizations for Probabilistic Processes. Proc. CONCUR'90, LNCS 458, pp 367-383, 1990.
25. P. Kanellakis, S. Smolka: CCS Expressions, Finite State Processes, and Three Problems of Equivalence. Information and Computation, Vol. 86, pp 43-68, 1990.
26. K. Larsen, A. Skou: Bisimulation through Probabilistic Testing. Information and Computation, Vol. 94, pp 1-28, 1991.
27. K. Larsen, A. Skou: Compositional Verification of Probabilistic Processes. Proc. CONCUR'92, LNCS 630, pp 456-471, 1992.
28. R. Milner: Calculi for Synchrony and Asynchrony. Theoretical Computer Science, Vol. 25, pp 269-310, 1983.
29. R. Milner: Communication and Concurrency. Prentice Hall, 1989.
30. R. Paige, R. Tarjan: Three Partition Refinement Algorithms. SIAM Journal of Computing, Vol. 16, No. 6, pp 973-989, 1987.
31. A. Pnueli, L. Zuck: Verification of Multiprocess Probabilistic Protocols. Distributed Computing, Vol. 1, No. 1, pp 53-72, 1986.
32. A. Pnueli, L. Zuck: Probabilistic Verification. Information and Computation, Vol. 103, pp 1-29, 1993.
33. R. Segala, N. Lynch: Probabilistic Simulations for Probabilistic Processes. Proc. CONCUR 94, LNCS 836, pp 481-496, 1994.
34. M. Vardi: Automatic Verification of Probabilistic Concurrent Finite-State Programs. Proc. FOCS'85, pp 327-338, 1985.
35. M. Vardi, P. Wolper: An Automata-Theoretic Approach to Automatic Program Verification. Proc. LICS'86, pp 332-344, 1986.
36. S. Yuen, R. Cleaveland, Z. Dayar, S. Smolka: Fully Abstract Characterizations of Testing Preorders for Probabilistic Processes. Proc. CONCUR'94, LNCS 836, pp 497-512, 1994.
37. W. Yi, K. Larsen: Testing Probabilistic and Nondeterminsitic Processes. Protocol Specification, Testing and Verification XII, Elsevier Science Publishers, IFIP, pp 47-61, 1992.

Towards a Mechanization of Cryptographic Protocol Verification

Dominique Bolignano

Dyade, B.P.105 78153 Le Chesnay Cedex France, Dominique.Bolignano@dyade.fr

Abstract. We revisit the approach defined in [2] for the formal verification of cryptographic protocols so as to allow for some mechanization in the verification process. In the original approach verification uses theorem proving. Here we show that for a wide range of practical situations and properties it is possible to perform the verification on a finite and safe abstract model.

1 Introduction

Formal verification of cryptographic protocols has recently received increased consideration due to the importance of cryptographic protocols in the design of new security or electronic commerce architectures. Many proof-based verification techniques have been proposed (see [2] for a discussion of this issue) to perform systematic analysis of large protocols. Model-checking based techniques have recently been applied [11, 7] to the verification of such protocols. Verification is performed on a finite model that corresponds to an abstraction of the initial specification. The verification is thus automatic. But the proof that such abstractions are safe and do not compromise the generality and accuracy of the verification process has not yet been formalized in the case of cryptographic protocols. In the case of electronic commerce protocols, for which the coherence of data (e.g. price, order or payment information, etc.) is critical, finding a safe abstraction is a particularly crucial issue. In this paper we propose a safe abstraction that can be incorporated into the framework proposed in [2] and further extended in [3]. Similar abstractions based on abstract interpretation techniques have been developed for the verification of temporal properties expressed using various branching-time temporal logics (e.g. [6, 4, 10, 5, 8, 9, 12]). Here we transpose some of the results of [4, 9, 12] to the verification of security properties. We also automate the construction of the abstract model and the translation of security properties into abstract ones for a large class of practical situations. As opposed to other uses of abstraction which typically guarantee the preservation of a whole logic or of a whole class of properties, here a specific abstraction function is selected for each given property and is thus only to guarantee the property at hand. The requirements are consequently much less demanding and the model reduction can be much more important. The proposed approach is currently being applied for the verification of large electronic commerce protocols.

2 Basics

Encryption is the transformation of data into a form unreadable by anyone without a secret decryption key. Decryption is the inverse function, which recreates the original data in its form prior to encryption. A cryptographic key system is said to be symmetric if, and only if, the same key can be used for both encryption and decryption. A cryptographic key system is said to be asymmetric when different keys are used for encryption and decryption. In this latter case, one of the key is only known by a particular principal and is known as the private key of this principal, whereas the other one is not confidential and is known as the public key of this principal. For illustration purposes we use a very simple two message key distribution protocol:

$$\boxed{(1)\ A \rightarrow S : (A, B)\ (2)\ S \rightarrow A : (K_B, B)_{K_S^{-1}}}$$

This protocol description can be read as follows: (1) A sends a message to S to tell him that he is A and wants to get B's public key K_B; no encryption is used; (2) S replies to the request by sending A B's public key K_B; this message is encrypted with the S's private key K_S^{-1} which S is the only one to know and which thus authenticates the producer (this kind of encryption is thus called a signature). Following the approach of [2] we first have to identify the different principals involved. Principals receive messages at one end and emit other messages at another end. Some principals will be considered to be "trustable" (i.e. to work according to their role in the protocol) and some not. Communications media are typically considered to be non-trustable, because messages can usually be intercepted, replayed, removed, or created by intruders. We will consider that this is the case in the following discussion. The set of untrustable principals is modelled as a single (black box) agent which is called the "external world" or, more concisely, the intruder. The intruder is modelled as a principal that may know some data initially and that will store and try to decrypt all data passed to him and thus in particular all information circulating on the communications media. The intruder will also be able to encrypt data to create new messages that will be sent to mislead other principals. But the intruder will be able to decrypt and encrypt data only with keys he knows. This modeling will in particular allow us to determine at any time which data are potentially known to the intruder under the chosen "trustability" hypothesis. The same protocol can be studied in terms of many different hypotheses. According to [2], the knowledge of the intruder is formalized as a set of data components. Data components range over domain C and sets of data components over domain S. Data components can be:

- basic data, which may be (1) cryptographic keys which take their values in domain KA (for asymmetric keys) or KS (for symmetric ones), (2) other basic data which will take their values in domain D;
- data obtained by composition (1) using the pair operator which takes some data c_1 and some c_2 and returns the pair (c_1, c_2), (2) or by encryption of some data c using key k which is noted c_k.

Messages that are exchanged over communication media are of type C. The domains S and C are formalized as:

$$
\begin{array}{|c|}
\hline
C = C_K | (C, C) | B \\
B = K | D \\
K = KA | KS | K^{-1} \\
\hline
\end{array}
$$

figure (1)

$$
\begin{array}{|c|}
\hline
S = C \cup S | \emptyset \\
\hline
\end{array}
$$

figure (2)

C is in fact defined modulo (i.e. quotiented by) the two axioms $\forall k. k \in KS \Rightarrow k^{-1} = k$, and $\forall k. k \in KA \Rightarrow (k^{-1})^{-1} = k$. Similarly $\cup$ is an ACUI operator with neutral $\emptyset$ (i.e. associative, commutative, unitary and idempotent). It is used to describe "flat" sets. The pair operator is used to represent reversible constructors such as the sequence, set, or aggregate constructors. The fact that a given data component c can be derived from the intruder knowledge s is formalized and axiomatized in [2] and is noted: c *known_in* s. In the sequel, we will adopt the following conventions: variables $s, s', s'', ..., s_1, s_2, ...$ take their values in S by default; variables $k, k', k'', ..., k_1, k_2, ...$ take their values in K.

3 Formalizing the Protocol

We then need to formally specify the protocol itself. This specification consists in the description of the role of each trustable agent. The formal specification of the protocol consists of a set of atomic actions. The sending and reception of a message are not synchronous. Consequently the transmission of a message is considered as two atomic actions, one for sending and one for receiving. More precisely, the formalization is based on the chemical reaction paradigm [1]: a system is described as a set of atomic actions which may be applied repeatedly, in any order and whenever their pre-condition holds. Our modeling of the key distribution protocol will thus distinguish 4 different kinds of atomic actions. These actions will be identified using the labels drawn from $\mathcal{A} = \{1_A, 1_S, 2_S, 2_A\}$. Each of the 4 labels n_X of $\mathcal{A}$ stands for one action: principal X sends or receives message n. The system is defined as a pair (s_0, r) where s_0 is the initial global state, and r is a relation binding the global state before applying an action to the global state after applying the action. The relation r is defined using a predicate or logic formula p, defined on $(S \times (\mathcal{A} \times C) \times S)$ where the domain for global states S is defined as the Cartesian product, $S_A \times S_S \times S_I$, of local state domains, i.e. S_A and S_S for the two trustable principals, A and S, and S_I for the intruder. By definition $p(s, (l, m), s')$ is true if and only if the global state s is modified into s' upon firing the action labelled l for sending or receiving of message m. The set S_I is the domain S of data components defined in the previous section. Intuitively the state of the intruder is the set of data components that have been listened to on the communication line and that the intruder may use to build new messages. The state of a trustable principal is defined as an aggregate or a tuple describing the value of each local state variable. We will use tuples to simplify the presentation. The local state of the key server S is a triple containing a key directory mapping principal identifiers to public keys, the value of the last principal for which the public key was requested when relevant and the value of the program counter. The third state variable is useful in the case where control constraints have to be specified. The local-state of A is a pair containing the directory of known keys and the local program counter. The directory held by A is empty initially and is updated each time a new association is received from S. The directory held by S is never changed. For more conciseness in the sequel, we drop the program counter information from the local state of A and from the local state of S. The formula p is thus expressed as the disjunction of 4 sub-formulae, i.e. one for each action:

$$p\left((d_A, (d_S, x), s_I), (l, m), (d'_A, (d'_S, x'), s'_I)\right) =$$
$$(l = 1_A \wedge m = (A, id) \wedge s'_I = s_I \cup m \wedge d_A = d'_A \wedge d_S = d'_S) \vee$$
$$(l = 1s \wedge m = (\_, x') \wedge m \; known\_in \; s_I \wedge s'_I = s_I \wedge d_A = d'_A \wedge d_S = d'_S) \vee$$
$$(l = 2s \wedge m = (k, x)_{K_S^{-1}} \wedge s'_I = s_I \cup m \wedge (x, k) \in d_S \wedge d_A = d'_A \wedge d_S = d'_S) \vee$$
$$(l = 2_A \wedge m = (k, id)_{K_S^{-1}} \wedge m \; known\_in \; s_I \wedge s'_I = s_I \wedge d_A = d'_A \cup (id, k) \wedge d_S = d'_S)$$

The first action (i.e. 1_A) describes A sending a pair composed of the identification of A and of the identification of the principal id for which the public key is requested. Each sending of a message m increases the knowledge of the intruder, i.e. $s'_I = s_I \cup m$. The value of id is not constrained in any way. This allows A to request any public key he wishes. The second action (i.e. 1_S) describes S receiving a pair of data. This pair can be the pair just sent by A or any pair of data known by the intruder. The second situation is only meaningful if this can go undetected by A: here there is no particular checking other than on the form of the message. The third action (i.e. $2s$) describes S sending a pair composed of the public key of d and of the identifier d stored previously[1]. Receiving a message m does not change the state of the intruder (i.e. $s'_I = s_I$), but the message should be deducible from the knowledge of the intruder (i.e. $m \; known\_in \; s_I$). The fourth action (i.e. 2_A) implicitly specifies that the received message is to be signed using K_s^{-1}.[2]

4 Proving security properties

Most security properties are safety properties[3]. They mainly rely on the fact that the intruder does not know some private data or is not able to construct the expected message. This is in both cases formalized as an invariant property, $\neg(c \; known\_in \; s_I)$, where c stands for the private data in the first case and is the message to construct in the second, and where s_I is the data collected by the intruder. Confidentiality properties which are the simplest security properties, correspond to the situation where c is either a key or a basic

---

[1] As we have decided to represent data constructors such as the sequence, set, or aggregate constructors using the pair operators, sets and set operators are supposed to be coded in a Lisp-like manner.

[2] Because we have chosen not to store the value of the chosen id in local state of A, there is no possibility here for A to check that the key he receives is the key he requested.

[3] The only liveness property is denial of service, which current cryptographic protocols do not guarantee.

data (e.g. a nonce, a credit card number, etc.). As an example, K_S^{-1} should remain unknown to the intruder. This is written $\neg(K_S^{-1} \ known\_in \ s_I)$. But some security properties cannot be written so as to fit into the general form above. As an illustration we will use in the sequel two representative invariant properties drawn from [2]. The first one will be referred to as invariant (1): $\forall k, \ x. \ (k, x) \in d_A \Rightarrow (k, x) \in d_S$, i.e. the directory of A should always be coherent with the master directory held by S. The second one will be referred to as invariant (2): $\forall k, x.(k, x)_{K_S^{-1}} \ known\_in \ s_I \Rightarrow (x, k) \in d_S$ i.e. any data of the form $(k, x)_{K_S^{-1}}$ that the intruder can replay or produce corresponds to a valid identifier-key association.

5 Using a finite state machine

One of the keys to mechanization is to transform a system model into a model that only uses a finite number of keys and basic data values: these keys and basic data are defined as part of a finite subset B_0 of B. The corresponding subsets of C and S will be noted C_0 and S_0. The transformation is defined using a function $h : B \to B_0$ which will intuitively associate each element of B to one of its representative in B_0. We then define the homomorphic extension $\hat{h} : S \to S_0$ of h (i.e. $\hat{h}((c_1, c_2)) = (\hat{h}(c_1), \hat{h}(c_2))$, $\hat{h}(c_k) = \hat{h}(c)_{h(k)}$, etc.).

Given a model $M = (s_0, r)$, let us consider a finite abstract model M_a such that for any finite run $s_0 \xrightarrow{(l_1, m_1)} s_1 \dots \xrightarrow{(l_k, m_k)} s_k$ of M then $\hat{h}(s_0) \xrightarrow{(l_1, \hat{h}(m_1))} \hat{h}(s_1) \dots \xrightarrow{(l_k, \hat{h}(m_k))} \hat{h}(s_k)$ is a run of M_a: in other words, $M_a = (\hat{h}(s_0), r_a)$, with r_a such that $(s, (l, m), s') \in r \Rightarrow (\hat{h}(s), (l, \hat{h}(m)), \hat{h}(s')) \in r_a$. Let us note $\mathcal{R}(M)$ (resp. $\mathcal{R}(M_a)$) the set of reachable states of a transition system M (resp. M_a). By construction $\hat{h}(\mathcal{R}(M)) \subseteq \mathcal{R}(\hat{h}(M_a))$.

Thus in order to prove that an invariant property inv holds on $M = (s_0, r)$ it is sufficient, (a) to provide r_a such that $(s, (l, m), s') \in r \Rightarrow (\hat{h}(s), (l, \hat{h}(m)), \hat{h}(s')) \in r_a$, (b) to provide an invariant property inv_a on $M_a = (\hat{h}(s_0), r_a)$ such that $\forall s.inv_a(\hat{h}(s)) \Rightarrow inv(s)$, and (c) to check inv_a on $M_a = (\hat{h}(s_0), r_a)$. This can be seen as a direct reformulation in our framework of results presented in [9, 12][4] and based on ideas and theoretical results presented in [4]. The steps (a) and (b) generate proof obligations that should be discharged using formal provers, whereas step (c) can be performed using model checking techniques. This was already the case in [9]. The benefit of this approach comes from the fact that both kinds of proof obligations are much simpler to perform than the proof of invariant inv for the initial concrete model M.

But in order to perform step (c) we need to be able to perform the checking of inv_a automatically on each reachable state of M_a. The problem here comes from the fact that even when a limited number of keys and of basic data components is used, the computations that the intruder may perform (or the data that he can generate) are unbounded: e.g. starting from k the intruder can generate k_k,

---

[4] In [9, 12] this was proved for the AG operator of CTL.

k_{k_k}, etc. In this section we thus provide a decision procedure for the *known_in* predicate in the case where the parameters of *known_in* are explicit (described by extension using a variable free expression). The five basic operations that an intruder may use in order to exploit data were defined in [2] and referred to as γ, γ', π, π' and ξ operations: γ for the encryption of a known data component using a known key, γ' for the decryption of a known data component using a known key, π for the pairing of two known data components, π' for the decomposition of a pair (i.e. obtaining the first or second projection); and ξ for data extraction. Each action was formalized as a state transformation relation:

$$s \xrightarrow{\gamma} s' \stackrel{def}{=} \{(s,s')|(\exists c,k \,.\, k \cup c \subseteq s \wedge s' = s \cup (c)_k\}$$

$$s \xrightarrow{\gamma'} s' \stackrel{def}{=} \{(s,s')|(\exists c,k \,.\, k^{-1} \cup (c)_k \subseteq s \wedge \ s' = s \cup c\}$$

$$s \xrightarrow{\pi} s' \stackrel{def}{=} \{(s,s')|(\exists c_1,c_2 \,.\, c_1 \cup c_2 \subseteq s \wedge s' = s \cup (c_1,c_2))\}$$

$$s \xrightarrow{\pi'} s' \stackrel{def}{=} \{(s,s')|(\exists c_1,c_2 \,.\, (c_1,c_2) \subseteq s \wedge s' = s \cup c_1 \cup c_2)\}$$

$$s \xrightarrow{\xi} s' \stackrel{def}{=} \{(s,s')|s' \subseteq s\}$$

where $\subseteq$ is defined on $S \times S$ as: $s' \subseteq s \stackrel{def}{=} \exists s''.s' \cup s'' = s$. The exploitation of a given knowledge (i.e. a given set of data components) to deduce new information (i.e. new data) consists in the application of zero or more of the above operations in any order and any number of times. A set of data components s' (or a single data components) is thus said to be deducible from a set of data component s if and only if there exists a sequence of applications of the five basic operations which allows us to obtain s' from s. Given any subset[5] $E = \{x_1, .., x_n\}$ of $\{\gamma, \gamma', \pi, \pi', \xi\}$, $\xrightarrow{E}$ is defined as the reflexive-transitive closure of the relation $\xrightarrow{x_1} \cup ... \cup \xrightarrow{x_n}$. The predicate *known_in* is defined as follows: c *known_in* s if and only if $s \xrightarrow{\{\gamma,\gamma',\pi,\pi',\xi\}} c$: c *known_in* s if and only if c is deducible from s. We recall here some of the properties that were proved in [2] and that we will use in the sequel.

Lemma 1. *If* $E \subseteq \{\gamma, \gamma', \pi, \pi', \xi\}$ *then* $\forall s, s', s''.(s \xrightarrow{E} s') \Rightarrow (s \cup s'' \xrightarrow{E} s' \cup s'')$

Proposition 2 Confluence. *Relation* $\xrightarrow{E}$ *is confluent for any given subset* E *of* $\{\gamma, \gamma', \pi, \pi'\}$: *i.e.* $s \xrightarrow{E} s_1$ *and* $s \xrightarrow{E} s_2$ *then there exists* s_3 *such that* $s_1 \xrightarrow{E} s_3$ *and* $s_2 \xrightarrow{E} s_3$. *Furthermore* $s_3 = s_1 \cup s_2$ *is always a solution.*

Proposition 3. *If* $s \xrightarrow{\{\gamma,\gamma',\pi,\pi',\xi\}} s'$, *then there exists* s'' *such that* $s \xrightarrow{\{\gamma,\gamma',\pi,\pi'\}} s''$ *and* $s'' \xrightarrow{\{\xi\}} s'$. *More generally for any non-empty subset* E *of* $\{\gamma, \gamma', \pi, \pi'\}$ *if* $s \xrightarrow{E \cup \{\xi\}} s'$, *then there exists* s'' *such that* $s \xrightarrow{E} s''$ *et* $s'' \xrightarrow{\{\xi\}} s'$.

Proposition 4. *If* $s \xrightarrow{i} s''$ *and* $s'' \xrightarrow{j} s'$, *with* $i \in \{\gamma, \pi\}$ *and* $j \in \{\gamma', \pi'\}$ *then there exists* s''' *such that* $s \xrightarrow{\{j\}} s'''$ *and* $s''' \xrightarrow{i} s'$.

---

[5] Only non empty subsets are useful in practice.

Corollary 5. *If* $s \xrightarrow{\{\gamma,\gamma',\pi,\pi'\}} s'$, *then there exists* s'' *such that* $s \xrightarrow{\{\gamma',\pi'\}} s''$ *and* $s'' \xrightarrow{\{\gamma,\pi\}} s'$.

We then define a first algorithm described using the chemical reaction paradigm. The algorithm is supposed to stop whenever a fixed point is reached[6]. The algorithm performs a decomposition of s into components obtained by applying only decomposition operations γ', π', ξ. The returned value, $decomp(s)$, is by definition the last value of s_1:

$$
\begin{array}{l}
(Init)\ s_1:=s \\
(Act1)\ \text{If}\ \exists\ k,c.(k \subseteq s_1 \wedge c_{k-1} \subseteq s_1)\ \text{Do}\ s_1:=s_1 \cup c\ \text{End} \\
(Act2)\ \text{If}\ \exists\ c,c'.((c,c') \subseteq s_1)\ \text{Do}\ s_1:=s_1 \cup c \cup c'\ \text{End}
\end{array}
$$

(Decomposition algorithm: decomp)

Proposition 6. *For any* s *with an explicit value, the previous algorithm terminates and the returned value* s_1 *is the set of all data components* c *such that* $s \xrightarrow{\{\gamma',\pi',\xi\}} c$.

Proof. The proof of termination is quite straightforward: each step consumes one sub-tree of the abstract syntactic tree that corresponds to the value of s. The fact that the returned value s_1 is the set of all data components c such that $s \xrightarrow{\{\gamma',\pi',\xi\}} c$ is proved in two steps. First we prove that any component c of s_1 is such that $s \xrightarrow{\{\gamma',\pi',\xi\}} c$, next we prove the converse. The first part is straightforward, and the second is a direct application of propositions 3 and 2.

Let us now consider the following algorithm which uses the previous one:

$$
\begin{array}{l}
(Init)\ s_1:=decomp(s);\ s_1':=s' - s_1 \\
(Act1)\ \text{If}\ \exists\ c,k.c_k \subseteq s_1'\ \text{Do}\ s_1':=(s_1' \cup c \cup k) - s_1 - c_k\ \text{End} \\
(Act2)\ \text{If}\ \exists\ c,c'.(c,c') \subseteq s_1'\ \text{Do}\ s_1':=(s_1' \cup c \cup c') - s_1 - (c,c')\ \text{End}
\end{array}
$$

(Decision Algorithm)

Proposition 7. *The previous algorithm is a decision procedure which takes two explicitly defined parameters* s *and* $s' = \{c\}$ *and returns an empty set* s_1' *whenever* c *known in* s *and a non empty set otherwise.*

Proof. The proof for the termination of the algorithm is similar to that of proposition 6. The proof of correctness and the proof of completeness both use the same invariant property: $s_1 \cup s_1' \xrightarrow{\{\gamma,\pi,\xi\}} s'$. Thus when $s_1' = \emptyset$ then $s \xrightarrow{\{\gamma',\pi'\}} s_1 \xrightarrow{\{\gamma,\pi,\xi\}} s'$ which proves the correctness. If the last value of s_1' is not $\emptyset$ then we can easily prove by contradiction using propositions 3, 2, 6 and corollary 5 that $s \cup s_1' \xrightarrow{\{\gamma,\gamma',\pi,\pi',\xi\}} s'$ but that $s \xrightarrow{\{\gamma,\gamma',\pi,\pi',\xi\}} s'$ is false: it is not possible to build s' from s without using an element of s_1' (in fact all elements of s_1' are necessary).[7]

---

[6] The algorithm can be implemented by only firing actions which *effectively* change the state, and by terminating when no more action can be fired.

[7] More detailled proofs can be found in the extended version of this paper.

6   Computing the abstract model and the abstract properties

Now we improve on the approach proposed in the previous section by bringing some automation for steps (a) and (b). In step (a), given a logical formula p (e.g. $p : (S \times (A \times C) \times S) \rightarrow Bool$ defined in section 3 we are looking for an abstract logical formula p_a such that $\forall x.p(x) \Rightarrow p_a(\hat{h}(x))$ (i.e. we consider that h is the identity function on labels of A). In step (b) given a logical formula p (e.g. p is inv) we are looking for an abstract logical formula p_a (i.e. p_a is inv_a) such that $\forall x.p_a(\hat{h}(x)) \Rightarrow p(x)$. The main difference in both cases comes from the direction of the implication (i.e. it goes from concrete to abstract in the first case and from abstract to concrete in the second). The goal will be said to be negative in the first case and positive in the second. In both cases, formulae are supposed to be expressed in a very simple (typed) logical language defined on C and S using the operators and connectors of basic set theory, i.e. $\vee, \wedge, \in, \neg, \Rightarrow$, together with the predefined predicate $known\_in$. For the sake of simplicity, quantifiers are omitted and free variables are considered to be universally quantified. The homomorphic extension of $\hat{h}$ can now be defined on this new language. In the sequel we will use the same notation $\hat{h}$ to refer to it because it generalizes the previous extension $\hat{h}$[8]. We first consider the following preliminary result:

Proposition 8. $\forall c, s.c\ known\_in\ s \Rightarrow \hat{h}(c)\ known\_in\ \hat{h}(s)$

Proof. $c\ known\_in\ s$ means by definition that $s \xrightarrow{\{\gamma,\gamma',\pi,\pi',\xi\}} c$, and thus that $s \xrightarrow{a_1} s_1 \xrightarrow{a_2} ... \xrightarrow{a_k} c$ where $a_1, a_2, ..., a_k$ are elements of $\{\gamma, \gamma', \pi, \pi', \xi\}$. $\hat{h}(c)$ has the same structure as c, and each component c' of s has its counterpart $\hat{h}(c')$ in $\hat{h}(s)$. In order to prove the proposition we just need to associate each step $s_i \xrightarrow{a_{i+1}} s_{i+1}$ with the corresponding step $\hat{h}(s_i) \xrightarrow{a_{i+1}} \hat{h}(s_{i+1})$.

We now describe the main steps of an algorithm for checking that given a formula p and a goal (i.e. positive or negative), we can use $\hat{h}(p)$ as an abstract formula (i.e. $p_a = \hat{h}(p)$). The algorithm is based on the ten rules of figure (3) below and works as follows: we use the initial formula p and its associated sign as an initial goal; at each step we try to match the current logical formula[9] and its associated sign to the *formula* and *sign* part of a rule; if one of the rules (1) to (4) is matched, then each matching sub-expression, i.e. the sub-expression matching x and/or y, forms a new sub-goal that has to be checked recursively using the sign specified by the rule for the corresponding sub-expression[10]; if one of the rules (5) to (10) is applied no new sub-goal is generated; the checking stops when

---

[8] We will assume that $\hat{h}(true)$ (resp. $\hat{h}(false)$) is defined and that $\hat{h}(true) = true$ (resp. $\hat{h}(false) = false$).

[9] The symbol a used in rules (9) and (10) can only match by convention a variable free element of C. The symbols x and y can match any formula.

[10] Each rule (1), (2), (3), (4), or (7) in fact specifies two rules: one for a positive sign and another for a negative one.

all sub-goals have been checked, or a sub-goal does not match any rule. In the first case the checking is said to be successful. The test, $\hat{h}^{-1}(a) = \{a\}$, can be checked automatically provided that the set $B_0^{injective} = \{b \in B_0 | \hat{h}^{-1}(b) = \{b\}\}$ (or a subset of it) is provided by some mean (typically $B_0^{injective}$ is provided by the user at the time a particular function h is proposed): the test is positive if only if a (which is variable free by definition) is only made of components of $B_0^{injective}$ (e.g. $a = (K_{any}, K_{any})_{K_{any}}$, with $B_0^{injective} = \{K_{any}\}$).

	Formula	Sign	x	y
(1)	$x \wedge y$	$+/-$	$+/-$	$+/-$
(2)	$x \vee y$	$+/-$	$+/-$	$+/-$
(3)	$\neg x$	$+/-$	$-/+$	
(4)	$x \Rightarrow y$	$+/-$	$-/+$	$+/-$
(5)	$x = y$	$-$		

	Formula	Sign
(6)	$x \in y$	$-$
(7)	$true, false$	$+/-$
(8)	$c\ known\_in\ s$	$-$
(9)	$x = a\ s.t.\ \hat{h}^{-1}(a) = \{a\}$	$+$
(10)	$a \in e\ s.t.\ \hat{h}^{-1}(a) = \{a\}$	$+$

figure (3)

Proposition 9. *The previous algorithms always terminates. Whenever it succeeds then taking p_a to be $\hat{h}(p)$ we have $\forall x.p_a(\hat{h}(x)) \Rightarrow p(x)$ if the goal was positive and $\forall x.p(x) \Rightarrow p_a(\hat{h}(x))$ otherwise.*

Proof. The proof of termination is straightforward. The proof of correctness is done by structural induction on p. This leads to one induction step per rule. For the positive side of rule (1) we have to prove that given any four logical formulae q, q', q_a, q'_a, that satisfy $\forall x.q_a(\hat{h}(x)) \Rightarrow q(x)$ and $\forall x.q'_a(\hat{h}(x)) \Rightarrow q'(x)$ then $\forall x.p_a(\hat{h}(x)) \Rightarrow p(x)$ where $p = q \wedge q'$ and $p_a = q_a \wedge q'_a$. For the negative side of rule (1) and for rules (2) to (7), the proof is similar. For rule (8) we just need to use proposition 8. For rule (9) (resp. for rule (10)) we use the fact that $\hat{h}^{-1}(a) = \{a\}$ to prove that $x' \in \hat{h}^{-1}(x) \Rightarrow x' = a$ (resp. that $e' \in \hat{h}^{-1}(e) \Rightarrow a \in e'$).

The algorithm will thus be used to automate steps (a) and (b) in all situations where the algorithm succeeds. In case of failure the unsatisfied sub-goals can still be discharged using theorem proving, or a new formula verifying the sub-goal can be proposed by the user. In practice it has always been quite easy to add new rules similar to rules (9) and (10) in the rare cases of failure of the algorithm. As an illustration of the use of the proposed algorithm let us first consider the first kind of security properties identified in section 4, i.e. $\neg(c\ known\_in\ s)$. The algorithm proceeds as follows: the initial goal is positive as it used for step (b); rule (3) is applied with a positive sign and with x matching sub-expression $c\ known\_in\ s$; in the column for x, we find a negative sign associated to a positive goal (i.e. the sign of the goal is in the column "Sign", here on the left side of the column); thus a new negative sub-goal $c\ known\_in\ s$ is generated; this negative sub-goal matches rule (8) and the checking succeeds. Thus the only problem here is to find an adequate function h. We propose, h such that $h(k) = if\ k = K_S^{-1} then\ K_S^{-1}\ else\ K_{other}$ and $\hat{h}(d) = D_{any}$, where d is a typed variable that is supposed to range over domain D. For keys, h will return either

K_S^{-1} or K_{other}. The second key, K_{other}, will necessarily be part of the intruder knowledge for $\hat{h}(M)$ (i.e. $K_{other} \subseteq \hat{h}(s_I)$), but the first one K_S^{-1} should not be deducible from $\hat{h}(s_I)$. It is private. The distinction between these two kinds of keys is essential here: at least one key must be private; the other ones which can be represented using (i.e. collapsed into) a single key K_{other} may be known by the intruder. The same distinction between private and non private data is on the other hand not useful here for basic data. Thus h will return the same value for all data in D_{any}, and this basic data does not need to be private (i.e. D_{any} known_in $\hat{h}(s_I)$). After a few steps the knowledge of the intruder will thus typically be $\hat{h}(s_I) = K_{other} \cup D_{any} \cup (K, D)_{K_S^{-1}}$. The previous discussion is quite representative of issues that have to be considered during the identification of h. A misconception in h results in the identification of non existent flaws, and can easily be fixed by reducing some of the collapses formalized by h.

Let us now consider the example of invariant (1): $\forall\, k,\ x.\ (k, x) \in d_A \Rightarrow (k, x) \in d_S$. First the formula is transformed into an equivalent quantifier free formula. This is done by introducing two constants (i.e. *eigenvariables*), let us say K_{this} and D_{this}. Then we define h such that $h(k) = if\ k = K_S^{-1} then\quad K_S^{-1}\ elseif\ k = K_{this} then\quad K_{this}\ else\ K_{other}$ and $h(d) = if\ d = D_{this}\ then\quad D_{this}\ else\ D_{other}$. Thus $B_0^{injective} = \{D_{this}, K_{this}, K_S^{-1}\}$. The previous algorithm terminates successfully using rule (10) in particular, where a matches (D_{this}, K_{this}). The same invariant $(D_{this}, K_{this}) \in d_A \Rightarrow (D_{this}, K_{this}) \in d_S$, can thus be used on M and $\hat{h}(M)$. The automatic checking of the invariant completes successfully on $\hat{h}(M)$. Indeed if the d_S directory is chosen to be both functional and injective then $\hat{h}(d_S) = (D_{this}, K_{this}) \cup (D_{other}, K_{other})$ and $\hat{h}(d_A) \subseteq \hat{h}(d_S)$ on all states of $\mathcal{R}(\hat{h}(M))$.

Now for invariant (2), i.e. $\forall k, x.(k, x)_{K_S^{-1}}$ known_in $s_I \Rightarrow (x, k) \in d_S$, we can use the same function h as for invariant (1). For similar reasons, the algorithm terminates successfully and the abstract invariant, i.e. $(K_{this}, D_{this})_{K_S^{-1}}$ known_in $\hat{h}(s_I) \Rightarrow (D_{this}, K_{this}) \in d_S$, can be checked automatically on $\hat{h}(M)$.

7 Conclusion

We have shown how to automate the formal verification of cryptographic protocols for a large variety of security properties. The proposed approach relies on the general theorem proving framework originally proposed in [2] and incorporates abstract interpretation inspired facilities, thus applying techniques developed for the verification of general temporal properties (i.e. [6, 4, 5, 9, 12]). We have first transposed work in [4, 9, 12] to the framework of verification of security properties proposed in [2]. This entails providing a decision procedure for the intruder's (unbounded) knowledge. But we have also significantly improved the mechanization proposed in [9] by providing an algorithm for computing the abstract model and the abstract properties, given an abstraction function. The algorithm may fail to show that a particular sub-expression meets the sub-goal. In this situation, which is very rare in practice the user should then either prove manually that the problematic sub-expression indeed meets the sub-goal, or should provide a new sub-expression himself. An alternative, more restrictive, but probably more elegant approach would be to characterize the precise language for which the abstract property can be computed automatically and restrict the logic language that can be used for describing the protocol and for expressing security properties. We would then consider the checking algorithm of section 6 as a typing or static inference algorithm. In doing so we would obtain a complete mechanization in all cases once the abstraction function is provided. The approach that is proposed here for the verification of cryptographic protocols is somewhat more complex than the two model-checking based approaches proposed so far (i.e. [11] and [7]). This is mainly because the latter approaches do not encompass the first abstraction phase, and the user has to provide the simplified finite model directly. There is thus a risk that the informal abstraction step implicitly performed by the user is unsafe and compromises the result of the analysis itself (by validating problematic protocols). The main objective of the proposed approach is indeed to prove the absence of flaws, and not only to identify flaws. The two kinds of approaches are thus complementary in their objectives. In order to cope with the abstraction problem, some guidelines are provided in [11] and are informally justified for the writing of the finite model. For example, the number of different keys that the intruder may use is specified. This number is independent of the protocol or of the property at hand. Even if this is acceptable in practice for many authentication protocols it is a severe limitation for more general cryptographic protocols, as it is quite easy to exhibit protocols for which problematic scenarios require larger numbers of distinct keys. In the proposed approach, the number of distinct keys (featured by the size of the set $h(K)$, e.g. 2 and 3 in the examples of the previous section) will typically depend on the property and the protocol at hand. Finally we believe that some of the results presented here are quite general and could also be used with pure model checking approaches. In [11] and [7], for example, the number of internal steps that the intruder may perform in order to deduce new data from existing one is implicitly bounded so as to keep the model finite. In many cases (i.e. for many protocols) this decision could be justified formally using the model and the results of [2]. But the decision algorithm proposed in section 5 in fact suppresses the need for such limitation of the number of steps, and could be used in conjunction with approaches like [11] and [7]. The approach is currently being applied successfully for the verification of large electronic commerce protocols[11]. The abstracted models experimented so far have always been very small in terms of the number of states. This is mainly due to the fact that in the proposed approach an abstract function has only to preserve the particular property for which it is provided and not for a whole logic or a class of properties as it is the case in other approaches such as [11], [7], or [6, 10, 8] for example.

---

[11] *http://www.dyade.fr/actions/VIP/vip.html*

References

1. J.-P. Banâtre and D. Le Métayer. Gamma and the chemical reaction model: ten years after. In *Coordination programming: mechanisms, models and semantics*. World Scientific Publishing, IC Press, 1996.
2. D. Bolignano. Formal verification of cryptographic protocols. In *Proceedings of the third ACM Conference on Computer and Communication Security*, 1996.
3. D. Bolignano. Towards the Formal Verification of Electronic Commerce Protocols. In *Proceedings of the 10 th IEEE Computer Security Foundations Workshop*. IEEE, June 1997.
4. Edmund M. Clarke, Orna Grumberg, and David E. Long. Model checking and abstraction. *ACM Transactions on Programming Languages and Systems*, 16(5):1512–1542, September 1994.
5. Rance Cleaveland, Purush Iyer, and Daniel Yankelevich. Optimality in abstractions of model checking. In *Proceedings of SAS'95*. LNCS, 1995.
6. Dennis Dams, Orna Grumberg, and Rob Gerth. Abstract interpretation of reactive systems: Abstractions preserving ∀CTL*, ∃CTL* and CTL*. In E.-R. Olderog, editor, *Proceedings of the IFIP WG2.1/WG2.2/WG2.3 Working Conference on Programming Concepts, Methods and Calculi (PROCOMET)*, IFIP Transactions, Amsterdam, June 1994. North-Holland/Elsevier.
7. G.Leduc, O. Bonaventure, E. Koerner, L. Léonard, C. Pecheur, and D. Zanetti. Specification and verification of a ttp protocol for the conditional access to services. In *Proceedings of the 12th Workshop on the Application of Formal Methods to System Development (Univ Montreal)*, 1996.
8. S. Graf. Verification of a distributed cache memory by using abstractions. In *Workshop on Computer-Aided Verification, CAV'94, Stanford*. LNCS 818, Springer Verlag, jun 1994.
9. Klaus Havelund and N. Shankar. Experiments in theorem proving and model checking for protocol verification. In *Formal Methods Europe FME '96*, volume 1051 of *Lecture Notes in Computer Science*, pages 662–681, Oxford, UK, March 1996. Springer-Verlag.
10. C. Loiseaux, S. Graf, J. Sifakis, A. Bouajjani, and S. Bensalem. Property preserving abstractions for the verification of concurrent systems. *Formal Methods in System Design Volume 6, Issue 1*, 1995.
11. G. Lowe. An attack on the needham-schroeder public-key protocol. In *Information Processing Letters*, 1995.
12. S. Owre, S. Rajan, J.M. Rushby, N. Shankar, and M.K. Srivas. PVS: Combining specification, proof checking, and model checking. In Rajeev Alur and Thomas A. Henzinger, editors, *Computer-Aided Verification, CAV '96*, volume 1102 of *Lecture Notes in Computer Science*, pages 411–414, New Brunswick, NJ, July/August 1996. Springer-Verlag.

Efficient Model Checking Using Tabled Resolution*

Y.S. Ramakrishna, C.R. Ramakrishnan, I.V. Ramakrishnan,
Scott A. Smolka, Terrance Swift, David S. Warren

Department of Computer Science
SUNY at Stony Brook
Stony Brook, NY 11794–4400, USA

Abstract. We demonstrate the feasibility of using the XSB tabled logic programming system as a programmable fixed-point engine for implementing efficient local model checkers. In particular, we present XMC, an XSB-based local model checker for a CCS-like value-passing language and the alternation-free fragment of the modal mu-calculus. XMC is written in under 200 lines of XSB code, which constitute a declarative specification of CCS and the modal mu-calculus at the level of semantic equations.
In order to gauge the performance of XMC as an algorithmic model checker, we conducted a series of benchmarking experiments designed to compare the performance of XMC with the local model checkers implemented in C/C++ in the Concurrency Factory and SPIN specification and verification environments. After applying certain newly developed logic-programming-based optimizations (along with some standard ones), XMC's performance became extremely competitive with that of the Factory and shows promise in its comparison with SPIN.

1 Introduction

Model checking [CE81, QS82, CES86] is a verification technique aimed at determining whether a system specification possesses a property expressed as a temporal logic formula. Model checking has enjoyed wide success in verifying, or finding design errors in, real-life systems. An interesting account of a number of these success stories can be found in [CW96b].

Model checking is the main verification technique deployed by the Concurrency Factory [CLSS96], NCSU Concurrency Workbench [CS96], SMV [CMCHG96], SPIN [HP96], and TempEst [JPO95] specification and verification environments. These tools use similar, but slightly different, system specification languages and property specification logics: the Concurrency Factory supports local model checking with partial order reductions in the alternation-depth-2 fragment of the modal mu-calculus for processes specified in a CCS-like value passing language; the NCSU Concurrency Workbench offers global model checking in the alternation-free modal mu-calculus for processes specified in pure CCS; SMV supports BDD-based symbolic model checking in CTL (with fairness) for a state-machine specification language;

* Research supported in part by NSF grants CDA–9303181, CCR–9404921, CCR–9505562, CDA–9504275, and AFOSR grants F49620-95-1-0508 and F49620-96-1-0087. Email correspondence: sas@cs.sunysb.edu

SPIN implements on-the-fly LTL model checking with partial order reductions for processes specified in Promela, a guarded-command language with buffered communication; and TempEst provides model checking of LTL with past operators for the Esterel synchronous language.

As is clear from this short list, there is a plethora of temporal logics and specification languages currently in use, and building a model checker for a particular combination involves having to confront the low-level computational details of the underlying model checking algorithm. One thing, however, these logics and process languages typically have in common is that their semantics are specified via structural recursion as fixed points of certain types of functionals.

To deal with the complexity of implementing model checkers, we would like ideally to focus only on declaratively specifying the semantics of the temporal logic and process language, while leaving the computational details to an efficient underlying engine. Such an ideal can be realized by the availability of engines that (i) compute fixed points, since from a computational viewpoint, model checking can be formulated in terms of computing fixed points, and (ii) are efficient enough to generate systems competitive with hand-crafted model checkers. One way to attain the second goal is for the fixed-point engine to provide *programmability*, so that optimizing program transformations can be made directly to the model checker specifications. Programmability also allows direct encoding of traditional model checking optimizations such as partial order reduction [HPP96].

Recent advances in *tabled resolution* [TS86, CW96a] offer significant promise towards achieving the above objective. At a high-level, tabled resolution augments Prolog-style SLDNF resolution for evaluating normal logic programs (with default negation). Tabled evaluation overcomes the three major limitations of Prolog, namely, weak termination, redundancy of computations, and weak semantics for negation. The XSB tabled logic programming system developed at SUNY Stony Brook is a practical embodiment of the power and enhanced functionality of tabled resolution.

When tabled resolution is used in XSB (by declaring particular predicates to be tabled), the system automatically maintains a table of predicate invocations and answers, using the table for all equivalent invocations after the first one. Many programs that would loop infinitely in Prolog will terminate in XSB because XSB calls a tabled predicate with the same arguments only once, whereas Prolog may call such a predicate infinitely often. For these terminating programs XSB efficiently computes the least model, which is the least fixed point of the program rules understood as "equations" over sets of atoms. More precisely, XSB is based on SLG resolution [CW96a], which computes queries to normal logic programs (containing default negation) according to the well-founded semantics.

This paper shows that by using XSB as a programmable fixed-point engine, one can construct an efficient model checker in under 200 lines of code. In particular, we have specified the syntax and semantics of a CCS-like value passing language similar to one supported by the Concurrency Factory, along with the syntax and semantics of the alternation-free fragment of the modal mu-calculus. The specification is based on a parallel constant-time reduction from the alternation-free modal mu-calculus to Datalog with negation presented in [ZSS94]. Not surprisingly, the XSB specification directly reflects the structural operational semantics of CCS and the fixed-point semantics of the modal mu-calculus. The direct execution of these declarative specifications yields a local (on-the-fly) model checker, which we refer to as XMC.

In order to gauge the performance of XMC as an algorithmic model checker, we conducted a number of benchmarking experiments designed to compare the performance of XMC with the local model checkers implemented in the Concurrency Factory and SPIN. The model checking benchmarks we considered include Milner's "scheduler of cyclers" [Mil89] and the leader election and sieve algorithms from the SPIN benchmark suite.[2] After applying certain newly developed logic-programming-based optimizations (along with some standard ones—see Section 3), XMC's performance became extremely competitive with that of the Factory and shows promise in its comparison with SPIN.

These results, discussed further in Section 4, are somewhat surprising since the Factory's and SPIN's model checkers are written in low-level languages (C/C++) with the express purpose of temporal logic model checking, while XSB is a general-purpose logic programming system. Our experimental results provide evidence that writing efficient model checkers for various process languages and logics in XSB can be a viable idea.

Concerning related work, XMC can be viewed as an algorithmic model checker in a deductive setting (XSB, after all, is a system to deduce theorems from normal logic programs). The recent literature contains a number of proposals for combining deductive methods with algorithmic model checking techniques in order to prove temporal properties of concurrent systems. For example, the STeP system [BBC+96] combines the deductive methods of [MP95] with decision procedures for automatically checking the validity of a large class of first-order and temporal formulas. [PS96] uses deduction to establish an invariant that is then used to constrain the state space exploration performed in model checking. [RSS95] embeds a symbolic model checking decision procedure into the PVS higher-order prover, and [SUM96] employs first-order linear temporal-logic formulas to construct an abstract representation of the state space to be explored, and deductive methods to successively refine this representation until an answer to the model checking problem can be ascertained.

In other related work, [SHIR96] also uses Horn logic to specify model checking (for a basic, non-value-passing process specification language) but reports no effort to implement or evaluate this approach. Toupie [Rau95] is a mu-calculus interpreter that utilizes a combination of constraint logic programming (over finite domains) and BDDs to perform model checking. Constraint logic programming is also used in [Ost91] for semi-automatic verification of possibly infinite-state systems. In [SCK+95], an efficient "fixpoint-analysis machine" (FAM) is presented which can be used on a variety of fixed point computation problems, including model checking.

The structure of the rest of this paper is as follows. Section 2 describes our encoding in XSB of a value-passing language and the alternation-free modal mu-calculus. The logic-based optimizations we performed on the XMC model checker are the subject of Section 3, and our expermental results are discussed in Section 4. Section 5 concludes and presents directions for future work.

---

[2] The XMC and benchmark sources can be found at http://www.cs.sunysb.edu/~ysr/xmc.

2 Value-Passing Language and Modal Mu-Calculus Encoding

As described in the Introduction, we encoded in XSB a model checker for a CCS-like value-passing language and the alternation-free modal mu-calculus. The syntax of processes in our value-passing language is the following:[3]

```
P  ::=   X   |  a?Y  |  a!Y  |  P o P  |  if X then P else P
     |  P # P  |  P || P |  P\L   |  P@f  |  C(Z1,...,Zn)
```

In the above, X is a Prolog formula. Thus, for example, the formula length(Buf, Len) is the process that binds Len to the length of list Buf. Note that this process performs no actual transitions. Process a?Y inputs a value over port a into Y, where Y is a Prolog term. Similarly, a!Y outputs the value of Y over port a. Operator o is generalized prefixing. The remaining operators are like their CCS counterparts (modulo occasional changes in syntax to avoid clashes with Prolog lexicon). E.g., process if X then P else Q behaves like P if X succeeds and otherwise like Q; # is nondeterministic choice; P||Q is the parallel composition of P and Q; @ is relabeling, where f is a list of substitutions represented as Prolog terms; and C(Z1,...,Zn) is a process constant C, parameterized by $Z1,...,Zn$ (C and the Zi are Prolog atoms). Recursion is provided by *defining equations* of the form C(Z1,...,Zn) :== P.

The formal semantics of our language is given using structural operational semantics. Due to space limitations, we present here the axioms and inference rules for a few key constructs. In order to emphasize the highly declarative nature of our encoding, these are presented exactly as they are encoded in the Prolog syntax of XSB.

```
trans(a?Y, a?Y, nil).
trans(a!Y, a!Y, nil).
trans(X, nil, nil) :- call(X).

trans(P1 o P2, Act_a, Q) :- trans(P1, Act_b, Q1),
          (Act_b == nil -> trans(P2, Act_a, Q);
          (Act_a = Act_b, (Q1 == nil -> Q = P2 ; Q = Q1 o P2))).

trans(if X then P1 else P2, Act_a, Q) :-
          call(X) -> trans(P1, Act_a, Q) ; trans(P2, Act_a, Q).

trans( P || Q, Act_a, P1 || Q ) :- trans(P, Act_a, P1).
trans( P || Q, Act_a, P  || Q1) :- trans(Q, Act_a, Q1).
trans( P || Q, tau,    P1 || Q1) :- trans(P, Act_a, P1),
                       trans(Q, Act_b, Q1), comp(Act_a, Act_b).
```

In the above, A -> B ; C is Prolog syntax for if A then B else C. The trans predicate is of the form trans(P, Act_a, Q) meaning that process P performs an

---

[3] To increase readability, we use here a slightly sugared version of the syntax actually interpreted by XMC.

Act_a transition to become process Q. The axiom for input says that a?Y can execute an a?Y transition and then terminate; similarly for the output axiom. The axiom for internal computation forces the evaluation of X and then terminates (without exercising any transition). The rule for generalized prefix states that P1 o P2 behaves like P1 until P1 terminates; at that point it behaves as P2. The conditional process if X then P1 else P2 behaves like P1 if evaluation of X succeeds, and like P2 otherwise. Finally, the rules for parallel composition state that P|Q can perform an autonomous Act_a transition if either P or Q can (the first two rules), and P|Q can perform a synchronizing tau transition if P and Q can perform "complementary" actions (the last rule); i.e., actions of the form a?Y and a!Y.

To illustrate the syntax and semantics of our value-passing language, consider the following specification of a channel chan (with input port in and output port out) implemented as a bounded buffer of size N.

```
chan(N, Buf) :== length(Buf, Len) o
                 if (Len == 0) then receive_only(N, Buf)
                 else if (Len == N) then send_only(N, Buf)
                 else receive_only(N, Buf) # send_only(N, Buf).
```

```
receive_only(N, Buf) :== in?Msg o chan(N, [Msg|Buf]).
send_only(N,Buf) :== rm_last(Buf,Msg,RBuf) o out!Msg o chan(N,RBuf).
```

Our encoding of the modal mu-calculus uses the following syntax for formulas:

```
F  ::=  Z  | tt | ff | F \/ F | F /\ F | diam(Act_a,F) | box(Act_a,F)
```

In the above, Z, which is a Prolog atom, is a mu-calculus logical variable; tt and ff are propositional constants; \/ and /\ are standard logical connectives; and diam(Act_a,F) (possibly after action Act_a formula F holds) and box(Act_a,F) (necessarily after action Act_a formula F holds) are dual modal operators. Additionally, logical variables can be given defining equations of the form X :== mu(F) (least fixed point) or X :== nu(F) (greatest fixed point). For example, a basic property, the absence of deadlock, is expressed in this logic by the formula Z :== nu(box(-,Z) /\ diam(-,tt)), where '-' stands for any action. The formula states, essentially, that from every reachable state (box(-,Z)) a transition is possible (diam(-,tt)).

As in the case of our value-passing language, the semantics of the modal mu-calculus is specified declaratively in XSB by providing a set of rules for each of the operators of the logic. For example, the semantics of \/, diam, and mu are encoded as follows:

```
State_s |= F_1 \/  _      :- State_s |= F_1.
State_s |=  _  \/ F_2      :- State_s |= F_2.

State_s |= diam(Act_a, F) :- trans(State_s, Act_a, State_t),
                             State_t |= F.

State_s |= Z              :- Z :== mu(F), State_s |= F.
```

Consider the rule for diam. It states that a state State_s (of a process) satisfies a formula of the form diam(Act_a,F) if State_s has an Act_a transition to some state State_t and State_t satisfies F. As for mu, the semantics of logic programs are based on minimal models, and accordingly XSB directly computes least fixed points. Thus, the encoding of mu is straightforward as shown above.

To compute greatest fixed points in XSB, we exploit its capability to handle normal logic programs: programs with rules whose right-hand side literals may be negated using XSB's tnot, which performs negation by failure in a tabled environment. In particular, we make use of the duality nu(F) = ¬ mu(¬F). The "not models" predicate |/= performs this negation, and appears below for the same sampling of operators as given above.

```
State_s |/= F_1 \/ F_2          :- State_s |/= F_1, State_s |/= F_2.

State_s |/= diam(Act_a, F)      :-
        tfindall(State_t, trans(State_s, Act_a, State_t), State_ts),
        lnotModels(State_ts, F).

lnotModels([],_).
lnotModels([State|LState], F) :- State |/= F, lnotModels(LState, F).

State_s |/= Z                   :- Z :== mu(F), tnot(State_s |= F).
```

where tfindall finds all solutions of a predicate in a tabled environment. The semantics of nu is then defined by:

```
State_s |= Z    :- Z :== nu(F), tnot(State_s |/= F).     % Nu -- models

State_s |/= Z   :- Z :== nu(F), State_s |/= F.           % Nu -- not models
```

This encoding provides a sound method for model checking any modal mu-calculus formula that is alternation free [EL86]. In the alternation-free case, fixed points are computed "inside out," with an inner fixed point computed before an outer fixed point in whose scope it lies. The proof of correctness rests on showing that the XSB program for model checking an alternation-free formula is *dynamically stratified* with respect to negation and to tfindall/3, and has a two-valued minimal model. Dynamic stratification ensures that the program's dynamic dependency graph can be evaluated without loops through negation. In [SSW96] it was shown that the evaluation method underlying XSB correctly computes this class of programs.

Tabling ensures that each explored system state is visited only once in the evaluation of a modal mu-calculus formula. Consequently, the XSB program will terminate under XSB's tabling method when there are a finite number of states in the transition system.

3 Logic-Based Optimization Techniques

XMC benefits from optimization techniques developed for deductive-database-style applications, such as literal reordering and clause resolution factoring, as well as from source-code representational changes of process terms.

Literal Reordering Literal reordering (see, for example, [Ull88]) is a common technique for optimizing computation by changing the order in which literals on the right hand sides of clauses are selected for resolution. The selection strategy controls the search space needed to evaluate the rule regardless of whether the rule is evaluated top-down or bottom-up. Consider the computation of tau transitions using trans:

```
trans(par(P, Q), tau, par(P1, Q1)) :- trans(P, Act_a, P1),
                      trans(Q, Act_b, Q1), compAct(Act_a, Act_b).
```

In general, the number of solutions to the predicate compAct(Act_a, Act_b) is much smaller than the number of solutions to trans(Q, Act_b, Q1), and hence it pays to rewrite the rule as:

```
trans(par(P, Q), tau, par(P1, Q1)) :-    trans(P, Act_a, P1),
                      compAct(Act_a, Act_b), trans(Q, Act_b, Q1).
```

Clause Resolution Factoring Clause resolution factoring, introduced in [DRRS95], is a newer optimization that is geared specifically to deductive databases having a tightly linked top-down and bottom-up evaluation strategy. Clause resolution factoring shares elementary match and unification operations across program and answer clause resolution steps. An important aspect of this optimization is that it enables individual clauses (instead of whole predicates) to be tabled, improving the space and time efficiency of programs. Consider the following fragment of the trans relation:

```
:- table trans/3.
trans(C, Act_a, Q) :-  C :== P, trans(P, Act_a, Q).
trans(Act_a o P, Act_a, P).
trans(P1 # P2, Act_a, Q) :- trans(P1,Act_a,Q) ; trans(P2,Act_a,Q).
```

Observe that the rules for trans have structural recursion, and to ensure termination, only the recursive case (i.e., the first rule) needs to be tabled. Applying clause resolution factoring with this information results in the following fragment:

```
:- table trans_rec/3.
trans_rec(P, Act_a, Q) :- trans(P, Act_a, Q).

trans(C, Act_a, Q) :-  C :== P, trans_rec(P, Act_a, Q).
trans(Act_a o P, Act_a, P).
trans(P1 # P2, Act_a, Q) :- trans(P1,Act_a,Q) ; trans(P2,Act_a,Q).
```

In the above fragment, only trans_rec is tabled; this results in considerable savings in table space as well as computation time because terms which do not need to be tabled do not incur the overhead of tabling. The model checking predicate models, which also has structural recursion, is also subject to this optimization.

Optimizing Representation of Process States As mentioned in Section 2, processes are represented in XMC using a CCS-like value passing language. For instance in the six-agent sieve benchmark, a generator process and six tester processes communicate along a linear chain. As an XSB term, the sieve process might be specified in source code as:

```
sieve :==
  (gen || chan0 || test1 || chan1 || test2 || chan2 || test3 || chan3
   || test4 || chan4 || test5 || chan5 || test6 || chan6 || cons) \
 {gen_out(X), in1(X), in2(X), in3(X), in4(X), in4(X), in5(X), in6(X), in7(X),
  con_in(X), out1(X), out2(X), out3(X), out4(X), out5(X), out6(X), out7(X)}.
```

XMC runtime states directly reflect this specification. For instance, a runtime state might have the form:

```
  (generator1(4,31) @ 1  || chan_1([]) @ 10 || tester2(2,4) @ 2
 || chan_1([3]) @ 11 || test2 || chan2 || test3 || chan3 || test4
 || chan4 || test5 || chan5 || test6 || chan6 || cons) \ 1
```

Taken as Prolog terms, these runtime states are relatively large. This situation is inefficient not only in terms of memory, but also in terms of time, since each state encountered must be checked against the table and inserted if it is not there. To reduce state size source code representation can be "folded" as below:

```
    sieve :== (gen || chan0 || sieve1) \ {gen_out(X), ...,   out7(X)}.

    sieve1 :== (test1 || sieve2).   ...   sieve6 :== (test6 || chan6).
```

This representation leads to smaller runtime terms such as

```
    (generator1(4,31) @ 1  || chan_1([]) @ 10 || tester2(2,4) @ 2
 || chan_1([3]) @ 11 || sieve2) \ 1
```

Optimizing process states leads to a 50% reduction in memory required to represent states in the leader and sieve examples of Section 4.

4   Experimental Results

In this section, we compare the performance of XMC with that of the Concurrency Factory and SPIN in terms of time and memory. Figure 1 shows the space and time used by XMC and the Factory on Milner's scheduler for the formula Z :== nu(box(-,Z) /\ diam(-,tt)), for a scheduler of n cyclers, $4 \leq n \leq 10$. The formula, which asserts the absence of deadlock, forces exploration of the entire state-space of the system, thus allowing us to assess the scalability of the two implementations. As is clear from the figure, XMC performs better than the Factory in terms of speed, and is quite competitive in terms of space.

The example of Milner's scheduler does not involve value-passing. For examples involving value-passing, we compared the performance of XMC with SPIN, rather than with the Factory, since the latter does not yet have efficient support for value-passing processes. (This problem is expected to be remedied in the next release of the Factory, slated for Fall '97.)

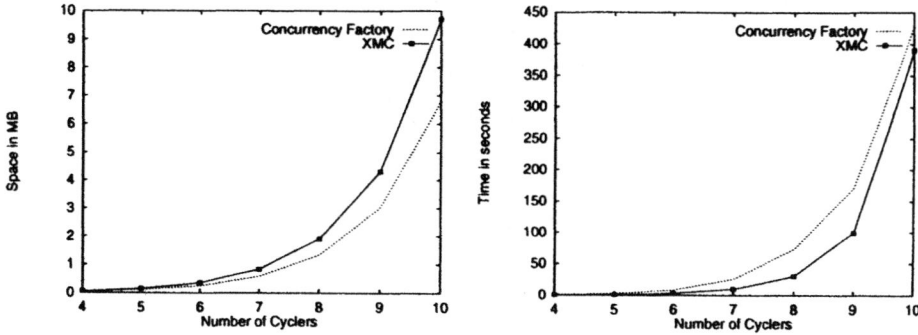

Fig. 1. Performance comparison with the Concurrency Factory on Milner's scheduler of cyclers.

To assess XMC's ability to model check in a value-passing language, and to assess the effects of the optimizations described in the previous section, we used the leader election example from the SPIN benchmark suite. As in the case of the scheduler, we benchmarked the system for several different ring sizes. The "leader5" system corresponds to the system used in the SPIN suite. Table 1 gives the space and time figures for two different formulas, F1 being a least fixed point formula stating that in every run of the system a leader is eventually elected, and F2 being a nested fixed point formula stating that in every run of the system at most one leader is elected. In this table, for a system of given size, the first line indicates the space and time figures with the naive encoding without any of the optimizations of the previous section, and the second line gives the corresponding figures with all the optimizations in place.

To compare XMC to SPIN we also implemented in XMC, a simple transitive closure algorithm to search and store all the reachable states of leader5 as well as sieve6, also from the SPIN benchmark suite. The results in Table 2 indicate that XMC has good memory usage as compared to SPIN, but that the speed of XMC appears uneven.[4] Two features account for the good memory usage of XMC. First, tabled terms in the underlying XSB engine are stored using a trie-like data structure that provides good structure sharing for variant subterms. Second, the scheduling strategy of XSB allows left-linear transitive closure to be performed using a minimum of runtime stack space.

An important feature of SPIN is that it combines on-the-fly model checking with *partial order reduction*, a technique for combating the combinatorial explosion that results from interleaving concurrent independent transitions in all possible orders. Roughly speaking, partial order reduction partitions the state space into equivalent search paths; (dis)proving a given property then requires exploring only one

---

[4] The sieve benchmark of Table 2 was run on an SGI challenge for both XMC and SPIN; SPIN results are from [GKPP97]. All other figures for XMC and the Concurrency Factory were performed on a sparc10 with about 500 MB available main memory; the leader benchmark for SPIN was also run on a sparc10 with 128 MB main memory [HP95].

Program	F1		F2	
	Time (sec)	Space (MB)	Time (sec)	Space (MB)
leader2 (unopt)	0.23	0.817	0.22	0.768
(opt)	0.10	0.209	0.11	0.198
leader3 (unopt)	1.21	4.593	1.18	4.342
(opt)	0.46	0.581	0.51	0.596
leader4 (unopt)	8.51	37.366	8.39	35.604
(opt)	2.93	3.079	3.23	3.239
leader5 (unopt)	39.09	170.608	37.51	163.405
(opt)	11.87	11.396	12.87	12.139

Table 1. Illustrating the effect of logic-based optimizations.

Program	System	Time (sec)	Space (MB)
leader5	SPIN	8.1	9.60
	XMC	5.5	0.78
sieve6	SPIN	1.8	2.31
	XMC	10.4	1.23

Table 2. Performance comparison with SPIN on value-passing examples.

path in each equivalence class. The results quoted above for SPIN (and for XMC) were obtained without the use of partial order reduction, and the numbers go down appreciably (especially for sieve) with the use of this technique. The programmability of XSB should, however, allow the implementation of partial order reduction techniques within XMC, a topic currently under investigation.

5 Conclusions and Future Work

We have provided experimental evidence that writing efficient algorithmic model checkers in a tabled logic programming system is a viable idea. Our work on XMC reveals a number of directions for future work. For example, we have not considered *alternating* fixed points [EL86] in this paper. The logic-programming-based approach to model checking, however, suggests a promising technique in which inner fixed points are computed *symbolically*, thereby avoiding their repeated computation.

Traditionally, model checking has been viewed as an *algorithmic* technique, although there is initial activity on combining model checking with *deductive* methods (see our discussion of related work in Section 1). Observe that (optimized) XSB meta-interpreters can be used to execute arbitrary deductive systems. Hence, the XSB-based approach offers a unique opportunity to fully and flexibly integrate algorithmic and deductive model checking. Demonstrating the feasibility of this idea is another direction for future work.

XSB's unification mechanism handles interpreted and uninterpreted variables in a value-passing language as ground and non-ground logical variables, respectively. Moreover, XSB automatically offers *lazy grounding* of variables. Since grounding can increase the search space of a query (every possible valuation must be considered), lazy grounding can result in substantial savings. As future work, we plan to experimentally measure the impact of lazy grounding on performance and investigate how it can be used to effectively realize Wolper's *data independence* scheme [Wol86].

References

[AH96]   R. Alur and T. A. Henzinger, editors. *Computer Aided Verification (CAV '96)*, volume 1102 of *Lecture Notes in Computer Science*, New Brunswick, New Jersey, July 1996. Springer-Verlag.

[BBC⁺96]   N. Bjørner, A. Browne, E. Chang, M. Colón, A. Kapur, Z. Manna, H. B. Sipma, and T. E. Uribe. STeP: Deductive-algorithmic verification of reactive and real-time systems. In Alur and Henzinger [AH96], pages 415–418.

[CE81]   E. M. Clarke and E. A. Emerson. Design and synthesis of synchronization skeletons using branching-time temporal logic. In D. Kozen, editor, *Proceedings of the Workshop on Logic of Programs*, Yorktown Heights, volume 131 of *Lecture Notes in Computer Science*, pages 52–71. Springer-Verlag, 1981.

[CES86]   E. M. Clarke, E. A. Emerson, and A. P. Sistla. Automatic verification of finite-state concurrent systems using temporal logic specifications. *ACM TOPLAS*, 8(2), 1986.

[CLSS96]   R. Cleaveland, P. M. Lewis, S. A. Smolka, and O. Sokolsky. The Concurrency Factory: A development environment for concurrent systems. In Alur and Henzinger [AH96], pages 398–401.

[CMCHG96]   E. M. Clarke, K. McMillan, S. Campos, and V. Hartonas-GarmHausen. Symbolic model checking. In Alur and Henzinger [AH96], pages 419–422.

[CS96]   R. Cleaveland and S. Sims. The NCSU concurrency workbench. In Alur and Henzinger [AH96], pages 394–397.

[CW96a]   W. Chen and D.S. Warren. Tabled evaluation with delaying for general logic programs. *Journal of the ACM*, 43(1):20–74, January 1996.

[CW96b]   E. M. Clarke and J. M. Wing. Formal methods: State of the art and future directions. *ACM Computing Surveys*, 28(4), December 1996.

[DRRS95]   S. Dawson, C.R. Ramakrishnan, I.V. Ramakrishnan, and T. Swift. Optimizing clause resolution: Beyond unification factoring. In *International Logic Programming Symposium*, pages 194–208. MIT Press, 1995.

[EL86]   E. A. Emerson and C.-L. Lei. Efficient model checking in fragments of the propositional mu-calculus. In *Proceedings of the First Annual Symposium on Logic in Computer Science*, pages 267–278, 1986.

[GKPP97]   R. Gerth, R. Kuiper, W. Penczek, and D. Peled. A partial order approach to branching time model checking. *Information and Computation*, 1997.

[HP95]   G. J. Holzmann and D. Peled. An improvement in formal verification. In *Seventh Int. Conf. on Formal Description Techniques (FORTE '94)*, pages 177–194. Chapman and Hall, 1995.

[HP96]   G. J. Holzmann and D. Peled. The state of SPIN. In Alur and Henzinger [AH96], pages 385–389.

[HPP96]   G. Holzmann, D. Peled, and V. Pratt, editors. *Partial-Order Methods in Verification (POMIV '96)*, DIMACS Series in Discrete Mathematics and Theoretical Computer Science, New Brunswick, New Jersey, July 1996. American Mathematical Society.

[JPO95]   L. J. Jagadeesan, C. Puchol, and J. E. Von Olnhausen. Safety property verification of ESTEREL programs and applications to telecommunications software. In Wolper [Wol95], pages 127–140.

[Mil89]   R. Milner. *Communication and Concurrency*. International Series in Computer Science. Prentice Hall, 1989.

[MP95]   Z. Manna and A. Pnueli. *Temporal Verification of Reactive Systems: Safety*. Springer-Verlag, 1995.

[Ost91]   J. S. Ostroff. Constraint logic programming for reasoning about discrete event processes. *Journal of Logic Programming*, 11(2/3):243–270, Oct./Nov. 1991.

[PS96]   A. Pnueli and E. Shahar. A platform for combining deductive with algorithmic verification. In Alur and Henzinger [AH96], pages 184–195.

[QS82]   J. P. Queille and J. Sifakis. Specification and verification of concurrent systems in Cesar. In *Proceedings of the International Symposium in Programming*, volume 137 of *Lecture Notes in Computer Science*, Berlin, 1982. Springer-Verlag.

[Rau95]   A. Rauzy. Toupie = μ-calculus + constraints. In Wolper [Wol95], pages 114–126.

[RSS95]   S. Rajan, N. Shankar, and M. K. Srivas. An integration of model checking with automated proof checking. In Wolper [Wol95], pages 84–97.

[SCK$^+$95]   B. Steffen, A. Classen, M. Klein, J. Knoop, and T. Margaria. The fixpoint-analysis machine. In I. Lee and S. A. Smolka, editors, *Proceedings of the Sixth International Conference on Concurrency Theory (CONCUR '95)*, Vol. 962 of *Lecture Notes in Computer Science*, pages 72–87. Springer-Verlag, 1995.

[SHIR96]   S. K. Shukla, H. B. Hunt III, and D. J. Rosenkrantz. HORNSAT, model checking, verification and games. In Alur and Henzinger [AH96], pages 99–110.

[SSW96]   K. Sagonas, T. Swift, and D.S. Warren. An abstract machine to compute fixed-order dynamically stratified programs. In *International Conference on Automated Deduction (CADE)*, 1996.

[SUM96]   H. B. Sipma, T. E. Uribe, and Z. Manna. Deductive model checking. In Alur and Henzinger [AH96], pages 208–219.

[TS86]   H. Tamaki and T. Sato. OLDT resolution with tabulation. In *Third Int'l Conf. on Logic Programming*, pages 84–98, 1986.

[Ull88]   J. D. Ullman. *Principles of Data and Knowledge-base Systems, Volume I*. Computer Science Press, Rockville, MD, 1988.

[Wol86]   P. Wolper. Expressing interesting properties of programs in propositional temporal logic. In *Proc. 13th ACM Symp. on Principles of Programming*, pages 184–192, St. Petersburgh, January 1986.

[Wol95]   P. Wolper, editor. *Computer Aided Verification (CAV '95)*, volume 939 of *Lecture Notes in Computer Science*, Liége, Belgium, July 1995. Springer-Verlag.

[ZSS94]   S. Zhang, O. Sokolsky, and S. A. Smolka. On the parallel complexity of model checking in the modal mu-calculus. In *Proceedings of the 9th IEEE Symposium on Logic in Computer Science*, London, England, July 1994.

Containment of Regular Languages in Non-Regular Timing Diagram Languages is Decidable

Kathi Fisler*

Department of Computer Science
Rice University
6100 S. Main MS 132
Houston TX 77005-1892
kfisler@cs.rice.edu

Abstract. Parametric timing constraints are expressed naturally in timing diagram logics. Algorithmic verification of parametrically constrained timing properties is a difficult problem known to be undecidable in most general cases. This paper establishes that a class of parametrically constrained timing properties can be verified algorithmically against finite-state systems; alternatively stated containment by a regular language is shown decidable for a class of language properties (regular and non-regular) expressible in our timing diagram logic.

1 Introduction

Timing diagrams provide a linear-time temporal logic that is well suited to expressing timing constraints. When variables can appear in timing constraints the resulting timing diagram logic can express context-free and context-sensitive language properties. Algorithmic verification of such non-regular properties against finite-state system specifications is generally known to be undecidable. Timing diagrams however can only express non-regular languages with particular structural characteristics. This raises the question of whether the class of timing diagram languages is amenable to algorithmic verification. This paper establishes that containment by a regular language is decidable for a class of timing diagram languages implying that certain non-regular language properties expressible as timing diagrams can be algorithmically tested against finite-state systems.

Timing diagrams have been used formally in a variety of hardware reasoning tasks. Brzozowski Gahlinger and Mavaddat provided algorithms for testing consistency and satisfiability of timing specifications given as timing diagrams in the context of interfacing components [3]; similar efforts have been undertaken by Cerny and Khordoc [4]. Several researchers have proposed using algebras of timing diagrams annotated with various programming language constructs for

---

* This research was conducted while the author was a graduate student at Indiana University with financial support from AT&T Bell Laboratories under the PhD Fellowship Program.

the behavioral specification of designs [6 9 10]. Algorithmic verification has been applied to requirements expressed as timing diagrams by translating the diagrams into existing formalisms such as VHDL [11] and timed automata [2]. Although some of these efforts support quantitative timing constraints (those using numeric constants) none support *parametric* timing constraints (those allowing variables over numerals).

Alur Henzinger and Vardi have studied parametric timing constraints for real-time systems [1]. They defined a theory of parametric timed automata with multiple clocks for tracking parametric values and established that language emptiness is decidable when one clock is constrained by parameters undecidable when three or more clocks are constrained by parameters and an open problem when two clocks are so constrained. The timing diagrams considered in this work can correspond to problems that would require multiple parameterized clocks. We do not solve the general question of decidability of language emptiness for two clock systems. Rather this work shows that timing diagrams correspond to a class of parameterized timing problems potentially requiring multiple clocks for which containment by a regular language is decidable.

2   Timing Diagrams and Their Languages

This work uses a formal logic of timing diagrams (called TDL) developed as part of our study of diagrammatic representations as formal specification languages for design and verification [5]. Starting from fairly common timing diagram notations we define timing diagram semantics relative to formal languages. TDL is expressively incomparable to existing temporal logics such as LTL. In particular LTL cannot express parametric timing constraints while TDL cannot express properties such as Fp and $G(p \rightarrow q)$; reasons for this are given in Section 2.2.

2.1   Syntax

Waveforms depict transitions between low and high voltage levels; timing diagrams depict relations over the levels and transitions appearing within a set of waveforms. TDL supports two relations: synchronization and temporal ordering. Temporal ordering relationships may be constrained with discrete-time lower and upper bounds. We allow these bounds to contain variables that range over the natural numbers; these variables introduce parametric timing constraints as shown in the following example.

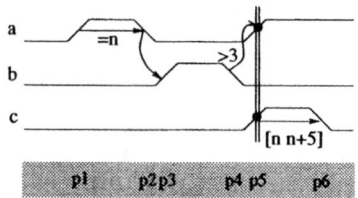

Vertical parallel lines indicate synchronization of the levels or transitions on which the circles appear. The term *event* refers to a transition on a waveform or a synchronization. The arrows indicate temporal ordering while the annotations on the arrows indicate the lower and upper bounds on the time passing between the related events: annotation "=n" (shorthand for [nn]) indicates that the lower and upper bounds are the same while annotation "> 3" (shorthand for [3 ∞]) indicates a lower bound of 3 but no upper bound. Unannotated arrows have time bound [1 ∞] by default. *Valid bound expressions* consist of natural numbers variables and arbitrary addition and subtraction expressions over them as well as the symbol ∞. The labels in the shaded area are for explanatory purposes only and are not part of the timing diagram.

Formally a timing diagram contains three components: (1) an ordered sequence P of *time points* which are abstract moments of time at which events occur; (2) a function N from names to *waveforms* defined as functions from P to voltage level designators of type H (for high level) L (for low level) F (for falling transition) and R (for rising transition); and (3) a ternary relation O on $N \times P \times B$ capturing temporal ordering synchronization and time bounds where B consists of time bound expressions of the form $[l, u]$ such that l is a non-∞ valid bound expression and u is any valid bound expression.

As an example we construct tuple $\langle P, N, O \rangle$ to capture the above timing diagram. P contains time points $\{p_1, p_2, p_3, p_4, p_5, p_6\}$ as shown in the shaded area. N is constructed from the levels on each waveform at each time point.

$$N = \{(a, \{(p_1, R), (p_2, F), (p_3, L), (p_4, L), (p_5, R), (p_6, H)\}),$$
$$(b, \{(p_1, L), (p_2, L), (p_3, R), (p_4, F), (p_5, L), (p_6, L)\}),$$
$$(c, \{(p_1, L), (p_2, L), (p_3, L), (p_4, L), (p_5, R), (p_6, F)\})\}$$

Relation O contains five elements the first four corresponding to the arrows and the fifth to the synchronization line:

$$O = \{((a, p_1), (a, p_2), [n, n]), ((a, p_2), (b, p_3), [1, \infty]), ((b, p_4), (a, p_5), [3, \infty]),$$
$$((c, p_5), (c, p_6), [n, n + 5]), ((a, p_5), (c, p_5), [0, 0])\}$$

Although we have provided only an example here the process of representing a timing diagram in this tuple form can be formalized as a straightforward parsing procedure. In the remainder of the paper the term "timing diagram" refers to the tuple form rather than the original picture.

2.2 Semantics

Timing diagrams are modeled by (finite or infinite) words over an alphabet containing all possible assignments of boolean values to the names labeling waveforms. Intuitively a word models a timing diagram when the transition patterns in the diagram reflect the changes in values assigned to names in the word. One difficulty in formalizing timing diagrams is that their intended meanings differ widely between contexts and among users. Rather than fix one interpretation TDL has been parameterized to allow user customization of the semantics. These parameters are illustrated using the following timing diagram and word.

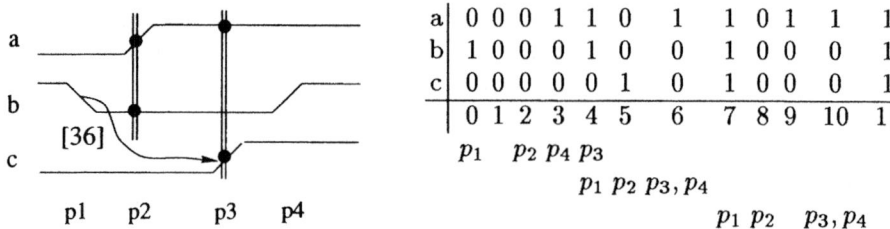

	0	1	2	3	4	5	6	7	8	9	10	11
a	0	0	0	1	1	0	1	1	0	1	1	1
b	1	0	0	0	1	0	0	1	0	0	0	1
c	0	0	0	0	0	1	0	1	0	0	0	1

$$p_1 \quad p_2\ p_4\ p_3$$
$$p_1\ p_2\ p_3, p_4$$
$$p_1\ p_2 \quad p_3, p_4$$

The word is presented in tabular form: the rows are labeled with waveform names and the columns with the indices into the word. The three lines containing time points beneath the table indicate three separate assignments of indices to time points as explained in the example below.

We allow timing diagrams to specify assume-guarantee relationships between their events. One parameter indicates those time points that comprise the "assume" portion. For purposes of this example take p_1 as the only such time point. Semantically we will begin to match the word against the timing diagram starting at the first index that matches the events in the assumed portion in this case index 0. Next we walk the word looking for the smallest indices that match any events that can immediately follow the falling transition on b in this case the first synchronization line (p_2).

A second parameter is motivated by the attempt to assign an index to the first synchronization line. The line itself requires that b be low when a rises; however is b required to be low *until* a rises? The desirability of the "until" interpretation is heavily context-dependent. Therefore the user may indicate segments of waveforms that should be matched exactly within words. Such segments are called *fixed-level constraints* and have the form (n, p, p') where n is a waveform name and p and p' are time points such that the waveform corresponding to n shows a single voltage level between p and p'. For this example assume we have only one such constraint: (a, p_2, p_3). Then the first synchronization line is matched at index 2 while the rising transition on b is matched at index 3 and the second synchronization line at index 4: this assignment appears in the first line below the table. Note that despite the appearance that the rising transition on b must follow the one on c the semantics does not enforce this since the relationship was not indicated explicitly using an arrow.

TDL requires timing diagrams to be matched repeatedly in a word. Two notions of repetition appear useful: one in which the next repetition starts after the previous one has been completed and the other in which a new repetition starts in any index satisfying the "assume" portion of the diagram. We therefore define two semantic relationships: $\models_{\text{Iter}}$ (for iterative) and $\models_{\text{Inv}}$ (for invariant) respectively. Under the invariant semantics the next match would begin at index 4 while under the iterative semantics the next match would begin at index 5; these matches are shown in the next two lines beneath the table. Note that the match attempted from index 4 is not valid since the assigned indices violate the bounds on the arrow. This word would therefore model the diagram under the iterative semantics but not under the invariant semantics.

This example provides insight into the expressive nature of TDL. For example TDL can express context-sensitive languages such as $(a^n b^n c^n)^*$ (taking a^n to mean $\langle a = 1, b = 0, c = 0 \rangle$ with similar interpretations of b^n and c^n). TDL can not express more general non-regular languages such as "the number of a's equals the number of b's". Relative to temporal logic TDL can not express LTL formula Fp because there is no way to stop the repeated searches at a particular point. TDL can not express $G(p \rightarrow q)$ because it is not possible to make disjunctive statements within a TDL timing diagram. In separate work we are investigating calculi over timing diagrams that would relax these restrictions [5].

Due to space constraints only the invariant semantics is defined in the remainder of this section. The iterative semantics is defined formally in [5]. Tuples $\langle T, S, X \rangle$ capture a timing diagram its set of assumed time points and its fixed-level constraints; the term "timing diagram" is henceforth overloaded to also refer to one of these tuples.

Given a timing diagram we can derive a partial order on its time points from the ordering of events within individual waveforms and the temporal ordering relationships. For a time point p the *enabling points* of p are those time points p' such that p' precedes p in this partial order. If the order is total the timing diagram is called *temporally unambiguous*.

An *index assignment* is a partial function I from time points to natural numbers indexing a word; if I is not total the time points on which it is defined must form a prefix of the partial order on time points. Defn. 1 details the conditions an index assignment must meet in order to satisfy the requirements of a prefix of time points. Intuitively the assigned indices must satisfy the events occurring at each time point while respecting the fixed-level constraints and time bounds on all events defined within those time points. For index i into a word W $W_i(n)$ denotes the value of W on the signal named n at index i.

Definition 1 Let $D = \langle \langle P, N, O \rangle, S, X \rangle$ be a timing diagram. Let U be a prefix of the partial order of P and let I be an index assignment for U over a word W. I *satisfies the constraints of U relative to D* iff

1. For each time point $p \in U$ $I(p)$ satisfies p; *i.e.* for every waveform name n in N $W_{I(p)}(n) = 0$ (resp. 1) and $W_{I(p)+1}(n) = 1$ (resp. 0) if n has a rising (resp. falling) transition at p and $W_{I(p)}(n) = 0$ (resp. 1) if n has a low (resp. high) level at p and there is a synchronization line through n at p.
2. Each variable appearing in a time-bound expression in O can be replaced by a natural number such that for each $((a, p), (a', p'), [l, u])$ in O if p and p' are both in U then $l \leq I(p') - I(p) \leq u$.
3. For each fixed-level constraint (n, p, p') in X if p and p' are both in U then for each index i such that $I(p) < i < I(p')$ $W_i(n) = 0$ (resp. 1) if n has a low (resp. high) level between p and p'.

It follows from part 2 of this definition that variables in timing constraints are treated as existentially quantified within a single index assignment. However the instantiations of variables need not be consistent across the many index assignments produced while repeatedly matching the diagram against the word.

Starting from a given index there are potentially many index assignments satisfying Defn. 1. The semantic definitions must rely on a particular such index assignment. We have chosen to use the one that assigns to each time point the smallest index that satisfies it while respecting the partial order among the time points; this index assignment will be called *minimal*.

Definition 2 Let $D = \langle\langle P, N, O \rangle, S, X \rangle$ be a timing diagram W be a word i be an index into W and U be a prefix of the partial order on P. Index assignment I is *minimal* for D W i and U iff I satisfies the constraints of U relative to D and for each time point $p \in U$ $I(p) \geq i$ and $I(p)$ is the smallest index of W that satisfies p and is larger than all indices assigned to the enabling points of p.

The semantics places one other restriction on index assignments in addition to minimality: they must be defined on as large a prefix of the time point partial order as possible. An index assignment is called *fully minimal* if it is minimal and cannot be extended to a minimal index assignment for the same timing diagram word and starting index but with a larger prefix of time points. Fully minimal index assignments are unique for temporally unambiguous timing diagrams.

Given a timing diagram $\langle T, S, X \rangle$ and a word W the invariant semantics starts from each index of W in turn and locates the fully minimal index assignment. If that assignment is defined for all time points in S the semantics requires that it be defined for all time points in T. If this property fails for some index of W then W fails to model $\langle T, S, X \rangle$.

Definition 3 Let $D = \langle T, S, X \rangle$ be a timing diagram and let W be a word. D *invariantly describes* W (denoted $W \models_{\text{Inv}} D$) iff for all indices i into W whenever the fully minimal index assignment for D W i and S is defined for all time points in S it is defined for all time points in T. Given a language L D *invariantly describes* L (denoted $L \models_{\text{Inv}} D$) iff for every word $W \in L$ $W \models_{\text{Inv}} D$. The set of all words that invariantly describe D is denoted $\mathcal{L}(D)^{\text{Inv}}$.

3 Decidability

This section establishes that containment of a regular language in a temporally unambiguous timing diagram language is decidable; we refer to the general problem of containment by a regular language as the *regular containment problem*. Formally a *timing diagram language* is any language that can model a timing diagram under either the iterative or the invariant semantics. The proof for the invariant semantics is discussed in detail; the proof for the iterative semantics is outlined. Our decision procedures are based on a correspondence between temporally unambiguous timing diagram languages and the languages accepted by deterministic two-way 1-counter machines (1-2DCM). Given a temporally unambiguous timing diagram our algorithm creates one 1-2DCM if the diagram is interpreted invariantly and two such machines if the diagram is interpreted iteratively. Then given a finite automaton we determine whether the language of the automaton models the timing diagram by computing relations on the states of the automaton using the counter machine(s). The algorithms discussed here operate on finite-state automata accepting by final state. With a slight modification they can be tailored to operate on Büchi automata; the Büchi construction is not presented here for lack of space.

A 1-2DCM has a finite-state control a two-way read-only head over a finite bounded-length input tape and one counter which can store any natural number. Transitions are based on the current state the letter being read and whether the counter contains zero; the transition indicates a next state which direction if any to move the input head and whether to increment decrement or hold the value of the counter. The following formal definition is adapted from [7].

Definition 4

1. A two-way 1-counter machine M is a tuple $\langle K, \Sigma, \triangleleft, \triangleright, \delta, q_0, F \rangle$ where K Σ $\triangleleft$ $\triangleright$ q_0 and F are the states inputs left and right endmarkers initial state and accepting states respectively. δ is a mapping from $K \times (\Sigma \cup \{\triangleleft, \triangleright\}) \times \{0, 1\}$ into $K \times \{-1, 0, 1\} \times \{-1, 0, 1\}$.

2. A *configuration* of M on an input $\triangleleft x \triangleright$ for $x \in \Sigma^*$ is given by a tuple $(q, \triangleleft x \triangleright, i, c)$ denoting the fact that M is in state q with the input head reading the ith symbol of $\triangleleft x \triangleright$ and value c is in the counter.

3. Relation $\Rightarrow$ is defined between configurations as follows: $(q, \triangleleft x \triangleright, i, c) \Rightarrow (p, \triangleleft x \triangleright, i + d, c + d_c)$ if a is the ith symbol of $\triangleleft x \triangleright$ and $\delta(q, a, \lambda(c))$ contains (p, d, d_c) where $\lambda(c) = 0$ if $c = 0$ and $\lambda(c) = 1$ if $c \neq 0$. $\Rightarrow^*$ denotes the transitive closure of $\Rightarrow$.

4. A string $x \in \Sigma^*$ is *accepted* by M if $(q_0, \triangleleft x \triangleright, 1, 0) \Rightarrow^* (q, \triangleleft x \triangleright, i, c)$ for some $q \in F$ $1 \leq i \leq | \triangleleft x \triangleright |$ and non-negative integer c. The set of strings accepted by M form the *language* of M and will be denoted $\mathcal{L}(M)$.

Languages accepted by 1-2DCM can be characterized by the number of times the counter changes between incrementing and decrementing while reading the input tape. Denoting this parameter by r the following results about 1-2DCM(r) are due to Ibarra *et al.* [8]:

Theorem 1 (Ibarra *et al.* 1993)

- *The emptiness problem for 1-2DCM(r) is decidable for every $r \geq 1$.*
- $\bigcup_r$ *1-2DCM(r) is effectively closed under complementation intersection and union.*
- *The containment and equivalence problems for $\bigcup_r$ 1-2DCM(r) are decidable.*

This result indicates that we can use 1-2DCM in decision procedures if we can bound the number of counter reversals made while processing any input. Such machines are called *reversal bounded*.

Given a timing diagram $\langle T, S, X \rangle$ we construct a 1-2DCM called M_{FAIL} that accepts exactly those words for which the fully minimal index assignment starting from the first position of the word is defined for all the time points in S but undefined for some time point in T. Intuitively the machine walks the word from the starting index looking for indices to assign to time points; the transitions used to search for each time point's index also check for violations of the fixed-level constraints. If an index satisfying the time point is found the machine tests any time-bounds on temporal ordering arrows whose target is at the recently matched time point. Constraints are tested one at a time by repeatedly sweeping over the input word. M_{FAIL} moves into an accepting state as soon as a violation of either the fixed-level constraints or the time-bound requirements is found. If indices corresponding to all of the time points are located M_{FAIL} moves into a looping state from which nothing is accepted.

By construction M_{FAIL} rejects certain words that do not model $\langle T, S, X \rangle$. In particular this applies to words for which the fully minimal index assignment from position 0 is defined for all time points in T but the fully minimal index assignment from some later starting position is undefined for some time point in T. The restriction of M_{FAIL} to accepting only words failing on the index assignment from the first position is important for the decidability of the problem. Based on the syntax of T we can bound the number of counter reversals required for a 1-2DCM to test the time bound constraints of T over an arbitrary word; this follows from results in [5]. Therefore we can bound the number of counter reversals required in a test of some fixed number of index assignment searches over a given timing diagram. As there is no fixed upper bound for the number of searches required in testing an entire word our algorithm must perform searches only in finite increments. The restriction to single searches is sufficient for either semantics since it follows from the definitions that any word failing to model a timing diagram has a suffix accepted by M_{FAIL}.

The decision procedure for the invariant semantics is fairly simple: the language generated by DFA A is contained in the language of timing diagram $\langle T, S, X \rangle$ iff no reachable state of A can generate a word accepted by M_{FAIL}. Formally let $A = \langle Q, \Sigma, \delta, q_0, Q_F \rangle$ be a DFA that accepts by final state. Notation $A|_{(q, q')}$ denotes A modified to have q as the only start state and q' as the only final state where q and q' are both in Q. We define a set Avoid containing exactly those states of A from which a word in M_{FAIL} is accepted as follows:

$$\text{Avoid} =_{\text{def}} \{q \in Q \mid \exists q_f \in Q_F : \mathcal{L}(A|_{(q, q_f)}) \cap \mathcal{L}(M_{\text{FAIL}}) \neq \emptyset\}$$

Theorem 2 *Let $A = \langle Q, \Sigma, \delta, q_0, Q_F \rangle$ be a finite automaton and $D = \langle T, S, X \rangle$ be a timing diagram. Let M_{FAIL} be the machine constructed for D as described above. Let Avoid be computed as defined above for A. $\mathcal{L}(A) \subseteq \mathcal{L}(D)^{\text{Inv}}$ iff no state reachable from q_0 under δ is in Avoid.*

Proof

1. Assume $\mathcal{L}(A) \subseteq \mathcal{L}(D)^{\text{Inv}}$. From Defn. 3 every suffix of every word accepted by A invariantly describes D. Hence there does not exist a state of A reach-

able from q_0 from which a word can be generated such that the fully minimal index assignment for S is defined for all time points in S but for which the fully minimal index assignment for all time points in T is undefined for some time point. By construction any states in Avoid cannot be reachable from q_0 so Theorem 2 holds.

2. Assume $\mathcal{L}(A) \not\subseteq \mathcal{L}(D)^{\mathrm{Inv}}$. From Defn. 3 there must exist some index i into W from which the fully minimal index assignment for S is defined for all time points in S but undefined for some time point in T. By construction the suffix of W starting at index i is accepted by M_{FAIL}. Let q_i be the state A was in when it processed index i; q_i must be in Avoid by construction. The existence of W proves that q_i is reachable from q_0 so containment is correctly determined to fail. □

Theorem 2 suggests a decision procedure. Both M_{FAIL} and the set Avoid are constructible. Any DFA can be converted into a 1-2DCM by augmenting the transitions of the DFA with a counter whose value is never changed. The intersection of two reversal-bounded 1-2DCMs is effectively constructible and is also a reversal-bounded 1-2DCM by Theorem 1. The emptiness test on the intersection machine is decidable by Theorem 1.

We outline the decision procedure for the iterative semantics via an example. The set Avoid is also used in deciding containment under the iterative semantics. However the procedure for the iterative semantics is harder because the existence of a reachable state of A from which a word in M_{FAIL} is generated is not sufficient. The iterative semantics only starts a test in an index if the previous test ended in the preceding index. The decision procedure therefore needs a way to track which states in Avoid can serve as starting states for tests under the iterative semantics. We accomplish this by constructing a second 1-2DCM called M_{EXACT} which accepts those words meeting two conditions: (1) the fully minimal index assignment constructed from the first position in the word is either undefined for some time point in S or it is defined for all time points in T; (2) the last index of the word is the index in which the subsequent index assignment search must start. The justification for the first position search is the same as it was for M_{FAIL}. The restriction on the final index of the word is necessary so that we can compose words accepted by M_{EXACT} into longer words iteratively modeled by the timing diagram.

Given DFA A that accepts by final state we use M_{EXACT} to compute a binary relation TD-Reach on the states of A such that $(q, q') \in$ TD-Reach iff $A|_{(q,q')}$ accepts some word in M_{EXACT}. Formally

$$\mathsf{TD\text{-}Reach} =_{\mathrm{def}} \{(q, q') \mid \mathcal{L}(A|_{(q,q')}) \cap \mathcal{L}(M_{\mathrm{EXACT}}) \neq \emptyset\}$$

Intuitively once TD-Reach and Avoid are computed we decide iterative description by checking whether there exists a state q of A such that q is in Avoid and (q_0, q) is in the transitive closure of TD-Reach. The language of A models $\langle T, S, X \rangle$ iteratively iff no such state exists. As examples consider the following two finite automata A_1 (left) and A_2 (right) and timing diagram T with the time point of the rising transition on a in S and nothing in X. Let $D = \langle T, S, X \rangle$.

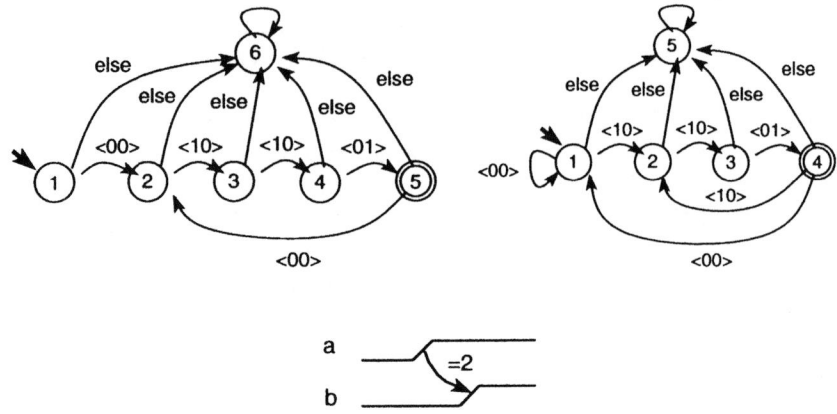

The language of D is

$$\left(\left(\left(\langle 0,1\rangle + \langle 1,0\rangle + \langle 1,1\rangle\right)^* \langle 0,0\rangle^+ \langle 1,0\rangle \langle 1,0\rangle \left(\langle 0,1\rangle + \langle 1,1\rangle\right)\right)\right)^*$$

where each pair $\langle x, y \rangle$ denotes that $a = x$ and $b = y$. Furthermore note that

$$\mathcal{L}(A_1) = \left(\langle 0,0\rangle \langle 1,0\rangle \langle 1,0\rangle \langle 0,1\rangle\right)^* \qquad \mathcal{L}(A_2) = \left(\langle 0,0\rangle^* \langle 1,0\rangle \langle 1,0\rangle \langle 0,1\rangle\right)^*$$

The language of A_1 is contained in the language of D. By definition Avoid $= \{2,3,4\}$ and TD $-$ Reach $= \{(1,5),(5,5),(1,6),(2,6),(3,6),(4,6),(5,6),(6,6)\}$. The only states accessible from the start state (1) in the closure of TD-Reach are 5 and 6. As neither of these is in Avoid $\mathcal{L}(A_1) \subseteq \mathcal{L}(D)$. The language of A_2 however is not contained in the language of D. By definition Avoid $= \{1,2,3,4\}$ and TD $-$ Reach $= \{(1,4),(4,4),(1,5),(2,5),(3,5),(4,5),(5,5)\}$. The start state is listed in Avoid indicating that $\mathcal{L}(A_2) \not\subseteq \mathcal{L}(D)$.

4 Future Work

Although we have proven that the regular containment problem is decidable for temporally unambiguous timing diagram languages we do not yet have an efficient decision procedure. Testing containment of a regular language in a 1-2DCM language lies in PSPACE. Our decidability proof relied on quadratically many such tests with respect to the number of states in the automaton for the regular language. Methods for reducing the number of containment tests required remains an important problem for future work as does the empirical analysis of the overall procedure. In addition our current restriction to temporally unambiguous timing diagrams can likely be removed by altering the construction algorithms for M_{FAIL} and M_{EXACT}.

We are also interested in the general problem of language containment for timing diagram languages. Although the results presented here could be used to test containment of a regular-language timing diagram in an arbitrary timing diagram they do not decide the general problem since arbitrary 1-2DCM have an unbounded number of states. It is possible to build a 1-2DCM that accepts the entire language rather than just a single pass of any timing diagram. Intuitively the machine is a modification of M_{EXACT} that begins a subsequent check in the appropriate index into the word after the previous check has been completed and allows the previous pass check to walk off the end of a word. Unfortunately this machine is not guaranteed to have bounded counter reversals. Results governing the undecidability of language containment for 1-2DCM with unbounded reversals are also inapplicable because there exist 1-counter non-reversal-bounded languages that cannot be captured in any timing diagram. Consider the "timing diagram"

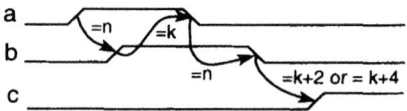

which is not well-formed in our syntax due to the disjunction in the time-bound expression. Although no well-formed timing diagram has exactly the same language as this one a 1-2DCM could be constructed to accept the language of this diagram using techniques similar to those used in constructing M_{FAIL} and M_{EXACT}. Therefore the undecidability of language containment for 1-counter non-reversal bounded languages does not prove the undecidability of containment for timing diagram languages. We are investigating this general problem as well as possible syntactic characterizations of general timing diagram language containment.

5 Conclusions

This paper has established that the regular containment problem is decidable for any temporally unambiguous timing diagram language regardless of where it falls in the Chomsky hierarchy. This result holds for both finite regular languages and infinite regular languages accepted by Büchi automata. We see two main implications of this result. First there is the practical implication that certain non-regular language properties are amenable to algorithmic verification against finite-state systems; an implementation of these ideas would extend the scope of algorithmic verification as existing logics such as LTL express only regular language properties.

The second implication is more foundational in nature. The formal methods community has largely treated diagrams as interface tools. Diagrammatic representations certainly have advantages in this regard as evidenced by their popularity. Unfortunately the interface approach to diagrams has lead us to focus more on how diagrams can be used to represent existing sentential logics rather than on the computational models suggested by the diagrams in their own right. This work establishes that the structure naturally imposed by diagrammatic representations also offers advantages on a theoretical level thus making diagrammatic representations worthy of investigation outside of the realm of interface design.

Acknowledgements

The author thanks Moshe Vardi and the anonymous reviewers for their helpful comments on this paper.

References

1. Rajeev Alur Thomas A. Henzinger and Moshe Y. Vardi. Parametric real-time reasoning. In *Proc. of the 25th ACM Symposium on the Theory of Computing* pages 592–601 1993.
2. Bachi Berkane Simona Gandrabur and Eduard Cerny. Timing diagrams: semantics and timing analysis. LASSO Laboratory University of Montreal 1996.
3. J.A. Brzozowski T. Gahlinger and F. Mavaddat. Consistency and satisfiability of waveform timing specifications. *Networks* **21**:91–107 1991.
4. E. Cerny and K. Khordoc. Interface specifications with conjunctive timing constraints: realizability and compatibility. In *Second AMAST Workshop on Real-Time Systems* June 1995.
5. Kathryn Fisler. *A Unified Approach to Hardware Verification Through a Heterogeneous Logic of Design Diagrams.* PhD thesis Indiana University August 1996.
6. Werner Grass *et al.* Transformation of timing diagram specifications into VHDL code. In *Proc. of Computer Hardware Description Languages and Their Applications* pages 659–668 August 1995.
7. Oscar H. Ibarra. Reversal-bounded multicounter machines and their decision problems. *Journal of the ACM* 25(1):116–133 January 1978.
8. Oscar H. Ibarra Tao Jiang Nicholas Tran and Hui Wang. New decidability results concerning two-way counter machines and applications. In *Proc. of the 20th International Colloquium on Automata Languages and Programming* 1993. Lecture Notes in Computer Science 700.
9. K. Khordoc M. Dufresne E. Cerny P. A. Babkine and A. Silburt. Integrating behavior and timing in executable specifications. In *Proc. of Computer Hardware Description Languages and their Applications* pages 385–402 April 1993.
10. Philippe Mooeschler Hans Peter Amann and Pausto Pellandini. High-level modeling using extended timing diagrams. In *Proc. of the European Design Automation Conference* pages 494–499 1993.
11. Rainer Schlör. A prover for VHDL-based hardware design. In *Proc. of Computer Hardware Description Languages and Their Applications* August 1995.

An Improved Reachability Analysis Method for Strongly Linear Hybrid Systems (Extended Abstract)

Bernard Boigelot*, Louis Bronne* and Stéphane Rassart

Université de Liège
Institut Montefiore, B28
B-4000 Liège Sart-Tilman, Belgium
{boigelot,bronne,rassart}@montefiore.ulg.ac.be

Abstract. This paper addresses the exact computation of the set of reachable states of a strongly linear hybrid system. It proposes an approach that is an extension of classical state-space exploration. This approach uses a new operation, based on a cycle analysis in the control graph of the system, for generating sets of reachable states, as well as a powerful representation system for sets of values. The method broadens the range of hybrid systems for which a finite and exact representation of the set of reachable states can be computed. In particular, the state-space exploration may be performed even if the set of variable values reachable at a given control location cannot be expressed as a finite union of convex regions. The technique is illustrated on a very simple example.

1 Introduction

Hybrid systems are dynamical systems whose variables change both discretely and continuously over time, which makes them well-suited for modeling real-life systems such as embedded controllers and clocked systems. Techniques have been developed for analyzing various properties of hybrid systems [ACHH93, HH94, HNSY94, ACH⁺95, LPY95, Hen96], and some of them have been implemented as tools such as HyTech [HH95, HHWT95a, HHWT95b], Kronos [DOTY96, DY95, MY96], and UP-PAAL [BLL⁺95]. All the current analysis methods are based on symbolic state-space exploration. Thanks to various search strategies and approximations, a wide range of properties can be decided or semi-decided for some restricted classes of hybrid systems [KPSY92, ACD93, AD94, HKPV95, AHH96].

This paper deals with exact reachability analysis of hybrid systems, i.e., computing an exact and finite representation of their set of reachable states. We restrict our study to strongly linear hybrid systems, which are systems whose discrete variable changes are linear, and whose continuous variable changes obey constant-slope laws. Reachability analysis is traditionally done by performing a search in the state space of the system, while representing sets of reachable states with the help of some symbolic representation system. The usual representation consists of a finite set of

* "Aspirants" (Research Assistants) for the National Fund for Scientific Research (Belgium)

pairs (control location, region), where a region is a convex set of variable values bounded by conjunctive linear constraints. Regions are themselves represented by formulas expressed in some simple arithmetic, or specific mathematical objects such as convex polyhedra. This approach suffers from a major drawback: the exploration algorithm never terminates for systems whose reachable part of the state space cannot be expressed as a finite set of pairs (control location, region). There are however numerous examples of such systems which seem to be analyzable without resorting to approximation techniques, in spite of the fact that the general reachability problem is undecidable for the whole class of strongly linear hybrid systems.

In Section 3, we show how the classical state-space search algorithm can be improved in order to be able to analyze systems with an infinite number of reachable regions. Although our improved algorithm does not always terminate, which is not surprising since it addresses an undecidable problem, it makes it possible to broaden the class of systems for which an exact reachability analysis is possible. In particular, our analysis method is not limited to systems for which every reachable state is reachable by an exploration path of bounded length. Our technique relies on a powerful representation system for sets of values, the *Real Vector Automaton (RVA)*, which is described in Section 4. The technique is illustrated on a very simple example in Section 5.

2 Hybrid Systems

A hybrid system is a dynamical system with discrete and continuous components. It is modeled by a *hybrid automaton*, which consists of a finite-state automaton associated to a set of real variables. The control locations of a hybrid automaton are labeled with *evolution laws* (differential equations) that govern the continuous change of the variables with time, as well as with *invariant conditions* that must hold when the control resides in that location. The transitions of a hybrid automaton are labeled with *guarded assignments*. A transition is *enabled* when the values of the variables satisfy the guard. Following an enabled transition modifies the values of the variables according to the assignment labeling the transition.

In this paper, we restrict ourselves to *strongly linear hybrid systems*, which are hybrid systems with particular restrictions on their evolution laws, invariant conditions, and guarded assignments. A strongly linear hybrid system is composed of the following elements:

- A finite set C of *control locations*.
- A vector $\mathbf{x} = (x_1, \ldots, x_n) \in \mathbf{R}^n$ of *variables*.
- An *initial location* $c_0 \in C$ and an *initial variable value* $\mathbf{x}_0 \in \mathbf{Z}^n$.
- A labeling function *inv* that assigns to each control location $c \in C$ an *invariant condition* $inv(c)$, which is a predicate over the domain $\mathbf{R}^n$ of the variables. Invariant conditions of strongly linear hybrid systems are of the form $P\mathbf{x} \leq \mathbf{q}$, where $P \in \mathbf{Z}^{m \times n}$ and $\mathbf{q} \in \mathbf{Z}^m (m \geq 0)$.
- A labeling function *eq* that assigns to each control location $c \in C$ a *control law* $eq(c)$, which consists of a differential equation involving the variables. Control laws of strongly linear hybrid systems are of the form $\dot{\mathbf{x}} = \mathbf{d}$, where $\mathbf{d} =$

$(d_1, \ldots, d_n) \in \mathbf{Z}^n$ contains the rates $d_1, \ldots, d_n$ according to which the variables $x_1, \ldots, x_n$ change with time. The vector $\mathbf{d}$ of rates associated to c is denoted $rates(c)$.

- A finite set T of *transitions*. Each transition is a triple (c, a, c'), where $c, c' \in C$ are respectively *source* and *target* locations, and a is a *guarded assignment*. Guarded assignments of strongly linear hybrid systems are of the form $P\mathbf{x} \leq \mathbf{q} \rightarrow \mathbf{x} := A\mathbf{x} + \mathbf{b}$, with $P \in \mathbf{Z}^{m \times n}$, $\mathbf{q} \in \mathbf{Z}^m$ $(m \geq 0)$, $A \in \mathbf{Z}^{n \times n}$, and $\mathbf{b} \in \mathbf{Z}^n$. The guard $P\mathbf{x} \leq \mathbf{q}$ and the assignment $\mathbf{x} := A\mathbf{x} + \mathbf{b}$ of a are respectively denoted by $guard(a)$ and $assgn(a)$.

A *state* of a strongly linear hybrid system is a pair $(c, \mathbf{v})$, where c is a control location and $\mathbf{v}$ is a value for the variables. The state of the system can change in two ways:

- A time delay can modify the value of the variables according to the control law of the current control location, without changing this location. Let $c \in C$ be a control location and $\mathbf{v}, \mathbf{v}' \in \mathbf{R}^n$ be variable values. The state $s' = (c, \mathbf{v}')$ is a *time-step* successor of the state $s = (c, \mathbf{v})$, which we note $s \rightarrow_{ti} s'$, if there exists $t \in \mathbf{R}^+$ such that $\mathbf{v}' = \mathbf{v} + t.rates(c)$ and both $\mathbf{v}$ and $\mathbf{v}'$ satisfy the invariant condition $inv(c)$.
- Following a transition can change the control location and modify the values of the variables according to the guarded assignment of the transition. If $(c, a, c') \in T$ is a transition and $\mathbf{v}, \mathbf{v}' \in \mathbf{R}^n$ are variable values, then the state $s' = (c', \mathbf{v}')$ is a *transition-step* successor of the state $s = (c, \mathbf{v})$, which we note $s \rightarrow_{tr} s'$, if $guard(a)$ is satisfied by $\mathbf{v}$ and $assgn(a)$ transforms $\mathbf{v}$ into $\mathbf{v}'$.

Consider two states s and s'. We say that s' is a *step-successor* of s, which we note $s \rightarrow_s s'$, if either we have $s \rightarrow_{ti} s'$, or there exists $s'' \in C \times \mathbf{R}^n$ such that $s \rightarrow_{ti} s''$ and $s'' \rightarrow_{tr} s$. Let $\rightarrow_s^*$ denote the transitive closure of the relation $\rightarrow_s$. The state s' is said to be *reachable* from the state s if we have $s \rightarrow_s^* s'$. A *reachable state* is a state that is reachable from the initial state $(c_0, \mathbf{v}_0)$.

3 Reachability Analysis

3.1 Principles

In this section, we address the problem of computing an exact and finite representation of the set of reachable states of a strongly linear hybrid system. The classical method consists of performing a state-space exploration of the system, starting from a set containing only the initial state and spreading reachability information along control locations and transitions until a stable set is obtained. Reachability information is propagated by executing time-step and transition-step operations from the current set of reachable states. Stabilization is detected by testing if the current set is included in the union of the sets obtained at previous steps. Various search strategies [Eve79] can be used for the exploration (depth-first, breadth-first, ...).

A time-step operation may generate an infinite number of reachable states from a finite number of them. It follows that state-space exploration techniques require

a symbolic representation system for the sets of states that have to be manipulated. Traditionally, sets of states are represented with the help of *regions*, which,
for strongly linear hybrid systems, are sets of variable values bounded by conjunctive linear constraints. The idea is to represent a set of states by associating to each
control location a finite number of regions corresponding to the variable values that
are reachable at that location. Regions are themselves represented by mathematical
formulas, or by specific objects such as convex polyhedra. For strongly linear hybrid systems, there exist simple algorithms for computing the effect of time-step and
transition-step operations on a set of states represented by a pair (control location,
region).

A major drawback of this approach is that state-space exploration will not terminate if there are reachable states that cannot be reached from the initial state by a
bounded sequence of time-step and transition-step operations. In particular, this happens when the set of reachable values at some control location cannot be expressed
as a finite union of convex regions. An example of such a system is given at Figure 1.
Its set of reachable states is given at Figure 2 (solid and dashed lines respectively
correspond to values that are reachable at control locations c_0 and c_1).

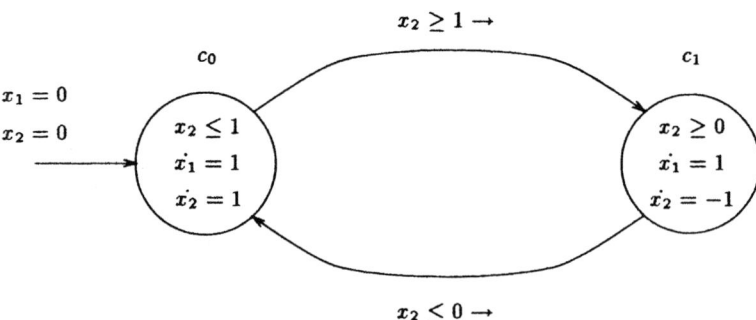

Fig. 1. Example of strongly linear hybrid system.

Let us show how to extend the classical state-space exploration algorithm such
as to be able to analyze systems with an infinite number of reachable regions. The
main idea, inspired by [BW94] and [BG96], consists of adding a *cycle-step* operation,
whose purpose is to capture discrete periodicity. Specifically, given a cycle in the
control graph of a hybrid automaton, a cycle-step operation is able to generate all
the variable values that could be obtained by performing an unbounded number of
times the sequence of time-step and transition-step operations corresponding to the
cycle. This makes it possible to generate an infinite number of convex regions in a
finite number of steps. As a consequence, cycle-step operations may generate sets
of states that are not representable by a finite set of pairs (control location, convex
region). It follows that a more powerful representation system is needed. Such a
system will be described in Section 4.

171

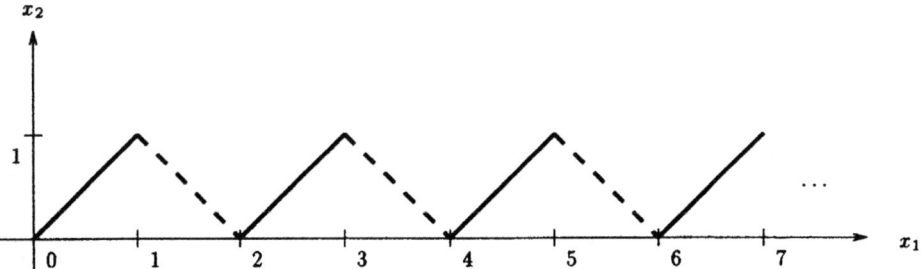

Fig. 2. Reachable states.

3.2 Cycle-step Operations

Let $C = (c_1, a_1, c_2), (c_2, a_2, c_3), \ldots, (c_{k-1}, a_{k-1}, c_k), (c_k, a_k, c_1)$ be a cycle of transitions. This cycle is said to be *composable* if for all $1 \leq i \leq k$, the conjunction $inv(c_i) \wedge guard(a_i)$ is a predicate of the form $\mathbf{p}_i.\mathbf{x} = q_i$, with $\mathbf{p}_i \in \mathbf{Z}^n$, $q_i \in \mathbf{Z}$, and $\mathbf{p}_i.rates(c_i) \neq 0$. Intuitively, a cycle is composable if for every visited control location and values of the variables at this location, there is exactly one amount of time one can spend at the location that allows to follow the next transition. Determining whether a cycle is composable can be performed by a simple algorithmic check.

Composable cycles have a nice property. If C is composable, then there exists a guarded assignment $a \equiv P\mathbf{x} \leq \mathbf{q} \to \mathbf{x} := A\mathbf{x} + \mathbf{b}$, with $P \in \mathbf{Z}^{m \times n}$, $\mathbf{q} \in \mathbf{Z}^m$ ($m \geq 0$), $A \in \mathbf{Q}^{n \times n}$ and $\mathbf{b} \in \mathbf{Q}^n$, whose effect is equivalent to following C. In other words, executing a from a given set of variable values would yield the same result as performing a time step at the location c_1, followed by a transition step along (c_1, a_1, c_2), then a time step at c_2, and so on until the transition step associated to the last transition (c_k, a_k, c_1) of the cycle. There is a simple algorithm for computing the equivalent guarded command of a composable cycle. It proceeds by first expressing at each control location the only possible time delay at this location as a linear function of the variables, and then by composing the linear transformations undergone by the variables at the control locations and transitions visited by the cycle.

Definition 1 *Let $a \equiv P\mathbf{x} \leq \mathbf{q} \to \mathbf{x} := A\mathbf{x} + \mathbf{b}$ be the equivalent guarded assignment of some composable cycle C, and $r > 1$ be an integer. The guarded assignment a is said to be* iterable *in base r if there exist $p \in \mathbf{N}_0$ and $m \in \mathbf{N}$ such that the matrix A^p is diagonalizable, and all its eigenvalues belong to $\{0, r^m\}$.*

Iterable guarded assignments have two important properties. First, one can algorithmically check for iterability:

Theorem 2. *There is a decision procedure, based on simple integer arithmetic, for checking whether a guarded assignment is iterable or not.*

Proof The algorithm is left for the full paper. □

Second, one can compute the image of a set of values by the transitive closure of an iterable guarded assignment:

Theorem 3. *There exists a representation system for sets of variable values, such that:*

- *Any finite union of convex regions can be represented.*
- *For every guarded assignment a and represented set V of values, one can compute a representation of the image $V' = a^*(V)$ of V by the transitive closure of a (in other words, V' contains the values obtained by executing repeatedly a any number of times from elements of V).*

Proof A suitable representation system is described in Section 4. The proof that $a^*(V)$ is computable on represented sets is left for the full paper. $\square$

The classical state-space exploration algorithm is extended in the following way. Given a composable cycle $\mathcal{C} = (c_1, a_1, c_2), \ldots, (c_k, a_k, c_1)$ such that its equivalent guarded assignment a is iterable, we simply add to the set of transitions of the system a *meta-transition* (c_1, a^*, c_1), whose effect is to transform a set of values $V \subseteq \mathbf{R}^n$ into $a^*(V)$ without changing the control location c_1. Performing a *cycle-step* operation simply consists of executing a meta-transition. We do not impose an exploration order; however, a breadth-first search will always reach a stable set whenever there is a search order that reaches such a set. Since cycle-step operations generate all the values that could be produced by following repeatedly their underlying cycle, they do not influence the result of a state-space exploration if it terminates. However, they may force the search to terminate, or lower dramatically the number of exploration steps needed before stabilization occurs.

4 Real Vector Automata

In this section, we describe a symbolic representation system well suited to the sets of values that are manipulated by the improved reachability analysis method described in the previous section. The requirements on this system are linked to the operations that are performed during the analysis. Specifically, the representation system has to be able to represent single vectors of integers (such as the set of initial variable values) as well as convex regions. It must be closed over time-step, transition-step, cycle-step, and elementary set-theory operations (union, intersection, ...), and allow an easy computation of their effect on represented sets. Moreover, inclusion of represented sets must be decidable.

4.1 Principles and Definitions

The main idea, inspired by [WB95] and [BG96], consists of representing a set of values by a finite-state automaton accepting encodings of those values as strings of symbols over some alphabet. Since we deal here with sets of vectors with real components, the first step is thus to give an encoding scheme for such vectors.

Let $x \in \mathbf{R}$ be a real number and $r > 1$ be an integer. We encode x in base r, most significant digit first, using r's complement for negative numbers. The result is a word of the form $w = w_i.w_f$, where w_i encodes the integer part of x as a finite word over the alphabet $\{0, \ldots, r-1\}$, the symbol "." is a separator, and w_f encodes the fractional part of x as a infinite word over the alphabet $\{0,\ldots,r-1\}$. We do not fix the length p of w_i, but only require it to be such that $-r^{p-1}-1 \le x \le r^{p-1}+1$. Hence, the most significant digit of a number will be "0" if and only if this number is positive. For simplicity, we require the length of w_f to be infinite (this is not a severe restriction, since an infinite number of "0" symbols can always be appended harmlessly to w_f). The encoding w of x is thus an infinite word over the alphabet $\{0,\ldots,r-1,.\}$. We define its *integer-part length* $|w|_i$ as the number of symbols in w_i. It is noteworthy to remark that for some $x \in \mathbf{R}$ and $p \in \mathbf{N}$, there exist two encodings of x of integer-part length p. For instance, choosing $r = 10$, $x = 11/2$ and $p = 3$ yields the two words $005.5(0)^\omega$ and $005.4(9)^\omega$. Such encodings are said to be *dual*.

To encode a vector of real numbers, we encode each of its components with words of identical integer-part length. This length can be chosen arbitrarily, provided that is sufficient for encoding the vector component with the highest magnitude. It follows that any vector has an infinite number of possible encodings. An encoding of a vector of reals $\mathbf{x} = (x_1,\ldots,x_n)$ can indifferently be viewed either as a tuple $(w_1,\ldots,w_n)$ of words of identical integer-part length over the alphabet $\{0,\ldots,r-1,.\}$, or as a single word w over the alphabet $\{0,\ldots,r-1\}^n \cup \{.\}$.

Since a real vector has several possible encodings, we have to choose which of these the automata we define will recognize. A natural choice is to accept all encodings. This leads to the following definition.

Definition 4 *Let $n \ge 0$ and $r > 1$ be integers. A* Real Vector Automaton (RVA) $\mathcal{A}$ *in base r for vectors in $\mathbf{R}^n$ is a Büchi automaton [Büc62] over the alphabet $\{0,\ldots,r-1\}^n \cup \{.\}$, such that:*

- *Every word w accepted by $\mathcal{A}$ is of the form $w = w_i.w_f$, with $w_i \in (\{0,\ldots,r-1\}^n)^*$ and $w_f \in (\{0,\ldots,r-1\}^n)^\omega$.*
- *For every vector $\mathbf{x} \in \mathbf{R}$, $\mathcal{A}$ accepts either all the encodings of $\mathbf{x}$ in base r, or none of them.*

A RVA is said to *represent* the set of vectors encoded by the words belonging to its accepted language. Remark that the representation is not canonical, for different Büchi automata may accept the same language.

4.2 Elementary RVA

RVA representing sets of real vectors satisfying elementary predicates are easy to obtain. We have the following result.

Theorem 5. *Let $n \ge 0$ and $r > 1$ be integers. There exist RVA for representing in base r the sets:*

- $\mathbf{Z}^n$;
- $\{\mathbf{v}\}$, *for any $\mathbf{v} \in \mathbf{Q}^n$;*
- $\{(x_1,x_2) \in \mathbf{R}^2 \mid x_1\theta x_2\}$, *for any $\theta \in \{=,\ne,<,>,\le,\ge\}$;*
- $\{(x_1,x_2,x_3) \in \mathbf{R}^3 \mid x_1+x_2 = x_3\}$.

Proof The RVA will be given in the full paper. □

4.3 Elementary Operations on RVA

We consider operations on sets of real vectors and study their implementation by operations on the RVA representing those sets. We have the following result.

Theorem 6. *Let $r > 1$ and $m \geq 0$ be integers, V_1, V_2 be sets of real vectors of respective arities (number of components per vector) n_1 and n_2, and A_1, A_2 be RVA representing respectively V_1 and V_2. There exist algorithms for computing RVA representing:*

- *The union $V_1 \cup V_2$ and intersection $V_1 \cap V_2$, provided that $n_1 = n_2$;*
- *The complement $\overline{V_1}$;*
- *The Cartesian product $V_1 \times V_2 = \{(\mathbf{x}_1, \mathbf{x}_2) \mid \mathbf{x}_1 \in V_1 \wedge \mathbf{x}_2 \in V_2\}$;*
- *The projection $\exists x_i V_1 = \{(x_1, \ldots, x_{i-1}, x_{i+1}, \ldots, x_{n_1}) \mid (\exists x_i)(x_1, \ldots, x_{n_1}) \in V_1\}$;*
- *The reordering $\pi V_1 = \{(x_{\pi(1)}, \ldots, x_{\pi(n_1)}) \mid (x_1, \ldots, x_{n_1}) \in V_1\}$, where π is a permutation of $\{1, \ldots, n_1\}$;*
- *The expansion $expand(V_1, m) = \{r^{mk}\mathbf{x} \mid \mathbf{x} \in V_1 \wedge k \in \mathbf{N}\}$.*

Moreover, there are algorithms for deciding if V_1 is empty, and if $V_1 \subseteq V_2$.

Proof The algorithms are left for the full paper.   □

An important consequence of this result and those of the previous section is that any set of real vectors definable in the structure $\langle \mathbf{R}, +, \leq, Z \rangle$, where Z is the predicate defined as

$$Z(x) \equiv \begin{cases} \text{True if } x \in \mathbf{Z} \\ \text{False if } x \in \mathbf{R} \setminus \mathbf{Z} \end{cases}$$

is representable by a RVA (in any base). Moreover, any set operation expressed in the structure $\langle \mathbf{R}, +, \leq, Z \rangle$ is computable on RVA. Remark that the reciprocal is not true, since the expansion operation is not definable in $\langle \mathbf{R}, +, \leq, Z \rangle$. A similar result appears in [Büc62].

4.4 Performing Step Operations with RVA

Using RVA in the context of our improved reachability analysis method as described in Section 3 requires to be able to perform time-step, transition-step, and cycle-step operations on sets of states represented by a finite union of pairs (control location, RVA). This can be done thanks to the following result:

Theorem 7. *Let $c \in C$ be a control location and $V \subseteq \mathbf{R}^n$ be a set of variable values represented by a RVA $\mathcal{A}$.*

- *One can compute a RVA representing the result*

$$\{\mathbf{v}' \mid (\exists \mathbf{v} \in V, t \in \mathbf{R}^+)(\mathbf{v}' = \mathbf{v} + t.\text{rates}(c) \wedge \text{inv}(c)(\mathbf{v}) \wedge \text{inv}(c)(\mathbf{v}'))\}$$

of a time-step operation performed at c.
- *Let $t = (c, a, c')$ be a transition. One can compute a RVA representing the result $a(V)$ of a transition-step operation performed along t.*

- *Let $m = (c, a^*, c')$ be a meta-transition. One can compute a RVA representing the result $a^*(V)$ of a cycle-step operation performed along m, provided that a is iterable in the base r of A.*

Proof The idea is to express the results in terms of the elementary sets and operations concerned by Theorems 5 and 6. The complete proof is left for the full paper.

□

5   Example of Use

Let us show how the improved reachability analysis method presented in Section 3 can be applied to the very simple system depicted at Figure 1.

The first step consists of adding meta-transitions. The hybrid automaton contains the cycle $C = (c_0, a_0, c_1), (c_1, a_1, c_0)$, with $a_0 \equiv x_2 \geq 1$ and $a_1 \equiv x_2 \leq 0$. This cycle is composable. Indeed, $(x_2 \leq 1 \wedge x_2 \geq 1) \equiv (x_2 = 1)$ and $(x_2 \geq 0 \wedge x_2 \leq 0) \equiv (x_2 = 0)$ have both the form $\mathbf{p}_i.\mathbf{x} = q_i$, $i = 0, 1$, where each $\mathbf{p}_i$ is such that $\mathbf{p}_i.rates(c_i) \neq 0$. Since C is composable, there exists a guarded assignment a whose effect is equivalent to following C. In order to compute the components of a, we express at each control location the (unique) time delay that can be spent there as a linear function of the variables. If one spends the time t_0 at location c_0, the evolution law will cause the variable values to undergo the transformation

$$\begin{bmatrix} x_1 \\ x_2 \end{bmatrix} := \begin{bmatrix} x_1 \\ x_2 \end{bmatrix} + t_0 \begin{bmatrix} 1 \\ 1 \end{bmatrix}. \tag{1}$$

Since the result of this transformation must satisfy the output condition $x_2 = 1$, we obtain $t_0 = 1 - x_2$. Replacing this value in (1), we obtain that the effect of a time-step operation at c_0 is equivalent to the guarded assignment

$$a_{c_0} \equiv x_2 \leq 1 \rightarrow \begin{bmatrix} x_1 \\ x_2 \end{bmatrix} := \begin{bmatrix} x_1 + 1 - x_2 \\ 1 \end{bmatrix}.$$

Similarly, one obtains for the control location c_1 the guarded assignment

$$a_{c_1} \equiv x_2 \geq 0 \rightarrow \begin{bmatrix} x_1 \\ x_2 \end{bmatrix} := \begin{bmatrix} x_1 + x_2 \\ 0 \end{bmatrix}.$$

Finally, the sequential composition of a_{c_0}, a_0, a_{c_1} and a_1 yields the guarded assignment

$$a \equiv x_2 \leq 1 \rightarrow \begin{bmatrix} x_1 \\ x_2 \end{bmatrix} := \begin{bmatrix} x_1 - x_2 + 2 \\ 0 \end{bmatrix},$$

which therefore captures the effect of C. The last expression can be rewritten in the canonical form $P\mathbf{x} \leq \mathbf{q} \rightarrow \mathbf{x} := A\mathbf{x} + \mathbf{b}$:

$$a \equiv \begin{bmatrix} 0 & 1 \end{bmatrix} \begin{bmatrix} x_1 \\ x_2 \end{bmatrix} \leq 1 \rightarrow \begin{bmatrix} x_1 \\ x_2 \end{bmatrix} := \begin{bmatrix} 1 & -1 \\ 0 & 0 \end{bmatrix} \begin{bmatrix} x_1 \\ x_2 \end{bmatrix} + \begin{bmatrix} 2 \\ 0 \end{bmatrix}.$$

Since A is diagonalizable and has the eigenvalues 0 and 1, the guarded assignment a is iterable (in any base). We can therefore add the meta-transition (c_0, a^*, c_0) to the system.

We are now ready for exploring the state space of the system. Let us simply show that there exists a single exploration path of finite length that visits all the reachable states (the existence of such a path implies that a breadth-first search would terminate at a depth less or equal to the length of the path). The results are given at Figure 3. For clarity, each computed set of states is prefixed by the operation that produced it, and is expressed as a pair (control location, set of values). In the actual computation, the sets of variable values are represented by RVA.

(initial set of states) $S_0 = (c_0, \{(0,0)\})$
(cycle step, (c_0, a^*, c_0)) $S_1 = (c_0, \{(2\lambda, 0) \mid \lambda \in \mathbf{N}\})$
(time step, c_0) $S_2 = (c_0, \{(2\lambda + \delta, \delta) \mid \lambda \in \mathbf{N} \wedge 0 \leq \delta \leq 1\})$
(transition step, (c_0, a_0, c_1)) $S_3 = (c_1, \{(2\lambda + 1, 1) \mid \lambda \in \mathbf{N}\})$
(time step, c_1) $S_4 = (c_1, \{(2\lambda + 1 + \delta, 1 - \delta) \mid \lambda \in \mathbf{N} \wedge 0 \leq \delta \leq 1\})$
(transition step, (c_1, a_1, c_0)) $S_5 = (c_0, \{(2\lambda + 2, 0) \mid \lambda \in \mathbf{N}\}) \subseteq S_1$

Fig. 3. State-space exploration path.

6   Conclusions and Comparison with Other Work

We give an algorithm for computing an exact and finite representation of the set of reachable states of a strongly linear hybrid system. Our algorithm can be seen as a strict extension of existing methods [HNSY94, ACH+95, Hen96], which are based on state-space exploration. The improvement consists of a new operation for generating sets of reachable states, that is based on a cycle analysis in the control graph of the system, combined with an original representation system for sets of variable values. Our algorithm considerably broadens the class of systems for which an exact reachability analysis is possible. In particular, it is not limited to systems such that the set of reachable values at each control location can be expressed as a finite union of convex regions. When it terminates, our algorithm allows to decide properties such as reachability of isolated states, or reachability of sets of states expressed as a finite union of pairs (control location, set of values defined in the structure $\langle \mathbf{R}, +, \leq, Z \rangle$).

Of course, since reachability of a given state is undecidable for strongly linear hybrid systems [HKPV95], our algorithm does not necessarily terminate. From a theoretical point of view, this might seem unsatisfactory, but from a practical point of view, this is not at all troublesome. Indeed, our algorithm always terminates whenever existing techniques succeed in producing an exact representation of the reachable part of the state space, and may give out an exact answer when traditional algorithms must resort to approximations methods [HH94]. Moreover, it may produce a faster result for systems having a finite but large number of reachable regions.

Expressing sets of real vectors as finite automata is a very old idea [Büc62], which has originally been introduced as a tool for establishing decidability results in arithmetic. However, the use of finite automata as actual representations of sets of real vectors is original, and generalizes previous results [WB95, BG96] which were obtained for very different systems. The idea of using meta-transitions for speeding up reachability analysis was proposed in [BW94, BG96]. Interesting future work will be to generalize to hybrid systems ongoing work concerning symbolic exploration with meta-transitions (for instance, analyzing a larger class of properties than plain reachability). Another interesting subject will be to study the complexity and practical usefulness of the manipulation algorithms for RVA discussed in Section 4, and evaluating the benefits of the overall method on an actual implementation.

7 Acknowledgments

We wish to thank Pierre Wolper for helpful comments on a preliminary version of this paper.

References

[ACD93]   R. Alur, C. Courcoubetis, and D. Dill. Model-checking in dense real-time. *Information and Computation*, 104(1):2–34, May 1993.

[ACH+95]   R. Alur, C. Courcoubetis, N. Halbwachs, T. A. Henzinger, P.-H. Ho, X. Nicollin, A. Olivero, J. Sifakis, and S. Yovine. The algorithmic analysis of hybrid systems. *Theoretical Computer Science*, 138(1):3–34, 6 February 1995.

[ACHH93]   R. Alur, C. Courcoubetis, T.A. Henzinger, and P.-H. Ho. Hybrid automata: an algorithmic approach to the specification and verification of hybrid systems. In R.L. Grossman, A. Nerode, A.P. Ravn, and H. Rischel, editors, *Hybrid Systems I*, volume 736 of *Lecture Notes in Computer Science*, pages 209–229. Springer-Verlag, 1993.

[AD94]   R. Alur and D. L. Dill. A theory of timed automata. *Theoretical Computer Science*, 126(2):183–235, 25 April 1994. Fundamental Study.

[AHH96]   R. Alur, T.A. Henzinger, and P.-H. Ho. Automatic symbolic verification of embedded systems. *IEEE Transactions on Software Engineering*, 22(3):181–201, 1996.

[BG96]   B. Boigelot and P. Godefroid. Symbolic verification of communication protocols with infinite state spaces using QDDs. In *Proc. Computer Aided Verification*, volume 1102 of *Lecture Notes in Computer Science*, pages 1–12, New-Brunswick, NJ, USA, July 1996. Springer-Verlag.

[BLL+95]   J. Bengtsson, K. G. Larsen, F. Larsson, P. Pettersson, and W. Yi. UPPAAL - a tool suite for automatic verification of real-time systems. In *Proceedings of the 4th DIMACS Workshop on Verification and Control of Hybrid Systems*, New Brunswick, New Jersey, October 1995.

[Büc62]   J. R. Büchi. On a decision method in restricted second order arithmetic. In *Logic, Methodology and Philosophy of Science*, Proceedings of the 1960 International Congress, Stanford, California, 1962. Stanford Univ. Press.

178

[BW94] B. Boigelot and P. Wolper. Symbolic verification with periodic sets. In *Computer Aided Verification, Proc. 6th Int. Conference*, Stanford, California, June 1994. Lecture Notes in Computer Science, Springer-Verlag.

[DOTY96] C. Daws, A. Olivero, S. Tripakis, and S. Yovine. The tool Kronos. In *Hybrid Systems III, Verification and Control*, volume 1066 of *Lecture Notes in Computer Science*. Springer-Verlag, 1996.

[DY95] C. Daws and S. Yovine. Two examples of verification of multirate timed automata with Kronos. In *Proceedings of the 1995 IEEE Real-Time Systems Symposium*, Pisa, Italy, 1995. IEEE Computer Society Press.

[Eve79] S. Even. *Graph Algorithms*. Computer Science Press, 1979.

[Hen96] T. A. Henzinger. The theory of hybrid automata. In *Proceedings, 11th Annual IEEE Symposium on Logic in Computer Science*, pages 278–292, New Brunswick, New Jersey, 27–30 July 1996. IEEE Computer Society Press.

[HH94] T.A. Henzinger and P.-H. Ho. Model-checking strategies for linear hybrid systems. Technical Report CSD-TR-94-1437, Cornell University, 1994. Presented at the Seventh International Conference on Industrial and Engineering Applications of Artificial Intelligence and Expert Systems (Austin, TX).

[HH95] T.A. Henzinger and P.-H. Ho. HyTech: The Cornell Hybrid Technology Tool. In P. Antsaklis, A. Nerode, W. Kohn, and S. Sastry, editors, *Hybrid Systems II*, volume 999 of *Lecture Notes in Computer Science*, pages 265–293. Springer-Verlag, 1995.

[HHWT95a] T.A. Henzinger, P.-H. Ho, and H. Wong-Toi. HyTech: the next generation. In *Proceedings of the 16th Annual Real-time Systems Symposium*, pages 56–65. IEEE Computer Society Press, 1995.

[HHWT95b] T.A. Henzinger, P.-H. Ho, and H. Wong-Toi. A user guide to HyTech. In E. Brinksma, W.R. Cleaveland, K.G. Larsen, T. Margaria, and B. Steffen, editors, *TACAS 95: Tools and Algorithms for the Construction and Analysis of Systems*, volume 1019 of *Lecture Notes in Computer Science*, pages 41–71. Springer-Verlag, 1995.

[HKPV95] T.A. Henzinger, P.W. Kopke, A. Puri, and P. Varaiya. What's decidable about hybrid automata? In *Proceedings of the 27th Annual Symposium on Theory of Computing*, pages 373–382. ACM Press, 1995.

[HNSY94] T.A. Henzinger, X. Nicollin, J. Sifakis, and S. Yovine. Symbolic model checking for real-time systems. *Information and Computation*, 111(2):193–244, 1994. Special issue for LICS 92.

[KPSY92] Y. Kesten, A. Pnueli, J. Sifakis, and S. Yovine. Integration graphs: a class of decidable hybrid systems. In *Proceedings of Workshop on Theory of Hybrid Systems*, volume 736 of *Lecture Notes in Computer Science*, pages 179–208, Lyngby, Denmark, 1992. Springer-Verlag.

[LPY95] K. G. Larsen, P. Pettersson, and W. Yi. Model-checking for real-time systems. In Horst Reichel, editor, *Proceedings of the 10th International Conference on Fundamentals of Computation Theory*, volume 965 of *Lecture Notes in Computer Science*, pages 62–88, Dresden, Germany, August 1995. Springer-Verlag.

[MY96] O. Maler and S. Yovine. Hardware timing verification using Kronos. In *Proceedings of the IEEE 7th Israeli Conference on Computer Systems and Software Engineering, ICCBSSE'96*. IEEE Computer Society Press, 1996.

[WB95] P. Wolper and B. Boigelot. An automata-theoretic approach to Presburger arithmetic constraints. In *Proc. Static Analysis Symposium*, Lecture Notes in Computer Science, Glasgow, September 1995. Springer-Verlag.

Some Progress in the Symbolic Verification of Timed Automata*

Marius Bozga[1], Oded Maler[1], Amir Pnueli[2], Sergio Yovine[1]

[1] VERIMAG, Centre Equation, 2, av. de Vignate, 38610 Gières, France,
{bozga, maler, yovine} @imag.fr
[2] Dept. of Computer Science, Weizmann Inst. Rehovot 76100, Israel,
amir@wisdom.weizmann.ac.il

Abstract. In this paper we discuss the practical difficulty of analyzing the behavior of timed automata and report some results obtained using an experimental BDD-based extension of KRONOS. We have treated examples originating from timing analysis of asynchronous boolean networks and CMOS circuits with delay uncertainties and the results outperform those obtained by previous implementations of timed automata verification tools.

1 Introduction

The computational burden associated with the verification of discrete systems consists in representing and calculating the set of reachable states of a transition system, usually described as a product of small interacting systems. Timed systems were introduced in order to provide a more detailed level of modeling in which it is possible to refine a statement such as *"a is followed by b"* into *"a is followed by b within t time units"*. Timed formalisms for describing systems (timed automata [AD94], [D89], timed Petri nets [BD91], timed transition systems [HMP92a] or real-time process algebras [NS92]) and for specifying behaviors (real-time temporal logics [AH92], timed regular expressions [ACM96]) allow the intuitive expression of real-life phenomena. Among these is the hard fact that *it takes some time between the initiation and a completion of a change* and that quantitative timing information may matter in the future evolution of a system.

In fact, after playing with timed models for some time, one starts wondering about the underlying assumptions that make "classical" untimed reasoning valid and useful. What class of real-timed systems is hiding behind each and every untimed automaton? How are discrete transitions embedded in the real time axis? Without getting too much into the details one can suggest two kinds of answers:

Asynchronous answer: we assume that changes in various system components may take arbitrary amount of time to be accomplished. From this perspective

---

* This research was supported in part by the European Community projects HYBRID EC-US-043 and INTAS-94-697. VERIMAG is a joint laboratory of CNRS and UJF.

an untimed system can be viewed as a timed system with trivial $[0, \infty]$ bounds on the duration of a transition. Clearly, such an abstraction will create much more executions than a real system would.

Synchronous answer: certain assumptions are made and certain precautions are taken in order to ensure that most of the timing information can be ignored. This is the principle underlying clocked realization of sequential machines: we are not interested in the intermediate states of the next-state logic, nor whether one state variable has changed before the other. What is important is that everybody has stabilized until the next time their values are sampled.

When one is not satisfied with the type of answers suggested by the abstract untimed models or with the performance of clocked systems, timed models seem to be the next logical step (see also [BS94]). It has been shown elsewhere ([D89], [L89], [MP95]) how a very general model of non-clocked circuits with delays can be translated into timed automata, on which one can ask all sorts of interesting timing questions ([ACD93], [HNSY94] [AMP95]). The only problem with these models is the amount of time (and space) that might elapse between posing the question and obtaining the answer. Indeed, it is the performance bottleneck that prevents the transfer of timing verification technology from theory to practice. In this paper we describe some attempts to push forward the performance limitations of current timed automata verification tools by augmenting the tool KRONOS [DOTY96] with an additional BDD-based capability.

The rest of the paper is organized as follows: in Section 2 we discuss, via generic examples, the computational difficulty of timed automata analysis methods and present an alternative data-structure, NDD which is used to analyze the examples in this paper. NDDs are essentially nothing more than BDDs over the bits of discretized clocks. In Section 3 we show the performance of the NDD implementation on benchmark examples coming from asynchronous boolean networks and compare them with other implementations, while in Section 4 we apply NDDs to realistic (but small) examples of MOS circuits with up to 5 inputs and 16 transistors, in order to answer a question motivated by noise problems. We assume that the reader is familiar with the basic definitions of timed automata and with BDDs.

2 The Difficulty of Timing Analysis

Consider a system which can generate events out of a set $\mathcal{T} = \{\tau_1, \ldots, \tau_n\}$, such that every two consecutive occurrences of τ_i must be separated by l_i time units, while every occurrence of τ_i must be followed by another one within u_i units. Such a system can be modeled by the simple one-state timed automaton $\mathcal{A}$ depicted in Figure 1-a having n clocks and n transitions. Calculating the set of reachable clock configurations is needed in order to determine which $\mathcal{T}$-sequences are realizable by the system. An illustration of the calculation of the set of reachable clock configurations for $n = 2$ is given in Figure 2. At the beginning, Time progresses until it reaches the smallest lower-bound (in this case, l_1). Since then, until the first upper-bound is encountered (in this case, u_1) the transition

τ_1 can be taken while resetting C_1 to zero. After crossing the lower bound l_2, transition τ_2 can be, as well, taken, and so on. Although it might look simple for two clocks, this set can become rather complex in more dimensions!

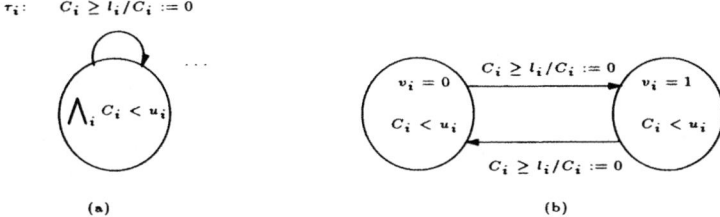

Fig. 1. (a) A one-state automaton $\mathcal{A}$ with n transitions and n clocks. (b) A two-state automaton $\mathcal{B}$ for representing a set of input signals satisfying upper and lower bounds on the distance between two switching points.

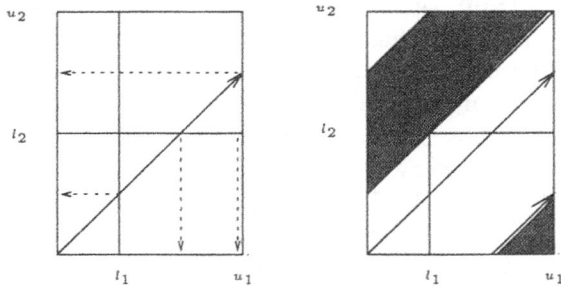

Fig. 2. The initial sets of reachable clock configurations of the automaton in Figure 1-(a) starting from $(0,0)$.

In general, the sets of reachable clock configurations obtained this way can be expressed as a union of *zones*, that is, convex polyhedra generated by half-spaces of the form $C_i < k$ or $C_i - C_j < k$ for k in some finite subset of the integers.[3] Zones admit an efficient representation using difference-bounds matrices (DBM, [D89]) on which it is easy to calculate intersection and the progress of time. As it often happens in computational geometrical problems, the difficulty comes from the need to manipulate *non-convex* sets. In this case the representation is not canonical and a lot of work is needed in order to determine whether all the reachable states have already been encountered. It may turn out, for example,

---

[3] We ignore intentionally some technicalities concerning strictness of inequalities.

that a union of zones stored in memory is, in fact, convex and can be replaced by a single zone, but testing this possibility at every iteration is costly. Some authors ([H93], [AIKY95] [B96], [WD94]) try to use various sorts of approximations, e.g. to use convex hulls instead of unions, but these over-approximations often tend to become too large and hence not useful.

The problem aggravates when the untimed state-space is non-trivial. Consider the two-state automaton $\mathcal{B}$ of Figure 1-(b). Such automaton represents a boolean input signal whose only constraint is that every two changes in its value are separated by some time $t \in [l_i, u_i)$. An array of such automata is an unavoidable component in any model for analyzing the behavior of circuits under *all possible inputs*. When two such automata work in parallel, the reachable clock configurations are "distributed" among the discrete states $\{00, 01, 10, 11\}$ as shown in Figure 3. This raises several problems: there might be a lot of redundancy if we represent reachable configurations for every state separately because two states might share zones. In addition, if we use symbolic methods ([BCM$^+$93], [McM93]) to overcome the discrete state-explosion problem, how should they be combined[4] with the DBM representation? Finally, the convergence of the set of reachable configurations into a convex zone is usually slower than in the case of a one-state automaton.

In order to overcome these problems we have devised and implemented an alternative representation scheme for sets of clock configurations, the *Numerical Decision Diagrams* (NDD, [ABK$^+$97]) and tested its performance on these and other examples. This scheme has some major advantages over DBMs (canonicity, natural combination with discrete symbolic representations) but, of course, has its own disadvantages, most notably, the sensitivity to time granularity.

The idea behind NDDs is trivial. Suppose that each clock can take values in the range $[0, k)$, and consider a *discretization* of time such that the possible clock values are $K = \{0, \ldots, k - 1\}$. Each clock can be treated as a bounded integer variable and any of its possible values can be encoded in binary using $\log k$ bits. Consequently, any subset of K^n can be viewed as a subset of $\{0, 1\}^{n \log k}$ and represented by a BDD over $n \log k$ boolean variables. Given a fixed variable ordering, this representation is canonical regardless of convexity, and it offers BDD-based boolean operations as well as the calculation of the passage of time by simple arithmetical operations.

For dense time models, two discretization schemes has been proposed in [GPV94]. They are based on taking a rational constant Δ, depending on the number of clocks such that by cutting space and time into a Δ-grid, one obtains a discrete-time automaton which is equivalent (for all interesting purposes) to the given dense-time automaton. These two schemes require $\Delta = 1/(n + 1)$ and $\Delta = (1/2n)$ respectively, and involve some distortion of the passage of time or of the reset operator in order to preserve the properties of the original dense-time system (a more detailed description appears in [GPV94] and [ABK$^+$97]).

---

[4] This problem has been addressed by Wong-Toi and Dill [WD94], who combined DBMs and BDDs and recently by Balarin [B96] who encoded matrices using BDDs. Both used the representations for *approximate* reachability analysis.

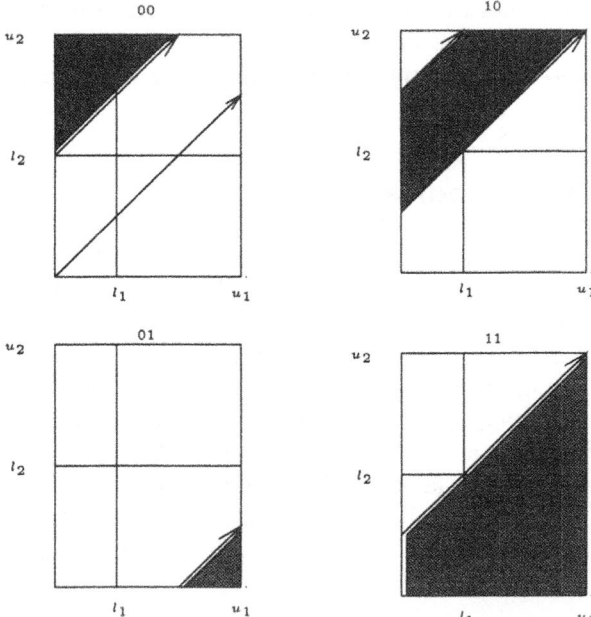

Fig. 3. The initial sets of reachable clock configurations of the automaton in Figure 1-(b) starting from the discrete state 00 and the clock configuration $(0, 0)$.

We have observed, however, that the special class of automata obtained from circuits ([MP95]), where all the clock conditions are of the form $C \geq l$ or $C < u$, admits a slightly simpler and coarser region graph (see also [HMP92]). For these automata, a discretization with $\Delta = 1/n$, where the passage of time is simply the addition of Δ to all the clocks, is sufficient.

Consequently, although all the reported experiments have been performed with respect to the discrete time interpretation, they can be viewed as if we used a dense time interpretation with all the constants divided by n. Approximations are used anyway in order to tackle the complexity of timing analysis ([AIKY95], [H93], [WD94], [B96]), and we believe that playing with the granularity of time might prove to be an alternative approximation strategy.

Note that the NDD-based method is different from calculating the region graph of the timed automaton and *then* trying to encode its transition relation using some choice of boolean state variables (see also [AK96] [CC95]). We build a *uniform discretized state-space* which happens to contain one or more concrete representative of every region, and on which the passage of time is calculated by adding a time unit Δ to every clock variable simultaneously.

We have implemented NDD-based verification algorithms for timed automata by using a system developed at VERIMAG for representing and manipulating communicating automata augmented with bounded integer variables [BFK96].

This system takes such automata and translates them into BDDs using one of several publicly-available BDD packages. We have used the CUDD package [S95] of Colorado University. The experimental results are reported in the following sections.

3   Asynchronous Boolean Circuits

With the NDD representation we were able to calculate within 12 hours all reachable states of the automaton A (Figure 1-a) with 18 clocks and transitions, while a DBM-based implementation could not treat more than 5 clocks. The relative weakness of DBM in this apparently-trivial example is due to the fact that the set of reachable configurations of this automaton converges finally to the whole clock space, by accumulating more and more zones. We were able to treat products of up to 9 B automata (Figure 1-b). The results[5] are illustrated in Figure 3. It should be noted, for the fairness of the comparison, that we have used the discrete time interpretation and have chosen clock values in the range $\{0,\ldots,15\}$ – NDDs are much more sensitive to the granularity of time than DBMs.

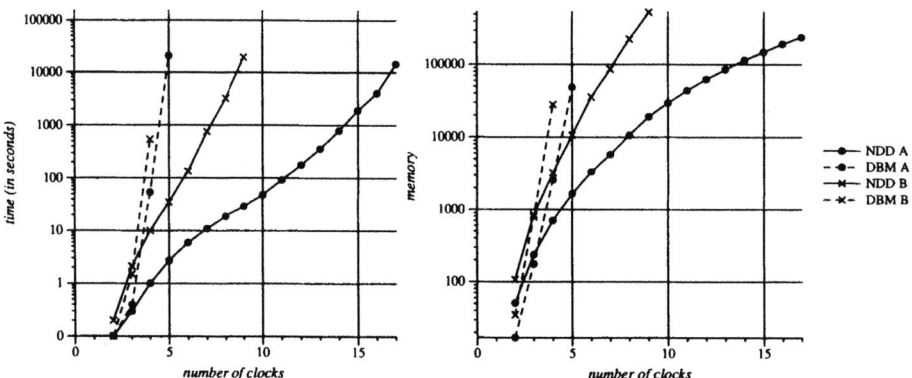

Fig. 4. Comparative performance of NDDs and DBMs for the automata A and B.

A more complicated example is the family of circuits depicted in Figure 5. For every $i \in \{0,\ldots,n-1\}$ we let the XOR of x_i and x_{i-1} pass through a non-deterministic inertial delay buffer (the exact definitions and the translation procedure from circuits to timed automata are described in [MP95]). Every such gate is modeled by the four-state timed automaton appearing in Figure 6. The states are encoded using two Boolean variables v_i and v_i, the former denoting the value observed at the exit of the delay element while the latter represents the "hidden" value of the XOR. When both variables are equal we say that the state is *stable* and that it is *excited* otherwise.

---

[5] Unless otherwise stated, all the results reported here were obtained using a SUN Ultra-Sparc 1 with 256MB of memory.

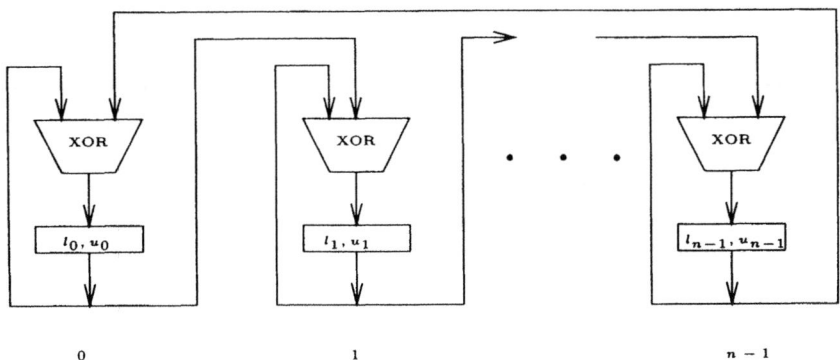

Fig. 5. A cascade of XOR gates with delays.

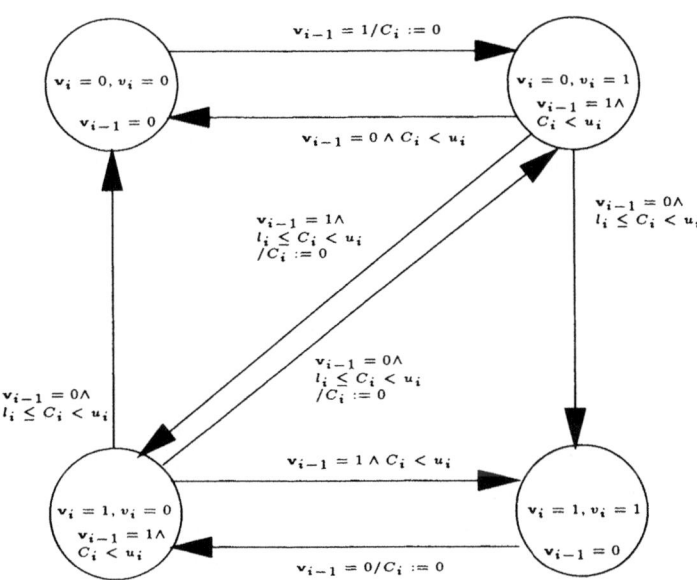

Fig. 6. The automaton for every XOR gate, $i \in \{0, \ldots, n-1\}$.

When n such automata are composed together we obtain a timed automaton $\mathcal{C}$ with 4^n discrete states and n clocks, which we let range in $\{0, \ldots, 7\}$. Note that the feed-back loops make this class of automata rather hard to analyze as all the variables depend on each other. We have managed to calculate all the states reachable from the unstable state $(1, 1, \ldots, 1)$ for a cascade of up to 10 components in less than 2 hours. These results outperformed those of the DBM implementation which could handle only up to 6 gates, using the clock minimization techniques described in [DY96]. Note that in both implementations it was easier to treat the more logically-involved XOR network $\mathcal{C}$ than the n "independent" inputs of $\mathcal{B}$. This can be explained by the fact that in timed systems, independence of components is an illusion as there is a common shared variable, Time, observed and manipulated by *all* the components. This explains why the BDD results were more modest than initially expected. Nevertheless, the ability to analyze such a non-trivial circuit is remarkable and we could verify that under certain l and u parameters, the stable state $(0, 0, \ldots, 0)$ is never reached.

Concerning variable-ordering, we have found it most efficient to arrange the variables by component such that every discrete variable is followed by the bits of its associated clock with the most significant bit first.

4 MOS Circuits

The next example, motivated by problems related to noise and power consumption, illustrates some pragmatic trade-offs between accuracy and efficiency as well as the effect of other simplifying assumptions on verification performance.

Consider a 4-AND gate implemented by the MOS circuit of Figure 7. We assume that the system is governed by a clock with a period u_X and that the inputs are static, or more precisely: each of the inputs can change its value *at most once* in the sub-interval $[0, l_X)$ and remain constant in the sub-interval $[l_X, u_X)$. Concerning the transistors, we assume that they change their states t pico-seconds after the change of their inputs where $t \in [l_P, u_P)$ for the P-MOS elements (A,B,I and J) and $t \in [l_N, u_N)$ for the N-MOS elements (C,D,L and K). A 4-state timed automaton, similar to the one of Figure 6 can be constructed to model every such transistor.

Although such a circuit is supposed to work in a synchronous environment, some practical problems motivate us to look at what happens on a smaller time scale. A particular question one might want to ask is: "what is the maximal (over all legal input patterns) number of transitions that may take place *simultaneously?*" By a transition we mean the opening or closing of a transistor, which is the main energy consumer. When two many transitions occur simultaneously, it might create noise affecting the behavior of the chip.

While this question might be answered manually for a small circuit, it is not at all clear how to do it for a 8-AND made of 28 transistors, not to mention a 16-AND with 60 transistors, where the internal elements can "change their mind" several times within a clock cycle. It should be emphasized that unlike commonly-used SPICE simulations, where the simulation is done *once* for each input pattern, here the results of the calculations cover *all* possible legal input patterns and all delay uncertainties.

We have transformed the 4-AND circuit into 16 timed automata: 12 for the transistors and 4 for the inputs (the latter share the same clock in the range 0 to u_X), and attempted to calculate the set of reachable clock configurations.

We have kept $(l_N, u_N) = (8, 16)$ throughout the experiments. By taking $(l_P, u_P) = (10, 20)$ and dividing all the constants by $\mathrm{lcm}\{10, 20, 8, 16\} = 2$ we

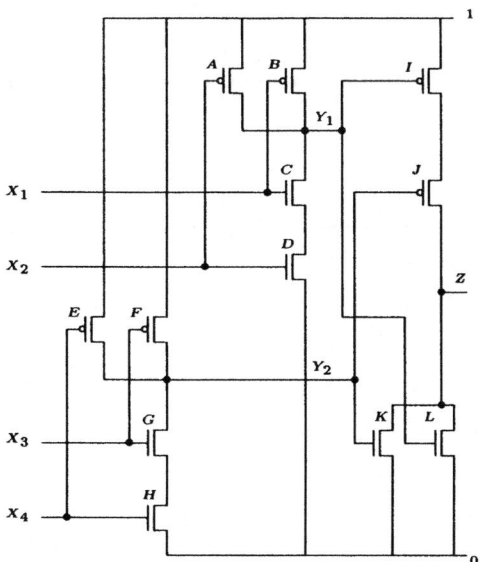

Fig. 7. A MOS realization of the 4-AND function.

had to code all the transistor clocks using 4 bits. Changing l_P from 10 to 8, the lcm becomes 4 and we could use only 3 bits for the clocks. Another factor which influenced performance was the partition of the central clock period into active and non-active phases. Not surprisingly, the results were much better for $(l_X, u_X) = (20, 60)$ than for $(l_X, u_X) = (40, 60)$.

We have constructed an auxiliary automaton for counting the number of transitions taking place at the same time and could test whether there is an input pattern generating more than a given number of simultaneous transitions. For example, concerning the 4-AND circuit, under the parameters $(l_P, u_P) = (8, 20)$ and $(l_X, u_X) = (40, 56)$ we asked whether 9 simultaneous transitions are possible starting from the initial stable state where all the inputs are 0. The system gave (in 1:15 hours) a positive answer and provided the following witness sequence:

$$(X_2 \uparrow, 0) \rightarrow (\{A \downarrow, D \uparrow\}, 8) \rightarrow (X_1 \uparrow, 88) \rightarrow (X_2 \downarrow, 96) \rightarrow (\{B \downarrow, C \uparrow\}, 100) \rightarrow$$

$$(D \downarrow, 104) \rightarrow (I \uparrow, 108) \rightarrow (A \uparrow, 112) \rightarrow (\{X_1 \downarrow, X_2 \uparrow, X_3 \uparrow, X_4 \uparrow\}, 120) \rightarrow$$

$$(\{A \downarrow, B \uparrow, C \downarrow, D \uparrow, E \downarrow, F \downarrow, G \uparrow, H \uparrow, I \downarrow\}, 128)$$

where each pair of the form (S, t) indicates the occurrence of the event (or set of events) S after t pico-seconds since the beginning. The results of the experiments with 3-AND, 4-AND and 5-AND circuits are given in Table 4.[6]

We have also detected the possibilities of short-cuts (a wire connected to both 0 and 1) as we did in [MY96] for a simpler example of a MOS circuit

---

[6] The results for the 5-AND circuit (17 clocks!) were obtained on a 200MHz PentiumPro with 512MB of memory.

#	test	$(l_p,u_p)=(8,20)$ $(l_n,u_n)=(8,16)$		$(l_p,u_p)=(10,20)$ $(l_n,u_n)=(8,16)$	
		$(l_X,u_X)=(24,56)$	$(l_X,u_X)=(40,56)$	$(l_X,u_X)=(20,60)$	$(l_X,u_X)=(40,60)$
3	reach	31.7	1:09.9	1:53.8	5:52.5
	seq#6	(*) 3.7		(*) 6.1	
	#7	1:09.8	(*) 2:21.0	3:23.4	(*) 8:57.7
	#8		2:32.2		10:37.1
4	reach	5:24.7	18:39.4	17:26.1	1:20:04.7
	seq#8	(*) 25.3		(*) 43.0	(*) 56.4
	#9	45:02.1	(*) 1:15:38.6	1:33:07.6	MO
	#10		1:43:02.8		
5	reach	28:24.5	1:45:36.2	1:08:41.7	MO
	seq#10	(*) 2:09.6		(*) 3:02.5	(*) 4:15.3
	#11	9:07:52.4	(*) 4:24:04.4	MO	MO
	#12		(*) 5:02:16.0		

Table 1. A summary of the MOS results. The lines denoted by "reach" correspond to the calculation of the reachable states. The lines of the form "seq#n" correspond to the time it takes to answer whether there exist a sequence of n simultaneous transitions – a positive answer is indicated by (*) and MO denotes memory overflow.

using the DBM version of KRONOS. While some of the assumptions we made in the modeling of transistors deviate from the physical reality (for example, we have adopted a "lazy evaluation" approach concerning transistors whose input becomes "floating", that is, they maintain their previous status), we believe that the approach presented here can be integrated into the design methodology of MOS circuits. Once a suspicious input pattern has been detected by a tool like ours, a full-fledged SPICE simulation, focused around that pattern, can be invoked in order to determine whether or not the alarm is false.

5 Additional Examples

Other experimental results will be reported elsewhere due to lack of space. They include Fischer's mutual exclusion protocol which has become a traditional benchmark for timed automata verification tools ([DOY94], [WD94], [LPY95], [B96]). We managed to calculate the reachable states for 14 such processes. We have also verified (in few minutes) the manufacturing example due to A. Puri, described in [DY95], where timed automata are used as an abstraction of hybrid systems.

6 Conclusions

We have suggested, implemented and tested an alternative method for efficient verification of timed automata. The essence of this method is a canonical representation of discretized sets of clocks configurations using BDDs. This method can take advantage of the symbolic representation of the untimed state-space. We were able to treat some examples that could not be treated by state-of-the-art DBM-based tools. Looking more closely at the "bit-structure" of the clock-space allows us to make an informed choice concerning the trade-off between model accuracy and computational hardness, as was demonstrated in the CMOS case-study.

Notwithstanding the achievements, this is still not *the* breakthrough in timed verification. The main reason, as mentioned in this paper, is the hidden dependency between "syntactically-independent" components, which makes the BDDs of the clock part of a system rather big.

Acknowledgement: We have benefitted from the CMOS know-how of Israel Wagner and Ken McMillan.

References

[AD94]   R. Alur and D.L. Dill, A Theory of Timed Automata, *Theoretical Computer Science* 126, 183–235, 1994.

[ACD93]   R. Alur, C. Courcoubetis, and D.L. Dill, Model Checking in Dense Real Time, *Information and Computation* 104, 2–34, 1993.

[AH92]   R. Alur and T.A. Henzinger, Logics and Models for Real-Time: A survey, J.W. de Bakker et al (Eds.), *Real-Time: Theory in Practice*, LNCS 600, 74-106, Springer, 1992.

[AIKY95]   R. Alur, A. Itai, R.P. Kurshan and M. Yanakakis, Timing Verification by Successive Approximation, *Information and Computation* 118, 142-157, 1995.

[AK96]   R. Alur, and R.P. Kurshan, Timing Analysis in COSPAN, in R. Alur, T.A. Henzinger and E. Sontag (Eds.), *Hybrid Systems III*, LNCS 1066, 220-231, Springer, 1996.

[ABK+97]   E. Asarin, M. Bozga, A. Kerbrat, O. Maler, A. Pnueli and A. Rasse, Data-Structures for the Verification of Timed Automata, in O. Maler (Ed.), *Proc. HART'97*, LNCS 1201, 346-360, Springer, 1997.

[ACM96]   E. Asarin, P. Caspi and O. Maler, A Kleene Theorem for Timed Automata, *Proc. LICS'97*, 1997.

[AMP95]   E. Asarin, O. Maler and A. Pnueli, Symbolic Controller Synthesis for Discrete and Timed Systems, in P. Antsaklis et al (Eds.), *Hybrid Systems II*, LNCS 999, 1-20, Springer, 1995.

[B96]   F. Balarin, Approximate Reachability Analysis of Timed Automata, *Proc. RTSS'96*, 52-61, IEEE, 1996.

[BD91]   B. Berthomieu and M. Diaz, Modeling and Verification of Time Dependent Systems using Time Petri Nets, *IEEE Trans. on Software Engineering* 17, 259-273, 1991.

[BFK96]   M. Bozga, J.-C. Fernandez and A. Kerbrat, *A Symbolic μ-calculus Model Checker for Automata with Variables*, Unpublished Manuscript, VERIMAG, 1996. http://www.imag.fr/VERIMAG/DIST_SYS/SMI/

[Bry86]   R.E. Bryant, Graph-based Algorithms for Boolean Function Manipulation, *IEEE Trans. on Computers* C-35, 677-691, 1986.

[BS94]   J.A. Brzozowski and C-J.H. Seger, *Asynchronous Circuits*, Springer, 1994.

[BCM⁺93] J.R. Burch, E.M. Clarke, K.L. McMillan, D.L. Dill, and L.J. Hwang, Symbolic Model-Checking: 10^{20} States and Beyond, *Proc. LICS'90*, Philadelphia, 1990.

[CC95] S.V. Campos and E.M. Clarke, Real-time Symbolic Model Checking for Discrete Time Models, in T. Rus and C. Rattray (Eds.), *Theories and Experiences for Real-Time System Development*, World Scientific, 1995.

[DOTY96] C. Daws, A. Olivero, S. Tripakis, and S. Yovine, The Tool KRONOS, in R. Alur, T.A. Henzinger and E. Sontag (Eds.), *Hybrid Systems III*, LNCS 1066, 208-219, Springer, 1996.

[DOY94] C. Daws, A. Olivero and S. Yovine, Verifying ET-LOTOS Programs with KRONOS, *Proc. FORTE'94*, Bern, 1994.

[DY95] C. Daws and S. Yovine, Two Examples of Verification of Multirate Timed Automata with KRONOS, *Proc. RTSS'95*, 66-75, IEEE, 1995.

[DY96] C. Daws and S. Yovine, Reducing the Number of Clock Variables of Timed Automata, *Proc. RTSS'96*, 73-81, IEEE, 1996.

[D89] D.L. Dill, Timing Assumptions and Verification of Finite-State Concurrent Systems, in J. Sifakis (Ed.), *Automatic Verification Methods for Finite State Systems*, LNCS 407, 197-212, Springer, 1989.

[GPV94] A. Göllü, A. Puri and P. Varaiya, Discretization of Timed Automata, *Proc. 33rd CDC*, 1994.

[H93] N. Halbwachs, Delay Analysis in Synchronous Programs, in C. Courcoubetis (Ed.), *Proc. CAV'93*, LNCS 697, 333-346, Springer, 1993.

[HMP92a] T. Henzinger, Z. Manna, and A. Pnueli, Timed Transition Systems, in J.W. de Bakker et al (Eds.), *Real-Time: Theory in Practice*, LNCS 600, 226-251, Springer, 1992.

[HMP92] T. Henzinger, Z. Manna, and A. Pnueli. What Good are Digital Clocks?, in W. Kuich (Ed.), *Proc. ICALP'92*, LNCS 623, 545-558, Springer, 1992.

[HNSY94] T. Henzinger, X. Nicollin, J. Sifakis, and S. Yovine, Symbolic Model-checking for Real-time Systems, *Information and Computation* 111, 193–244, 1994.

[LPY95] K.G. Larsen, P. Pettersson and W. Yi, Compositional and Symbolic Model-Checking of Real-time Systems, *Proc. RTSS'95*, 76-87, IEEE, 1995.

[L89] H.R. Lewis, Finite-state Analysis of Asynchronous Circuits with Bounded Temporal Uncertainty, TR15-89, Harvard University, 1989.

[MP95] O. Maler and A. Pnueli, Timing Analysis of Asynchronous Circuits using Timed Automata, in P.E. Camurati, H. Eveking (Eds.), *Proc. CHARME'95*, LNCS 987, 189-205, Springer, 1995.

[MY96] O. Maler and S. Yovine. Hardware Timing Verification using KRONOS, In *Proc. 7th Israeli Conference on Computer Systems and Software Engineering*, Herzliya, Israel, June 1996.

[McM93] K.L. McMillan, *Symbolic Model-Checking: an Approach to the State-Explosion problem*, Kluwer, 1993.

[NS92] X. Nicollin and J. Sifakis, An Overview and Synthesis of Timed Process Algebra, in J.W. de Bakker et al (Eds.), *Real-Time: Theory in Practice*, LNCS 600, 526-548, Springer, 1992.

[S95] F. Somenzi, CUDD: CU Decision Diagram Package, 1995.

[WD94] H. Wong-Toi and D.L. Dill, Approximations for Verifying Timing Properties, in T. Rus and C. Rattray (Eds.), *Theories and Experiences for Real-Time System Development*, World Scientific Publishing, 1994.

STARI: A Case Study in Compositional and Hierarchical Timing Verification

Serdar Taşıran*   Robert K. Brayton

Department of Electrical Engineering and Computer Sciences,
University of California at Berkeley.

Abstract. In [TAKB96], we investigated techniques for checking if one real-time system correctly implements another and developed theory for hierarchical proofs and assume-guarantee style reasoning. In this study, using the techniques of [TAKB96], we verify the correctness of the timing of the communication chip STARI.

1 Introduction

We describe the application of the techniques and tools described in [TAKB96] to the verification of the high-bandwidth communication chip, STARI [G93].

STARI (by Greenstreet, [G93, G96]) is a self-timed FIFO that interfaces a transmitter and a receiver that operate at the same clock frequency but may have some skew between their clock signals (Figure 1). STARI can compensate for large, time varying skews and makes high bandwidth synchronous operation possible by eliminating the need for handshakes between the transmitter and the receiver. However, because there are no handshakes, certain timing properties need to be verified to show that the interface functions correctly. In particular, it needs to be shown that no data is duplicated or dropped by the interface.

The FIFO in STARI consists of a cascade of identical stages and thus, the complexity of automatically verifying a monolithic model of an n stage STARI circuit is roughly $O(k^n)$, where k is the size of the model for a single stage. If the circuit is modeled at the gate level, k is rather large, and this limits automatic verification methods to very small n. As long as the circuit is modeled at this level of detail, improvements to verification algorithms are not likely to have a significant effect, since adding a single stage multiplies the resource requirements by k. Hence, one needs to perform verification on a more abstract representation to be able to handle larger n.

The initial proof of correctness for STARI was performed using a theorem-prover ([G93, LG95]). An automatic proof was also published ([HBAB93]). Neither of these studies verified the actual circuit. They operated on simplified, abstract models for STARI which were not proven to be correct and which ignored certain aspects of the circuit implementation. Such simplifications were necessary for these approaches, otherwise the techniques would have become inapplicable or unmanageably complicated.

Our approach provides a formal guarantee of correctness for the circuit itself, and models the implementation more faithfully. We proceed as follows:

(i) We construct an abstract model for one stage of STARI, which we prove to be correct in the environment that it operates in.

(ii) By composing n of these abstract models, we obtain an abstract model for STARI on which we prove that the timing properties are satisfied.

---

* Supported by SRC under contract DC-324-026.

(i) implies that the properties are also satisfied by the circuit itself. To achieve (i), we made use of the following, which we had developed in [TAKB96]:

- An algorithm for checking if a real-time system is a correct abstraction for another: In [TAKB96] we provided a sufficient condition under which a given untimed mapping preserves timed behavior, and gave an algorithm for checking if this condition is satisfied. This algorithm was implemented as part of the verification tool COSPAN.
- Assume-guarantee style reasoning for real-time systems: While proving that the abstract model for the FIFO stage was correct, we needed to make assumptions about the environment that it operates in. To discharge these assumptions in a sound way, assume-guarantee reasoning needs to be employed.

The use of multiple levels of abstraction and an inductive argument together with assume-guarantee style reasoning for (i) makes this case study an interesting combination of model checking and theorem proving. The assume-guarantee argument, the abstract model, and the mappings that relate abstract models with the gate level descriptions need to be constructed manually, whereas the abstraction check and the verification of the timing properties on the abstract model are performed automatically by COSPAN. The automation afforded by COSPAN eliminates the need for having oversimplified abstract models.

In Section 2 we describe the STARI circuit. Section 3 presents the verification of the timing properties and contrasts our method with previous ones. Section 4 summarizes the experience from this study and suggests further research.

2 STARI

2.1 Operation of the Interface

Most digital electronic circuits are synchronous, i.e., they make use of a clock signal to define the time step. A high frequency clock signal can be safely distributed over relatively large distances, however, it is hard to control the exact phase of the clock at different points in the distribution network. The difference between the phases of the clock signals at two such points is referred to as *skew*. For systems that are not built on a single chip, such as board level designs, ATM networks, etc., skew can be large and time-varying, which makes it a limiting factor on the performance of purely synchronous systems. Self-timed systems avoid this problem by using handshake protocols. For self-timed systems, if no assumptions are made about the delays of circuits and wires, for each data item that is communicated between two parts of a circuit, an acknowledgment needs to be sent back to the transmitter before another data item can be sent. This can limit the communication bandwidth severely, since only one data item can be in transit at a given time, i.e., two pieces of data need to be separated by the round-trip time between the transmitter and receiver in addition to the response time of the receiver.

STARI (Self-Timed At Receiver's Input) is a hybrid-scheme: it is a self-timed first-in first-out queue (FIFO) that connects a transmitter and receiver. The two

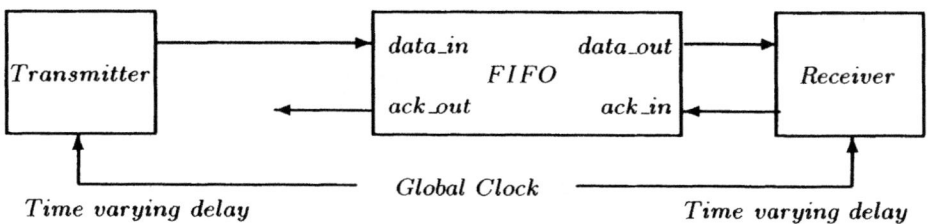

Fig. 1. The STARI interface

communicate as though they were part of an ideal synchronous system (Fig. 1 from [G96]) despite a possibly time-varying skew. The FIFO is initialized to be roughly half-full, and during each period of the clock, one value is inserted to the FIFO by the transmitter and one value is removed by the receiver. Because data is inserted and removed at the same rate, no control signals are required to prevent underflow and overflow. However, because of variations in clock skew, there can be short term fluctuations in the clock rate at the receiver or transmitter and it can appear that one of them is working faster than the other. STARI responds to these fluctuations by building up more data in the FIFO when the transmitter is working faster and by supplying data from the FIFO when the receiver is working faster.

For correct operation of the STARI interface, the following two properties need to be proven[2]:

(i) Each data value output by the transmitter must be inserted into the FIFO before the next one is output.

(ii) A new value must be output by the FIFO before each acknowledgment from the receiver.

Intuitively, the longer and faster the FIFO, the more skew it can tolerate. The correctness of the properties above depend on the length of the FIFO, the clock speed, the magnitude of the skew and the speed of operation of FIFO stages. [G93, LG95] verify that if a certain relationship holds between these parameters, then properties (i) and (ii) hold.

In the rest of Section 2 we present the implementation of the STARI circuit and the operation of the interface.

2.2 Dual-rail Coding

In the STARI circuit, each Boolean signal **x** is represented by the dual-rail code depicted in Fig. 2. The "empty" value is needed to distinguish between two consecutive data items of the same value and one data value asserted for a long time.

---

[2] In this study, we focus on timing related properties only and do not consider other properties which need to be proved to ensure correct operation.

x.t	x.f	x
0	0	E (empty)
0	1	F (false)
1	0	T (true)
1	1	illegal

Fig. 2. Dual rail encoding

2.3 A high-level view of STARI

According to the STARI scheme, the transmitter outputs a data stream, updating the value of *data_in* in Fig. 1 at each rising edge of its clock input. After each time the transmitter outputs a T or F, it outputs an E to separate the current data item from the next one. The receiver samples its input (*data_out* in Fig. 1) each time its clock signal goes high, and updates its acknowledge signal after some delay (*ack_in* in Fig. 1).

The FIFO consists of n identical stages, each of which holds a single data value (See Fig. 3 for an example). Suppose that stage k of the FIFO holds data value d_{old} and that a new data value d_{new} is applied at its inputs by stage $k - 1$. Stage k is "enabled" to read and hold the value d_{new} if stage $k + 1$ has copied the value d_{old} and has notified stage k. After some delay, stage k takes on the value d_{new} and sends an acknowledgment of this fact to stage $k - 1$. Stage k holds this value until a different value is applied to its input by stage $k - 1$ and stage $k + 1$ has acknowledged reading d_{new}. The same data value in the input sequence can be held by many adjacent stages simultaneously, which is what enables the FIFO to hold fewer than n data values (Fig. 3).

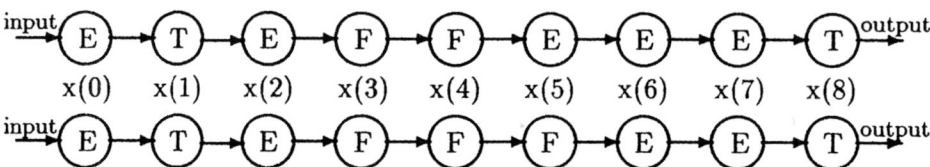

$$x(0) \quad x(1) \quad x(2) \quad x(3) \quad x(4) \quad x(5) \quad x(6) \quad x(7) \quad x(8)$$

Fig. 3. The FIFO holds the sequence "E,T,E,F,E,T". Stage 5 is enabled and copies the data value "F".

2.4 One stage of the FIFO

Each stage of the FIFO consists of two Muller C-elements that hold the value of the .t and .f components of a data item, and a **NOR** gate that computes the acknowledge output signal of the stage (Fig. 5). A Muller C-element works as follows: when the two inputs are the same, the output takes on this value, when the inputs are different, the output retains its previous value (Fig. 4). To

Input 1	Input 2	Output
0	0	0
0	1	unchanged
1	0	unchanged
1	1	1

Fig. 4. Muller C-element functionality.

understand how data flows down the FIFO, first note that stage k is said to have "acknowledged" the data it holds if its ack_out output is equal to the **NOR** of x(k).t and x(k).f. Thus, the copying of data value E is acknowledged by asserting ack_out = 1 and data values T and F are acknowledged by ack_out = 0. Let us consider a situation where stages k and $k+1$ hold the value E and stage $k-1$ has the value T. Stage k is enabled to copy the new data from stage $k-1$. We have ack_out(k+1) = ack_in(k) = 1 and x(k-1).t = 1 and x(k-1).f = 0. Therefore, both inputs to the C-element that computes x(k).t are 1, while the output of the C-element, x(k).t = 0. After some delay, x(k).t becomes 1 while x(k).f remains unchanged, and, in this way, the value T gets copied to stage k. Transitions from a T or F to E happen similarly.

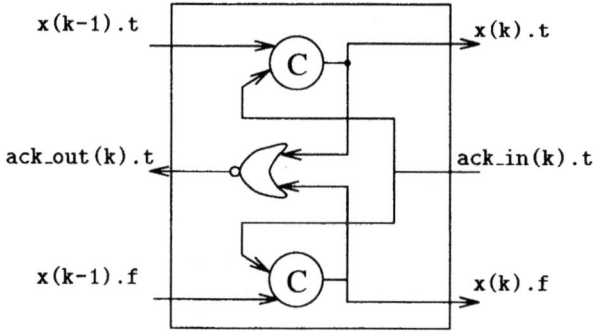

Fig. 5. Stage k of the FIFO.

Given this circuit description for STARI, we now proceed to verify the two timing properties mentioned earlier.

3 Verification of STARI

3.1 Background

The formalism and tools used in the verification of STARI are described in detail in [TAKB96]. In this section, we review the essential facts.

Modeling timed systems: Timed processes. For an example of a *timed process*, refer to Figure 6. A timed process has a set of locations S, where $S_0 \subseteq S$ is designated as initial. The sets of input and output variables are I and O. At each location a unique value is specified for each output variable. *Clocks* are real-valued variables that can be reset when edges are taken, and they increase at the same rate. Edges are conditioned on *clock* and *input predicates*. A *clock* *predicate* is a positive Boolean combination of inequalities $x \diamond k$ where $k \in \mathbb{N}$ and $\diamond$ is $\leq$ or $\geq$. An *input predicate* is a condition of the form $i' = i_{new}$, $i = i_{old}$ which denotes the fact that the input variable i has switched to value i_{new} from i_{old}. At each location there is a clock predicate, called an *invariant*, that needs to be satisfied while the process remains at that location.

The set of input/output waveforms that a process can exhibit constitute the *language* of the process.

The delay model. We model the C-elements and the NOR gates used in the STARI circuit as ideal delayless elements followed by inertial delay buffers, in a fashion similar to [MP95]. The output of an inertial delay buffer follows the input with a delay in the range $[d_{min}, d_{max}]$, i.e., input transitions are reflected at the output with a delay in the given range. The timed process modeling an

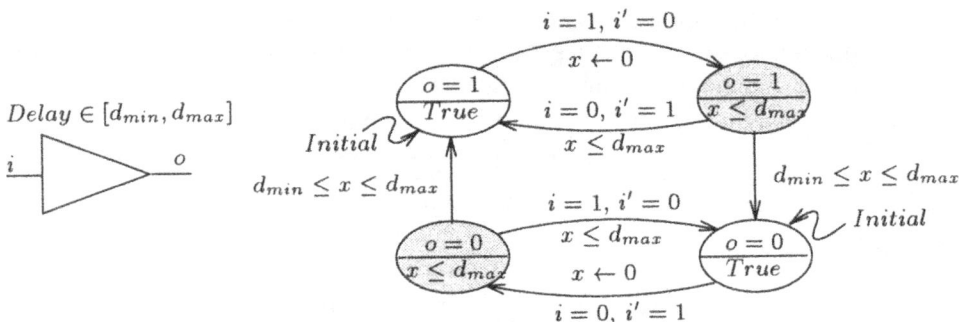

Fig. 6. An inertial delay buffer with delay in the range $[d_{min}, d_{max}]$. The locations where an output change is pending are shaded.

inertial delay buffer is given in Figure 6. If an input pulse lasts less than d_{min}, it is not reflected at the output. If it lasts longer than d_{max}, then it is guaranteed to cause a pulse at the output. Pulses lasting between d_{min} and d_{max} may or may not result in an output pulse: Suppose a transition occurs at the input, and before the corresponding output transition takes place (shaded locations in Fig. 6), the input returns to its original value. Then the output can either remain unchanged (by taking the edges marked $x \leq d_{max}$ from the shaded locations) or reflect both input transitions (by taking the edges marked $d_{min} \leq x \leq d_{max}$).

Abstractions of timed systems. In [TAKB96], we examined three notions for a timed system being a correct abstraction (or implementation) of another: (i) timed language inclusion, (ii) timed simulation, and (iii) the existence of timed behavior preserving mappings. We write $A \preceq B$ to denote the fact that A implements B. For timed processes A and B, a mapping between the locations $h : S^A \to S^B$ is said to *preserve timed behavior*, iff for each run[3] of A, the image of the run under h is a run of B. The existence of such a map implies that B is a correct abstraction of A. We gave an algorithm for checking this condition and implemented it as part of COSPAN. We use this algorithm extensively at several stages of the verification of STARI.

---

[3] A *run* is a sequence of locations, where the time spent at each location is specified.

Compositional and assume-guarantee style reasoning. An implementation relation $\preceq$ is *compositional* iff the following holds

For all i, $1 \leq i \leq n$, $R_i \preceq A_i$ implies $(\|_{1 \leq i \leq n} R_i) \preceq (\|_{1 \leq i \leq n} A_i)$

With the stronger *assume-guarantee style reasoning*, one can prove $(\|_{1 \leq i \leq n} R_i) \preceq (\|_{1 \leq i \leq n} A_i)$ by proving for all i, $1 \leq i \leq n$, that

$$A_1 \| \dots \| A_{i-1} \| R_i \| A_{i+1} \| \dots \| A_n \preceq A_1 \| \dots \| A_{i-1} \| A_i \| A_{i+1} \| \dots \| A_n$$

This style of reasoning is often more useful, since, while showing $R_i \preceq A_i$ one often needs to make assumptions about the environment that R_i and A_i operate in, and $A_1, ..., A_{i-1}$ and $A_{i+1}, ..., A_n$ encapsulate the strongest such set of assumptions.

In [TAKB96] it was shown that timed language inclusion, denoted by $\preceq_L$ is compositional and that assume-guarantee style reasoning can be used in conjunction with it correctly, provided that all timed processes are non-blocking. The other two implementation relations mentioned imply timed language inclusion, and thus one can apply assume-guarantee style reasoning using these relations as well.

3.2 Verification Steps

The verification of STARI consisted of the following two steps:
- Constructing an abstraction for a FIFO stage and verifying its correctness within the environment that it operates.
- Verifying properties (i) and (ii) of Section 2 using the abstract model for the entire circuit.

The latter of these steps was performed using the existing timing verification capabilities of COSPAN ([AK96]). The former step is the novel part of our approach and will be detailed below.

The abstract model for a stage. The abstract model for the FIFO stage describes its behavior at a high level, as in Section 2.3, and expresses bounds on certain response times. The abstract model A (depicted in Figure 7) makes use of only one clock variable. Let us focus on stage k. At location **stable**, the FIFO stage has read and acknowledged its current input. If new data arrives at the inputs of stage k, A moves to location **wait_for_ack**, waiting for stage $k + 1$ to acknowledge having copied the current data. If stage $k + 1$ sends an acknowledgment before the new data arrives at stage k, stage k moves to location **wait_for_data** from location **stable** instead. After new data and an acknowledgment for the old data from stage $k + 1$ has been received, A moves to location **out_pend** from where, after some delay, it moves to **ack_out_pend** and copies the new data to its output. Again after some delay, an acknowledgment is sent to stage $k - 1$ and A moves to location **stable** (see [W3] for COSPAN code describing A).

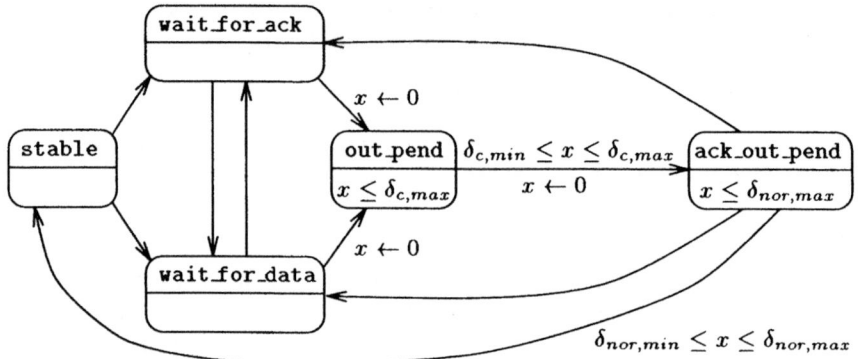

Fig. 7. The timed process A describing the abstract model for a FIFO stage. The minimum and maximum response times of the C-element and the NOR gate are given by $\delta_{c,min}$, $\delta_{c,max}$ $\delta_{nor,min}$ and $\delta_{nor,max}$ respectively. Input predicates labeling the edges and output labels on the locations have been omitted to simplify the figure.

Note that it has been possible to capture the timing information about the stage using one clock only, since only one of the three circuit elements forming the stage can have a pending output change at any given time. Intuitively, this is guaranteed by the fact that the inputs to a stage will not change unless the stage has acknowledged the previous inputs. This assumption about the environment of a stage is crucial for the correctness of the abstraction, and is taken into account in our verification by the use of assume-guarantee reasoning.

Let F denote the timed process describing one stage of the FIFO at the gate level. F is the composition of processes representing two Muller C-elements and a NOR-gate as described by Figure 5 and Section 3.1. Let F_i and A_i denote the detailed and abstract models for the ith FIFO stage. F_i and A_i have structures identical to those of F and I. Also let Tx and Rx be the timed processes describing the transmitter and the receiver. Refer to [W3] for COSPAN models of Tx and Rx. We would like to prove that

$$Tx \parallel F_1 \parallel F_2 \parallel ... \parallel F_n \parallel Rx \preceq_L Tx \parallel A_1 \parallel A_2 \parallel ... \parallel A_n \parallel Rx \qquad (1)$$

which will enable us to prove properties using the abstract description for the circuit given by the right-hand side. We would like to achieve this by showing that for all i, A_i is a correct abstraction for F_i. As noted above, this is true only within the environment that F_i and A_i operate in. For an arbitrary environment $F_i \leq_L A_i$ does not hold: if the inputs to F are unconstrained, then F_i does not behave like a FIFO element. Therefore, we need to employ assume-guarantee reasoning to carry out the proof. We must prove, for all i, $1 \leq i \leq n$, that

$$Tx \parallel A_1 \parallel ... \parallel A_{i-1} \parallel F_i \parallel A_{i+1} \parallel ... \parallel A_n \parallel Rx \preceq$$
$$Tx \parallel A_1 \parallel ... \parallel A_{i-1} \parallel A_i \parallel A_{i+1} \parallel ... \parallel A_n \parallel Rx$$

Since the environment of each FIFO stage is different, for each i, the condition to be checked is different. To avoid performing a separate check for each i, we would like to have one set of environment assumptions that is sufficient for showing $F_i \preceq A_i$ and show that this set of assumptions is true for the environment of each module i. Towards this end, we define timed processes E_{left} and E_{right} and show the following:

(I) For all i, $Tx \parallel A_1 \parallel A_2 \parallel ... \parallel A_{i-1} \preceq E_{left}$
(II) For all i, $A_{i+1} \parallel A_{i+2} \parallel ... \parallel A_n \parallel Rx \preceq E_{right}$

(I) and (II) guarantee that E_{left} and E_{right} are correct abstractions for the left and right sides of the environment of stage i. By the assume-guarantee rule, showing that $F \preceq A$ in the environment defined by E_{left} and E_{right}, i.e.,

$$E_{left} \parallel F \parallel E_{right} \preceq E_{left} \parallel A \parallel E_{right}$$

suffices to prove the containment in Equation 1.

Proving correctness of environment abstractions. E_{left} encapsulates the restrictions on the behavior of the left side of F for it to function correctly and for A to be a correct abstraction. The essential features of E_{left} are that it always outputs a valid data value, and that it does not change this value until the next stage acknowledges having copied this value. We use induction on i to prove that E_{left} is a correct abstraction for $Tx \parallel A_1 \parallel A_2 \parallel ... \parallel A_{i-1}$. More precisely, we show the following

1. $Tx \preceq E_{left}$ [4]
2. Assuming $Tx \parallel A_1 \parallel A_2 \parallel ... \parallel A_{i-1} \preceq_L E_{left}$ we show $Tx \parallel A_1 \parallel ... \parallel A_i \preceq E_{left}$. By the induction assumption, it suffices to prove $E_{left} \parallel A_i \preceq E_{left}$.

For both steps we specify mappings from the locations of the left-hand side process to those of the right-hand side process, and show that this mapping preserves timed behavior using the COSPAN implementation mentioned in Section 3.1. COSPAN code describing the modules and the mappings is provided at [W3].

The essential feature of E_{right} is that it samples the data at its inputs periodically and after a certain delay, acknowledges having read the data. We proved that E_{right} is a correct abstraction in exactly the same manner as E_{left}. The COSPAN code for E_{right} and the untimed mappings can be found at [W3].

Proving that A is a correct abstraction for F. Given E_{left} and E_{right}, it was rather straightforward to prove that $E_{left} \parallel F \parallel E_{right} \preceq E_{left} \parallel A \parallel E_{right}$ COSPAN code for the untimed mapping is given in [W3].

Time and memory consumption. We report the resource usage for the following checks (Table 1):

---

[4] Some technicality is involved here. To prove the basis case, we disallow the transmitter to change its data output if the first FIFO stage has not copied the previous value. Later on, while proving that the interface works correctly, we prove that it is never the case that the transmitter wants to modify the data output and the FIFO is not ready to receive new data.

(I) $Tx \preceq E_{left}$

(II) $E_{left} \parallel A \preceq E_{left}$

(III) $Rx \preceq E_{right}$

(IV) $A \parallel E_{right} \preceq E_{right}$

(V) $E_{left} \parallel F \parallel E_{right} \preceq E_{left} \parallel A \parallel E_{right}$

(VI) $Tx \parallel A_1 \parallel ... \parallel A_8 \parallel Rx$ satisfies timing properties (i) and (ii) of Section 2.

For all of these checks the following parameters were used: $\delta_{c,min} = 1$, $\delta_{c,max} = 2$, $\delta_{nor,min} = 1$, $\delta_{nor,max} = 2$, the clock period $\pi = 12$. The delays from the clock to the transmitter and the receiver (see Figure 1) were allowed to be time varying and bounded by 1 time unit.

To serve as a comparison, we tried to verify properties (i) and (ii) of Section 2 using the gate level model for STARI, i.e., using F as the model for a FIFO stage. At this level of detail, we ran out of space using 1 GB of memory for a three stage FIFO. Improvements to our timing verification algorithm could enable us to verify larger FIFOs at the gate level, however, any method working on a monolithic description at the circuit level is bound to run out of resources for a FIFO with a large enough number of stages. Using abstractions as we demonstrated above, one is able to handle larger FIFOs, although not an unbounded number of them, since the number of FIFO elements still enters into the computation (VI).

	Num. of clocks	Memory (MB)	CPU time (seconds)
I	3	0.02	1.3
II	3	0.02	4.9
III	3	0.02	13.4
IV	6	3.18	92.7
V	7	6.33	158.6
VI	12	92.4	6014.1

Table 1.

Comparison with previous approaches. The most important benefit of our approach is the correctness guarantee that it provides for the actual circuit, whereas [LG95] and [HBAB93] based their proofs on oversimplified abstractions of the circuit. Their tools do not provide a mechanism for checking the correctness of abstractions, therefore there is no formal guarantee that the properties they proved at a high level are satisfied by the circuit.

[LG95] and [HBAB93] neglect the time taken by the NOR gate (see Figure 5) to compute the acknowledgment output and, furthermore, use a delay model that is less realistic than the inertial delay model that we employ. Since verification of properties on the abstract model is performed automatically in our approach, we did not need to resort to such simplifications.

The proof of [LG95] is for all FIFO lengths n, and makes it easier to see the trade-off between circuit parameters, whereas our approach is still limited by n. However, the proof of [LG95] is rather involved, and one needs to have an in-depth understanding of why the properties are satisfied. The abstraction proofs and environment abstractions that we used were rather straightforward and intuitive.

4 Conclusion

We demonstrated the use of compositionality and hierarchy on the verification of the STARI communication circuit. By using the timed refinement checking algorithm that we had implemented as part of COSPAN in a compositional framework, we were able to divide the verification problem into smaller pieces, which enabled us to automatically verify a larger circuit than was previously possible.

This case study demonstrated once more that abstractions are indispensable for verifying large systems, and that compositional and assume-guarantee style reasoning are not only useful techniques for verifying the correctness of abstractions, but are almost always necessary.

The size of our abstract model for STARI, $Tx \parallel A_1 \parallel ... \parallel A_n \parallel Rx$ still has an exponential dependency on n, although less severe than the gate level model. One problem that remains is the construction of an abstract model for STARI that is parametrized with respect to n. One would then prove the correctness of this abstraction using induction. Parametrized real-time systems have been studied before ([AHV93]) and there is indication that this problem is rather complex.

Acknowledgments

We thank Rajeev Alur and Robert Kurshan for helpful discussions and support with COSPAN.

References

[AHV93] R. Alur, T.A. Henzinger, M.Y. Vardi. Parametric real-time reasoning. In *Proceedings of the 25th ACM Symposium on Theory of Computing*, pp. 592-601, 1993.

[AK96] R. Alur and R.P. Kurshan. Timing analysis in COSPAN. In *Hybrid Systems III*, Lecture Notes in Computer Science. Springer-Verlag, 1996.

[G93] M. R. Greenstreet STARI: A Technique for High-Bandwidth Communication. PhD thesis, Princeton University, 1993.

[G96] M. R. Greenstreet STARI: Skew Tolerant Communication. Unpublished manuscript.

[HBAB93] H. Hulgaard, S. M. Burns, T. Amon, and G. Borriello Practical Applications of an Efficient Time Separation of Events Algorithm In *Digest of Technical Papers of the 1993 IEEE Intl. Conf. on Computer-Aided Design*, November 1993.

[LG95] C. Leung, M. Greenstreet A Simple Proof Checker for Timing Verification. In *ACM Intl. Workshop on Timing Issues in the Specification and Synthesis of Digital Systems*, pages 294-305, November 1995.

[MP95] O. Maler, A. Pnueli Timing Analysis of Asynchronous Circuits Using Timed Automata In *ACM Intl. Workshop on Timing Issues in the Specification and Synthesis of Digital Systems*, pages 249-257, November 1995.

[TAKB96] S. Taşıran, R. Alur, R. P. Kurshan, and R. K. Brayton Verifying Abstractions of Timed Systems. In *Proc. of the 7th Intl. Conf. on Concurrency Theory, CONCUR '96*, LNCS 1119, pages 546-562, Springer-Verlag, 1996.

[W3] http://www-cad.eecs.berkeley.edu/~serdar/stari.html

A Provably Correct Embedded Verifier for the Certification of Safety Critical Software

Alessandro Cimatti[1], Fausto Giunchiglia[1], Paolo Pecchiari[1], Bruno Pietra[2],
Joe Profeta[3], Dario Romano[2], Paolo Traverso[1], Bing Yu[3]

[1]IRST - Institute for Scientific and Technological Research
38050 - Povo - Trento, Italy
[2]Ansaldo Trasporti Spa
Via dei Pescatori, 35 - 16100 - Genova, Italy
[3]Ansaldo Signal
1000 Technology Drive, Pittsburgh, PA 15219-3120

Abstract. VFRAME is one of ANSALDO's software driven vital architectures for safety critical products. This paper describes a project whose result is the development of an "embedded verifier", i.e. a system integrated within VFRAME and able to certify the correctness of one of VFRAME components, a compiler. The embedded verifier satisfies two precise requirements. First, the compiler must be certified in a fully automatic and efficient way. Second, the embedded verifier must be itself certified, in a way which can be easily understood and validated by end users.

1 Introduction

This paper describes the results of a project where theorem proving techniques have been applied to the certification of the correctness of a component of VFRAME [9], one of ANSALDO's software driven vital architectures for safety critical products. VFRAME is used for the development of rail transportation industrial applications. The VFRAME component under consideration can be thought of as a compiler which, given in input a (source) program, has to generate a "semantically equivalent" (target) program as its output. The goal of the project was the development of an "embedded verifier", i.e. a system integrated within the VFRAME architecture and able to certify the correctness of the compiler. More precisely, every time a compilation is performed, the Verifier must take in input the actual source program, the actual target program generated by the compiler, and prove that the latter is a correct translation of the former[1]. Being part of VFRAME, the Verifier had to meet the following requirements.
Requirement 1. The Verifier must be fully *automatic*, since it must be used by VFRAME end users, and *efficient*, as in general the final installations on-the-field are subject to time constraints.

---

[1] A well known alternative approach, the (mechanical) "once for all" verification of the correctness of the VFRAME compiler for all its possible inputs (see for instance [7]), has been rejected since the compiler's environment platform is not guaranteed to be fail-safe and can not assure the correct execution of verified software. See also [1], which describes a further approach.

Requirement 2. As any other component of the vital architecture, the Verifier must be itself certified, i.e. there must be a way to guarantee that the Verifier is itself correct. An additional requirement is that the certification of the Verifier and the proof of the correctness of the compilations must be easily understood and validated by end users.

The design of the Verifier was characterized by the following key steps:

Step 1. A formal semantics has been defined for the source and target languages of the VFRAME compiler, and a notion of semantic equivalence has been devised.

Step 2. The Verifier has been functionally specified as a system capable of proving a set of "Syntactic Verification Conditions" over source and target programs. These conditions have been formally proved to imply the semantic equivalence of the programs.

Step 3. The architecture of the Verifier has been specified in terms of two independent programs, a Logger and a Checker. The Logger generates a Log, containing the proof that the Syntactic Verification Conditions are satisfied. The Checker certifies the correctness of the proof by checking that some "Checking Conditions" hold of the Log, the source program and the target program. The Checking Conditions have been formally proved to imply the Syntactic Verification Conditions.

Requirement 1 was addressed by reducing the (hard) task of proving the semantic equivalence of the input programs to the (easier) task of proving the Syntactic Verification Conditions (step 2 above). Indeed, the direct proof of the semantic equivalence of the two programs would require complex theorem proving techniques, and therefore interaction with a user and high computation time. On the contrary, the Syntactic Verification Conditions can be analyzed automatically and efficiently. The proof of the correctness of this step was performed a priori, once for all.

Requirement 2 was achieved through the decomposition of the Verifier into the Logger and the Checker (step 3 above). The independence of the Logger and the Checker guarantees that the Logger is non critical, and the correctness of the Verifier relies only on the correctness of the Checker. Indeed, if the Logger generates a wrong proof, and the Checker is correct, the Verifier will not accept the compilation. This decomposition is motivated by the fact that the task performed by the Checker (i.e. checking a proof) is in general much simpler than the task of the Logger (i.e. finding a proof). Hence the Checker is a small portion of the Verifier, and can be easily validated. The proof of the correctness of this decomposition was performed a priori, once for all. Since the task of the Verifier has been reduced to proving some syntactic properties of the two programs, the proof steps in the Log (e.g. substitutions) are presented to end users as information on the syntactic structures of the two programs (e.g. the two programs corresponding instructions). As a consequence, the logical steps performed by the Checker can be presented to end users with no experience of logic or theorem proving as simple tests on the syntactic structures of the two programs.

The paper is structured as follows. Section 2 is a brief overview of VFRAME.

Section 3 describes, through an example, the source and target programs of the VFRAME compiler and their semantics. Section 4 describes the functional specifications of the Verifier. Section 5 describes how the Verifier specifications are refined into the specifications of the Logger and the Checker. Section 6 discusses some issues and assumptions about the certification requirements of the Verifier. Since the work done involved proprietary information not all of the details can be disclosed in this paper.

2   Overview of VFRAME

VFRAME (Vital Framework) [9] is one of ANSALDO software driven vital architectures used to develop safety-critical applications from commercial, off-the-shelf hardware and software. VFRAME can be thought of as a virtual logical and arithmetic machine that executes a vital algorithm on a vital platform. This virtual machine is a cyclic, finite state machine designed to have fail safe behavior independent of the physical implementation. In this way system vitality does not depend on knowing how the processor might fail. The software which implements this virtual machine is called the cyclic Runtime Executive. Figure 1 shows an overview of VFRAME. At the software level, VFRAME is partitioned into the Off-line and Runtime systems.

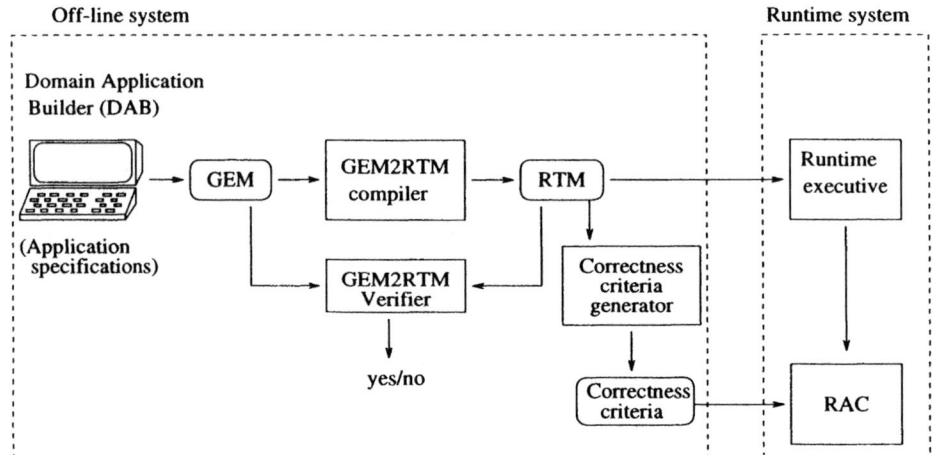

Fig. 1. VFRAME overview

The Off-line system provides an application programming environment in the form of a Domain Application Builder (DAB), i.e. a graphical interface designed to allow specification of both the system hardware and application algorithms. A visual language compiler translates graphical specifications into a unique generic and domain independent form, called the Generic Entity Model (GEM), which represents the application in terms of standard operations, like boolean and arithmetic operations, access to tables, etc. The GEM is not yet in a form which can be executed by the Runtime Executive. A compiler, called the GEM2RTM compiler, translates a GEM into a loadable and executable program, called a Run Time Model (RTM). The compiler decomposes the GEM into a sequence of primitive executable operations. At the RTM level, information is stored in form of "codewords", i.e. words protected with CRC (Cyclic Redundant Checksum) to detect data corruptions. The RTM is loaded onto the Runtime Executive. A correctness criteria generator independently processes the RTM and generates precomputed data describing what the correct result of each primitive operation should be. These correctness criteria are loaded onto a Realtime Application Checker (RAC), a simple, fail-safe hardware checker which performs concurrent checking of the results of the runtime execution against the correctness criteria. The on-line architecture allows for safety quantification: a "probability of undetected error" [9] can be determined which depends on the length of the CRC in the codewords. As a consequence, run time execution can be guaranteed to be performed with a small probability of undetected error by means of techniques based on information encoding and concurrent checking by independent hardware.

The remaining problem is the correctness of the off line translations, where the techniques used for the runtime execution cannot be applied. A project under development is dealing with the formal verification of the correctness of the visual compiler [9, 4]. In this paper we describe the project on the certification of the GEM2RTM compiler. The goal is to embed the (GEM2RTM) Verifier (see Figure 1) within the off-line part of the vital architecture. The Verifier can be thought of as a black box which takes in input the source and target programs and answers "yes" only if the target program (generated by the compiler) is a semantically equivalent correct translation of the source program (in input to the compiler). A future project will apply the same methodology developed in this project to the formal verification of the correctness criteria generator.

3 GEM and RTM Programs

GEM and RTM programs can be thought of as "embedded programs", i.e. programs which are embedded in an external environment (at different abstraction levels). After (variable) initialization, embedded programs are executed cyclically. At each cycle, values are acquired from the external environment (e.g. information from sensors such as train speed) and stored in input variables. Then, the instructions of the program are executed (e.g. to compute a control algorithm), and the computed values are stored in output variables and then delivered to the external environment (e.g. information for actuators such as control to a breaking device).

Embedded programs are composed of (variable) declarations and instructions. A GEM variable declaration contains a variable identifier, its initial value, information about whether it is an input or an output variable, and its type (e.g. boolean or integer). For example, in Figure 2, the GEM program contains the

```
- GEM PROGRAM              - RTM PROGRAM
- DECLARATIONS             - DECLARATIONS
1. A, 1,  Output, bool     1. A1, 1, Output
2. B, 21, Input,  int      2. B1, 1, Input
3. C, 17, Input,  int      3. B2, 0, Input
                           4. C1, 2, Input
                           5. C2, 3, Input
                           6. tmpequ, 0
- INSTRUCTIONS             - INSTRUCTIONS
1. A <- B == C             1. tmpequ <- B1 EQU C1      – operation #1 –
                           2. A1    <- tmpequ OR tmpequ – operation #2 –
                           3. tmpequ <- B2 EQU C2      – operation #3 –
                           4. A1    <- A1  AND tmpequ  – operation #4 –
```

Fig. 2. Examples of GEM and RTM programs.

declarations of the variables A,B,C, which are initialized to 1, 21, 17, respectively (in the case of boolean variables 0 and 1 stand for **false** and **true**, respectively). A is a boolean output variable and B,C are integer input variables. GEM instructions have type restrictions, and can have multiple arguments and multiple results. The GEM program in Figure 2 contains only one instruction, A <- B == C, which tests if the two integer variables B and C are equal and assigns the boolean result to A.

RTM programs are not typed. In order to prevent undetected data corruptions, information is manipulated in form of codewords, uniform data structures containing, among other things, a numerical value, the identifier of the variable where the codeword is stored, and a CRC protection. RTM variables can be thought of as the result of an "expansion" of GEM variables. [2] This expansion depends on some configuration parameters of the compiler, the most important being a sequence of relatively prime numbers, which can change from compilation to compilation. Let us assume that this sequence is $\langle p_1, ..., p_n \rangle$. Then, an integer GEM variable is translated into n RTM variables. These RTM variables correspond to the residues modulo p_1, ..., p_n, respectively, of the integer GEM variable. Boolean GEM variables are translated into single RTM variables. For simplicity, in the rest of the paper we assume that the sequence of relatively prime numbers is fixed and is equal to $\langle 5, 7 \rangle$. For instance, in the programs in Figure 2 the integer variables B and C are expanded into two pairs of variables, B1,B2 and C1,C2, respectively. The boolean variable A is translated into the single variable A1. RTM instructions are expansions of GEM instructions as well. In the example, the GEM instruction A <- B == C gets expanded into the four RTM instructions. operation #1 compares the first two pairs (B1 and C1) and the boolean result is assigned to a variable introduced by the compiler (tmpequ). The result is stored in A1 (operation #2). The second pair is compared and the result is stored in tmpequ (operation #3). The result (A1) is the conjunction of the results of the two equality comparisons (operation #4). The intuition underlying this expansion is that the two GEM variables B and C are equal if and only if the RTM corresponding variables are pairwise equal, i.e. B1 is equal

---

[2] The motivation underlying this expansion is to simplify the check of consistency of arithmetic calculations (to be performed by the RAC, see Section 2).

to C1 and B2 is equal to C2 (this fact is guaranteed by the Chinese Remainder Theorem, under the condition that B and C are less than 35, i.e. the product of the two relatively prime numbers chosen for the translation).

For simplicity and readability, in this paper we have written RTM programs "symbolically". RTM programs are, actually, sequences of hexadecimal numbers. A somewhat more "realistic" presentation of the instructions of the RTM program in Figure 2 is reported below (lines starting with – are comments). For instance, consider **operation #1**. 0x00000002 and 0x00000014 identify the variables B1 and C1, respectively, 0x0000000d identifies the operator EQU, and 0x00000019 identifies **tmpequ**.

```
- operation #1 -
0x00000002 0x00000014 0x0000000d 0x00000019
- operation #2 -
0x00000019 0x00000019 0x0000000b 0x00000001
- operation #3 -
0x00000003 0x00000015 0x0000000d 0x00000019
- operation #4 -
0x00000001 0x00000019 0x0000000a 0x00000001
```

GEM and RTM programs were given semantics by formalizing the cyclic execution process informally presented above. The basic entities are *computation states*, mapping the variables of a program on the corresponding values. In the following, we write the value of a variable v in the computation state s as $v(s)$. Each execution step - initialization, input acquisition, execution of instruction, output delivery - is formalized as an operation on the (computation) state. Initialization is a function mapping a program into the initial state s such that for each variable v, $v(s)$ is the initial value of v. Input acquisition is the function mapping the computation state s and an input vector $I = \langle i_1, ..., i_m \rangle$, i.e. a tuple of (input) values, into the computation state s', such that, for $1 \leq j \leq m$, $v_j(s') = i_j$, where $v_1, ..., v_m$ are the input variables of the program, and for every other variable w, $w(s') = w(s)$. Output delivery is a function from a state into an output vector, i.e. a function from a state s into the tuple of the values $\langle v_1(s), ..., v_k(s) \rangle$, where $v_1, ..., v_k$ are the output variables of the program. Each (GEM and RTM) instruction is semantically interpreted as a function mapping states into states. For instance, the interpretation of the GEM operation $v_1 \texttt{<-} v_2 == v_3$ is the function $[\![v_1 \texttt{<-} v_2 == v_3]\!](s) = s'$, where $v_1(s')$ is 1 iff $v_2(s)$ and $v_3(s)$ are equal, 0 otherwise, and for all v other than v_1, $v(s') = v(s)$.

Intuitively, the (state) semantics of an embedded program p, written $[\![p]\!]$, is a function from the set of all finite sequences of input vectors into state sequences, such that for every input sequence of length l, $\overline{I} = \langle I_1, ..., I_l \rangle$, the sequence of states is obtained by composing initialization, input acquisition and the execution of the sequence of instructions.

4   Functional Specification of the Verifier

A correct compilation is defined by a set of *Syntactic Verification Conditions*, i.e. conditions on how source programs are mapped syntactically into target programs. The Verifier is thus formally specified as a system which, given in input

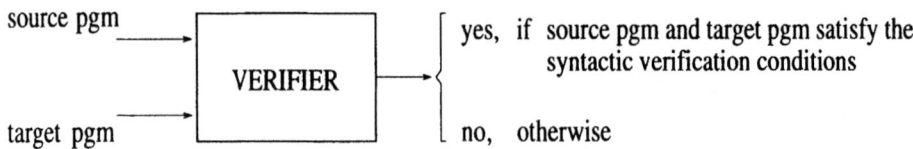

Fig. 3. The Verifier

the two programs, answers "yes" only if the two programs satisfy the Syntactic Verification Conditions (see Figure 3). Let g and r be a GEM and an RTM program, respectively. Intuitively, g and r satisfy the Syntactic Verification Conditions (written as $g \sim_M r$) iff they correspond through a mapping M from GEM variable declarations into RTM variable declarations, and from GEM instructions into RTM instructions. The following are some of the conditions which must hold of the GEM and RTM programs. If v is an integer variable in g, then $M(v)$ must be a pair $\langle M_1(v), M_2(v) \rangle$ of distinct variables in r (in the following we write $M_i(v)$ as the i-th element of $M(v)$). For each integer input [output, resp.] variable v in g, $\langle M_1(v), M_2(v) \rangle$ are input [output] variables in r, and for each input [output, resp.] variable v' in r, there exists an input [output] variable v in g such that, either $M_1(v) = v'$ or $M_2(v) = v'$. The GEM and RTM programs in Figure 2 satisfy the conditions above. For instance, $M(\text{B}) = \langle \text{B1}, \text{B2} \rangle$ and all and only GEM input/output variables are mapped into RTM input/output variables.

Each instruction in the GEM program must correspond to a sequence of instructions in the RTM program. Not only does this correspondence depend on the operator of the instruction (e.g. ==), but also on the types of GEM variables (e.g. integer or boolean). For instance, if v_2 and v_3 are integer variables, a GEM instruction of the form $v_1 \leftarrow v_2 == v_3$ must be mapped by M into the sequence of RTM instructions reported below, where t is an RTM (temporary) variable which does not correspond to any GEM variable. Comparison between boolean variables would be translated in a different way.

$$
\begin{aligned}
M(v_1 \leftarrow v_2 == v_3) = \quad & t & \leftarrow M_1(v_2) \text{ EQU } M_1(v_3), \\
& M(v_1) \leftarrow \quad t \quad \text{ OR } \quad t, \\
& t & \leftarrow M_2(v_2) \text{ EQU } M_2(v_3), \\
& M(v_1) \leftarrow M(v_1) \text{ AND } \quad t
\end{aligned}
$$

The instructions of GEM and RTM programs in Figure 2 satisfy the above conditions, the (temporary) variable t being `tmpequ`.

The functional specification of the Verifier through the Syntactic Verification Conditions makes it possible to satisfy Requirement 1 (see Section 1). Indeed, the problem of verifying the Syntactic Verification Conditions is decidable and not computationally complex. As a consequence, the Verifier can be implemented as a fully automatic and efficient system.

The next step was to make sure that this specification is actually such that correct compilations generate target programs which are semantically equivalent to source programs. Two (GEM and RTM) programs are semantically equivalent when, given two sequences of "equivalent" input vectors, they compute two sequences of "equivalent" output vectors. The notion of equivalent (sequences of) input vectors is formalized by extending the mapping M to input vectors. If $I = \langle i_1, ..., i_m \rangle$ is a GEM input vector, $M(I)$ is the vector $M(i_1)\| ... \|M(i_m)$, where $\|$ denotes concatenation of sequences, $M(i_j)$ is $\langle i_j \rangle$ if the input variable v_j of the GEM program is a boolean, and $\langle i_j \bmod 5, i_j \bmod 7 \rangle$ otherwise. The notion of equivalent output vectors and equivalent states is formalized similarly.

We formally prove that, for any possible individual compilation, the Syntactic Verification Conditions imply semantic equivalence. This result is a direct consequence of the following theorem, stating that the Syntactic Verification Conditions imply that the GEM and RTM programs are state equivalent. The intuitive meaning is that the execution of the programs when given corresponding inputs proceeds through sequences of pairwise corresponding states.

Theorem 1 State equivalence between programs. *Let g and r be a* GEM *and an* RTM *program, such that $g \sim_M r$. Then they are state equivalent, i.e. for every input vector sequence $\overline{I}$ for g,*

$$[\![g]\!](\overline{I}) \sim_M [\![r]\!](M(\overline{I}))$$

The proof of Theorem 1 is done by induction on the length of sequences of inputs $\overline{I}$. The base case, corresponding to the null sequence of inputs, follows from the equivalence between the initial states of GEM and RTM. The step case states that, if the sequences of states generated by any input sequence of length n are equivalent, then the sequences of states generated by any input sequence of length $n + 1$ are. We prove this by showing that each state transition (e.g. input acquisition, execution of instructions) preserves the equivalence. This was done for each possible GEM instruction and legal typing configuration of GEM operands and results.

As an example, let us consider the proof that the GEM instruction $v_1 \text{ <- } v_2 \text{ == } v_3$ and the RTM instruction sequence $M(v_1 \text{ <- } v_2 \text{ == } v_3)$ preserve equivalence. Part of this proof consists in showing that the value of v_1 in the final state is equal to the value of $M(v_1)$ in the final state. We have two cases. If (the values of) v_2 and v_3 are equal, then v_1 has value 1 and, by induction hypothesis, $M_1(v_2)$ is equal to $M_1(v_3)$ and $M_2(v_2)$ is equal to $M_2(v_3)$. This implies that, after the first RTM state transition, t has value 1, after the second $M(v_1)$ has value 1, after the third t has value 1, and at the end of the final transition $M(v_1)$ has value 1. The other case is similar.

5 Functional Specification of the Logger/Checker

The formal specification of the Verifier is refined into the specification of a system (see Figure 4) composed of two independent programs, a Logger and a Checker. The Logger generates a Log containing the proof that the Syntactic Verification Conditions are satisfied. The Checker certifies that the proof is correct by checking that some *Checking Conditions* on the source program, on the target program and on the Log, are satisfied. This decomposition allows for the

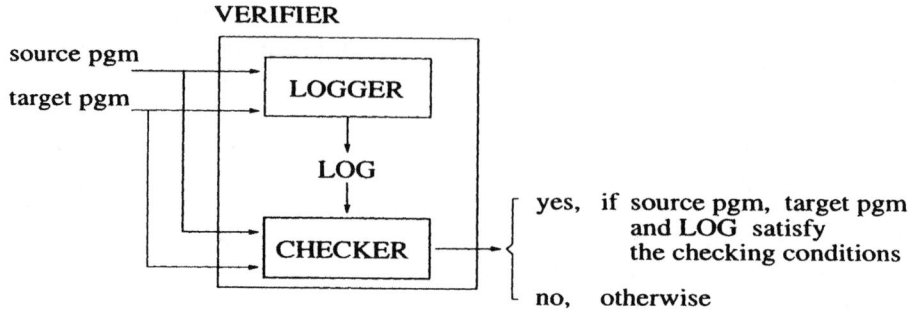

Fig. 4. The VFRAME Logger/Checker Architecture

achievement of Requirement 2 (see Section 1), being the Checker the only critical component of the Verifier.

The first step is to provide a formal characterization of the output of the Logger, i.e. the Log. Intuitively, the Logger tries to build a proof that the GEM program and the RTM program in input to the Verifier satisfy the Syntactic Verification Conditions, and writes it in the Log. In particular, the Log contains a description of the mapping M from the GEM program into the RTM program, as described in previous section. As an example, let us consider the following Log, generated by the Logger when its inputs are the two programs in Figure 2.

```
- LOG HEADER
3   - GEM decl length
1   - GEM instr length
6   - RTM decl  length
4   - RTM instr length
- DECLARATION MAPPING
1 1                 - 1. bool decl
2 <2,3>             - 2. int decl
3 <4,5>             - 3. int decl
- INSTRUCTION MAPPING
1 <1,2,3,4>     - 1. int instr
- ABSTRACT GEM INSTRUCTIONS
EQUALITY-II  1 2 3    - 1. abstract gem instr
- ABSTRACT RTM INSTRUCTIONS
EQU 6 2 3  - 1. abstract rtm instr
OR  1 6 6  - 2. abstract rtm instr
EQU 6 3 5  - 3. abstract rtm instr
AND 1 1 6  - 4. abstract rtm instr
```

The log header states the length of the GEM and RTM declarations and instructions. The declaration mapping and the instruction mapping are a description of the M which has been found by the Logger. Variables are (abstractly) referred to in terms of indexes indicating the position of the corresponding declaration in the declaration list. For instance, the GEM integer variable B is referred to as 2, while the corresponding RTM variables B1 and B2 are referred to as 2 and 3. Instruction indexes are defined analogously. For instance, the GEM instruction at index 1, i.e. A <- B == C, is mapped into the four RTM instructions at indexes 1, 2, 3 and 4. The abstract GEM/RTM instructions provide an abstract description of the (concrete) instructions of the GEM/RTM programs. For instance, EQUALITY-II 1 2 3 is the abstract instruction corresponding to the GEM concrete instruction A <- B == C. EQUALITY-II stands for an equality operation between two integer variables and 1 2 3 are the indexes of the declarations of the variables A,B,C, respectively.

Notice that the Log can be validated by end users which have no experience of logic and theorem proving (part of Requirement 2). Indeed, the logical proof steps actually performed by the Logger (e.g. substitutions, universal bounded quantifications) are presented to the users as information on the syntactic structures of the two programs, e.g. the two programs corresponding instructions (corresponding to substitution), the lengths of the two programs (corresponding to the bound on universal quantification).

Let us consider now the Checking Conditions. Intuitively, they make sure that the Log is syntactically correct. For instance, the Checker must check that the abstract instructions are well formed and well typed, that the indexes of the variables in the abstract GEM/RTM instructions are consistent with the log header, and that there is an appropriate mapping, say M^{ai}, from abstract GEM instructions into corresponding abstract RTM instructions. For instance, in the case of EQUALITY-II, M^{ai} is defined as follows:

$$M^{ai}(\text{EQUALITY-II } i_1 \ i_2 \ i_3) = < \text{EQU } rd \ M_1^d(i_2) \ M_1^d(i_3),$$
$$\text{OR } M^d(i_1) \ rd \ rd,$$
$$\text{EQU } rd \ M_2^d(i_2) \ M_2^d(i_3),$$
$$\text{AND } M^d(i_1) \ M^d(i_1) \ rd >,$$

(1)

M^d is the mapping from GEM variable indexes to RTM variable indexes as reported in the declaration mapping. In the example, $M^d(2) = < 2,3 >$. $M_1^d(i)$ and $M_2^d(i)$ are the first and second elements of the sequence $M^d(i)$, e.g. $M_1^d(2) = 2$. rd is the index of the RTM variable tmpequ. Notice that the Log actually satisfies the Checking Conditions, e.g. M^{ai} maps the first abstract GEM instruction into the corresponding abstract RTM instructions 1, 2, 3, and 4.

However, knowing that the Log is well formed is not enough. The Checker must make sure that the Log is a proof of the theorem we are interested in, i.e. the equivalence of the two GEM and RTM programs in input to the verifier. This amounts to verifying that the Log applies to the actual GEM and RTM programs. For instance, the Checker must check that the actual programs contain as many instructions and declarations as stated in the log header, and that there is a bijective correspondence between GEM/RTM abstract instructions (contained in the Log) and the concrete GEM/RTM instructions (parsed directly from the actual GEM/RTM). For each possible type of GEM and RTM abstract instruction, the mapping M^c determines the structure of the corresponding concrete instruction. For instance, in the case of EQUALITY-II, it holds:

$M^c(\text{EQUALITY-II } i_1 \ i_2 \ i_3) = v_1 \ \texttt{<-} v_2 \ \texttt{==} \ v_3$, where v_j is the variable of the i_j-th GEM declaration.

The correctness of the decomposition of the Verifier in the logging/checking schema presented above is guaranteed by proving that, for any possible individual compilation, the Checking Conditions imply the Syntactic Verification

Conditions. The proof is done by constructing a mapping M from the M^d, M^{ai} and M^c obtained from the Log. This proof is not difficult and we omit to comment it for lack of space.

6 Certification Assumptions

As any other form of certification, the certification provided by the Verifier is not absolute. First of all, it depends on the assumption that the formal models of GEM and RTM computation are accurate with respect to the actual GEM and RTM computation. This problem has been tackled with a strict integration between IRST and ANSALDO in the development of the formal model.

Second, it depends on the correctness of the formal results. The proofs have been performed manually and, though not technically complex, they are rather long. In order to improve the confidence on their correctness, a further step will be the mechanization of these proofs by means of an industrial-strength prover (e.g. [8, 5]). A prover can be much more accurate than a human in working out the details of fifty pages of proofs. Of course, the mechanization would not give a 100% certification, because in principle the prover itself could be questioned. Several approaches to this problem are under development. Some of these aim at the development of logging/checking mechanisms for full blown provers (e.g. [6]). Others aim at the development of a provably correct prover, see for instance [2] and [3].

Finally, the certification provided by the Verifier depends on the correct implementation and execution of the Checker. The confidence in this assumption is rather high, as the Checker has been designed to be validated by end users, and given its simplicity also the compilation and the execution platform can be trusted.

However, our approach does not rely on the accuracy of the correspondence between the actual GEM and RTM programs in input to the Verifier and their formal model. This correspondence is guaranteed by the Checker itself. As explained in previous section, a large part of the Checking Conditions are intended to make sure that there is a one-to-one correspondence between the actual programs and their model. This innovative feature is due to the requirement that the Verifier must be integrated in VFRAME, and therefore a manual intervention to generate the formal model would not be feasible.

7 Conclusion and Results

We have developed a Verifier which is able to certificate a real industrial safety critical software component. The Verifier is embedded within the safety critical architecture. As required by the industrial application, it is fully automatic and efficient. The Verifier has verified the translation of thousands of instructions in a few seconds. The certification requirement has been satisfied. The correctness of the Verifier depends only on an extremely simple and short portion of its code (a few hundred lines of C code) which can be easily understood and validated by end users.

The project has provided further results and benefits. First, the development of the formal proofs of the semantic equivalence sketched in Section 4 revealed that one of the specified translations performed by the compiler was not semantically preserving. More precisely, the translation of GEM instructions of the form v_1 <- v_1 == v_2, where v_1 is boolean, had been specified as the mapping presented in Section 4. This bug was discovered while failing to prove the corresponding case for Theorem 1.

Second, by running the Verifier on substantial examples of GEM to RTM translations, implementation bugs were detected in the compiler. These bugs were pinpointed by the Checker failure to certify the correctness of the translation.

The approach followed in this project is completely general and independent of the fact that it is used to certify a particular component of VFRAME. Moreover, in spite of the fact that some of the modules of the Logger and the Checker depend on the compiler, the architecture of the Verifier can be re-used for the certification of different systems. Such an architecture can be devised for several safety critical systems which need a certification of translations of data/programs/models/specifications, such as compilers, translators, and specification editors.

References

1. B. Boyer and Yu Y. Automated Correctness Proofs of Machine Code Programs for a Commercial Microprocessor. In *Proc. of the 11th Conference on Automated Deduction*, number 607 in Lecture Notes in Computer Science, pages 416–430. Springer-Verlag, 1992.
2. R.S. Boyer and J.S. Moore. A Theorem Prover for a Computational Logic. In M. E. Stickel, editor, *Proc. of the 10th Conference on Automated Deduction*, pages 1–15, Kaiserlautern, Germany, July 1990. Published as Springer LNAI, number 449.
3. F. Giunchiglia, P. Pecchiari, and C. Talcott. Reasoning Theories: Towards an Architecture for Open Mechanized Reasoning Systems. Technical Report 9409-15, IRST, Trento, Italy, 1994.
4. D. Guaspari, C. Barbash, and D. Hoover. Checking critical code. Technical Report ORA TM-95-0081, Odyssey Research Associates, Ithaca, NY 14850 USA, September 1995.
5. M. Kaufmann and J S. Moore. Design Goals for ACL2. Technical Report 101, Computational Logic Inc., Austin, Texas, 1994.
6. S. Kromodimoeljo, B. Pase, M. Saaltink, D. Craigen, and I. Meisels. The EVES system. In *Proceedings of the International Lecture Series on "Functional Programming, Concurrency, Simulation and Automated Reasoning" (FPCSAR)*. McMaster University, August 1992.
7. J.S. Moore, editor. *Special Issue on Systems Verification, Journal of Automated Reasoning*. Vol. 5, n. 4, 1989.
8. S. Owre, J. Rushby, N. Shankar, and F. von Henke. Formal verification for fault-tolerant architectures: Prolegomena to the design of PVS. *IEEE Transactions on Software Engineering*, 20(2):107–125, February 1995.
9. J. Profeta, N. Andrianos, B. Yu, B. Jonson, T. DeLong, D. Guaspari, and D. Jamsek. Safety Critical Systems Built with COTS. *Computer*, 29(11):54–60, November 1996.

Model Checking in a Microprocessor Design Project

Geoff Barrett and Anthony McIsaac

SGS-Thomson Microelectronics Limited
1000 Aztec West, Almondsbury, Bristol BS12 4SQ, UK
{geoffb, mcisaac}@bristol.st.com

Abstract. This paper gives an account of the use of model checking in a large-scale microprocessor development project. It describes the tools, methods and techniques used, the way the work was organized, and some of the problems encountered, as well as the results achieved. The verification of a bus arbiter is presented as a case study illustrating the abstraction techniques required in order to achieve results for large designs.

1   Introduction

The Chameleon program is a family of next-generation microprocessors being developed by SGS-Thomson Microelectronics. It is based on a modular, core-based 64-bit superscalar architecture. The first products are targeted at the consumer computing market. It implements multi-media features, as well as common microprocessor capabilities.

The overall verification methodology in Chameleon [5] is based on conventional simulation methods for the register transfer level (RTL) model of the design, using advanced techniques and tools for acceleration, emulation and test generation. This is supplemented by model checking in areas where coverage is thinnest. The circuit design is verified by formal equivalence checking, with the structural RTL as reference model. The purpose of this paper is to describe the experience of implementing this methodology, as far as model checking is concerned. We describe the successes and the problems that have arisen in the course of using technology that is still a novelty in such a large and complex development, and we illustrate some techniques for overcoming the problems.

In Section 2 we give a general account of the tools and methods used, and in Section 3 we describe their application to one particularly important example, the verification of a bus arbiter.

We compare our experiences with other accounts of industrial use of model checking [9, 4, 2].

2   Model checking in the design process

Model checking has been applied to a RTL model of the design. The model-checking activity has spanned a period of some 18 months, during which this level of the design has been developed, refined and modified. The scope of the activity has been to supplement verification by simulation; thus it has concentrated on areas where design errors are likely to be shown up only by particular sequences of signal values over several cycles, for example where there is complex interaction of competing demands for resources.

The work has been carried out by members of the verification team, with experience of the tools and specification formalisms used. Each such person has been associated with some part of the design, and has been responsible for: specifying those properties that will be checked, in conjunction with both the relevant designers, and other members of the verification team responsible for developing test suites for the components; carrying out the model-checking task; interpreting the results; and, when a property failure indicates a genuine bug, working with the designer to identify and correct it.

2.1 Methods, tools, and techniques

Given a component for which temporal properties are to be checked, the strategy is, first to construct a representation of that component as a Mealy machine, with boolean input, state and ouput variables, and then to use automated model checkers to test the properties. In view of the limitations on the size of systems for which current model-checking technology can produce a result, the components were of the order of 10000 transistors.

Specification of properties There are two questions: what properties to check, and what formalism to use to specify them. The properties were identified by the designer of the component, as being particularly important, and ones whose contravention might not be detected, at least at an early stage. For example, a component in the unit handling memory instructions was required to have the property that it didn't indefinitely stall a buffer that supplied it with data; the withdrawal of this stall signal depended on complex interactions among the ways in which the resources used by the unit became available, and it was conceivable (and indeed, for an early version of the design, true!), that the stall might never be withdrawn. Only a small number (2 or 3) of crucial properties was chosen for each component; no attempt was made to cover its whole functionality. These properties were concerned with control aspects of the components (arbitration, snooping mechanisms, interaction of state machines).

Along with the properties, assumptions about the environment of the component were specified, such that the properties were only required to hold if the environment did satisfy these assumptions. It was not usually possible to identify all these assumptions first up; they would emerge, as properties were found to fail under circumstances that would never in fact occur. It was also acceptable, and indeed necessary, to include assumptions that made restrictions among those behaviours of the environment that could occur, for example by making certain input values zero. This enabled one to focus on the behaviour of those signals that really did stress the design, in the same way as is done in selecting tests for simulation.

Both properties and assumptions were expressed in terms of interface signals of the component. The properties specified in this way, with the appropriate assumptions, were to be checked for each revision of the design.

The formalism for expressing properties was CTL, with fairness constraints [6]. This was chosen because there are efficient model-checking algorithms for it, implemented in several modern tools, such as the SMV system [10]. CTL is relatively inexpressive, as regards properties of runs of a system, but this was not a problem, since further elements could be added to the specification. For example, a new variable can be introduced, whose value on any cycle is equal to the value of some other variable on the previous cycle.

Given a Mealy machine representing the component, a property specification for it comprises:

1. Sets of new input and state variables, with transition functions for the state variables;
2. A set of *axioms*, boolean expressions in the system's variables, where the quantifiers in the CTL formula are interpreted as ranging over paths on which all the axioms are true at all points;
3. A set of *fairness constraints*, boolean expressions in the system's variables, where the quantifiers in the CTL formula are interpreted as ranging over paths on which each fairness constraint is true infinitely often;
4. A CTL formula.

Using this formalism, it was possible to express all the properties we wanted, although very occasionally their formulation looked contrived. The axioms could be incorporated in the formula, but it is convenient to specify them separately, and our model-checking tool has a special way of dealing with them (see below).

Tools The RTL model is written in the hardware description language VHDL. Given a VHDL description of a component, the first stage is to construct a Mealy machine representing the cycle-by-cycle behaviour of the component. This is done using part of the Compass equivalence-checking tool suite VFormal. VFormal includes a tool which takes as input a VHDL description, and yields a finite state machine (FSM) in which the transition functions for the state variables, and the output functions, are represented as typed decision graphs (TDGs) [8].

This FSM is used as one input to the model-checking tool, Shadow, which has been developed within SGS-Thomson. Shadow also represents FSMs as collections of TDGs for the transition and output functions. The other input to Shadow is the property specification along with axioms, fairness constraints, and definitions of extra variables. Shadow has similar functionality to SMV: it reports whether the property holds or not, and gives a counter-example if not. Its implementation differs from SMV in two major respects: it uses the representation of the FSM as vectors of functions, and does not build the transition relation; and it treats the axioms in a special way [1]. It constructs a new environment for the component, with a new set of unconstrained inputs; the old inputs are defined in terms of them in such a way that all the axioms hold. It gives warnings if the axioms are inconsistent, in the sense that there is no infinite path from the initial state on which the axioms are always true.

We have also implemented a simple translation of the FSM output of VFormal into SMV, and have experimented with using SMV for the property checks. In some cases, Shadow is able to complete tasks where SMV cannot build the transition relation (or fails to complete the proof with a partitioned transition relation). In other cases, SMV is more efficient. We have found that, for large designs, where the transition relation is large, but the property only depends on a small part of the design, Shadow is preferable; while for smallish designs, where there are complex relationships between the signals, and the property depends on the entire design, SMV is preferable. The size of FSM for which Shadow can produce results is comparable with the 300 state and input variables reported for the RuleBase tool [2], but we have found that the number of state variables (latches) is usually the most crucial indicator of computational complexity. In some cases, Shadow can handle over 100 latches, whereas in others it struggles with 20. SMV is more uniform: it has rarely failed in our examples with under 30 latches, and rarely succeeded in those with over 60.

Abstraction The numbers of variables in the FSMs for the components we have considered are an order of magnitude greater than this, and it is necessary to perform some abstraction. Three techniques have been used.

- black-boxing: when the component has a hierarchical design, and there are subcomponents whose behaviour has no relevance to the property under consideration, VFormal can construct an FSM in which the state variables of the subcomponents are eliminated, and their outputs are just considered as inputs to the component.
- projection: given the FSM for a design, Shadow can construct an abstraction of this FSM containing only those inputs and state variables that influence, directly or indirectly, the outputs appearing in the property, axioms and fairness constraints. (A variable influences an output directly if it appears in the value function for that output, indirectly if it appears in the transition function for a state variable that influences the output directly or indirectly.) The output and transition functions in the abstracted FSM are the same as in the original FSM.
- liberalization: allowing a state variable to have arbitrary behaviour, by removing its transition function and converting the state variable to an input variable. Shadow will perform this operation for a list of state variables provided by the user.

In each case, the abstracted FSM can be viewed as the image of the original system under a homomorphism in the sense of [7] and therefore all these techniques yield *safe* abstractions: if a property in ∀CTL (the formulae in CTL whose positive normal form has only universal path quantifiers) holds for the abstracted FSM, it holds for the original FSM. Projection also produces an *exact* abstraction: a CTL property holds for the abstracted FSM if and only if it holds for the original FSM. Projection and liberalization correspond to the use of the *essential* and *cutting* attributes in the RuleBase system developed at IBM Science and Technology, Haifa [3].

Projection is performed as a matter of course in all property checks. It usually removes a large number of data registers, and commonly reduces the number of state variables by a factor of 10. Black-boxing and liberalization require some understanding of the design, to identify those parts which, though they influence the variables appearing in the property, are not relevant to its validity. These two techniques also have the disadvantage that, when a property check fails, further investigation is needed to see whether there is a genuine bug, or too liberal an abstraction has been made. However, they are very effective, as proofs are much easier when state variables are converted to inputs.

Liberalization (and black-boxing) can be performed in conjunction with adding axioms. If there is some set of state variables such that the validity of the property only depends on these variables in so far as there is some boolean function of them that is an invariant of the system, then these variables can be liberalized, and the invariant imposed as an axiom on their new incarnation as inputs. Of course, it is also necessary to prove that the axiom is indeed an invariant.

2.2 Experiences

There have been four phases in the model-checking work in Chameleon. The first few months were devoted to establishing the tools, and such results as were obtained were not reliable. When a working tool chain was achieved, the design was still at an early stage, and provided fruitful ground for model checking, the components being small and not yet subjected to thorough testing that removed all but the most recondite errors. Two successes were particularly noteworthy: the discovery of the bug in the memory unit mentioned earlier (Section 2.1), and work on an early version of the arbiter for the chip's internal bus. A straightforward check of a property of the form $AG(\text{request} \rightarrow AF(\text{grant} \vee \neg\text{request}))$ showed that continuous requesters were not always granted the bus, and identified a deadlock scenario. At that time, the scenario had not occurred during simulation, although the model had been running for several weeks. Investigation revealed that the bus protocol was flawed, and there were no implementations of the arbiter that avoided something as serious as this deadlock; this led to work on the formal specification of the protocol.

At this stage, projection was the only abstraction technique needed. The two bugs were dicovered using SMV on a SPARC 10, and took under half an hour each to discover, using not more than 30 MB of memory.

Designers who were unfamiliar with these techniques were impressed by these results, and the potential they revealed in formal verification. The successes perhaps also led to some subsequent problems in the model-checking activity, raising expectations that were not fulfilled. For, as the design developed, components became increasingly complex, the sizes of FSMs rose from 20 to 50 or more state variables, and property checks that had once been done in a few minutes would take several days, eventually running out of memory. Further, when the designs were revised, even in small ways, property specfications needed to be changed, abstraction techniques that had once worked were no longer sufficient, and each successive new release required almost as much work as the previous one, so that it was not possible to establish an effective automated regression procedure.

Work was concentrated on a small number of properties, for which designers felt least confident that simulation covered all possible interactions. The hardest property checked during this stage (which revealed another subtle bug in the memory unit, that it could under some circumstances lose its data) required runs of a week and more on an UltraSPARC, and up to a gigabyte of memory. Liberalization combined with the use of axioms was essential.

The most recent work has been on system-level properties. It has tried to avoid large computations as described above; the approach has been to study the design and try to understand why a property is expected to hold, then to break proofs into stages, with sub-properties expressed in terms of internal signals of the components. This is only worthwhile when the designs are mature, and the internal signals and structure are not expected to change. Some of this work is described in the case study in Section 3.

2.3 Comparison with other work

Eiriksson and McMillan [9] describe verification of a cache protocol within an industrial project. They describe the system directly in SMV, whereas we start from an implementation of the system, and construct an FSM representation using automated tools. We have been concerned not so much with verifying protocols, as with checking that they are implemented as intended. We have always derived FSMs from the VHDL exactly as written by designers.

The CVE system used in Siemens [4] has a specification language, CIL, that is less expressive, but more intuitive than CTL. In the examples described, reduction is achieved by considering small-scale instances, rather than the automated abstractions described here.

The way the RuleBase tool is applied in IBM [2] is very similar to our approach, as are the abstractions used. Several interesting and impressive examples are described. In this paper, we have tried to illustrate the place of model checking in a large project, not just on individual examples, and we have been concerned with the problems of tracking designs as they develop, and the relationship of model checking to more general specification and proof.

3 The bus arbiter

Some of the most successful work has been on system-level properties. There are two reasons for this: the system interfaces are common to all parts of the design, and so have to be fixed at an early stage; and the properties are hard to test by simulation.

As an illustration, we describe the work done on the chip's internal bus. The component comprises a bus and arbiter; their combination is called the router. Several client modules are attached to the router, and all communication between modules is via the bus. There is arbitration first for bus access, and then senders can control the rate of transmission. The protocol allows implementations with one or several buses. There is a refinement of the arbitration in order to maximize bus usage; a consequence of this is that there are a large number of memory elements in the arbiter, and there is a complex arbitration algorithm.

3.1 Specification

There are 13 properties that the router must satisfy, defined in terms of values of control signals, and expressed in CTL. They cover issues such as only connecting modules to the bus when they are prepared to be connected, transmitting data faithfully to the correct destination, and not indefinitely ignoring requests to use the bus. Two examples are given in Section 3.2 below. From these low-level properties, it was possible to prove that the router satisfied a set of requirements at a higher level, for example that there is a strategy by which any module can be sure to send a packet.

The properties are only required to hold under certain assumptions about its environment, i.e. the client modules. The full specification consists of an interrelated set of properties of the router and the modules, with care being taken to avoid circularity. An example of a rule for a module is that, once it has started a transmission, it must eventually terminate it. For safety, modules should obey their rules even when some things happen that aren't supposed to (especially if software can make them happen). Using simulation, it is hard to test that modules behave correctly in these error cases (as they don't occur!). Formal verification came to the fore in these issues, and made a substantial contribution to the specification of precisely what limits to misbehaviour were insisted upon when modules were the victims of errors.

3.2 Verification

VFormal aims to construct *canonical* FSMs, in which there is some fixed order of the input and state variables, and each transition and output function is represented as a canonical TDG in these variables. If such an FSM were constructed for the router, it would be huge; it was estimated that there was no way of avoiding TDGs of at least a hundred million nodes. The solution to this problem is to keep a small number of intermediate variables in the FSM. These variables, called breakpoints, are functions of the input and state variables, and the output and transition functions of the FSM are expressed in terms of these variables, as well as input and state variables. VFormal in fact starts by constructing an FSM containing functions for state transitions, outputs, and breakpoints, these last typically corresponding to internal signals. To obtain a canonical representation, the breakpoints are substituted in the output and transition functions. VFormal can output an FSM in which not all the breakpoints have been substituted.

Shadow requires canonical FSMs, but, by starting with a non-canonical one and making abstractions at suitable points, one can ensure that one has a tractable FSM by the time the breakpoints have to be substituted.

The strategy used in the verification of the router was to break properties into smaller ones, and to supplement the model checking with reasoning that the properties that were checked did indeed imply those in the specification. Ideally, these arguments would have been formalised using a proof assistant, but this was not a priority in allocation of resources: the reasoning was thoroughly reviewed, and in fact the main target of this verification activity was not the correctness of the mechanisms the designers had used to ensure the validity of the individual properties in the specification, for it was clear how these mechanisms achieved their purpose, and some were well-known algorithms. What needed to be tested was that the designers were aware of all the properties in the specification; that the mechanisms were correctly implemented and encoded; and that the mechanisms for different properties did not interfere with each other.

The aim was to use model checking on properties that only depended on small parts of the design; thus Shadow was used for most of the checks, although SMV was still found to be better for one or two of them. Many of the checks took less than 1 minute, and none more than 30 minutes.

We illustrate the techniques used in the verification of two properties.

Use of intermediate variables The property checked was: The arbiter must not give a grant to a sender that hasn't made a request.

$$AG(\neg request \rightarrow AX \neg grant)$$

First, the subcomponents of the router that were not expected to influence the property were identified, and an FSM was constructed with these subcomponents treated as black boxes. 12 breakpoints were retained in this FSM, to keep its size within reasonable bounds. Projection was then performed with respect to the output $grant$. This resulted in an FSM with 250 input variables and 49 state variables. The breakpoints remained in the FSM after projection. An FSM of this size is on the borderline for the model-checking tools. However, there was reason to suppose that many of the state variables, although they influenced the value of $grant$, did not affect its relationship with $request$. These variables were liberalized, yielding an FSM with 246 input variables and 21 state variables. For an FSM of this size, if the individual outputs were not too complex as functions of the inputs, model checking would be expected to be fairly straightforward. Unfortunately, there were still 12 breakpoints, and there was no way of avoiding vast TDG representations of the output functions if these were substituted.

The property was proved by treating the breakpoints as inputs (liberalizing them), and imposing an axiom of the form

$$\neg request \rightarrow \bigwedge f_i(b_i, \vec{x})$$

where b_i ranges over the breakpoints, and each f_i is a function of b_i and the vector of inputs $\vec{x}$. It was then necessary to prove that the axiom was always true; this could be done for each breakpoint separately. Thus, each of the formulae

$$AG(\neg request \rightarrow f_i(b_i, \vec{x}))$$

was proved. In each case, an output was added that was set equal to the break-point b_i, and projection relative to this output was performed. The other break-points did not appear in the resulting FSM, and the one that was present could be substituted without any difficulty.

The whole proof took 20 minutes using Shadow.

Abstract views of the transition system The property checked was: Requests to send are eventually granted.

$$AG(AF(\neg request \vee grant))$$

There were fairness constraints expressing the fact that any other module that started a transmission on the bus eventually finished that transmission. This property is simple to formulate, but the proof presents huge problems. No components could be black-boxed: constructing an FSM and projecting with respect to the relevant outputs yielded an FSM with 226 input and 129 state variables. Even using liberalization and axioms, it was impossible to check the property directly, and it had to be deduced from properties of smaller systems.

The clearest and most economical way that was found to do this was not to consider properties of subcomponents, but rather to build *abstract views* of the whole system: the idea was to define transition systems that, in an intuitive sense, represented the behaviour of the system from the point of view of one or two distinguished modules. The relationship of abstraction and model checking in this method is very different from that in the methods described so far: instead of using the tools to perform an abstraction, and then checking properties on the abstracted system, here model checking is used to prove that the abstract views are in some sense abstractions of the original system. The properties that are actually proved, which we shall call the implementation properties, define the exact sense in which the abstract views are abstractions. Then ordinary reasoning (such as could be carried out in a higher-order logic proof system) is used to prove that the implementation properties imply the specification properties, those that the system is required to satisfy.

The guiding principles in choosing abstract views to represent the system are that the number of implementation properties should not be too large; that the individual implementation properties should be simple (often of the form $AG(P \rightarrow AXQ)$); that the line of reasoning from the implementation properties to the specification properties should be clear; that large parts of this reasoning should be applicable in a wide variety of cases, not just the example under consideration; and that the abstract views should be expected to remain substantially unchanged as the design develops, even if the details of the implementation and the coding change.

The features of abstract views are:

1. The states of the abstract view are sets of states of the original system (in fact, partitions under an equivalence relation, so that there is a map f from the original states to the abstract states).

2. Some of the transitions of the original system are deemed to be *invisible* in the abstract view. If it is possible for a visible transition from s_1 to s_2 to occur in a run of the original system, then there must be a transition from $f(s_1)$ to $f(s_2)$ in the abstract view; and if it is possible for an invisible transition from s_1 to s_2 to occur, then $f(s_1) = f(s_2)$.

Then if a run of the original system contains infinitely many visible transitions, it is mapped by f to a run of the abstract view (ignoring the invisible transitions in the first run). This map will preserve the validity of LTL path formulae not involving the next state operator, if the interpretation of each atomic proposition in the original system respects the equivalence relation.

We describe a simplification, sufficient for the purposes of illustration, of the abstract views that were used for the property under consideration. Let A be the module we want to prove eventually gets granted, and let B be any other module. We denote the abstract view from the point of view of A and B (in that order) by $V_{A,B}$. The visible transitions for the abstract view $V_{A,B}$ are chosen to be those on which either the grant or the request signal for A or B change, or B is using the bus. There are six abstract states in $V_{A,B}$: Idle (when A is not using the bus and not requesting it), Granted (when A is using the bus), and four Requesting states in which A is requesting the bus and not using it. The subdivisions of Requesting are indicated by -In and -Out (when B is respectively using or not using the bus) and -Earlier and -Later (when A is respectively earlier or later in the queue for the bus than B).

The abstract view is:

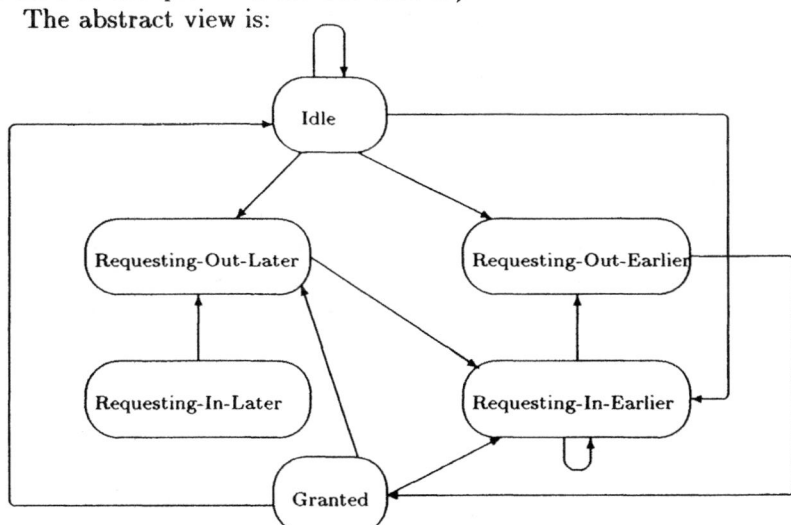

Shadow is used to prove the following:

A1 On any run of the system, if a transition occurs that is visible in $V_{A,B}$, the states before and after that transition are in sets that are related by an arrow in $V_{A,B}$.

A2 On any run of the system, if a transition occurs that is invisible in $V_{A,B}$, then the states before and after that transition are in the same set in $V_{A,B}$.

A3 On any run of the system, if A is requesting in some state, then there is some B such that the transition to the next state is visible in $V_{A,B}$.

A4 On any run of the system, the visible transition from Requesting-In-Earlier to itself in $V_{A,B}$ cannot occur infinitely often without some other visible transition in $V_{A,B}$ occurring.

The first three of these involve only properties relating one state and the next. For example, part of A1 is the property $AG(($Requesting-Out-Later $\wedge\ grant_B) \rightarrow AX($Requesting-In-Earlier$))$. A4 is the property $AG(AF\neg$Requesting-In-Earlier$)$. For this property, we make use of the fairness constraint that B finishes all the transmissions it starts, but this is not enough to make the property trivial; the property tests the fact that B does not indefinitely reclaim the bus as soon as it has finished a transmission.

All except A3 consist of properties referring to a single abstract view, which allows one to reduce the system considerably. A3 could have been a stumbling block, but its proof was in fact very rapid (less than 2 minutes).

No further part is played by VFormal and Shadow. The property is proved by direct reasoning. Suppose that there is a run of the system in which, from some point on, A continuously requests but is never granted. By A3, since there are only finitely many modules, there must be some B such that the run of the system includes infinitely many transitions that are visible in $V_{A,B}$. By A1 and A2, this run can be mapped as above to a run of $V_{A,B}$ (consisting just of visible transitions), which must remain within the Requesting states from some point onwards. By examination of the diagram, it is immediate that any infinite loop that consists entirely of visible transitions in $V_{A,B}$ and is confined to the Requesting states must contain infinitely many repetitions of the visible transition from Requesting-In-Earlier to itself. (This could of course be treated as a simple model-checking task.) Such loops are ruled out by A4.

Here A1 and A2 define the sense in which the abstract view is an abstraction, and allow one to argue that certain properties of runs are preserved in the abstract view. A3 is the key to proving liveness properties of this sort, and its analogue can be used in many similar examples. Only A4 is peculiar to this particular example.

4 Conclusions

Model checking has a part to play in a large-scale microprocessor development, and in particular areas its contribution is hard to replace by other means. It is suitable for checking complex control properties of components of moderate size: almost every such task can be done somehow, but flexibility in approach is essential. Simple abstraction techniques such as projection and liberalization can easily be incorporated in tools, and they are cheap and highly effective in tasks of moderate size. For larger tasks, a combination of model checking and proof can almost always achieve results; it is costly, but brings benefits such as clear and precise specifications.

A welcome development would be a framework for managing proofs: relating properties of one component to assumptions about the environment of another; splitting proofs into stages; reasoning about properties of a system in terms of properties of different abstract views; and establishing justifications of abstractions and other operations.

5 Acknowledgements

The authors wish to thank the members of the Chameleon team involved in this work, in particular Christian Berthet, Mohammed Belhadj, Mike Bartley, Giovanni Castorina, Margaret Gearty, Will Barnes.

References

1. Geoff Barrett. Modelling nondeterminism with transition functions. Technical report, ST Internal Report, SHD AX 0.0, 1996.
2. Ilan Beer, Shoham Ben-David, Cindy Eisner, and Avner Landver. RuleBase: An industry-oriented formal verification tool. In *Proceedings of the 33rd Design Automation Conference, Las Vegas*, pages 655–660, 1996.
3. Ilan Beer, Shoham Ben-David, Daniel Geist, Raanan Gewirtzman, and Michael Yoeli. Methodology and system for practical formal verification of reactive hardware. In D.Dill, editor, *CAV'94, Lecture Notes in Computer Science 818*, pages 182–193, 1994.
4. Jörg Bormann, Jörg Lohse, Michael Payer, and Gerd Venzl. Model checking in industrial hardware design. In *Proceedings of the 32nd Design Automation Conference, San Francisco*, pages 298–303, 1995.
5. Françoise Casaubieilh, Anthony McIsaac, Mike Benjamin, et al. Functional verification methodology of Chameleon processor. In *Proceedings of the 33rd Design Automation Conference, Las Vegas*, pages 421–426, 1996.
6. E.M. Clarke, E. Emerson, and A.P. Sistla. Automatic verification of finite state concurrent systems using temporal logic specifications. *ACM Transactions on Programming Languages and Systems*, 8(2):244–263, April 1986.
7. E.M. Clarke, O. Grumberg, and D.E.Long. Model checking and abstraction. In *Proceedings of the 19th Annual ACM Symposium on Principles of Programming Languages*, pages 343–354, 1992.
8. O. Coudert, C. Berthet, and J.C. Madre. Verification of sequential machines using boolean functional vectors. In *Proceedings of the Workshop on Applied Formal Methods for Correct VLSI Design, Houlathen, Belgium, November 1989, in Formal VLSI Correctness Verification vol. II*. North-Holland, 1990.
9. A.T. Eiriksson and K.L. McMillan. Using formal verification/analysis methods on the critical path in system design: A case study. In P.Wolper, editor, *CAV'95, Lecture Notes in Computer Science 939*, pages 367–380. Springer Verlag, 1995.
10. K.L. McMillan. *Symbolic Model Checking*. Kluwer Academic Publishers, 1993.

Some Thoughts on Statecharts, 13 Years Later

(Summary of Talk)

David Harel*

Abstract: The talk describes the background and motivation for the language of statecharts, discusses some of the semantic issues it raises, shows how statecharts have been embedded in structured-analysis and object-oriented frameworks, and describes the supporting tools, STATEMATE and RHAPSODY, from i-Logix, Inc. Some peripheral research is also mentioned.

Introduction

Statecharts were conceived of in late 1983. In the (belatedly published) paper that first presented them [H1], statecharts were portrayed in isolation, as a visual formalism for specifying 'raw' reactive behavior. They were described rather informally there, and several semantic issues were discussed only very briefly.

In the years that have elapsed since, much work has been carried out around statecharts. In this talk we attempt to survey some of the main lines of this work, which can be divided up as follows:

1. Semantics of statecharts.
2. Embedding in a structured analysis framework.
3. The STATEMATE tool.
4. Embedding in an object-oriented framework.
5. The RHAPSODY tool.
6. Variants of the language.
7. Related research topics.

Item 3 essentially implements the ideas in item 2, and, similarly, item 5 implements the ideas in item 4. In this note we shall say a few words about items 1, 4 and 7.

Semantics

A rigorous semantics was first defined for statecharts in [HPSS]. Since then, many variants of statecharts have been proposed in the literature, and several papers include definitions of semantics too. Some examples are [HR, KP, L+, M, PS]. A recent survey [vB] discusses around 20 variants. Subtle issues arise when

---

* The Weizmann Institute of Science, Rehovot, Israel, and i-Logix, Inc., Andover, MA 01810. Email: harel@wisdom.weizmann.ac.il.

one tries to define a semantics for this language, and there is no consensus on the "right" way to go about the task.

In a recent paper [HN], we describe the semantics of statecharts as implemented in the STATEMATE system [H$^+$, HP]. The initial version of this semantics was developed by several people about 10 years ago. With the added experience of the users of the system it has since been extended and modified. This executable semantics has been in operation in driving the simulation, dynamic tests and code generation tools of STATEMATE since 1987, and a technical report describing it was written in 1989. We decided to revise and publish the report so as to make it more widely accessible, to alleviate some of the confusion about the "official" semantics of the language, and to counter a number of incorrect comments made in the literature about the way statecharts have been implemented.[2]

Being an unofficial language, statecharts clearly has no official semantics, and researchers are free to propose semantics as they see fit. However, for better or worse, the only implemented and working semantics for statecharts has for many years been the one described in [HN]. One of the main issues in defining a semantics for statecharts, and one that was the central topic of our often heated deliberations when working on the problem, is whether changes that occur in a given step (such as generated events or updates to the values of data items) should take effect in the current step or in the next one. The semantics we finally adopted, in contrast to those of [HPSS, PS], for example, takes the latter approach.

The main consideration behind the definitions in [HN] is to provide a semantics for the specification and design of real-world complex systems, coming from a variety of disciplines. As such, the semantics has to be rich enough to support different styles of modeling, yet it should be relatively simple and intuitive. It must also be technically straightforward enough to enable fast simulation of models, and to generate useful hardware and software code out of these models. Clearly, these desires cannot be satisfied in full, but they served to guide the process that led to [HN].

Since the publication of [HN] a number of papers have been written, in which more formal descriptions of this semantics have been proposed. They include [EGKP, MLPS, PU].

Object modeling with statecharts

For large systems, statecharts cannot be used as the sole specification technique, even if behavior is the central concern. Rather, one should use statecharts as the

---

[2] For example, the survey [vB] does not mention the STATEMATE implementation of statecharts or the semantics adopted for it at all, although this semantics is different from the ones surveyed therein (and was developed earlier than all of them except for [HPSS]).

behavioral component of a general system-modeling approach. This is a nontrivial matter, since the links between the various aspects of a system's description can be subtle and slippery, especially if full behavior is to be part of the specification. Since modeling approaches must be detailed and precise enough to enable model execution, dynamic analysis and code synthesis, the language set must be rigorously defined and 'closed up': Any possible combination of graphical and/or textual constructs must be clearly characterized as syntactically legal or illegal, and all legal combinations must then be given unique and formal meaning.

About a decade ago, a language set was built around statecharts, based on the function-oriented structured-analysis paradigm (SA). Statecharts, used for behavioral description, were closely integrated with a structured language for functional decomposition and data-flow, called activity-charts. A third language, module-charts, was used to specify physical decomposition. See [H3] for the motivation and 'philosophical' aspects of this effort, and [HP] for a full description of the languages. This language set underlies the STATEMATE tool, built to enable executability, analysis and full code-generation [H+]. However, since SA methods are widely regarded as suffering from a discontinuity problem in transition to design and reuse, many people recommend approaches that follow the object-oriented paradigm. This change is one of the most significant in software engineering in recent years. Accordingly, we recently embarked on an effort to develop a set of languages for object modeling, built around statecharts, and to construct a supporting tool (called RHAPSODY) with full executability and code-synthesis capabilities. This effort is reported on in [HG].

The basic idea is to model the structural properties of classes in a hierarchical manner, and to integrate the resulting description with a precise specification of behavior over time, using statecharts. Since classes represent collections of concrete objects (instances), and since the instances and their relationships change dynamically over time, the model must address issues like the initialization of, and the reference to, actual object instances, the delegation of messages, the creation and destruction of instances, the initialization, modification and maintenance of links representing association relationships, etc. We must also define aggregation and inheritance from a behavioral point of view. All this makes the problem of combining structure and behavior much harder than in an SA-based framework. And it is particularly delicate in the realm of reactive systems, which are characterized not by data-intensive computation but by control-intensive, often time-critical, behavior [HPn].

Most object-oriented modeling methodologies (for example [B, CD, R+, SGW, SM]) offer graphical notations for specifying the model. They typically have ER-style diagrams for specifying classes of objects and their inter-relationships, and means for describing the interface and capabilities of the objects themselves. A state-based formalism is usually adopted for specifying behavior, and the methodologies listed above recommend statecharts (or some sublanguage thereof) for this. However, in many cases such methodologies do not address dynamic semantics adequately, so that the precise behavior of models over time is not always well-defined. One major motivation for our work in [HG] was to eliminate this crucial shortcoming.

The approach in [HG] involves two constructive modeling languages, *object-model diagrams* and *statecharts*, and a reflective language, *message sequence charts* (MSC's; also called sequence diagrams).[3] Object-model diagrams specify the structure of the system, by identifying classes of objects (i.e., object types) and their multiplicities, object relationships and roles, subtyping and inheritance. Especially noteworthy in this language is the provision for specifying composite objects, which capture a strong form of aggregation; they are depicted by higraph-like encapsulation [H2].[4]

A statechart attached to a class specifies the behavior of all instances thereof. It captures not only the state of the object in terms of its willingness, as a server, to respond to events or requests for services, but also the dynamics of its internal behavior in carrying out those responses, and in maintaining its relationships as a client (or aggregate) with other objects.

One of the main technical issues that arise in devising the setup concerns the choice of mechanisms to be used for inter-object interaction. There is a tradeoff between high-level mechanisms that are easier to model, and lower-level ones that are easier to translate into efficient code. We have tried to compromise in [HG], adopting a two-kind approach — asynchronous *events* and synchronous *operations* — and in the process make careful distinctions between them. An object can generate an event, which is queued, to be "plucked" from the queue by the target server object in its turn, and an object can also directly invoke an operation of another object, thus causing it to carry out an appropriate method, and perhaps return a value. Interestingly, one of the upshots of our hierarchical modeling of composite structure is that these interactions can be arranged to take on the form of either direct communication or broadcast.

The description in [HG] concentrates on a single-thread approach to 'event-driven' concurrency, which makes the exposition somewhat easier. For example, we need not concern ourselves there with the issue of multiple event queues. And while the presentation of both the syntax and semantics of the languages in [HG] is informal (for clarity) and not totally exhaustive (for brevity), we do have a full-fledged definition of both. This definition is reflected in the algorithm that

---

[3] A language is constructive if it contributes to the dynamic semantics of the model. That is, its constructs contain information needed in executing the model or in translating it into executable code. Other languages are reflective or assertive, and can be used by the system modeler to capture parts of the thinking that go into building the model — behavior included —, to derive and present views of the model, statically or during execution, or to set constraints on behavior in preparation for verification.

[4] The joint work we have been doing recently with the UML team, which is led by rational Corp. (see [Ra]), has resulted in full consistency between our object-model diagrams and the object models of UML. In particular, the semantics of composite objects is now defined in UML as it is in [HG].

RHAPSODY uses to translate any syntactically legal model into executable code. The current target language of RHAPSODY's code-synthesis is C^{++}, but we hope that other languages will follow.

Spinoff research

Time permitting, this part of the talk will mention a few research topics we have been involved in, which were triggered in one way or another by the work on statecharts. Among them are (i) the question of succinctness of behavioral models (e.g., it is shown in [DH] that the kind of cooperative concurrency present in statecharts provides an exponential saving in size), (ii) the formalism of higraphs [H2], which is an extension and combination of graphs and hypergraphs, and (iii) the problem of drawing graphs and higraphs nicely [DaH, HS].

References

[B]   Booch, G., *Object-Oriented Analysis and Design, with Applications* (2nd edn.), Benjamin/Cummings, 1994.

[CD]   Cook, S. and J. Daniels, *Designing Object Systems: Object-Oriented Modelling with Syntropy*, Prentice Hall, New York, 1994.

[DaH]   Davidson, R. and D. Harel, "Drawing Graphs Nicely Using Simulated Annealing", *ACM Transactions on Graphics* 15 (Oct. 1996), 301–331. (Also, Technical report, The Weizmann Institute of Science, Rehovot, Israel, 1989.)

[DH]   Drusinsky, D. and D. Harel, "On the Power of Bounded Concurrency I: Finite Automata", *J. Assoc. Comput. Mach.* 41 (1994), 517–539.

[EGKP] Ehrig, H., R. Geisler, M. Klar and J. Padberg, "Horizontal and Vertical Structuring Techniques for Statecharts", *Proc. CONCUR '97*, to appear.

[H1]   Harel, D., "Statecharts: A Visual Formalism for Complex Systems", *Sci. Comput. Prog.* 8 (1987), 231–274. (Preliminary version appeared as Tech. Report CS84-05, The Weizmann Institute of Science, Rehovot, Israel, Feb. 1984.)

[H2]   Harel, D., "On Visual Formalisms", *Comm. ACM* 31 (1988), 514–530.

[H3]   Harel, D., "Biting the Silver Bullet: Toward a Brighter Future for System Development", *Computer* (Jan. 1992), 8–20.

[HG]   Harel, D. and E. Gery, "Executable Object Modeling with Statecharts", *Computer*, to appear. (Also, *Proc. 18th Int. Conf. Soft. Eng.*, Berlin, IEEE Press, March, 1996, pp. 246–257.)

[H$^+$] Harel, D., H. Lachover, A. Naamad, A. Pnueli, M. Politi, R. Sherman, A. Shtull-Trauring, and M. Trakhtenbrot, "STATEMATE: A Working Environment for the Development of Complex Reactive Systems", *IEEE Trans. Soft. Eng.* 16 (1990), 403–414. (Preliminary version appeared in *Proc. 10th Int. Conf. Soft. Eng.*, IEEE Press, New York, 1988, pp. 396–406.)

[HN]   Harel, D. and A. Naamad, "The STATEMATE Semantics of Statecharts", *ACM Trans. Soft. Eng. Method.* 5:4 (Oct. 1996), 293–333. (Preliminary version appeared as Tech. Report, i-Logix, Inc., 1989.)

[HPn]   Harel, D. and A. Pnueli, "On the Development of Reactive Systems", in *Logics and Models of Concurrent Systems*, (K. R. Apt, ed.), NATO ASI Series, Vol. F-13, Springer-Verlag, New York, 1985, pp. 477-498.

[HP] Harel, D. and M. Politi, *Modeling Reactive Systems with Statecharts*, McGraw-Hill, to appear. (Early version titled *The Languages of* STATEMATE, Tech. Report, i-Logix, Inc. (250 pp.), 1991.)

[HPSS] Harel, D., A. Pnueli, J.P. Schmidt and R. Sherman, "On the Formal Semantics of Statecharts", *Proc. 2nd IEEE Symp. on Logic in Computer Science*, IEEE Press, New York, 1987, pp. 54-64.

[HS] Harel, D. and M. Sardas, "Randomized Graph Drawing with Heavy-Duty Preprocessing", *J. Visual Lang. and Comput.* **6** (1995), 233-253.

[HR] Huizing, C. and W. P. deRoever, "Introduction to design choices in the semantics of Statecharts", *Inf. Proc. Lett.* **37** (1991), 205-213.

[KP] Kesten, Y. and A. Pnueli, "Timed and Hybrid Statecharts and their Textual Representation", In *Formal Techniques in Real-Time and Fault-Tolerant Systems* (J. Vytopil, ed.), Lecture Notes in Computer Science, Vol. 571, Springer-Verlag, Berlin, 1992, pp. 591-619.

[L+] Leveson, N.G., M.P.E. Heimdahl, H. Hildreth and J.D. Reese, "Requirements Specification for Process-Control Systems", *IEEE Trans. Soft. Eng.* **20** (1995),684-707.

[MLPS] Mikk, E., Y. Lakhnech, C. Petersohn and M. Siegel, "On Formal Semantics of Statecharts as Supported by STATEMATE", Manuscript, 1996.

[M] Maraninchi, F., "Operational and Compositional Semantics of Asynchronous Automaton Compositions", *Proc. CONCUR '92*, Lecture Notes in Computer Science, Vol. 630, Springer-Verlag, Berlin, 1992, pp. 550-564.

[PU] Petersohn, C., and L. Urbina, "A Timed Semantics for the STATEMATE Implementation of Statecharts", Manuscript, 1996.

[PS] Pnueli, A. and M. Shalev, "What is in a Step: On the Semantics of Statecharts", *Proc. Symp. on Theoret. Aspects of Comput. Soft.*, Lecture Notes in Computer Science, Vol. 526, Springer-Verlag, Berlin, 1991, pp. 244-264.

[Ra] Rational Corp., Documents on UML (the Unified Modeling Language), Version 1.0 (http://www.rational.com/ot/uml/1.0/), 1996.

[R+] Rumbaugh, J., M. Blaha, W. Premerlani, F. Eddy and W. Lorensen, *Object-Oriented Modeling and Design*, Prentice Hall, 1991.

[SGW] Selic, B., G. Gullekson and P. T. Ward, *Real-Time Object-Oriented Modeling*, John Wiley & Sons, New York, 1994.

[SM] Shlaer, S. and S. J. Mellor, *Object Lifecycles: Modeling the World in States*, Yourdon Press, 1992.

[vB] von der Beek, M., "A Comparison of Statechart Variants", in *Formal Techniques in Real-Time and Fault-Tolerant Systems* (Langmaack, de Roever and Vytopil, eds.), Lecture Notes in Computer Science, vol. 863, Springer-Verlag, New York, 1994, pp. 128-148.

On-the-Fly Model Checking Under Fairness That Exploits Symmetry *

Viktor Gyuris[1] and A. Prasad Sistla[2]

[1] Mathematics, Statistics and Computer Science Department, The University of
Illinois at Chicago, USA
[2] Electrical Engineering and Computer Science Department, The University of
Illinois at Chicago, USA

Abstract. An on-the-fly algorithm, for model checking under fairness,
is presented. The algorithm utilizes symmetry in the program to reduce
the state space, and employs new novel techniques that make the on-
the-fly modelchecking feasible. The algorithm uses state symmetry and
eliminates paralle edges in the reachability graph. Experimental results,
demonstrating dramatic reductions in both the running time and memory usage, are presented.

1 Introduction

The state explosion problem is one of the major bottlenecks in temporal logic
model checking. Symmetry based techniques have been proposed in [CFJ93,
ES93, ID93] for combating the state explosion problem. In these methods the
reachability graph is collapsed by identifying states that are equivalent under
symmetry, and model checking is performed on the reduced graph. Although
the initial methods of [CFJ93, ES93] could only handle a limited set of liveness
properties, a more generalized approach for checking liveness properties under
various notions of fairness has been proposed in [ES95]. This method constructs
an *Annotated Quotient Structure* (AQS), computes a product graph and explores
the product for existence of fair paths that violate the correctness property.

Many traditional model checking algorithms ([BCG95, G96, HP96, K94]) use
on-the-fly techniques to avoid storing the complete reachability graph in the main
memory. However, none of these techniques employ symmetry. [ID93] uses on-
the-fly techniques together with symmetry for model checking. There the focus is
on reasoning about a simple but basic type of correctness, i.e., safety properties
expressible in temporal logic CTL by an assertion of the form AG¬error.

In this paper, we present an on-the-fly model checking algorithm that checks
for correctness under fairness and that exploits symmetry. The algorithm explores the product graph at the same time as it constructs it and terminates
early if it finds an incorrect fair computation. Thus, it may terminate early even
before it completes the construction of the product graph. Furthermore, it only
saves the states in the partially constructed product graph but not the edges.

---

* This work is partly supported by the NSF grants CCR-9623229, CCR-9633536

The paper develops additional theory that leads to new novel techniques that make the on-the-fly model-checking feasible. Our algorithm also uses another technique, called *state symmetry* [ES93], for reducing the running time as well as memory usage. The on-the-fly model checking algorithm has been implemented and experimental results indicate substantial improvement in performance compared to the original method.

The fairness that we consider in this paper is the traditional weak fairness (a computation is said to be weakly fair if every process is either infinitely often disabled or is executed infinitely often). The algorithm for fairness, given in [ES95], works as follows. It constructs the AQS $\overline{M}$ and then computes the product $\overline{B}$ of $\overline{M}$ and A where A is the automaton that accepts exactly all the incorrect computations. It explores $\overline{B}$ checking for existence of "subtly fair" and "final" strongly connected components; in order to check if a strongly connected component C is subtly fair, it resolves C into a threaded graph C^{thr} and then checks if each of the connected components in C^{thr} is "obviously fair", i.e., contains a good node. The nodes of the threaded graph are of the form (v, j) where v is a node in $\overline{B}$ and j is a process index.

Our on-the-fly algorithm works as follows. It incrementally constructs $\overline{B}$ as and when required, and at the same time runs a modified algorithm for computing the strongly connected components (*scc*) using depth first search [AHU74]. During the depth first search, with each vertex on the stack, it maintains a partition vector. If u is a state in $\overline{B}$ belonging to the *scc* C then the partition vector associated with u captures information about the strongly connected components of the threaded graph C^{thr} (intuitively, if the ith and j^{th} components of the partition vector are equal then it indicates that the nodes (u, i) and (u, j) are in the same *scc* in C^{thr}). Whenever, an edge to an already visited node in the same *scc* is explored then the corresponding partition vectors are merged, and whenever a new vertex in the same *scc* is visited then the corresponding partitions are combined. After each combine or merge operation, it is checked if all the components in the partition vector are weakly fair, and if the strongly connected component contains a final automaton state; if so, the algorithm terminates indicating that an incorrect fair computation has been found.

In addition to the above, our algorithm uses state symmetry [ES93] to reduce the size of the constructed AQS. A permutation $\pi \in Aut\,M$ on process indices is a state symmetry of a representative state s, if $\pi(s) = s$. The state symmetry is exploited in different forms in our algorithms. When checking the correctness of the execution of a single process, in [ES93], $\overline{B}$ is constructed as the product $M \times I \times A$ where A is the automaton. However, we construct $\overline{B}$ as the product $\overline{M} \times \overline{I} \times A$; the new product can have potentially fewer states. State symmetry is also used to reduce the number of edges in $\overline{B}$ and $\overline{M}$; especially, parallel edges between the same nodes are eliminated. This reduces memory usage. (For example, in any state s of $\overline{M}$, if many processes are in the same local state then it is enough if we execute one of them and store the corresponding transitions.)

Our paper is organized as follows. Section 2 contains notation and preliminaries. In Sect. 3 we develop the necessary theory and present the on-the-fly algorithm. We describe various modifications of the algorithm that take state symmetry into consideration. Section 4 presents experimental results showing the effectiveness of our algorithm and dramatic improvements in time as well as memory usage. Section 5 contains concluding remarks.

2 Preliminaries

2.1 Programs, Processes, Global State Graph

Let I be a set of *process indices* and *Sym I* denote the set of all permutations on I. We consider a system $P = \|_{i \in I} K_i$ of processes running parallel. Each process K_i is a set of transitions. We assume that all variables of P are indexed by indices from I that denote the processes that share the variable. A system P, that meets the above description, is called an *indexed transition system* (or briefly program).

A *global state* of an indexed transition system is an assignment of values to the variables. We assume that the domain of every variable is finite. This assumption is motivated by the applications and yields that there are only finitely many global states. We can define an indexed graph M on the set of global states that captures the behavior of the program. The *indexed global state graph* is $M = \langle S, R, s_0 \rangle$ where S is the set of global states, s_0 is the initial state, and $R \subseteq S \times I \times S$ is the transition relation, i.e., $s \xrightarrow{i} t \in R$ if there is a transition in process i that is enabled in state s and its execution leads to state t.

2.2 Annotated Quotient Structure, Threaded Graph

For a permutation π, we define the action of π on the set of global states. For a global state s, we define the global state $\pi(s)$ as follows; for every variable $v_{i_1,\ldots,i_k}$, its value in the state s is given to the variable $v_{\pi(i_1),\ldots,\pi(i_k)}$ in the state $\pi(s)$; of course, if $v_{\pi(i_1),\ldots,\pi(i_k)}$ is not a variable then $\pi(s)$ is undefined. We say that π is an *automorphism* of the indexed global state graph M if the action of π is defined on S, $\pi(s_0) = s_0$ and $s \xrightarrow{i} t \in R$ exactly when $\pi(s) \xrightarrow{\pi(i)} \pi(t) \in R$. The set of automorphisms of M is denoted by $Aut\,M$. Certainly, $Aut\,M$ is a subgroup of $Sym\,I$. Given any subgroup G of $Aut\,M$, we can define an equivalence relation on S. State s is equivalent to t if there is a $\pi \in G$ such that $\pi(s) = t$. M can be compressed using G as follows. The *annotated quotient structure* (AQS) for M is $\overline{M} = \langle \overline{S}, \overline{R}, s_0 \rangle$ where $\overline{S}$ is a set of *representative states* that contains exactly one state from each equivalence class of S/G, $\overline{R} = \{s \xrightarrow{\pi,i} t \; : \; \pi \in G, s, t \in \overline{S}, s \xrightarrow{i} \pi(t) \in R\}$.

In order to check correctness of a program under fairness, processes need to be traced in the compressed graph $\overline{M}$, that is, $\overline{M}$ needs to be partially unwound. This leads to the notion of a threaded graph. Let $H = \langle V, E \rangle$ be any graph whose edges are labelled with permutations of a set I. The *threaded graph* H^{thr} corresponding to H is $\langle V \times I, E^{\text{thr}} \rangle$ where $E^{\text{thr}} = \{(s, k) \to (t, l) \; : \; s \xrightarrow{\pi} t \in E$ for some permutation $\pi, l = \pi^{-1}(k)\}$. If H has further labels on its edges then H^{thr} inherits them. For further details consult [ES95].

2.3 Strongly Connected Subgraphs

The set of states that appear infinitely often in an infinite computation of a finite state program forms a strongly connected subgraph of M. Many properties, such as fairness, can be checked by checking properties of reachable strongly connected components (scc for short) of M. Let C be a subgraph of M. Define $\overline{C}$ to be the image of C in $\overline{M}$, that is, to be $\{s \in \overline{S} : \pi(s) \in C$ for some permutation $\pi\}$.

Lemma 1. *1. If C is a scc of M then $\overline{C}$ is a scc of $\overline{M}$.*
2. If $\overline{C}$ is a scc of $\overline{M}$ then there is a scc D of M with $\overline{D} = \overline{C}$.
3. If $\overline{C}$ is a scc of $\overline{M}$ then $\overline{C}^{\mathrm{thr}}$ is a disjoint union of scc of $\overline{M}^{\mathrm{thr}}$.

2.4 Fairness

In this paper we consider the traditional weak fairness. A computation is said to be *weakly fair* if every process is either infinitely often disabled or executed. This condition leads to the following definitions on M.

Definition 2. A scc C of M is weakly fair if every process is either disabled in some state of C or executed in C. (Process i is executed in C if there are states s,t in C such that $s \xrightarrow{i} t \in R$.)

Definition 3. A scc C of $\overline{M}^{\mathrm{thr}}$ is weakly fair if there is a state (s,k) in C such that process k is disabled in s or C has an edge of type $(s,k) \xrightarrow{k} (t,l)$.

Lemma 4. *Let C be a scc of M. Then C is weakly fair if and only if $\overline{C}^{\mathrm{thr}}$ consists of weakly fair sccs of $\overline{M}^{\mathrm{thr}}$.*

2.5 Model Checking

Let A be an automaton that accepts exactly the incorrect computations. The problem of checking whether the program P has any incorrect weakly fair computation can be decided by looking at the product graph B_0 of M and A. If B_0 has a weakly fair scc with a final automaton state then P has a weakly fair incorrect computation.

Let $i_1^0, \ldots, i_k^0$ be the indices that are referred to in A. In [ES95], it is shown that we can take the smaller product $\overline{B}_0$ of $\overline{M}$, I^k and A and perform the search for a scc in $\overline{B}_0$. Formally, $\overline{B}_0 = \langle \overline{S} \times I^k \times A, \overline{R}_{\mathrm{pr}}, s_{\mathrm{pr}} \rangle$ where $s_{\mathrm{pr}} = (s_0, i_1^0, \ldots, i_k^0, a_0)$, $\overline{R}_{\mathrm{pr}}$ consists of edges $(s, i_1, \ldots, i_k, a) \xrightarrow{\pi,l} (t, j_1, \ldots, j_k, a')$ such that $s \xrightarrow{\pi,l} t \in \overline{R}$, $j_1 = \pi^{-1}(i_1), \ldots, j_k = \pi^{-1}(i_k)$, and the automaton A moves from state a to a' on the input gained from s after simultaneously interchanging the indices $i_1, \ldots, i_k$ with $i_1^0, \ldots, i_k^0$ respectively. Lemmas 1 and 4, mutatis mutandis, hold to $\overline{B}_0^{\mathrm{thr}}$.

Theorem 5. *P satisfies the complement of the property defined by A if and only if there is no scc C of $\overline{B}_0$ such that C contains a final automaton state and C^{thr} consists of weakly fair sccs.*

3 On-the-Fly Model Checking

The original algorithm constructed $\overline{B}_0$ together with the threaded graphs $\overline{B}_0^{\text{thr}}$. This method can be improved by applying the following three new ideas.

First, note that the symmetry of $M \times I^k$ was not fully utilized. Instead of compressing M to $\overline{M}$ and then taking the product with $I^k \times A$, we can first compress $M \times I^k$ to $\overline{M \times I^k}$ and then take the product with A. This product graph is denoted by $\overline{B}$. It is possible for two states of the form $(s, i_1, \ldots, i_k)$ and $(s, j_1, \ldots, j_k)$ to be equivalent and be represented by a single state in $\overline{M \times I^k}$. Thus, $\overline{M \times I^k}$ is possibly smaller than $\overline{M} \times I^k$.

The second improvement is the application of an on-the-fly algorithm. Here we incrementally construct $\overline{B}$ and simultaneously explore it. By this exploration we analyze the threaded graphs without constructing them. If the partially explored $\overline{B}$ contains a required subgraph then the algorithm immediately exits saving further computation time. Because of the on-the-fly nature of the algorithm, we do not need to store the complete $\overline{B}$. Specially, no edges need to be stored.

Finally, the third idea is to use the symmetry of a single global state. Up till this point we did not change the number of edges, $\overline{B}$ has as many edges as $\overline{B}_0$. Using state symmetry we can reduce the number of edges by eliminating the redundant parallel ones. Such redundant parallel edges can be removed from $\overline{M}$ also. This results further reduction in memory usage.

For keeping the presentation simple, we assume that we are tracking only one process. Doing so, we do not loose generality. All the results, that are presented below, apply (with the obvious modifications) to the case with many tracked processes. In the actual implementation of the algorithm given below, we used the general case.

3.1 Compressing $M \times I$

In Subsect. 2.2 we defined an equivalence relation on S. Now, we extend it to $S \times I$: $u = (s, i)$ and $v = (t, j)$ are equivalent if there is a permutation $\pi \in G$ such that $\pi(u) = v$, that is, $\pi(s) = t$ and $\pi(i) = j$. Let $\overline{S}_{\text{aqsi}}$ be a set of *representative* states that contains exactly one state from each equivalence class. To ensure that $\overline{S}_{\text{aqsi}}$ and $\overline{S}$ are closely related we adopt the obvious convention that $(s, i) \in \overline{S}_{\text{aqsi}}$ implies $s \in \overline{S}$, that is, $\overline{S}_{\text{aqsi}} \subseteq \overline{S} \times I$. The *annotated quotient structure with tracked indices* (AQSI) of $M \times I$ is $\overline{M \times I} = \langle \overline{S}_{\text{aqsi}}, \overline{R}_{\text{aqsi}}, s_{\text{aqsi}} \rangle$ where $\overline{R}_{\text{aqsi}} = \{(s, i) \xrightarrow{\pi, l} (t, j) : s \xrightarrow{\pi, l} t \in \overline{R}, j = \pi^{-1}(i)\}$, and s_{aqsi} is (s_0, i_0). In a state (s, i), i is called the *tracked process*. Note that $\overline{M \times I}$ is the subgraph of $\overline{M} \times I$ spanned by $\overline{S}_{\text{aqsi}}$. Hence $\overline{M \times I}$ is considerably smaller than $\overline{M} \times I$.

Let $\overline{B}$ be the product of $\overline{M \times I}$ and A. In the actual algorithm presented below we will construct $\overline{B}$ from $\overline{M}$ (instead of $\overline{M \times I}$) and A. The reason for that inconvenience is that we do not want to store $\overline{M \times I}$. During the construction of the product graph $\overline{B}$, we can locally construct $\overline{M \times I}$ from the stored $\overline{M}$. This is done in command 7 of the algorithm presented below.

3.2 Partitions

As explained earlier, our on-the-fly model-checking algorithm will explore $\overline{B}$ simultaneously as it constructs it. During this process, in order to analyze the threaded graph without explicitly constructing it, we will maintain a partition of I with each $\overline{B}$ node on the stack; this partition will be represented as an n-vector.

First, we would like to adopt the following conventions concerning partitions. We identify equivalence relations and the corresponding partitions on a given set. In that sense, we say that a partition contains another partition if the equivalence relation corresponding to the first partition is a superset of the equivalence relation corresponding to the second partition.

Let $r = (s, l, a)$ be a state in $\overline{B}$ and C be the *scc* of $\overline{B}$ that contains r. By the analogue version of Lemma 1, C^{thr} is a collection of disjoint *sccs*. Thus, if a node in C^{thr} is reachable from both (r, i) and (r, j) then (r, i) and (r, j) are in the same *scc* of C^{thr}. Now we define the equivalence relation $\overset{*}{\sim}_r$ on I as follows:

$$i \overset{*}{\sim}_r j \quad \text{if} \quad (r, i) \text{ and } (r, j) \text{ are in the same component of } C^{\mathrm{thr}}.$$

It is easy to see that a class of the partition $\overset{*}{\sim}_r$ identifies a unique component of C^{thr}, and every component of C^{thr} is identified by a class of $\overset{*}{\sim}_r$. Thus, we will use these partitions to represent the *sccs* of C^{thr}. A class of $\overset{*}{\sim}_r$ is called weakly fair if the corresponding *scc* of C^{thr} is weakly fair. Note that the tracked process l in r always forms a class of size 1.

Suppose that if r and r' are nodes in the same *scc* in $\overline{B}$. The partitions of $\overset{*}{\sim}_r$ and $\overset{*}{\sim}_{r'}$ are unfortunately not equal, but one can be obtain from the other by a permutation in G. This problem can be overcome if we use a common referential base. The perfect nominee for this is the initial state s_{pr} of $\overline{B}$.

Let T be a depth first search spanning tree of $\overline{B}$ with root s_{pr}. For each node $u \in \overline{B}$, let π_u denote the product of the permutations on the unique $s_{\mathrm{pr}} \rightsquigarrow u$ path in T. Now, for each state r in $\overline{B}$, we define an equivalence relation $\sim_r$ on I as follows.

$$i \sim_r j \quad \text{if} \quad \pi_r^{-1}(i) \overset{*}{\sim}_r \pi_r^{-1}(j).$$

With this definition we achieved that $\sim_r = \sim_{r'}$ whenever r and r' are states in the same *scc* of $\overline{B}$. Intuitively, $i \sim_r j$ indicates that the threads of (s_{pr}, i) and (s_{pr}, j) enter the same *scc* of the threaded graph after they passed r.

Next, we show how to compute $\sim_r$ by exploring $\overline{B}$ using depth first search. For each edge $e = u \xrightarrow{\pi, i} v$ in $\overline{B}$, let π_e denote the permutation $\pi_u \circ \pi \circ \pi_v^{-1}$. Note that if e is an edge of T then π_e is the identity permutation. The permutation π_e satisfies the following property.

Proposition 6. *If e is an edge in the scc containing r, then $\pi_e(i) = j$ implies $i \sim_r j$.*

Let ρ be a permutation on I. We define the *orbit partition of ρ* on I to be the smallest partition containing $(i, \rho(i))$ for all $i \in I$. Now Claim 6 can be reformulated as: *If e is an edge in the scc of r, then the orbit partition of π_e is smaller than or equal to $\sim_r$.* The following stronger result characterizes $\sim_r$.

Theorem 7. $\sim_r$ *is the smallest partition that contains the orbit partition of* π_e, *for every edge e in the strongly connected component of r.*

The next theorem is a necessary and sufficient condition for checking if a class of $\sim_r$ is weakly fair. Let C be the *scc* of r in $\overline{B}$.

Theorem 8. *A class K of the partition* $\sim_r$ *is weakly fair if and only if there is an* $i \in K$ *and* $u \in C$ *such that process* $\pi_u^{-1}(i)$ *is disabled in u or it is executed (that is, there is an edge* $u \xrightarrow{\pi,\pi_u^{-1}(i)} v$ *in C).*

We have gathered together all the necessary tools to present the on-the-fly algorithm.

3.3 The Algorithm

Our algorithm in Table 1 is a modification of the strongly connected component computation using depth first search presented e.g. in [AHU74]. For each vertex $u = (s, l, a)$ of the product graph $\overline{B}$, we maintain the following information.

u.dfnum is a unique id (or *depth first number*) of the node, used for the strongly connected component computation.

u.lowlink is the id of a reachable node lower than u itself.

u.onstack is a flag indicating that u is still on stack.

u.perm is the vector π_u as defined in the previous subsection.

u.partition is an approximation of $\sim_u$.

u.status is a vector of flags that indicate which partition classes are known to be weakly fair.

u.final is a flag that indicates if u is in a *scc* that contains a final automaton state. This information is propagated down on the depth first tree.

The variables u.dfnum, u.lowlink and u.onstack are maintained as in the algorithm given in [AHU74]. Command 3 initializes u.status and u.final appropriately. The two "for" loops in commands 5 and 6, generate the successors of the $\overline{B}$ state u. In command 7, we construct the product state v. To do this, we consider the state $(t, \pi^{-1}(l))$ of $\overline{M} \times I$ and find an already generated state of the form (t, l') and a permutation ρ such that $(t, \pi^{-1}(l))$ is equivalent to (t, l') under ρ. If no such equivalent state has already been generated, then l' is taken as $\pi^{-1}(l)$ and ρ is taken as the identity permutation. Here the same equivalence checking function can be used as in the construction of $\overline{M}$. (It is to be noted that we need this equivalence checking since we are constructing $\overline{B}$ to be the product of $\overline{M} \times I$ and the automaton A, and we are doing this using $\overline{M}$ and A; however, if we want to construct $\overline{B}$ to be $\overline{M} \times I \times A$, as in [ES95], then we do not need this equivalence checking, and in this case we may have more states in the resulting $\overline{B}$.)

In command 8, we check if the edge $u \to v$ is a non-tree edge (i.e., v has already been visited) and v is in the same *scc* as u. In this case, it merges the orbit partition of π_e with u.partition. Commands 11 through 14 are executed if the edge $u \to v$ is a tree edge, i.e., v is constructed (and hence visited) for the

ON-THE-FLY MODEL CHECKING
M1. Construct $\overline{M}$.
M2. Construct A.
M3. Set u to be the initial state s_{pr} of $\overline{B}$.
     Set u.perm to be the identity permutation.
     Set the depth-first-counter to zero.
     Conduct DF-Search(u).

DF-Search(u)   (Note that $u = (s, l, a)$).
1.   Push u in the stack, set u.onstack.
     Set u.dfnum and u.lowlink to the depth-first-counter.
     Increase the depth-first-counter.
2.   Initialize u.partition to be the identity partition.
3.   Initialize u.status with the information on disabled processes stored
     in the AQS state s.
     Set u.final if a is a final automaton state.
4.   (Idle command. Later modification will use it.)
5.   For each automaton transition $a \to a'$ that is enabled in s do
6.   For each AQS edge $e = s \xrightarrow{\pi, i} t$ do
7.   Find an already generated AQSI state of the form
             (t, l') that is equivalent to $(t, \pi^{-1}(l))$ and
             find the permutation $\rho \in G$ that maps $(t, \pi^{-1}(l))$ to (t, l').
             Let $v = (t, l', a')$.
8.   If v is already constructed and v.onstack is set do
9.   Merge u.partition with the orbit partition of π_e.
                 Update u.status using that process i was executed.
                 Update u.lowlink to be the minimum of u.lowlink
                 and v.lowlink.
10.   If v is not constructed yet then do
11.   Set v.perm $= u$.perm $\circ \pi \circ \rho$.
12.   Conduct DF-Search(v).
13.   If v.onstack is still set then do
14.   Combine v.partition to u.partition.
                     Combine v.status to u.status.
                     Update u.status using that process i was executed.
                     Update u.lowlink to be the minimum of u.lowlink
                     and v.lowlink.
                     Set u.final if v.final is set.
15.   If all the partition classes are weakly fair (use u.status)
             and u.final is set then exit with *Yes* answer.
16. If u.dfnum $= u$.lowlink then do
17.   Pop all elements above u (inclusive) from the stack and mark
         the popped vertices off–stack.
18. Return with *No* answer.

Table 1. The Algorithm

first time. In command 11, v.perm is set; in command 12, DF-search is invoked on v. If v and u are in the same *scc* (indicated by the condition in command 13) then the partitions are combined, the *status* vector of u is updated and other updates are carried out. After processing the edge $u \to v$, in command 15, we check if the partially explored *scc* containing u is weakly fair and has a final state; if so the algorithm exits with an "yes" answer indicating a fair computation accepted by the automaton A is found. In command 17, after detecting the *scc*, we pop all the states of the *scc* from the stack.

Theorem 9. *The algorithm described above outputs* Yes *if and only if the original program has a weak fair computation that is accepted by A. The algorithm runs in time $O(|\overline{M \times I}| \cdot |I| \cdot |A|)$.*

3.4 State Symmetry, Partition Initialization

Let $u = (s, l, a)$ be a vertex of the product graph $\overline{B}$. Process i and j are called u–*equivalent*, denoted by $i \overset{*}{\approx}_u j$, if there is a permutation $\rho \in G$ such that $\rho(i) = j$ and $\rho(u) = u$. Intuitively, $i \overset{*}{\approx}_u j$ shows that process i and j are identical in state u. Let $u \xrightarrow{\pi, l} v$ be an edge of $\overline{B}$. Then $u \xrightarrow{\rho \circ \pi, \rho(l)} v$ is also an edge yielding that $(v, \pi^{-1}(i))$ is a successor of both nodes (u, i) and (u, j) in the threaded graph $\overline{B}^{\text{thr}}$. Therefore, (u, i) and (u, j) are in the same *scc* of $\overline{B}^{\text{thr}}$. Hence, $i \overset{*}{\sim}_u j$.

Lemma 10. *The partition $\overset{*}{\approx}_u$ is smaller than $\overset{*}{\sim}_u$.*

This fact allows an improvement to the algorithm. First we need to project down $\overset{*}{\approx}_u$ to the common referential base. We define $i \approx_u j$ if $\pi_u^{-1}(i) \overset{*}{\approx}_u \pi_u^{-1}(j)$. Command 2 in DF-Search can be changed to

2'.   Initialize u.partition to be $\approx_u$.

3.5 Parallel edges in $\overline{B}$

Let $e = u \xrightarrow{\pi, l} v$ and $e' = u \xrightarrow{\pi', l'} v$ be edges in $\overline{B}$. We call e and e' *parallel* if there is a permutation $\rho \in G$ such that $\rho(u) = u, \rho \circ \pi = \pi', \rho(l) = l'$. Surely, being parallel is an equivalence relation on the edges. Let $\overline{R}_{\text{pr}}^r$ be a set of *representative edges* that contains at least one edge from each parallel class. Having the partitions initialized as presented in command 2', the orbit partition of $\pi_{e'}$ does not give any new information after the orbit partition of π_e was considered. It is reflected in the next lemma.

Lemma 11. *If u is in a scc of $\overline{B}$ then $\sim_u$ is the smallest partition that contains $\approx_v$ (the initial value of v.partition) for every v in the scc of u as well as the orbit partition of π_e for every edge $e \in \overline{R}_{\text{pr}}^r$.*

These ideas can be applied as follows. ¿From each class of $\approx_u$ pick a representative process and call it the *leader* of that class. Put $\overline{R}_{\text{pr}}^r = \{u \xrightarrow{\pi,l} v \in \overline{R}_{\text{pr}} :$ l is a leader}. Since every edge is parallel to one that was caused by a leader process, this $\overline{R}_{\text{pr}}^r$ is a satisfactory set of representative edges. We introduce the new vector $u.\texttt{leader}$ of flags. The next improvement in the algorithm is the introduction of command 4 and the modification of command 6.

4.   Initialize $u.\texttt{leader}$.

5.   For each automaton transition $a \rightarrow a'$ that is enabled in s do

6′.   For each AQS edge $e = s \xrightarrow{\pi,i} v$ if $u.\texttt{leader}[i]$ is set do

3.6   Redundant edges in $\overline{M}$

In this subsection we show that the edges of $\overline{M}$ can be stored in a more compact way. For that we define state equivalence for every AQS state s.

$$i \overset{*}{\approx}_s j \text{ if there is a } \mu \in G \text{ with } \mu(s) = s, \mu(i) = j.$$

Note that in Subsect. 3.4 we introduced state equivalence for $\overline{B}$ states. The state equivalence relation for $u = (s, l, a)$ was denoted by $\overset{*}{\approx}_u$. We recall that $i \overset{*}{\approx}_u j$ if there is a $\mu \in G$ with $\mu(s) = s, \mu(l) = l$ and $\mu(i) = j$. It follows that $i \overset{*}{\approx}_u j$ implies $i \overset{*}{\approx}_s j$.

Let $s \xrightarrow{\pi,i} t$ be an edge of $\overline{M}$, $\mu(s) = s, \mu(i) = j$. Then $s \xrightarrow{\mu\circ\pi,j} t$ is an edge as well. This simple observation shows that we need not store both $s \xrightarrow{\pi,i} t$ and $s \xrightarrow{\mu\circ\pi,j} t$ provided that μ can be efficiently computed from s, i and j.

We are ready to present the last improvement to our algorithm.

M1′. Construct $\overline{M}$ with the following modifications. When a new node s is created, compute $\overset{*}{\approx}_s$. Define a vector $s.\texttt{repr}$ that, for every index i, points to a representative of the $\overset{*}{\approx}_s$-class of i. By the construction of the edges of $\overline{M}$, store only those edges that are caused by a representative process. (So $s \xrightarrow{\pi,i} t$ is stored if $s.\texttt{repr}[i] = i$.)

6″.   For each stored AQS edge $e = s \xrightarrow{\pi,i} t$ and each process j with $s.\texttt{repr}[j] = i$ and $u.\texttt{leader}[j]$ is set, compute $\mu \in G$ with $\mu(s) = s$ and $\mu(i) = j$, and then do

11′   Set $v.\texttt{perm} = u.\texttt{perm} \circ \mu \circ \pi \circ \rho$.

4   Implementation

We have developed a prototype of the on-the-fly model checker implementing the above presented algorithm. We used the implemented system to check for the correctness of the *Resource Controller* example with various number of users. We were able to check many properties including the liveness property that every user process that requests a resource will eventually access the resource, and the mutual exclusion property.

We contrasted our new system with the old model checker that implements the results presented in [ES95] on the Resource Controller example. Dramatic improvement was detected in all performance measures as indicated in table 2 below. The product graphs constructed by the old and new model checker are referred to as $\overline{B}_0$ and $\overline{B}$ respectively. Each statistics is given as a/b where a and b are the numbers corresponding to the old and new model checker respectively.

Liveness Prop.	10	50	100
AQS states	38 / 38	198 / 198	398 / 398
AQS transitions	235 / 107	6175 / 1567	24850 / 5642
AQS const. time (sec)	0 / 0	16 / 5	149 / 39
Explored $\overline{B}_0/\overline{B}$ states	385 / 91	9943 / 91	39893 / 91
$\overline{B}_0/\overline{B}$ const. time (sec)	0 / 0	19 / 0	330 / 0
Total memory used (kbyte)	31 / 13	1219 / 216	6878 / 830
Total CPU time used (sec)	0 / 0	37 / 6	481 / 42
Mutual Excl. Prop.	10	50	100
AQS states	38 / 38	198 / 198	398 / 398
AQS transitions	235 / 107	6175 / 1567	24850 / 5642
AQS const. time (sec)	0 / 0	16 / 5	149 / 39
Explored $\overline{B}_0/\overline{B}$ states	38 / 38	198 / 198	398 / 398
$\overline{B}_0/\overline{B}$ const. time (sec)	0 / 0	1 / 0	7 / 2
Total memory used (kbyte)	11 / 10	481 / 221	2903 / 857
Total CPU time used (sec)	0 / 0	18 / 6	158 / 44

Table 2. Statistics for the model checker

The liveness property we checked is not satisfied by the Resource Controller. Both model checkers found a fair incorrect computation. ¿From the table, we see that the number of AQS states are the same, while the number of AQS transitions is much smaller in the new model checker due to the use of state symmetry. The number of product states explored in the on-the-fly system is much smaller since it terminated early. On the other hand the original model checker constructed the whole $\overline{B}$ before checking for an incorrect fair computation.

For the mutual exclusion property, both model checkers indicated that the resource controller satisfies the mutual exclusion property. In this case, early termination does not come into effect. Furthermore, since we do not track any process (mutual exclusion is a global property), the number of states explored in $\overline{B}_0$ and $\overline{B}$ are the same. However, the number of transitions are much smaller in $\overline{M}$ as well as in $\overline{B}$ due to the effect of state symmetry. The over all CPU time and the memory usage are substantially smaller for the new model checker.

5   Conclusions

In this paper, we have presented an on-the-fly model checking system that exploits symmetry (between states as well as inside a state) and checks for correctness under fairness.

As part of future work, it plan to explore techniques to automatically detect symmetries and integrate these techniques with the model checker. Also, algorithms for checking equivalence of global states under other types of symmetry need to be further explored.

References

[AHU74] Aho, A. V., Hopcroft, J., Ullman, J. D.: The Design and Analysis of Computer Algorithms. Addison-Wesley (1974)

[BCG95] Bhat, G., Cleaveland, R., Grumberg, o.: Efficient On-the-Fly Modelchecking for CTL. International Conference on Logic in Computer Science, San Diego, California, 1995

[CES83] Clarke, E. M., Emerson, E. A., Sistla, A. P.: Automatic Verification of Finite State Concurrent Programs. using Temporal Logic: A Practical Approach, Proceedings of the ACM Symposium on Principles of Programming Languages, January 1983, Austin, Texas, Also appeared in *ACM TOPLAS*, April 1986

[CFJ93] Clarke, E. M., Filkorn, T., Jha, S.: Exploiting Symmetry in Temporal Logic Model Checking. 5th International Conference on Computer Aided Verification, Crete, Greece, June 1993.

[ES93] Emerson, E. A., Sistla, A. P.: Symmetry and Model Checking. 5th International Conference on Computer Aided Verification, Crete, Greece, June 1993

[ES95] Emerson, E. A., Sistla, A. P.: Utilizing Symmetry when Model Checking under Fairness Assumptions: An Automata-theoretic Approach. 7th International Conference on Computer Aided Verification, Leige, Belgium, July 1995

[G96] Godefroid, P.: Partial-Order Methods for the Verification of Concurrent Systems. Lecture Notes in Computer Science **1032** Springer, 1996

[HP96] Holzmann, G.J., Peled, D.: The State of SPIN. 8th Intl. Conference on Computer Aided Verification, July 1996

[ID93] Ip, C. N., Dill, D. L.: Better Verification through Symmetry. Intl. Symposium on Computer Hardware Description Languages and their Application, April 1993. Also in Formal Methods in System Design **9** 1/2 (1996) 41–75

[K94] Kurshan, R. P.: Computer Aided Verification of Coordinated Processes: The Automata Theoretic Approach. Princeton Univerity Press, Princeton NJ (1994)

Exploiting symmetry when verifying transistor-level circuits by symbolic trajectory evaluation

Manish Pandey and Randal E. Bryant

School of Computer Science, Carnegie Mellon University, Pittsburgh, PA-15213, USA.

Abstract. In this paper we describe the use of symmetry for verification of transistor-level circuits by symbolic trajectory evaluation. We show that exploiting symmetry can allow one to verify systems several orders of magnitude larger than otherwise possible. We classify symmetries in circuits as *structural symmetries*, arising from similarities in circuit structure, *data symmetries*, arising from similarities in the handling of data values, and *mixed* structural-data symmetries. We use graph isomorphism testing and symbolic simulation to verify the symmetries in the original circuit. Using *conservative approximations*, we partition a circuit to expose the symmetries in its components, and construct reduced system models which can be verified efficiently. We have verified Static Random Access Memory circuits with up to 1.5 Million transistors.

1 Introduction

In this paper we have focussed on exploiting symmetry in the verification of transistor-level circuits by symbolic trajectory evaluation (STE). Many high performance hardware designs are custom designed at the transistor-level to optimize their area and performance, and this makes it necessary to verify them directly at the transistor-level. Common examples of such hardware units include static random access memory (SRAM) arrays which are found in instruction and data caches of microprocessors, cache tags, and TLBs, to name a few. These circuits exhibit considerable symmetry. By exploiting symmetry with the use of STE, we show that it is possible to verify systems that are orders of magnitude larger than previously possible[9, 4]. We present empirical results for the verification of SRAM circuits of varying sizes, including one with over 1.5 million transistors. Furthermore, our results show that our techniques scale up linearly or sub-linearly with SRAM size, and one can verify circuits that are much larger than our benchmarks.

Our verification approach builds on the following three ideas — *circuit partitioning*, *structural analysis*, and *conservative modeling*. Many systems, viewed as a whole, do not possess symmetries that can easily be exploited, but they are made up of smaller components which can. One can exploit the symmetry in the components by partitioning the larger system, verifying the smaller components, and composing the verification results.

We describe two forms of symmetries. *Structural symmetries* arise from similarities in the structure of a system, e.g., by replication of system components. *Data symmetries* arise from similarities in handling of data values in the system.

---

* This research is sponsored by the Defense Advanced Research Projects Agency (DARPA) under contract number DABT63-96-C-0071 and by a grant from Motorola.

Most previous work exploiting symmetry in formal verification to date [6, 8, 7] focussed on aspects of structural rather than data or mixed structural-data symmetry. We have found these other forms of symmetry useful in verifying many common digital building blocks like decoders. We verify structural symmetries in a transistor-level circuit through a purely *structural analysis* of the system by doing circuit graph isomorphism checks.

Our work is related in many ways to recent symmetry work by others, including that by Clarke [6], Emerson [7], and Ip [8]. In [6], Clarke et al. describe the symmetry of a system as a transition relation preserving state permutation. In [7] Emerson et al. describe the symmetry of a system as a group of graph automorphisms acting on the global state transition graph. Both [6] and [7] establish a result which states that there is a correspondence between the original state transition graph, and the symmetry reduced graph which preserves the correctness of CTL* formulae. We define symmetries as excitation function preserving state transformations, and in this paper we state a correspondence result for STE assertions. In [8], Ip and Dill discuss the verification of systems, where the symmetry in the system is identified by a special scalar-set datatype in the system description language. In contrast, to exploit symmetry, we do not constrain the user to explicitly give symmetry as a part of the system description. In [1], Aggarwal et al. exploit symmetry between 0 and 1 values to verify the alternating bit protocol. Our work formalizes the notion of such a similarity in the handling of data values as data symmetry.

2 Background

Symbolic trajectory evaluation (STE) was originally formulated as a formal verification method using a symbolic ternary simulator as the verification "engine" [5]. With ternary simulation, each state variable may have value 0, 1, or X, where X indicates an unknown or indeterminate state. With symbolic simulation, the state values are encoded using BDDs, allowing one simulation run to effectively evaluate circuit operation under many possible operating conditions.

With STE, the three state values are partially ordered by their "information content" with $X < 0$ and $X < 1$. The simulator is used to verify assertions of the form $[A \Longrightarrow C]$, where A and C are formulas containing (possibly symbolic) values for state variables, conjunctions, and the temporal logic "next time" operator. Intuitively, antecedent A defines a stimulus for the circuit inputs and initial state, while consequent C defines the expected response for the circuit outputs and new state. The simulator then proves that for any initial state and input sequence satisfying stimulus A, the circuit will generate outputs and new state satisfying C.

In a later formulation of STE [10], the states and their ordering was generalized to any complete lattice, and a slightly more general class of assertions was allowed. In this presentation, we will take a middle ground, using a lattice-structured state set, but with these states closely matching the ternary values of the original formulation. This particular formulation is chosen to allow a clear expression of symmetry properties.

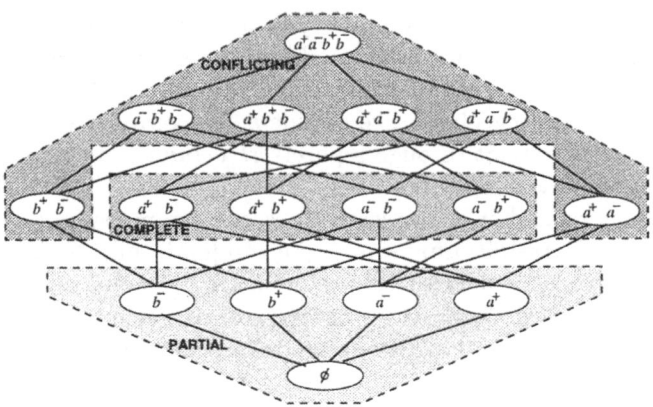

Fig. 1. Structure of State Lattice for Two Node Circuit

2.1 State Domain

Let N denote the nodes (i.e., signal points) of a circuit. For each node n we define two *atoms*, written n^+ and n^-, indicating that node n has value 1 or 0, respectively. Let $\mathcal{A}$ denote the set of all atoms. We define a circuit state S to be any subset of $\mathcal{A}$, and $\mathcal{S}$ to be the set of all possible states, i.e., $\mathcal{S} = 2^{\mathcal{A}}$.

State set $\mathcal{S}$, together with the subset ordering $\subseteq$ forms a complete lattice, where states are ordered according to their "information content," i.e., how much they restrict the values of the circuit nodes. For example, the structure of the state domain for a circuit having nodes a and b is illustrated in Figure 1. In this diagram we indicate the set of atoms in each state. As the shaded regions indicate, states can be classified as being "partial", "complete", or "conflicting". In a partial state, some nodes have no corresponding atoms while others have at most one. In a complete state, there is exactly one atom for each node. In a conflicting state, there is some node n for which both atoms n^- an n^+ are present. Such a state is physically unrealizable—it requires a signal to be both 0 and 1 simultaneously. Conflicting states are added to the state domain only for mathematical convenience. They extend the semilattice derived from a ternary system model into a complete lattice.

We view the operation of a circuit as an infinite sequence of states. A partial ordering $\sqsubseteq$ is defined over such sequences as the pointwise extension of the state ordering $\subseteq$. That is, for state sequences $S_0 = s_0^0 s_0^1 \ldots$, and $S_1 = s_1^0 s_1^1 \ldots$, $S_0 \sqsubseteq S_1$ iff $\forall i \geq 0. s_0^i \subseteq s_1^i$.

2.2 Model Structure

The behavior of a circuit is defined by its *excitation function* $Y: \mathcal{S} \rightarrow \mathcal{S}$. This function serves a role similar to the transition relation or next-state functions of temporal logic model checkers. We require this function to be monotonic over the information ordering, i.e., if two states are ordered $s_1 \subseteq s_2$, then their excitations must also be ordered: $Y(s_1) \subseteq Y(s_2)$.

We will define a circuit model $\mathcal{M}$ to be the combination of a lattice-structured state set and a monotonic excitation function, i.e., $\mathcal{M} = \langle \mathcal{S}, Y \rangle$. The behavior of a circuit can be represented as an infinite sequence of states. We define a *circuit trajectory* to be any state sequence $\sigma = \sigma^0 \sigma^1 \ldots$ such that $Y(\sigma^i) \subseteq \sigma^{i+1}$ for all

$i \geq 0$. That is, the state sequence obeys the constraints imposed by the circuit excitation function.

2.3 Representation of the Excitation Function

Our verifier computes the excitation function by evaluating logic expressions derived from the transistor circuit structure. These expressions are generated by the Anamos symbolic switch-level analyzer [3]. The analysis and the resulting excitation expressions capture a variety of low-level MOS circuit effects such as dynamic charge storage, different signal strengths, and bidirectional signal transmission.

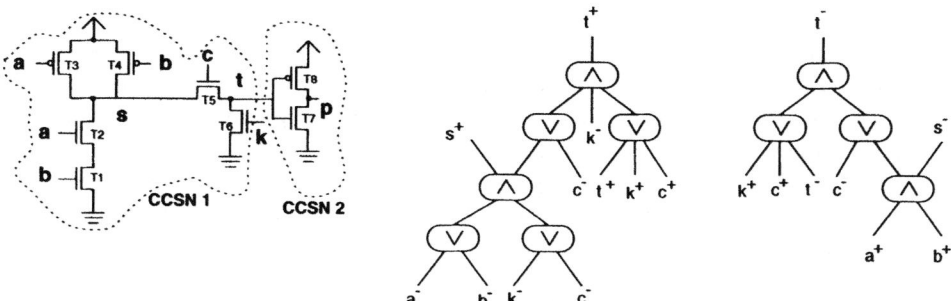

Fig. 2. Switch-level analysis of a circuit with pass logic and stored charge.

As an example, consider the CMOS circuit shown in Figure 2. The first step in the symbolic switch-level analysis of the circuit is to partition it into *channel connected subnetworks* (CCSNs), each consisting of a set of storage nodes connected by the source-drain terminals of the transistors. In our circuit, this yields two subnetworks: CCSN1 containing nodes s and t, and CCSN2 containing node p. The analyzer derives the excitation expressions for each CCSN separately.

Figure 2 also shows the expressions describing the excitation for CCSN1 in the example circuit. These expressions are represented as a directed acyclic graph where the leaves indicate possible atoms in the set s and the roots indicate possible atoms in the set $Y(s)$. That is, for state s, a leaf labeled by atom a evaluates to true if $a \in s$ and to false otherwise. The Boolean operations indicated by the intermediate vertices are then evaluated. If a root labeled by atom a evaluates to true, then a is included in $Y(s)$.

For a large class of circuits, including the memory circuits we have verified, it can be shown that the DAGs describing the excitation functions have complexity linear in the number of circuit transistors. The constant factors can be significant, however. For example, a static RAM (SRAM) requires about 6 transistors for each memory bit. The DAGs generated by Anamos require around 73 vertices per memory bit. Moreover, the entire memory array consists of just two CCSNs. Hence the time and memory required to generate these DAGs limits the size of the memory circuit that can be analyzed. We will show how our symmetry reduction techniques can be used to verify the circuit using a reduced circuit model.

2.4 Trajectory Evaluation

In STE the system specification consists of a set of *trajectory assertions*, each having the form $[A \Longrightarrow C]$, where A and C are *trajectory formulas*. Antecedent

A describes the stimulus to the circuit over time, while consequent C describes its expected response. Trajectory formulas (TFs) have the following recursive definition:

1. **Atoms**: For any node n, atoms n^+ and n^- are TFs.
2. **Conjunction**: $(F_1 \wedge F_2)$ is a TF if F_1 and F_2 are TFs.
3. **Domain restriction**: $(E \to F)$ is a TF if F is a TF and E is a Boolean expression.
4. **Next time**: $(\mathbf{X}F)$ is a TF if F is a TF.

$\mathbf{X}$ is the *next time* temporal operator which causes advancement of time by one unit.

The truth of a scalar trajectory formula F is defined relative to a state sequence. Due to the restricted form of our temporal formulas, it can be shown that for every scalar formula F, there is unique *defining sequence* δ_F. Any sequence S satisfying F must satisfy the relation $\delta_F \sqsubseteq S$.

We can combine a (scalar) trajectory formula and the circuit excitation function to generate a *defining trajectory* τ_F consisting of a sequence of states $\tau_F^0 \tau_F^1 \ldots$ given by:

$$\tau_F^i = \begin{cases} \delta_F^0 & \text{if } i = 0 \\ \delta_F^i \cup Y(\tau_F^{i-1}) & \text{otherwise} \end{cases}$$

It can be shown that τ_F is the unique minimum trajectory satisfying F. That is, τ_F satisfies F, and for any σ satisfying F, must obey the ordering $\tau_F \sqsubseteq \sigma$.

For an assertion $[A \Longrightarrow C]$ where both A and C are scalar formulas $\models_{\mathcal{M}} [A \Longrightarrow C]$ if every trajectory of $\mathcal{M}$ satisfying A also satisfies C. Such an assertion can be verified by showing that $\delta_C \sqsubseteq \tau_A$. Essentially, this involves simulating the circuit applying the constraints given in antecedent A and checking the constraints given in the consequent C at the appropriate time points.

3 Symmetry

We express symmetries in a circuit and the corresponding transformations of the specification in terms of bijective mappings over atoms. A state transformation, σ, is a bijection over the set of atoms: $\sigma : \mathcal{A} \to \mathcal{A}$. We can extend σ to be a bijection over states by defining $\sigma(s)$ for state s as $\cup_{a \in s} \sigma(a)$.

Two types of state transformations are particularly interesting. A *data* transformation involves swapping the two atoms for a single node. For node n, we write $n^{\pm}$ to denote the transformation consisting of the swapping of n^+ with n^-. A *structural* transformation involves swapping the atoms for two different nodes. For nodes n_1 and n_2, we write $n_1 \leftrightarrow n_2$ to denote the transformation consisting of the swappings: n_1^+ with n_2^+ and n_1^- with n_2^-. By composing transformations of these two forms, we can express a variety of circuit transformations. We will denote more complex transformations as a list of elementary transformations.

A state transformation σ is a *symmetry property* of a circuit with excitation function Y when $\sigma(Y(s)) = Y(\sigma(s))$ for every state s. That is, the excitation of the circuit on the transformed state $\sigma(s)$ matches the transformation of the excitation of s. One can readily show that σ is a symmetry property if and only if its inverse σ^{-1} is a symmetry property. Furthermore, if σ_1 and σ_2 are symmetry properties, then so is their composition $\sigma_1 \sigma_2$.

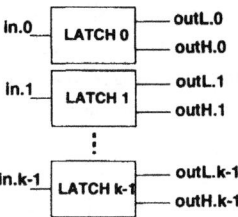

Fig. 3. Illustration of the symmetries of a circuit

If a *symmetry property* consists entirely of structural transformations, it is termed *structural symmetry*, and if it consists entirely of data transformations, it is termed *data symmetry*. A symmetry involving a combination of the two transformation types is called a *mixed symmetry*.

Consider, for example, the circuit shown in Figure 3. This circuit consists of k identical latches. In each latch outL is a complement of the input, and outH has the same value as the input. Since the latches are identical, this circuit has a structural symmetry corresponding to the swapping of any pair of latches i and j, such that $0 \le i, j < k$:

$$[\text{in}.i \leftrightarrow \text{in}.j, \text{outL}.i \leftrightarrow \text{outL}.j, \text{outH}.i \leftrightarrow \text{outH}.j] . \tag{1}$$

Each individual latch also stores data values 0 and 1 in a symmetric way, expressed for Latch 0 by the data symmetry:

$$[\text{in}.0^{\pm}, \text{outL}.0^{\pm}, \text{outH}.0^{\pm}] . \tag{2}$$

Finally, each latch can also be viewed as a one-bit decoder—it sets one of its outputs high based on its input data. Such behavior for Latch 0 is expressed by a mixed symmetry:

$$[\text{in}.0^{\pm}, \text{outL}.0 \leftrightarrow \text{outH}.0] . \tag{3}$$

We can extend state transformation σ to be a bijection over temporal formulas by defining $\sigma(F)$ to be the result of replacing every atom a in F by $\sigma(a)$. Similarly, we can extend σ to be a bijection over state sequences by applying σ to each state in the sequence. One can readily show that if temporal formula F has defining sequence δ_F, then its transformation $\sigma(F)$ will have defining sequence $\delta_{\sigma(F)} = \sigma(\delta_F)$. In addition, if σ is a symmetry property of a circuit model $\mathcal{M}$, then its defining trajectories for any temporal formula F will obey the symmetry: $\tau_{\sigma(F)} = \sigma(\tau_F)$. From this, one can conclude that for any assertion $[A \implies C]$ and any symmetry property σ of model $\mathcal{M}$, $\models_{\mathcal{M}} [A \implies C]$ if and only if $\models_{\mathcal{M}} [\sigma(A) \implies \sigma(C)]$.

Thus, proving that σ is a symmetry property of a circuit allows us to infer the validity of a transformed assertion once we verify the original. For example, suppose we verify that Latch 0 in Figure 3 operates correctly for input value 1, and also prove that the transformations defined by Equations 1 and 2 are indeed symmetry transformations. Then we can infer from Equation 1 that for all j, Latch j operates correctly for input value 1, and from Equation 2 that Latch 0 operates correctly for input value 0. Furthermore, by composing these two transformations, we can infer that for all j, Latch j will operate correctly for input value 0.

The fact that symmetry properties may be composed makes it possible to prove the correctness of an entire set of assertions by simply verifying that each member of a set of "generators" for a group of transformations is a symmetry property. For example, Equation 1 represents a total of $k(k-1)/2$ symmetry transformations, corresponding to the pairwise exchange of any two latches. In general, one could argue that this circuit would remain invariant for any permutation π of the latches. Consider the transformation σ_π mapping the 6 atoms for each Latch i (two each for nodes in.i, outL.i and outH.i) to their counterparts in Latch $\pi(i)$. We could prove that each such transformation is a symmetry property, but this would require $k!$ tests. Instead, we can exploit the fact that any permutation π can be generated by composing a series of just two different permutation types. The "exchange" permutation swaps values 0 and 1, while the "rotate" permutation maps each value i to $i+1 \bmod k$. Thus, proving that the state transformations given by these two permutations are symmetry properties allows us to infer that σ_π is a symmetry property for an arbitrary permutation π.

4 Conservative Approximations

Let $\mathcal{M}'$ and $\mathcal{M}$ be circuit models over the same state set, having excitation functions Y' and Y, respectively. We say that $\mathcal{M}'$ is a *conservative approximation* of $\mathcal{M}$ if for every state s, $Y'(s) \subseteq Y(s)$. In such a case, one can readily show that for any assertion $[A \Longrightarrow C]$, if $\models_{\mathcal{M}'} [A \Longrightarrow C]$, then $\models_{\mathcal{M}} [A \Longrightarrow C]$. Thus, proving an assertion for a conservative approximation to a circuit model allows us to infer that the assertion holds for the original circuit.

Conservative approximations provide a systematic way to reason about partitioned circuits, allowing us to verify the complete circuit by proving properties about each partition. This is particularly useful when the partitioning can expose highly symmetric regions of the circuit. In addition, if we can prove that a circuit has some structural symmetry, then we can create a "weakened" version of the circuit containing just enough circuitry to verify the behavior for one representative of the symmetry group.

Let N' be a subset of the set of circuit nodes N, and $\mathcal{A}'$ be the corresponding set of atoms. Then we can view the removal of those nodes not in N' as yielding a conservative approximation to the circuit with an excitation function Y' such that:

$$Y'(s) = Y(s \cap \mathcal{A}') \cap \mathcal{A}'. \tag{4}$$

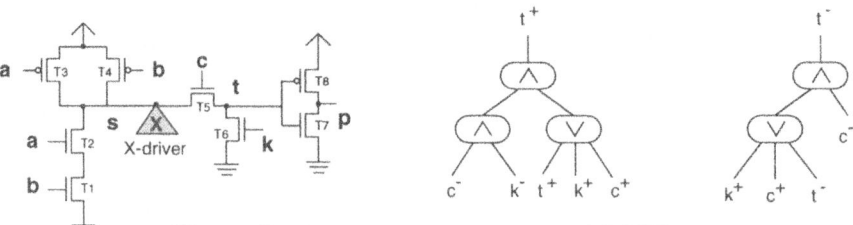

Fig. 4. Conservative approximation of CCSN1.

As an example, suppose we wish to create a reduced model for the circuit in Figure 2 by eliminating nodes a, b, and s. Then we could describe the remaining portions of CCSN1 by the excitation expressions shown in Figure 4. One can see that these expressions were obtained from those of Figure 2 by simplifying the result of setting the leaves for all eliminated atoms to false. This conservative approximation could be used to verify circuit operation for the cases where node c is set to 0. We have modified Anamos to generate these simplified expressions directly, avoiding the need to ever generate a complete model. In particular, we would replace node s in the example circuit by a "X-driver," consisting of an input node set to constant value X.

We can view the partitioning of a circuit into different components as a process of creating multiple conservative approximations. For example, suppose we partition a circuit with nodes N into two components having nodes N_1 and N_2, respectively. The set of nodes forming the interface between the components comprise the set $N_1 \cap N_2$. In this example, we assume the communication is purely unidirectional—N_1 generates signals for N_2. Suppose we wish to prove a property described by an assertion $[A \implies C]$, where the atoms of C are contained only in N_2. We could then create conservative models $\mathcal{M}_1$ and $\mathcal{M}_2$ using the subset construction given by Equation 4.

Using a technique we term *waveform capture*, we can record the output values generated by model $\mathcal{M}_1$ and use them in verifying the assertion with model $\mathcal{M}_2$. In particular, let τ_A^1 be the defining trajectory generated by model $\mathcal{M}_1$ for antecedent A. Construct a temporal formula W describing the occurrence of the atoms corresponding to the nodes in $N_1 \cap N_2$ at the appropriate time points.[2] We have therefore proved that $\mathcal{M}_1$, and therefore $\mathcal{M}$, satisfies the assertion $[A \implies W]$. Using model $\mathcal{M}_2$, we then verify the assertion $[A \wedge W \implies C]$. Effectively, we "play back" the waveforms on the interface nodes. One can readily show that for any model $\mathcal{M}$ and any temporal formula F, if $\models_{\mathcal{M}} [A \implies F]$ and $\models_{\mathcal{M}} [A \wedge F \implies C]$, then $\models_{\mathcal{M}} [A \implies C]$, and therefore this pair of verifications is sufficient to prove the desired property.

5 Verification of a SRAM

Consider the 16-bit (1 bit/word) SRAM circuit shown in Figure 5. This circuit consists of the the following major components — row decoder, column address latches, column multiplexer (Mux) and the memory cell array core. To simplify discussion many essential SRAM components have not been shown here. In order to verify this circuit we must show that the read and write operations work correctly. We express these operations as STE assertions. Ahead, we show the use of symmetry to verify these operations efficiently.

5.1 Symmetries of a SRAM

Consider the decoder in Figure 6. For any memory operation, the value of the row address assigned to nodes a.2 and a.3, causes one of the word lines wl.0, wl.1, wl.2 and wl.3 to be active. The figure shows that wl.0 is active for row

---

[2] Although the sequence τ_A^1 is infinite, we only need record the values up to the maximum depth of the next-time operators in C.

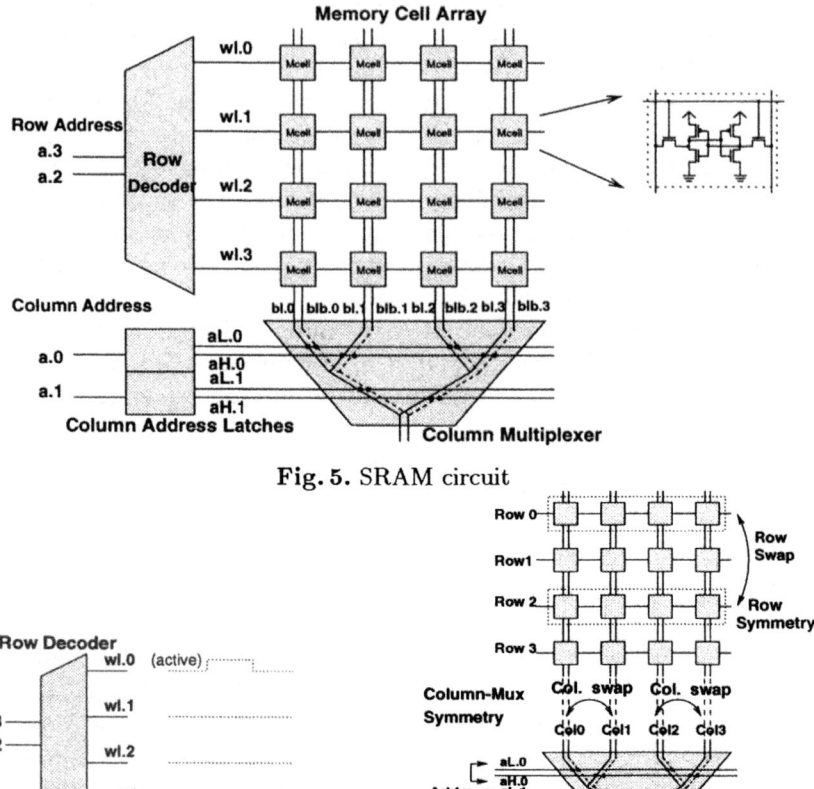

Fig. 5. SRAM circuit

Fig. 6. Row decoder and word line waveforms.

Fig. 7. SRAM core structural symmetries.

address 00. The same waveform occurs on the active word line regardless of the address. This mixed symmetry of the decoder is expressed by the group of transformations generated by transformations σ_0 and σ_1:

$$\sigma_0 = [\text{a.2}^{\pm}, \text{wl.0} \leftrightarrow \text{wl.1}, \text{wl.2} \leftrightarrow \text{wl.3}]$$
$$\sigma_1 = [\text{a.3}^{\pm}, \text{wl.0} \leftrightarrow \text{wl.2}, \text{wl.1} \leftrightarrow \text{wl.3}]$$

Transformation σ_i indicates that complementing bit i of the row address causes an exchange of signal waveforms for each pair of word lines j and k such that the binary representations of j and k differ at bit position i. The column address latches obey the "decoder" symmetry expressed by Equation 3.

The mixed symmetries of the decoder and the column address latches can be verified by symbolic simulation. For example, to verify that σ_0 is a symmetry of the decoder, we symbolically simulate the decoder with symbolic values s_0 and s_1 at the decoder inputs a.2, and a.3 in Figure 6. As the simulation proceeds, we check that a substitution of $\overline{s_0}$ for s_0 in the symbolic waveform for wl.0 (resp., wl.2) matches the symbolic waveform on wl.1 (resp., wl.3).

Figure 7 illustrates the two structural symmetries of the SRAM core and column Mux combination. The *row symmetry* arises from the invariance of the core-mux circuit structure under permutations of the rows of the core. The *column-mux symmetry* arises from the invariance of the circuit structure under a swap of column address latch output pairs accompanied by a corresponding exchange of columns. For example, in Figure 7, a swap of aH.0 and aL.0 accompanied by a swap of column 0 with 1, and a swap of column 2 with 3 is a symmetry of the circuit.

We verify the core-Mux symmetries in two parts. First we verify that arbitrary row and column permutations are symmetries of the core. Verification that the exchange and rotate permutation generators for rows and columns are symmetries suffices for this. This gives a total of 4 symmetry checks for the core. Next we verify the column-mux symmetry for the Mux. In the figure, the generators of the four different column address line pair permutations are the two permutations associated with each column address latch output pair. Therefore, two symmetry checks verify the column-mux symmetry. In general n symmetry checks must be done for the Mux in a SRAM with n column address line pairs.

5.2 Verification steps

To verify the SRAM circuit we partition the circuit into two components — the decoder with the column address latches, and the memory core with the column Mux. Using symbolic simulation and circuit graph isomorphism checks, respectively, we verify the symmetries of these two components.

Next, we create two conservative approximations of the SRAM. In the first model, the memory core and the column Mux are disabled. In the second model, the decoder, the column address latches are disabled, and all the memory cells except that for location 0 are disabled. Given the assertion $[A \Longrightarrow C]$ specifying an operation for memory location 0, we use the antecedent A to symbolically simulate the first conservative approximation. and we record the signal waveforms on the outputs of the decoder and the column address latches. We construct a trajectory formula W, which captures the recorded signal values on the outputs.

Finally, with the second conservative approximation, we show that given the waveform W, and the antecedent A, the consequent C is true, i.e., $[A \wedge W \Longrightarrow C]$. From earlier discussion, since $[A \Longrightarrow W]$ and $[A \wedge W \Longrightarrow C]$ are both true, we can conclude that $[A \Longrightarrow C]$ is true, i.e., the memory operation is verified for location 0. Given the symmetries of the circuit we can then conclude that the operation works correctly for every memory location.

6 Experiments and Results

All the time and memory figures in this paper have been measured on a Sun SparcStation-20. We used the Anamos switch-level analyzer to generate switch-level models [3]. We modified Anamos to make it possible to attach *X-drivers* to circuit nodes to generate reduced models (conservative approximations) of switch-level circuits. Table 1 shows the results of model generation for SRAM circuits of varying sizes. For circuits larger than 16K, it was not possible to generate the full circuit model within reasonable time or memory bounds (empty table entries). Conservative approximations of SRAM circuits, on the other hand, can be generated for much larger circuits for a miniscule fraction of the cost of the full model. The reduced model size grows proportional to the square root of the SRAM size, and its generation time and memory is proportional to the SRAM size.

SRAM size (bits)	No. of Transistors	Model Size (Bool. ops)		Anamos Time (CPU Secs.)		Anamos Memory (MB)	
		Full	Reduced	Full	Reduced	Full	Reduced
1K	6690	79951	2781	120	4.1	9.6	0.9
4K	25676	307555	5462	863	14.1	36.8	2.1
16K	100566	1205239	10895	7066	43.2	144.2	6.0
64K	397642	—	21960	—	170.7	—	22.0
256K	1581494	—	44545	—	732.7	—	80.0

Table 1. Generation of SRAM model: Full vs. Reduced model.

To verify a structural symmetry, we take the original circuit, and swap the circuit nodes specified in the symmetry. Then we verify if the new circuit is symmetric to the original circuit by verifying that the circuit graphs for the two circuits are isomorphic by using a graph vertex coloring technique [2]. Columns 2 and 3 in Table 2 show the total time and the memory required to do all the isomorphism checks for the memory core and the column multiplexer circuits. Columns 4 and 5 of this table report the resources required to check the decoder and column address latch symmetries by symbolic simulation. The last two columns of this table report the running time and the memory required for verifying the write operation for location 0. In addition, we verify two other properties — that the read operation reads the value stored at the specified cell, and that operations at other addresses do not change the data in a given cell, and these take resources similar to that of writes (figures not reported here). The total verification time for a SRAM circuit is the sum of the times in columns 2, 4 and 6, in addition to the times required to verify the two other properties. For example, to verify a 64K SRAM, the total verification time equals 170.7 secs.(generate reduced circuit model) + 955.5 secs.(symmetry checks) + 6.0 + 6.6 + 6.1 secs. (verify all three operations) = 1145.0 secs. It is interesting to note that symmetry checks dominate much of this time. In the verification process, the only time we ever work with the complete circuit is the symmetry check phase. This partially explains the reason for the relatively large time and memory requirements of this phase. However, the circuit isomorphism code we have used is a simple modification of that in Anamos. There is considerable scope for reducing time and memory by developing a specialized circuit isomorphism checker.

7 Conclusion

We believe that with our work the problem of SRAM verification is solved. With more computational resources, and some fine-tuning of our programs, the results of our experiments indicate that we can verify multi-megabit SRAM circuits. The techniques we have presented can be used in a rather straightforward manner to exploit symmetries in other hardware units like set associative cache tags, where

SRAM Size bits	Mem. Core+Col. Mux Symm.		Decoder+Col. latch		Reduced Write Verif.	
	CPU Time (Secs.)	Memory (MB)	CPU Time (Secs.)	Memory (MB)	CPU Time (Secs.)	Memory (MB)
1K	11.9	1.6	1.7	0.69	1.5	0.79
4K	47.4	6.5	2.1	0.74	2.0	1.05
16K	214.1	26.0	2.5	0.88	3.0	1.80
64K	952.4	104.0	3.2	1.10	6.0	2.84
256K	4601.8	416.0	4.2	1.52	18.5	4.26

Table 2. Symmetry checks and reduced SRAM write verification.

every set is identical in structure. One direction for future work in the short run would be to extend these ideas to verify content addressable memories. In the longer run, it would be interesting to apply these ideas to verify hardware units other than memory arrays. Candidates for such an application include a processor datapath, where one can find the presence of structural symmetries because of bit-slice repetition, and data symmetries arising from the datapath operations.

References

1. S. Aggarwal, R. P. Kurshan, and K. Sabnani. A calculus for protocol specification and validation. In *Protocol Specification, Testing and Verification*, volume 3, 1983.
2. Derek L. Beatty and Randal E. Bryant. Fast incremental circuit analysis using extracted hierarchy. In *25th ACM/IEEE Design Automation Conference*, pages 495–500, June 1988.
3. Randal E. Bryant. Boolean analysis of MOS circuits. *IEEE Transactions on Computer-Aided Design*, CAD-6(4):634–649, July 1987.
4. Randal E. Bryant. Formal verification of memory circuits by switch-level simulation. *IEEE Transactions on Computer-Aided Design*, CAD-10(1):94–102, January 1991.
5. Randal E. Bryant and Carl-Johan H. Seger. Formal verification of digital circuits using symbolic ternary system models. In Robert P. Kurshan, editor, *Computer Aided Verification*, pages 121–146, 1990.
6. Edmund M. Clarke, Robert Enders, Thomas Filkorn, and Somesh Jha. Exploiting symmetry in temporal logic model checking. *Formal Methods in System Design*, 9:77–104, 1996.
7. E. Allen Emerson and A. Prasad Sistla. Symmetry and model checking. *Formal Methods in System Design*, 9:105–131, 1996.
8. C. Norris Ip and David L. Dill. Better verification through symmetry. *Formal Methods in System Design*, 9:41–75, 1996.
9. Manish Pandey, Richard Raimi, Derek L. Beatty, and Randal E. Bryant. Formal verification of PowerPC(TM) arrays using symbolic trajectory evaluation. In *33rd ACM/IEEE Design Automation Conference*, pages 649–654, June 1996.
10. Carl-Johan H. Seger and Randal E. Bryant. Formal verification by symbolic evaluation of partially-ordered trajectories. *Formal Methods in System Design*, 6:147–189, 1995.

Parallelizing the Murφ Verifier

Ulrich Stern* and David L. Dill

Department of Computer Science, Stanford University,
Stanford, CA 94305
{uli@verify, dill@cs}.stanford.edu

Abstract. With the use of state and memory reduction techniques in verification by explicit state enumeration, runtime becomes a major limiting factor. We describe a parallel version of the explicit state enumeration verifier Murφ for distributed memory multiprocessors and networks of workstations that is based on the message passing paradigm. In experiments with three complex cache coherence protocols, parallel Murφ shows close to linear speedups, which are largely insensitive to communication latency and bandwidth. There is some slowdown with increasing communication overhead, for which a simple yet relatively accurate approximation formula is given. Techniques to reduce overhead and required bandwidth and to allow heterogeneity and dynamically changing load in the parallel machine are discussed, which we expect will allow good speedups when using conventional networks of workstations.

1 Introduction

Complex protocols are often verified by examining all reachable protocol states from a set of possible start states. This reachability analysis can be done using two different methods: the states can be explicitly enumerated by storing them individually in a table, or a symbolic method can be used, such as representing the reachable state space with a binary decision diagram (BDD) [3]. Both methods have application domains in which they outperform the other; explicit state enumeration has worked better for the types of industrial protocols examined in our group [11].

There have been two approaches to improve explicit state enumeration. First, state reduction methods have been developed that aim at reducing the size of the reachability graph while ensuring that protocol errors will still be detected. Examples would be exploiting symmetries, utilizing reversible rules and employing repetition constructors [13]. These methods directly tackle the main problem in reachability analysis: the very large number of reachable states of most protocols. The second approach aims at reducing the amount of memory needed to perform the reachability analysis. Examples would be bitstate hashing [9] and hash compaction [26, 20].

---

* Ulrich Stern was supported during parts of this research by a scholarship from the German Academic Exchange Service (DAAD-Doktorandenstipendium HSP-II).

In this paper, we explore a third approach to improve explicit state enumeration: parallel processing. With the use of state and memory reduction techniques, runtime becomes a major limiting factor [26, 20]. For example, when verifying complex protocols with the Murφ verifier [7] using symmetry reduction in combination with hash compaction, a single verification run that does not expose new errors typically takes several days.

We present a parallel version of the Murφ verifier for distributed memory multiprocessors and networks of workstations that uses the message passing paradigm. Parallel Murφ was originally developed on a network of workstations (NOW) at UC Berkeley (SPARC20s connected via Myrinet) using generic active messages [6] as the message passing layer; later it was ported with little effort to an SP2 at IBM Watson.

In parallel Murφ, the state table, which stores all reached protocol states, is partitioned over the nodes of the parallel machine. Thus, the table can be larger than on a single node. Each node maintains a work queue of unexplored states. When a node generates a new state, the "owning" node for this state is calculated with a hash function and the state is sent to this node; this policy implements randomized load balancing. On reception of a state descriptor, a node first checks if the state has been reached before (with the local part of the state table). If the state is new, it is inserted in the state table and the local work queue. Special algorithms for termination detection and error trace generation have to be employed in this distributed setting. Due to space constraints, however, only the termination detection algorithm will be discussed in this paper. We also show analytically that the state space is typically very evenly distributed over the nodes.

We measured the speedup of parallel Murφ when verifying three complex cache coherence protocols: SCI [12], DASH [17] and FLASH [16]. On a 63 node SP2 the speedup was 44.2 for SCI and 53.7 for DASH, while we obtained speedups of 26.6 for SCI, 27.8 for DASH, and 29.4 for FLASH on a 32 node NOW in Berkeley. Thus, our algorithm achieves close to linear speedup. In addition, experiments performed at Berkeley [18] show that the runtime of parallel Murφ is largely insensitive to increased communication latency and reduced bandwidth. There is, however, some sensitivity to communication overhead. We give a simple formula for the expected runtime on a parallel machine depending on the communication overhead. We show empirically that the formula accurately predicts parallel speedup.

Aggarwal, Alonso and Courcoubetis [1] also presented a distributed reachability algorithm. Their algorithm seems more complicated than ours, has not been implemented and the correctness of the termination detection relies on timing assumptions that may be difficult to guarantee. One potential advantage of their method is that it might be usable under dynamically changing load conditions on a network of heterogeneous workstations. We propose an extension of our algorithm, however, that also allows heterogeneous systems with dynamically changing load and, at the same time, reduces the communication volume by typically one or two orders of magnitude.

Kumar and Vemuri [15] proposed and implemented a distributed algorithm to check the equivalence of two finite state machines, which essentially does a reachability analysis of the product machine. Their algorithm synchronizes after each breadth-first level and does not overlap communication and computation. Although the examples they present require only infrequent communication with very small messages, the reported speedups are worse than the ones reported here. In addition, their algorithm seems to have a high overhead, since it is only faster than a sequential one when running on four nodes.

Parallel Murφ, however, when running on one node is as fast as the most recent version (3.0) of sequential Murφ, for which the runtime was optimized. In fact, parallel Murφ is based on this version of sequential Murφ, which contains symmetry reduction and hash compaction.

There have also been some efforts to parallelize BDD-based verification methods. Stornetta and Brewer [23, 22] and Ranjan et al. [19] have presented distributed memory BDD algorithms. Both algorithms only achieve speedups in comparison to sequential versions if the sequential versions run out of memory and are forced to do swapping, but they enable the use of the total memory of the parallel machine. Kimura and Clarke [14] presented BDD algorithms for a shared memory machine and reported a speedup of roughly 10 on 15 nodes, while efficiently using the total available memory.

2 Active Messages

Active messages [24] have been introduced to reduce the communication costs in message passing and can be thought of as a fast message passing library. In contrast to a message in traditional message passing, an active message also contains the address of a procedure, called *handler*, that will be called on the destination node after the arrival of the message. For example, when a state descriptor s is to be sent to some node n, we will send the active message "Receive(s)" to n, indicating that the handler Receive() should be called on node n with the state descriptor s as argument.

When sending an active message, the sender does not wait for the message to arrive at the receiver but continues immediately. Upon arrival of the message, the receiver's current stream of control is not interrupted. Instead, the receiver has to periodically call poll(), which, in turn, calls all handlers for the active messages that have arrived since the last call to poll(). We will say that a message is *received* after the corresponding handler has returned. The use of handlers and polling enables efficient implementations of the active message scheme.

All nodes have to execute the same program when using active messages. Each node, however, is assigned a unique node number from $\{0, \ldots, N-1\}$, where N denotes the number of nodes in the parallel machine. To implement a "master" node with special responsibilities like, for example, startstate generation, an if statement can be used with the condition that the node number is 0. The barrier() command synchronizes all the nodes running the parallel program by waiting until every node has reached the barrier.

3 Parallel Explicit State Enumeration

The Basic Algorithm

The basic algorithm that runs on each node of the parallel machine is given in Figure 1 and described in this paragraph. Note that the global variables are local to each node since we assume distributed memory. The state enumeration is started by calling Search() on each node. The master node generates the startstates and distributes them by calling Send(). In the Send() procedure, the state is first canonicalized (for symmetry reduction) and then sent to the owning node, whose node number is calculated by a hash function $h()$. The handler Receive() checks a state against the local state table and potentially inserts it into the state table and queue. The search loop dequeues a state, generates its successors and sends them to the owning nodes. Note that this loop calls poll() to execute the handlers for newly arrived messages. The search loop is exited as soon as termination is detected. Termination detection is described in more detail in the next subsection.

Termination Detection

The parallel search has terminated when the following two conditions hold: there are no more messages in progress (i.e. sent but not received) and there are no more states in the queues Q. Note that the latter condition also implies that no state is currently being expanded, since states being expanded are removed from the queue only after their expansion.

Figure 2 shows the termination detection algorithm used. The algorithm is only invoked after the master has been idle for longer than a certain threshold value. Setting this value to, say, 0.1s results in negligible runtime overhead for termination detection. The correctness proof is similar to the one presented in [25] and is omitted here.

Randomized Load Balancing

We now examine how well the hash function balances the state space over the individual state tables. We look at a particular node and assume that for each state the probability that it is sent to this node is $1/N$, i.e., that the hash function distributes states uniformly. (Universal hashing [4], used in Murφ [20], can be shown to distribute at least as well as uniformly.) Let n denote the number of reachable states and Y the random variable describing the number of states sent to our node, which has the expected value $\bar{Y} = n/N$. For a large n, Y is distributed according to a normal distribution because of the central limit theorem. To bound the probability that the relative error of Y in comparison to $\bar{Y}$ is larger than a certain constant r, we use that for every $x > 0$, $1 - \Phi(x) < \phi(x)/x$, where $\Phi(x)$ and $\phi(x) = e^{-x^2/2}/\sqrt{2\pi}$ denote the standard normal distribution and density functions [8]. Using basic calculations one obtains that

$$\Pr(|Y/\bar{Y} - 1| > r) < 2\,\phi(z)/z \quad \text{with } z = r\,\sqrt{n/(N-1)}\ .$$

```
var      // global variables, but local to each node
  T: hash table;       // state table
  Q: FIFO queue;       // state queue
  StopSend: boolean;       // for termination detection
  Work, Sent, Received: integer;

Search()      // main routine
begin
  T := ∅;  Q := ∅;       // initialization
  StopSend := false;  Sent := 0;  Received := 0;
  barrier();
  if I am the master then       // master generates startstates
    for each startstate s₀ do
      Send(s₀);
    end
  do      // search loop
    if Q ≠ ∅ then begin
      s := top(Q);
      for all s' ∈ successors(s) do
        Send(s');
      end
      Q := Q − {s};
    end
    poll();
  while not Terminated();
end

Send(s: state)      // send state s to "random" node h(s)
begin
  s_c := canonicalize(s);       // symmetry reduction
  while StopSend do       // wait for StopSend = false
    poll();                // (for termination detection)
  end
  Sent++;
  send active message Receive(s_c) to node h(s_c);
end

Receive(s: state)      // receive state (active message handler)
begin
  Received++;
  if s ∉ T then begin
    insert s in T;
    insert s in Q;
  end
end
```

Fig. 1. Parallel Explicit State Enumeration

```
Terminated(): boolean
begin
   if I am the master then        // master initiates termination check
      if idletime exceeds threshold then begin
         Work := 0;
         send active message ReportCounters() to all nodes;
         wait for all replies (i.e., calls to SumCounters());
         if Work > 0 then        // continue search
            send active message Continue() to all nodes;
         else        // terminate search
            notify all nodes of termination (details omitted);
      end
   return termination status;
end


// active message handlers
ReportCounters()        // report counter values
begin
   StopSend := true;
   send active message SumCounters(Sent − Received + |Q|) to master;
end

SumCounters(w: integer)        // master sums counter values
begin
   Work := Work + w;
end

Continue()        // continue with search
begin
   StopSend := false;
end
```

Fig. 2. Termination Detection

For example, when $n=10^8$ and $N=32$, the probability that the relative error exceeds $r=0.1\%$ is smaller than 8.85% and the probability that the relative error exceeds $r=0.5\%$ is smaller than $2.73 \cdot 10^{-19}$. Generally, if the number of reachable states n is large and the number of nodes N is not too large, the state space will be distributed very evenly over the nodes.

Results

Figures 3 and 4 show the measured speedup of parallel Murφ on a 63-node SP2 at IBM Watson and on a 32-node UltraSPARC/Myrinet NOW at Berkeley, for instances of the SCI, DASH and FLASH protocols. Some parameters of these instances are shown in Table 1. The protocols were scaled to both provide interesting data and make the process of running the examples not too time-consuming. The speedup graphs show that the Murφ verifier can be parallelized quite efficiently.

Table 1. Example protocols

protocol	reachable states	successors generated	bytes/ state	diameter	single-node runtime NOW	SP2
SCI	1179 942	2973 536	124	46	717s	2804s
DASH	254 937	2646 647	532	64	1287s	5204s
FLASH	1021 464	4556 496	136	45	2477s	n/a

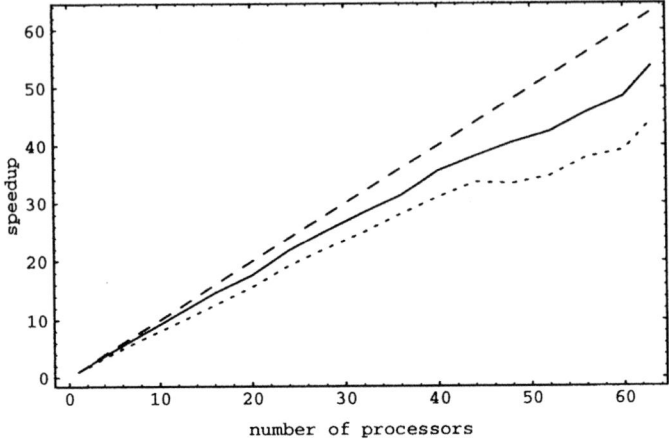

Fig. 3. Speedups for the SCI (dotted) and DASH (solid) protocols, calculated from the average runtime over two runs on an SP2, in comparison to linear speedup (dashed)

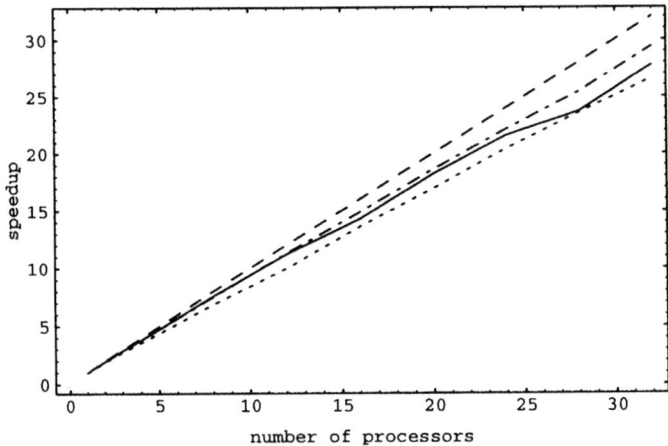

Fig. 4. Speedups for the SCI (dotted), DASH (solid) and FLASH (dashed and dotted) protocols, calculated from the average runtime over five runs on the Berkeley NOW, in comparison to linear speedup (dashed)

4 Estimating the Speedup

Rich Martin et al. [18] have performed a study on the Berkeley NOW of the impact of communication performance on several parallel applications including Murφ. They characterized communication performance based on the LogGP model [5, 2] with four parameters: latency L, overhead o, gap g and time-per-byte G. The latency is the delay in communicating a small message, the overhead is the average time consumed in sending or receiving a message, the gap is the minimum time between two messages, i.e. the reciprocal message bandwidth, and the time-per-byte is the reciprocal bulk transfer bandwidth.

The communication layer of the NOW was modified so that each of these parameters could be slowed down independently, starting from the following values of the unmodified communication layer: $o=3.5\mu s$, $g=7.0\mu s$, $L=5.5\mu s$ and $G=38MB/s$. Parallel Murφ, when verifying the SCI example, showed only negligible slowdown when either increasing latency or gap by up to $100\mu s$ or when reducing the bulk transfer bandwidth to 1MB/s. The insensitivity to latency can be explained by observing that if there are enough states in the state queues, all latency is overlapped with computation. Parallel Murφ is not sensitive to increased gap since it does not send messages in bursts. Finally, the bandwidth requirement per node is smaller than 1MB/s (roughly 0.5MB/s).

The runtime of parallel Murφ, however, showed some dependency on the overhead, for which we now derive an approximation formula. We assume that each node sends m/N messages, where m denotes the total number of messages sent. On the average, a fraction of $(N-1)/N$ of these messages will be sent to nodes different from the sender, each resulting in an overhead of $4o$, which stems from the sending and receiving of the message and its (automatically generated) reply message. Assuming linear speedup if there were no overhead, we approximate the runtime t_N on N nodes as

$$t_N = 4o\,m\,(N-1)/N^2 + t_1/N \ , \tag{1}$$

where t_1 denotes the runtime on a single node. Table 2 shows that (1) quite accurately predicts the measured runtimes for a range of different overhead values and numbers of nodes. Note that the numbers of messages sent are (slightly) smaller than the number of generated successors ($2.974 \cdot 10^6$), which is due to a small cache of recently sent states.

5 Improvements of the Basic Algorithm

Message Aggregation

By packing several states into one message, one can reduce the overhead per state. This well-known technique basically trades excess parallelism for communication performance. As shown in Figure 5, each of our three sample protocols provides a high degree of parallelism measured in the number of states in each

Table 2. Measured $(t_{N,m})$ and predicted $(t_{N,p})$ runtimes for the SCI protocol (in seconds) when varying the overhead. Measurements are averaged over five runs.

	messages sent m [million]	added overhead [μs]									
		0		25		50		100		200	
N		$t_{N,m}$	$t_{N,p}$	$t_{N,m}$	$t_{N,p}$	$t_{N,m}$	$t_{N,p}$	$t_{N,m}$	$t_{N,p}$	$t_{N,m}$	$t_{N,p}$
1	1.983	705.8									
2	2.534	372.2	361.8	432.1	425.1	496.1	488.5	617.4	615.2	891.7	868.6
16	2.697	52.7	46.3	66.5	62.1	81.6	77.9	114.1	109.5	177.2	172.7
32	2.706	26.2	23.2	34.6	31.4	43.1	39.6	59.4	56.0	92.8	88.7

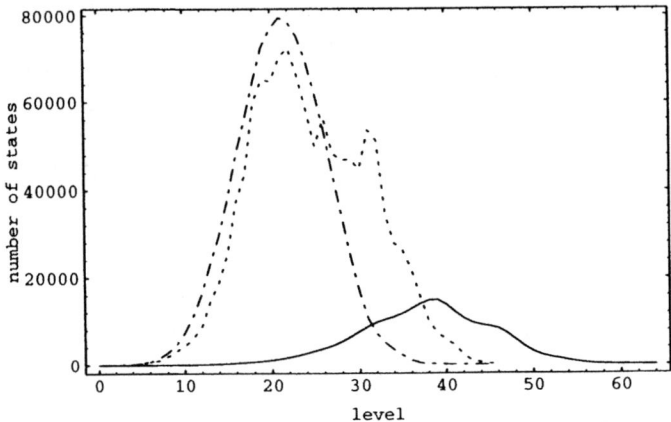

Fig. 5. Number of states in each breadth-first level for the SCI (dotted), DASH (solid) and FLASH (dashed and dotted) protocols

level of a breadth-first search, which enabled the efficient parallelization in the first place.

Table 3 shows the effect of message aggregation on runtime t_N and the number of messages sent m for the unmodified NOW and with an additional overhead of $100\mu s$. An overhead of $100\mu s$ is typical for message passing libraries based on TCP/IP. In both cases, the number of messages sent is strongly reduced. Our implementation packs 10 states into each message given that there are more than 20 states in the local queue. We have not tried to optimize these values or even make the message size vary with the number of states in the queue. While the reduction in runtime is small in the case of the unmodified NOW (as expected), in the high overhead case we achieve approximately a factor of two reduction, approaching the runtime on the unmodified NOW.

Aiming for a Conventional NOW

The bandwidth requirement of parallel Murφ becomes a problem on a conventional NOW, like workstations connected by Ethernet. For example, when veri-

Table 3. Measured $(t_{N,\mathrm{m}})$ and predicted $(t_{N,\mathrm{p}})$ runtimes and messages sent m (in million) for the SCI protocol when using message aggregation in comparison to the basic scheme. Measurements are averaged over six runs.

	added overhead [μs]								
	0				100				
	basic scheme		aggregation			basic scheme		aggregation		
N	$t_{N,\mathrm{m}}$	m	$t_{N,\mathrm{m}}$	m	$t_{N,\mathrm{p}}$	$t_{N,\mathrm{m}}$	m	$t_{N,\mathrm{m}}$	m	$t_{N,\mathrm{p}}$
16	52.3s	2.692	47.9s	.334	43.9s	114.1s	2.692	54.8s	.315	51.3s
32	25.7s	2.708	25.9s	.400	22.0s	58.9s	2.703	29.8s	.350	26.2s

fying the DASH protocol, each node requires a bandwidth of roughly 0.5MB/s, which would make an implementation even on top of switched Ethernet (where each node gets 10Mb/s for itself) difficult. In addition, the presented algorithm only works optimally if the state table size is proportional to the speed for each of the nodes, and thus allows only limited heterogeneity. Also, randomized load balancing performs poorly if the load on the nodes changes dynamically, since the hash function is fixed.

The algorithm can, however, be adapted to the situation of a slow network, heterogeneity and dynamically changing load. Instead of sending a full state s, each node only sends a (hash) signature $c(s)$ to the owning node $h(s)$, which, in turn, returns a bit indicating whether the state had been reached before. It can be shown in a similar fashion to [20] that this scheme will typically enable a reduction in bandwidth requirements of one or two orders of magnitude at the cost of a small probability that the search becomes incomplete. Note that in this scheme each node generates its work (new states to explore) by itself, which has the effect that a fast node needing much work will also generate much work for itself. Thus, the scheme is well suited for situations of dynamically changing load. To provide each node with initial work and to "restart" a node that runs out of states, a load balancing protocol similar to the one described in [25] can be employed. Also, heterogeneous systems are allowed since the tabulation of states is now independent of their expansion.

6 Conclusions and Future Research

Runtime has been becoming a major bottleneck in verification. We show that the Murφ verifier can be parallelized quite efficiently. The resulting algorithm is shown to run with close to linear speedup on a wide range of distributed memory multiprocessors and networks of workstations. In addition, we give a formula with which the speedup of parallel Murφ can be predicted depending on the communication performance. Since the state table is partitioned over the parallel machine, the algorithm also allows the verification of larger protocols.

The methods used to parallelize Murφ could also be used for other explicit state verification tools like SPIN [10]. The architectures for which parallel Murφ

was developed – distributed memory multiprocessors and networks of workstations – are becoming more common. Techniques to reduce overhead and required bandwidth and to allow heterogeneity and dynamically changing load in the parallel machine are discussed, which we expect will allow good speedups when using conventional networks of workstations.

The algorithm presented is compatible with the two newer reduction techniques in Murφ [13], reversible rules and repetition constructors, which were not yet available in the public release. It is also compatible with the latest version of hash compaction [21].

The most recent version of sequential Murφ, on which the parallel version is based, does not support the checking of temporal properties because of difficulties combining this checking with symmetry reduction. Thus, we did not put high priority on parallelizing the verification of temporal properties. This seems, however, to be an interesting area for future research.

Acknowledgments

We are grateful to the Berkeley active message group and all the people at IBM Watson that assisted with the SP2 port. In particular, Joefon Jann and Yarsun Hsu from IBM Watson helped in many ways. We would especially like to thank Rich Martin from Berkeley for making his modified communication layer available to us and for his invaluable assistance on active message issues.

References

1. S. Aggarwal, R. Alonso, and C. Courcoubetis. Distributed reachability analysis for protocol verification environments. In *Discrete Event Systems: Models and Applications. IIASA Conference*, pages 40–56, 1987.
2. A. Alexandrov, M. F. Ionescu, K. E. Schauser, and C. Scheiman. LogGP: incorporating long messages into the LogP model – one step closer towards a realistic model for parallel computation. In *7th Annual ACM Symposium on Parallel Algorithms and Architectures*, pages 95–105, 1995.
3. J. R. Burch, E. M. Clarke, K. L. McMillan, and D. L. Dill. Sequential circuit verification using symbolic model checking. In *27th ACM/IEEE Design Automation Conference*, pages 46–51, 1990.
4. J. L. Carter and M. N. Wegman. Universal classes of hash functions. *Journal of Computer and System Sciences*, 18(2):143–54, 1979.
5. D. Culler, R. Karp, D. Patterson, A. Sahay, K. E. Schauser, E. Santos, R. Subramonian, and T. von Eicken. LogP: towards a realistic model of parallel computation. In *4th ACM SIGPLAN Symposium on Principles and Practice of Parallel Programming*, pages 1–12, 1993.
6. D. Culler, K. Keeton, C. Krumbein, L. T. Liu, A. Mainwaring, R. Martin, S. Rodrigues, K. Wright, and C. Yoshikawa. *Generic Active Message Interface Specification*. UC Berkeley, 1995. Version 1.1.
7. D. L. Dill. The Murφ verification system. In *Computer Aided Verification. 8th International Conference*, pages 390–3, 1996.

8. W. Feller. *An Introduction to Probability Theory and Its Applications*, volume 1. John Wiley & Sons, 3rd edition, 1968.

9. G. J. Holzmann. On limits and possibilities of automated protocol analysis. In *Protocol Specification, Testing, and Verification. 7th International Conference*, pages 339–44, 1987.

10. G. J. Holzmann and D. Peled. The state of SPIN. In *Computer Aided Verification. 8th International Conference*, pages 385–9, 1996.

11. A. J. Hu, G. York, and D. L. Dill. New techniques for efficient verification with implicitly conjoined BDDs. In *31st Design Automation Conference*, pages 276–82, 1994.

12. *IEEE Std 1596-1992, IEEE Standard for Scalable Coherent Interface (SCI)*.

13. C. N. Ip. *State Reduction Methods for Automatic Formal Verification*. PhD thesis, Stanford University, 1996.

14. S. Kimura and E. M. Clarke. A parallel algorithm for constructing binary decision diagrams. In *IEEE International Conference on Computer Design*, pages 220–3, 1990.

15. N. Kumar and R. Vemuri. Finite state machine verification on MIMD machines. In *European Design Automation Conference*, pages 514–20, 1992.

16. J. Kuskin, D. Ofelt, M. Heinrich, J. Heinlein, R. Simoni, K. Gharachorloo, J. Chapin, D. Nakahira, J. Baxter, M. Horowitz, A. Gupta, M. Rosenblum, and J. Hennessy. The Stanford FLASH multiprocessor. In *21st Annual International Symposium on Computer Architecture*, pages 302–13, 1994.

17. D. Lenoski, J. Laudon, K. Gharachorloo, W.-D. Weber, A. Gupta, J. Hennessy, M. Horowitz, and M. S. Lam. The Stanford DASH multiprocessor. *Computer*, 25(3):63–79, 1992.

18. R. P. Martin, A. M. Vahdat, D. E. Culler, and T. E. Anderson. Effects of communication latency, overhead, and bandwidth in a cluster architecture. In *24th Annual International Symposium on Computer Architecture*, 1997.

19. R. K. Ranjan, J. V. Sanghavi, R. K. Brayton, and A. Sangiovanni-Vincentelli. Binary decision diagrams on network of workstations. In *International Conference on Computer Design*, pages 358–64, 1996.

20. U. Stern and D. L. Dill. Improved probabilistic verification by hash compaction. In *Advanced Research Working Conference on Correct Hardware Design and Verification Methods*, pages 206–24, 1995.

21. U. Stern and D. L. Dill. A new scheme for memory-efficient probabilistic verification. In *Joint International Conference on Formal Description Techniques for Distributed Systems and Communication Protocols, and Protocol Specification, Testing, and Verification*, pages 333–48, 1996.

22. T. Stornetta. Implementation of an efficient parallel BDD package. Master's thesis, UC Santa Barbara, 1995.

23. T. Stornetta and F. Brewer. Implementation of an efficient parallel BDD package. In *33rd Design Automation Conference*, pages 641–4, 1996.

24. T. von Eicken, D. E. Culler, S. C. Goldstein, and K. E. Schauser. Active messages: a mechanism for integrated communication and computation. In *19th Annual International Symposium on Computer Architecture*, pages 256–66, 1992.

25. C.-P. Wen. A distributed task queue for load balancing on the CM5. Unpublished paper written in Katherine Yelick's group at UC Berkeley.

26. P. Wolper and D. Leroy. Reliable hashing without collision detection. In *Computer Aided Verification. 5th International Conference*, pages 59–70, 1993.

A New Heuristic for Bad Cycle Detection Using BDDs

R. H. Hardin[1]   R. P. Kurshan[1]
S. K. Shukla[2]   M. Y. Vardi[3]

Abstract. We describe a new heuristic for detecting bad cycles (reachable cycles that are not confined within one or another designated sets of model states), a fundamental operation for model-checking algorithms. It is a variation on a standard implementation of the Emerson-Lei algorithm, which our experimental data suggests can result in a significant speed-up for verification runs that pass. We conclude that this heuristic can be used to advantage on "mature" designs for which the anticipated result of the verification is *pass*.

1 Introduction

It is well known that the model-checking problem for the linear-time temporal logic LTL, the branching time temporal logic CTL, and ω-automaton specifications are all solvable in time that is linear in the size of the model [CES86, LP85, VW86]. In most existing approaches, the model-checking problem is reduced to the graph problem of finding a "bad" cycle, *i.e.*, a reachable cycle that is not contained in one or more designated set of nodes [CES86, CVWY91, Kur94, LP85]. Since this graph problem has a well known linear-time solution using depth-first search [Kur94], the linear-time complexity of the model-checking problems follows.

In this paper, we concentrate on the bad cycle detection problem. Our experimental data derives from our implementation of the titled heuristic in the verification tool COSPAN [HHK96, Kur94]. COSPAN applies to a model-checking paradigm in which both the program and the specification are represented by ω-automata. Fairness is captured by automata acceptance conditions, and model-checking consists of checking that the language of the program is contained in the language of its specification (in terms of their respective representations as automata). As with the other model-checking paradigms cited above, COSPAN performs this check by searching a derived reachable state space for "bad" – or more specifically, unfair – cycles, captured as reachable cycles not contained in

---

[1] Bell Labs, Murray Hill, NJ 07974, {rhh,k}@research.bell-labs.com

[2] Computer Science Department, State University of New York at Albany, NY 12222 sandeep@cs.albany.edu

[3] Department of Computer Science, Rice University, Houston, TX 77005-1892, vardi@cs.rice.edu, http://www.cs.rice.edu/~vardi. Supported in part by NSF grant CCR-9628400. Part of this work was done in Bell Laboratories during the DIMACS Special Year on Logic and Algorithms.

one or more specified sets of states [Kur94]. In COSPAN, the derived state space is formed from the product of the automata representing the program and the complement of the specification, and the specified sets of states are the *cycle sets* defined as part of the respective automata acceptance structures. The language containment check is verified if and only if there are no bad cycles in this derived state space (hence the name).

Model checking algorithms can be classified broadly according to the method of state reachability employed: *explicit* state enumeration, in which states are generated as explicit data addresses, or *implicit* (or "symbolic") state enumeration, in which states are represented implicitly as a solution of an equation. An obvious apparent advantage of implicit over explicit is that the size of the model state space that can be verified is not intrinsically limited by a linear function of the available computational space: a syntactically small equation can define a very large set of states. Unfortunately, in the worst case, the reachability problem in both paradigms is PSPACE-complete in the number of program variables. Nonetheless, implicit state enumeration has found many applications in industrial-scale verificational problems, on account of its potential to search very large state spaces [BCM+92].

The most successful implementation of implicit state enumeration currently is in terms of binary decision diagrams (BDDs) [BCM+92, McM93, TBK91, TBK95]. Thus, many modern verification tools, for example SMV [McM93] and COSPAN [HHK96], employ implicit state enumeration implemented with BDDs. (COSPAN also employs explicit state enumeration that in some circumstances is more efficient, and can be used effectively in concert with implicit state enumeration.)

In model-checking based upon explicit state enumeration, cycle detection may be done in time linear in the size of the program state space, by using depth-first search to find the strongly connected components of a graph derived from the product of the automata representing the program and the specification [Kur94]. All reachable cycles are contained in the strongly connected components of the graph (which are cycles themselves), and and it is enough to check that no strongly connected component is a bad cycle.

In BDD-based model-checking, a depth-first search is incompatible with the routines used to efficiently manipulate the BDDs. Instead, the cycle detection algorithms in BDD-based algorithms [McM93, TBK91, TBK95] generally employ some form of the Emerson-Lei algorithm for model checking [EL86]. These algorithms have time complexity quadratic in the size of the underlying state space because the Emerson-Lei algorithm employs a double nesting of fixed-point computations. Each inner fixed-point computation involves a number of iterations that is linear in the diameter of the state space, and the number of times the inner fixed-point is computed is linear in the size of the state space. Thus, even for small-size BDDs ($O(\log n)$), the time complexity is $O(n^2 \log^2 n)$. In principle, one may think it is possible in implicit state enumeration to detect bad cycles more efficiently by means of a transitive-closure computation, which requires only a linear number of steps to find bad cycles, following a logarithmic number of BDD-manipulation iterations to compute the transitive closure of a state space of size n, using successive path doubling. For small BDDs, the time complexity of the transitive-closure algorithm is polylogarithmic. In practice, however, the BDDs that define the transitive-closure become rather large, and empirical results have demonstrated that whatever time may be saved in a cycle-detection algorithm employing a transitive-closure subroutine is more than lost in manipulating the larger-size BDDs required to represent it [HTBK93, TBK91, TBK95]. In most applications, the Emerson-Lei algorithm advantageously trades the quadratic increase in algorithmic steps for a decrease in the number of steps required to manipulate the associated BDDs, resulting in fewer steps over-all (and requiring less space than the transitive-closure algorithm, as well). Thus, current implementations based upon the Emerson-Lei algorithm not only require less space than an implementation based upon transitive closure, but are empirically much faster as well.

In practice, the Emerson-Lei algorithm is often quite slow and is acceptable only for lack of a better algorithm. It is not unusual to find examples in which bad-cycle detection takes 2-10 times longer than reachability. It is known that the Emerson-Lei formula cannot be expressed as an alternation-free fixed-point formula [EL86], (which would have yielded a linear-time algorithm for the implicit state cycle detection also [Cle93]). It is an open question whether there is an algorithm for implicit-state cycle detection that has an over-all time complexity better than Emerson-Lei, when manipulation of the underlying data-structure (say, BDDs) is taken into account. We do not solve this problem in this paper; rather we focus on heuristics to improve the performance of the Emerson-Lei algorithm for cycle detection.

We present a heuristic and experimental evidence based upon running 10K randomly generated models, that this heuristic can significantly speed up bad cycle detection in the case that no bad cycle in fact is present. When there is no bad cycle, which implies that the system satisfies its specification, our heuristic outperforms the Emerson-Lei algorithm in almost all the longer-running models we tried, sometimes very significantly (performance measured in terms of running time). On the other hand, when there is a bad cycle, which means that the property being checked is not satisfied by the system, the normal implementation performs generally better. (The new heuristic and the normal implementation require comparable BDD sizes and space.) This consistent comparative performance suggests a guided use of model-checking in the following fashion. If the user has a reasonable expectation that the verification will result in a positive answer, use the new heuristic. If there is a reason to believe otherwise, use the existing algorithm. Often the user has a reasonable expectation of the outcome of verification: if the design is "green", it likely has many bugs and failure is anticipated; if the design already has been verified and a small change is made to the model, it may be anticipated that the verification most likely will pass. In the latter case, the new heuristic is recommended. A particular example of this latter case is regression verification [HKM+96], for which the choice of the new heuristic may be automated. Moreover, in any case, both algorithms may be run concurrently on separate processors to yield an average speedup over all.

2 Previous work

For perspective, we state the two basic algorithms for bad cycle detection in the context of implicit state enumeration: transitive closure and the Emerson-Lei algorithm. As stated in the Introduction, experimental evidence [HTBK93] suggests that transitive closure not only results in a larger memory requirement, but also in an empirically slower bad cycle check, on account of the added overhead of manipulating larger-sized BDD's. It is hard to find an example in which the transitive-closure algorithm outperforms the Emerson-Lei algorithm.

2.1 Bad Cycle Detection Based on Transitive Closure

Let $R(x, y)$ denote the Boolean function representing the transitive closure of the transition relation $T(x, y)$ determining the set of transitions from a state x to a state y. Then $(R(x, y) \wedge R(y, x))$ implicitly defines the set of cycles involving both x and y. Let $\{C_1, \ldots, C_n\}$ denote the *cycle sets* of states in which cycles are allowed. For each C_i, a set NC_{C_i} is computed as follows:

$$NC_{C_i}(x) = \exists y((R(x, y) \wedge R(y, x)) \wedge \overline{C_i(y)})$$

A state x belongs to NC_{C_i} if and only if there is a cycle involving x that is not entirely contained in C_i.

Theorem 1. [TBK91, TBK95] *Every reachable cycle is contained in at least one of the cycle sets C_i iff the set NC is empty, where $NC = \cap_{1 \leq i \leq n} NC_{C_i}$.*

The transitive-closure relation can be computed using a number of iterations that is logarithmic in the size of the state space, using successive path-doubling. Nevertheless, in practice the transitive-closure computation is very expensive and it was shown experimentally that even with various implementations of the transitive-closure computation, transitive-closure-based algorithms were much slower than the algorithms based on the Emerson-Lei formula described in the next subsection [TBK91, TBK95].

2.2 Bad Cycle Detection Based on The Emerson-Lei Formula

In [EL86] Emerson and Lei introduced a μ-calculus formula of alternation depth 1, which expressed an FCTL fairness constraint. In [TBK91, TBK95] this formula was used to find bad cycles in the context of checking language containment. The main idea is to compute the set NC_μ of reachable states from which set NC can be reached. Hence, emptiness of NC is equivalent to the emptiness of NC_μ.

NC_μ is obtained as the greatest fixed point of the following function F:

$$F(c)(x) = c(x) \wedge \bigwedge_{i=1}^{n} \exists y(T(x, y) \wedge lfp(G_i^c)(y))$$

Evaluation of F requires the computation of n least fixed points (lfp), one per function of G_i^c, for each iteration of F. For a given set c, G_i^c is defined as follows:

$$G_i^c(d)(x) = c(x) \wedge (\overline{C_i}(x) \vee \exists y(T(x,y) \wedge d(y)))$$

The following theorem is central to the correctness of the methods based on the Emerson-Lei formula.

Theorem 2. [TBK95] NC_μ *is the set of reachable states from which* NC *can be reached.*

It is clear from the alternation of the fixed points that the complexity of these algorithms will be quadratic in the size of the underlying structure (BDD nodes, and in the worse case, states). Moreover, it was shown that this fixed point formula cannot be expressed in the alternation-free fragment of the μ-calculus [EL86]. Thus, it does not seem that a linear-time algorithm will be possible based on this formalism. Instead, we propose a heuristic that is based upon the idea of computing quickly the set of *bad states*: states lying on some bad cycle, by successive approximation. Our heuristic strategy can be described as a *catch-them-young* strategy as explained in the next section.

3 New Heuristics

In this section we describe our *catch-them-young* heuristic for faster refinement of the set of bad states. The central idea is to use combined forward and backward reachability to find out if there is a C_i that contains the set of all bad states relative to $\{C_1, ..., C_{i-1}\}$. If that is the case for some i, then there is no bad cycle.

3.1 Description of the Basic Heuristic and Correctness Proof

Let S be the state space of the system and $\{C_1, C_2, ..., C_n\}$ be the set of cycle sets. We may assume that all relations are restricted to the set of reachable states. Now construct the BDDs for the complements of cycle sets and call them $F_1, F_2, ..., F_n$. So $F_i = S \setminus C_i$. A bad cycle must pass through all the F_i's.

We now describe the successive steps for constructing the set B of *bad states* (states lying on some bad cycle). B will be the set limit of its monotonically decreasing successive approximations $B^\#$. In any iteration, $B^\#$ is the set of states through which some bad cycle potentially may pass. Let

$$^*F_i = \{x \mid \text{there is a path from state } x \text{ to some state in } F_i\} ,$$

$$F_i^* = \{x \mid \text{there is a state in } F_i \text{ from which there is a path to } x\} .$$

These sets can be computed using standard backward and forward reachability (respectively), using a linear number of iterations. Let $F_i^\# = {}^*F_i \cap F_i^*$, $F^\# = \bigcap_{i=1}^n F_i^\#$.

If we now denote by f_i, f_i^*, ${}^*f_i$, and $f^\#$ the characteristic functions of F_i, F_i^*, ${}^*F_i$, and $F^\#$, respectively, then $f^\#$ can be computed as follows:

$f\# := true$
for all i do
$\quad f_i := f_i \wedge b$
$\quad f\# := f\# \wedge f_i^* \wedge^* f_i$

Here b is the characteristic function of $B^\#$, which is initially *true*. Note that if there is a cycle through x that visits some state in F_i, then $x \in F_i^\#$. Hence all the states on a bad cycle, must be in $F^\#$. Our first approximation to the set of bad states is thus given as $B^\# = F^\#$.

Lemma 3. $F^\#$ *contains all the bad states.*

Note, however, that $F^\#$ is only an approximation to B, as there may be some states in $F^\#$ that are not on any bad cycle. Hence, we have now to refine the set $B^\#$ to discard at least some of those states until either we can cover $B^\#$ by one of the C_i's, at which point we can stop since no bad cycle can exist, or the approximation reaches a fixed point where no more states can be thrown out of $B^\#$.

At this point we apply our *catch-them-young* strategy. The strategy is based on the observation in Lemma 4, which helps us to identify *early on* some states that provably do not belong to the set of bad states.

Lemma 4. *If $s \in B$ then there must be a predecessor s' of s in the state reachability graph such that $s' \in B$. Similarly, if $s \in B$ then there must be a successor s' of s in the state reachability graph such that $s' \in B$.*

Due to Lemma 4, we may identify those states that have none of their predecessors and none of their successors in $B^\#$ to be the ones that cannot be bad states. So we throw these states out of the set $B^\#$. Note that this is possible because of the monotonicity of our approximation (refinement) and Lemma 4. Hence the next step is to change the characteristic function of $B^\#$ to a new one as follows:

$$B^\#(x) := B^\#(x) \wedge (\exists y(T(x,y) \wedge B^\#(y))) \wedge (\exists y(T(y,x) \wedge B^\#(y))).$$

If this step changes $B^\#$ then we keep deleting more such states repeating the above BDD manipulation until a fixed point is reached.

Let b, b^+ and ^+b denote the characteristic functions of $B^\#$, the set of successor of states in $B^\#$, and the set of predecessors of states in $B^\#$. Then the next approximation $B^\#$ can be computed as follows.

$b := f\#$
while b changes do
$\quad b := b \wedge b^+$
$\quad b := b \wedge^+ b$

Now we have a better approximation of B. However, at this point we throw out from each F_i, the states that have already been known not to be bad states. This is accomplished by $F_i := F_i \cap B^\#$.

Then we again compute $F^\#$. If there are bad cycles, this set will contain all the states on those cycles. It may contain, however, also some good states. Thus, we need to repeat the calculation of $B^\#$ as described above, starting with $B^\# := F^\#$. By repeating this approximation of B several times, when we reach a fixed point, we check if there is some C_i that fully covers $B^\#$. If there is one, then we know that there is no bad cycle, and if there is none, then there is a bad cycle.

The correctness of the algorithm depends on the following proposition.

Proposition 5

- *If there are no bad cycles, then the fixed point of $B^\#$ is empty.*
- *If there are bad cycles, then the fixed point of $B^\#$ contains a strongly connected component with states from each F_i.*

Since the sequence of successive approximations to B is monotonic, the operations on $B^\#$ are iterated a number of times that is only linear in the size of the state space. Note, however, that this does not eliminated the doubly nested loop of the Emerson-Lei algorithm; at best this might speed up the convergence of the algorithm.

3.2 Implementational Improvements by transformational design

The heuristic approach explained in the previous section gives rise to the following implementation.

1. $b := S$
2. $f\# := true$
   for all i do
   $\qquad f_i := f_i \wedge b$
   $\qquad f\# := f\# \wedge f_i^* \wedge^* f_i$
3. $b := f\#$
   while b changes do
   $\qquad b := b \wedge b^+$
   $\qquad b := b \wedge^+ b$
4. If b is changed then go to step 2 else go to step 5;
5. If $b = \emptyset$ then there is no bad cycle else b contains bad cycle.

The correctness of this implementation follows from the correctness argument of the previous subsection. However, we did a few more correctness preserving transformation on this implementation to optimize the performance.

Note that in the above implementation, we have created a BDD for b, and a BDD for $f\#$, but eventually, b is assigned the same BDD as $f\#$. Hence, we can do the computations on b in step 2, rather than creating an intermediate representation $f\#$. This speeds up the implementation quite a bit.

We get the final version of our heuristic by using a simple technique in David Long's implementation in COSPAN of the Emerson-Lei algorithm: if at any point of our successive refinement of $B^\#$, we find an F_i such that $B^\# \subseteq F_i$ and that is not the only F_i that is left, we can drop this F_i from the further steps of the algorithm. The reason is that since the refinement of $B^\#$ is monotonic, after $B^\# \subseteq F_i$ holds, any further refinement of $B^\#$ will still be a subset of F_i. This means that at this point, it is guaranteed that if there is any bad cycle then it certainly passes through F_i. Hence in the computation of bad states, C_i is an irrelevant cycle set.

3.3 Experimental Results and their Interpretations

In order to test the performance of the new heuristic against the standard Emerson-Lei algorithm, we randomly generated 10K small models and ran them in COSPAN, using the two algorithms in succession. The random models were generated as one to seven processes which follow each other in identical graphs, one process making a transition at a time. The identical graphs contain from 1 to 17 nodes, and are randomly connected with a fanout of 1 to 3. The number of processes, the fanout at a node, and the number of nodes all were chosen uniformly. Each model had a passing version, where each strongly connected component was exactly matched by cycle sets or canceled by *recur edges* [Kur94] (another part, together with cycle sets, of the automaton acceptance structure for the type of automata used with COSPAN), and a failing version, where one of these cycle sets or recur edges was omitted. The generated data shows that whereas the ordinary Emerson-Lei algorithm is generally faster than the new heuristic on models that fail, the new heuristic tends to be better on models that pass (see Figure 1). For longer passing runs, when the Emerson-Lei algorithm runs slowly, the new heuristic can be as much as 10× faster, whereas for the top third longest runs, the Emerson-Lei algorithm was almost never faster than the heuristic. For passing runs, the Emerson-Lei algorithm outperformed the new heuristic by a factor of 3× or more in fewer than .001 of the models, and almost all of those were among the shorter runs. The new heuristic outperformed the Emerson-Lei algorithm by a factor of 3× or more in .04 of the models, mostly among the longer runs. The new heuristic thus seems to be much less likely to get into whatever difficulty is causing long runs, for passing runs. Overall, as an arithmetic average, the heuristic ran 18 percent faster for passing runs, and 36 percent slower for failing runs.

The size of the models, measured in number of bdd nodes, was essentially unchanged as a function of algorithm or pass/fail.

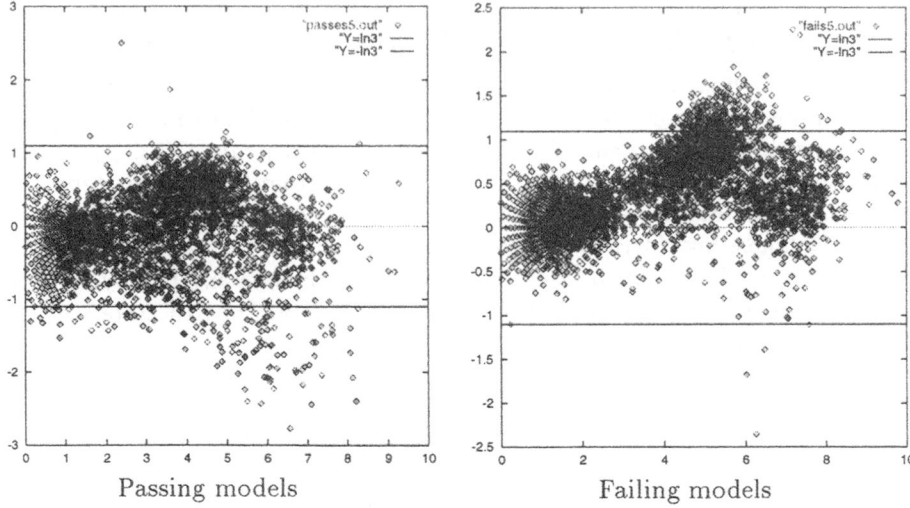

Passing models   Failing models

Fig. 1. Plotted points are of the form $(ln(r/r_0), ln(t_1/t_0))$, one point for each randomly generated model, where t_1 is the run time for the new heuristic and t_0 is the run time for the ordinary Emerson-Lei algorithm. r is $sqrt(t_1^2 + t_0^2)$ and represents a sort of average run time, and finally r_0 is 0.1 seconds. The horizontal lines show run time ratios of 3 and 1/3. The "fish tails" at small r indicate the timing granularity of .01 seconds. After eliminating from the plots runs with times reported as "0 seconds" or with r less than r_0, 3929 models passed and 5724 models failed.

We also ran the new heuristic on some longer-running hardware and software design models. While the number of models was too small to have experimental significance, the results were consistent with the randomly generated models, with one possible exception: there was some indication in these design-model runs that the incremental benefit of the new heuristic may be directly related to the number of cycle sets in the model.

4   Conclusion and Future work

We have described a variation of the Emerson-Lei algorithm applied to "bad" cycle detection. It uses a combination of backward and forward reachability limited to a successively restricted subset of the reachable states, and successively eliminates irrelevant cycle sets. This heuristic has been implemented in COSPAN, and run on approximately 10K randomly generated models. The results of these runs suggest that the new heuristic can be much faster than the Emerson-Lei algorithm on models that pass the verification, and essentially never slower on the longer-running models. On the other hand, the Emerson-Lei algorithm seems generally faster for models that fail. Therefore, it is recommended that this new heuristic be applied to models which are expected to pass verification, for example, models which have already been verified but need to be reverified on account of a small change in the model. If two computers are available, the two algorithms could be run in parallel, decreasing the expected termination time.

It is not known how well this heuristic does on models which derive from rationally generated (non-random) designs, although some preliminary experiments suggest that the heuristic will be beneficial on real designs as well, especially those with many cycle sets (fairness constraints). We plan to do further experimentation using commercial models. More investigation is needed to understand why this heuristic is skewed in favor of models which pass, something which is not understood by the authors.

This heuristic supports the general model-checking strategy of creating different algorithms for different special cases. This is useful as long as the applicable case can be predicted in advance, and is especially useful when the choice of heuristic can be automated. The heuristic presented here joins a number of such special-case algorithms which have been implemented to considerable advantage in COSPAN. In the case of this heuristic, it is a natural choice for regression verification [HKM+96] in which the verification is anticipated to pass. We hope there will be more work in the direction of special-purpose heuristics such as this one.

References

[BCM+92] J. R. Burch, E. M. Clarke, K. L. McMillan, D. L. Dill, and L. J. Hwang. Symbolic model checking: 10^{20} states and beyond. *Information and Computation*, 98(2):142–170, June 1992.

[CES86] E. M. Clarke, E. A. Emerson, and A. P. Sistla. Automatic verifications of finite-state concurrent systems using temporal logic specifications. *ACM Transactions on Programming Languages and Systems*, 8(2):244–263, April 1986.

[Cle93] R. Cleaveland. A linear-time model-checking algorithm for the alternation-free modal μ-calculus. *Formal Methods in System Design*, 2:121–147, 1993.

[CVWY91] C. Courcoubetis, M. Y. Vardi, P. Wolper, and M. Yannakakis. Memory efficient algorithms for the verification of temporal properties. *Lecture Notes in Computer Science*, 531:233–245, 1991.

[EL86] E. A. Emerson and C. L. Lei. Efficient model checking in fragments of the propositional modal mu-calculus. In *Proceedings of LICS 1986*, pages 267–278, 1986.

[HHK96] R. H. Hardin, Z. Har'El, and R. P. Kurshan. COSPAN. *Lecture Notes in Computer Science*, 1102:423–427, 1996.

[HKM+96] R. H. Hardin, R. P. Kurshan, K. L. McMillan, J. A. Reeds, and N. J. A. Sloane. Efficient regression verification. *IEE Proc. WODES'96*, pages 147–150, 1996.

[HTBK93] R. Hojati, H. J. Touati, R. K. Brayton, and R. P. Kurshan. Efficient ω-regular language containment. In *Proceedings of CAV 93, LNCS 663*, pages 396–409, 1993.

[Kur94]   R. P. Kurshan. *Computer Aided Verification of Coordinating processes :
          An Automata Theoretic Approach.* Princeton University Press, 1994.
[LP85]   O. Lichtenstein and A. Pnueli. Checking that finite state concurrent pro-
          grams satisfy their linear specifications.   In *Conference Record of the
          Twelfth Annual ACM Symposium on Principles of Programming Lan-
          guages*, pages 97–107. ACM, ACM, January 1985.
[McM93]   K. L. McMillan. *Symbolic Model Checking.* Kluwer Academic Publishers,
          1993.
[TBK91]   H. J. Touati, R. K. Brayton, and R. P. Kurshan. Testing language con-
          tainment for omega-automata using BDD'S. In *Proceedings of The 1991
          International Workshop on Formal Methods in VLSI Design*, January 1991.
[TBK95]   H. J. Touati, R. K. Brayton, and R. P. Kurshan. Testing language con-
          tainment for ω-automata using BDD's. *Information and Computation*,
          118(1):101–109, April 1995.
[VW86]   M.Y. Vardi and P. Wolper. An automata-theoretic approach to automatic
          program verification. In *Proceedings of the First Symposium on Logic in
          Computer Science*, pages 322–331, Cambridge, June 1986.

Efficient Detection of Vacuity in ACTL Formulas

Ilan Beer, Shoham Ben-David, Cindy Eisner and Yoav Rodeh

IBM Science and Technology
Haifa Research Laboratory, Matam, Haifa, Israel
shoham@vnet.ibm.com

Abstract. Propositional logic formulas containing implications can suffer from antecedent failure, in which the formula is true trivially because the pre-condition of the implication is not satisfiable. In other words, the post-condition of the implication does not affect the truth value of the formula. We call this a vacuous pass, and extend the definition of vacuity to cover other kinds of trivial passes in temporal logic. We define w-ACTL, a subset of CTL and show by construction that for every w-ACTL formula φ there is a formula $w(\varphi)$, such that: both φ and $w(\varphi)$ are true in some model M iff φ passes vacuously. A useful side-effect of $w(\varphi)$ is that if false, any counter-example is also a non-trivial witness of the original formula φ.

1 Introduction

Beatty and Bryant [BB94] have noted that antecedent failure is a problem in any application of formal verification, as it is an inherent problem in the use of logic, rather than of a particular approach (model checking or theorem proving). Antecedent failure means that a formula is trivially true because the pre-condition (antecedent) of the formula is not satisfiable in the model. We call this a vacuous pass, and extend the definition of vacuity to cover other kinds of trivially true formulas. If vacuity is not indicated to the user, the usefulness of formal verification is compromised, since a trivially true formula is not intentionally part of a specification (and therefore indicates a problem in the design or an error in the specification).

Several years of experience in practical formal verification of hardware at IBM [BB+96] have shown us that vacuity is a serious problem in the day-to-day use of formal verification. While it is possible to check vacuity using hand-written auxiliary formulas, the process is time-consuming and error prone, especially for long formulas containing many nested levels of pre-conditions.

In this paper we extend the notion of vacuity to cover many kinds of trivial passes in temporal logic. We then define a subset of ACTL [GL91] formulas, w-ACTL, for which it is possible to construct a single formula, $w(\varphi)$, which detects all vacuous passes of φ. In addition, $w(\varphi)$ has the useful side-effect that if no vacuity is detected, the model-checker produces a non-trivial witness to the original formula φ. We have implemented automatic generation of witness formulas as a feature of RuleBase [BB+96], the formal verification tool developed at the IBM Haifa Research Laboratory.

Detecting trivial passes of even relatively straightforward formulas is not in itself a trivial task. We use a typical Sugar[1] formula as an example:

---

[1] Sugar is a syntactic sugaring of CTL [CE81] formulas, and is the specification language used by the RuleBase formal verification tool. In [BB+96] we outlined its basic features.

$$AG(request \rightarrow next\_event(data)[4](last\_data)) \tag{1}$$

Formula 1 states that last_data should be asserted with the fourth data after a request. The translation into CTL is:

$$AG(request \rightarrow !E[!dataU(data \wedge EXE[!dataU(data \wedge$$
$$EXE[!dataU(data \wedge EXE[!dataU(data \wedge !last\_data)])])])]) \tag{2}$$

A trivial pass of Formula 2 would be a pass in a model in which either request never occurs, or a request is never followed by four datas. A hand-written check of a trivial pass of Formula 2, which verifies that it is possible to receive a request followed by four datas, might look like the following:

$$EF(request \wedge (EF(data \wedge EXEF(data \wedge EXEFdata \wedge (EXEFdata)))))) \tag{3}$$

Our goal was to automate the checking of trivial passes so as to free the user from coding Formula 3 or its equivalent.

A nice side-effect of our method is that the same witness formula $w(\varphi)$ which detects trivial passes of the original formula when true, will provide a non-trivial witness (one instance of the truth of the formula) to φ when false. Witnesses are important because a formula may pass as the result of an error in the formula, rather than as a result of the design conforming to the formula that was intended by the user. Thus, examining a witness provides some confidence that the formal specification accurately reflects the intent of the user, one of the weak links in the practical application of formal verification to hardware design.

Note that simply negating the original formula will not provide a non-trivial witness. For instance, consider the CTL formula:

$$AG(p \rightarrow AX(q \rightarrow AXr)) \tag{4}$$

If we negate Formula 4, we get:

$$EF(p \wedge EX(q \wedge EX\neg r)) \tag{5}$$

Obviously, since Formula 5 is the negation of Formula 4, Formula 5 is false if Formula 4 is true. However, because Formula 5 is an existential formula, there is no trace which can show it is false, and the counter-example mechanisms of [HBK93] and of SMV [McM93, CG+95] will not generate a trace. We would like, however, to see a witness of Formula 4 which contains a sequence of states on which p occurs, followed by q in the next state, followed by r in the next.

Negating the single operand of the AG operator in Formula 4 as follows:

$$AG\neg(p \rightarrow AX(q \rightarrow AXr)) \tag{6}$$

will also not guarantee an interesting witness. For instance, a valid counter-example to Formula 6 is a path to a state in which p does not occur. Once again, this is a trivial positive example of the truth of the original Formula 4.

Both the ability to detect trivial passes and the ability to generate interesting witnesses are of great importance in the practical application of formal verification to hardware design. Our experience has shown that typically 20% of formulas pass vacuously during the first formal verification runs of a new hardware design, and that vacuous passes always point to a real problem in either the design or its specification or environment. Of the formulas which pass non-vacuously, examination of the witness traces discovers a problem for approximately 10% of the formulas. Of course, once the formula itself has been debugged by examination of a witness, there is no need to examine the witness on later runs. Thus, the model checking stays a fully automated process in the sense that a non-vacuous pass after a formula has been debugged requires no hand check by the user.

The remainder of this paper is organized as follows. In Section 2 we compare our work with related work. In Section 3 we give some background. Section 4 is the heart of the paper, and describes the theory and results. In Section 5 we conclude, and point to future directions for research.

2 Comparison with Related Work

Previous works, including [BB94] and [PP95], have noted the problem of trivial passes, and shown how to avoid them using hand-written checks. This work is, we believe, the first attempt to automatically detect trivial passes under symbolic model checking.

In this paper, we use the term interesting witness to mean a computation path showing one non-trivial example of the truth of the formula. In [HBK93], Hojati, Brayton and Kurshan describe counter-example generation for model checking using CTL and language containment using L-automata [Kur90]. They do not use the term witness, and do not produce a counter-example for a CTL formula containing an existential operator. In [CG+95], Clarke, Grumberg, McMillan and Zhao describe the counter-example and witness generation algorithm of SMV [McM93]. In their terminology, a witness is a computation path that shows that a formula with an existential path quantifier is true. For true formulas not containing an existential operator, no trace at all is generated.

Thus, neither [HBK93] nor [CG+95] produce witnesses for ACTL formulas. To the best of our knowledge, this work is the first to address the problem of generating a witness, in the sense of a positive non-trivial example for non-existential formulas, under symbolic model checking.

3 Preliminaries

CTL, or Computation Tree Logic [CE81], is a temporal logic useful for reasoning about the ongoing behavior of reactive systems, and is the logic used by the symbolic model checker SMV [McM93]. In CTL, temporal operators occur in pairs consisting of A or E, followed by F, G, U, or X, as follows:

1. Every atomic proposition is a CTL formula, and
2. If f and g are CTL formulas, then so are $\neg f, (f \wedge g), AXf, EXf, A[fUg], E[fUg]$

The remaining operators are viewed as abbreviations of the above, as follows: $f \vee g = \neg(\neg f \wedge \neg g), AFg = A[trueUg], EFg = E[trueUg], AGf = \neg E[trueU\neg f]$ and $EGf = \neg A[trueU\neg f]$.

The semantics of a CTL formula is defined with respect to a model M. A model is a quadruple (S, S_0, R, L), where S is a finite set of states, $S_0 \subseteq S$ is a set of initial states, $R \subseteq S \times S$ is the transition relation, and L is the valuation, a function mapping each state with a set of atomic propositions true in that state. We require that there is at least one transition from every state. A computation path of a model M is an infinite sequence of states $(s_0, s_1, s_2, \cdots)$ such that $R(s_i, s_{i+1})$ is true for every i.

The notation $M, s \models f$ means that the formula f is true in state s of model M. The notation $M \models f$ is equivalent to $\forall t \in S_0\ M, t \models f$. The semantics of a CTL formula is defined as follows:

$M, s \models p \Longleftrightarrow p \in L(s)$, where p is an atomic proposition

$M, s \models \neg f \Longleftrightarrow M, s \not\models f$

$M, s \models f \wedge g \Longleftrightarrow M, s \models f$ and $M, s \models g$

$M, s_i \models AX\ f \Longleftrightarrow$ for all paths $(s_i, s_{i+1}, ...), M, s_{i+1} \models f$

$M, s_i \models EX\ f \Longleftrightarrow$ for some path $(s_i, s_{i+1}, ...), M, s_{i+1} \models f$

$M, s_i \models A[fUg] \Longleftrightarrow$ for all paths $(s_i, s_{i+1}, ...), \exists k \geq i$ such that $M, s_k \models g$, and $\forall j$ such that $i \leq j < k, M, s_j \models f$

$M, s_i \models E[fUg] \Longleftrightarrow$ for some path $(s_i, s_{i+1}, ...), \exists k \geq i$ such that $M, s_k \models g$ and $\forall j$ such that $i \leq j < k, M, s_j \models f$

ACTL is a subset of CTL defined by Grumberg and Long in [GL91], and can be informally described as CTL without the "E" operators, in which the $\neg$ operator modifies only atomic propositions. ACTL includes an additional operator, "AV", where A[p V q] $\equiv \neg$ E[$\neg$ p U $\neg$ q]. A[p V q] can intuitively be understood as "p releases q", in the sense that q must hold up to and including the time that p holds, at which point q is "released". If p never occurs, then q must hold forever. Thus, the "AV" operator is a weak operator, in contrast to the "AU" operator, which is strong: A[p U q] requires that q eventually occur. Notice that because some of the "A" operators can be defined in terms of the "E" operators, and vice versa, a CTL formula containing the "E" operator may still be an ACTL formula if the "E" operator is negated. The formal description can be found in [GL91].

4   Detection of vacuity in w-ACTL formulas

In this section, we describe the detection of vacuity in w-ACTL formulas. First, we define vacuity, w-ACTL and interesting witnesses. Then we define witness formulas to be formulas which detect vacuity and provide interesting witnesses. We then give the main result of this paper, an algorithm for constructing witness formulas for w-ACTL formulas, and prove that it is correct. Finally, we show some examples.

4.1 Vacuity

In this section, we will define vacuity, first intuitively and then formally.

Propositional antecedent failure means that a formula trivially passes because some pre-condition is not satisfiable, where a pre-condition is the left-hand-side of an implication. Another way to think of the same thing is to say that the right-hand-side of the implication does not affect the validity of the formula. This gives an intuitive extension of vacuity to any operator: vacuity occurs when one of the operands does not affect the validity of the formula. We first define what we mean by a sub-formula not affecting the truth value of the formula, then define vacuous passes.

Definition 1 (Does Not Affect). *A sub-formula χ of formula φ does not affect the truth value of φ in model M if for every formula $\chi\prime$, the truth value of $\varphi\prime$ in model M is the same as the truth value of φ in model M, where $\varphi\prime$ is the formula obtained by replacing χ with $\chi\prime$ in φ.*

Definition 2 (Vacuous Passes). *Formula φ passes vacuously in model M if it passes, and contains a sub-formula χ such that χ does not affect the truth value of φ in M.*

As an example, consider the following formula:

$$AG(p \rightarrow AX(q \rightarrow AXr)) \tag{7}$$

Some trivial passes of Formula 7 are passes in which either p never occurs, and thus $AX(q \rightarrow AXr)$ does not affect the validity of Formula 7, or q never occurs at a next state of p, and thus AXr does not affect the validity of Formula 7. Thus, the idea of vacuity includes a notion of when q should occur, and not just that it should occur. For instance, if $M \models \text{EF q}$, but also $M \models \text{AG } (p \rightarrow AX \neg q)$, a pass of Formula 7 is still trivial.

4.2 w-ACTL

We now define w-ACTL, a subset of ACTL which, in our experience, is sufficient for expressing most of the formulas used by engineers to specify their designs. In addition, we will show that we can efficiently detect vacuity of w-ACTL formulas using CTL model checking. Informally, w-ACTL formulas are ACTL formulas in which for all binary operators ($\wedge$, $\vee$, AU, AV), at least one of the operands is a propositional formula. Formally, w-ACTL is the set of state formulas described by the following:

Definition 3 (w-ACTL).

1. *If p is an atomic proposition, then p and $\neg p$ are simple formulas.*
2. *If f and g are simple formulas, then $f \wedge g$ and $f \vee g$ are simple formulas.*
3. *If ψ is a simple formula, it is a state formula.*
4. *If ψ is a simple formula, and χ is a state formula, then $\psi \wedge \chi, \chi \wedge \psi, \psi \vee \chi, \chi \vee \psi$, are state formulas.*
5. *If ψ is a simple formula, and χ is a state formula, then $AF \chi$, $AG \chi$, $A[\chi U \psi]$, $A[\psi U \chi]$, $A[\chi V \psi]$, $A[\psi V \chi]$, and $AX \chi$ are state formulas.*

Note that simple formulas are conjunctions and disjunctions of atomic propositions and their negations. In the sequel, we will usually use φ to designate some w-ACTL formula, ψ to designate a simple w-ACTL formula, and χ to designate a possibly non-simple w-ACTL formula.

We call our method efficient because it can detect vacuity of many sub-formulas simultaneously. However, our algorithm requires us to choose one operand of every binary operator, for which vacuity will be detected. We call this operand the important operand, and choose it as follows.

Definition 4 (Important Operand).

1. *If φ is a simple formula, its operands are not important[2].*
2. *If φ is a non-simple formula of the form $\psi \vee \chi$, $\chi \vee \psi$, $\psi \wedge \chi$ or $\chi \wedge \psi$, where ψ is simple and χ is non-simple, then χ is the important operand.*
3. *If φ is a formula of the form $A[\psi\ U\ \chi]$, $A[\chi\ U\ \psi]$, $A[\psi\ V\ \chi]$ or $A[\chi\ V\ \psi]$, where ψ is simple and χ is non-simple, then χ is the important operand.*
4. *If φ is a formula of the form $A[\psi_1\ U\ \psi_2]$ or $A[\psi_1\ V\ \psi_2]$, where both ψ_1 and ψ_2 are simple, then ψ_1 is the important operand[3].*
5. *If φ is a non-simple formula of the form $AX\ \chi$, $AF\ \chi$ or $AG\ \chi$, where χ is either simple or non-simple, then χ is an important operand.*

The following lemma follows directly from Definition 4, because only one operand of every binary operator can be important:

Lemma 5. *For every w-ACTL formula φ, there is a smallest important sub-formula s_φ, such that s_φ contains no important sub-formulas, and s_φ is a sub-formula of every other important sub-formula of φ.*

We justify choice of the non-simple operand of $\vee$ and $\wedge$ as the important operand as follows. The choice is simply a reflection of how engineers tend to use CTL to code a specification, as well as how they tend to design their hardware. For instance, consider the following specification:

$$AG(request \rightarrow AX(req\_accepted \rightarrow AXAX(read\_busy \vee write\_busy))) \quad (8)$$

---

[2] Actually, if the $\vee$ operator is derived from the use of the $\rightarrow$ operator by the user, we consider the right-hand-side of the original formula to be important even if it is simple. Similarly, we consider the second operand of the next_event operator [BB+96] to be important if both are simple. Since these are implementation details, we ignore them in the rest of this paper.

[3] This is counter-intuitive. The reason that only ψ_1 is important is that ψ_2 is the only operand that can cause vacuity. For $A[\psi_1\ U\ \psi_2]$, ψ_2 can cause vacuity of ψ_1 if it is always true immediately. However, ψ_1 cannot cause vacuity of ψ_2 because even if ψ_1 is always true forever, the AU operator still requires something of ψ_2: that eventually it occurs. For the AV operator, ψ_2 can cause vacuity of ψ_1 if it is always true forever, because then nothing is required of ψ_1. However, ψ_1 cannot cause vacuity of ψ_2 if it is always true immediately, because in that case, the AV operator still requires something of ψ_2: that it occurs at the same time.

which expresses the requirement that if a request is accepted (which happens or not one cycle after it appears), then two cycles later either the read_busy signal is asserted, or the write_busy signal is asserted. Logically, this is equivalent to the formula:

$$AG(\neg request \lor AX(\neg req\_accepted \lor AXAX(read\_busy \lor write\_busy)))\quad(9)$$

A trivial pass of 8, in which it is detected that $M \models AG(\neg request)$ would probably detect a problem in the model, because otherwise the signal called request is meaningless. However, a trivial pass in which it is detected that $M \models AG(AX(\neg req\_accepted \lor AXAX(read\_busy \lor write\_busy)))$ is quite often useless to the engineer, as it is highly likely that she has designed her logic intentionally for this to be so, and prevents read_busy or write_busy from being asserted spuriously by not asserting req_accepted if there was not a request the previous cycle.

Thus, for the binary operators, we have chosen the non-simple operand to be the important operand. We now define important vacuous passes as follows:

Definition 6 (Important Vacuous Passes). *If formula φ passes in model M, and contains an important sub-formula χ such that χ does not affect the truth value of φ in M, we say that the vacuous pass is an important vacuous pass.*

In the remainder of this paper, we will use the term "passes vacuously" to refer to important vacuous passes as defined above.

4.3 Witnesses for w-ACTL formulas

In the previous section we defined vacuity, the main motivation of this paper. In this section, we define interesting witnesses, which is the second motivation. Informally, an interesting witness is a path showing one instance of the truth of the formula, on which every important sub-formula affects the truth of the formula. In the formal definition of an interesting witness we make use of the fact that every computation path can be viewed as a model.

Definition 7 (Interesting Witness). *An interesting witness of a passing formula φ in model M is a computation path C in M such that $C \models \varphi$ non-vacuously.*

In the following, we define a witness formula, and show how to construct one for any given w-ACTL formula. Because our generation of a witness makes use of the counter-example mechanism of SMV [CG+95], we first define a counter-example as follows.

Definition 8 (Counter-example). *A counter-example of a failing formula φ in model M is a computation path C in M such that $C \not\models \varphi$.*

It should be noted that according to Definition 8, there are w-ACTL formulas for which no counter-example exists in some models. For example, there is no counter-example for the formula $\varphi = AFAGp$ in a model $M = (S, S_0, R, L), S = \{s_0, s_1, s_2\}$, $S_0 = s_0, R = \{(s_0, s_0), (s_0, s_1), (s_1, s_2), (s_2, s_2)\}, L(s_0) = L(s_2) = \{p\}, L(s_1) = \{\}$.

This is because despite the fact that $M \not\models \varphi$, $C \models \varphi$ for any computation path C in model M. Despite this fact, Definition 8 captures the essence of what we mean by a counter-example, in a succinct and intuitive manner, for the vast majority of w-ACTL formulas and models encountered in the day-to-day verification of hardware.

We now define a witness formula, which is the main definition of this paper. A witness formula is a formula which performs a dual function: it both detects vacuity, and, if not vacuous, induces a positive example to the original formula. Formally,

Definition 9 (Witness Formula). *A formula w is a witness formula of formula φ, denoted by $w(\varphi)$, if, for any model M,*

1. *$(M \models \varphi$ and $M \models w(\varphi)) \iff \varphi$ passes vacuously in M.*
2. *If $M \models \varphi$ and $M \not\models w(\varphi)$ then any counter-example of $w(\varphi)$ in M is also an interesting witness of φ in M.*

4.4 Construction of Witness Formulas

The main result of this paper is now presented. We show construction of a witness formula $w(\varphi)$ for any w-ACTL formula φ, and then prove that $w(\varphi)$ is indeed a witness formula of φ, according to Definition 9.

Algorithm 10 (Construction of Witness Formulas).

1. *If φ is a simple important formula, $w(\varphi) = FALSE$.*
2. *If φ is non-simple, and has the form $\psi \wedge \chi$ or $\chi \wedge \psi$, where χ is important, $w(\varphi) = \psi \wedge w(\chi)$.*
3. *If φ is non-simple, and has the form $\psi \vee \chi$ or $\chi \vee \psi$, where χ is important, $w(\varphi) = \psi \vee w(\chi)$.*
4. *If φ has the form $AF \chi$, $w(\varphi) = AF w(\chi)$.*
5. *If φ has the form $AG \chi$, $w(\varphi) = AG w(\chi)$.*
6. *If φ has the form $AX \chi$, $w(\varphi) = AX w(\chi)$*
7. *If φ has the form $A[\chi U \psi]$, where χ is important, $w(\varphi) = A[w(\chi) U \psi]$[4].*
8. *If φ has the form $A[\psi U \chi]$, where χ is important, $w(\varphi) = A[\psi U w(\chi)]$.*
9. *If φ has the form $A[\chi V \psi]$, where χ is important, $w(\varphi) = A[w(\chi)V\psi]$.*
10. *If φ has the form $A[\psi V \chi]$, where χ is important, $w(\varphi) = A[\psi V w(\chi)]$.*

---

[4] Actually, we produce $A[w\prime(\chi) U \psi]$, where $w\prime(\chi)$ is similar to $w(\chi)$, except that we replace a simple important formula with AF FALSE rather than FALSE. The reason for this is practical rather than theoretical. In theory, a computation path is infinite and therefore, every witness is infinite. In practice, however, the algorithm of [CG+95] will sometimes give finite counter-examples, when a finite counter-example is enough to show that the formula is false. In every case but one, the finite counter-example given by [CG+95] is "interesting enough" for our purposes. The exception is the AU operator. As a witness to $A[\chi U \psi]$, we would like to see a trace on which ψ occurs, but [CG+95] may give us a counter-example to $A[w(\chi) U \psi]$ which ends before ψ has occurred. Therefore, we use AF FALSE to get an infinite counter-example, just as [CG+95] uses EG TRUE to get an infinite witness. Since this is an implementation detail, we ignore it in the rest of this paper.

Note that the witness construction algorithm replaces the smallest important sub-formula by FALSE.

In order to prove that Algorithm 10 produces a witness formula, the following two lemmas are needed.

Lemma 11. *Let φ be an ACTL formula, M be a model and C a computation path in M. If $M \models \varphi$ then $C \models \varphi$.*

The proof follows directly from [Lon93].

Lemma 12. *For every ACTL formula φ, and every χ, a sub-formula of φ which is not an operand of ¬: let $\chi\prime$ be any formula, and $\varphi\prime$ be the formula obtained by replacing χ with $\chi\prime$ in φ. Then, for any model M, $M \models (\chi\prime \rightarrow \chi) \Longrightarrow M \models (\varphi\prime \rightarrow \varphi)$.*

The proof is by induction on the length of φ.

We are now ready to prove the correctness of our algorithm:

Theorem 13. *If φ is a w-ACTL formula, then $w(\varphi)$ given by Algorithm 10 is a witness formula of φ.*

Proof. Let $sub(\chi, \chi\prime)\varphi$ be the formula obtained by replacing χ with $\chi\prime$ in φ. Let s_φ be the smallest important sub-formula of φ. It is easy to see that by Algorithm 10,

$$w(\varphi) = sub(s_\varphi, FALSE)\varphi.$$

Furthermore, by Lemma 5, s_φ is a sub-formula of every important sub-formula χ of φ, so for every such χ,

$$w(\varphi) = sub(\chi, sub(s_\varphi, FALSE)\chi)\varphi.$$

In order for $w(\varphi)$ to be a witness formula we should prove that the two conditions of Definition 9 hold:

1. First we prove that $(M \models \varphi$ and $M \not\models w(\varphi)) \Longleftrightarrow \varphi$ passes vacuously.
   ($\Longleftarrow$)
   Let φ pass vacuously in M. By Definition 6, $M \models \varphi$, and $\exists\chi$, an important sub-formula of φ, such that $\forall\chi\prime$, $M \models sub(\chi, \chi\prime)\varphi$. For this χ, let $\chi\prime$ be $sub(s_\varphi, FALSE)\chi$. Then by the definition of vacuity, $M \models sub(\chi, \chi\prime)\varphi$, but as shown in the beginning of this proof, $w(\varphi) = sub(\chi, \chi\prime)\varphi$. Thus $M \models w(\varphi)$.
   ($\Longrightarrow$)
   Let $M \models \varphi$ and $M \not\models w(\varphi)$. We must show that φ passes vacuously in M, that is, we must show that $\exists\chi$ important sub-formula of φ, such that $\forall\chi\prime$, $M \models sub(\chi, \chi\prime)\varphi$. We choose χ to be s_φ.
   By Lemma 12, $\forall M$, $M \models (FALSE \rightarrow \chi\prime) \Longrightarrow M \models (sub(s_\varphi, FALSE)\varphi \rightarrow sub(s_\varphi, \chi\prime)\varphi)$.
   Since $\forall\chi\prime$, $\forall M$, $M \models (FALSE \rightarrow \chi\prime)$, it follows that

   $$\forall\chi\prime\forall M, \ M \models (sub(s_\varphi, FALSE)\varphi \rightarrow sub(s_\varphi, \chi\prime)\varphi)$$

   As shown in the beginning of this proof, $w(\varphi) = sub(s_\varphi, FALSE)\varphi$. Since we are given that $M \not\models w(\varphi)$, it follows that $\forall\chi\prime$, $M \models sub(s_\varphi, \chi\prime)\varphi$. Thus φ passes vacuously in M.

2. Now, we prove that if $M \models \varphi$ and $M \not\models w(\varphi)$ then any counter-example of $w(\varphi)$ in M is also an interesting witness of φ in M.

   By Definition 8, any counter-example produced for an ACTL formula, is a computation path in M. Let $CE_{w(\varphi)}$ be a computation path which is a counter-example for $w(\varphi)$ in M. By Lemma 11, $CE_{w(\varphi)} \models \varphi$. We have to show that $CE_{w(\varphi)} \models \varphi$ non-vacuously, that is, for every χ important sub-formula of φ, χ affects the truth value of φ in $CE_{w(\varphi)}$.

   As shown at the beginning of this proof, for every χ important sub-formula of φ

   $$w(\varphi) = sub(\chi, sub(s_\varphi, FALSE)\chi)\varphi.$$

   Since $CE_{w(\varphi)} \models \varphi$ and $CE_{w(\varphi)} \not\models w(\varphi)$, we have found for any important sub-formula χ of φ, a formula $\chi\prime = sub(s_\varphi, FALSE)\chi$ which affects the value of φ in $CE_{w(\varphi)}$. Thus φ passes non-vacuously in $CE_{w(\varphi)}$. $\qquad\qquad$ $\square$

4.5 Examples

We now show the generation of the witness formula for Formula 1 from Section 1. We first convert Formula 2 (the CTL equivalent of Formula 1) into normal form:

$$AG(\neg request \lor A[dataV(\neg data \lor AXA[dataV(\neg data \lor$$
$$AXA[dataV(\neg data \lor AXA[dataV(\neg data \lor last\_data)])])])]) \qquad (10)$$

Since last_data is considered to be non-simple (because it is the second operand of a next_event operator, see Footnote 2) the witness formula is:

$$AG(\neg request \lor A[dataV(\neg data \lor AXA[dataV(\neg data \lor$$
$$AXA[dataV(\neg data \lor AXA[dataV(\neg data \lor FALSE)])])])]) \qquad (11)$$

It is easy to see that Formula 11 will pass iff either a request never occurs, or no request is ever followed by four datas. Also, it is clear that if Formula 11 fails, the counter-example will be an interesting witness of Formula 1, on which a request followed by four datas will occur.

Now examine the following formula, which expresses the fact that we require q to occur an infinite number of times:

$$AG\,AF\,q \qquad (12)$$

The witness formula for Formula 12 is:

$$AG\,AF\,FALSE \qquad (13)$$

If Formula 12 passes, it cannot pass vacuously unless there are no fair paths, and indeed Formula 13 will fail in all models unless there are no fair paths. If Formula 12 passes, the counter-example to Formula 13 will be a computation path, on which q will appear infinitely many times (because Formula 12 passed).

4.6 Discussion

If a vacuous pass is detected by a witness formula, there is no indication of which of the pre-conditions caused the vacuous pass. This can easily be determined by multiple formulas, each of which checks one pre-condition. It should be noted that these multiple formulas need be run only if both the original formula and the witness formula passed. The RuleBase [BB+96] formal verification tool makes this decision automatically.

It should be noted that determination of vacuity is intrinsically entwined with the model checking algorithm: because vacuity is dependent on the context of a pre-condition, it is natural to discover it by model checking another formula with identical pre-conditions. An attempt to discover vacuity by directly manipulating BDDs would end up mimicking many of the model checking steps. Thus, while the vacuity of AG (p $\rightarrow$ q) can be found by simply intersecting the BDD of the states for which $M, s \models p$ with the reachable states, the direct detection of the vacuity of AG (p $\rightarrow$ AX (q $\rightarrow$ AX r)) would need as well to intersect the BDD of the states in which $M, s \models q$ with the states which are reachable in one step from the states for which $M, s \models p$.

5 Conclusions and future directions

We have shown a method for efficient detection of vacuity in w-ACTL formulas, a subset of ACTL [GL91] formulas. In addition, we have shown that our algorithm has the capability, as a side-effect, of providing an interesting witness, one positive non-trivial example of the truth of the formula. As discussed above, the ability to detect vacuity and provide an interesting witness are extremely important in the practical application of model checking to industrial hardware designs.

Although w-ACTL formulas define, in our experience, almost all of the CTL formulas used by engineers to specify their designs, there are useful formulas not included in w-ACTL. Therefore, we would like to have a general method for generating witness formulas for any CTL formula, in particular formulas containing a combination of existential and universal operators.

Acknowledgements

We thank Danny Geist and Shmuel Ur for important remarks on early drafts of this paper. We thank an anonymous referee for very important observations, which improved the quality of the final version of this paper.

References

[BB94] D. Beatty and R. Bryant, "Formally verifying a microprocessor using a simulation methodology", Design Automation Conference '94, pp. 596-602.

[BB+96] I. Beer, S. Ben-David, C. Eisner, A. Landver, "RuleBase: an Industry-Oriented Formal Verification Tool", in Proc. 33rd Design Automation Conference 1996, pp. 655-660.

290

[CE81] E.M. Clarke and E.A. Emerson, "Design and synthesis of synchronization skeletons using Branching Time Temporal Logic", in Proc. Workshop on Logics of Programs, Lecture Notes in Computer Science, Vol. 131 (Springer, Berlin, 1981) pp. 52-71.

[CE81b] E.M. Clark and E.A. Emerson, "Characterizing Properties of Parallel Programs as Fixed-point", in Seventh International Colloquium on Automata, Languages, and Programming, Volume 85 of LNCS, 1981.

[CG+95] E. Clarke, O. Grumberg, K. McMillan, X. Zhao, "Efficient Generation of Counterexamples and Witnesses in Symbolic Model Checking", Design Automation Conference 1995, pp. 427-432.

[GL91] O. Grumberg and D. Long, "Model checking and modular verification." In J.C.M. Baeten and J.F. Groote, editors, Proccedings of CONCUR '91: 2nd International Conference on Concurrency Theory, Volume 527 of LNCS, 1991.

[HBK93] R. Hojati, R.K. Brayton and R.P. Kurshan, "BDD-based debugging of designs using language containment and fair CTL." CAV '93, pp. 41-58.

[Kur90] R. Kurshan, "Analysis of Discrete Event Coordination," LNCS 1990.

[Lon93] D. Long, "Model Checking, Abstraction and Compositional Verification", Ph.D. Thesis, CMU, 1993.

[McM93] K.L. McMillan, "Symbolic Model Checking", Kluwer Academic Publishers, 1993.

[PP95] B. Plessier and C. Pixley, "Formal Verification of a Commercial Serial Bus Interface", International Phoenix Conference on Computers and Communications, 1995, pp. 378-382.

[SG90] G. Shurek, O. Grumberg, "The Computer-Aided Modular Framework - Motivation, Solutions and Evaluation Criteria", Workshop on Computer Aided Verification, 1990.

Model Checking and Transitive-Closure Logic[*]

Neil Immerman[**][1] and Moshe Y. Vardi[***][2]

[1] Computer Science Dept., University of Massachusetts, Amherst, MA 01003,
http://www.cs.umass.edu/~immerman, immerman@cs.umass.edu
[2] Computer Science Dept., Rice University, Houston, TX 77005-1892,
http://www.cs.rice.edu/~vardi, vardi@cs.rice.edu

Abstract. We give a linear-time algorithm to translate any formula from computation tree logic (CTL or CTL*) into an equivalent expression in a variable-confined fragment of transitive-closure logic FO(TC). Traditionally, CTL and CTL* have been used to express queries for model checking and then translated into μ-calculus for symbolic evaluation. Evaluation of μ-calculus formulas is, however, complete for time polynomial in the (typically huge) number of states in the Kripke structure. Thus, this is often not feasible, not parallelizable, and efficient incremental strategies are unlikely to exist. By contrast, evaluation of any formula in FO(TC) requires only NSPACE[$\log n$]. This means that the space requirements are manageable, the entire computation is parallelizable, and efficient dynamic evaluation is possible.

1 Introduction

Model checking, proposed first as a paradigm for computer-aided verification of finite-state programs in [CE81] and developed further in [BCM92, CES86, LP85, QS81, VW86] has been gaining widespread acceptance lately (see [BBG94]). The approach is especially appropriate for the design and verification of circuits and distributed protocols. The detailed, low-level design can be automatically translated into a logical structure called a Kripke structure $\mathcal{K}$. We can then write a series of short correctness conditions $\varphi_1, \varphi_2, \ldots$ concerning the behavior of the Kripke structure. The conditions are written in a formal language such as computation tree logic (CTL) or the more expressive CTL*. Given $\mathcal{K}$ and φ_i, the model-checking program will automatically test whether or not $\mathcal{K}$ satisfies φ_i. If it does, then confidence in the design is improved. If $\mathcal{K}$ does not satisfy some φ_i, then the checking program will usually present a counter example which thus exposes a bug in the design.

The Kripke structures used in model checking usually have a state for each possible configuration of the circuit or protocol being designed. For this reason they are often of size exponential in the size of the design. In this case,

---

[*] Part of the research reported here was conducted while the authors were visiting DIMACS during the Special Year on Logic and Algorithm.
[**] Research partly supported by NSF grant CCR-9505446.
[***] Research partly supported by NSF grant CCR-9628400

one usually represents the Kripke structure symbolically rather than explicitly, often using ordered binary decision diagrams (OBDDs). The model checking performed using these symbolic representations is called symbolic model checking [BCM92, McM93].

The correctness conditions φ_i described above can be thought of as queries to the Kripke structure. In fact, in this paper we emphasize the close relationship between model checking and database query evaluation (cf. [Var97]). Optimization of the queries is crucial. For this reason, the tradeoff between the expressive power of the query language and the complexity of doing model checking is important.

A powerful query language for model checking is the branching-time logic CTL*. Consider the model checking problem for CTL* in which we fix a query $\varphi \in$ CTL* and vary the Kripke structure $\mathcal{K}$. The complexity of this problem, called *program complexity* in [VW86] and *data complexity* in [Var82], is known to be NSPACE[log n] [BVW94] for CTL*. Here n is the size of the Kripke structure – as we have mentioned, n is often exponential in the size of the design being verified.

The standard way to perform symbolic model checking using CTL* is to translate the query to the modal μ-calculus [Koz83, EL86]. A problem with this is that the data complexity of the modal μ-calculus is polynomial-time complete [BVW94] (cf. [I86, Var82]). This means that evaluation of modal μ-calculus queries most likely requires polynomial space, is not parallelizable, and efficient incremental evaluation strategies are unlikely to exist.

We give here a linear-time algorithm to translate any formula from CTL* into an equivalent expression in a variable-confined fragment of transitive-closure logic FO(TC). In fact, the resulting formulas have only two first-order variables. The resulting logic, denoted FO^2(TC), is known to have a data complexity of NSPACE[log n] [I87, Var82]. This means that the space requirements are manageable, the entire computation is parallelizable, and entire computation is parallelizable, and efficient incremental evaluation is possible (see, for example, [PI94, ZSS94]). Thus, it is very promising to do model checking and symbolic model checking using the language FO^2(TC) rather than the more complex modal μ-calculus.

2 Background on Temporal Logic and the Modal μ-calculus

Let $\Phi = \{p_1, \ldots, p_r\}$ be a finite set of propositional symbols. A *propositional Kripke structure*, $\mathcal{K} = (S, R, \pi)$, is a tuple consisting of a finite set of states S, a binary transition relation $R \subseteq S^2$, and a labeling function $\pi : \Phi \to 2^S$, where intuitively, $\pi(p_i)$ is the set of states at which p_i is true. S is often called the set of possible worlds, but we call it the set of states because in model checking applications it usually represents the set of global states of the circuit or protocol being designed. Typically, we are interested in infinite computation paths, so in this paper we restrict our attention to Kripke structures in which every state has at least one successor, which may be itself. We can meet this condition by adding the loop $R(s, s)$ to each state that has no other successors. A Kripke structure may be thought of as a directed graph whose vertices are the states, labeled by the set of propositional symbols they satisfy.

The propositional Kripke structure $\mathcal{K}$ may also be thought of as a finite relational structure, i.e., relational database, $\mathcal{K}^\star = (S, R, p_1^{\mathcal{K}^\star}, \ldots, p_r^{\mathcal{K}^\star})$. The universe of $\mathcal{K}^\star$ is the set of states S. The binary relation $R \subseteq S^2$ is the transition relation, and a unary relation $p_i^{\mathcal{K}^\star} = \pi(p_i)$ is the set of states at which the proposition p_i holds. For any first-order formula φ, we will use the notation $\mathcal{K}^\star \models \varphi$ to mean that φ is true in $\mathcal{K}^\star$.

We use in this paper the computation tree logics CTL and CTL*. For definitions of syntax and semantics of these logics see [Eme90].

The modal μ-calculus is a propositional modal logic that includes the least-fixed point operator (μ) [Koz83, Eme97]. The modal μ-calculus is strictly more expressive than CTL*, and has polynomial-time data complexity (see next section). As an example, we can write the CTL formula $\mathbf{EF}p$ as a least fixed point,

$$\mathbf{EF}p \quad \equiv \quad \mu Y (p \vee \langle R \rangle Y) \tag{1}$$

Equation 1 can be generalized to show that all of CTL* can be interpreted in the modal μ-Calculus. See [Eme97, Var97] for details.

Fact 2

- *There is a linear time algorithm that translates any formula in CTL into an equivalent formula in the modal μ-calculus.*

- *There is an exponential time algorithm that translates any formula in CTL* into an equivalent formula in the modal μ-calculus.*

Symbolic model checking is typically carried out by first translating the CTL correctness condition into the μ-calculus [McM93]. A drawback of this approach is that model checking of the μ-calculus uses space polynomial in the size of the usually huge Kripke structure. In the next section we describe transitive-closure logic. We will see that although transitive-closure logic has lower complexity than the μ-calculus, it still suffices to interpret CTL*.

3 Background on Descriptive Complexity

In descriptive complexity, we study finite logical structures — relational databases — such as the Kripke structures,

$$\mathcal{K}^\star \quad = \quad (S, R, p_1^{\mathcal{K}^\star}, \ldots, p_r^{\mathcal{K}^\star}) \, .$$

The complexity of computing queries on such structures is intimately tied to the power of variants of first-order logic needed to describe these queries. This has been studied in great detail. See for example [EF95, I89, LR96, Var82].

Let FO be the set of first-order expressible properties. For example, consider the first-order formula,

$$\varphi \quad \equiv \quad (\forall x)(p(x) \rightarrow (\exists y)(R(x, y) \wedge p(y))) \ .$$

A Kripke structure $\mathcal{K}^\star$ satisfies φ — in symbols, $\mathcal{K}^\star \models \varphi$ — iff every state satisfying p has a successor state that also satisfies p.

The class FO captures the complexity class AC^0 consisting of those properties checkable by bounded depth polynomial-size circuits. This is equal to the set of properties computable in constant time on a concurrent parallel random access machine that has at most polynomially many processors [I89a].

To obtain a richer class of queries, let FO(LFP) be first-order logic extended by a least-fixed-point operator. This is the closure of first-order logic under the power to define new relations by induction. We can view the modal μ-calculus as a restriction of FO(LFP) in which all fixed points are taken over monadic relations, and such that only two domain variables are used. Let FO^k be the restriction of FO such that the only domain variables are $x_1, \ldots, x_k$. Let LFP^r be the restriction of LFP to act only on inductive definitions of arity at most r. Then there is a linear-time mapping of each formula from the modal-mu calculus to an equivalent formula in $FO^2(LFP^1)$ [Var97].

As an example, consider the μ-calculus formula, $\psi \equiv \mu Y(p \vee \langle R \rangle Y)$. Recall from Equation 1 that ψ is equivalent to the CTL formula $\mathbf{EF}p$. This can be interpreted in FO(LFP) as the formula,

$$\psi' \quad \equiv \quad \mathrm{LFP}_{Y,y}(p(y) \vee \exists y'(R(y, y') \wedge Y(y')))\,(y) \ . \tag{3}$$

The equivalence between ψ and ψ' is that for any propositional Kripke structure $\mathcal{K}$ and state s,

$$(\mathcal{K}, s) \models \psi \quad \Leftrightarrow \quad (\mathcal{K}^\star, s/y) \models \psi' \ .$$

It is well known that FO(LFP) captures polynomial time. The following facts assume that structures in question are finite and include a total ordering on their universes.

Fact 4 ([I86, Var82]) *The queries computable in polynomial time are exactly those expressible in* FO(LFP).

While the modal μ-calculus is a proper subset of FO(LFP), it still contains problems complete for polynomial-time [BVW94]. Since the model checking problem for $CTL^\star$ is contained in NSPACE[$\log n$], it would be much better to interpret $CTL^\star$ in a logic with this lower complexity.

Let the formula $\varphi(x_1, \ldots x_k, y_1, \ldots y_k)$ represent a binary relation on k-tuples. We express the reflexive, transitive closure of this relation using the transitive-closure operator (TC), as follows: $TC_{\overline{x}, \overline{y}}\varphi$. Let FO(TC) be the closure of first-order logic under the transitive-closure operator. For example, the following formula is equivalent to ψ' (Equation 3) and thus interprets the CTL formula,

EFp. It does so directly, by saying that there is an R-path to a state satisfying p.

$$\psi'' \equiv (\exists y')[(TC_{y,y'} R(y, y'))(y, y') \wedge p(y')]$$

We will see in the next section that every formula in CTL* can be so interpreted.

Transitive closure logic exactly captures nondeterministic logspace:

Fact 5 ([I87, I88]) *The queries computable in* NSPACE[log n] *are exactly those expressible in* FO(TC).

The number of variables used is an important descriptive resource. Each domain variable x_i ranges over the universe of its input structure. In the definition of FO^k, we allow an unbounded number of *boolean variables*, $b_1, \ldots, b_c$ in addition to the k domain variables. Boolean variables are essentially first-order variables that are restricted to range only over the first two elements of the universe, which we fix as 0 and 1. Including also boolean variables makes the definition of FO^k more robust [I91]. As a simple example, we can interpret the conjunction **EF**$p \wedge$ **EF**q using a universally quantified boolean variable,

$$(\forall b)(\exists y')[(TC_{y,y'} R(y, y'))(y, y') \wedge (b \wedge p(y') \vee \neg b \wedge q(y'))] \; .$$

We note, however, that the inclusion of boolean variables has a nontrivial complexity-theoretic consequence. While "pure" (i.e., boolean-variable-free) queries in FO^k(TC) can be evaluated in *uniform* polynomial time, the space required to evaluate queries in FO^k(TC) is polynomial in the number of boolean variables.

We sometimes want a *strict* transitive closure operator: TC$^s(\varphi)$ denotes the transtive closure of φ, as opposed to the reflexive, transitive closure of φ. The strict and reflexive transitive closure operators are definable from each other, as follows. Note that no extra variables are needed:

$$TC(\varphi(y, y'))(y, y') \equiv y = y' \quad \vee \quad TC^s(\varphi(y, y'))(y, y')$$
$$TC^s(\varphi(y, y'))(y, y') \equiv (y \neq y' \quad \wedge \quad TC(\varphi(y, y'))(y, y'))$$
$$\vee \quad (y = y' \quad \wedge \quad (\exists y')(\varphi(y, y') \wedge TC(\varphi(y, y'))(y', y)))$$

4 Transitive Closure Logic Suffices

In this section we present an algorithm that translates any formula in CTL* to an equivalent formula in FO^2(TC), i.e., first-order logic with only two first-order variables, extended by the transitive-closure operator. We first do the case of CTL, which is significantly simpler.

Theorem 6. *There is a transformation f from state formulas in* CTL *to formulas in* $\mathrm{FO}^2(\mathrm{TC})$ *that preserves meaning. That is, for all state formulas* $\varphi \in$ CTL *and all Kripke structures* $\mathcal{K}$, *and states s,*

$$(\mathcal{K}, s) \models \varphi \quad \Leftrightarrow \quad (\mathcal{K}^\star, s/y) \models f(\varphi) \tag{7}$$

Proof. We define f by induction on φ,

- $f(p) = p(y)$, for predicate symbol p
- $f(\neg\varphi) = \neg f(\varphi)$
- $f(\varphi \wedge \psi) = f(\varphi) \wedge f(\psi)$
- $f(\mathbf{E}(\varphi \mathbf{U} \psi)) = (\exists y')(\mathrm{TC}(M_{f(\varphi)})(y, y') \wedge f(\psi)(y'))$
  where, $M_\alpha(y, y') \equiv R(y, y') \wedge \alpha(y)$
- $f(\mathbf{E}(\varphi \mathbf{B} \psi)) = (\exists y')(\mathrm{TC}(M_{f(\psi)})(y, y') \wedge ((f(\varphi)(y') \wedge f(\psi)(y')) \vee \mathrm{TC}^\bullet(M_{f(\psi)})(y', y')))$

It is easy to show by induction that Equation 7 holds. The interesting cases are the last two: For "Until", note that there is a path starting at y along which $\varphi \mathbf{U} \psi$ holds iff there is some point y' at which ψ holds and there is a path from y to y' along which φ holds. For "Before", there is a path starting at y along which $\varphi \mathbf{B} \psi$ holds iff there is some point y' for which there is a path from y to y' along which ψ holds, and either φ and ψ both hold at y', or there is an infinite path, i.e., a cycle, starting at y' along which ψ remains true. □

Note that the formulas $f(\varphi)$ does not use boolean variables. We would be happier if the above f were linear-time computable. The problem is that the formula $f(\psi)$ occurs more than once in the definition of $f(\mathbf{E}(\varphi \mathbf{B} \psi))$. This could cause an exponential blowup in the size of the resulting formula. We will defer this problem to Corollary 11.

The difficulty in extending Theorem 6 to CTL* occurs in a formula such as

$$\alpha = \mathbf{E}((p \to q\mathbf{U}r)\mathbf{U}t)$$

As before, we can express that at some state y', t holds, and that there is a path from y to y' along which $(p \to q\mathbf{U}r)$ holds. The problem is that we must remember our obligations along this path, i.e., whether we need to preserve $q\mathbf{U}r$, and we may need to preserve this along the same path, beyond y'.

To solve this problem we introduce a new boolean variable b, whose purpose is to remember our obligation concerning the formula $q\mathbf{U}r$. The following formula $\alpha^\star$ asserts that there is a path to a future state y' and a boolean value b' such that $(p \to q\mathbf{U}r)$ holds along the path, t holds at y', and if b' holds, i.e., we are still obliged to fulfill $q\mathbf{U}r$, then there is a continuation of the path along which $q\mathbf{U}r$ holds,

$$\alpha^\star \equiv (\exists y'b')(\mathrm{TC}(\gamma)(y, \mathbf{false}, y', b') \wedge t(y') \wedge$$
$$b' \to (\exists y)(\mathrm{TC}(M_q)(y', y) \wedge r(y))$$
$$\gamma(y, b, y', b') \equiv ((p \vee b) \to (r \vee (q \wedge b'))) \wedge R(y, y')$$

Observe that as desired, for all Kripke structures $\mathcal{K}$ and states s,

$$(\mathcal{K}, s) \models \alpha \quad \Leftrightarrow \quad (\mathcal{K}^\star, s/y) \models \alpha^\star)$$

Reiterating the main point, in addition to the $\log n$ bits needed to name y – the current state in our n-state Kripke structure – we use one additional bit b to record our obligations concerning the truth of a formula along the remainder of a path.

We now describe this construction in general so that we may extend Theorem 6 to CTL*. Let $\mathbf{E}(\varphi)$ be a CTL* formula. Define the *closure* of φ ($cl(\varphi)$) to be the set of path subformulas of φ. We introduce a boolean variable b_α for each $\alpha \in cl(\varphi)$. Intuitively, we use the boolean variables to encode the state of the automaton that runs along a path and checks that the path satisfies a path formula (see [VW94]).

We inductively define a mapping g from state formulas $\mathbf{E}(\varphi)$ in CTL* to equivalent formulas in FO^2(TC). Let $\bar{b}$ be a tuple of all the boolean variables b_α, for $\alpha \in cl(\varphi)$. Define the transition relation $R_\varphi^0(y, \bar{b}, y', \bar{b}')$ as follows. In each case, the comment on the right is the condition underwhich the given conjunct is included in the formula. (We assume that φ is written in positive-normal form.)

$$R(y, y')$$

$\wedge$	$b_\alpha \rightarrow g(\alpha)(y)$	for any state formula $\alpha \in cl(\varphi)$
$\wedge$	$b_{\alpha \wedge \beta} \rightarrow b_\alpha \wedge b_\beta$	for any path formula $\alpha \wedge \beta \in cl(\varphi)$
$\wedge$	$b_{\alpha \vee \beta} \rightarrow b_\alpha \vee b_\beta$	for any path formula $\alpha \vee \beta \in cl(\varphi)$
$\wedge$	$b_{\mathbf{X}\alpha} \rightarrow b_\alpha'$	for any path formula $\mathbf{X}\alpha \in cl(\varphi)$
$\wedge\, b_{\alpha \mathbf{U}\beta}$	$\rightarrow b_\beta \vee (b_\alpha \wedge b_{\alpha \mathbf{U}\beta}')$	for any path formula $\alpha\mathbf{U}\beta \in cl(\varphi)$
$\wedge\, b_{\alpha \mathbf{B}\beta}$	$\rightarrow b_\beta \wedge (b_\alpha \vee b_{\alpha \mathbf{B}\beta}')$	for any path formula $\alpha\mathbf{B}\beta \in cl(\varphi)$

It follows by an inductive proof from the definition of R_φ^0 that if the structure $\mathcal{K}^\star$ satisfies the formula,

$$(\exists y'\, \bar{b}\,\bar{b}')(b_\varphi \quad \wedge \quad \mathrm{TC}(R_\varphi^0)(y, \bar{b}, y', \bar{b}') \quad \wedge \quad \mathrm{TC}^s(R_\varphi^0)(y', \bar{b}', y', \bar{b}')) \tag{8}$$

then there is a path from y to y' along which φ may be true. The reason we say, "may be," is that there may be some booleans $b_{\alpha \mathbf{U}\beta}'$ that are true, promising that eventually β will become true, but in fact as we walk around the cycle, α remains true but β never becomes true. Essentially, the boolean variables encode only the states of the "local automaton" in [VW94], which does not guarantee the satisfaction of "Until" formulas.

In order to solve this problem, let $\bar{m}$ be a tuple of bits $m_{\alpha \mathbf{U}\beta}$, one for each "Until" formula, $\alpha\mathbf{U}\beta \in cl(\varphi)$. We use the "memory bit" $m_{\alpha \mathbf{U}\beta}$ to check that β actually occurs on the path from y' back to itself. We do this by starting the cycle with $m_{\alpha \mathbf{U}\beta}$ being false and only letting it become true when β holds. Essentially, the memory bits encode the state of the "eventuality automaton" in [VW94].

Define the relation $R_\varphi(y, \bar{b}, \bar{m}, y', \bar{b}', \bar{m}')$ as follows,

$$R_\varphi^0(y, \bar{b}, y', \overline{b'})$$
$$\wedge \ m'_{\alpha \mathbf{U} \beta} \ \rightarrow (m_{\alpha \mathbf{U} \beta} \ \vee \ b_\beta) \qquad \text{for any formula } \alpha \mathbf{U} \beta \in cl(\varphi)$$

Finally, we define the desired mapping g from CTL* state formulas to FO^2(TC) as follows:

$$g(p) = p(y)$$
$$g(\alpha \wedge \beta) = g(\alpha) \wedge g(\beta)$$
$$g(\neg \alpha) = \neg g(\alpha)$$
$$g(\mathbf{E}(\varphi)) = (\exists y' \, \bar{b} \, \overline{b'} \, \overline{m})(\ b_\varphi$$
$$\wedge \ \mathrm{TC}(R_\varphi)(y, \bar{b}, \mathbf{false}, y', \overline{b'}, \mathbf{false})$$
$$\wedge \ \mathrm{TC}^s(R_\varphi)(y', \overline{b'}, \mathbf{false}, y', \overline{b'}, \overline{m})$$
$$\wedge \ b'_{\alpha \mathbf{U} \beta} \ \rightarrow \ m_{\alpha \mathbf{U} \beta} \qquad \text{for any formula } \alpha \mathbf{U} \beta \in cl(\varphi)$$

The following can now be proved by induction on φ,

Theorem 9. *The map g defined above translates CTL* state formulas to equivalent formulas in FO^2(TC). That is, for all Kripke structures $\mathcal{K}$, states s, and CTL* state formulas φ,*

$$(\mathcal{K}, s) \models \varphi \qquad \Leftrightarrow \qquad (\mathcal{K}^\star, s/y) \models g(\varphi) \tag{10}$$

The transformation g suffers from a similar problem as the transformation f of Theorem 6. The problem is that the formula R_φ is written twice in the definition of $g(\mathbf{E}(\varphi))$. This may cause the size of the formula $g(\gamma)$ to grow exponentially in the nesting depth of path quantifiers $(\mathbf{E}, \mathbf{A})$ in γ. In practice there is little reason for this nesting depth to be greater than one or two. We can, however, alleviate this problem in general as follows:

Corollary 11. *The mapping g above may be modified to run in linear time and thus produce linear size output, in any of the following ways:*

1. *Modify the mapping allowing another variable, that is, map to FO^3(TC).*
2. *Allow the definition of R_φ to be written once and reused, that is, we represent the formula as a first-order circuit.*
3. *Allow the construction, "$R' := \mathrm{TC}^s(R_\varphi)$," that is, whenever we compute the transitive closure of a relation we may reuse it.*

Proof. Items 2 and 3 simply change our mode of representation and are thus obvious. The idea in item 1 is that with an extra state variable t and a universal quantifier, we can eliminate the extra occurrence of R_φ. For example, we can rewrite the definition of $G(\mathbf{E}(\varphi))$ as follows:

$$g'(\mathbf{E}(\varphi)) = (\exists y'\,\bar{b}\,\overline{b'}\,\overline{m})(\forall t\bar{c}\bar{d})(b_\varphi \wedge$$
$$(t = y \wedge \bar{c} = \bar{b} \wedge \bar{d} = \overline{\mathbf{false}} \vee t = y' \wedge \bar{c} = \overline{b'} \wedge \bar{d} = \overline{m}) \rightarrow$$
$$\mathrm{TC}^s(R_\varphi)(t,\bar{c},\overline{\mathbf{false}},y',\overline{b'},\bar{d})$$
$$\wedge\quad b'_{\alpha\mathbf{U}\beta} \rightarrow m'_{\alpha\mathbf{U}\beta} \qquad \text{for any formula } \alpha\mathbf{U}\beta \in cl(\varphi)$$

Note: In all of the cases of Corollary 11, the resulting formulas remain in FO(TC) and thus have data complexity NSPACE[$\log n$]. In addition, conditions 2 and 3 are quite feasible from a symbolic model checking point of view: we would naturally compute the OBDD for the relation R_φ and its transitive closure only once.

The use of the finiteness of the Kripke structures, $\mathcal{K}^\star$, in our proofs of Theorems 6 and 9 is crucial. It is known that CTL cannot be translated to FO(TC) over all structures [Ott].

5 Applications to Symbolic Model Checking

The main application of this work is to symbolic model checking. In this situation, the Kripke model is too large to be represented in memory and is instead represented symbolically, often via an OBDD.

From a descriptive point of view, this corresponds to a Kripke structure determined by a set of n boolean variables. Let,

$$\mathcal{A} = \langle\{x_1, x_2, \ldots, x_n\}, \delta, p_1, \ldots, p_r\rangle .$$

Here the universe of $\mathcal{A}$ is a set of n boolean variables. A state in the corresponding Kripke structure $\mathcal{K}(\mathcal{A})$ is a unary relation S over $\mathcal{A}$, i.e., a truth assignment to the elements of $|A|$. The formula, δ, which might be represented as an OBDD, expresses the transition relation, $\delta(S_1, S_2)$, on states of $\mathcal{K}(\mathcal{A})$. Similarly, the formulas $p_1, \ldots, p_r$ represent the relevant unary relations that are true or false at each state S of $\mathcal{K}(\mathcal{A})$.

Above, we expressed CTL or CTL* conditions concerning a Kripke structure $\mathcal{K}$ in FO^2(TC), that is, in first-order logic with two variables, and a transitive closure operator. In the symbolic setting, such a formula concerning $\mathcal{K}(\mathcal{A})$ is best thought of as a second-order, monadic formula concerning the structure $\mathcal{A}$. That is, the elements of the universe of $\mathcal{K}(\mathcal{A})$ are unary relations over $\mathcal{A}$. Thus, the correctness conditions in question are queries to $\mathcal{A}$ in the language MSO^2(TC) — monadic, second-order formulas, with only two second-order variables, and a transitive closure operator.

It is not hard to see that

Fact 12 NSPACE[n] = MSO(TC).

Thus, the CTL and CTL* queries are all checkable in nondeterministic linear space [BVW94]. Here the space is linear in n, the size of the design of the circuit or protocol to be verified, not 2^n, the size of the Kripke structure $\mathcal{K}(\mathcal{A})$.

It is important in our simulations that we used as few variables as possible. With two second-order, monadic variables, the paths to be checked can have length at most 2^n. Each boolean variable that we add, can at most double the length of such a path, whereas adding another second-order, monadic variable is essentially n boolean variables, and could thus increase the length of paths to be searched by a factor of 2^n. We suspect that the number of boolean variables needed for typical CTL* queries is quite small. It is an interesting open open question how many boolean variables are needed in the worst case. (For example, in the context of linear temporal logic, analogous translations are known that use no boolean variables [EVW97].)

Experiments need to be performed concerning practical aspects of using FO(TC) as a language for expressing correctness queries. While the straight-forward approach for adopting transitive-clousre algorithms to symbolic model checking have failed [TBK95], more sophisticated transitive-closure algorithms (see [Ya90]) might be quite useful for symbolic model checking.

This work suggests a new paradigm for model checking: One can write the conditions to be checked in a very expressive language, e.g., second-order logic or first-order logic with least-fixed point operators or FO(LFP). Next, if the Kripke structure is small, we may be able to check this condition automatically. If not, we may need to break our correctness conditions down into simpler conditions which may be expressed in simpler languages, e.g., FO(TC), which can be automatically checked in a feasible amount of time. Even within FO(TC), there is a hierarchy of how many varables we need, and how many boolean variables in $FO^2(TC)$. There is a well-developed theory in the context of finite-model theory of the relationship between descriptive complexity and computational complexity [I89]. This understanding could be also important in computer-aided verification.

6 Conclusions and Future Work

We have shown that every formula in CTL* may be translated in linear time to an equivalent formula in transitive closure-logic, FO(TC). Since the language FO(TC) has data complexity NSPACE[$\log n$], it admits more efficient model checking algorithms than the modal μ-calculus, which has a polynomial-time-complete data complexity

There are several open questions concerning the number of variables needed for the resulting formulas in FO(TC):

1. We have shown that the resulting formulas are linear size when we allow three domain variables, that is they are in $FO^3(TC)$. It is open whether linear size can be maintained when we map to $FO^2(TC)$, or indeed, whether an exponential blow-up is required.

2. We would like to know how many boolean variables are needed to interpret CTL^* in $FO^2(TC)$ (our construction allows a linear number of such boolean variables).

Finally, our approach of using transitive-closure logic rather than the much more complex μ-calculus for model checking might be useful in practice. This requires further investigation and testing. Part of the program of Descriptive Complexity is that the computational complexity of query evaluation should be apparent just from looking at the syntax of the query under consideration. Translating CTL^* queries into transitive-closure logic rather than μ-calculus facilitates this approach.

Acknowledgements: Thanks to Kousha Etessami and Thomas Wilke for helpful comments, corrections, and suggestions.

References

[BBG94] I. Beer, S. Ben-David, D. Geist, R. Gewirtzman and M. Yoel, "Methodology and System for Practical Formal Verification of Reactive Hardware," in *Computer Aided Verification, Proc. 6th Int. Conference*, D. L. Dill, ed., LNCS 818, 1994, Springer-Verlag, 182–193.

[BVW94] O. Bernholtz, M.Y. Vardi and P. Wolper, "An Automata-Theoretic Approach to Branching-Time Model Checking," in *Computer Aided Verification, Proc. 6th Int. Conference*, D. L. Dill, ed., LNCS 818, 1994, Springer-Verlag, 142–155.

[BCM92] J.R. Burch, E.M. Clarke, K.L. McMillan, D.L. Dill and L.J. Hwang, "Symbolic Model Checking: 10^{20} States and Beyond," *Information and Computation* 98(2) (1992), 142–170.

[CE81] E.M. Clarke and E.A. Emerson, "Design and Synthesis of Synchronization Skeletons Using Branching Time Temporal Logic," in *Proc. Workshop on Logic of Programs*, LNCS 131, 1981, Springer-Verlag, 52–71.

[CES86] E.M. Clarke, E.A. Emerson and A.P. Sistla, "Automatic Verification of Finite-State Concurrent Systems Using Temporal Logic Specifications," *ACM Transactions on Programming Languages and Systems*, 8(2) (1986), 244-263.

[EF95] H.-D. Ebbinghaus, J. Flum, *Finite Model Theory* 1995, Springer 1995.

[Eme90] E.A. Emerson, "Temporal and modal logic," in *Handbook of theoretical computer science*, 1990, 997-1072.

[Eme97] E. A. Emerson, "Model Checking and the Mu-Calculus," in *Descriptive Complexity and Finite Models*, N. Immerman and Ph. Kolaitis, eds., 1997, American Mathematical Society.

[EL86] E.A. Emerson and C.-L. Lei, "Efficient Model Checking in Fragments of the Propositional mu-Calculus," *Proc. 1st Symp. on Logic in Computer Science* (1986), 267-278.

[EVW97] K. Etessami, M.Y. Vardi, and T. Wilke, "First-Order Logic with Two Variables and Unary Temporal Logic," *Proc. 12th IEEE Symp. on Logic in Computer Science*, July 1997.

[I86] N. Immerman, "Relational Queries Computable in Polynomial Time," *Information and Control*, 68 (1986), 86-104.

[I87]   N. Immerman, "Languages That Capture Complexity Classes," *SIAM J. Comput.* 16(4) (1987), 760-778.

[I88]   N. Immerman, "Nondeterministic Space is Closed Under Complementation," *SIAM J. Comput.* 17(5) (1988), 935-938.

[I89]   N. Immerman, "Descriptive and Computational Complexity,"in *Computational Complexity Theory,* ed. J. Hartmanis, Lecture Notes for AMS Short Course on Computational Complexity Theory, *Proc. Symp. in Applied Math.* 38, American Mathematical Society (1989), 75-91.

[I89a]   N. Immerman, *Expressibility and Parallel Complexity, SIAM J. of Comput* 18 (1989), 625-638.

[I91]   N. Immerman, "DSPACE[n^k] = VAR[$k+1$]," *Sixth IEEE Structure in Complexity Theory Symp.* (July, 1991), 334-340.

[Koz83] D. Kozen, "Results on the Propositional μ-Calculus," *Theoretical Computer Science,* 27 (1983), 333–354.

[LR96]   R. Lassaigne and M. de Rougemont, *Logique et Complexité,* 1996, Hermes.

[LP85]   O. Lichtenstein and A. Pnueli, "Checking that Finite State Concurrent Programs Satisfy their Linear Specification" *Proc. 12th ACM Symp. on Principles of Programming Languages* (1985), 97-107.

[McM93] K. McMillan, *Symbolic Model Checking,* 1993, Kluwer.

[Ott]   M. Otto, private communication.

[PI94]   S. Patnaik and N. Immerman, "Dyn-FO: A Parallel, Dynamic Complexity Class," *Proc. ACM Symp. on Principles of Database Systems* (1994), 210-221.

[QS81]   J.P. Queille and J. Sifakis, "Specification and Verification of Concurrent Systems in Cesar," *Proc. 5th Int'l Symp. on Programming,* LNCS 137, 1981, Springer-Verlag, 337–351.

[TBK95] H. J. Touati, R. K. Brayton, and R. P. Kurshan, "Testing language containment for ω-automata using BDD's," *Information and Computation,* 118(1):101–109, 1995.

[Var82] M.Y. Vardi,   "Complexity of Relational Query Languages," *ACM Symp. Theory Of Comput.* (1982), 137-146.

[Var97] M.Y. Vardi, "Why is Modal Logic So Robustly Decidable?"in *Descriptive Complexity and Finite Models,* N. Immerman and Ph. Kolaitis, eds., 1997, American Mathematical Society.

[VW84]   M.Y. Vardi and P. Wolper, "Yet Another Process Logic," in *Logics of Programs,* LNCS 164, 1984, Springer-Verlag, 501–512.

[VW86]   M.Y. Vardi and P. Wolper, "An Automata-Theoretic Approach to Automatic Program Verification," *Proc. 1st Symp. on Logic in Computer Science* (1986), 322–331.

[VW94]   M.Y. Vardi and P. Wolper, "Reasoning about Infinite Computations," *Information and Computation* 115(1) (1994), 1-37.

[Ya90]   M. Yannakakis, "Graph-theoretic methods in database theory", *Proc. 9th ACM Symp. on Principles of Database Systems,* 230–242, 1990.

[ZSS94] S. Zhang, S.A. Smolka, and O. Sokolsky, "On the Parallel Complexity of Model Checking in the Modal μ-Calculus," *Proc. 9th IEEE Symp. on Logic in Computer Science,* 1994, 154-163.

Boolean and 2-adic Numbers Based Techniques for Verifying Synchronous Designs

Gerard Berry
Centre de Mathematiques Appliquees (CMA)
Ecole des Mines de Paris
2004, Route des Lucioles
06902 Sophia-Antipolis, France

We present two distinct techniques to verify synchronous designs. The first technique applies to controllers written in Esterel or similar imperative languages. The problem is to efficiently compute the reachable state space (RSS) of large FSMs. We use structural information extracted from the program to cheaply compute an over-approximation of the RSS. This over-approximation can be used to simplify the logic and to remove registers, which makes the exact RSS computation much easier. We present other crucial optimizations implemented in the TiGeR BDD package we use for Esterel verification. The second technique is the usage of 2-adic number theory for verification of sequential arithmetic circuits, introduced by Jean Vuillemin. Infinite bitstreams are seen as numbers written low-order bits first. This makes it possible to consider the sequential transfer function of a circuit as a standard numerical function and to make sequential circuit correctness proofs by straight numerical calculations. Finally, we suggest to explore more deeply the relation between Boolean and number-based techniques.

Programs with Quasi-Stable Channels are Effectively Recognizable
(Extended Abstract)

Gérard Cécé   Alain Finkel

LSV, CNRS URA 2236; ENS de Cachan, 61 av. du Pdt. Wilson
94235 Cachan Cedex, FRANCE.
{Gerard.CECE, Alain.FINKEL}@lsv.ens-cachan.fr

Abstract. We consider the analysis of infinite half-duplex systems which consists of finite state machines that communicate over unbounded channels. The property half-duplex for two machines and two channels (one in each direction) says that each reachable state has at least one channel empty.

The contributions of this paper are (a) to give a finite description of the reachability set of such systems, which happens to be effectively recognizable; this description allows us to solve classical verification problems such as: whether a given state is reachable, whether there exist deadlock states, whether the reachability set is finite and whether a specified action is useless; (b) to propose an extension of these results for a new class, systems with quasi-stable channels, which includes systems with similar behavior but which implies more than two machines.

1 Introduction

There are several models which can be used to study distributed algorithms and communicating protocols. The model we use in this paper is that of systems of communicating finite states machines (CFSMs). It consists of programs represented by finite state machines which communicate over unbounded channels. This model is widely used both for verification and validation in languages such ESTELLE, SDL and LOTOS [15]. It has also its own theoretical interest as shown by the literature it has generated in the last few years [1,2,6,9] .

However, this model has the power of Turing machines since it's possible to simulate them by a system of two communicating finite state machines [5,10], thus verification is undecidable for non-trivial problems. This limitation motivates the study of classes of systems for which verification algorithms are possible [1,2,6,8,9,12,14].

The class introduced by Pachl [14], systems with a recognizable reachability set, is interesting since it covers a wide number of protocols and since the reachability problem is solved for it. However, the need to list recognizable sets makes this algorithm inefficient! Moreover, it's not possible to decide whether a given system has a recognizable reachability set, which is the starting point for using Pachl's result.

The term half-duplex is used to qualify communication between two machines which don't send messages simultaneously. We show in this paper that many verification problems are solvable for systems of two machines using this kind of communication. More precisely, we give a recognizable description of their reachability sets and show that the property of being half-duplex for systems with two machines and two channels is decidable. These results are quite surprising since one might think that the half-duplex property doesn't really reduce the power of the model as each machines can transfer data each one in turn. But this hypothesis is precisely too restrictive to simulate a Turing machine since it forbids the possibility of storing the content of the tape in the channels: when an automaton sends messages, since it is not able to receive information from the other automaton, its possible future states are fixed and of finite number. The information it sends must thus be recognizable and we use this fact to describe the reachability set.

The remaining of the paper is as follows. In section 2, we define the model and the problems we want to verify on it. In section 3, we show that half-duplex systems with two machines and two channels are verifiable, we give a recognizable representation of their reachability sets and show that this result is useable since we can also decide whether any system with two machines and two channels is half-duplex. Then in section 4, we suggest a generalization of the half-duplex property, quasi-stable systems. Section 5 is the conclusion.

For lack of space, we mostly give only the ideas of proofs. The complete presentation can be found in the technical report [7].

2   System of Communicating Finite State Machines

2.1   Preliminaries and properties

Let us consider the communicating protocol of Fig. 1. It involves two machines: a sender and a receiver. When the sender has a message to transmit, it first advices the receiver by sending a starting symbol *start*. Then, it sends the main message over an alphabet of two letters, $\{a, b\}$. When this is complete, it advises the receiver by sending an *end* symbol and then waits for an acknowledgment, *ack*. The receiver has a symmetrical behavior. Formally we have:

Definition 1. A *Communicating Finite State Machine* (CFSM) is a finite transition system given by a 4-tuple $M = (Q, q_0, \Sigma, \delta)$ where : Q is a finite set of *states*, $q_0 \in Q$ is the *initial state*, Σ is a finite *alphabet*, and $\delta \subseteq Q \times (\{+, -\} \times \Sigma \times \mathbb{N}) \times Q$ is a finite set of *transitions*. We also consider δ as an application from $Q \times (\{+, -\} \times \Sigma \times \mathbb{N})$ to 2^Q.

Note that the alphabet of M in the usual transition system sense is $(\{+, -\} \times \Sigma \times \mathbb{N})$ rather than Σ, i.e. M sees $(+, a, i)$ and $(-, a, i)$ as single symbols, which we henceforth write as $+a$ and $-a$ respectively when there is no ambiguity about the identity of the channel. Intuitively, $(-, a, i)$ denotes the emission of a in channel i, and $(+, a, i)$ denotes the reception of a from channel i. Furthermore, we do

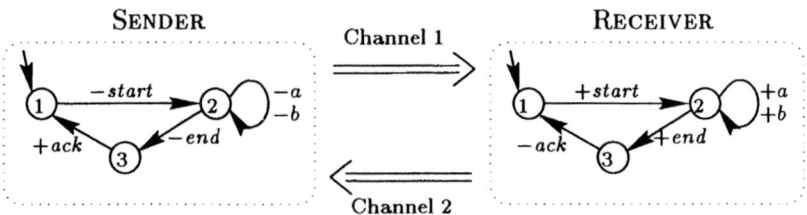

Fig. 1. The protocol S_1

not allow a machine to send and receive messages in/from the same channel, which could then be used as an auxiliary memory. We will need to consider transitions of δ which correspond only to sending actions (receiving actions) whence $\delta^- = \delta \cap Q \times (\{-\} \times \Sigma \times \mathbb{N}) \times Q$, $\delta^+ = \delta \cap Q \times (\{+\} \times \Sigma \times \mathbb{N}) \times Q$. We want now to group communicating machines together in order to deal with systems. Formally, we have:

Definition 2. A *system S of n CFSMs* is a n-tuple of CFSMs $S = (M_1, \ldots, M_n)$ with $M_i = (Q_i, q_{0i}, \Sigma, \delta_i)$ such that there is at most one machine which sends messages to a given channel. And conversely, there is at most one machine which receives messages from a given channel.

In the remainder of the paper and if not state otherwise, S will refer to a system $S = (M_1, \ldots, M_n)$ of CFSMs such that $M_i = (Q_i, q_{0i}, \Sigma, \delta_i)$; we also define $Q = \cup_{i=1,\ldots,n} Q_i$ and $\delta = \cup_{i=1,\ldots,n} \delta_i$ as the set of all transitions of the system. Let p be the number of channels used in S, we can rename the channels in $\{1, \ldots, p\}$. Then a *global state* (abbreviated to a *state*) of S is a $(n+p)$–tuple $s = (\mathbf{q}; \mathbf{x})$ with $\mathbf{q} = (q_1, \ldots, q_n)$, $q_i \in Q_i$ and $\mathbf{x} = (x_1, \ldots, x_p)$, $x_i \in \Sigma^*$. We note λ the empty word of Σ^* and $G(S)$ the *set of all global states* of S. An element $\mathbf{q} \in Q_1 \times \ldots \times Q_n$ is a *control state* and an element $q \in Q_i$ for $i \in \{1, \ldots, n\}$ is a *local state* (of machine i).

The operational semantics associated with a system of CFSMs is defined by the firing of a transition which changes the current global state in one step.

Definition 3. Let S be a system. A state $s' = (q'_1, \ldots, q'_n; x'_1, \ldots, x'_p)$ is *reachable* from another state $s = (q_1, \ldots, q_n; x_1, \ldots, x_p)$ *by the firing of the transition* t, written $s \rightarrow s'$, or redundantly $s \xrightarrow{t} s'$, if one of the following two cases hold :

1. $t = (q_i, (-, a, j), q'_i) \in \delta_i$ such that:
   (a) $q'_k = q_k$ for all $k \neq i$; (b) $x'_j = x_j.a$ and $x'_l = x_l$ for all $l \neq j$.
2. $t = (q_i, (+, a, j), q'_i) \in \delta_i$ such that:
   (a) $q'_k = q_k$ for all $k \neq i$; (b) $a.x'_j = x_j$ and $x'_l = x_l$ for all $l \neq j$.

Condition 1. above describes the output of message a by the machine M_i in channel j. Condition 2. describes the reception of message a by the machine M_i from channel j.

As usual, we extend relation $\rightarrow$ to its reflexive and transitive closure $\overset{*}{\rightarrow}$. Furthermore, we note $s_1 \overset{t_1 t_2 \ldots t_m}{\longrightarrow} s_{m+1}$ whenever we have $s_1 \overset{t_1}{\rightarrow} s_2 \overset{t_2}{\rightarrow} \ldots \overset{t_m}{\rightarrow} s_{m+1}$. The *initial state* is $s_0 = (\mathbf{q_0}; \boldsymbol{\lambda})$ with $\mathbf{q_0} = (q_{01}, \ldots, q_{0n})$, and $\boldsymbol{\lambda} = (\lambda, \ldots, \lambda)$. A state s is said *reachable* if $s_0 \overset{*}{\rightarrow} s$ and the *reachability set* of S is the set $\mathrm{RS}(S) = \{s \in \mathrm{G}(S) | s_0 \overset{*}{\rightarrow} s\}$ of all reachable states.

Example 4. $\mathrm{RS}(S_1) = \{(1, 1; \lambda, \lambda), (2, 1; (start)\{a, b\}^*, \lambda), (3, 1; (start)\{a, b\}^*$ $(end), \lambda), (2, 2; \{a, b\}^*, \lambda), (3, 2; \{a, b\}^*(end), \lambda), (3, 3; \lambda, \lambda), (3, 1; \lambda, (ack)) \}$.

Since S can be viewed as a transition system, we also define its reachability tree and its reachability graph:

- the *reachability tree* of S is the labelled tree $RT(S)$ with root labelled s_0 such that a node labelled s has a child labelled s' and the arc (s, s') is labelled by transition t iff $s \overset{t}{\rightarrow} s'$.
- the *reachability graph* of S is the labelled graph $\mathrm{RG}(S)$ whose nodes are $\mathrm{RS}(S)$ labelled by their corresponding states in $\mathrm{RS}(S)$. A node labelled s has a successor labelled s' and the arc (s, s') is labelled by transition t iff $s \overset{t}{\rightarrow} s'$.

The term half-duplex is commonly used to characterize a channel, between two machines, which can transmit messages in both directions but not simultaneously. The direction of the transmission can be set for a fixed amount of time and then be switched. A consequence is that the reachability graph of the system is finite since channels are bounded in function of the duration of each sending period and of the transmission's rate. We will use the term half-duplex with a less restrictive sense, without notion of elapsed time.

Definition 5. A system $S = (M_1, M_2)$ of two machines with two channels (one in each direction) is *half-duplex* if each reachable state has at least one channel empty.

Example 6. System S_1 of Fig. 1 is half-duplex.

2.2 Properties and decidability for systems of CFSMs

Usually, the verification of systems requires to solve the following kinds of problems: *reachability problems* which are to determine whether a given global state or local state or transition is reachable or executable; *boundedness problems* which are to determine whether the system requires unbounded channels and which ones.

The following theorem states how difficult verification of systems is.

Theorem 7 (Brand & Zafiropulo [5], Finkel & McKenzie [10]). *Systems of CFSMs have the power of Turing's machines. Hence, general verification is undecidable.*

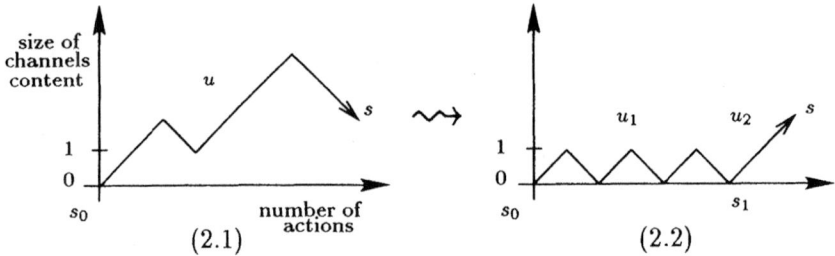

Fig. 2. Transformation of executions

In [13,14], Pachl shows that reachability problems are decidable under the sole assumption that the reachability set is recognizable. Remember that the notion of recognizable set is the natural extension (see [3]) for set of tuple of words of the classical notion of recognizable or regular languages. But we've seen in the introduction that these results are not useable in practice. Furthermore, *knowing that a reachability set is recognizable is not sufficient* to give a description of that set or even to decide the boundedness problem. One example of this point is given by the case of *lossy channel systems* [6]. On the other hand, having an effective recognizable description of the reachability set makes all of the problems just stated, easy to solve [7]. So we have:

Theorem 8. *For a system S of n CFSMs whose reachability set is recognizable and from which we have an effective description, the problems of interest are decidable.*

3 Half-duplex systems with two machines are verifiable

3.1 A Symbolic Reachability Graph

In this subsection and in the two following ones, we restrict ourselves to systems $S = (M_1, M_2)$ with two machines and two channels, the first one from M_1 to M_2 and the second one in the opposite direction. First of all, we show that each reachable state of such half-duplex systems is reached by a particular execution which we use to give a recognizable description of the reachability set.

Example 9. Let's consider the half-duplex system S_1 of Fig. 1. The sequence of actions $u = (-start)(-a) \ (+start)(-b)(-b)(-a)(+a)(+b)$ leads to the state $s = (2, 2; ba, \lambda)$. A representation of u is given by Fig. (2.1). But as shown by Fig.(2.2), u can be reordered in an execution split in two part, $u_1 = (-start)(+start) \ (-a)(+a)(-b)(+b)$ and $u_2 = (-b)(-a)$, such that u_1 is "bounded" by 1 and leads to a stable state s_1, and u_2 is exclusively made by sending messages in the same channel. We will show that this transformation is always available for such half-duplex systems. Hence, we can compute the reachability set in two steps. The first one computes the finite set of all stable states reached by a "1-bounded" execution. For each of these states, the second step gives all states reached by carrying out sending actions in a given channel. Because this last step uses only one machine, we obtain a recognizable set. What follows proves and formalizes this informal description.

We first need to give a more precise description of executions and states reached by "bounded" executions.

Definition 10. Let S be a system.

- an *execution* is a sequence of the form $s_1, t_1, s_2, t_2, \ldots, t_{m-1}, s_m$ such that $s_1 \overset{t_1}{\to} s_2 \overset{t_2}{\to} \ldots \overset{t_{m-1}}{\to} s_m$. Given a starting state s we also consider a sequence of transitions $t_1 t_2 \ldots t_m$ as an *execution* whenever there exists a sequence of states $(s_k)_{k=1,\ldots,m}$ such that $s, t_1, s_1, \ldots, t_m, s_m$ is an execution. If not set otherwise, the starting state will supposed to be the initial one s_0. Given a sequence of transitions representing an execution u, we note $u|_i$ the projection of this sequence on transitions of machines i. Thus, the projection $u|_i$ is the local execution induced by u on machine i.
- an execution $u = s_1, t_1, s_2, \ldots, t_{m-1}, s_m$ of S is *k-bounded* if the sizes of each channel's content of all intermediate states s_i visited by u is less than k.
- the *k-reachability* set of S with $k \in \mathbb{N}$ is the largest subset $\mathrm{RS}_k(S)$ of $\mathrm{RS}(S)$ in which, each state s is reached by a k-bounded execution from s_0.

Remark 11. Given a system S, for every integer $k \in \mathbb{N}$ the set $\mathrm{RS}_k(S)$ is finite and computable.

From an execution, we want to extract the sequence of messages involving a given channel j into an execution; so we define for each j, the morphism proj_j : $\delta^* \to \Sigma^*$ such that $\mathrm{proj}_j((q, (-, a, j), q')) = \mathrm{proj}_j((q, (+, a, j), q')) = a$ and for $k \neq j$, $\mathrm{proj}_j((q, (-, a, k), q')) = \mathrm{proj}_j((q, (+, a, k), q')) = \lambda$.

Lemma 12. *Let $S = (M_1, M_2)$ be a half-duplex system. For every reachable state $s = (q_1, q_2; x_1, x_2)$ of S, there exists an execution $u_1 u_2$ and a state s_1 such that the three following conditions hold:*

1. $s_0 \overset{u_1}{\to} s_1 \overset{u_2}{\to} s$,
2. *u_1 is 1-bounded, s_1 is a stable state, and,*
3. *$\exists i \in \{1, 2\}$ such that $u_2 \in (\delta_i^-)^*$, $x_i = \mathrm{proj}_i(u_2)$ and $x_{3-i} = \lambda$.*

Proof. By induction on the length of an execution u ending at s. There are two cases depending whether the last action of u is a receiving or a sending one.

Definition 13. From a given system, $S = (M_1, M_2)$, we distinguish the following subset of global states:

$$
\mathrm{H}(S) = \bigcup_{\substack{(q_1', q_2'; \lambda, \lambda) \in \mathrm{RS}_1(S), \\ (q_1, q_2) \in Q_1 \times Q_2}} \{q_1\} \times \{q_2\} \times L_1(q_1', q_1) \times L_2(q_2', q_2)
$$

where $L_i(q_i', q_i)$ is the recognizable language defined by the automaton $M_i(q_i', q_i)$ $= (Q_i, q_i', \Sigma, \{q_i\}, \delta_i')$ with q_i' the initial state, q_i the single final state and $\delta_i' = \{(q, a, q') | (q, (-, a, i), q') \in \delta_i\}$ the transition's relation.

Remark 14. $H(S)$ is recognizable as a finite union of products of recognizable languages [3]. Secondly, the description of $H(S)$ is effective since those of the different $L_i(q_i', q_i)$ are.

Lemma 15. *The reachability set* $RS(S)$ *of a half-duplex system* S *is equal to* $H(S)$.

Proof. The set $H(S)$ describes states reached by a specific execution, hence $H(S) \subseteq RS(S)$. The converse part, $RS(S) \subseteq H(S)$, is straightforward from Lemma 12 ■

Example 16. Let's consider system S_1, the reader can verify that $RS(S_1) = H(S_1)$. In particular, the subset $(2, 2; \{a, b\}^*, \lambda)$ is obtained by taking $(q_1', q_2') = (q_1, q_2) = (2, 2)$ in Definition 13.

From this Lemma, we deduce the main result of this section.

Theorem 17. *The reachability set of a half-duplex system is* recognizable and computable *in time:*
$$O(|(\Sigma + 1)^3 \times Q_1 \times Q_2|(|Q_1| + |Q_2|)).$$

Proof. The recognizability and computability of $RS(S)$ is proved by the preceding Remark and Lemma. Let us now consider the complexity. From Definition 13, we only need to compute stable states of $RS_1(S)$ since from these states a simple run through sending actions of one of the machine gives other states. Computing of $RS_1(S)$ is done by a simple reachability search from the starting state s_0. Knowing that $|RS_1(S)| = |Q_1 \times Q_2 \times (\Sigma + 1)^2|$ and that a reachable state has at most $|\Sigma \times Q_1| + |\Sigma \times Q_2|$ successors, we deduce the complexity. ■

Corollary 18. *For half-duplex systems, the problems of interest are decidable.*

Proof. Straightforward from Theorems 17 and 8. ■
    Having a recognizable description of the reachability set of a given half-duplex system S allows us the following definition.

Definition 19. Let S be a system.

- the *symbolic reachability set* of S, SRS(S), is a set whose elements have two parts. The first one is a control state and the second one the restriction on the channels of the recognizable description of the reachability set on this control state.
- the *symbolic reachability graph* of S, SRG(S), is a graph whose nodes are labelled by elements of SRS(S) and such that there is an edge labelled by $t \in \delta$ from $(\mathbf{q}; \mathbf{X})$ to $(\mathbf{q}'; \mathbf{X}')$ if and only if every successor, by the execution of transition t, of elements of $(\mathbf{q}, \mathbf{X})$ are in $(\mathbf{q}', \mathbf{X}')$.

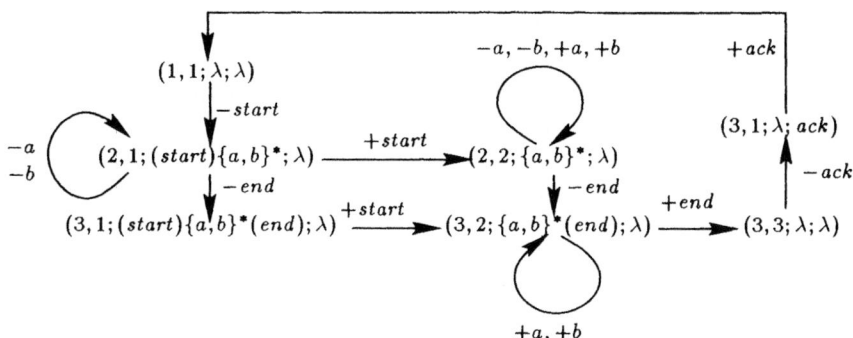

Fig. 3. The symbolic reachability graph of S_1

The symbolic reachability graph of a system is closely related to the minimal coverability graph (MCG) of a Petri net, in the sense that every execution of a system S is a path in $\mathrm{SRG}(S)$ and every reachable state is covered by (i.e. is an element of) a node of this graph. However, the SRG contains more information since its nodes describe exactly the reachability set, which is not the case for the minimal coverability graph of a Petri net.

Example 20. The symbolic reachability graph of system S_1 is given in Fig. 3.

3.2 Decidability of the half-duplex property

In the previous subsection, we gave a mean to describe the reachability set of a half-duplex system. But to be useful, we need to know on which systems these results may be applied. In other words, we have to decide whether a system of two machines S is half-duplex.

Obviously, since a system may have an infinite reachability set, we have to reduce the domain of interest to a finite one. Then, we will be able to verify the half duplex property.

Lemma 21. *A system $S = (M_1, M_2)$ is not half-duplex if and only if there exist* $s = (q_1, q_2; \lambda, \lambda) \in \mathrm{RS}_1(S)$ *and* $a_1, a_2 \in \Sigma$ *such that* $\delta_1(q_1, (-, a_1, 1)) \neq \emptyset$ *and* $\delta_2(q_2, (-, a_2, 2)) \neq \emptyset$.

Proof. The if part is straightforward. For the only if part, we consider one of the smallest execution u leading to a state which contradicts the half-duplex property. Then the state we're looking for is the stable one obtained by using lemma 12 on u truncated of its last action. ∎

Theorem 22. *The half-duplex property is decidable in time:*
$$O(|(\Sigma + 1)^3 \times Q_1 \times Q_2|(|Q_1| + |Q_2|)).$$

Proof. Since $\mathrm{RS}_1(S)$ is finite and computable, the property of Lemma 21 is checkable. The complexity comes from that of Theorem 17 ∎

4 Generalization for more than two machines

In the preceding section we showed how half-duplex systems with two machines and two channels can be verified. In this section, we look for a generalization of these nice results for systems with more than two machines and more than two channels. One way is to consider a generalization of the half-duplex notion. We see two possibilities: (a) the *natural generalization* and (b) the *restricted generalization*. We will see that neither of them satisfies our requirements. This will lead us to define a new class of systems whose restriction for systems of two machines and two channels corresponds to this of half-duplex.

First of all, let's consider the two generalizations.

(a) The *natural generalization* is to define as half-duplex all systems in which each pair of machines linked by two channels have a half-duplex communication. Unfortunately, this class allows the simulation of a Turing machine, with such a system of three machines, by the following construction. Let's consider the simulation of a Turing machines in [5]. It involves two machines which don't have half-duplex communication since each machine can send messages while its input channel is not empty. Let's add a third machine which will act only as a repeater of a channel . Then, we have three machines and three channels forming a cycle. Let's add three dummy channels in the opposite direction. We obtain a half-duplex system which still simulates a Turing machine. Thus we have.

Theorem 23. *Half-duplex systems with three machines are able to simulate Turing Machines.*

So this generalization is not analyzable and we cannot adopt the approach used in the previous sections.

(b) The *restricted generalization* is to consider systems in which each reachable state has at most one non-empty channel. This kind of communication is often used in radio communications where transceivers use the same frequency (at a given moment only one machine is allowed to send messages). And this condition is sufficient to describe the reachability set of such systems by use of the same techniques explained in the previous sections. However, consider now two independent subsystems satisfying this generalization. We would have liked the whole system to satisfy it too. But this is not the case since two channels (respectively in each subsystem) can be simultaneously non-empty.

Another possibility is to start from the good property of half-duplex system with two machines and two channels saying this of Lemma 12. This leads us to the following Definition 24. In what follows we note j^- the unique machine allowed to send messages in channel j, $T_j^- = \delta \cap Q \times (\{-\} \times \Sigma \times \{j\}) \times Q$ (resp. $T_j^+ = \delta \cap Q \times (\{+\} \times \Sigma \times \{j\}) \times Q$) the set of sending (resp. receiving) transitions in (resp. from) channel j, $T_j = T_j^- \cup T_j^+$ and ⊎ the shuffle operator of two words e.g. $x ⊎ y = \{y_1 x_1 y_2 \ldots y_n x_n y_{n+1} | x = x_1 \ldots x_n,\ y = y_1 \ldots y_{n+1}\}$.

Definition 24. Let S be a given system with p channels.

 – An execution u is said to be *quasi-stable* if:

313

(a) $u \in v_1'v_1'' \, \sqcup \ldots \sqcup v_p'v_p''$ with $v_j' \in (T_j^-T_j^+)^*$ and $v_j'' \in (T_j^-)^*$. The sequence v_j' is called the *quasi-stable part* of channel j and the sequence v_j'' its *increasing part*. Fig.(2.2) is also an illustration of the change in size of the content of a given channel during a quasi-stable execution.

(b) For each decomposition $u = u_1tu_2$ with t a transition belonging to the increasing part of channel j then $u_2|_{j-} \in (T_j^-)^*$. In other words, the machine which sends messages during the increasing part of a channel j, doesn't execute any action involving other channels during its future actions.

  – A system is said to be *quasi-stable*, or to have quasi-stable channels, if every reachable state can be reached by a quasi-stable execution.

Remark 25. The reader can verify using Lemma 12 that half-duplex systems with two machines and two channels are quasi-stable systems.

Quasi-stable systems can be characterized by a more effective property which will allow us to effectively compute their reachability sets.

Lemma 26. *Let $s = (\mathbf{q}; x_1, \ldots, x_p)$ be a state of a system S with n machines and p channels. The state s is reachable by a quasi-stable execution if and only if s can be reached by an execution u such that:*

1. $u = u_0u_1u_2\ldots u_p$,
2. u_0 is 1-bounded and leads to a stable state,
3. $\forall j, k \in \{1, \ldots, p\}, j \neq k, (u_j \neq \lambda$ and $u_k \neq \lambda \Longrightarrow j^- \neq k^-)$,
4. $\forall j \in \{1, \ldots, p\}$ $x_j = \text{proj}_j(u_j)$.

Proof. The if part is straightforward. For the only if part, we show, by the independence of the actions involved that a quasi-stable execution can be reordered in an execution satisfying the requirements.

Definition 27. From a given system S with n machines and p channels, we distinguish the following subset of global states:

$$Q(S) = \bigcup_{\substack{(\mathbf{q}'; \, \boldsymbol{\lambda}) \in \text{RS}_1(S) \text{ and} \\ J \subseteq \{1, \ldots, p\} \text{ such that} \\ \forall j, k \in J, \, j \neq k \Rightarrow j^- \neq k^-}} \left\{ (\mathbf{q}; \mathbf{x}) \, \middle| \, \begin{array}{l} j \in J \Rightarrow x_j \in L(j, q_{j-}', q_{j-}) \\ j \notin J \Rightarrow x_j = \lambda \\ \forall i \notin \{j^- | j \in J\}, q_i' = q_i \end{array} \right\}$$

With $L(j, q_{j-}', q_{j-})$ the regular language recognized by the machine M_{j-} considered as an finite automaton and such that: q_{j-}' is the initial state; q_{j-} is the unique final state; each edge labeled by $(-, a, j)$ in M_{j-} is labeled by the corresponding message (i.e. a); other edges are removed.

Since $Q(S)$ is a finite union of products of regular languages, the set $Q(S)$ is recognizable [3]. Furthermore, its description is computable.

Lemma 28. *For any quasi-stable system S, $\mathrm{RS}(S) = \mathcal{Q}(S)$.*

Proof. Lemma 26 says that a reachable state s is reachable from a stable state s' of $\mathrm{RS}_1(S)$ such that from s' to s there is an execution with each machine sending messages in at most one channel. The definition of $\mathcal{Q}(S)$ describes exactly all states reached by this procedure.

Theorem 29. *The reachability set of a quasi-stable system $S = (M_1, \ldots, M_n)$ with $M_i = (Q_i, q_{0i}, \Sigma, \delta_i)$ and p channels is recognizable and computable in time:* $O((\prod_{i=1}^{n} |Q_i|)|(\Sigma + 1)|^{n+1}(\sum_{i=1}^{p} |Q_i|))$.

Proof. Similar to that of Theorem 17.
From this theorem, we deduce that.

Corollary 30. *For a quasi-stable system, the problems of interest are decidable.*

The property of quasi-stability is decidable but needs a different approach than that of Lemma 21.

Theorem 31. *The quasi-stable property for a system S is decidable.*

Proof. From Definition 27 and Lemma 26, the problem of showing that a system S is quasi-stable amounts to that of showing that $\mathrm{RS}(S) = \mathcal{Q}(S)$. Because $\mathcal{Q}(S) \subseteq \mathrm{RS}(S)$, we have only to verify whether $\mathcal{Q}(S)$ is a fixpoint of the successor function. This is possible by the recognizability of $\mathcal{Q}(S)$.

Example 32. Here is an example of a quasi-stable system which is not half-duplex (the two machines can send a message to each other simultaneously):

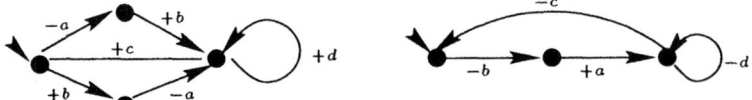

5   Conclusion

In this paper, we have shown that half-duplex systems with two machines have a effectively recognizable reachability set. Which allows us to define a symbolic reachability set and graph for this class of systems. However, half-duplex systems with more than two machines happen to be Turing powerful. This has led us to define a new class: quasi-stable systems, whose reachability set stays effectively recognizable for systems of any number of machines and channels. The restriction of this class for systems of two machines includes the half-duplex one.

Compared to general systems with recognizable channels [13] and lossy channel systems [1,2], our results are effective. We have applied these results to a class, systems with compatible communication, defined by Gouda et al. [11]. Only the boundedness problem was solved for it and we proved that this class is included in the half-duplex one with two machines and two channels. Hence reachability problems are also solvable.

Symbolic reachability sets and graphs are classical notions to represent infinite transition systems. Boigelot and Godefroid [4] used a symbolic reachability graph which approximates by recognizable sets the reachability set of any given system. Nodes of their graph are labelled by recognizable sets and edges by transitions or cycle of transitions of the underlying system. The approach we've used in this paper has led us to consider a similar construction but with recognizable languages as symbolic transitions, which is strictly more general. We intend to investigate the decidability of temporal logic such as LTL for quasi-stable systems.

References

1. P. Abdulla and B. Jonsson. Verifying Programs with Unreliable Channels. In *Proc. 8th Annual IEEE Symposium of Logic in Computer Science*, 1993.
2. P. Abdulla and B. Jonsson. Undecidable Verification Problems for Programs with Unreliable Channels. in *Proc. of ICALP*, vol. 820 of LNCS pp.316- 1994.
3. J. Berstel. Transductions and Context-Free Languages. *B.G. Teubner Stuttgart*, 1979.
4. B. Boigelot and P. Godefroid. Symbolic Verification of Communication Protocols with Infinite State Spaces Using QDDs. In *Proc. of 8th CAV (August), USA* LNCS 1102,pp.1–12, 1996.
5. Daniel Brand and Pitro Zafiropulo. On communicating finite-state machines. *JACM*, 30(2):323–342, 1983.
6. G. Cécé, A. Finkel and S. Purushothaman Iyer. Unreliable Channels Are Easier to Verify Than Perfect Channels. In *Information and Computation*, vol.124, No 1,20-31, 1996
7. G. Cécé and A. Finkel Programs with Quasi-Stable Channels are Effectively Recognizable. Technical Report, LSV, ENS de Cachan, 1997 (available via the authors)
   grenade
8. A. Finkel. Reduction and covering of Infinite Reachability Trees. *Information and Computation*, vol.89, n° 2, pp. 144–170, 1990.
9. A. Finkel. Decidability of the termination problem for completely specified protocols. *Distributed Computing*, 7:129–135, 1994.
10. A. Finkel and P. McKenzie. Verifying identical communicating Processes is undecidable. *to appear in TCS* 1997
11. M. G. Gouda, E. G. Manning and Y. T. Yu. On the Progress of Communication between Two Finite State Machines. *Information and Control*, 63:217–225, 1984.
12. T. Jéron and C. Jard. Testing for unboundedness of fifo channels. *Theoretical Computer Science* 113, pp.93-117, 1993.
13. J. K. Pachl. Reachability Problems for Communicating Finite State Machines *Research Report CS-82-12*, University of Waterloo, Dpt. of Computer Science, 1982.
14. J. K. Pachl. Protocol description and analysis based on a state transition model with channel expressions. In *Proc. of Protocol Specification, Testing and Verification, VII*, May 1987.
15. Kenneth J. Turner. Using Formal Description Techniques; an introduction to ESTELLE, LOTOS and SDL. © *John Wiley & Son Ltd.*, 1993.

Combining Constraint Solving and Symbolic Model Checking for a Class of Systems with Non-linear Constraints

William Chan[*], Richard Anderson, Paul Beame, David Notkin

Computer Science and Engineering, University of Washington, Box 352350
Seattle, WA 98195-2350, U.S.A.
{wchan,anderson,beame,notkin}@cs.washington.edu

Abstract. We extend the conventional BDD-based model checking algorithms to verify systems with non-linear arithmetic constraints. We represent each constraint as a BDD variable, using the information from a constraint solver to prune the BDDs by removing paths that correspond to infeasible constraints. We illustrate our technique with a simple example, which has been analyzed with our prototype implementation.

1 Introduction

Although symbolic model checking [BCM+90] based on Binary Decision Diagrams [Bry86], or BDDs, has been remarkably successful for verifying finite state systems, it fails when complex arithmetic constraints are present. For example, if the bits of the integers x, y and z are represented as BDD variables, the BDD for the non-linear constraint $xy = z$ has exponential size [LS81]. In this paper, we tightly couple a constraint solver with a BDD-based model checker to verify systems with possibly non-linear arithmetic constraints.

A large class of embedded, reactive systems consist of a finite-state *control* component together with *numeric data inputs* that measure quantities such as velocity, temperature, etc. In these systems, state transitions depend on predicates, or *constraints*, on these numerical values.

We have been studying the practicality of model checking for specifications of large and complex reactive software systems of this type. Our major effort has been directed at the preliminary requirements of one such system, TCAS II, an airborne collision avoidance system used on many commercial aircraft. In [ABB+96] we applied BDD-based model checking to about one third of the TCAS II specification, discovering a number of violations of desirable properties. The full specification—expressed in RSML [LHHR94], a dialect of Statecharts [Har87]—comprises about 400 pages.

Our approach for handling constraints exploited finiteness of the data input domains, representing each bit of data input as a BDD variable and constraints by BDDs in these variables. This worked well when dealing with purely linear

---

[*] Supported by a Microsoft Graduate Fellowship

constraints but did not extend efficiently to non-linear constraints, such as those found in the remaining portions of TCAS II.

In this paper, we propose to represent each (linear or non-linear) constraint, instead of each bit, as a BDD variable. For soundness and completeness, infeasible combinations of constraints have to be detected, which we do using an auxiliary constraint solver.

The class of systems we consider is defined by a restriction on the updates to data values: a transition must either set all new data values based only on absolute properties of their current values, or else leave them unchanged. A key property of such systems is that the decision to take a transition depends on the current data only via Boolean combinations of the constraints originally present in the specification. This restriction was also partly motivated by the semantics of RSML and, although it cannot handle all of TCAS II, it does allow modeling of a significant portion of it. We define our system model and show the key property of the restrictions on the transitions in Sect. 2.

Given the key property, a simple approach to combining the model checker and constraint solver is to test all combinations of constraints for feasibility before applying model checking. We develop a potentially more efficient approach whereby we prune the infeasible paths from the BDDs on the fly. We present our model checking algorithms in Sect. 3. and give a simple example that has been analyzed with our prototype implementation in Sect. 4.

Related Work. We have opted to augment BDD-based model checking to deal with non-linear constraints. The main reason is that we are interested in systems with large and complex control logic, for which only BDD-based model checking has proven to work well. The high dependence between control and data paths also prevents us from separating them for verification, a technique that is sometimes used in microprocessor verification.

Most work on handling non-linearity in verification has been focused on arithmetic circuits. One approach is to use BMDs or *BMDs [BC95] and their variants, such as HDDs [CFZ95]. Although they can represent the product xy concisely, representing the constraint $xy = z$ still requires exponential size. In fact, Thathachar [Tha96] shows that small variations of these representations are not likely to solve the problem. Our approach can deal with not only integral multiplicative constraints but also arbitrarily complex (e.g. trigonometric) constraints over finite or infinite domains, provided an appropriate constraint solver is available.

Abstracting a constraint as a single Boolean variable is not a new idea (e.g., [CDV96]). However, since infeasible combinations of constraints are not automatically detected, either the approach is incomplete for safety properties, or it requires substantial manual abstraction. Wang et al. [WME93] also represent certain timing constraints in distributed real-time systems as BDD variables. However, to ensure soundness and completeness, their method requires building a BDD in exponential time before running the fixed-point algorithm. We try to avoid a similar preprocessing by restricting the class of systems that we deal with and by filtering the BDDs on the fly.

Note that the work on nonlinear hybrid systems [HH95] differs from ours since it is concerned with constraints that are non-linear *differential equations*.

2 Models

We first give the definitions of basic transition systems, bisimulation equivalence, and quotient systems. Then we present our system model, whose semantics can be defined in terms of a basic transition system, and then show that certain restrictions on the transitions give rise to a natural bisimulation.

2.1 Basic Transition Systems

A reactive system can be modeled as a *basic transition system* $\langle Q, Q_0, \rightarrow, \Sigma, L \rangle$, where Q is a set of states, $Q_0 \subseteq Q$ is a set of initial states, $\rightarrow \subseteq Q \times Q$ is the transition relation, Σ is a set of atomic propositions, and $L: Q \mapsto 2^\Sigma$ labels each state with the set of atomic propositions in Σ that are true in that state. If we have $q \rightarrow q'$, then the state q' is called a *successor* of q.

Intuitively, an observer sees the label of the current state, but not the state itself. Two states are indistinguishable if their labels are the same and their successors are again indistinguishable. Formally, we say that an equivalence relation $\approx$ of Q is a *bisimulation* (cf. [Mil80, pp. 42]) if for all states q_1 and q_2, we have that $q_1 \approx q_2$ implies (1) $L(q_1)$ equals $L(q_2)$ and (2) for all q_1' in Q with $q_1 \rightarrow q_1'$, there exists a q_2' in Q with $q_2 \rightarrow q_2'$ and $q_1' \approx q_2'$.

The quotient system of $\langle Q, Q_0, \rightarrow, \Sigma, L \rangle$ with respect to a bisimulation $\approx$ is a basic transition system $\langle Q^\approx, Q_0^\approx, \rightarrow^\approx, \Sigma, L^\approx \rangle$. The quotient state space $Q^\approx$ is the set of equivalence classes induced by $\approx$. For all S and S' in $Q^\approx$, we have $S \rightarrow^\approx S'$ if and only if there exist an s in S and an s' in S' with $s \rightarrow s'$. We define $L^\approx(S) = L(s)$ for any s in S, and $Q_0^\approx = \{S \in Q^\approx \mid S \cap Q_0 \neq \emptyset\}$. We say that $\approx$ is *finite* if $Q^\approx$ is finite.

Many properties of $\langle Q, Q_0, \rightarrow, \Sigma, L \rangle$ can be expressed in the temporal logic CTL* [EH86] as formulas whose atomic propositions are taken from Σ. CTL* is strictly more expressive than CTL and LTL, commonly used in model checking. For our methods we need the following theorem (see, for example, [BCG88] for a proof of a similar theorem):

Theorem 1. *Any CTL* formula f is true in a basic transition system M if and only if f is true in the quotient system of M with respect to any bisimulation.*

2.2 System Model

We are interested in reactive systems with a finite control component and a finite or infinite numeric data component. The control component is represented by a finite set N of *control nodes*. The data component is represented by a finite vector $\mathbf{x}$ of *data variables*, and the domain of each variable is a finite or infinite subset of $\mathbb{R}$, the set of reals. Let D be the Cartesian product of the domains of the data variables. An assignment to $\mathbf{x}$ denotes a point in D, and a *constraint* on $\mathbf{x}$ denotes a subset of D. More explicitly, a constraint $c(\mathbf{x})$ is a predicate of the form $g(\mathbf{x}) \bowtie 0$ with $g \colon D \mapsto \mathbb{R}$ and $\bowtie$ is one of $\{<, \leq, =, \neq, \geq, >\}$. If we have $g(\mathbf{x}) \equiv \mathbf{a} \cdot \mathbf{x} + b$ for some vector $\mathbf{a}$ and constant b, then the constraint is *linear*. We are interested in both linear and non-linear constraints. We also call any finite Boolean combination of constraints a constraint. We denote by $[\![c(\mathbf{x})]\!]$ the set of points in D that satisfy $c(\mathbf{x})$. The constraint $c(\mathbf{x})$ is *feasible* if and only if $[\![c(\mathbf{x})]\!]$ is not empty. We write c for $c(\mathbf{x})$ when there is no ambiguity.

Our *system model* is a tuple $\langle N, N_0, \mathbf{x}, D, \Delta, C \rangle$, where N, $\mathbf{x}$, and D are defined as above, $N_0 \subseteq N$ is a set of initial control nodes, Δ is a mapping from N^2 to $2^{D \times D}$, and C is a finite set of constraints on $\mathbf{x}$. The system model defines a basic transition system $\langle Q, Q_0, \rightarrow, \Sigma, L \rangle$ as follows. The state space Q is $N \times D$. The set of initial states Q_0 is $N_0 \times D$. We define $L(v, a) = \{v\} \cup \{c \in C \mid a \in [\![c]\!]\}$ and $\Sigma = N \cup C$. Intuitively, this choice of labeling implies that the control nodes are fully observable, while data points are only distinguishable through the constraints in C.

The transition relation $\rightarrow$ is defined so that for all (v, a) and (v', a') in $N \times D$, $(v, a) \rightarrow (v', a')$ if and only if (a, a') is in $\Delta(v, v')$. If we define $\mathbf{x}' = (x'_1, x'_2, \ldots, x'_m)$, the "next-state" version of $\mathbf{x} = (x_1, x_2, \ldots, x_m)$, then we can think of Δ as specifying as a mapping from pairs of nodes to joint constraints on $\mathbf{x}$ and $\mathbf{x}'$. That is, for any v and v' in N, we have $\Delta(v, v') = [\![\alpha(\mathbf{x}, \mathbf{x}')]\!]$ for some constraint $\alpha(\mathbf{x}, \mathbf{x}')$. For example, if $\Delta(v, v')$ is $[\![x_1 > 0 \ \wedge \ x'_1 = x_1 + 1]\!]$ and the domain of x_1 is $\mathbb{R}$, then $(1, 2) \in \Delta(v, v')$ so $(v, 1) \rightarrow (v', 2)$ is a possible transition.

2.3 Restrictions on Transitions

The system model defined above is very general and contains classes of systems that are undecidable or intractable for model checking. We restrict our attention to system models with the following property on Δ.

Property 2. *For all (v, v') in N^2, $\Delta(v, v')$ is either*

1. $[\![\alpha_1(\mathbf{x}) \ \wedge \ \alpha_2(\mathbf{x}')]\!]$, *or*
2. $[\![\alpha_1(\mathbf{x}) \ \wedge \ \alpha_2(\mathbf{x}') \ \wedge \ \mathbf{x}' = \mathbf{x}]\!]$

where $\alpha_1(\mathbf{x})$ and $\alpha_2(\mathbf{x})$ are some Boolean combinations of constraints from C.

In the above definition, $\alpha_2(\mathbf{x}')$ is the renaming of $\alpha_2(\mathbf{x})$ with the occurrences of $\mathbf{x}$ replaced by $\mathbf{x}'$. We call the first kind of transition above *data-memoryless*. The idea is that the value of $\mathbf{x}'$ is independent of $\mathbf{x}$. For example, $\Delta(v, v') = [\![x_1 < 3 \ \wedge \ x'_1 > 5]\!]$ satisfies the property (if the constraints $x_1 < 3$ and $x_1 > 5$ are in C). The second kind of transition is called *data-invariant* since the values of all the data variables remain unchanged after the transition.

Property 2 may seem quite restrictive. Even the simple constraint $x'_1 = x_1 + 1$ mentioned earlier is ruled out. However, it does allow complex "guarding conditions", like $x_1 x_2 < x_3$ or $x_1 > \sin x_2$, etc. As we will see in Sect. 4, this property is naturally exhibited by certain Statecharts machines whose internal steps, while responding to particular changes in their environment, may be modeled as data-invariant transitions and whose environment may be modeled conservatively via data-memoryless transitions.

The key observation is that for any system model with the above property, the equivalence relation induced by the labeling is a bisimulation. Furthermore, the bisimulation is finite even if D is infinite.

Theorem 3. *Given a system model with state space $N \times D$ and labeling function L, let $\sim$ be the equivalence relation of $N \times D$ such that for all (v_1, a_1) and (v_2, a_2) in $N \times D$, we have $(v_1, a_1) \sim (v_2, a_2)$ if and only if $L(v_1, a_1)$ equals $L(v_2, a_2)$. The relation $\sim$ is a finite bisimulation for system models that satisfy Property 2.*

3 Model Checking

As a result of Theorems 1 and 3, given a system model with Property 2 and a CTL* formula, it is sufficient to verify the quotient system with respect to $\sim$. In this section, we first describe a Boolean encoding of the quotient system, and give a straightforward model checking algorithm which requires an exponential-time preprocessing stage to build a special BDD. Then we explain how that may be avoided by an operation we call filtering. Although the worst-case time complexity of filtering BDDs is also exponential, the hope is that the actual time required is less than the worst case.

We assume that we have a constraint solver that given a set of constraints can determine whether their conjunction is feasible. This problem has been studied by the constraint logic programming (CLP) community to extend CLP languages for non-linear constraints, and also by the operations research community to solve constrained optimization problems by first finding a feasible point.

3.1 A Boolean Encoding for Model Checking

Given a system model $\langle N, N_0, \mathbf{x}, D, \Delta, C \rangle$, the quotient state space with respect to $\sim$, i.e. the set of equivalence classes of $N \times D$ induced by $\sim$, is of the form $N \times D^\sim$ where $D^\sim$ is a collection of disjoint subsets of D, which we call *regions*, defined by the set of constraints in C that are true on those data points.

Our goal is to encode the quotient system symbolically by a set of Boolean variables so that BDDs can be used. The control part is encoded in a conventional manner: we encode the node $v \in N$ in some convenient way as an assignment $\psi_N(v)$ to a vector $\mathbf{v}$ of n Boolean variables with $n \geq \lceil \log |N| \rceil$, e.g. as the binary encoding of a number between 1 and $|N|$.

The way we handle the data part, $D^\sim$, distinguishes our approach from others. For $C = \{c_1, \ldots, c_m\}$, each region is of the form $[\![\alpha]\!]$ with $\alpha \equiv \bigwedge_{1 \leq i \leq m} l_i$ where l_i is either c_i or $\neg c_i$. This suggests a natural embedding ψ_D of $D^\sim$ into $\{0, 1\}^m$ in which an assignment to a vector $\mathbf{k}$ of m Boolean variables $k_1, k_2, \ldots, k_m$ encodes a region $[\![\alpha]\!]$ if k_i is set to 1 exactly when c_i occurs positively in

α. We also define a Boolean function $Feas(\mathbf{k})$ such that $Feas(\overline{k}) = 1$ if only if $\overline{k} \in \mathrm{Im}\psi_D$, i.e. $\overline{k}$ encodes a feasible constraint.

A state in the quotient system is encoded as an assignment to $(\mathbf{v}, \mathbf{k})$, and a set of states can be represented in the standard way as a Boolean function $S(\mathbf{v}, \mathbf{k})$, such that a state $(\overline{v}, \overline{k})$ is in the set if and only if $S(\overline{v}, \overline{k}) = 1$. (As is usual, we will think of S as a function and as a set interchangeably.) In general an arbitrary S may contain *infeasible states* — assignments to $(\mathbf{v}, \mathbf{k})$ with $Feas(\mathbf{k}) = 0$ — that we can remove by computing $S \wedge Feas$.

We now define a transition relation R on $\{0, 1\}^{n+m}$ that encodes the transitions of the quotient system on $N \times D^{\sim}$. That is, we define a Boolean function $R(\mathbf{v}, \mathbf{k}, \mathbf{v}', \mathbf{k}')$, where $\mathbf{k}' = (k_1', k_2', \ldots, k_m')$ and $\mathbf{v}'$ are the next-state versions of $\mathbf{k}$ and $\mathbf{v}$ respectively, that represents the transition relation of the quotient system. A natural condition in doing this would be to restrict $R(\overline{v}, \overline{k}, \overline{v'}, \overline{k'})$ to be 1 only if $(\overline{v}, \overline{k})$ and $(\overline{v'}, \overline{k'})$ each encode elements of $N \times D^{\sim}$; however this may lead to a very large BDD for R if the BDD for $Feas$ is large. Instead, we permit R to be 1 for values of $\overline{k}$ and $\overline{k'}$ that encode infeasible constraints and rely on manipulation of the state representations to eliminate infeasible states.

More precisely, let $\Delta(v, v')$ be $[\![\alpha_{v,v'}(\mathbf{x}, \mathbf{x}')]\!]$ for some constraint $\alpha_{v,v'}(\mathbf{x}, \mathbf{x}')$ which satisfies Property 2. If we replace each $c_i(\mathbf{x})$ and $c_i(\mathbf{x}')$ in $\alpha_{v,v'}(\mathbf{x}, \mathbf{x}')$ with k_i and k_i' respectively (just as in our encoding of quotient states) and conjoin $k_i = k_i'$ for $i = 1, \ldots, m$ if the transition is data-invariant, we obtain a Boolean function $\chi_{v,v'}(\mathbf{k}, \mathbf{k}')$. It can be shown that if $(\overline{v}, \overline{k})$ and $(\overline{v'}, \overline{k'})$ encode states $(v, [\![\alpha]\!]), (v, [\![\alpha']\!]) \in N \times D^{\sim}$, then $(\overline{v'}, \overline{k'})$ is a successor of $(\overline{v}, \overline{k})$ if and only if $\chi_{v,v'}(\overline{k}, \overline{k'}) = 1$. The relation $R(\mathbf{v}, \mathbf{k}, \mathbf{v}', \mathbf{k}')$ is then

$$\bigvee_{(v,v')\in N^2} (\mathbf{v} = \psi_N(v) \wedge \mathbf{v}' = \psi_N(v') \wedge \chi_{v,v'}(\mathbf{k}, \mathbf{k}')).$$

The BDD for R is easy to build from the system model description and thus conventional model checking algorithms can now be used to compute in the quotient system, provided that we also conjoin each set of states encountered with $Feas$ to remove infeasible states.

However, even if the BDD for $Feas$ is small, in general there may be no efficient way of computing it. The naive method enumerates all 2^m assignments to $\mathbf{k}$ and invokes the constraint solver to check the feasibility of each case. This method may work well if the number of constraints m is small.

3.2 Filtering

We can avoid building the BDD for $Feas$ if we have some other way of removing infeasible states. One solution is *filtering* the functions on the fly. We represent an arbitrary function S by a BDD in the implementation which, to simplify the terminology when explaining filtering, we think of as simply a DNF formula representing S, consisting of the disjunction of all the paths from the root to the leaf 1. The idea of filtering is that, instead of computing $S \wedge Feas$, we remove every disjunct d of S with $d \wedge Feas \equiv 0$. We denote the resulting function as $Filter_{Feas} S$. (Note that the value of $Filter_{Feas} S$ depends on the particular DNF representation for S.)

Since every disjunct d is a conjunction, we can determine whether d is feasible using the constraint solver, without computing $Feas(\mathbf{k})$. Note also that $Filter_{Feas}S$ and $S \wedge Feas$ are not necessarily the same function. For example, let S be the constant function 1, which can also be its DNF representation. Then, we have $S \wedge Feas \equiv Feas$ but $Filter_{Feas}S \equiv 1$. In general, we have $(S \wedge Feas) \subseteq Filter_{Feas}S \subseteq S$ (the inclusion is referring to the sets represented by the Boolean functions). Although $Filter_{Feas}S$ still contains some infeasible states, we will show that it is sufficient for model checking.

The algorithms for symbolic model checking [BCM+90] involve four types of operations on sets of states: Boolean operations, emptiness checking, image (or pre-image) computation, and finding elements in non-empty sets (for counterexample traces). The lemma below is easy to prove and implies that for Boolean operations we can delay the removal of infeasible states until the end (S and T are arbitrary Boolean functions).

Lemma 4. *We have the following equalities:*

(i) $(S \wedge Feas) \wedge (T \wedge Feas) \equiv (S \wedge T) \wedge Feas$.
(ii) $(S \wedge Feas) \vee (T \wedge Feas) \equiv (S \vee T) \wedge Feas$.
(iii) $(\neg(S \wedge Feas)) \wedge Feas \equiv (\neg S) \wedge Feas$.

The functions on the left hand side are the straightforward way of doing the operations. On the right hand side, we do the same operations but remove infeasible states only in the final result. The next lemma implies that if we only care whether the set is empty, then even the final result does not need to be intersected with $Feas$; instead, we can check the emptiness of the filtered result.

Lemma 5. $S \wedge Feas \equiv 0$ *if and only if* $Filter_{Feas}S \equiv 0$.

The next lemma gives a way of computing the image (i.e., successors) of a set of states without using $Feas$ (pre-image computation is similar).

Lemma 6. *We have the following equality:*

$$\exists \mathbf{v}. \exists \mathbf{k}. \ (Feas(\mathbf{k}) \wedge S(\mathbf{v}, \mathbf{k}) \wedge R(\mathbf{v}, \mathbf{k}, \mathbf{v}', \mathbf{k}'))$$
$$\equiv \exists \mathbf{v}. \exists \mathbf{k}. \ \left(Filter_{Feas(\mathbf{k})} \left(S(\mathbf{v}, \mathbf{k}) \wedge R(\mathbf{v}, \mathbf{k}, \mathbf{v}', \mathbf{k}') \right) \right).$$

As a result of the above three lemmas, the only necessary change to the conventional symbolic model checking algorithms is to use the right hand sides of Lemmas 5 and 6 to detect convergence and compute images respectively. Finally, the following lemma implies a way of finding a feasible state in a set.

Lemma 7. *If we have* $Filter_{Feas}S \not\equiv 0$, *then for each disjunct d of* $Filter_{Feas}S$, *there exists an assignment to the input variables of S with* $d \wedge Feas = 1$.

So to find a feasible state in S, we compute $Filter_{Feas}S$ and pick an arbitrary disjunct d, which corresponds to a partial assignment to the variables. To get a complete assignment, the unassigned variables not in $\mathbf{k}$ can be set arbitrarily. For the unassigned variables in $\mathbf{k}$, we can set them one by one using information

FILTER(B: BDD): BDD
  LABEL(B,*true*)
  return PRUNE(B)

PRUNE(B: BDD): BDD
  if $B = 0$ **or** $B = 1$ **then return** B
  let $y_j = B.\,Var$
  if $j > l$ **then return** B
  if $\langle B, B' \rangle$ is in cache, **return** B'
  if $B.Ledge = \top$
    then $B_0 \leftarrow$ PRUNE($B.Lchild$)
    else $B_0 \leftarrow 0$
  if $B.Redge = \top$
    then $B_1 \leftarrow$ PRUNE($B.Rchild$)
    else $B_1 \leftarrow 0$
  $B' \leftarrow$ ITE-BDD($B.\,Var, B_0, B_1$)
  insert $\langle B, B' \rangle$ and $\langle B', B' \rangle$ in cache
  return B'

LABEL(B: BDD, α: Constraint): $\{\top, \bot\}$
  if $B = 0$ **then return** $\bot$
  if $B = 1$ **then return** $\mathcal{FEAS}(\alpha)$
  let $y_j = B.\,Var$
  case
    $j < u$: .... (case 1: upper layer)
      if $B.Ledge = ?$ **then**
        $r_0 \leftarrow$ LABEL($B.Lchild, \alpha$)
        $B.Ledge \leftarrow r_0$
      else $r_0 \leftarrow B.Ledge$
      if $B.Redge = ?$ **then**
        $r_1 \leftarrow$ LABEL($B.Rchild, \alpha$)
        $B.Redge \leftarrow r_1$
      else $r_1 \leftarrow B.Redge$
    $u \leq j \leq l$: ... (case 2: middle layer)
      $r_0 \leftarrow$ LABEL($B.Lchild, \alpha \wedge \mathcal{I}(\neg y_j)$)
      if $r_0 = \top$ **then** $B.Ledge \leftarrow \top$
      $r_1 \leftarrow$ LABEL($B.Rchild, \alpha \wedge \mathcal{I}(y_j)$)
      if $r_1 = \top$ **then** $B.Redge \leftarrow \top$
    $j > l$: .... (case 3: lower layer)
      return $\mathcal{FEAS}(\alpha)$
  endcase
  if $r_0 = \top$ **or** $r_1 = \top$ **then return** $\top$
  else return $\bot$

Fig. 1. A BDD filtering algorithm

from the constraint solver: pick an unassigned variable and arbitrarily set it to 0, and if the extended assignment is not feasible, revert it to 1 (the new extended assignment is guaranteed to be feasible). Repeat until all the variables are set.

3.3 Filtering BDDs

Filtering a BDD amounts to removing all paths from the root to the leaf 1 that correspond to infeasible constraints. Figure 1 shows a BDD filtering algorithm FILTER. We assume that the given BDD is a function of **v** and **k**, which is being filtered with respect to *Feas*(**k**). (What we will describe can be easily generalized to handle functions of $(\mathbf{v}, \mathbf{k}, \mathbf{v}', \mathbf{k}')$ and filtering with respect to *Feas*(**k**′).) The algorithm consists of two phases: in the labeling phase, it labels the edges along all feasible paths with $\top$, and in the pruning phase, it redirects the edges not labeled with $\top$ to the leaf 0.

Each non-leaf BDD node has five fields. The *Var* field stores the BDD variable. The *Lchild* field points to the 0-child BDD. The *Ledge* field is the label of the left edge, which is either $\top$ (feasible), $\bot$ (infeasible), or ? (unknown, the initial value). The *Rchild* and *Redge* fields are symmetric. Suppose the BDD variables in order are $y_1, y_2, \ldots, y_u, \ldots, y_l, \ldots, y_{m+n}$, where y_u and y_l are the first and last variables in $\mathbf{k}$. We call the part of the BDD with variables y_1 through y_{u-1} the upper layer, y_u through y_l the middle layer, and y_{l+1} through y_{m+n} the lower layer. Therefore, only the middle layer contains variables in $\mathbf{k}$.

The routine LABEL traverses the paths in a depth-first manner, keeping track of the corresponding constraint α as it walks down a path. Case 2 is important for correctness, while cases 1 and 3 are for optimizations—each node in the upper layer is not visited more than once (case 1), and nodes in the lower layer are not explored at all (case 3). The constraint solver $\mathcal{FEAS}$ takes a constraint α, and returns $\top$ if α is feasible, or $\bot$ otherwise. The function $\mathcal{I}$ "interprets" the BDD variables as data constraints. For each v_i in $\mathbf{v}$, we have $\mathcal{I}(\neg v_i) = \mathcal{I}(v_i) = true$, and for each k_i in $\mathbf{k}$, we have $\mathcal{I}(k_i) = c_i$ and $\mathcal{I}(\neg k_i) = \neg c_i$. The routine PRUNE performs the pruning phase. The function $ITE\text{-}BDD$ takes a BDD variable y and two BDDs B_0 and B_1, and returns a BDD with top variable y, 0-child B_0 and 1-child B_1.

Assuming that $\mathcal{FEAS}$ takes constant time, the time complexity of FILTER is linear in the number of nodes in the upper layer, and in the number of *paths* in the middle layer (which is the major bottleneck of the algorithm).

A Refinement. It makes sense to filter the BDDs instead of building *Feas* only if the number of paths checked is smaller than 2^m. Unfortunately, filtering $S \wedge R$ as suggested by Lemma 6 may be very expensive. To see this let $R(\mathbf{v}, \mathbf{k}, \mathbf{v}', \mathbf{k}')$ be $R_1(\mathbf{v}, \mathbf{k}, \mathbf{v}', \mathbf{k}') \vee (R_2(\mathbf{v}, \mathbf{k}, \mathbf{v}', \mathbf{k}') \wedge \mathbf{k}' = \mathbf{k})$, where R_1 and $R_2 \wedge \mathbf{k}' = \mathbf{k}$ represent the data-memoryless and data-invariant transitions respectively. The constraint $\mathbf{k}' = \mathbf{k}$ conjoined with R_2 introduces a path for each possible assignment to $\mathbf{k}$, so there may be 2^m paths to check. However, the observation is that we can rename each k_i' in R_2 to k_i without changing the function $R_2 \wedge \mathbf{k}' = \mathbf{k}$, thus eliminating $\mathbf{k}'$ from R_2. We have the following lemma.

Lemma 8. *The following equality holds:*

$$\left(\exists \mathbf{v}.\, \exists \mathbf{k}.\, \left(Filter_{Feas(\mathbf{k})}\left(S(\mathbf{v}, \mathbf{k}) \wedge R(\mathbf{v}, \mathbf{k}, \mathbf{v}', \mathbf{k}'))\right)\right)\right) \wedge Feas(\mathbf{k}')$$
$$\equiv (U(\mathbf{v}', \mathbf{k}') \vee V(\mathbf{v}', \mathbf{k}')) \wedge Feas(\mathbf{k}')$$

with

$$U(\mathbf{v}', \mathbf{k}') = \exists \mathbf{v}.\, \exists \mathbf{k}.\, Filter_{Feas(\mathbf{k})}\left(S(\mathbf{v}, \mathbf{k}) \wedge R_1(\mathbf{v}, \mathbf{k}, \mathbf{v}', \mathbf{k}')\right)$$
$$V(\mathbf{v}', \mathbf{k}) = \exists \mathbf{v}.\, Filter_{Feas(\mathbf{k})}\left(S(\mathbf{v}, \mathbf{k}) \wedge R_2(\mathbf{v}, \mathbf{k}, \mathbf{v}'))\right).$$

So we compute $U \vee V$, handling the constraint $\mathbf{k} = \mathbf{k}'$ implicitly.

4 Implementation and Example

We implemented the above algorithms in SMV [McM93]. The constraint solver used was QUAD-CLP($\mathbb{R}$) [PB94], a less incomplete solver than CLP($\mathbb{R}$) for quadratic constraints. We had access only to the executable of the solver, so it was integrated with SMV through interprocess communication.

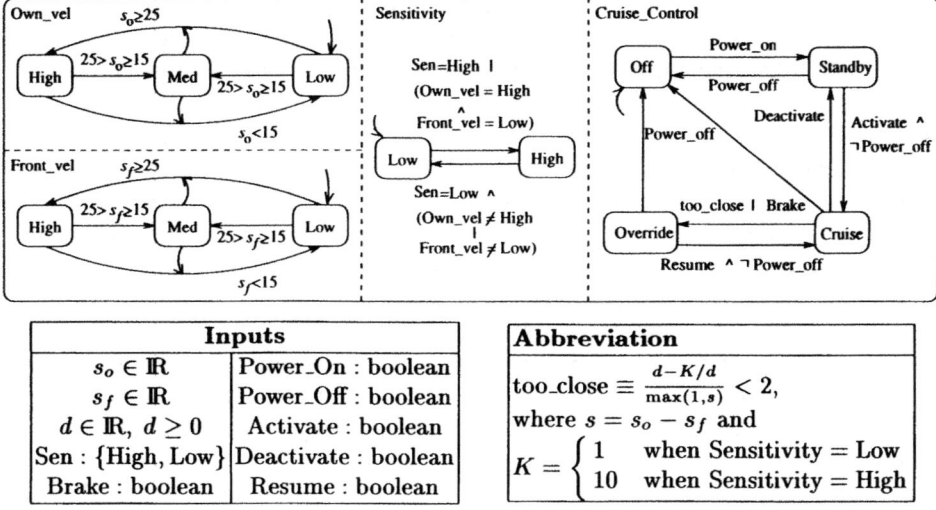

Fig. 2. A hypothetical automobile cruise control system with collision avoidance

Because a motivation of this work is to analyze the TCAS II requirements, we illustrate our technique with a simple Statecharts-like system shown in Fig. 2. It is a hypothetical automobile cruise control system with collision avoidance. The idea is that when the automobile is too close to the vehicle in front, the cruise control system will automatically deactivate itself. (In addition to TCAS, the example was influenced by the one used by Atlee and Gannon [AG93].)

Three inputs to the system are s_o, the velocity of the vehicle; s_f, the velocity of the front vehicle; and $d \geq 0$, the distance between the vehicles. (In reality, s_f may be estimated from the current and previous values of s_o and d.) The closeness of the two vehicles is based on time rather than distance. Let s be $s_o - s_f$. The estimated time to collision is d/s. If this quantity is less than some threshold t, the two vehicles may be considered too close. However, if s is positive but small, the two vehicles can get very close without triggering the condition. To fix this problem, the following condition can be used instead:

$$\frac{d - K/d}{\max(\epsilon, s)} < t.$$

The max function is for avoiding division-by-zero. Subtracting K/d from the numerator makes the inequality true when d is tiny, regardless of the value of s. The positive value K depends on the "sensitivity level" (large K for high sensitivity). Although this example is naive, the inequality is exactly the one used in TCAS II for threat detection. We arbitrarily chose $\epsilon = 1$ and $t = 2$.

As shown in Fig. 2, the system is divided into four components. In Statecharts and RSML, different components are synchronized by *events* (signals). We omit this mechanism in the figure and assume the components execute in the following order: in the first *micro-step*, Own_vel and Front_vel execute concurrently (i.e., each takes one enabled transition, or stays unchanged if none is enabled); in the second and third micro-steps, Sensitivity and Cruise_Control execute respectively. The three micro-steps together form a *super-step*. Transitions in a component are guarded by assertions on the inputs and/or other components. It should be clear that we can construct the product system of the components in the usual manner and represent it with a system model (Sect. 2.2). The values of all the inputs are nondeterministic at the beginning of a super-step, but during a super-step they are assumed to be unchanged by the so-called *synchrony hypothesis*. Therefore this system satisfies Property 2: micro-step transitions are data-invariant, while transitions across super-steps are data-memoryless.

We verified several safety properties of a model of this system using our prototype implementation. In the model, there are (at least) six Boolean variables representing constraints: $s_o \geq 25, s_o < 15, s_f \geq 25, s_f < 15, ((d - 1/d)/\max(1, s_o - s_f)) < 2, ((d - 10/d)/\max(1, s_o - s_f)) < 2$. Additional Boolean variables are used when the property being verified contains other constraints. We focused on verifying that Cruise_Control is never in the Cruise node under certain conditions, for example, when d is less than 2, (That is, in CTL, AG !($d < 2$ & Cruise_Control = Cruise).) This property is false because the two transitions into the Cruise node are not guarded by ¬too_close. The model checker correctly showed a counterexample. After strengthening the guards on the two transitions, the property was verified true. Two other related properties were also successfully verified: Cruise_Control is never in the Cruise node when either (1) d is less than 4 and Sensitivity is High, or (2) d is less than 20, Sensitivity is High, and Sen is Low. Each of the above specifications was evaluated within a second by our prototype implementation. The numbers of calls made to the constraint solver were at most about 30% of the number of calls required to construct *Feas*.

5 Conclusion

The technique described in this paper can be generalized in various ways. The idea can be applied to systems with transitions annotated by assertions in any theory, if a decision procedure for the theory is available. Allowing transitions that are not data-memoryless or data-invariant can make the technique more useful, but that would probably require computing a bisimulation before applying model checking, or approximating one on the fly. Doing so may blow up the number of BDD variables. There are also many open questions for the short term. We need to experiment with larger systems like TCAS II to see whether the technique is practical. The choice of variable ordering also needs investigation because it affects both the BDD size and the number of paths traversed.

References

[ABB+96] R. J. Anderson, P. Beame, S. Burns, W. Chan, F. Modugno, D. Notkin, and J. D. Reese. Model checking large software specifications. In *Pro-*

ceedings of the Fourth ACM SIGSOFT Symposium on the Foundations of Software Engineering, pages 156–166, October 1996.

[AG93] J. M. Atlee and J. Gannon. State-based model checking of event-driven system requirements. *IEEE Transactions on Software Engineering*, SE-19(1):24–40, January 1993.

[BC95] R. E. Bryant and Y.-A. Chen. Verification of arithmetic circuits with Binary Moment Diagrams. In *Proceedings of the 32nd ACM/IEEE Design Automation Conference*, pages 535–541, June 1995.

[BCG88] M. C. Browne, E. M. Clarke, and O. Grümberg. Characterizing finite Kripke structures in propositional temporal logic. *Theoretical Computer Science*, 59:115–131, 1988.

[BCM⁺90] J. R. Burch, E. M. Clarke, K. L. McMillan, D. L. Dill, and L. J. Hwang. Symbolic model checking: 10^{20} states and beyond. In *Proceedings of the Fifth Annual Symposium on Logic in Computer Science*, pages 428–439. IEEE Computer Society Press, June 1990.

[Bry86] R. E. Bryant. Graph-based algorithms for boolean function manipulation. *IEEE Transactions on Computers*, C-35(6):677–691, August 1986.

[CDV96] J. Crow and B. L. Di Vito. Formalizing space shuttle software requirements. In *Proceedings of the ACM SIGSOFT Workshop on Formal Methods in Software Practice*, pages 40–48, January 1996.

[CFZ95] E. M. Clarke, M. Fujita, and X. Zhao. Hybrid Decision Diagrams overcoming the limitations of MTBDDs and BMDs. In *1995 IEEE/ACM International Conference on Computer-Aided Design, Digest of Technical Papers*, pages 159–163. IEEE Computer Society Press, November 1995.

[EH86] E. A. Emerson and J. Y. Halpern. "Sometimes" and "Not Never" revisited: On branching versus linear time temporal logic. *Journal of the ACM*, 33(1):151–178, 1986.

[Har87] D. Harel. Statecharts: A visual formalism for complex systems. *Science of Computer Programming*, 8:231–274, 1987.

[HH95] T. A. Henzinger and P.-H. Ho. Algorithmic analysis of nonlinear hybrid systems. In *Proceedings of the 7th International Conference on Computer Aided Verification*, pages 225–238. Springer-Verlag, July 1995.

[LHHR94] N. G. Leveson, M. P. E. Heimdahl, H. Hildreth, and J. D. Reese. Requirements specification for process-control systems. *IEEE Transactions on Software Engineering*, SE-20(9), September 1994.

[LS81] R. J. Lipton and R. Sedgewick. Lower bounds for VLSI. In *Conference Proceedings of the Thirteenth Annual ACM Symposium on Theory of Computing*, pages 300–307, May 1981.

[McM93] K. L. McMillan. *Symbolic Model Checking*. Kluwer, 1993.

[Mil80] R. Milner. *A Calculus of Communicating Systems*. Springer-Verlag, 1980.

[PB94] G. Pesant and M. Boyer. QUAD-CLP(IR): Adding the power of quadratic constraints. In *Second International Workshop, Principles and Practice of Constraint Programming*, pages 95–108. Springer-Verlag, May 1994.

[Tha96] J. S. Thathachar. On the limitations of ordered representations of functions. Technical Report CSE-96-09-03, University of Washington, September 1996.

[WME93] F. Wang, A. Mok, and E. A. Emerson. Symbolic model checking for distributed real-time systems. In *Proceedings of the First International Symposium of Formal Methods Europe*, pages 632–651, April 1993.

Relaxed Visibility Enhances Partial Order Reduction

Ilkka Kokkarinen[1] and Doron Peled[2] and Antti Valmari[1]

[1] Tampere University of Technology, Software Systems Laboratory,
PO Box 553, FIN-33101 Tampere, FINLAND,
email: {imk,ava}@cs.tut.fi
[2] Bell Laboratories, Lucent Technologies,
700 Mountain Ave., Murray Hill, NJ 07974, USA,
email: doron@research.bell-labs.com

Abstract. State-space explosion is a central problem in the automatic verification (model-checking) of concurrent systems. Partial order reduction is a method that was developed to try to cope with the state-space explosion. Based on the observation that the order of execution of concurrent (independent) atomic actions is in many cases unimportant for the checked property, it allows reducing the state space by exploring fewer execution sequences. However, to be on the safe side, partial order reductions put constraints about commuting the order of atomic actions that may change the value of propositions appearing in the checked specification. In this paper we relax this constraint, allowing a weaker requirement to be imposed, achieving a better reduction. We demonstrate the benefits of our improved reduction with experimental results.

1 Introduction

During the recent years, many practical techniques for the automatic verification of concurrent systems have been developed. One group of such techniques is the *partial order reduction* [3, 5, 10, 11, 13, 14], based on the observation that executing concurrent atomic transitions is commutative. It is then sufficient in many cases to check only a subset of their execution orders instead of all of them. There are two main factors for the effectiveness of such techniques: (a) the amount of commutativity (reflecting independence or concurrency) among atomic program transitions and (b) the number of *visible* atomic transitions, i.e. transitions whose execution may change a predicate in the checked property.

Some attempts with asymmetric or global-state-sensitive dependency relations have been made to reduce the dependency between atomic actions [4, 7, 13] to allow constructing better reduced state spaces. However, only little attention has been made to study the visibility obstacle. In this paper we tackle the problem of relaxing the visibility condition for partial order reduction. Some earlier attempts to make the reduction more sensitive to the checked property eliminate the need of the visibility condition by increasing the dependency according to the checked property. In [5] and [15], the specification was given as an automaton over *operations*, rather than states as in our case. Then any two operations that can change the state of the property automaton become interdependent. However, this is almost equivalent to the visibility condition (see also [16]). In [10] it is shown that by making a certain fairness assumption and rewriting the property as a Boolean combination of simpler properties, some dependencies between operations that affect the checked property can be eliminated.

We propose a more flexible use of visibility, where the set of visible transitions may diminish during the progress in the construction. We present an improved partial order reduction for model checking that uses this idea. We provide experimental results that show that the new algorithm can achieve substantial improvement over the existing ones.

2 Preliminaries

2.1 Modeling Systems

A *finite state system* P is a triple $\langle S, T, \iota \rangle$, where S is a finite set of *states*, T is a finite set of deterministic *transitions*, and $\iota \in S$ is the *initial state*. For each transition $a \in T$ we associate a partial function $a : S \mapsto S$. A transition a is *enabled* from s, if $a(s)$ is defined. Then, executing a from s results in the state $a(s)$. The set of transitions enabled at a state s is denoted by $enabled(s)$.

The full *state-space* of P contains the states reachable from the initial state ι by repeatedly executing the transitions T.

A *transition sequence* is a finite or infinite sequence of transitions $a_0 a_1 a_2 \ldots$ such that there exists a sequence of states $s_0 s_1 s_2 \ldots$ satisfying that (1) $s_0 = \iota$, (2) for each $i \geq 0$, $s_{i+1} = a_i(s_i)$, and (3) the sequence is maximal, namely it is either infinite, or ends with a state s such that $enabled(s) = \emptyset$. To save space, we discuss only the case of infinite transition sequences.

A *dependency relation* $D \subseteq T \times T$ is a symmetric and reflexive relation such that if $(a, b) \notin D$, then

- If $a \in enabled(s)$, then $b \in enabled(s)$ iff $b \in enabled(a(s))$.
- If $a, b \in enabled(s)$ then $a(b(s)) = b(a(s))$.

Transitions $(a, b) \in D$ are said to be *dependent*, otherwise they are *independent*.

If $\mathcal{P}$ is a finite set of propositional variables, let L be an interpretation function $L : S \mapsto 2^{\mathcal{P}}$, which assigns a boolean value to each proposition in $\mathcal{P}$ for every state in S. We will use the letter ξ to denote the sequence of program states that is induced by a transition sequence. Applying the interpretation function L to each state of ξ, we obtain the *propositional sequence* $L(\xi)$.

Definition 1. We assume that the set of transitions has been divided into *visible* and *invisible* such that if (but not necessarily only if) the execution of a transition from any state of the system can change the value assigned to at least one of the propositions from $\mathcal{P}$, then the transition is visible [14]. □

That is, if there exists a state s and a successor state $s' = a(s)$ such that $L(s) \neq L(s')$, then a is visible. The set of visible transitions is thus some upper approximation of the set of transitions that can modify values of propositions.

An upper approximation is used although it may give less reduction, because the exact set is often too hard to determine.

One of the most popular specification formalisms for concurrent systems is Linear Temporal Logic (LTL) [12]. Its syntax is as follows:

$$\varphi ::= (\varphi_1) \mid \neg\varphi_1 \mid \varphi_1 \vee \varphi_2 \mid \varphi_1 \wedge \varphi_2 \mid \bigcirc \varphi_1 \mid \Box\varphi_1 \mid \Diamond\varphi_1 \mid \varphi_1 \, \mathcal{U} \, \varphi_2 \mid p$$

where $p \in \mathcal{P}$. We denote a propositional sequence over $2^\mathcal{P}$ by σ, and its suffix starting from the ith state (where the first state is numbered 0) by $\sigma^{(i)}$. The boolean operators have their usual interpretations, while the modal operators $\bigcirc$ (nexttime), $\Box$ (always), $\Diamond$ (eventually) and $\mathcal{U}$ (until) are interpreted as follows:

- $\sigma \models \bigcirc\varphi$ iff $\sigma^{(1)} \models \varphi$.
- $\sigma \models \Box\varphi$ iff for each $i \geq 0$, $\sigma^{(i)} \models \varphi$.
- $\sigma \models \Diamond\varphi$ iff there exists $i \geq 0$ such that $\sigma^{(i)} \models \varphi$.
- $\sigma \models \varphi\,\mathcal{U}\,\psi$ iff $\sigma^{(j)} \models \psi$ for some $j \geq 0$ so that for each $0 \leq i < j$, $\sigma^{(i)} \models \varphi$.

Two propositional sequences w and w' are considered to be *stuttering equivalent*, denoted by $w \equiv w'$, if they differ in at most the number of times the state labeling may adjacently repeat. Every "$\bigcirc$"-free LTL formula obtains the same truth value on any two stuttering equivalent sequences [9], i.e., LTL without nexttime is *stuttering-closed*.

2.2 Partial Order Reduction Algorithms

Many versions have been suggested for partial order reduction algorithms. Most of them have a common basis of doing a search (usually a depth-first search or its variation) on the state space of the checked system (or, in the case of on-the-fly verification, over the combination of program and property states). At each state in the search, only a subset of the successors obtained by executing the enabled transitions is constructed.

Some conditions and algorithms apply to selecting a subset of the enabled transitions from the current state. These conditions must guarantee that the generated state space, albeit smaller than the full state space, preserves the checked property. Developed by different researchers, such subsets adhere to different names: *stubborn* sets [14], *ample* sets [11], *persistent* sets [5] or faithful decompositions [6]. Although their definitions differ, they have much in common. We will call them generically *stamper* sets. For every state s, $stamper(s) \subseteq enabled(s)$, and we call a state s with $stamper(s) = enabled(s)$ *fully expanded*.

It would be futile to try to capture all the subtleties of the various suggested algorithms, some of which take advantage of confining themselves to a more restricted set of properties. We will describe a general algorithm which resembles some of the versions, and can be changed accordingly to capture others. We use the following four conditions.

Non emptiness $stamper(s)$ is empty iff $enabled(s)$ is empty.

Consistency In every finite path of the system that starts from s and does not contain a transition from $stamper(s)$, only transitions independent of the ones in $stamper(s)$ can appear.

Non ignorance Every cycle of the reduced state space contains at least one node t for which $stamper(t) = enabled(t)$.

Visibility If $stamper(s) \neq enabled(s)$, then $stamper(s)$ may not contain transitions that are visible with respect to $\mathcal{P}$.

Let $Seq(P, t)$ be the set of propositional sequences of the concurrent system P, starting from a (not necessarily initial) state t, and $Red(P, t)$ be the corresponding set of propositional sequences of the reduced state space.

Theorem 2. *Let t be a state of the reduced state space. Then $Red(P, t) \subseteq Seq(P, t)$, and for each $\xi \in Seq(P, t)$, there exists a sequence $\xi' \in Red(P, t)$ such that $L(\xi) \equiv L(\xi')$.*

This is the main theorem [11, 14], which holds for many variations of the above rules. We immediately obtain that the reduced state space preserves the correctness of every stuttering-closed property, as follows:

Corollary 3. *For every stuttering-closed property φ, there is a sequence satisfying φ in $Seq(P, t)$ iff there is a sequence satisfying φ in $Red(P, t)$.*

2.3 Translating LTL formulas to automata

In this section we sketch the algorithm presented in [2] for translating an LTL formula φ into a Büchi automaton $\mathcal{A}$.

As a preparatory step, we bring the formula φ into a normal form. First, we push negation inwards, so that only propositional variables can appear negated. To do that, we use LTL equivalences, such as $\neg\Diamond\psi = \Box\neg\psi$. One problem is that pushing negations into until ($\mathcal{U}$) subformulas can explode the size of the formula. For that, we use the operator *release* ($\mathcal{V}$), which is the dual of the operator until, namely $\neg(\mu\,\mathcal{U}\,\eta) = (\neg\mu)\,\mathcal{V}\,(\neg\eta)$. Then we remove the eventuality ($\Diamond$) and always ($\Box$) operators, using the until and release operators and the equivalences $\Diamond\psi = \mathbf{True}\,\mathcal{U}\,\psi$ and $\Box\psi = \mathbf{False}\,\mathcal{V}\,\psi$.

The algorithm uses the following fields for every generated node of $\mathcal{A}$:

id A unique identifier of the node.

incoming The set of edges that are pointed into the node.

new A set of subformulas of the translated formula, which need to hold from the current node and have not yet been processed.

old A set of subformulas as above, which have been processed.

next A set of subformulas of the translated formula, which have to hold for every successor of the current node.

The algorithm starts with a single node, with one incoming edge from a dummy node called *init*. Its field *new* includes the translated formula φ in the above normal form, and the fields *old* and *next* are empty. A list *completed-nodes* is initialized as empty. The algorithm proceeds recursively: for a node x not yet in *completed-nodes*, it moves a subformula η from *new* to *old* [3]. The algorithm

---

[3] The algorithm can be improved a bit by storing in *old* only subformulas that are atomic propositions, their negations, or of the form $\mu\,\mathcal{U}\,\eta$. The latter are needed for determining the acceptance sets, as explained in the sequel.

then splits the node x into left and right copies while adding subformulas to the fields *new* and *next* according to the following table. The fields *old* and *incoming* retain their previous values in both copies. The algorithm continues recursively with the split copies.

Formula	New left	Next left	New right	Next right
$\mu\,\mathcal{U}\,\eta$	$\{\mu\}$	$\{\mu\,\mathcal{U}\,\eta\}$	$\{\eta\}$	$\emptyset$
$\mu\,\mathcal{V}\,\eta$	$\{\eta\}$	$\{\mu\,\mathcal{V}\,\eta\}$	$\{\mu,\eta\}$	$\emptyset$
$\mu\vee\eta$	$\{\mu\}$	$\emptyset$	$\{\eta\}$	$\emptyset$
$\mu\wedge\eta$	$\{\mu,\eta\}$	$\emptyset$	—	—

When there are no more subformulas in the field *new* of the current node x, x is compared against the nodes in the list *completed-nodes*. If there is a node y that agrees with x on the fields *old* and *next*, one adds to the field *incoming* of y the incoming edges of x (hence, one may arrive to the node y from new directions). Otherwise, one adds x to that list and a new node is initiated with a new identifier in *id*, an incoming edge from x, and its *new* field the set of the subformulas in the *next* field of x.

When new nodes can no longer be generated, the set of initial nodes I is identified as those which have an incoming edge from the dummy node *init*. Also an *accepting set* for each subformula of the form $\mu\,\mathcal{U}\,\eta$ contains the nodes such that either their *old* field contains the subformula η, or does not contain $\mu\,\mathcal{U}\,\eta$. The accepting condition is that of *generalized Büchi* [1], namely, an accepting computation has to traverse *for each accepting set* through at least one of its nodes infinitely often. Each node x is *labeled* by the propositions and negated propositions in its field *old*.

In order to reason about the automaton construction, we use the following notation: let $Next(x)$, $Old(x)$ and $New(x)$ be the subformulas that are in the fields *next*, *old* and *new*, at a specified given point. The conjunction of a set of formulas F will be denoted by $\bigwedge F$, and similarly $\bigvee F$ denotes disjunction. If a node x is repeatedly split to obtain a node y, then x is an *ancestor of y*.

Denote $Form(x) = \bigwedge Old(x) \wedge \bigcirc \bigwedge Next(x)$, at the end of the construction. The above construction has several properties which we exploit for improving the partial order reduction. The following property [2] will be used in the sequel.

Theorem 4. *Let x be a node of the constructed automaton $\mathcal{A}$. Consider the automaton $\mathcal{A}_x$ which is otherwise like $\mathcal{A}$, but has x as its (only) initial state. Then $\mathcal{A}_x$ accepts exactly the sequences satisfying $Form(x)$. Furthermore, for the translated formula φ, $\varphi \leftrightarrow \bigvee_{x\in I} Form(x)$.*

Let $\mathrm{eff}(x)$, the *effective set* of x, be the propositions that appear in the formulas $Old(x) \cup Next(x)$. The following is obvious from the construction:

Lemma 5 Monotonicity. *Let $x \longrightarrow y$ be an edge of $\mathcal{A}$. Then $\mathrm{eff}(y) \subseteq \mathrm{eff}(x)$.*

Lemma 6. *Let x' be an ancestor node of x. If during the translation of a temporal formula into an automaton we have $\psi \in New(x')$, then at the end of the construction $Form(x) \longrightarrow \psi$.*

Proof. We prove by induction on the number of splits that for an ancestor x' of y, we have $(\bigwedge New(y) \wedge Form(y)) \rightarrow \bigwedge New(x')$. We then use the fact that at the end of the construction, the field new is empty, i.e. **True**. The inductive step of the proof is by cases. For example, let $\psi_1 \vee \psi_2$ be in $New(y)$, and y is split into y_1 and y_2 such that $\psi_1 \in New(y_1)$ and $\psi_2 \in New(y_2)$. Then, $\psi_1 \rightarrow \psi_1 \vee \psi_2$. Hence, $(\bigwedge New(y_1) \wedge Form(y_1)) \rightarrow (\bigwedge New(y) \wedge Form(y))$ and by the inductive hypothesis, $(\bigwedge New(y_1) \wedge Form(y_1)) \rightarrow \bigwedge New(x')$. The proof for node y_2 is similar. □

3 An Improved Algorithm

In Section 2.3, the properties attached to the nodes of the constructed automaton are of the form $\eta = \psi_1 \wedge \bigcirc \psi_2$, with ψ_1, ψ_2 nexttime free. It is not necessarily the case that a property $Form(x)$ attached to an automaton node x is nexttime free. For example, this is not the case when $Old(x) = p$, and $Next(x) = p \, \mathcal{U} \, q$. Then $Form(x)$ allows the sequence $(p, q), (p, q), (\neg p, \neg q), \ldots$, but does not allow the sequence $(p, q), (\neg p, \neg q), \ldots$, which is stuttering equivalent to it.

This is not a problem for the classic on-the-fly stamper set method, because it works at the level of the property. However, to prove the correctness of the new method that will be presented below, it is necessary that each node behaves correctly with respect to the set of transitions that it considers visible. Motivated by this, we investigate closer both the partial order reduction and the automaton construction.

3.1 More Insight About the Reduction

We start by defining a relation between infinite sequences that is stronger than stuttering equivalence.

Definition 7. Let ρ, $\sigma \in \Sigma^\omega$ for some finite alphabet Σ, and let $\alpha \in \Sigma$. Denote $\rho \angle \sigma$ iff there are γ and γ' such that $\rho = \alpha\gamma$, $\sigma \in \alpha^+\gamma'$, and $\gamma \equiv \gamma'$ (where $\alpha^+ = \{\alpha, \alpha\alpha, \ldots\}$). □

Note that for α, $\beta \in \Sigma$, $\alpha \neq \beta$ and $\gamma \in \Sigma^\omega$, although $\alpha\alpha\beta\gamma \equiv \alpha\beta\gamma$, it does not hold that $\alpha\alpha\beta\gamma \angle \alpha\beta\gamma$. We can now strengthen the second half of Theorem 2:

Theorem 8. *Let t be a state of the reduced state space. For each $\xi \in Seq(P, t)$, there exists a sequence $\xi' \in Red(P, t)$ such that $L(\xi) \angle L(\xi')$.*

Proof. Let s be the first state of ξ, and $L(\xi) = \alpha\gamma$. Consider first the case where $stamper(s) = enabled(s)$. Choose a transition τ such that executing τ from s results in s', which is the second state of ξ. Write $\xi = ss'\tilde{\xi}$. Then apply Theorem 2 from s', obtaining a sequence $\tilde{\xi}'$ such that $\gamma = L(s'\tilde{\xi}) \equiv L(s'\tilde{\xi}') = \gamma'$. Then, $\alpha\gamma \angle \alpha\gamma'$, hence, $L(\xi) \angle L(ss'\tilde{\xi}')$.

In the second case, we have $stamper(s) \subset enabled(s)$ and all the transitions in $stamper(s)$ are invisible. Now, according to Theorem 2, there is a sequence ξ' such that $L(\xi) \equiv L(\xi')$ constructed from s. Let $\tau \in stamper(s)$ be the first transition taken to construct ξ'. Since τ is invisible, $L(\xi')$ is of the form $\alpha\alpha\delta$. Since $L(\xi) \equiv L(\xi')$, $\alpha\gamma \equiv \alpha\alpha\delta$. Now, if γ begins with α, let $\gamma' = \alpha\delta$; otherwise, let $\gamma' = \delta^{(i)}$, where i is the smallest value such that $\delta^{(i)}$ does not begin with α. In both cases, by Definition 7, $\alpha\gamma = L(\xi) \angle L(\xi') = \alpha\alpha\delta$. $\quad\square$

Lemma 9. *Let x be a node of the automaton $\mathcal{A}$, and $\rho \angle \sigma$. If $\rho \models Form(x)$, then $\sigma \models Form(x)$.*

Proof. Let $\rho = \alpha\gamma$, with $\alpha \in \Sigma$. Consider first the case where $\sigma = \alpha\gamma'$, with $\gamma \equiv \gamma'$. Then, since both $\bigwedge Old(x)$ and $\bigwedge Next(x)$ are nexttime-free, hence closed under stuttering, we have that $\alpha\gamma \models Form(x)$ iff $\alpha\gamma' \models Form(x)$.

Consider now the case where $\sigma \in \alpha\alpha^+\gamma'$, with $\gamma \equiv \gamma'$. Since any sequence in $\alpha^+\gamma'$ is stuttering equivalent to $\alpha\gamma'$, we can use the above argument to show that $\sigma \models Form(x)$ iff $\alpha\alpha\gamma' \models Form(x)$. Thus, we obtain the claim if we prove $\alpha\alpha\gamma' \models Form(x)$ assuming that $\alpha\gamma \models Form(x)$.

Since $\bigwedge Old(x)$ is nexttime-free, we have that $\alpha\gamma \models Form(x)$ implies that $\alpha\gamma \models \bigwedge Old(x)$, which in turn implies $\alpha\alpha\gamma' \models \bigwedge Old(x)$. Any conjunct in $\bigwedge Next(x)$ can be only of the form $\mu \,\mathcal{U}\, \eta$ or $\mu \,\mathcal{V}\, \eta$. We handle only the latter; the former is similar with η replaced by μ except in $\mu \,\mathcal{U}\, \eta$. When the nexttime-free $\mu \,\mathcal{V}\, \eta$ was added to $Next(x')$, for some ancestor x' of x, η was added to $New(x')$. By Lemma 6, $Form(x) \rightarrow \eta$. Thus, $\alpha\gamma \models \eta$. Since η is nexttime-free, also $\alpha\gamma' \models \eta$. Since $\gamma \models \mu \,\mathcal{V}\, \eta$ and $\mu \,\mathcal{V}\, \eta$ is nexttime-free, $\gamma' \models \mu \,\mathcal{V}\, \eta$. Combining these, we have that $\alpha\gamma' \models \mu \,\mathcal{V}\, \eta$, and by the nexttime-freeness of $\mu \,\mathcal{V}\, \eta$, further that $\alpha\alpha\gamma' \models \mu \,\mathcal{V}\, \eta$. $\quad\square$

Consider the on-the-fly version of the stamper set algorithm. Each state of the state space is of the form $\langle s, x \rangle$, where s is a state of P and x is a state of $\mathcal{A}$. Moreover, $L(s)$ must agree with all propositions and negated propositions in the set $Old(x)$. Transition from $\langle s_1, x_1 \rangle$ to $\langle s_2, x_2 \rangle$ is only allowed when s_2 is the successor of s_1 under some atomic transition of T, x_2 is a successor of x_1 under the construction of $\mathcal{A}$, and $L(s_2)$ agrees with $Old(x_2)$. Acceptance of a combined state $\langle s, x \rangle$ equals the acceptance of the component x in $\mathcal{A}$. Initial states are of the form $\langle \iota, x \rangle$, where $x \in I$ and $L(\iota)$ agrees with $Old(x)$. The automaton $\mathcal{A}$ is the translation of the *negation* of the checked property φ. A counterexample for φ is obtained by finding a strongly connected component with at least one state for each accepting set of $\mathcal{A}$.[4]

When talking about the on-the-fly algorithm, we will use $stamper(s, x)$ to denote the stamper set used at the joint state with program component s and property component x. Similarly, we denote by $Seq(P, t, x)$ and $Red(P, t, x)$ the set of combined sequences (of system and automaton states) in the combined full and reduced state space, respectively, starting from the node $\langle t, x \rangle$. Such a sequence is accepting iff it passes through each accepting set infinitely often.

We obtain the following on-the-fly version of Theorem 8. The proof is similar to the one in [11], and uses Lemma 9.

---

[4] This can alternatively be conducted by a multiple depth-first search, with a 'separate' state space for each accepting set, implemented by adding one bit per accepting set [1].

Theorem 10. *Let $\langle t, x \rangle$ be a combined state of the on-the-fly reduced state space. For each accepting sequence ξ in $Seq(P, t, x)$ such that $L(\xi) \models Form(x)$, there exists an accepting sequence ξ' in $Red(P, t, x)$ such that $L(\xi) \angle L(\xi')$ (and hence $L(\xi') \models Form(x)$).*

3.2 An Improved Algorithm

We can now describe the improved algorithm. The only change is to relax the visibility condition. It allows reducing the set of visible transitions, according to the property component x. As the search progresses, the effective propositions in $Form(x)$ may diminish (see Lemma 5), hence less transitions remain visible.

Relative visibility If $stamper(s, x) \neq enabled(s)$, then $stamper(s, x)$ may not contain transitions that are visible w.r.t. the set of propositions $\mathrm{eff}(x)$.

Thus, in the improved algorithm, we start with a set of propositions $\mathcal{P}$, but with each state $\langle s, x \rangle$ in the reduced state space, the set of effective visible transitions is calculated with respect to $\mathrm{eff}(x)$. In Section 4 we show how this can affect the reduction. To prove the improved algorithm correct, we first give two easily provable Lemmas:

Lemma 11. *The improved algorithm finds only correct counterexamples.*

Lemma 12. *Let $\langle s_1, x_1 \rangle$, $\langle s_2, x_2 \rangle$ be two nodes in the same strongly connected component in the combined reduced state space. Then, $\mathrm{eff}(x_1) = \mathrm{eff}(x_2)$.*

The following theorem is stated with respect to the improved reduction, hence the set of joint sequences from $\langle t, x \rangle$ will be denoted by $Imp\_Red(P, t, x)$.

Theorem 13. *Let $\langle t, x \rangle$ be a combined state of the improved on-the-fly reduced state space. For each accepting sequence ξ in $Seq(P, t, x)$ such that $L(\xi) \models Form(x)$, there exists an accepting sequence ξ' in $Imp\_Red(P, t, x)$ such that $L(\xi) \angle L(\xi')$ (and hence $L(\xi') \models Form(x)$).*

Sketch of proof. By induction on the order of finishing strongly connected components. For the induction basis, consider the last finished strongly connected component. From Lemma 12, there is only one effective set of propositions labeling all the states in that component. Thus, for this component, one can simply use Theorem 10, with visible operations calculated w.r.t. that effective set.

For the inductive step, consider the current component, with edges of the form $\langle s_1, x_1 \rangle \longrightarrow \langle s_2, x_2 \rangle$, where $\langle s_1, x_1 \rangle$ is in the current strongly connected component, and $\langle s_2, x_2 \rangle$ is outside it. By the inductive hypothesis, the theorem already holds for the node $\langle s_2, x_2 \rangle$. The search of the current component uses visible operations relative to the single effective set of propositions for all of its nodes. It is modified to treat already completed searches from nodes outside the current component, such as $\langle s_2, x_2 \rangle$, as oracles about the existence of a desired sequence. Notice that the search from $\langle s_2, x_2 \rangle$ is already completed, and has a disjoint set of states from the current component. $\quad\square$

4 Case Study

The purpose of this case study is twofold: to demonstrate that relaxing visibility can yield significant savings, and to give an intuitive idea as to how and when that may be obtained. To achieve the latter goal, we chose a relatively simple example with only the necessary features for illustrating our point. Of course, its results do not generalize to all systems. A problem was that we have not yet implemented our new method and had to do the experiments by playing trickery with an existing tool. We used `ltspar`, a process-algebra-oriented stamper set tool developed by the first author [8]. It computes parallel compositions of synchronously communicating transition systems, and can also use the "transparent" (i.e., not on-the-fly) LTL-preserving stamper set method of Theorems 2 and 8 for computing a reduced parallel composition.

4.1 The Example System

The example concerns the termination of a token-ring system. The system consists of n stations, each of which is capable of sending signals out_i to the outside world and receivings commands $halt_i$ for stopping the system. A token circulates in the system, and only the station possessing it can send out-signals. The outside world can at any instant of time stop the system by sending some $halt_i$. The ith station then moves to a halted state and will not pass the token on any more. This will cause the token eventually to stop and the system to terminate.

Each of the stations is modeled by the automaton STATION$_i$ in Figure 1. In the figure, tkn_i and tkn_{i+1} denote the reception of the token from the previous station, and its delivery to the next station (for the nth one, tkn_{i+1} is replaced by tkn_1). The environment may halt the station at any time by executing $halt_i$. The label out_i denotes sending an out-signal to the environment. The edge labeled by τ corresponds to the possibility of the station deciding not to send an out-signal, although it has received the token. The station 1 initially has the token, so its initial state is 2 while the initial state of all other stations is 1.

The system is modeled by composing n instances of the station graph in parallel. We assume that communication between the stations is synchronous, so the tkn_i-transitions are executed simultaneously by stations i and $i-1$.

4.2 Encoding the Property

Informally, the property that we want to verify of the system is that it stops "soon" after it has been told to stop. More formally, we will verify that for each station i, after *any* station has received a $halt$-signal, the station i will send at most one out_i. We did the experiments in the case where $i = 1$. Except the initial position of the token, the other cases are symmetric.

The following LTL formula encodes the above property. In the formula, $halt_j$ and out_1 denote the atomic propositions "during its most recent transition, the

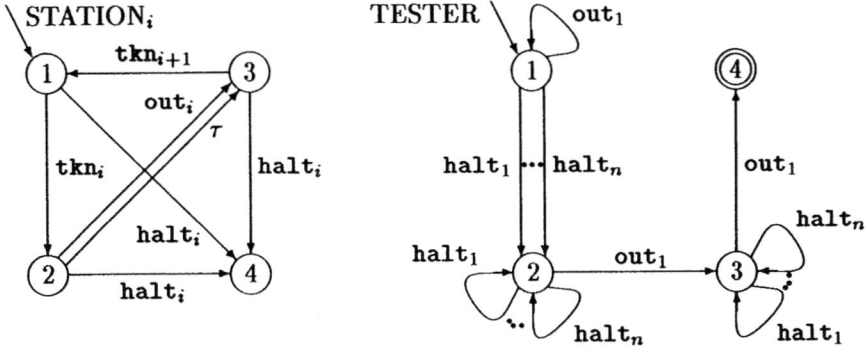

Fig. 1. The ith station process, and the tester process for n stations.

system did read / send the signal $\mathbf{halt}_j$ / $\mathbf{out}_1$".

$$\Box\left(\left(\bigvee_{j=1}^{n}\mathbf{halt}_j\right)\rightarrow\Box\left(\neg\mathbf{out}_1\vee(\mathbf{out}_1\,\mathcal{U}\,\Box\neg\mathbf{out}_1)\right)\right)$$

Unfortunately, ltspar does not contain support for Büchi automata. Therefore, we used the technique of *tester* processes [15]. We wrote a 4-state tester process, presented on the right in Figure 1, that mimics the negation of the above formula. From the point of view of partial order reductions, testers behave like ordinary processes. Their acceptance condition is different from Büchi automata, but this affects only the "reading" of the result from the reduced state space, not the partial order reduction. Relaxation of visibility affects testers the same way as Büchi automata.[5] Consequently, it was possible to do a first test of our improved on-the-fly algorithm with testers.

To test the performance of the old on-the-fly stamper set method it was sufficient just to add the tester process, declare all actions invisible, and switch the stamper set method on. To test the new method, a small source-level modification was made to ltspar, effectively cutting off the dependencies introduced by the tester when the tester is in any other state than the initial state.

4.3 Results

The measurements are shown in Table 1. The sizes of the ordinary state spaces obtained in the absence and presence of the tester process are shown in the columns labeled "full, no tester" and "full with tester". The latter sizes are what the ordinary on-the-fly method (i.e., without stamper set reduction) would yield. The number of states of the "full, no tester" case can be computed theoretically

---

[5] Actually, with testers the correctness of the relaxation is simpler to prove, because testers talk about the property in terms of transitions instead of propositional variables, and the problem with the nexttime operators needed in the construction of the Büchi automaton does not arise.

n	full, no tester states	trans.	reduced, no tester or vis. states	trans.	full with tester = old stamper states	trans.	new stamper states	trans.
2	11	24	9	16	13	25	13	25
3	31	87	17	28	42	106	36	77
4	79	268	28	43	117	367	79	165
5	191	755	42	61	300	1120	151	298
6	447	2010	59	82	731	3151	260	484
7	1023	5145	79	106	1722	8388	414	731
8	2303	12792	102	133	3961	21463	621	1047
9	5119	31095	128	163	8958	53320	889	1440
10	11263	74230	157	196	19959	129463	1226	1918
11	24575	174581	189	232	44022	308644	1640	2489

Table 1. Measurements

relatively easily, yielding $(n + 1)2^n - 1$. The "full with tester" state space sizes are more difficult to compute exactly, but they must be somewhat bigger than without the tester, because the tester adds some information of the past behavior to the state and does not restrict the behavior of the system.

The column "old stamper" was obtained in the presence of the tester using the classic on-the-fly stamper set method. The results turned out to be the same as in the column "full with tester", so these two columns were combined into one. This implies that the classic on-the-fly stamper set method gives no reduction in this example. This can be given a theoretical explanation: any station i that is ready to do something is also ready to do a halt$_i$-transition, and all halt$_i$-transitions depend on each other as they are all transitions that the tester is ready to make next, so all stamper sets contain all enabled transitions.

To see whether the absence of reduction was due to dependencies within the system, visibility, or both, we constructed also the stamper set state spaces with all transitions invisible and without the tester (remember that the presence of the tester corresponds to making the out$_1$ and halt$_i$-transitions visible). The results are shown in the column "reduced, no tester or vis." According to a theoretical analysis, the number of states is $\Theta(n^2)$. Indeed, the measured figures obey the formula $\frac{1}{2}(3n^2 + n + 4)$. The reduction is very good, so the failure of the classic on-the-fly stamper set method is apparently due to the dependencies caused by visibility.

Finally, the column "new stamper" shows the sizes with the new method. Although not as good as in the column "reduced, no tester or vis.", they are still far better than in "old stamper", demonstrating clearly the value of the new method. A theoretical analysis yields $\Theta(n^3)$ states. The measurements match $\frac{1}{6}(8n^3 - 9n^2 + 25n + 6)$ except for $n = 2$.

The results demonstrate that transition dependency caused by the property (i.e., visibility) can significantly hamper the verification of systems, but relaxation of visibility may substantially alleviate this problem.

Acknowledgement The authors would like to thank an insightful discussion of this subject with Amir Pnueli and Pierre Wolper. The work of the first author was partially funded by the Academy of Finland.

References

1. C. Courcoubetis, M. Vardi, P. Wolper, M. Yannakakis, Memory-efficient algorithms for the verification of temporal properties, *Formal Methods in System Design* 1 (1992) 275–288.
2. R. Gerth, D. Peled, M. Vardi, P. Wolper, Simple On-the-fly Automatic Verification of Linear Temporal Logic, *PSTV95, Protocol Specification Testing and Verification*, 3–18, Chapman & Hall, 1995, Warsaw, Poland.
3. P. Godefroid. Using partial orders to improve automatic verification methods. In Proc. *2nd Workshop on Computer Aided Verification*, LNCS 531, Springer-Verlag, New Brunswick, NJ, 1990, 176–185.
4. P. Godefroid, D. Pirottin, Refining dependencies improves partial order verification methods, *5th Conference on Computer Aided Verification*, Elounda, Greece, LNCS 697, Springer-Verlag, 1993, 438–449.
5. P. Godefroid, P. Wolper, A Partial Approach to Model Checking, *6th Annual IEEE Symposium on Logic in Computer Science*, 1991, Amsterdam, 406–415.
6. S. Katz, D. Peled, Verification of Distributed Programs using Representative Interleaving Sequences, *Distributed Computing* 6 (1992), 107–120.
7. S. Katz, D. Peled, Defining conditional independence using collapses, Theoretical Computer Science 101 (1992), 337–359.
8. I. Kokkarinen, *Reduction of Parallel Labelled Transition Systems with Stubborn Sets*, M. Sc. (Eng.) Thesis (in Finnish), 49 p.
9. L. Lamport, What good is temporal logic, *Information Processing 83*, Elsevier Science Publishers, 1983, 657–668.
10. D. Peled, All from one, one for all, on model-checking using representatives, *5th Conference on Computer Aided Verification*, Elounda, Greece, 1993, LNCS 697, Springer-Verlag, 409–423.
11. D. Peled. Combining partial order reductions with on-the-fly model-checking. *Formal Methods in System Design* 8 (1996), 39–64.
12. A. Pnueli, The temporal logic of programs, *18th FOCS, IEEE Symposium on Foundation of Computer Science*, 1977, 46–57.
13. A. Valmari, Stubborn sets for reduced state space generation, *10th International Conference on Application and Theory of Petri Nets*, Bonn, Germany, 1989, LNCS 483, Springer-Verlag, 491–515.
14. A. Valmari, A stubborn attack on state explosion. *Formal Methods in System Design*, 1 (1992), 297–322.
15. A. Valmari, On-the-fly Verification with Stubborn Sets, *5th Conference on Computer Aided Verification*, Elounda, Greece, 1993, LNCS 697, Springer-Verlag, 397–408.
16. B. Willems, P. Wolper, Partial-Order Methods for Model Checking: From Linear Time to Branching Time, *11th Annual IEEE Symposium on Logic in Computer Science*, 1996.

Partial-Order Reduction in Symbolic State Space Exploration*

R. Alur   R.K. Brayton   T.A. Henzinger   S. Qadeer   S.K. Rajamani

EECS Department, University of California, Berkeley, CA 94720, U.S.A.
Email: {alur, brayton, tah, shaz, sriramr}@eecs.berkeley.edu

Abstract. State space explosion is a fundamental obstacle in formal verification of designs and protocols. Several techniques for combating this problem have emerged in the past few years, among which two are significant: partial-order reductions and symbolic state space search. In asynchronous systems, interleavings of independent concurrent events are equivalent, and only a representative interleaving needs to be explored to verify local properties. Partial-order methods exploit this redundancy and visit only a subset of the reachable states. Symbolic techniques, on the other hand, capture the transition relation of a system and the set of reachable states as boolean functions. In many cases, these functions can be represented compactly using binary decision diagrams (BDDs). Traditionally, the two techniques have been practiced by two different schools—partial-order methods with enumerative depth-first search for the analysis of asynchronous network protocols, and symbolic breadth-first search for the analysis of synchronous hardware designs. We combine both approaches and develop a method for using partial-order reduction techniques in symbolic BDD-based invariant checking. We present theoretical results to prove the correctness of the method, and experimental results to demonstrate its efficacy.

1 Introduction

The number of states of a system grows exponentially with the length of its description. Commonly known as *state space explosion*, this is a fundamental problem in formal verification of systems like hardware designs, network protocols, and distributed algorithms. Techniques like model checking of temporal-logic properties, which depend on state space exploration, have been limited in their use because of this problem. A variety of heuristics have been proposed to combat state space explosion. Two significant solutions that are supported by existing tools are *symbolic model checking* and *partial-order reduction*:

- In synchronous hardware designs, state space explosion manifests itself in the number of states growing exponentially with the number of state variables in the design. Symbolic model checking [BCMD92, McM93] avoids explicit construction of the state space. The transition relation of the system and state sets are modeled as boolean functions and represented using binary decision diagrams (BDDs). Model checking of temporal-logic properties, then, reduces to symbolic fixpoint computation that uses BDD-based image computation as a primitive.

- In asynchronous systems consisting of a set of communicating concurrent processes (for example, network protocols and distributed algorithms), the behavior of the system can be

* This research was supported in part by the ONR YIP award N00014-95-1-0520, by the NSF CAREER award CCR-9501708, by the NSF grant CCR-9504469, by the AFOSR contract F49620-93-1-0056, by the ARO MURI grant DAAH-04-96-1-0341, by the ARPA grant NAG2-892, and by the Semiconductor Research Corporation contracts DC-324.036 and DC-324.005.

modeled as the set of all interleavings of the events in individual processes. One source of state space explosion are the $n!$ possible interleavings for n concurrent events. If the concurrent events are independent, then all interleavings are equivalent in that they lead to the same state. Partial-order semantics described in [Maz88] for the composition of concurrent processes group equivalent interleavings of concurrent events together into *traces*. It has been shown that sometimes it suffices to explore just one representative interleaving from each trace for verifying temporal-logic properties [Val91, Pel93, GW94]. Consequently, during state space exploration, in each state it suffices to search an *ample* subset of the enabled transitions, rather than all of them, leading to significant reduction in the explored state space for some asynchronous protocols [HP94, God96].

In this work, we address the problem of *combining* partial-order reduction methods with symbolic state space traversal for invariant checking. Such a combination is particularly useful in cases where the number of states that have to be explored remains exponential in the size of the system description, even after partial-order reduction. Consider, for example, a leader-election protocol, where the initial states of the processes are unknown. The correctness criterion asserts that *irrespective of the initial states* of the processes, the desired outcome must be ensured. Since the number of initial states is exponential in the number of processes, explicit state space search is forced to explore an exponential number of states, even with partial-order reduction. Partial-order reductions, however, give flexibility in the sets of states that need to be represented in symbolic search. Instead of computing images with the whole transition relation, it suffices to compute symbolically an ample set of successor states, or any set of successor states that contains an ample set. This flexibility adds a new dimension to heuristic techniques like modified search order [BCL91] and use of don't cares [RAP$^+$95], in symbolic state space exploration.

The following toy example illustrates the advantage of combining symbolic and partial-order methods. Consider n processes $P_1, P_2, \ldots, P_n$. Each process P_i increments a local variable x_i independent of all the other processes, until $x_i = N$, after which x_i remains equal to N. Each of the x_i's is initialized to 0. We assume interleaving semantics for process composition, that is, with each transition, only one process updates its local variable. There are n transitions out of each global state in which $x_i \neq N$ for all i. For the purpose of comparing symbolic and enumerative approaches we assume, without loss of generality, that the variable ordering is $x_1, x_2, \ldots, x_n$. A naive enumerative algorithm has to explore $O(N^n)$ states. If we perform symbolic search using MDDs^2 (multi-valued decision diagrams) on this example, the set of reached states after k steps ($k \leq N$) is defined by the relation $\sum_{i=1}^n x_i \leq k$, whose MDD representation has size $\Theta(nk)$. Suppose we are interested in checking a local invariant, such as $x_3 \leq N$. For checking such an invariant, it is not necessary to explore all transitions out of a state. In fact, using partial-order reduction, it suffices to first increment x_1 until $x_1 = N$, then increment x_2 until $x_2 = N$, and so on. Thus, the number of explored states is reduced to $O(Nn)$. Both methods improve significantly on naive state space exploration.

Moreover, if symbolic search is performed on the partial-order reduced state space, the MDD representation of the set of reached states after any number of steps has size $\Theta(n)$, which is an improvement over either method in isolation. This improvement becomes even more significant if the variables have nondeterministic initial values. Suppose that each x_i is initialized nondeterministically to either 0 or 1. An enumerative algorithm has to visit 2^n initial

---

^{2} MDDs are a generalization of BDDs in which the variables can take on values from any finite set instead of just $\{0,1\}$.

states, even with partial-order reduction.[3] In symbolic search, the set of reached states after k steps ($k \leq N$) is defined by the relation $\sum_{i=1}^{n} \langle x_i - 1 \rangle \leq k$, where $\langle x \rangle$ stands for x if $x \geq 0$, and for 0 otherwise. It can be shown that the size of the MDD representing the above relation is $\Omega(n^2 + nk)$. However, for symbolic state space traversal using the partial-order reduced transition relation, the MDD representing the set of reached states after any number of steps is only $\Theta(n)$. Similar improvements in search efficiency are obtained in two examples in Section 4—a leader-election protocol in a unidirectional ring and an asynchronous tree arbiter circuit.

Usually, partial-order reductions are implemented using a modified depth-first search algorithm. In Section 2, we show that correct partial-order reductions can be obtained on any search technique that has a certain property. Breadth-first search is shown to have this property. Consequently, partial-order reductions can be applied to symbolic search (which is inherently breadth-first). Partial-order methods explore only a subset of the enabled transitions at each state, called an *ample set*. For the automatic implementation of our method, ample sets have to be computed automatically in a symbolic setting. In Section 3, we present a symbolic version of a standard algorithm [God96] for computing ample sets.

2 Partial-Order Reduction for Breadth-First Search

In [Val91, Pel93, GW94], partial-order reductions are obtained by a modified depth-first search of the state space. We generalize their results to obtain a modified breadth-first search algorithm, which can then be used to explore the reduced state space symbolically. A similar generalization is also obtained by [CP96] in the context of mechanically verifying the partial-order reduction techniques implemented in the model checker SPIN [HP94].

A *labeled transition graph* is a 5-tuple $G = \langle V, S, \hat{S}, \Gamma, \rightarrow \rangle$ with the following components:

- A finite set V of binary *variables*.
- The set $S = 2^V$ of all possible valuations for the variables, called the *state set*.
- A set of *initial states* $\hat{S} \subseteq S$.
- A finite set Γ of *actions*.
- A *transition relation* $\rightarrow \subseteq S \times \Gamma \times S$, with the restriction that if (s, α, t) and (s, α, t') are in $\rightarrow$, then $t = t'$.

We write $s \xrightarrow{\alpha} t$ if $(s, \alpha, t) \in \rightarrow$, and $s \rightarrow t$ if there exists an action α such that $s \xrightarrow{\alpha} t$. The set of actions *enabled* in state s is defined as $enabled(s) = \{\alpha \mid \exists t. \ s \xrightarrow{\alpha} t\}$. An action sequence $\overline{\alpha} = \alpha_1 \alpha_2 \ldots \alpha_m$ in Γ^* is G-*enabled* in state s if there exist states $s_1, \ldots, s_{m-1}, t$ such that $s \xrightarrow{\alpha_1} s_1 \xrightarrow{\alpha_2} \cdots \xrightarrow{\alpha_{m-1}} s_{m-1} \xrightarrow{\alpha_m} t$. In this case, the state t is denoted by $succ(s, \overline{\alpha})$ and called the $\overline{\alpha}$-*successor* of s.

The algorithm to obtain a partial-order reduction performs a selective search. While exploring the successors of a state s, instead of considering all actions enabled in s, the algorithm chooses only a subset of the enabled actions, and thus, constructs a subgraph of the original graph. Let $G = \langle V, S, \hat{S}, \Gamma, \rightarrow \rangle$ be a labeled transition graph. A graph $G' = \langle V, S', \hat{S}, \Gamma, \rightarrow' \rangle$ is a subgraph of G if $S' \subseteq S$ and $\rightarrow' \subseteq \rightarrow$. A selective search can be specified by a function from states to subsets of actions. For a function Δ from S to 2^Γ, the subgraph

---

[3] In this particular example, since the processes are initialized independently and the behavior of the system from different initial states is identical, the system description could be modified so that enumerative search with partial-order reduction is efficient. But such a simplification is not possible in the general case.

$G_\Delta = \langle V, S_\Delta, \hat{S}, \Gamma, \to_\Delta \rangle$ of G is a *reduction* of G with respect to Δ if G_Δ is the smallest graph such that (1) $\hat{S} \subseteq S_\Delta$ and (2) for every state $s \in S_\Delta$, if $s \xrightarrow{\alpha} t$ for some $\alpha \in \Delta(s)$, then $s \xrightarrow{\alpha}_\Delta t$ and $t \in S_\Delta$. In the remainder of this section, we develop requirements on Δ so that the reduction G_Δ can be used for the verification of certain invariants.

Partial-order equivalence We proceed to define an equivalence relation over the action sequences of a labeled transition graph so that, when solving certain reachability problems, it suffices to explore only one representative from each equivalence class. The equivalence is defined using the notion of independence between actions.

Let α and β be two different actions of G. The two actions α and β are *independent*, written $\alpha \sim \beta$, if for all states $s \in S$, (1) if α is enabled in s, then β is enabled in s iff β is enabled in $succ(s, \alpha)$, (2) if β is enabled in s then, α is enabled in s iff α is enabled in $succ(s, \beta)$, and (3) if both α and β are enabled in s, then $succ(s, \alpha\beta) = succ(s, \beta\alpha)$. Intuitively, two actions are independent if they neither enable nor disable each other, and the order in which the two actions are executed does not affect the state that is reached. For every labeled transition graph G, the independence relation $\sim$ on the actions of G is irreflexive and symmetric.

For two action sequences $\overline{\gamma}$ and $\overline{\gamma}'$ of a labeled transition graph G, define $\overline{\gamma} \equiv \overline{\gamma}'$ if $\overline{\gamma} = \overline{\gamma_1}\alpha\beta\overline{\gamma_2}$ and $\overline{\gamma}' = \overline{\gamma_1}\beta\alpha\overline{\gamma_2}$, with $\alpha \sim \beta$. The *partial-order equivalence* $\equiv^*$ on the action sequences of G is the reflexive-transitive closure of $\equiv$. Intuitively, two action sequences are partial-order equivalent if one can be obtained from the other by repeatedly commuting adjacent independent actions. The set of all action sequences partial-order equivalent to an action sequence $\overline{\alpha}$ is represented by $[\overline{\alpha}]$. Such an equivalence class is called a Mazurkiewicz trace [Maz88].

Persistent functions The actions in the subset of actions selected to be explored from a state should be independent, not only of all the remaining actions enabled in state s, but also independent of all actions enabled in a state reachable from s by executing other actions. Such a subset of actions is called persistent. Formally, a function Δ from S to 2^Γ is *persistent* if for every state s of G the following holds: for all actions $\alpha \in \Delta(s)$, (1) α is enabled in s, and (2) if there is an action sequence $\overline{\beta} = \beta_1\beta_2 \ldots \beta_n \in (\Gamma \backslash \Delta(s))^*$ that is G-enabled in s, then α is independent of every action β_i in $\overline{\beta}$. We say that $\Delta(s)$ is a *persistent set* of actions at s.

A selective search based on exploring, from every state, only a persistent set of actions needs to ensure that an action is not delayed forever. Hence, if the persistent set at a state does not lead to a new state during the state space exploration, then all enabled actions need to be explored. Given a persistent function Δ, a mapping Ψ from the states of the reduction G_Δ to $\mathbb{N}$ is a *witness* for Δ if for all states s, if $\Delta(s) \neq enabled(s)$, then there exists an action $\alpha \in \Delta(s)$ such that $\Psi(succ(s, \alpha)) < \Psi(s)$. The well-foundedness of Ψ ensures that an action is not ignored everywhere in a loop. A *partial-order reduction* of G is a reduction of G with respect to a persistent function that has a witness.

Let $\overline{\alpha}$ and $\overline{\beta}$ be two action sequences. We say that $\overline{\beta}$ *subsumes* $\overline{\alpha}$ if there exists an action sequence $\overline{\gamma}$ such that $\overline{\alpha\gamma} \equiv^* \overline{\beta}$. The relationship between a graph and its partial-order reduction is captured by the following theorem, which states that every action sequence enabled in an initial state of the original graph is subsumed by some sequence enabled in the reduction.

Theorem 1. *Let s be a state in a partial-order reduction G_Δ of a labeled transition graph G, and let $\overline{\alpha}$ be an action sequence G-enabled in s. There exists an action sequence $\overline{\beta}$ that is G_Δ-enabled in s such that $\overline{\alpha}$ is subsumed by $\overline{\beta}$.*

```
σ_new := Ŝ
repeat
    /* σ is the current set of reached states */
    σ := σ_new
    Frontier F := {s ∈ σ | ∃t ∉ σ. s → t}
    Let Δ(s) be an ample set at s with respect to the history τ_B(s), for every s ∈ F
    σ_next := ∪_{s∈F} {t | ∃α ∈ Δ(s). s →^α t}
    σ_new := σ ∪ σ_next
until σ = σ_new
```

Fig. 1. Modified breadth-first search algorithm

Ample functions To compute partial-order reductions, we need persistent functions that can be shown to have witnesses. For this purpose, we consider a special class of persistent functions, called ample functions, which facilitate the construction of witnesses by taking into account the set of states visited so far during the selective search. A *history function* τ is a map from S to 2^S. We say that $\tau(s)$ is the *history* of s. A persistent function Δ is *ample* with respect to a history function τ if for every state s, either $\Delta(s) = enabled(s)$, or there is an action $\alpha \in \Delta(s)$ such that $succ(s, \alpha) \notin \tau(s)$. Thus, an ample function insists on exploring all enabled transitions or visiting some new state, which is not in the current history. If Δ is an ample function with respect to the history function τ, then $\Delta(s)$ is called an *ample set* at state s with respect to τ. Next, we define a history function τ_B and a numbering Ψ_B for breadth-first search so that Ψ_B is a witness for *any* ample function with respect to τ_B.

Partial-order reduction with breadth-first search The algorithm for constructing a partial-order reduction during BFS is a variation of the standard BFS algorithm. The idea is to use the current set of reached states as the history of a state. Further, since our aim is to perform the BFS symbolically, we simultaneously explore *all* states that are reachable in one step by the ample set of actions in the current frontier. More formally, let R_k be the set of reached states after the kth reachability step ($R_0 = \hat{S}$). Then define $\tau_B(s)$ as follows. If $s \in R_0$ then $\tau_B(s) = R_0$, else if $s \in R_{k+1} \backslash R_k$ then $\tau_B(s) = R_{k+1}$ (if $s \notin R_k$ for all k, the value of $\tau_B(s)$ is irrelevant). The pseudo code for the modified BFS algorithm is given in Figure 1.

Let G_B be the reduction of G with respect to the ample function chosen by the modified BFS. There are two types of states in the reduced state graph G_B—interior states that are never part of any search frontier, and frontier states that are part of some frontier exactly once. We define the mapping Ψ_B from the states of G_B to $\mathbb{N}$ as follows: (1) if s is never part of any frontier then $\Psi_B(s) = 1$, and (2) if s is part of the kth frontier and the total number of frontiers is N, then $\Psi_B(s) = N - k + 2$. Figure 2 illustrates the mapping Ψ_B for a reduced state graph with 4 frontiers. The shaded areas are the frontiers and the unshaded areas are the interior states. To prove that the modified BFS algorithm constructs a partial-order reduction G_B, it suffices to establish that the numbering Ψ_B is a witness for the ample function chosen by the algorithm.

Lemma 2. *Let Δ be an ample function with respect to the history function τ_B. If $\Delta(s) \neq enabled(s)$, then for some action $\alpha \in \Delta(s)$, we have $\Psi_B(succ(s, \alpha)) < \Psi_B(s)$.*

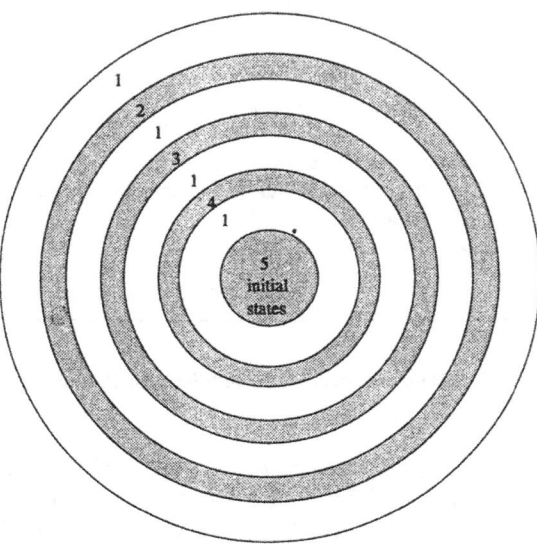

Fig. 2. Witness Ψ_B for states during BFS expansion

Theorem 3. *If G_B is the reduced graph obtained by the modified BFS algorithm from Figure 1, then G_B is a partial-order reduction of G.*

We note that depth-first search can also be used to construct a partial-order reduction. For this purpose, the set of states in the stack can be used as a history function [God96].

Verification using partial-order reductions Partial-order reductions are sound and complete for checking the invariance of local properties. We formalize local properties as independence-preserving regions. If there is an action sequence that originates at an initial state and leads to an independence-preserving region, then there exists some action sequence in any partial-order reduction that leads to the same region. A set $\sigma \subseteq S$ of states of a labeled transition graph G is an *independence-preserving region* if for all initial states s, whenever $succ(s, \overline{\alpha}) \in \sigma$ and $\overline{\beta}$ subsumes $\overline{\alpha}$, then there exists a prefix $\overline{\gamma}$ of $\overline{\beta}$ such that $succ(s, \overline{\gamma}) \in \sigma$. It follows that to verify that the given graph G satisfies an invariant σ (that is, no state outside σ is reachable in G), we can check whether some partial-order reduction of G satisfies the invariant σ, provided $S \backslash \sigma$ is an independence-preserving region of G.

3 Symbolic Computation of Ample Sets

Symbolic techniques capture transition sets and state sets of a labeled transition graph as boolean functions. The boolean functions are represented and manipulated as BDDs [BCMD92, McM93]. The functional representation of the transition relation is denoted by T, where $T(s, \alpha, t)$ is true iff $s \xrightarrow{\alpha} t$. Note that the BDD for T is built with variables that encode the present state, the next state, and the actions of G (these variables should not be confused with the variables of the labeled transition graph). In BFS, we denote the set of reached states by σ. First, we initialize σ to be the set of initial states. Second, the image σ_{new} of σ under T is computed:

```
σ_new := BDD representing Ŝ
repeat
     /* σ is the current set of reached states */
     σ := σ_new
     F := BDD representing the frontier of σ
     T^A := BDD representing the ample transition relation with respect to the history σ
     σ_next := image of F under T^A
     σ_new := σ ∨ σ_next
until σ = σ_new
```

Fig. 3. BDD-based modified breadth-first search algorithm

$\sigma_{new}(s) = \exists t.\exists\alpha.(\sigma(t) \land T(t,\alpha,s))$. The set of states that can be reached by the system in at most one step from σ is represented by $\sigma \lor \sigma_{new}$. The image computations are iterated until a fixpoint is reached. This fixpoint then represents the set of all reachable states. Figure 3 shows the modified BFS algorithm from Figure 1 (with partial-order reduction) rewritten with BDD operations. To implement this algorithm we need to produce an *ample transition relation* T^A at each reachability step.

A *persistent transition relation* T^P is a BDD encoding of a persistent function Δ such that $T^P(s,\alpha,t)$ iff $\alpha \in \Delta(s)$ and $s \xrightarrow{\alpha} t$. An ample transition relation T^A with respect to the history σ can be computed from T^P as

$$T^A(s,\alpha,t) = T^P(s,\alpha,t) \lor \left(\neg\exists\alpha'.\exists t'.(T^P(s,\alpha',t') \land \neg\sigma(t')) \land T(s,\alpha,t)\right).$$

It remains to be seen how we compute the persistent transition relation T^P. We now show that a heuristic for computing persistent sets in [God96] can be implemented symbolically to yield a persistent transition relation. We assume a model of the transition system annotated with processes and give a symbolic procedure for computing persistent sets in this model.

A *process structure* is a structured description of a labeled transition graph. Formally, it is a 4-tuple $\mathcal{P} = \langle \mathbb{P}, G, own, exec \rangle$ with the following components:

- A finite set $\mathbb{P} = \{p_1, p_2, \ldots, p_n\}$ of processes.
- A labeled transition graph $G = \langle V, S, \hat{S}, \Gamma, \rightarrow \rangle$.
- A function *own* from V to $\mathbb{P}$. We say that a variable v is *owned* by process $own(v)$.
- A function *exec* from Γ to $\mathbb{P}$, with the following restriction: for all states s and t, all actions α, and all variables v, if $s \xrightarrow{\alpha} t$ and v changes value from s to t, then $own(v) = exec(\alpha)$. We say that action α is *executed* by process $exec(\alpha)$.

Observe that in this model, variables are read-shared, but write-exclusive. We write $act(p_i)$ to denote the set $\{\alpha \mid exec(\alpha) = p_i\}$ of actions that are executed by process p_i. Since each action is executed by exactly one process, *act* induces a partition on the set Γ of actions. We differentiate between *global state* (valuations for all variables) and *local state* of a process (valuations for the variables owned by the process). A global state s is an n-tuple $(s_1, s_2, \ldots, s_n)$ of local states s_i, one for each process $p_i \in \mathbb{P}$. We say that s_i is the local state of process p_i in s. An action $\alpha \in act(p_i)$ is *enabled in the local state* s_i of process p_i if there exists a global state s containing s_i such that α is enabled in s.

```
/* Let s = (s₁, s₂, ..., sₙ) be the given global state */
P(s) := {pₖ}, where pₖ is some process enabled in s
repeat
    for every process pᵢ ∈ P(s) and every action α ∈ act(pᵢ) enabled in sᵢ do
        for every process pⱼ ∉ P(s) do
            if there exists an action β ∈ act(pᵢ) such that β is dependent with α then
                P(s) := P(s) ∪ {pⱼ}
            fi
        end
    end
until no more processes can be added to P(s)
```

Fig. 4. Algorithm for computing a persistent set $P(s)$ at state s

The algorithm for computing persistent sets is sketched in Figure 4. Given a state s, the algorithm finds a set of processes $P(s) \subseteq \mathbb{P}$ such that the set of actions executed by the processes in $P(s)$ is a persistent set at s. First, we initialize $P(s)$ with an arbitrary process p_k that executes an action enabled in s. Then we iteratively add more processes to $P(s)$, as follows, until no more processes can be added: for all processes $p_i \in P(s)$ and actions $\alpha \in act(p_i)$ that are enabled in the local state s_i of process p_i, we add process p_j to $P(s)$ if $act(p_j)$ executes an action β that is dependent with α. We call the resulting set $P(s)$ a *persistent set of processes* at s. The algorithm described above checks only a sufficient condition for persistence; it is possible to formulate more complex schemes that yield smaller persistent sets [God96].

Our aim is to compute a boolean function I such that $I(s, p)$ is true iff $p \in P(s)$ for the global state s. In effect, I encodes persistent sets of processes for all global states. For computing I, we make use of the following pre-computed relations:

- $enabledG(s, \alpha)$ is true iff action α is enabled in the global state s.
- $actionof(\alpha, p)$ is true iff $exec(\alpha) = p$.
- $enabledL(s, \alpha, p)$ is true iff $exec(\alpha) = p$ and α is enabled in the local state of p in s:

$$enabledL((s_1, s_2, s_3, ..., s_n), \alpha, p) = \bigvee_{1 \le i \le n}((p = p_i) \Rightarrow \\ \exists s_1' ... s_{i-1}' s_{i+1}' ... s_n'. \\ enabledG((s_1', s_2', ..., s_{i-1}', s_i, s_{i+1}', ..., s_n'), \alpha)).$$

- $dependent(\alpha, \beta)$ is true iff actions α and β are dependent. The dependence relation can be overapproximated by sufficient syntactic checks (e.g., disjointness of support variables) [God96].

For all i, $1 \le i \le n$, we compute $J_i(s, p)$ as follows:

$$J_i(s, p) = (p = p_i) \wedge \exists \alpha.(actionof(\alpha, p_i) \wedge enabledG(s, \alpha)).$$

The relation $J_i(s, p)$ is true iff $p = p_i$ and $act(p_i)$ contains at least action enabled in s. We then perform a fixpoint computation to compute the relation $I(s, p)$ as follows:

$$I_0(s, p) = J_1(s, p) \vee \\ (\neg \exists p.J_1(s, p) \wedge J_2(s, p)) \vee \\ (\neg \exists p.(J_1(s, p) \vee J_2(s, p)) \wedge J_3(s, p)) \vee ... \\ (\neg \exists p.(J_1(s, p) \vee J_2(s, p) \vee ... \vee J_{n-1}(s, p)) \wedge J_n(s, p)),$$

348

$$I_{k+1}(s,p) = I_k(s,p) \vee$$
$$\exists p'.\exists \alpha.\exists \beta.(I_k(s,p') \wedge enabledL(s,\alpha,p') \wedge actionof(\alpha',p) \wedge dependent(\alpha,\beta)).$$

The relation $I_0(s,p)$ is true iff p is the process of least index that executes an action enabled in state s. The computation of I_{k+1} from I_k mimics the repeat-until loop of the algorithm in Figure 4. Then, the desired relation I is I_m for the smallest m such that $I_{m+1} = I_m$. Now the persistent transition relation T^P can be computed from I as follows:

$$T^P(s,\alpha,t) = \exists p.(I(s,p) \wedge actionof(\alpha,p)) \wedge T(s,\alpha,t).$$

4 Experiments

We consider two examples for experiments—a protocol for electing a leader among a set of processes and an asynchronous tree arbiter circuit. In both cases, we built Verilog models for the original system as well as the reduced system obtained by considering only those actions from a state that form an ample set. To impose interleaving semantics on a Verilog description, we added a scheduler to the model which nondeterministically schedules one process at a time. The symbolic reachability computation was performed with VIS [BHSV+96]. The ample sets were manually computed as functions of global states and implemented using an "ample scheduler" that nondeterministically chooses one among a subset of enabled processes (corresponding to the ample set) at each state. While the algorithm given in Section 3 can be used to compute the ample sets automatically, the computations require the identification of actions in the representation of transition systems, which VIS does not support at present. The purpose of the experiments is to investigate if savings in BDD sizes could be obtained, if such ample sets were available, and the answer is in the affirmative.

4.1 Leader-election protocol

We consider the leader-election protocol described in [DKR82]. Extensive reduction in reachable state space sizes for this problem is reported by [HP94], using partial-order reductions with enumerative depth-first search of the state space.

There are N processes connected in a circular ring, with a finite FIFO unidirectional queue between adjacent processes. Each process has a unique id associated with it. A process receives messages from the queue immediately before it in the ring and can send messages to the queue immediately after it. Process p_i has a variable called $active_i$ associated with it. Initially, $active_i = 1$ for all processes. The objective of the protocol is to elect a unique leader process p_k such that $active_k = 1$. The messages put on the FIFO queues contain id's of processes currently active. Initially, each process sends its id to the next process and receives the id of the preceding process. Every process remembers the maximum id it has seen so far. As a result of comparing received process id's to the maximum id, a process may deactivate itself. Finally, only one process should remain active. To check the property that finally a unique leader exists using an independence-preserving invariant, we introduce a variable called $flag_i$ for each process p_i. As soon as process p_k knows that it is the leader, it asserts $flag_k$ and $flag_k$ does not change thereafter. The independence-preserving invariants to be checked are $\neg(flag_i \wedge flag_j)$, for all $i \neq j$.[4]

A process is enabled if there is at least one message in its input queue and at least one empty slot in its output queue. In every state, every enabled process has precisely one enabled

---

[4] This, of course, is not a complete specification of the protocol. A liveness property stating that eventually a process does become the leader is also needed.

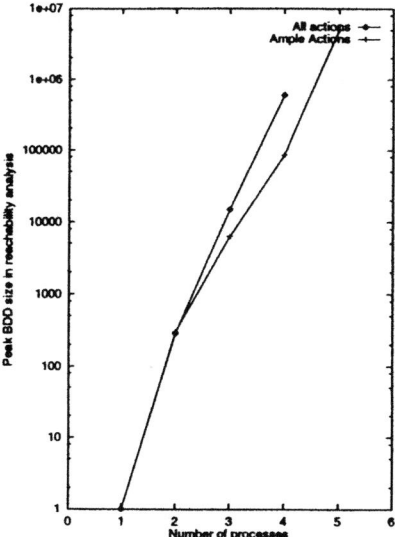

Fig. 5. Leader-election protocol: peak BDD sizes needed for reachability analysis

action. For each state, we consider the singleton set consisting of the action that is owned by the process with least index among the enabled processes. This set is a non-empty persistent set, because the protocol has the property that if multiple processes are enabled at the same time, the order in which the processes execute actions does not change the eventual outcome. The transition graph of the protocol is acyclic and hence every persistent set is ample.

Exponential partial-order reductions on this example are reported in [HP94] for a ring of 5 processes. There, however, the id's of the processes are assumed to be initialized to 0, 1, 2, 3, and 4 in circular order around the ring. Though the protocol is verified for this initial state, it is not verified for other initial states. For instance, if the id's are 0, 4, 1, 3, and 2, then the behavior of the protocol is very different. The former initialization requires a total of 15 messages passed around the ring before a leader is elected, whereas the latter requires 25 messages. In fact, there are certain lines of code in the protocol that are never exercised in the former case but are exercised in the latter. Our method verifies the correctness claim as stated in [DKR82], for *all* initial states.

Figure 5 shows the growth of peak BDD size during reachability analysis versus the number of processes. Two curves are shown—one for the entire transition relation and another for the ample transition relation. Note that reachability analysis with the entire transition relation runs out of memory for 5 processes. With partial-order reduction, in the case of 5 processes, VIS reports 3.76×10^{15} states visited. Thus, in this example, partial-order reduction coupled with symbolic search performs better than either method in isolation.

4.2 Asynchronous tree arbiter

The tree arbiter is an asynchronous circuit which solves the mutual-exclusion problem by building a tree of arbiter cells. The circuit does the arbitration in the form of an elimination tournament. An arbiter cell arbitrates between its two children. The leaves in the tree are processors that asynchronously demand access to a common resource. The n users at the

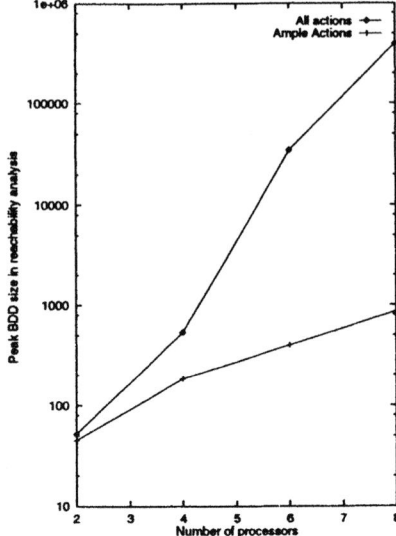

Fig. 6. Tree arbiter: peak BDD sizes needed for reachability analysis

lowest level in the tree are arbitrated by $\frac{n}{2}$ cells. The winners at this level are arbitrated at the next level and so on. If both children of an arbiter cell request, one of them is chosen nondeterministically. The requests propagate upward in the tree until the root cell is reached. It grants the resource to at most one of its children and the grant propagates downward to one of the processors. Similarly, when the resource is released by a processor, the request for release goes all the way up and is acknowledged all the way down. We model the arbiter cells as interacting asynchronously with each other. Four-phase signaling is used for communication between the arbiter cells. The circuit is verified in [Dil89].

We label all processes (processors and arbiter cells) by levels, starting at the leaves: at the lowest level, label the processors from left to right with the leftmost processor having the least label; then label the first level of arbiters from left to right; etc. Given such a labeling, it can be shown that at each state, the singleton set containing the enabled process with the least label is an ample set. Figure 6 shows the BDD sizes during reachability analysis, for the entire transition relation and the ample transition relation (8 processors induce a tree with three levels of arbitration). Note the log scale on the vertical axis of the plot. The memory requirement for the entire transition relation grows exponentially with the number of processors, whereas the memory for the ample transition relation grows polynomially. The difference in memory consumption also manifests itself in run time: for 8 processors, reachability analysis with the entire transition relation requires 1755 seconds, whereas the ample transition relation requires less than 1 second to complete.

4.3 Utilizing flexibility as "don't cares"

We implemented a new command in VIS called *ample_reach* that takes two transition relations (an ample transition relation and the entire transition relation) and does the following. At each step during reachability analysis, two images are computed, using the two transition relations. The image obtained by the ample transition relation is always a subset of the image obtained by the entire transition relation. Then, two new reached sets are computed, by taking the union of each of the two images with the reached set from the previous step. Finally, a heuristic BDD minimization function is called from the BDD package, to minimize the representation of a set that lies between the two reached sets. In both of the above examples, the heuristic minimization always returned the smaller reached set, that is, the one obtained from the ample transition relation. We believe that the reason for this is the exponential reduction in the number of states obtained using ample sets. However, if a system has asynchronous components operating with limited independence and there is limited partial-order reduction, this method might prove to be useful.

Acknowledgments Gerard Holzmann provided us with information on SPIN. Ken McMillan and Doron Peled contributed through discussions. The VIS group at UC Berkeley and Rajeev Ranjan in particular helped with the experiments.

References

[BCL91] J.R. Burch, E.M. Clarke, and D.E. Long. Symbolic Model Checking with Partitioned Transition Relations. In *Proc. of the 28th Design Automation Conference*, pages 403–407, 1991.
[BCMD92] J.R. Burch, E.M. Clarke, K.L. McMillan, and D.L. Dill. Symbolic Model Checking: 10^{20} States and Beyond. *Information and Computation*, 98:142–170, 1992.
[BHSV+96] R.K. Brayton, G.D. Hachtel, A. Sangiovanni-Vincentelli, F. Somenzi, A. Aziz, S.-T. Cheng, S. Edwards, S. Khatri, Y. Kukimoto, A. Pardo, S. Qadeer, R.K. Ranjan, S. Sarwary, T.R. Shiple, G. Swamy, and T. Villa. VIS: A System for Verification and Synthesis. In *Proc. of the 8th International Conference on Computer-Aided Verification*, vol. 1102 of *Lecture Notes in Computer Science*, pages 428–432. Springer, 1996.
[CP96] C.-T. Chou and D.A. Peled. Formal Verification of a Partial-Order Reduction Technique for Model Checking. In *Proc. of the Second International Workshop on Tools and Algorithms for the Construction and Analysis of Systems*, vol. 1055 of *Lecture Notes in Computer Science*, pages 241–257. Springer, 1996.
[Dil89] D.L. Dill. *Trace Theory for Automatic Hierarchical Verification of Speed-Independent Circuits*. MIT Press, 1989.
[DKR82] D. Dolev, M. Klawe, and M. Rodeh. An $O(n \log n)$ Unidirectional Distributed Algorithm for Extrema Finding in a Circle. *Journal of Algorithms*, 3:245–260, 1982.
[God96] P. Godefroid. *Partial-Order Methods for the Verification of Concurrent Systems: An Approach to the State-Explosion Problem*, vol. 1032 of *Lecture Notes in Computer Science*. Springer, 1996.
[GW94] P. Godefroid and P. Wolper. A Partial Approach to Model Checking. *Information and Computation*, 110:305–326, 1994.
[HP94] G.J. Holzmann and D.A. Peled. An Improvement in Formal Verification. In *Proc. of the 7th International Conference on Formal Description Techniques*, pages 197–211. Chapman & Hall, 1994.
[Maz88] A. Mazurkiewicz. Basic Notions of Trace Theory. In *Workshop on Linear Time, Branching Time, and Partial Order in Logics and Models for Concurrency*, vol. 354 of *Lecture Notes in Computer Science*, pages 285–363. Springer, 1988.
[McM93] K.L. McMillan. *Symbolic Model Checking*. Kluwer Academic Publishers, 1993.
[Pel93] D.A. Peled. All from One, One for All: On Model Checking Using Representatives. In *Proc. of the 5th International Conference on Computer-Aided Verification*, vol. 697 of *Lecture Notes in Computer Science*, pages 409–423. Springer, 1993.
[RAP+95] R.K. Ranjan, A. Aziz, B. Plessier, C. Pixley, and R.K. Brayton. Efficient Formal Design Verification: Data Structures + Algorithms. In *Workshop Notes of the International Workshop on Logic Synthesis*, 1995.
[Val91] A. Valmari. Stubborn Sets for Reduced State Space Generation. In *Advances in Petri Nets*, vol. 483 of *Lecture Notes in Computer Science*, pages 491–515. Springer, 1991.

Deadlock Checking Using Net Unfoldings*

Stephan Melzer and Stefan Römer**

Abstract. McMillan presented a deadlock detection technique based on unfoldings of Petri net systems. It is realized by means of a backtracking algorithm that has its drawback for unfoldings that increase widely. We present an approach that exploits precisely this property. Moreover, we introduce a fast implementation of McMillan's algorithm and compare it with our new technique.

1 Introduction

In the field of static analysis of concurrent systems deadlock freeness is almost always a desirable property. Many research has been carried out to propose methods that check this property [3]. One of these was presented by McMillan in [8]. It is based on net unfoldings of Petri net systems. A net unfolding is class of partial order semantics of Petri nets, also known as branching process [4]. The heuristic used in McMillan's algorithm is particularly good where the unfolding grows more deeply than widely and thereby only few end points of the unfolding (i.e., cut-off points) have to be considered. These kinds of unfoldings correspond to systems with a more deterministic behaviour. In contrast, highly non-deterministic systems tend to yield *wide* unfoldings that slow McMillan's algorithm down.

We introduce an approach that exploits the characteristic of wide unfoldings (i.e., the number of cut-off points is high). Moreover, we present an implementation of McMillan's algorithm and compare both approaches by means of several examples. We use Corbett's benchmark examples [3] as well as McMillan's examples [8] which allows a direct comparison between his LISP implementation and our carried out in C [12].

The paper is organized as follows: In section 2 we give a brief introduction of the basic concepts of Petri nets and net unfoldings. In this section we fall back on the introduction given in [5]. Section 3 presents the deadlock detection method using a linear algebraic approach. In section 4 we give an implementation of McMillan's deadlock algorithm [8]. In section 5 we show some results and compare both approaches. Section 6 serves as a conclusion and gives an outlook on further work. All proofs are presented in appendix A.

---

* This work was supported by the Sonderforschungsbereich SFB-342 A3 SAM.
** Institut für Informatik, Technische Universität München,
  e-mail: {melzers,roemer}@informatik.tu-muenchen.de

2   Basic Definitions

2.1   Petri Nets

A triple (P, T, F) is a *net* if P and T are disjoint sets and F is a subset of $(P \times T) \cup (T \times P)$. The elements of P are called *places* and the elements of T *transitions*. Places and transitions are generically called *nodes*. We identify F with its characteristic function on the set $(P \times T) \cup (T \times P)$. The *preset* of a node x, denoted by ${}^\bullet x$, is the set $\{y \in P \cup T \mid F(y, x) = 1\}$. The *postset* of x, denoted by $x^\bullet$, is the set $\{y \in P \cup T \mid F(x, y) = 1\}$. The generalization on sets of nodes $X \subseteq P \cup T$ is defined as ${}^\bullet X = \bigcup_{x \in X} {}^\bullet x$, respectively $X^\bullet = \bigcup_{x \in X} x^\bullet$. A *marking* M of a net (P, T, F) is a mapping $M : P \to \mathbb{N}$. We identify a marking M with the multiset containing $M(p)$ copies of p for every $p \in P$. A four-tuple $\Sigma = (P, T, F, M_0)$ is a *net system* if (P, T, F) is a net and M_0 is a marking of (P, T, F) (called the *initial marking* of Σ). A marking M *enables* a transition t if $\forall p \in P \colon F(p, t) \leq M(p)$. If t is enabled at M, then it can *occur*, and its occurrence leads to a new marking M' (denoted $M \xrightarrow{t} M'$), defined by $M'(p) = M(p) - F(p, t) + F(t, p)$ for every place p. A sequence of transitions $\sigma = t_1 t_2 \ldots t_n$ is an *occurrence sequence* if there exist markings $M_1, M_2, \ldots, M_n$ such that $M_0 \xrightarrow{t_1} M_1 \xrightarrow{t_2} \ldots M_{n-1} \xrightarrow{t_n} M_n$. M_n is the marking reached by the occurrence of σ, also denoted by $M_0 \xrightarrow{\sigma} M_n$. M is a *reachable marking* if there exists an occurrence sequence σ such that $M_0 \xrightarrow{\sigma} M$.

A marking M of a net is *n-safe* if $M(p) \leq n$ for every place p. A net system Σ is n-safe if all its reachable markings are n-safe.

A net system is called *deadlock-free* if every reachable marking enables at least one transition.

In this paper only nets with a finite number of places and transitions are considered. Moreover we assume that all transitions have neither an empty preset nor an empty postset.

2.2   Occurrence Nets

Let (P, T, F) be a net and let $x_1, x_2 \in P \cup T$. The nodes x_1 and x_2 are in *conflict*, denoted by $x_1 \# x_2$, if there exist distinct transitions $t_1, t_2 \in T$ such that ${}^\bullet t_1 \cap {}^\bullet t_2 \neq \emptyset$, and (t_1, x_1), (t_2, x_2) belong to the reflexive and transitive closure of F. In other words, x_1 and x_2 are in conflict if there exist two paths leading to x_1 and x_2 which start at the same place and immediately diverge (although later on they can converge again). For $x \in P \cup T$, x is in *self-conflict* if $x \# x$.

An *occurrence net* is a net $N = (B, E, F)$ such that:

- for every $b \in B$, $|{}^\bullet b| \leq 1$,
- F is acyclic, i.e. the (irreflexive) transitive closure of F is a partial order,
- N is finitely preceded, i.e., for every $x \in B \cup E$, the set of elements $y \in B \cup E$ such that (y, x) belongs to the transitive closure of F is finite, and
- no element $e \in E$ is in self-conflict.

The elements of B and E are called *conditions* and *events*, respectively. $Min(N)$ denotes the set of minimal elements of $B \cup E$ with respect to the transitive closure of F.

The (irreflexive) transitive closure of F is called the *causal relation*, and denoted by $<$. The symbol $\leq$ denotes the reflexive and transitive closure of F. Given two nodes $x, y \in B \cup E$, we say $x \, co \, y$ if neither $x < y$ nor $y < x$ nor $x \# y$.

2.3 Branching Processes

Branching processes are "unfoldings" of net systems containing information about both concurrency and conflicts. They were introduced by Engelfriet in [4]. We quickly review the main definitions and results of [4].

Let $N_1 = (P_1, T_1, F_1)$ and $N_2 = (P_2, T_2, F_2)$ be two nets. A *homomorphism* from N_1 to N_2 is a mapping $h: P_1 \cup T_1 \to P_2 \cup T_2$ such that:

- $h(P_1) \subseteq P_2$ and $h(T_1) \subseteq T_2$, and
- for every $t \in T_1$, the restriction of h to ${}^\bullet t$ is a bijection between ${}^\bullet t$ (in N_1) and ${}^\bullet h(t)$ (in N_2), and similarly for $t^\bullet$ and $h(t)^\bullet$.

In other words, a homomorphism is a mapping that preserves the nature of nodes and the environment of transitions.

A *branching process* of a net system $\Sigma = (N, M_0)$ is a pair $\beta = (N', h)$ where $N' = (B, E, F)$ is an occurrence net, and h is a homomorphism from N' to N such that

(i) The restriction of h to $Min(N')$ is a bijection between $Min(N')$ and M_0,
(ii) for every $e_1, e_2 \in E$, if ${}^\bullet e_1 = {}^\bullet e_2$ and $h(e_1) = h(e_2)$ then $e_1 = e_2$.

2.4 Configurations and Cuts

The central concept of branching processes is that of a configuration. It describes a possible partial run of an occurrence net. Accordingly, a configuration contains the whole history of the partial run, i.e., all events that have to occur during the run. Moreover, a configuration has to be conflict-free, because events that are in conflict lead to divergence which does not represent a single partial run. More precisely: A *configuration* C of an occurrence net is a set of events satisfying the two conditions: (i) C is causally closed, i.e., $e \in C \Rightarrow \forall e' \leq e : e' \in C$; (ii) C is conflict-free, i.e., $\forall e, e' \in C : \neg(e \# e')$.

A set B' of conditions of an occurrence net is a *co-set* if its elements are pairwise in *co* relation. A maximal co-set B' with respect to set inclusion is called a *cut*. Finite configurations and cuts are tightly related. Let C be a finite configuration of a branching process $\beta = (N, h)$. Then the co-set $Cut(C)$, defined below, is a cut: $Cut(C) = (Min(N) \cup C^\bullet) \setminus {}^\bullet C$. In particular, given a finite configuration C the set[3] of places $h(Cut(C))$ is a reachable marking, which we denote by $Mark(C)$.

---

[3] Remember that this is a multiset.

A marking M of a system Σ is *represented* in a branching process β of Σ if β contains a finite configuration C such that $Mark(C) = M$. It is easy to prove that every marking represented in a branching process is reachable, and that every reachable marking is represented in the unfolding of the net system.

In order to calculate a finite prefix of a branching process, a termination condition is required where the construction of the unfolding can be stopped. If an event is reached during the construction where something would be unfolded which is already represented in the already unfolded prefix, then the construction can be aborted at this event. We call these events *cut-off events*. More precisely: For a given event e, we define the local configuration $[e]$ by the set of all events e' such that $e' \leq e$. Moreover, we call an event a *cut-off* event of a branching process β if β contains a local configuration $[e']$ such that the corresponding markings are equal, i.e., $Mark([e]) = Mark([e'])$ and the configurations $[e']$ is smaller[4] than $[e]$, i.e., $[e'] \subset [e]$.

We say that a branching process β of a net system Σ is *complete* if and only if for every reachable marking M there exists a configuration C in β without any cut-off event such that:

- $Mark(C) = M$ (i.e., M is represented in β), and
- for every transition t enabled by M there exists a configuration $C \cup \{e\}$ such that $e \notin C$ and e is labelled by t.

Figure 1 shows a 1-safe net system (part (a)), a branching process (b) and a complete and finite prefix (c), where e_3, e_5 and e_6 are cut-off events. The homomorphism h is indicated by the corresponding place/transition names inside the nodes. Hereby, the set $\{e_1, e_3, e_4\}$ is a configuration while $\{e_1, e_2, e_3, e_4\}$ has a conflict and is thereby not a configuration.

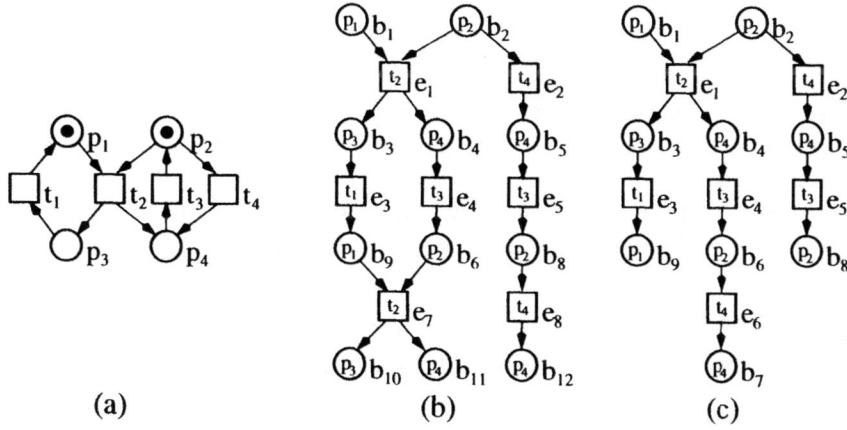

(a)   (b)   (c)

Fig. 1. A net system and two of its branching processes.

---

[4] In [5] a more precise definition of 'smaller' is given yielding a total order on configurations. For sake of simplicity we use the definition of McMillan [8].

Theorem 1. *Let $\Sigma = (P, T, F, M_0)$ be an n-safe net system. There exists a finite and complete branching process Unf_Σ of Σ.*

Proof. See [8] for the n-safe case and [5] for an improvement of the 1-safe case.

In the sequel we use the term *unfolding* to denote Unf_Σ if Σ is given by the context.

3 A new Method based on Linear Algebra

Each place p of a net is associated with a *token conservation* equation. Given an occurrence sequence $M_0 \xrightarrow{\sigma} M$, the number of tokens that p contains at the marking M is equal to the number of tokens it contains at M_0, plus the tokens added by (the firings of) the input transitions of p, minus the tokens removed by the output transitions. If we denote by $\nu(\sigma, t)$ the number of occurrences of a transition t in σ, then we can write the *token conservation* equation for p as:

$$M(p) = M_0(p) + \sum_{t \in \,^\bullet p} \nu(\sigma, t) F(t, p) - \sum_{t \in p^\bullet} \nu(\sigma, t) F(p, t).$$

The token conservation equations for every place are usually written in the following matrix form: $M = M_0 + \mathbf{N}. \overrightarrow{\sigma}$, where $\overrightarrow{\sigma} = (\nu(\sigma, t_1), \ldots, \nu(\sigma, t_m))$ is called the *Parikh vector* of σ, and $\mathbf{N}$ denotes the *incidence matrix* of N, a $P \times T$ integer matrix given by $\mathbf{N}(p, t) = F(p, t) - F(t, p)$.

If a given marking M is reachable from M_0, then there exists a sequence σ satisfying $M_0 \xrightarrow{\sigma} M$. So the following problem has at least one solution, namely $X := \overrightarrow{\sigma}$.

> *Variables: X: integer.*
> $M = M_0 + \mathbf{N}.X$
> $X \geq 0$

The equation $M = M_0 + \mathbf{N}.X$ (and, by extension, the whole problem) is called the *marking equation*. If the marking equation has no solution, then M is not reachable from M_0.

The inverse of the implication is not valid for arbitrary net systems, but we will see in the following theorem that the marking equation yields a sufficient condition for reachability in acyclic nets.

Theorem 2. *Let Σ be an acyclic net system and let M be a marking. M is reachable from the initial marking if and only if the marking equation has a nonnegative solution.*

Accordingly, we can use the marking equation for an algebraic representation of the set of reachable markings of an acyclic net system. We call a property $\mathcal{P}$ on markings *linear* if $\mathcal{P}$ can be expressed as a system of linear inequalities $L_{\mathcal{P}}$. A linear property is valid for all reachable markings of an acyclic net system if and only if the marking equation and $L_{\neg \mathcal{P}}$ have no common solution.

In 1-safe Petri nets each place can hold at most one token, and therefore a transition is enabled if and only if the total number of tokens in its input places is at least equal to the number of input places. In other words, the reachable deadlocked markings satisfy $\sum_{s \in {}^\bullet t} M(s) < |{}^\bullet t|$ for every transition t. We call these constraints *deadlock-inequalities*.

Proposition 3. *Given a 1-safe and acyclic net system* $\Sigma = (P, T, F, M_0)$, *an integer vector* M *is solution of the following system of inequalities if and only if* M *corresponds to a dead reachable marking of* Σ:

$$\text{Variables: } M, X: \text{integer.}$$
$$M = M_0 + \mathbf{N}.X$$
$$\sum_{p \in {}^\bullet t} M(p) \leq |{}^\bullet t| - 1 \qquad \text{for all } t \in T$$
$$X \geq 0$$

Observe that the application of proposition 3 to cyclic nets yields *just* a superset of reachable dead markings [9], because in cyclic nets the marking equation is not a sufficient condition for reachability. In this case we can interpret the solutions of the marking equation as a linear upper approximation of the state space.

Now we are able to apply proposition 3 to unfoldings of net systems. Since occurrence nets can be seen as acyclic and 1-safe net systems where all places of $Min(N)$ are initially marked we obtain the following theorem.

Theorem 4. *Let* $Unf_\Sigma = (N, h)$ *with* $N = (B, E, F)$ *be a finite and complete prefix of the branching process of a given n-safe net system* Σ. Σ *is deadlock-free if and only if the following system of inequalities has no solution:*

$$\text{Variables: } M, X: \text{integer.}$$
$$M = Min(N) + \mathbf{N}.X$$
$$\sum_{p \in {}^\bullet e} M(p) \leq |{}^\bullet e| - 1 \qquad \text{for all } e \in E$$
$$X(e) = 0 \qquad \text{for all cut-offs } e$$
$$X \geq 0$$

The key idea is based on the fact that all markings of Σ are represented in the unfolding Unf_Σ and moreover, the local net structure of each transition is preserved in Unf_Σ. Some dead markings conditional on the finiteness and acyclicity of Unf_Σ do not correspond to dead markings of Σ, because they are located beyond a cut-off event. But these *artificial* deadlocks are not solutions of the inequalities of theorem 4, because we only consider markings of Unf_Σ that can be reached without an occurrence of any cut-off event. Thereby we can identify dead markings of Σ with dead markings of Unf_Σ, and vice versa.

Now we want to focus our attention on implementation issues concerning the feasibility test of theorem 4. Since we know that $\mathbf{N}$ and $Min(N)$ are integers, we can conclude that if X is integer then so is M. Accordingly, we only have to demand that X has to be integer and M can be treated as a rational vector. Since we know that every event can only occur once, we can even demand X to be binary.

Since all variables of X which correspond to cut-off events are equal to zero, we can omit all these variables in the marking equation and thereby in the whole problem. The reader should note that we cannot remove any cut-off event from the prefix at all, because we need the information about its preset in order to formulate the *deadlock-inequalities* correctly.

Using a linear-program-solver like CPLEX [2] we obtain a straightforward implementation of the infeasibility test of theorem 4. Since the complexity of mixed-integer-programs (MIP), i.e., linear programs with rational as well as integer variables, is equal to the complexity of an algorithm to decide if the system of inequalities has a mixed-integer solution, we can make use of the good heuristic implemented in many MIP-solvers. The inherent complexity is NP-complete and more precisely, it is exponential in the number of integer variables.

As we mentioned in the previous paragraph we can formulate theorem 4 just with integer variables for non-cut-off events. Accordingly, the method for searching for a solution of the system of inequalities of the reformulated problem of theorem 4 using MIP-solvers like CPLEX, promises to yield good performance if the number of cut-off events is high regarding the total number of events.

4 McMillan's Method revisited

McMillan presented a way to detect deadlocks in an unfolding by means of looking at the configurations [8]. His observation was that there is no deadlock if each configuration of the unfolding can be extended to a configuration containing at least one cut-off event. In that case, all configurations can be infinitely often expanded.

In other words: The net contains a deadlock if and only if there exists a configuration being in conflict with every cut-off event of the unfolding. For that purpose we need the notion of *spoiler*: The set of all spoilers of a cut-off event e_c is defined as $S_{e_c} = \{e \in E \mid e \# e_c\} \cap ([e_c]^\bullet)^\bullet$, which contains all those events that are directly in conflict with an event from the local configuration of e_c.

McMillan described a branch and bound algorithm to construct a set of spoilers S that is in conflict with every cut-off element of the unfolding, if such a set exists. Then, S can be expanded to a configuration leading to a deadlock of the system. Otherwise, the set S is empty after termination of the algorithm, indicating the net as deadlock-free. This algorithm is sketched in figure 2.

The algorithm is exponential in the size of the unfolding in the worst case because of the backtracking. But by first taking the events with the smallest number of spoilers, this method quickly cuts down the number of possible choices in the average case.

For our implementation of both algorithms, the unfolding and the deadlock detection procedure, we used a special data structure to store and manipulate the nets in the C language [12]. Beside the improvements described in [5] concerning the size of the unfolding by introducing a total order of the configurations, we implemented some heuristic carried out in the combinatorial search of new

```
S := ∅; E_c := set of cut-off events;
while E_c ≠ ∅ do
    e_c := element of E_c with the fewest number of spoilers;
    if e_c has spoilers then
        choose an element e from the spoilers of e_c;
        S := S ∪ {e};
        delete all events in conflict with S
    else
        backtrack to the most recent choice of a spoiler
        and restore the deleted events
    endif
od
```

Fig. 2. McMillan's deadlock-detection algorithm.

events to be inserted in the finite prefix. The latter change drastically reduces the computation time: McMillan measured for the DME [7] consisting of 9 cells nearly 19000 seconds for the calculation of the unfolding in his LISP implementation, where we need only 132 seconds to construct the finite prefix, see Table 2. In this DME example, the size of the unfolding is independent from the chosen order of configurations, [8] or [5].

To check the deadlock property of DME(9), McMillan measured 6600 seconds; in our C implementation of his algorithm we get the result in 702 seconds.

5 Practical Results

In this section we want to compare both approaches. As already mentioned, the linear algebraic approach promises to be faster than McMillan's approach if the number of cut-off events is high w.r.t. the total number of events. In order to check our presumption we use the benchmark examples presented in Corbett's survey [3]. In Table 1 we use a representative subset of these examples to show the performance differences between both approaches w.r.t. the number of cut-off events. We use the abbreviations $\#c$,$\%c$, Unf, DC_{McM} and DC_{MIP} to denote the number of cut-off events, their percentage of cut-offs regarding to $|E|$, the time for the unfolding process[5], for McMillan's deadlock detection algorithm and for our approach, respectively. All results are measured on a SPARC 20/712 with 96 MBytes RAM. We used $CPLEX^{TM}$ (version 3.0) as underlying MIP-solver. Binaries of the programs described in the paper are available from the authors. We can directly observe that McMillan's algorithm is faster if the unfolding has only few cut-off events (cp. DPD, RING). In contrast to the examples DPH, ELEVATOR, FURNACE and RW where the new approach overtakes McMillan's method. However, these benchmark results are not strong enough to demonstrate

---

[5] We used the unfolding proposed in [5] which is smaller or equal to McMillan's.

[6] The example ELEVATOR has a deadlock; all others are deadlock free.

[7] $mem(n)$ indicates the process aborted due to a memory overflow after n seconds.

Problem(size)	States	Original net $\|P\|$	$\|T\|$	Unfolding $\|B\|$	$\|E\|$	#c	%c	Time [s] Unf	DC_{McM}	DC_{MIP}
DPD(4)	601	36	36	594	296	81	26	0.12	0.3	2.0
DPD(5)	3489	45	45	1582	790	211	26	0.58	1.9	17.3
DPD(6)	19861	54	54	3786	1892	499	27	3.35	20.2	82.8
DPD(7)	109965	63	63	8630	4314	1129	27	25.03	234.0	652.6
DPH(4)	513	39	46	680	336	117	35	0.15	0.3	1.8
DPH(5)	3113	48	67	2712	1351	547	40	1.48	10.5	42.9
DPH(6)	16897	57	97	14474	7231	3377	47	61.66	1907.6	1472.8
DPH(7)	79927	66	121	81358	40672	21427	53	1946.49	–	–
ELEVATOR(1)[6]	158	63	99	296	157	59	38	0.07	0.0	0.1
ELEVATOR(2)	1062	146	299	1562	827	331	40	0.65	0.9	2.3
ELEVATOR(3)	7121	327	783	7398	3895	1629	42	17.98	18.7	14.5
ELEVATOR(4)	43440	736	1939	32354	16935	7337	43	374.52	492.7	387.8
FURNACE(1)	344	27	37	535	326	189	58	0.12	0.2	0.3
FURNACE(2)	3778	40	65	5139	3111	1990	64	5.60	19.0	18.1
FURNACE(3)	30861	53	99	34505	20770	13837	67	270.02	$mem(811.1)$[7]	1112.5
RING(3)	87	39	33	97	47	11	23	0.02	0.0	0.1
RING(5)	1290	65	55	339	167	37	23	0.07	0.1	1.3
RING(7)	17000	91	77	813	403	79	20	0.23	0.3	17.1
RING(9)	211528	117	99	1599	795	137	17	0.93	1.1	71.2
RW(6)	72	33	85	806	397	327	82	0.08	0.5	0.7
RW(9)	523	48	181	9272	4627	4106	89	3.04	122.3	58.5
RW(12)	4110	63	313	98378	49177	45069	92	279.64	$mem(6004.9)$	24599.9

Table 1. Corbett's examples.

the advantages of both approaches, because all deadlock-free examples can be verified and even faster than via unfoldings by the application of proposition 3 to the original system. Although this corresponds *just* to a semi-decision method, it is strong enough for Corbett's examples. In other words, the gap between the state space and the linear upper approximation obtained by the marking equation is small enough to decide deadlock freeness.

Therefore we give two more case studies. Firstly, we take up the DME [7] example given in McMillan's original paper [8]. Secondly, we modelled the implementation of a readers/writers synchronization [6]. Both examples cannot be proved to be deadlock free by application of proposition 3 to the original system. Even a refinement of the marking equation that is proposed in [9] is not sufficient enough in this context, i.e., the gap between the state space and its upper linear approximation contains dead markings. This fact disables semi-decision methods based on the marking equation or its refinement.

Distributed Mutual Exclusion. In [7], an asynchronous circuit for distributed mutual exclusion (DME) is proposed. McMillan has already shown that the state space grows exponentially in the number of DME-cells while the unfolding increases just quadratically. Due to the fact that the unfolding has only few cut-off events the improvement fails. In Table 2 we list the results. The times DC_{McM} for the deadlock detection seem to increase exponentially, but the increment of DC_{McM} is much more slighter than the increment of DC_{MIP}. The new approach suffers from the small percentage of cut-off events and therefore we interrupted the example DME(7) after 12 hours.

The linear algebraic approach is not appropiated for these kind of systems. Asynchronous circuits do not have such an abundance of non-determinism which is required to yield wide unfoldings.

Problem(size)	States	Original net		Unfolding				Time [s]		
		$|P|$	$|T|$	$|B|$	$|E|$	#c	%c	Unf	DC_{McM}	DC_{MIP}
DME(2)	$> 10^2$	135	98	487	122	4	3	0.07	0.07	1.9
DME(3)	$> 10^3$	202	147	1210	321	9	3	0.27	0.50	64.6
DME(4)	$> 10^4$	269	196	2381	652	16	2	1.23	1.67	216.1
DME(5)	$> 10^5$	336	245	4096	1145	25	2	3.92	7.83	1968.3
DME(6)	$> 10^6$	403	294	6451	1830	36	2	10.37	26.43	13678.3
DME(7)	$> 10^7$	470	343	9542	2737	49	2	28.45	97.80	--
DME(8)	$> 10^8$	537	392	13465	3896	64	2	68.16	251.52	--
DME(9)	$> 10^9$	604	441	18316	5337	81	2	131.88	701.74	--
DME(10)	$> 10^{10}$	671	490	24191	7090	100	1	240.57	1801.48	--
DME(11)	$> 10^{11}$	738	539	31186	9185	121	1	420.12	4682.36	--

Table 2. Distributed mutual exclusion-examples.

Readers/Writers Synchronization. In [6], a scalable and bottleneck-free readers/writers synchronization algorithm for shared memory parallel machines is presented. We modelled a 4-bit implementation based on busy waiting semaphors. We used our methods to check deadlock freeness for a setting with one writer and two or three readers (SYNC). The results are depicted in Table 3. In contrast to the DME example we see that the application of the linear algebraic approach turns out to yield better results if the percentage of cut-off events is greater than one third.

Problem(size)	States	Original net		Unfolding				Time [s]		
		$|P|$	$|T|$	$|B|$	$|E|$	#c	%c	Unf	DC_{McM}	DC_{MIP}
SYNC(2)	17874	95	239	4007	2162	490	23	9.20	69.0	171.6
SYNC(3)	116446	106	270	29132	15974	5381	34	728.95	26621.7	11985.0

Table 3. Readers/writers-examples.

6 Conclusion

We have introduced a deadlock detection method based on net unfoldings using linear algebraic techniques. Moreover, we have presented an implementation of McMillan's deadlock algorithm and we pointed out the performance gap between McMillan's LISP implementation and our optimized C version. By means of several examples we have pointed out the strong and weak aspects of both approaches. The results show that the larger the percentage of cut-off events is, the more likely the new method will yield better performance than McMillan's. Our future work is to exploit some more CPLEX heuristic in order to speed up our implementation.

Acknowledgements. We thank Javier Esparza for drawing our attention to this problem and Ken McMillan for sending us his LISP sources of the DME generator.

References

1. E. Best and C. Fernández: Nonsequential Processes – A Petri Net View. EATCS Monographs on Theoretical Computer Science 13 (1988).
2. CPLEX 3.0 Manual, CPLEX Corp. (1995).
3. James C. Corbett: Evaluating Deadlock Detection Methods. University of Hawaii at Manoa (1994).
4. J. Engelfriet: Branching processes of Petri nets. Acta Informatica 28, pp. 575–591 (1991).
5. J. Esparza, S. Römer and W. Vogler: An Improvement of McMillan's Unfolding Algorithm. Proc. of *Tools and Algorithms for the Construction and Analysis of Systems*, LNCS 1055, 87–106 (1996).
6. H. Hellwagner: Scalable Readers/Writers Synchronization on Shared-Memory Machines, Esprit P5404 (GP MIMD), Working Paper (1993).
7. A.J. Martin: The Design of a self-timed Circuit of Distributed Mutual Exclusion. In Henry Fuchs, editor, 1985 *Chapel Hill Confernce on VLSI*, pp. 245–260. Computer Science Press (1985).
8. K.L. McMillan: Using Unfoldings to Avoid the State Explosion Problem in the Verification of Asynchronous Circuits. Proc. *4th Workshop on Computer Aided Verification*, LNCS 663, 164–174 (1992).
9. S. Melzer and J. Esparza: Checking System Properties via Integer Programming. In Proc. of *European Symp. on Programming*, LNCS 1058, 250–264 (1996).
10. T. Murata: Petri nets: Properties, Analysis and Applications. In Proc. of the IEEE 77(4), pp. 541–580 (1989).
11. M. Nielsen, G. Plotkin and G. Winskel: Petri Nets, Event Structures and Domains. Theoretical Computer Science 13(1), pp. 85–108 (1980).
12. S. Römer: Implementation of a Compositional Partial Order Semantics of Petri Boxes. Diploma Thesis (in German). Universität Hildesheim (1993).

A Proofs

Auxiliaries. Given a multiset or vector X, we denote by $\|X\| = \{x \mid X(x) > 0\}$ the *support* of X. Given a net system $\Sigma = (P, T, F, M_0)$ and a nonnegative transition vector X. We denote by Σ_x the subsystem generated by the transitions of $\|X\|$, their input and output places, i.e., $\Sigma_x = (P_x, T_x, F_x, M_{0x})$ with: $P_x = P \cap (^\bullet\|X\| \cup \|X\|^\bullet)$, $T_x = \|X\|$, $F_x = F \cap ((P_x \times T_x) \cup (T_x \times P_x))$, $M_{0x} = M_0 \cap P_x$. We use $\mathbf{e_t}$ to denote the transition vector with $\mathbf{e_t}(t) = 1$ and $\mathbf{e_t}(t') = 0$ for all $t' \neq t$.

Proof of theorem 2.

The following proof is a more detailed realization of the proof sketch given in [10]. It is well known that the marking equation is a necessary condition for reachability. Hence, we only have to show the sufficiency. Suppose that there exists a solution X of the marking equation. Now we consider the net system Σ_x. It is obvious that Σ_x is also acyclic and moreover if M_x is reachable from M_{0x} then it is also reachable by M_0. We show that M_x is reachable from M_{0x} by induction over the length of X, i.e., $n = \sum_{t \in \|X\|} X(t)$.

Induction Base: $n = 1$. Let t be the transition with $X(t) = 1$. Due to $F_X(t, p) = 0$ for all $p \in {}^\bullet t$, we obtain from the marking equation that $^\bullet t \subseteq M_{0x}$ and thereby

t is enabled at marking M_{0x}. Hence, $M_{0x} \xrightarrow{t} M_x$.

Induction Step: $n + 1$. We assume a transition t which is enabled at marking M_{0x}. The existence of such a transition is guaranteed by the acyclicity of Σ_x and by the fact that Σ_x is nonempty. Hence the occurrence of t yields a marking M'_x. Let $X' = X - \mathbf{e_t}$ be the vector where transition t fires one time less. Now we can conclude that $M_x = M_{0x} + \mathbf{N}.X = M_{0x} + \mathbf{N}.(X' + \mathbf{e_t})$. The last equation can be splitted into $M'_x = M_{0x} + \mathbf{N}.\mathbf{e_t}$ and $M_x = M'_x + \mathbf{N}.X'$. Since $\sum_{t \in \|X\|} X'(t) = n$ we can apply the induction hypothesis and get directly that M_x is reachable from M'_x. Together with the fact that $M_{0x} \xrightarrow{t} M'_x$ we finally get the reachability of M_x from M_{0x}. □

Proof of proposition 3.

Due to theorem 2 and the acyclicity of Σ, the set of reachable markings is represented by the solutions of the marking equation. Moreover, due to the 1-safeness we can express the fact that a transition t is enabled at a marking M by the linear constraint $\sum_{p \in {}^\bullet t} M(p) \geq |{}^\bullet t|$. Hence, a dead marking, i.e. a marking that enables no transition can be described by $\sum_{p \in {}^\bullet t} M(p) < |{}^\bullet t|$ for all $t \in T$ that is logically equivalent to $\sum_{p \in {}^\bullet t} M(p) \leq |{}^\bullet t| - 1$ since we are using integer variables for M. □

Proof of theorem 4.

We consider the net system $\Sigma' = (N, Min(N))$ with $N = (B, E, F)$. Since N is an occurrence net, Σ' is acyclic. Moreover, $Min(N)$ is a 1-safe marking and due to the acyclicity of N and the fact that each place has at most one incoming arc we can conclude that Σ' is a 1-safe system. Due to theorem 1 we know that each marking M of Σ is represented by a finite configuration C with $Mark(C) = M$ where C does not contain any cut-off event. Moreover, we know that the set of cuts corresponding to finite configurations without cut-off events coincides with the set of markings reachable from $Min(N)$ without occurring any cut-off event. Therefore it remains to show that a deadlocked system Σ' implies the existence of a finite configuration without cut-off events which corresponds to a cut where no event is enabled, and vice versa.

($\Rightarrow$) Suppose that the net system Σ is not deadlock-free, then there exists a reachable marking M such that no transition is enabled at M, i.e., for all $t \in T$, ${}^\bullet t \not\subseteq \|M\|$. Due to theorem 1 we know that there exists a finite configuration C without any cut-off events such that for all $t \in T$, ${}^\bullet t \not\subseteq \|Mark(C)\|$ still holds. Because $h(E) \subseteq T$, we can conclude that for all $e \in E$ ${}^\bullet h(e) \not\subseteq \|Mark(C)\|$ is also satisfied. Due to the monotony of h w.r.t. set inclusion we obtain that the preset of no transition is a subset of $Cut(C)$. Hence all events which are no cut-off event are disabled at $Cut(C)$.

($\Leftarrow$) Suppose the existence of a configuration C without cut-off events such that no event is enabled at marking $Cut(C)$. Then we can conclude that there exists no event $e \in E \setminus C$ such that its local configuration can be embedded in an extension of C by E, i.e., $[e] \not\subseteq C \cup \{e\}$. Hence there exists no configuration $C \cup \{e\}$ for an arbitrary event e. Due to theorem 1 we obtain that no transition $t \in T$ exists such that ${}^\bullet t \subseteq \|Mark(C)\|$. This means that the corresponding reachable marking $M = Mark(C)$ is a dead marking. □

Trace Table Based Approach for Pipelined Microprocessor Verification

Jun Sawada[1] and Warren A. Hunt, Jr.[2]

[1] Department of Computer Sciences, University of Texas, Austin, TX 78712, USA
E-mail: sawada@cs.utexas.edu
[2] Computational Logic, Inc., 1717 West 6th Street, Suite 290, Austin, TX 78703,
USA E-mail: hunt@cli.com

Abstract. This paper presents several techniques for formally verifying pipelined microprocessor implementations that contain out-of-order
execution and dynamic resolution of data-dependent hazards. Our principal technique models the trace of executed instructions using a table-
based representation called a MAETT. We express invariant properties
of pipelined implementations by specifying relations between fields in
the MAETT. To show the viability of this technique, we have proved the
correctness of a simple out-of-order completion pipelined microprocessor
design using the ACL2 theorem prover. This verification was performed
incrementally by proving that the specified relations hold for all micro-
architectural states reachable from a flushed implementation state, eventually permitting us to prove that the entire pipelined machine design
implements its ISA specification.

1 Introduction

In our project, we have been developing techniques to verify the correctness of
pipelined microprocessor implementations with relatively complex pipeline control logic. To achieve this goal, we designed an example microprocessor which
features out-of-order instruction completion, speculative instruction fetch, and
dynamic resolution of *read-after-write (RAW) dependencies* (also called *true dependencies*) and *write-after-write (WAW) dependencies* (also called *antidepen-
dencies*) [6, 8]. Our method employs a technique we call a *Micro-Architectural
Execution Trace Table (MAETT)*. With the help of the MAETT, we define various properties of our pipelined implementation, and incrementally prove that
each of them holds for all the reachable pipeline states. The correctness for our
pipelined implementation is then proved from these pipeline properties.

Our motivation is to permit the verification of complex pipelined microprocessor implementations. Although some measure of success has been achieved[7],
formal verification has not been widely applied to the micro-architectural design
of general-purpose microprocessors. Specifically, for pipelined machine designs

---

* This research was supported in part by the Semiconductor Research Corporation
under contract 96-DP-388.

there have been several efforts aimed at verifying pipelined implementations; however, most of the formally verified designs have a short and simple pipeline structure. An impediment to applying such proof techniques to commercial designs is the failure of current formal approaches to address the verification of today's processors with modern performance optimizations, including superscalar super-pipelining, out-of-order execution, and speculative execution.

2 Background

There have been a number of earlier efforts to verify pipelined microprocessor designs with interactive theorem provers[5, 10, 11, 13]. Typically in these projects, they show the equivalence of an *instruction-set architecture (ISA)* and a corresponding *micro-architectural* design. An ISA is a non-pipelined abstract machine which specifies the effects of individual instructions, while a micro-architectural design exposes the pipeline structure of an actual machine implementation. The equivalence between these levels is defined by a commutative diagram with an abstraction function mapping a micro-architectural state to an ISA state. In many cases, however, a pipeline state may not be directly mapped to an ISA state because of the *latency* of pipeline events.

One way to avoid this problem is to define a *skewed* [11] abstraction function, which relates multiple pipeline states to a single ISA state. Skewed abstraction functions are often complex, and they are vulnerable to minor design modifications because skewed abstraction functions are defined with the expectation that very specific timing properties are preserved between pipeline events.

Instead of defining an artificially-constructed skewed abstraction function, Burch and Dill[3] proposed a correctness criterion where they first flush the pipeline of the micro-architecture by stalling and then map the resulting microarchitectural state to an ISA-state. Diagram(a) in Fig. 1 shows their correctness criterion. Using induction, Diagram(a) can be extended to the more general criterion shown in Diagram(b). Diagram(b) suggests that the n-cycle micro-state transition which starts and ends with flushed pipeline states is equivalent to the m-cycle state transition at the ISA level, where m is the number of instructions executed in the micro-state transition.

Burch and Dill's approach is more robust to design modifications in the microarchitecture than the method with a skewed abstraction function, because it does not depend on specific timing between pipeline events. It is also applicable to pipelined machines with out-of-order execution without any modification.

Burch and Dill's automated verification procedure[3] is effective in verifying their correctness criteria for processors with a simple pipeline control logic, because it treats the data-path symbolically and only verifies the control. However, the procedure can fail for large and complex processor designs, because the number of examined cases explodes as the control part becomes complicated. Various studies have been done to improve the capability of the technique [8, 14]. Especially, [14] decomposed Diagram (a) to simpler diagrams, which were used in superscalar verification in [4]. However, it is still difficult to see how we can apply

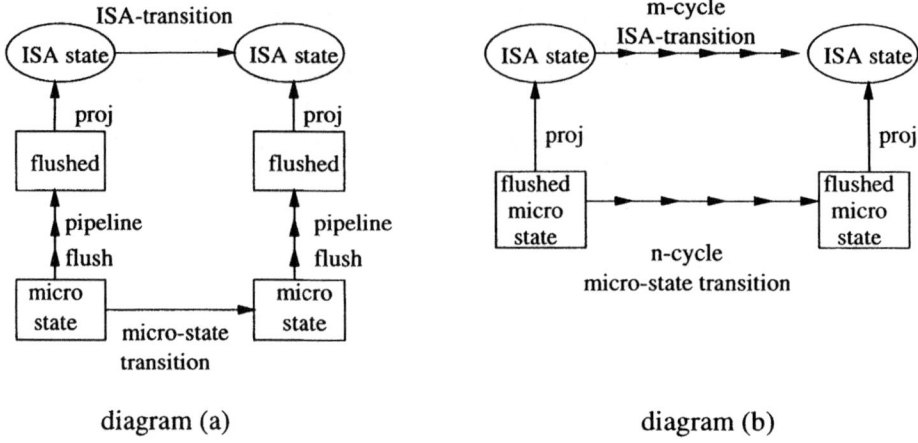

diagram (a)   diagram (b)

Fig. 1. Pipeline Correctness Criteria

the procedure to the verification of complex micro-architectural designs used in today's microprocessors.

Since we want to study the verification of out-of-order pipelined micro-architectural designs, we believe it will be necessary to use general and robust correctness criteria similar to the one used by Burch and Dill. We also think that dividing the complete verification problem into smaller subproblems is the key to the successful verification of complex processor implementations. In the verification of our example pipelined machine, we incrementally verify various pipeline properties first, from which we can prove our correctness criteria. An examples of such properties will be given in Sec. 3.2

Several earlier projects have focused on the verification of pipeline properties. Tahar and Kumar[12] verified that their DLX implementation does not have RAW hazards and other pipeline conflicts, but they didn't verify the equivalence between their ISA and micro-architecture. Agaard and Leeser[1] proposed a framework for pipeline verification focusing on structural hazards, which is similar in character to what we describe here; however, they did not mechanize its application. Our verification is complete in the sense that we mechanically verified pipeline properties and the more general criteria shown in Fig. 1.

3 Verification Approach

We first present our example machine in Subsection 3.1. Using the example, we discuss how to define and verify pipeline properties in Subsection 3.2, and how to prove the correctness criteria in Subsection 3.3. We briefly discuss the mechanization of the verification in Subsection 3.4.

3.1   An Example Pipelined Machine Design

We designed a new pipelined machine to study the verification of pipelined machines with out-of-order execution, where instructions may not be executed in the ISA program order. We did not use a published pipelined implementation such as DLX, because we wanted to study machine designs with a more complex control logic. A typical DLX implementation has a simple pipeline control with few pipeline interlocks. On the other hand, our example machine includes out-of-order execution and speculative instruction fetch. We also wanted our example machine to be as small as possible, so that we can rapidly try different approaches. Our example design has a very small instruction set and has neither external interactions nor interrupts.

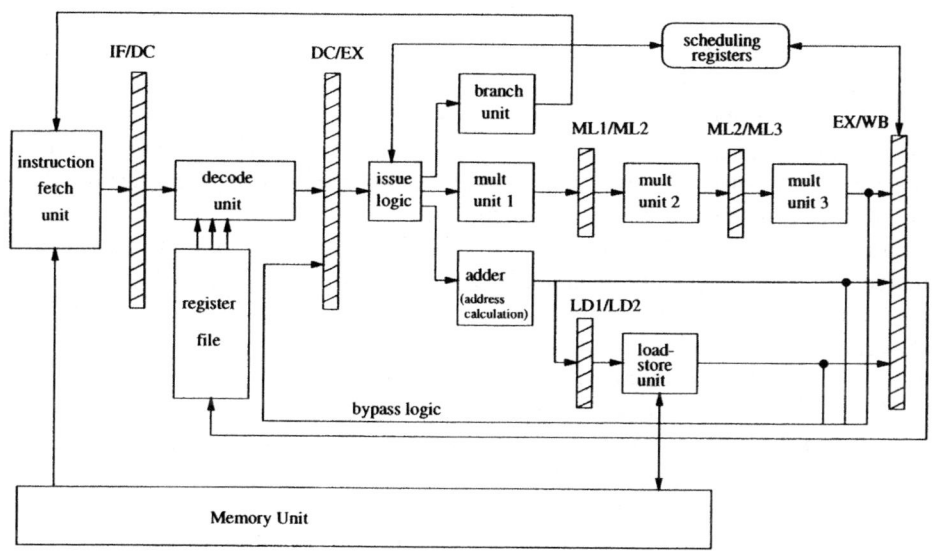

Fig. 2. A block diagram of our example processor.

A block diagram of our example pipelined machine is shown in Fig. 2. The maximum length of the pipeline is six stages and each stage is separated by pipeline latches shown as patterned rectangles. This machine has multiple execution units, including a simple adder and a pipelined multiplier. Different execution units have different numbers of pipeline stages; one stage for an addition, two for a load-store instruction, and three for a multiplication. Consequently, our example machine may complete the execution of instructions in an out-of-order fashion, even though the instructions are issued in order. Since our design does not have a re-order buffer, instructions retire immediately after their execution completes, and the register file may be updated in an out-of-order fashion.

A pipelined design with out-of-order register file updates may exhibit certain

368

hazards. Consider a code sequence including three assignment instructions:

$$R1 := R2 * R3 \qquad (i)$$
$$R5 := R1 + R4 \qquad (ii)$$
$$R1 := R6 + R7 \qquad (iii)$$

In this code, instruction (ii) uses the new value of register R1 which is returned by (i), and we say (ii) has a *read-after-write(RAW) dependency* on (i). A correct pipelined design has to postpone the execution of (ii) and/or bypass the result of (i) to earlier stages, so that (ii) obtains the correct value of R1. Otherwise, (i) may calculate an incorrect result, causing a *read-after-write(RAW) hazard.*

We can also see that (iii) updates the same register R1 as (i) does. We say (iii) has a *write-after-write(WAW) dependency* on (i). If (iii) updates register R1 earlier than (i) by out-of-order execution, (i) destroys the value stored by (iii), leaving R1 containing a wrong value. To prevent this incorrect behavior, which is called a *write-after-write(WAW) hazard,* (i) and (iii) must update R1 in program order.

A *structural hazard* occurs when multiple instructions simultaneously try to use the same hardware resource. With regard to our machine design, instructions may simultaneously occupy the write-back stage due to the various lengths of the execution units. Without proper arbitration or scheduling, the results of the execution of instructions may be corrupted.

In order to avoid these hazards, our issuing logic suspends the issue of any instruction that may cause a hazard. Once an instruction is issued, it is guaranteed that no hazard will occur due to the instruction. The scheduling registers shown in Fig. 2 keep track of the instructions in the execution units, and the issuing logic refers to them when deciding whether it can issue an instruction.

Using the ACL2 logic[2, 9], we have defined a ISA-level next-state function, ISA-state-step(), as an instruction interpreter and a micro-architectural next-state function, micro-state-step(), as a clock-by-clock cycle interpreter. The control of the pipeline is specified concretely, while the data-path is specified with abstract functions. For instance, our adder is represented by the ACL2 integer addition function, which is treated as an uninterpreted function during the verification process. One exception is our pipelined Wallace-tree multiplier, which is specified more concretely using carry-save adders and carry-propagate adders as primitive blocks. This is for studying data-path verification in the context of pipeline verification.

3.2   The MAETT and Pipeline Properties

Let us first discuss why the MAETT is useful with our verification approach for pipelined micro-architectural designs. We often wish to define invariants of the target design, but some pipeline properties are difficult to define as a predicate taking a micro-architectural state as its sole argument. This is because micro-architectural designs are usually optimized for speed and size, and a micro-architectural state may not contain enough information to directly define such predicates.

For example, an out-of-order pipelined machine design may suffer WAW hazards, and we would want to check that no such hazards occur in our micro-architectural design. However, a WAW hazard may involve an already retired instruction, so it is difficult to check for such a hazard by simply examining a micro-architectural state, because the machine may not contain information about retired instructions. This is why writing a WAW hazard-free predicate is easier if we have a richer and more redundant representation of the execution trace of the machine, that is, the MAETT.

A MAETT M is an *unbounded* list of all instructions $I_1, I_2, \ldots, I_n$ which are currently being executed or have already retired since the machine started:

$$M = (I_1 \ I_2 \ \cdots \ I_n) \ . \tag{1}$$

The ISA executes $I_1, I_2, \ldots, I_n$ in that order. Each instruction I_i is represented by a record like:

$$I_i = (Flg_i, PC_i, Inst_i, RA_i, RB_i, RC_i, Stg_i, Regs_i, Mem_i, Misc_i) \ , \tag{2}$$

where PC_i, $Inst_i$, RA_i, RB_i, RC_i, Stg_i, $Misc_i$ are respectively the instruction address; instruction word; operand register identifiers of RA, RB and RC; current stage of the instruction; and miscellaneous stage-dependent information. Flg_i is a flag indicating whether I_i is speculatively fetched. $Regs_i$ and Mem_i are the correct register file and memory states after completing all previous instructions $I_1, \ldots, I_{i-1}$ and before executing I_i with the ISA. Let $\texttt{ISA-state}(PC, Reg, Mem)$ denote the ISA state with PC, Reg, Mem as its program counter, register file and memory, respectively. We can define an "ideal" ISA state S_i corresponding to I_i by:

$$S_i = \texttt{ISA-state}(PC_i, Reg_i, Mem_i) \ . \tag{3}$$

The next ISA state S_{i+1} is related to S_i by:

$$S_{i+1} = \texttt{ISA-state-step}(S_i) \ . \tag{4}$$

In this sense, we say that a MAETT records an ISA execution sequence.

At the same time, a MAETT represents the current micro-architectural state, by recording the current status of each instruction. We define a MAETT updating function $\texttt{MAETT-step}()$ to simulate the micro-architectural state transition $\texttt{micro-state-step}()$. If s is a micro-architectural state and M is its MAETT representation, $\texttt{MAETT-step}(M,s)$ gives a MAETT representation of the next micro-state $\texttt{micro-state-step}(s)$. $\texttt{MAETT-step}$ updates appropriate fields of (2) for instructions already in a MAETT. It may also add a newly fetched instruction to a MAETT or delete speculatively fetched instructions if they are aborted.

The richness and regularity of the MAETT representation help us to define various pipeline properties. We can see this by looking at the definition of our WAW hazard-free predicate $\texttt{no-WAW-hazards?}$. The WAW hazard between the instructions I_k and I_l is defined as:

```
WAW-violation?(Iₖ,Iₗ) = (reg-writeback-inst?(entry-inst(Iₖ))
                         ∧ reg-writeback-inst?(entry-inst(Iₗ))
                         ∧ same-destination-reg?(Iₖ,Iₗ)
                         ∧ out-of-order-retire?(Iₖ,Iₗ)) .
```

This definition assumes that I_k is an earlier instruction than I_l, with regard to the ISA-execution order. The definition says that a WAW hazard between I_k and I_l occurs when both of the instructions are write-back instructions, they share the same destination register, and I_l retires earlier than I_k. Each of the predicates in the definition of **WAW-violation?** is further defined as a relation of the fields of I_k and I_l. For example, the **out-of-order-retire?** is defined as:

```
out-of-order-retire?(Iₖ,Iₗ)
= let Stgₖ be entry-stg(Iₖ) and
      Stgₗ be entry-stg(Iₗ)
  in
  (case Stgₖ of
         EX/WB:    Stgₗ ∈ {RETIRE}
         LD1/LD2:  Stgₗ ∈ {EX/WB RETIRE}
         ML2/ML3:  Stgₗ ∈ {EX/WB RETIRE}
         ML1/ML2:  Stgₗ ∈ {LD1/LD2 ML2/ML3 EX/WB RETIRE}
         otherwise: false ) ,
```

where **entry-stg**(I_i) returns Stg_i for I_i in (2). This definition checks for out-of-order retirements by considering different stages Stg_k for I_k. The first case specifies an out-of-order retirement occurring when I_k is still in the EX/WB latch while I_l has already retired. Finally, we can define our global WAW hazard-free property **no-WAW-hazards?** as a recursive predicate checking **WAW-violation?** for all the pairs of instructions in MAETT M:

$$\text{no-WAW-hazards?}(M) = \forall I_k, I_l \in M \text{ s.t. } I_k <_M I_l, \neg\text{WAW-violation}(I_k, I_l) ,$$

where $I_k <_M I_l$ means that I_k appears in M earlier than I_l.

In a similar manner, we have used the MAETT representation to define other pipeline properties which are essential to the correct operation of our design:

no-structural-hazard? : No structural hazards occur.

intermediate-values-ok? : Predicate checking that the intermediate values of the instruction at each stage are correct. This predicate entails the non-existence of RAW hazards. For instance, an instruction at the issue stage should have obtained the correct source register values from either the register itself or the bypass logic. The correct value of source register RA can be expressed as **read-reg**$(RA_i, Regs_i)$ for I_i in (2).

all-insts-in-MAETT? : All the partially executed instructions in the pipeline are in the MAETT.

consistent-scheduler? : The scheduling registers correctly keep track of instructions in the execution units.

`speculative-inst-not-issued?` : No speculatively fetched instructions are issued to the execution units.

`speculative-fetching-ok?` : All speculatively fetched instructions are abandoned before instructions are fetched from the correct branch.

`in-order-issue?` : Instruction issues are in-order.

`no-WAW-hazard?` : No WAW hazards occur.

`in-order-memory-accs?` : No out-of-order memory accesses are performed.

`sync-retires-insts?` : All instructions retire before a subsequent SYNC instruction retires.

`consistent-ISA-states?` : Equation (4) holds for all instructions except those speculatively fetched.

`correct-pc?` : The program counter is pointing to the next instruction to be fetched.

`correct-regs?` : The register file is correct. The correct register file is defined by scanning the MAETT and sequentially accumulating all the side-effects by the retired instructions on the initial register file. In other words, the register file should record all the updates caused by the retired instructions.

`correct-mem?` : The memory reflects all the memory writes by retired STORE instructions.

We define the conjunction of all of these properties to be predicate `MAETT-ok?`. Using this predicate, we proved two lemmas:

Lemma 1 Invariant property of MAETT-ok? . *Suppose s is a micro-architectural state and M is a corresponding MAETT satisfying* `MAETT-ok?`(M, s). *Then the next micro-architectural state* `micro-state-step`(s) *and the updated MAETT* `MAETT-step`(M, s) *satisfy:*

$$\text{MAETT-ok?}(\text{MAETT-step}(M, s), \text{micro-state-step}(s)).$$

Lemma 2 MAETT for a Flushed State. *Suppose s is a flushed micro-architectural state; that is, no partially executed instruction is in the pipeline of s. The empty MAETT* `nil` *is a correct MAETT representing s, and* `MAETT-ok?`(nil, s) *is true.*

From these two lemmas, we can conclude that `MAETT-ok?` is true for all the micro-architectural states reachable from a flushed state. Since the `MAETT-ok?` is a conjunction of pipeline properties, we can prove Lemma 1 and Lemma 2 by proving the pipeline properties one at a time. We do not have to examine the whole processor design to prove an individual property, because each property is relevant to a small part of the complete design. For instance, when we prove that our design invariantly satisfies the property `no-WAW-hazards?`, we can concentrate our effort on the issuing logic and ignore, for instance, the branching unit. Then, assuming no WAW hazard occurs, we can prove `correct-regs?` by concentrating our effort on the write-back stage to the register file. In this way, the complete verification problem is divided into local problems, which are verified incrementally. This incremental verification approach helped us avoid case explosions in our proof and reduced the computational cost of the verification process.

The proofs of Lemma 1 and 2 are the core part of our verification, because it required a great portion of our verification effort and profound analysis of the machine design. The proofs of individual properties vary, but it is often the case that the top-level proof goals are reduced, by induction, into simpler subproblems, which are then solved by case analysis and rewriting. We have been trying to verify these subproblems by more automatic procedures including BDD's, but with little success. We think improvements in this step will be important to make our approach more practical.

3.3 Equivalence Proof of ISA and Micro-architecture

We have proved the equivalence of our ISA and our micro-architectural design in two ways; one approach proves Diagram(a) in Fig. 1, and then we verify Diagram(b) from (a) by induction. Our second approach is a direct proof of the correctness criteria given in Diagram(b) without proving Diagram(a). Here we discuss only the latter approach, because it turned out to be simpler than the former approach.

We pictorially portray the proof of the correctness criteria using Fig. 3. Let us consider n micro-architectural state transitions $P_0, P_1, \ldots, P_n$. We assume that the initial state P_0 and the final P_n are flushed, as shown in Diagram (b). We further assume that m instructions $I_0, \ldots, I_{m-1}$ are executed in the micro-state transitions from P_0 to P_n. Let $S_0 = \texttt{proj}(P_0)$, that is, the ISA state projected from P_0. And let $S_1, \ldots, S_m$ be the m-step ISA-state transitions from S_0. Now we need to prove $\texttt{proj}(P_n) = S_m$ to satisfy Diagram(b).

From Lemma 1 and Lemma 2, micro-architectural states $P_0, P_1, \ldots, P_n$ have corresponding MAETT representations $M_0, M_1, \ldots, M_n$, and $\texttt{MAETT-ok?}(M_i, P_i)$ is satisfied by each pair of P_i and M_i. Figure 3 shows MAETT's $M_0, \ldots, M_n$, which contain instructions $I_0, \ldots, I_{m-1}$. In the figure, the current stages of instructions are shown; for instance, I_0 advances from stage IF/DC to DC/EX, and RETIRE's by the time it reaches M_n. M_n contains all of $I_0, \ldots, I_{m-1}$, and they are all retired since the corresponding micro-state P_n is flushed. The figure also shows the relations of instructions $I_0, \ldots, I_{m-1}$ and ideal ISA states $S_0, \ldots, S_m$ satisfying (3) and (4) ; the ISA-machine executes instruction I_i in the transition from S_i to S_{i+i}. In other words, S_{i+1} is the ideal ISA state after executing instruction I_i. We define a function $\texttt{final-state}(P_i, M_i)$ which returns the ideal ISA state after executing the last instruction in M_i. So $\texttt{final-state}(P_n, M_n) = S_m$, because I_{m-1} is the last instruction in M_n. The definition of $\texttt{final-state}$ is easy as a MAETT contains the ideal ISA states corresponding to the instructions. We then can prove:

Lemma 3. *If a micro state P_i and its MAETT M_i satisfy* $\texttt{MAETT-ok?}(P_i, M_i)$, *and all the instructions in M_i are retired, then* $\texttt{final-state}(P_i, M_i) = \texttt{proj}(P_i)$.

Lemma 3 can be proven from the invariant properties $\texttt{correct-pc?}$, $\texttt{correct-regs?}$ and $\texttt{correct-mem?}$, which are conjuncts of $\texttt{MAETT-ok?}$. Using Lemma 3

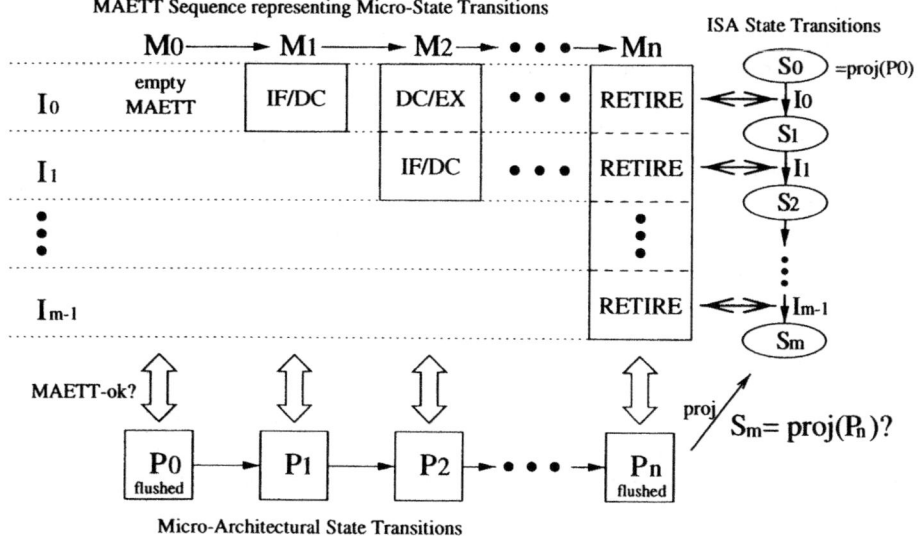

Fig. 3. Pictorial Description of the Proof of Diagram(b)

with M_n and P_n, we will get:

$$S_m = \texttt{final-state}(P_n, M_n) = \texttt{proj}(P_n).$$

The proof of the correctness criteria is performed by theorem proving techniques, and Diagram (b) in Fig. 1 has been shown to be valid for arbitrarily long micro-state transitions with any instruction sequences, provided that the initial and final states are flushed.

We also have to verify the liveness property of the pipelined machine, because the correctness criteria are vacuously true if the pipelined machine cannot reach a flushed state. We have shown that our pipelined design completes the execution of an arbitrary instruction sequence in finite cycles. The proof is done by constructing a measure function which returns the sum of the number of stages before each instruction retires, and then showing that the measure function decreases in each cycle. Such a measure function can be defined as a simple recursive function over a MAETT.

3.4 Mechanical Verification

Using ACL2 theorem prover, we have verified that the micro-architectural design of our example machine implements its ISA specification, by following the steps discussed in the previous subsections. The control logic of our micro-architectural design is proven correct with respect to the correctness criteria, but we did not concern ourselves with the correctness of the data-path elements, as in Burch and Dill's work. However, the pipelined multiplier was independently verified by showing the output from the unit is a wrap-around product of the inputs.

We demonstrated that this result can be integrated in our pipeline verification technique by proving the correctness criteria for the micro-architectural design with the detailed multiplier specification.

The verification effort took three months of manual effort. The replay of the whole proof takes about one hour of CPU time using a Pentium 133MHz. During the verification effort, we found two bugs which had not been discovered by running the ACL2 executable specification. One was a deadlock caused by undefined instructions, and the other was in the multiplier which returned wrong answers for certain inputs.

4 Conclusion

We have verified the correctness of the micro-architectural specification of a pipelined microprocessor with respect to its ISA-level specification by defining a table-based execution abstraction. Our technique introduced the MAETT as an execution trace model, which allows us to easily define various pipeline properties. We proved that such properties are invariantly held by all micro-architectural states reachable from a flushed state, and then used that fact to prove the final correctness criteria showing the micro-architecture implements the ISA.

Our proof approach is incremental. Properties of the micro-architectural design are identified and formally defined; for example, that the program counter should be pointing to the correct instruction. The definition of these properties often only involves a portion of the micro-architecture. Thus, proofs to ensure that these properties are maintained by the implementation do not require analyzing the entire implementation. Once we have established the correctness of these properties, we compose them to establish the correctness of the entire design.

We believe that this approach will allow us to verify deeper and more complex designs than is currently possible with automated approaches. The immediate focus of our future research is integrate exceptions and interrupts into our trace table based verification approach.

References

1. M. Agaard, M. Leeser, Reasoning About Pipelines with Structural Hazards, Pipelined Microprocessors, Theorem Provers in Circuit Design : theory, practice, and experience, Lecture Notes in Computer Science 901, Springer Verlag, 1995, page 13-32.
2. R. S. Boyer and J S. Moore. A Computational Logic Handbook. Academic Press, Boston, 1988.
3. J. R. Burch, D. L. Dill: Automatic Verification of Pipelined Microprocessor Control, In D. Dill Editor, Computer Aided Verification, Lecture Notes in Computer Science 818, Springer Verlag, 1994, page 68-80.
4. J. R. Burch. Techniques for verifying superscalar microprocessors. In Design Automation Conference, June 1996.

5. D. Cyrluk. Microprocessor verification in PVS: A methodology and simple example, Technical Report SRI-CSL-93-12, SRI Computer Science Laboratory, Dec. 1993

6. J. Hennessey, D. Patterson, Computer Architecture a Quantitative Approach, Morgan Kaufmann Publishers, Inc., 1996.

7. W. A. Hunt, Jr., B. Brock, A Formal HDL and Its Use in the FM9001 Verification. In C.A.R. Hoare and M.J.C. Gordon, editors, Mechanized Reasoning and Hardware Design, page 35-48. Prentice-Hall International Series in Computer Science, Englewood Cliffs, N.J., 1992

8. R. B. Jones, D. L. Dill, J. R. Burch, Efficient Validity Checking for Processor Verification, 1995 IEEE/ACM International Conference on Computer-Aided Design, pages 2-6.

9. M. Kaufmann, J S. Moore, ACL2: An Industrial Strength Version of Nqthm, Proceedings of the Eleventh Annual Conference on Computer Assurance (COMPASS-96), pages 23-34 , IEEE Computer Society Press, June 1996.

10. M. Srivas, M. Bickford, Formal Verification of a Pipelined Microprocessor, IEEE Software, September 1990, page 52-64.

11. M. K. Srivas, S. P. Miller, Formal Verification of a Commercial Microprocessor, Technical Report SRI-CSL-95-12, SRI Computer Science Laboratory, July 1995.

12. S. Tahar, R. Kumar, Formal Verification of Pipeline Conflicts in RISC Processors, Proc. European Design Automation Conference (EURO-DAC94), Grenoble, France, September 1994, IEEE Computer Society Press. page 285-289.

13. P. J. Windley, M. L. Coe, A Correctness Model for Pipelined Microprocessors, Theorem Provers in Circuit Design : theory, practice, and experience, Lecture Notes in Computer Science 901, Springer Verlag, 1995, page 33-51.

14. P. J. Windley, J. R. Burch: Mechanically Checking a Lemma Used in an Automatic Verification Tool, Formal Methods in Computer-Aided Design, Lecture Notes in Computer Science 1166, Springer Verlag, 1996, page 362-376.

On Combining Formal and Informal Verification

Jun Yuan*   Jian Shen**   Jacob Abraham**   Adnan Aziz**

Abstract. We propose algorithms which combine simulation with symbolic methods for the verification of invariants. The motivation is twofold. First, there are designs which are too complex to be formally verified using symbolic methods; however the use of symbolic techniques in conjunction with traditional simulation results in better "coverage" relative to the computational resources used. Additionally, even on designs which can be symbolically verified, the use of a hybrid methodology often detects the presence of bugs faster than either formal verification or simulation.

1 Introduction

In this paper we will be concerned with the problem of *design verification*; specifically, the problem of *invariant checking* over gate-level designs. Traditionally, designs have been verified by extensive simulation. While offering the benefits of simplicity and scalability, simulation offers no guarantees of correctness; for large designs, the fraction of the design space which can be covered in this methodology becomes vanishingly small. Indeed, there are many examples of designs that passed extensive simulation, but were still found to contain bugs [4]. This has led to the proposal of "formal methods" for design verification; the adjective formal refers to the unambiguous specification of the system and the properties being checked, together with the validation step generating a mathematically rigorous proof of correctness.

In theory the computational complexity of invariant checking on netlists is high; PSPACE-complete to be precise. In practise, many designs are well structured, and this can be exploited to devise heuristic procedures which perform well on specific classes of designs. One method which has been used to successfully verify a large number of complex designs is the use of "symbolic data structures" such as Binary Decision Diagrams (BDDs) to efficiently represent and manipulate the state spaces of designs [11]. The primary limitation of BDD based approaches to invariant checking is that for many designs, the BDDs constructed in the course of verification can grow extremely large, resulting in space-outs or severe performance degradation due to paging [12].

Practicing verifiers are less concerned with formally verifying designs than finding bugs in them as early as possible. As Henzinger has pointed out, "falsification" is a more accurate description of the endeavor called "verification" Faced

---

 * Motorola Inc., Austin TX yuan@adttx.sps.mot.com
** ECE Dept., Univ. of Texas, Austin TX {jshen | jaa | adnan} @ece.utexas.edu

with the twin dilemmas of diminished coverage through simulation and the inability of symbolic methods to formally verify large designs, it is natural to ask how best to combine symbolic methods with simulation, so as to find bugs as quickly as possible.

In this paper we provide two answers to the problem posed above. It is to be stressed that neither method is complete, i.e., guaranteed to provide a formal certificate of correctness if the invariant passes, or a counterexample if it fails. However, all reported violations of the invariant are true bugs.

We first develop the method of *saturated simulation*, wherein the designer designates a subset of the latches as being "interesting"; these could, for example, be the program counter and status bits in a microprocessor. The procedure performs a partial traversal of the state space. At each step, symbolic techniques are used to compute the image of current set of states, and only a minimal subset of the image is kept so that all control states seen thus far are represented; we also describe an extension that visits all controller edges. Heuristically, the control portion of the design, while being much smaller than the datapath, is the main source of design errors. Saturated simulation attempts to explore as much of the control state space, thus increasing the likelihood of finding bugs.

The efficiency of this approach comes from the observation that it is feasible to compute the symbolic image of a single state even for very large designs, coupled with the fact that the set of control states is typically much smaller than the entire state space. Additionally, fast BDD routines exist for generating and manipulating representative elements of equivalence classes [9].

We then describe an orthogonal approach referred to as *retrograde analysis* [15]. Starting from B_0, the complement of the invariant, successive preimages $B_0, B_1, B_2, \ldots$ are computed symbolically. This is done till the BDD for some B_n grows larger in size than a (user-specified) threshold value. Cycle simulation is performed from an initial state; simulation is halted if a state which lies B_n, since every state in B_n can reach a state in B_0. We describe greedy search strategies for finding paths to B_n from an initial state which use Hamming distance as a metric to be minimized. The primary benefit of retrograde analysis is that the set $\cup_i B_i$ is typically much larger (in the sense of cardinality) than B_0; hence, in a heuristic sense, B_n offers a much larger "target" for simulation.

These routines have been coded on top of the tool VIS [2]. Our experimental results underline the effectiveness that is suggested by the heuristic arguments given above.

To the best of our knowledge, the principles of saturated simulation and retrograde analysis are novel to this paper. We have been influenced by a number of related works. Thompson's [15] work on Retrograde Analysis provided the initial impetus. Additionally, we were influenced by the dramatic improvements made to cycle simulation by the use of BDDs by Ashar and Malik [1], and McGeer et al. [10], who made clear the importance of making maximum use of the physical memory available on the machine. Ravi et al. [13] attempt to pick subsets of state sets encountered during reachability analysis which have small BDDs but contain a large number of states. This is distinct from our approach, wherein a subset is chosen which attempts to maximize the number of distinct controller states. Cho et al. [5] pick nets to abstract into primary inputs, consequently obtaining super-sets of the set of reachable states. The work of Ho et al. [7] and Hoskote et al. [8] on creating simulation vectors which excite a large number of transitions on the controller states of a design suggested the usefulness of using transitions rather than states to obtain good coverage of controller behavior. However, they used designer supplied "translation functions", or test-based techniques to generate simulation input sequences which excited as much of the control as possible; our approach is rooted in symbolic methods.

2 Background — Invariant Verification

In order to be able to analytically reason about hardware, we first need to develop mathematical models for digital systems. Singhal [14] gives a detailed exposition for computational models for hardware.

Hardware designs can be modeled at the *structural* level using *netlists*, or at the *behavioral* level using *finite state machines* (FSMs). A netlist consists of an interconnected set of primary inputs, gates, and latches. Each gate has an associated Boolean function. A finite state machine can be represented by an edge-labeled directed graph, where the vertices correspond to *states*, and the labels are *input-output* pairs.

For a given a netlist η, there is a natural way of deriving a finite state machine from it; states are evaluations to the set of latch variables, and the next-state/output functions are derived by composing the gate functions.

Given a design D and a set of states A, the *image* of A (denoted by $Img(A)$) is the set of all states which can be reached from A by applying an input sequence of length one. Similarly, the *pre-image* of A (denoted by $PreImg(A)$) is the set off all states which can reach A in one step. The Img and Pre-image procedures can be implemented symbolically using Reduced Ordered Binary Decision Diagram [3].

A common verification problem for hardware designs is to determine if every state reachable from a designated set of initial states lies within a specified set of "good states" (referred to as the *invariant*). This problem is variously known as *invariant verification*, or *assertion checking*.

One straightforward solution to the invariant checking problem is to symbol-ically compute all states reachable from the initial states and determine that they all lie in the invariant. An alternate approach to checking invariants is based on *backward analysis*, wherein the symbolic *PreImg* operator is iteratively applied to determine all states which can reach the complement of the invariant; the invariant fails if the initial state lies in this set.

The primary limitation of both approaches is that the BDDs encountered in the course of image computations can grow very large.

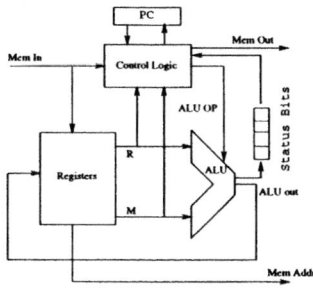

Fig. 1. Partitioning a design into Control and Datapath.

3 Saturated Simulation

Many designs can be separated into "control" and "datapath" as illustrated in Figure 1; furthermore, the designer is aware of this dichotomy. For most such designs, the number of latches in the controller is usually a small fraction of the total number of latches; however, the control portion is where bugs usually occur. In this section, we describe an approach we refer to as "saturate simulation"; this approach attempts heuristically to explore as much of the control portion of the design as possible.

As an example, consider the **viper** microprocessor [6]. It contains 9 latches which can be naturally designated control and 210 which are data. Hence, there are no more than 512 different possible values for the control state. It is feasible even for very large designs to compute the image of a small (in the sense of cardinality) set of states. In part, this follows from the fact that the construction of the BDD for the next-state logic can be restricted to the current set of states. This suggests that it may be possible to perform a "partial" reachability analysis, in which all distinct control states are preserved at each step.

Let the variables associated with the control portion of the design be X_c and the variables associated with the datapath be X_d. Thus the state of the design is given by an evaluation to $X_c \cup X_d$.

Definition 1. Let A be a set of states. A subset A' of A is *control-saturated* with respect to A if

$$(\forall \alpha_c . \forall \alpha_d) \left[(\alpha_c, \alpha_d) \in A \;\rightarrow\; (\exists \alpha_d')[(\alpha_c, \alpha_d') \in A'] \right]$$

Intuitively, A' is a control-saturated subset of A if every control state occurring in A occurs in A'. Thus control-saturated subsets of A preserve all the controller states present in A. Heuristically, a minimal control-saturated subset of A is a good representative set — it includes all the distinct controller configurations in A, and is as small as possible (in the sense of cardinality). An example of a control-saturated subset is given in Figure 2(a).

We now address the problem of computing minimal control-saturated subsets of A. Let f be a Boolean function on variables $X = \{x_1, x_2, \ldots, x_n\}$. Lin et

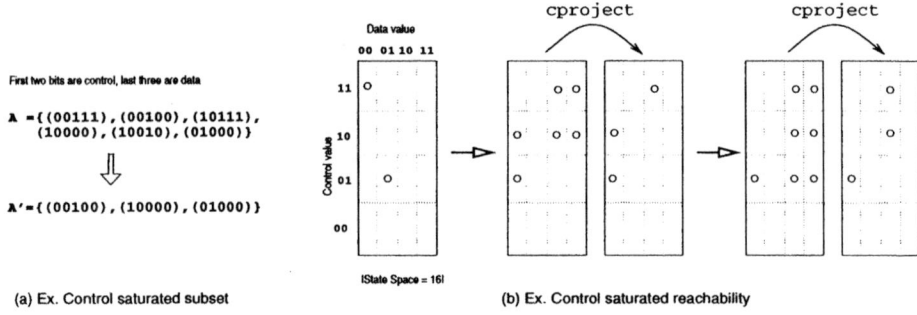

(a) Ex. Control saturated subset

(b) Ex. Control saturated reachability

Fig. 2. Minimal control saturated subsets.

```
/* A initialized to the BDD for the reset states. */
/* G is the BDD for the invariant.  */
BDD_t function Cntrl_Sat_Sim(A, Cntrl_Vars, G) {

    if (BDD_Intersects(A, Ḡ))  /* Invariant fails!! */
        assert FAIL;

    ImgA := BDD_Img(A);
    R := BDD_Or( A, ImgA );
    R* := BDD_Cproject( R, Cntrl_Vars );

    if (BDD_Equal( R*, A))
        return R*;

    return Cntrl_Sat_Sim(R*, Cntrl_Vars, G);
}
```

Fig. 3. Control-saturated simulation.

al. [9] presented an efficient algorithm (referred to as the `cproject` operator) which takes a BDD for f and a subset $X' \subset X$ of the variables, and returns a BDD for a function f^* which has the property that

1. for any assignment v to the variables in X, so that $f(v) = 1$, there is exactly one valuation v' which agrees with the valuation v over the variables in X' so that $f^*(v') = 1$, and furthermore
2. for all u, $f^*(u) = 1 \Rightarrow f(u) = 1$.

Since sets can be thought of in terms of characteristic functions, we will freely apply the `cproject` operator to sets. Observe that `cproject`(A, X_c) is a minimal control saturated subset of A.

In Figure 3 we sketch a simple symbolic procedure for invariant verification. Reachable states are iteratively computed using the Img operator; at each step, a control-saturated subset of the current reached state is computed using the `cproject` operator. This in turn is used as the current reached state set. The first few steps are illustrated in Figure 2(b). The procedure is incomplete, since it is greedy: minimal control-saturated subsets of the sets computed by the cproject operator will not necessarily be sufficient to cover all possible controller states.

One simple way of further enhancing the coverage achieved by control-saturated simulation is to generate several "representative" control states. There are simple modifications to the cproject operator which can achieve this effect. Another approach is to apply cproject only to the frontier of the reached states at each iteration.

3.1 Control-edge Saturated Simulation

A fundamental extension to obtain enhanced coverage is to perform a partial reachability analysis and at each step pick a subset of the image which preserves all "controller transitions" to the image from the current set. Ho et al. [7] and Abraham et al. [8] created simulation vectors which excite a large number of control transitions in designs; the high quality of their results in terms of finding bugs with these vectors underlines the usefulness of using transitions rather than states to obtain good coverage. As an example, consider a microprocessor where the control state is the value of the program counter. Two states which correspond to different lines in the program may both transition the same program line with different data values; in this case, it is natural to keep the resulting states different.

We now describe how to explore edges in the control state space.

Definition 2. Let A be a set of states. A subset B of $Img(A)$ is said to be *control-edge saturated* with respect to A if

$$(\forall \alpha_c.\forall \alpha_d.\forall \beta_c.\forall \beta_d)\big[\,[(\alpha_c,\alpha_d) \in A \;\wedge\; (\beta_c,\beta_d) \in Img(\{(\alpha_c,\alpha_d)\})] \;\rightarrow$$
$$(\exists \beta_d'.\exists \alpha_d')[(\beta_c,\beta_d') \in B \;\wedge\; (\alpha_c,\alpha_d') \in A \;\wedge\; (\beta_c,\beta_d') \in Img(\{(\alpha_c,\alpha_d')\})]\,\big]$$

In English, the above definition says that B is control-edge saturated when for every transition $(\alpha_C,\alpha_D) \rightarrow (\beta_C,\beta_D)$ from A to $ImgA$, there is a state (β_C,β_D') in B and a state (α_C,α_D') in A so that $(\alpha_C,\alpha_D') \rightarrow (\beta_C,\beta_D')$.

Thus in some sense, control-edge saturated subsets of $Img(A)$ preserve all the controller transitions originating at A. Heuristically, a minimal control-edge saturated subset of $Img(A)$ is a good representative set — it includes all the distinct controller configurations resulting in $Img(A)$ from transitions from A, and is as small as possible. An example of a minimal control-edge saturated subset is given in Figure 4.

Minimal control-edge saturated sets can be computed augmenting the design: for every control latch x_C, add a new latch x_S which "shadows" x_C, that is, the next state of x_S is the present state of x_C. Denote the set of shadow state variables thus introduced by X_s. Clearly the next-state of the latches indexed by $X_c \cup X_d$ is independent of that of the shadow latches. The following lemma demonstrates that minimal control-edge saturated sets can be computed from the augmented design.

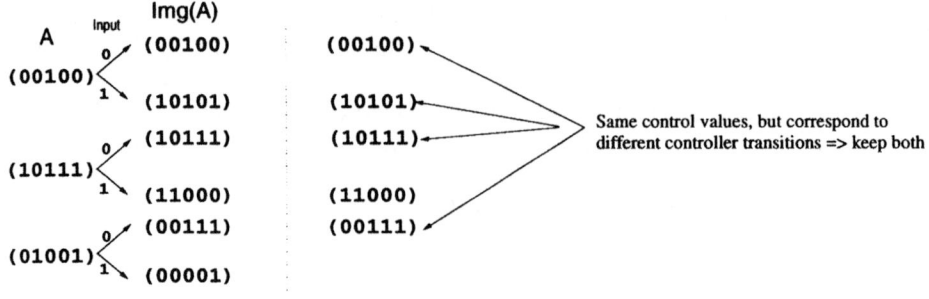

First two bits are control, last three are data

Fig. 4. A minimal control-edge saturated subset.

Lemma 3. Let A^* be A lifted from $X_c \cup X_d$ to $X_c \cup X_d \cup X_s$. Define B to be the existential quantification of $\mathtt{cproject}(Img(A^*), X_c \cup X_s)$ by X_s. Then B is minimal control-edge saturated with respect to A.

Proof. Observing that $\mathtt{cproject}(\Gamma, \theta)$ is always subset of Γ, it follows that $\mathtt{cproject}(Img(A^*), X_c \cup X_s)$ is a subset of $Img(A^*)$. Since the next state of non-shadow latches does not depend on the shadow latches, it follows that the existential quantification of $Img(A^*)$ by X_s is equal to $Img(A)$, and so B is a subset of $Img(A)$.

We now show B is control-edge saturated with respect to A. Let (α_C, α_D) and (β_C, β_D) satisfy the "if" portion of the implication in Definition 2. Then there is a transition from $(\alpha_C, \alpha_D) \in A$ to (β_C, β_D), i.e., $(\beta_C, \beta_D) \in Img(\{(\alpha_C, \alpha_D)\})$. ¿From the construction of the augmented design, $((\beta_C, \alpha_C), \beta_D)$ is in $Img((\alpha_C, \alpha_S), \alpha_D)$ for an arbitrary assignment α_S to the shadow latches. Hence $\mathtt{cproject}(Img(A^*), X_c \cup X_s)$ contains a state of the form $((\beta_C, \alpha_C), \beta'_D)$. Note $((\beta_C, \alpha_C), \beta_D')$ lies in $Img(A^*)$; let it lie in the image of $((\alpha_C, \alpha_S'), \alpha_D')$. Hence, on existentially quantifying the X_s variables from $\mathtt{cproject}(Img(A^*), X_c \cup X_s)$, the resulting set (namely B) will contain (β_C, β'_D). Since (β_C, β_D') lies in the image of (α_C, α_D'), α_D' and β_D' are existential witnesses for the "then" portion of the implication in Definition 2.

Minimality of B follows from the properties of $\mathtt{cproject}$ described in the previous section. ∎

3.2 Experimental Results – Saturated Simulation

We coded the routines described in the previous section as part of the VIS program [2]. Results are provided on two benchmarks – the *8085*, and *viper* microprocessors. The *8085* is approximately 4000 gate equivalents, and contains 242 latches, of which 33 were identified as being control. The *viper* is also 4000 gate equivalents, and contains 218 latches of which 9 were from the control. All experiments were conducted on an UltraSPARC 1, with a 170 MHz processor, and

Example	Rchd. States	Peak BDD	Control States	Control Edges	depth
viper	1.36×10^{19}	2033	23	31	4
8085	1.43×10^{7}	275641	1233	3723	10

Table 1. Complete BDD based reachability analysis.

Example	Peak BDD	Control States	Control Edges	depth
viper	160180	246	688	64
8085	81089	1846	4765	43

Table 2. Partial reachability analysis using control-state saturated subsets.

128 MBytes of main memory. A timeout of 2000 seconds was used for all *viper* experiments, and 1000 seconds for *8085* experiments. Sifting-based dynamic reordering was enabled throughout the experiments.

Table 1 presents results on the use of a complete BDD-based reachability analysis on the two benchmarks. Peak BDD is the number of nodes in the largest BDD encountered during reachability analysis. (The abnormally low peak BDD for *viper* in Table 1 stems from the fact that the program timed out after the first four reachability steps, which were easily performed.) Table 2 presents results on the use of a control-state saturated simulation (as given in Figure 3). For *8085*, we compute almost twice as many reachable control states and transitions; for *viper*, an order of magnitude more. Table 3 presents results on the use of control-edge saturated simulation. In the same time, more edges are visited; this comes at the expense of higher memory consumption with respect to control-state saturated simulation. Interestingly, fewer control states are visited; we ascribe this to the fact that the control-state saturated simulation is faster, and so manages to go deeper into the state space in the same amount of time; this is seen in the depth column.

We compare saturated simulation with fast lookup based cycle simulation [1, 10] in Table 4. For *viper*, we performed 1000 sets of simulations, each comprising of 200 vectors; for *8085* we performed 4000 sets of length 200. Even though we gave cycle simulation two orders of magnitude more time, it still performed far worse than saturated simulation.

Example	Peak BDD	Control States	Control Edges	depth
viper	71213	236	705	60
8085	81089	1696	6324	30

Table 3. Partial reachability analysis using control-edge saturated subsets.

Example	Saturated Simulation			Cycle Simulation			
	Time (sec)	Ctl States	Ctl Edges	Time	Size	Ctl States	Ctl Edges
viper	2000	236	705	86616	1000 × 200	121	288
8085	1000	1696	6324	99143	4000 × 200	705	2674

Table 4. Comparing saturated simulation with cycle simulation.

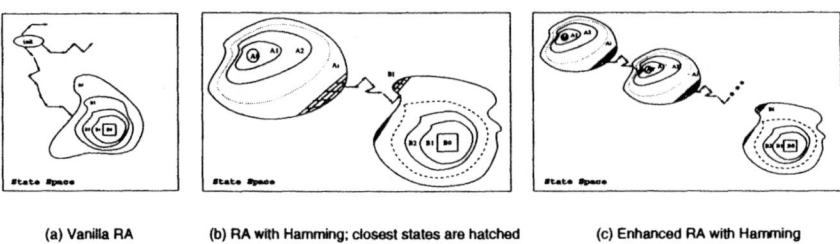

(a) Vanilla RA   (b) RA with Hamming; closest states are hatched   (c) Enhanced RA with Hamming

Fig. 5. Retrograde search for Invariant checking

4 Retrograde Analysis

Retrograde Analysis (RA) is an important search technique developed within the field of Artificial Intelligence. In its simplest form, RA first marks all end positions (e.g., checkmate), and then by making *unmoves* from the end positions works its way back to the positions farthest from the end position, on the way determining the game theoretic values of *all* positions in the search space.

RA can naturally be applied to invariant checking: construct the sets of states $B_0, B_1, \ldots$ where B_0 is the complement of the invariant and $B_{i+1} = PreImg(B_i)$. Analogously to the W_i's above, the B_i's are effectively bad states. The B_0's can grow very large in terms of cardinality; it is natural to use BDDs to represent them compactly. Finally, when main memory is nearly exhausted, say at the set B_l, search for an input sequence which takes an initial state to a state in B_l.

The simplest search strategy is the simulation of random input vectors starting from a random initial state; the search halts if some state reached in this fashion lies in B_l. This approach is illustrated in Figure 5(a). Note that checking if a state lies in the set defined by a BDD is very fast — it take time proportional to the number of bits in the state, and is independent of the size of the BDD.

A more sophisticated search strategy is to pick an initial state which is "close" to the target states, i.e., to B_l. We propose the use of Hamming distance as a measure of closeness.

Recall that the Hamming distance between $\alpha, \beta \in \{0,1\}^n$ (denoted by $\Delta(\alpha, \beta)$) is the number of positions in which the α and β vectors differ. Consider the relations $H_0, H_1, H_2, \ldots, H_n \subset \{0,1\}^{2n}$ where $(\alpha, \beta) \in H_k$ iff $\Leftrightarrow \Delta(\alpha, \beta) \leq k$. The relation H_1 can be constructed directly using BDDs. The relation H_{i+1} satisfies the following identity:

$$H_{i+1} = H_i \cup (\exists \gamma)[(\alpha, \gamma) \in H_i \wedge (\beta, \gamma) \in H_1]$$

Hence, the BDDs for $H_0, H_1, H_2, \ldots, H_n \subset \{0,1\}^{2n}$ can be easily constructed; furthermore a simple argument based on counting cofactors shows that they are small for the interleaved variable ordering.

The search for states in B_l can be enhanced by by first performing forward reachability from the initial states till the BDD for reached states reaches a threshold size. ¿From the outermost ring, pick a state (say α) which is closest to B_l, and then perform random cycle simulation from α. This is illustrated in Figure 5(b). Instead of cycle simulation from α, a combination of symbolic forward reachability analysis coupled with the the Hamming heuristic can be recursively applied. This illustrated in Figure 5(c).

4.1 Experimental Results – Retrograde Analysis

We coded the routines described in the previous section as part of the VIS program [2], and experimented with a number of examples. Representative results are provided on two benchmarks – *Mesh4* is a routing algorithm on a 4 by 4 mesh of nodes, and *Cube4* is hypercube based routing protocol. For both examples, we chose an invariant which fails.

Results on *Mesh4* are reported in Figure 6. We plot BDD size and cardinality after successive pre-images in Figure 6(a); both grow quickly. In Figure 6(b) we plot the number of simulation trials needed to reach a pre-image, starting from the initial state against the number of preimage steps taken; each trial consists of applying 100 random vectors. It is clear from the picture that this number decreases rapidly.

The effect of Hamming distance is given in Figure 7 for the *Cube4* example. Figures 7(a) and 7(b) are as before. In Figure 7(c), we show the effect of taking one forward step, and then picking a state in the image which is close to the target as opposed to a random state in the image; in Figure 7(d) we take two forward steps, and then pick a state which is close to the target. In both cases, there is an appreciable decrease in the number of simulation trials needed when Hamming distance is used. Interestingly, when a state in the image is picked at random, the performance is actually worse that simply starting at the initial state.

5 Conclusion

We investigated ways in which to combine symbolic verification with simulation. Specifically, we gave heuristic justification for saturated simulation and retrograde analysis. Experimental evidence corroborates that these approaches yield enhanced coverage and robustness. Thus the combination of formal and informal verification offers benefits not available in each independently.

In the future we intend to build upon the theme of relating formal and informal methods, particularly the problem of validating software for embedded controllers.

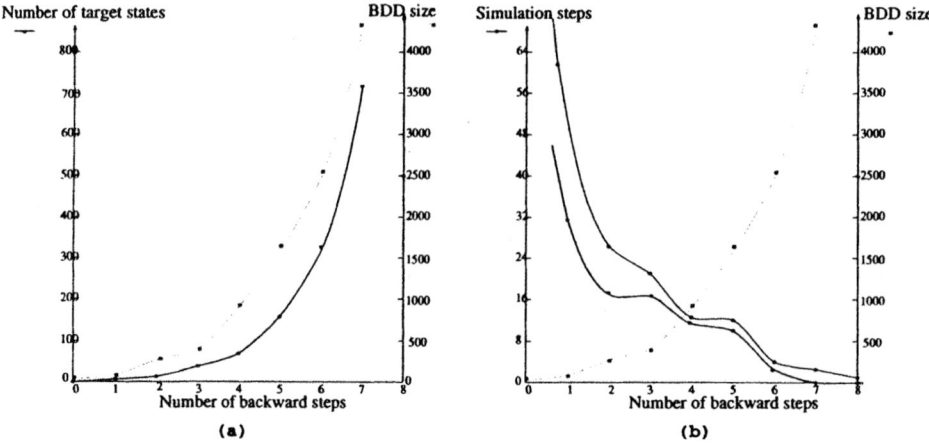

Fig. 6. Retrograde Analysis applied to *Mesh4*

References

1. P. Ashar and S. Malik. Fast Functional Simulation Using Branching Programs. In *Proc. Intl. Conf. on Computer-Aided Design*, November 1995.
2. R. K. Brayton, G. D. Hachtel, A. Sangiovanni-Vincentelli, F. Somenzi, A. Aziz, S.-T. Cheng, S. Edwards, S. Khatri, Y. Kukimoto, A. Pardo, S. Qadeer, R. K. Ranjan, S. Sarwary, T. R. Shiple, G. Swamy, and T. Villa. VIS: A system for Verification and Synthesis. In *Proc. of the Computer Aided Verification Conf.*, July 1996.
3. R. Bryant. Graph-based Algorithms for Boolean Function Manipulation. *IEEE Transactions on Computers*, C-35:677–691, August 1986.
4. B. Chen, M. Yamazaki, and M. Fujita. Bug Identification of a Real Chip Design by Symbolic Model Checking. In *Proc. European Conf. on Design Automation*, pages 132–136, March 1994.
5. H. Cho, G. D. Hachtel, E. Macii, M. Poncino, and F. Somenzi. A Structural Approach to State Space Decomposition for Approximate Reachability Analysis. In *Proc. Intl. Conf. on Computer Design*, October 1994.
6. W.J. Culler. *Implementing Safety Critical Systems: The VIPER microprocessor.* Kluwer Academic Publishment, 1987.
7. Richard C. Ho, C. Han Yang, Mark A. Horowitz, and David L. Dill. Architectural Validation for Processors. In *Proceedings of the International Symposium on Computer Architecture*, June 1995.
8. Y. Hoskote, D. Moundanos, and J. Abraham. Automatic Extraction of the Control Flow Machine and Application to Evaluating Coverage of Verification Vectors. In *Proc. Intl. Conf. on Computer Design*, Austin, TX, October 1995.
9. B. Lin and R. Newton. Implicit Manipulation of Equivalence Classes Using Binary Decision Diagrams. In *Proc. Intl. Conf. on Computer Design*, Cambridge, MA, October 1991.
10. P. McGeer, K. McMillan, A. Saldanha, A. Sangiovanni-Vincentelli, and P. Scaglia. Fast Discrete Function Evaluation. In *Proc. Intl. Conf. on Computer-Aided Design*, November 1995.

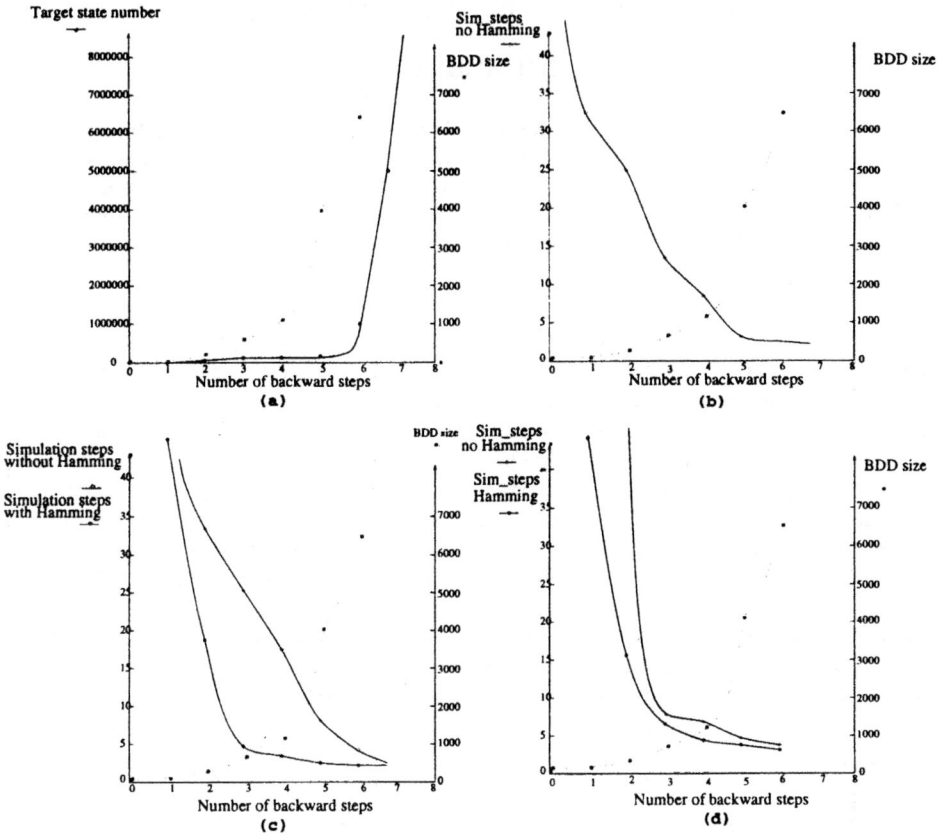

Fig. 7. Effect of Hamming Distance on *Cube4*

11. Kenneth L. McMillan. *Symbolic Model Checking.* Kluwer Academic Publishers, 1993.
12. R. Ranjan, J. Sanghavi, R. K. Brayton, and A. L. Sangiovanni-Vincentelli. High Performance BDD Package Based on Exploiting Memory Hierarchy. In *Proc. of the Design Automation Conf.*, Las Vegas, NV, June 1996.
13. K. Ravi and F. Somenzi. High Density Reachability Analysis. In *Proc. Intl. Conf. on Computer-Aided Design*, Santa Clara, CA, November 1995.
14. Vigyan Singhal. *Design Replacements for Sequential Circuits.* PhD thesis, University of California Berkeley, Electronics Research Laboratory, College of Engineering, University of California, Berkeley, CA 94720, 1996.
15. K. Thompson. Retrograde analysis of certain endgames. *ICCA Journal*, 9(3):131–139, 1986.

Efficient Modeling of MemoryArrays in Symbolic Simulation[1]

Miroslav Velev
Department of Electrical and
Computer Engineering
Carnegie Mellon University
Pittsburgh, PA 15213
mvelev@ece.cmu.edu

Randal E. Bryant
School of Computer Science
Carnegie Mellon University
Pittsburgh, PA 15213
randy.bryant@cs.cmu.edu

Alok Jain
Department of Electrical and
Computer Engineering
Carnegie Mellon University
Pittsburgh, PA 15213
alok.jain@ece.cmu.edu

Abstract. This paper enables symbolic simulation of systems with large embedded memories. Each memory array is replaced with a behavioral model, where the number of symbolic variables used to characterize the initial state of the memory is proportional to the number of memory accesses. The memory state is represented by a list containing entries of the form $\langle c, a, d \rangle$, where c is a Boolean expression denoting the set of conditions for which the entry is defined, a is an address expression denoting a memory location, and d is a data expression denoting the contents of this location. Address and data expressions are represented as vectors of Boolean expressions. The list interacts with the rest of the circuit by means of a software interface developed as part of the symbolic simulation engine. The interface monitors the control lines of the memory array and translates read and write conditions into accesses to the list. This memory model was also incorporated into the Symbolic Trajectory Evaluation technique for formal verification. Experimental results show that the new model significantly outperforms the transistor level memory model when verifying a simple pipelined data path.

1. Introduction

Simulation is widely used to validate systems at various levels of design abstraction such as the transistor, gate, and behavioral levels. The simulation models for memory arrays at all these levels explicitly represent each memory bit. This is not a problem for conventional simulation which uses a single logic value to denote the state of a memory bit. However, symbolic simulation would require a symbolic variable for every bit of the memory. In addition, bit-level symbolic model checking would need the next-state function for each memory bit. Therefore, the number of variables in symbolic computation is proportional to the size of the memory, and is prohibitive for large memory arrays.

This paper shows a way to overcome this limitation by replacing each memory array with an Efficient Memory Model (EMM). The EMM is a behavioral model, which allows the number of symbolic variables used to be proportional to the number of memory accesses rather than to the size of the memory. It is based on the observation that a single execution sequence typically contains a limited number of memory accesses.

Symbolic Trajectory Evaluation (STE) is an extension of symbolic simulation that has been used to formally verify circuits [8]. STE has been applied on the verifica-

---

1. This research was supported in part by the SRC under contract 96-DC-068.

tion of a simple pipelined data path [2]. Incorporation of the EMM in STE enabled us
to verify the pipelined data path with a significantly larger register file than previously
possible.

Symbolic model checking has also been used to verify a pipelined data path [3].
However, the limitation of the method is that it requires the next-state relation for the
entire circuit, which leads to introducing two symbolic variables for every state bit in
the circuit. Burch, Clarke, and Long [4] represent the transition relation as an implicit
conjunction of transition relations for parts of the circuit. In this way, they avoid building a monolithic BDD for the transition relation of the entire circuit, but still need two
symbolic variables for each memory bit. Clarke, Grumberg, and Long [6] propose a
method for using abstraction in order to reduce the complexity of symbolic model
checking. They show how abstraction functions can be applied to produce an abstract
model whose state space is a subset of that of the original model, such that if certain
properties hold on the abstract model, they will also be true for the original one. However, this requires a careful choice of abstraction functions by the user.

A symbolic representation of memory arrays has been used by Burch and Dill [5].
Their technique is also based on symbolic simulation. However, it verifies only the
control, assuming that the combinational logic in the data path is correct. On the other
hand, our method verifies the entire circuit. While Burch and Dill use uninterpreted
functions with equality, which abstract away the details of the data path, we use BDDs
and model fully the entire circuit, but that leads to greater memory and CPU time consumption. The logic of uninterpreted functions with equality allows them to introduce
only a single symbolic variable for denoting the initial state of a memory array. The
need to have data at the bit level in order to verify the data path, requires the user of
our method to introduce symbolic variables proportional to the number of memory
array accesses. Given a real circuit, their method would require the user to provide the
distinction between the control and the data path. Ours would need only an identification of the memory arrays. Finally, we perform the verification at the circuit level of
the implementation, while they operate on an abstracted high level model of the control and require the availability of an appropriate compiler to automatically extract the
control from the real circuit.

This paper advocates a two step approach for the verification of circuits with large
embedded memories. The first step is to use STE to verify the transistor level memory
arrays independently from the rest of the circuit. Pandey and Bryant have combined
symmetry reductions and STE to enable the verification of very large memory arrays
at the transistor level [7]. The second step is to use STE to verify the circuit after the
memory arrays are replaced by EMMs.

Section 2 describes the symbolic domain used in our algorithms. Section 3 gives a
brief overview of STE. Sections 4 presents the EMM and section 5 introduces its
underlying algorithms. Section 6 explains the way to incorporate the EMM into STE.
Experimental results are presented in Section 7, and plans for future work are outlined
in Section 8.

2. Symbolic Domain

We will consider three different domains - Boolean, address, and data - corresponding respectively to the control, address, and data information that can be applied at the inputs of a memory array. Symbolic variables will be introduced in each of the domains and will be used in expression generation. Address and data expressions will be represented by vectors of Boolean expressions having width n and w, respectively, for a memory with $N = 2^n$ locations, each holding a word consisting of w bits. The types **BExpr**, **AExpr**, and **DExpr** will denote respectively Boolean, address, and data expressions in the algorithms to be presented.

We will use the term *context* to refer to an assignment of values to the symbolic variables. A Boolean expression can be viewed as defining a set of contexts, namely those for which the expression evaluates to **true**.

The selection operator *ITE* (for "If-Then-Else"), when applied on three Boolean expressions, is defined as

$$ITE(b, t, e) \doteq (b \wedge t) \vee (\neg b \wedge e) \tag{1}$$

Address comparison is then implemented as:

$$A1 = A2 \doteq \neg \bigvee_{i=1}^{n} A1_i \oplus A2_i \tag{2}$$

while address selection $A1 \leftarrow ITE(b, A2, A3)$ is implemented by selecting the corresponding bits:

$$A1_i \leftarrow ITE_i(b, A2, A3) \doteq A1_i \leftarrow (b \wedge A2_i) \vee (\neg b \wedge A3_i), \quad i = 1, \dots, n \tag{3}$$

The definition of data operations is similar, but over vectors of width w.

Although we have used BDDs to represent the Boolean expressions in our implementation, there is nothing about this work that intrinsically requires it to be BDD based. Any canonical representation of Boolean expressions can be substituted.

3. STE Background

STE is a formal verification technique based on symbolic simulation. For the purpose of this paper, it would suffice to say that STE is capable of verifying circuit properties, described as *assertions*, of the form $A \overset{\text{LEADSTO}}{\Rightarrow} C$. The antecedent A specifies constraints on the inputs and the internal state of the circuit, and the *consequent* C specifies the set of expected outputs and state transitions. Both A and C are formulas that can be defined recursively as:

1) *a simple predicate*: the three possibilities being (**node** $n = boolean\_expression$), or (**node_vector** $N = address\_expression$), or (**node_vector** $N = data\_expression$), where in the last two cases each node of the node vector N gets associated with its corresponding bit-level Boolean expression of the given address or data expression;

2) *a conjunction of two formulas*: $F_1 \wedge F_2$ is a formula if F_1 and F_2 are formulas;

3) *a domain restriction*: (*boolean_expression* → *F*) is a formula if *F* is a formula, meaning that *F* should hold for the contexts in which *boolean_expression* is **true**;

4) *a next time operator*: N(*F*) is a formula if *F* is a formula, meaning that *F* should hold in the next time period.

A shorthand notation for k nested next time operators is N^k. A formula is said to be *instantaneous* if it does not contain any next time operators. Any formula F can be rewritten into the form $F_0 \wedge NF_1 \wedge N^2F_2 \wedge \ldots \wedge N^kF_k$, where each formula F_i is instantaneous. For simplicity in the current presentation, we will assume that the antecedent is free of self inconsistencies, i.e. it cannot have a node asserted to two complementary logic values simultaneously.

STE maintain two global Boolean expressions OK_A and OK_C, which are initialized to be **true**. The STE algorithm updates the circuit node values and the global Boolean expressions at every simulation time step. The antecedent defines the stimuli and the consequent defines the set of acceptable responses for the circuit. The expression OK_A maintains the condition under which the circuit node values are compatible with the values specified by the antecedent. The expression OK_C maintains the condition under which the circuit node values belong to the set of acceptable values specified by the consequent. The Boolean expression $\neg OK_A \vee OK_C$ defines the condition under which the assertion holds for the circuit.

4. Efficient Modeling of Memory Arrays

The main assumption of our approach is that every memory array can be represented, possibly after the introduction of some extra logic, as a memory with only write and read ports, all of which have the same numbers of address and data bits, as shown in Figure 1.

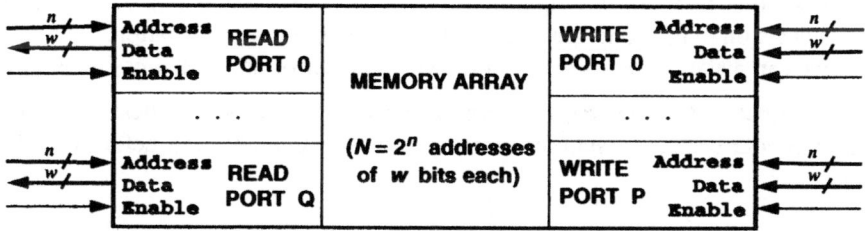

Figure 1. View of a memory array, according to our model.

The interaction of the memory array with the rest of the circuit is assumed to take place on the rising edge of a port Enable signal. In case of multiple port Enables having rising edges simultaneously, the resulting accesses to the memory array will be ordered according to the priority of the ports.

During symbolic simulation, the memory state is represented by a list containing entries of the form ⟨*c, a, d*⟩, where *c* is a Boolean expression denoting the set of contexts for which the entry is defined, *a* is an address expression denoting a memory location, and *d* is a data expression denoting the contents of this location. The context information is included for modeling memory systems where the *Write* and *Read* operations may be performed conditionally depending on the value of a control signal. Initially the list is empty.

The list interacts with the rest of the circuit by means of a software interface developed as part of the symbolic simulation engine. The interface monitors the port `Enable` lines. Should a rising edge occur at a port `Enable`, a *Write* or a *Read* operation will result, as determined by the type of the port. The Boolean expression *c* for the contexts of the memory operation will be formed as the condition for a rising edge on the port `Enable`. The operation will be performed if *c* is a non-zero Boolean expression. The `Address` and `Data` lines of the port will be scanned in order to obtain the address expression *a* and the data expression *d*, respectively. A *Write* operation completes with the insertion of the entry $\langle c, a, d \rangle$ in the list. A *Read* operation retrieves from the list a data expression *rd* that represents the data contents read from the memory at address *a* given the contexts *c*. The software interface completes the *Read* operation by asserting the `Data` lines of the port to the data expression *ITE(c, rd, d)*, i.e. to the retrieved data expression *rd* under the contexts *c* of the operation and to the old data expression *d* otherwise. The routines needed by the software interface for accessing the list are presented next.

5. Implementation of Memory Operations

5.1 Support Operations

The list entries are kept in order from *head* (low priority) to *tail* (high priority). Entries may be inserted at either end, using procedures *InsertHead* and *InsertTail*, and may be deleted using procedure *Delete*. The function *Valid*, when applied to a Boolean expression, returns **true** if the expression is valid, i.e., true for all contexts, and **false** otherwise. Note that in all of the algorithms, a Boolean expression cannot be used as a control decision in the code, since it will have a symbolic representation. On the other hand, we can make control decisions based on whether or not an expression is valid.

The function *GenDataExpr* generates a new data expression, whose variables are used to denote the initial state of memory locations that are read before ever being written.

5.2 Implementation of Memory *Read* and *Write* Operations

The *Write* operation, shown as a procedure in Figure 2, takes as arguments a memory list, a Boolean expression denoting the contexts for which the write should be performed, and address and data expressions denoting the memory location and its desired contents, respectively. As the code shows, it is implemented by simply inserting an element into the *tail* (high priority) end of the list, indicating that this entry should overwrite any other entries for this address. As an optimization, it removes any list elements that for all contexts are overwritten by this operation. Note that this optimization need not be performed, as will become apparent after the definition of the

Read operation. We could safely leave any overwritten element in the list.

procedure *Write*(**List** *mem*, **BExpr** *c*, **AExpr** *a*, **DExpr** *d*)
{ Write data *d* to location *a* under contexts *c* }
  { Optional optimization }
  for each $\langle ec, ea, ed \rangle$ **in** *mem* **do**
    if *Valid*($ec \Rightarrow [c \wedge a=ea]$) **then**
      Delete(*mem*, $\langle ec, ea, ed \rangle$)
  { Perform Write }
  InsertTail(*mem*, $\langle c, a, d \rangle$)

Figure 2. Implementation of the *Write* operation.

The *Read* operation is shown in Figure 3 as a function which, given a memory list, a Boolean expression denoting the contexts for which the read should be performed, and an address expression, returns a data expression indicating the contents of this location.

function *Read*(**List** *mem*, **BExpr** *c*, **AExpr** *a*): **DExpr**
{ Read from location *a* under contexts *c* }
  $g \leftarrow$ *GenDataExpr*()
  return *ReadWithDefault*(*mem*, *c*, *a*, *g*)

function *ReadWithDefault*(**List** *mem*, **BExpr** *c*, **AExpr** *a*, **DExpr** *d*): **DExpr**
{ Attempt to read from location *a*, using *d* for contexts where no value found }
  $rd \leftarrow d$
  found $\leftarrow$ **false**
  for each $\langle ec, ea, ed \rangle$ **in** *mem* from head to tail **do**
    match $\leftarrow ec \wedge a=ea$
    $rd \leftarrow$ *ITE*(*match*, *ed*, *rd*)
    found $\leftarrow$ *found* $\vee$ *match*
  if $\neg$*Valid*(*found*) **then**
    InsertHead(*mem*, $\langle c, a, d \rangle$)
  return *rd*

Figure 3. Implementation of the *Read* operation.

The main part of the *Read* operation is implemented with the function *ReadWith-Default*, which will also be used in the implementation of two STE procedures, to be presented in Section 6. The purpose of *ReadWithDefault* is to construct a data expression giving the contents of the memory location denoted by its argument address expression. It does this by scanning through the list from lowest to highest priority, adding a selection operator to the expression that chooses between the list element's data expression and the previously formed data expression, based on the match condition. It also generates a Boolean expression *found* indicating the contexts for which a matching list element has been encountered. *ReadWithDefault* has as its fourth argument a "default" data expression to be used when no matching list element is found. When this case arises, a new list element is inserted into the *head* (low priority) end of the list.

The *Read* operation is implemented by calling *ReadWithDefault* with a newly generated symbolic data expression g as the default. The contexts for which *ReadWith-Default* does not find a matching address in the list are those for which the addressed memory location has never been accessed by either a read or a write. The data expression g is then returned to indicate that the location may contain arbitrary data. By inserting the entry $\langle c, a, d \rangle$ into the list, we ensure that subsequent reads of this location will return the same expression. Note that computing and testing the validity of *found* is optional. We could safely insert the list element unconditionally, although at an increased memory usage.

6. Incorporation into STE

Efficient modeling of memory arrays in STE requires that formulas of the form $(c \rightarrow (mem[a] = d))$, where c is a Boolean expression, a is an Address expression, d is a Data expression, and *mem* is a memory array, be incorporated into the STE algorithm described in Section 3. When such formulas occur in the antecedent, they should result in asserting the memory state at location a to data d given contexts c, and are processed by procedure *AssertMem*, presented in Figure 6. Similarly, when such formulas occur in the consequent, they should result in checking the memory state at location a for having data d given contexts c, and are processed by procedure *CheckMem*, presented in Figure 7. The latter is a modified version of function *ReadWithDefault*, with the difference being that it does not insert a new entry into the list when the expression *found* is not valid.

> **procedure** *AssertMem*(**List** *mem*, **BExpr** *c*, **AExpr** *a*, **DExpr** *d*)
> { Determine conditions under which location a was asserted to data d given
> contexts c, and reflect them on OK_A, the Boolean expression indicating
> the absence of an antecedent failure }
> $rd \leftarrow ReadWithDefault(mem, c, a, d)$
> $OK_A \leftarrow OK_A \wedge (c \Rightarrow [rd = d])$

Figure 6. Implementation of the STE procedure *AssertMem*.

Procedure *AssertMem* uses the function *ReadWithDefault* in order to assert location a of *mem* to data d under the contexts c. OK_A maintains the condition under which the asserted value is consistent with the current state of the memory. In the case of procedure *CheckMem*, OK_C uses the Boolean expression *found* in order to maintain the condition under which *mem* has data d in location a given contexts c.

procedure *CheckMem*(**List** *mem*, **BExpr** *c*, **AExpr** *a*, **DExpr** *d*)

{ Determine conditions under which location *a* was checked to have data *d*

given contexts *c*, and reflect them on OK_C, the Boolean expression

indicating the absence of a consequent failure}

    rd ← *d*

    found ← **false**

    for each ⟨*ec, ea, ed*⟩ **in** *mem* from head to tail **do**

        match ← *ec* ∧ *a=ea*

        rd ← *ITE*(*match, ed, rd*)

        found ← *found* ∨ *match*

    OK_C ← OK_C ∧ *found* ∧ (*c* ⇒ [*rd* = *d*])

Figure 7. Implementation of the STE procedure *CheckMem*.

7. Experimental Results

Experiments were performed on the pipelined addressable accumulator shown in Figure 8. One mode of operation of the circuit is that of initialization of the register file with data from the input In, through the adder, and then through the Hold register. For this purpose the Clear signal is set to 1, so as to clear the value at the second input of the adder, while the destination location in the register file is specified by the address input Addr. A second mode of operation of the circuit is that of accumulation. Then, the address input Addr specifies a location in the register file, whose contents is to be added to the value supplied at the input In. In this case the Clear signal is set to 0, so as to ensure that the data value from the output of the register file will be passed unchanged to the adder.

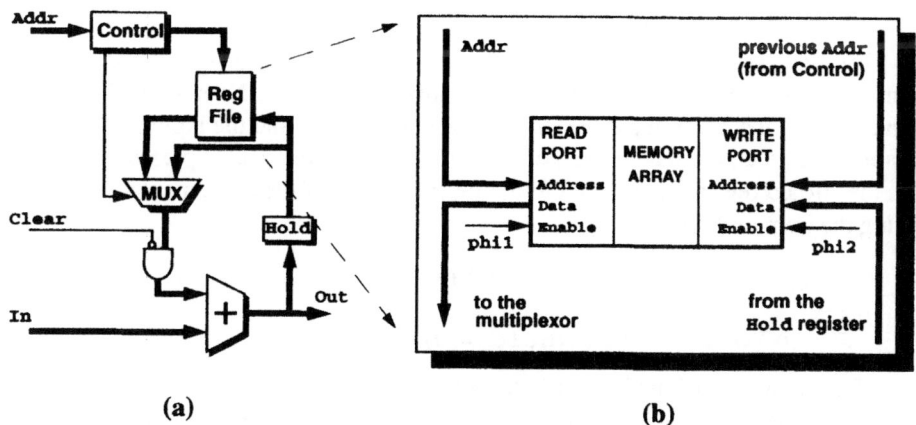

(a) (b)

Figure 8. (a) The pipelined addressable accumulator; (b) the connections of its register file when replaced by an EMM. The thick lines indicate buses, while the thin ones are of a single bit.

In order to speed up the accumulation mode by avoiding the latency of the register file, the addressable accumulator is pipelined by the introduction of a Hold register, a multiplexor (with the ability to choose between the outputs of the register file and the Hold register), and some extra circuitry in the control logic. This extra circuitry consists of a register to store the previous address and a comparator to determine whether that address is identical with the current address at the Addr input. Should the two addresses match, the control signal of the multiplexor is set so as to select the output of the Hold register. Hence, a bypassing of the register file takes effect.

For the experiments with the EMM, the dual-ported register file is removed from the circuit. The software interface ensures that a *Read* operation takes place on phi1 and a *Write* operation takes place on phi2, according to the register file connections shown in Figure 8.(b).

The specifications necessary for verifying the pipelined addressable accumulator, are presented in (4), (5), and (6). Note that Reg [i] and Reg [j] in (5) and (6), respectively, are instances of *symbolic indexing* [1], which results in the total number of symbolic variables being logarithmic in the number of address locations. We construct the antecedents by first defining the operation of the clocks. Shorthand notation for the possible signals applied to the clocks is presented next:

$$Clk01 \doteq (\texttt{phi1} = 0) \wedge (\texttt{phi2} = 1)$$
$$Clk00 \doteq (\texttt{phi1} = 0) \wedge (\texttt{phi2} = 0)$$
$$Clk10 \doteq (\texttt{phi1} = 1) \wedge (\texttt{phi2} = 0)$$

The clocking behavior of the entire circuit over 4, 8, and 12 time periods, respectively, is described by:

$$Clocks\_4 \doteq Clk01 \wedge N(Clk00) \wedge N^2(Clk10) \wedge N^3(Clk00)$$
$$Clocks\_8 \doteq Clocks\_4 \wedge N^4(Clocks\_4)$$
$$Clocks\_12 \doteq Clocks\_4 \wedge N^4(Clocks\_4) \wedge N^8(Clocks\_4)$$

The first assertion (4) verifies that the Hold register can be initialized with data from the input In of the pipelined addressable accumulator. Namely, if the Clear signal is high, the Addr input has an address expression i, and the input In has a data expression a, then the output Out of the adder will get the data expression a, and so will the Hold register, according to the timing details of the implementation (see the timing diagram on Figure 9).

$$Clocks\_8 \wedge N^2((\texttt{Clear} = 1) \wedge (\texttt{Addr} = i) \wedge (\texttt{In} = a))$$
$$\overset{\text{LEADSTO}}{\Rightarrow} N^4(\texttt{Out} = a) \wedge N^5(\texttt{Hold} = a) \tag{4}$$

The second assertion (5) verifies the adder in the pipelined addressable accumulator. It checks that if the Addr input has an address expression k and later, according to the timing details of the implementation, an address expression i, such that then the Clear signal is low, and the input In has a data expression a, the result will be that the output Out of the adder will get the data expression $a + b$, and so will the Hold register. Note that the Hold register is asserted to data expression b conditionally on the address equality $i == k$, and that location i of the register file is also asserted to data expression b, however conditionally on the address inequality $i \mathrel{!=} k$. If the control logic works properly, it should set the control signal of the multiplexor so as to select the data from the Hold register in the event that $i == k$ in order to bypass the register file. Otherwise, the data from location i of the register file will be selected. Altogether, the output of the multiplexor will be equal to $ITE(i == k, b, b) = b$, which will be the data expression at the second adder input. The timing diagram for this assertion can be seen on Figure 9.

$$Clocks\_12 \land N^2(\text{Addr} = k) \land N^5(i == k \;\rightarrow\; \text{Hold} = b) \land$$
$$N^6((\text{Clear} = 0) \land (\text{Addr} = i) \land (\text{In} = a) \land (i \mathrel{!=} k \;\rightarrow\; \text{Reg}[i] = b))$$
$$\overset{\text{LEADSTO}}{\Rightarrow} \quad N^8(\text{Out} = a + b) \land N^9(\text{Hold} = a + b) \tag{5}$$

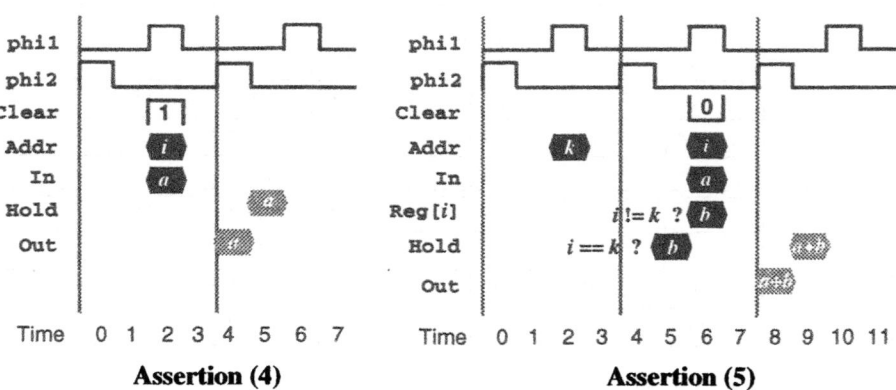

Figure 9. Timing diagrams for assertions (4) and (5). The solid areas denote asserted signals, while the shaded ones represent the expected results.

The last assertion (6) verifies that the register file can maintain its state in the pipelined addressable accumulator. If the Addr input has an address expression k and later, an address expression i, such that then a different location j of the register file has data expression b, then the data expression at that location will remain unchanged. The value b in the Hold register, asserted conditionally on $j == k$, allows testing the bus from the Hold register to the register file by using the same check of the memory state.

$$Clocks\_12 \land N^2(i \mathrel{!=} j \;\rightarrow\; \text{Addr} = k) \land N^5((i \mathrel{!=} j \land j == k) \rightarrow \text{Hold} = b) \land$$
$$N^6((i \mathrel{!=} j \;\rightarrow\; \text{Addr} = i) \land ((i \mathrel{!=} j \land j \mathrel{!=} k) \rightarrow \text{Reg}[j] = b))$$
$$\overset{\text{LEADSTO}}{\Rightarrow} \quad N^{10}(i \mathrel{!=} j \;\rightarrow\; \text{Reg}[j] = b) \tag{6}$$

The experiments were performed on an IBM RS/6000 58H running AIX 4.1.3 with 512 MB of physical memory. As can be seen from Table 1, the EMM outperforms the transistor level model (TLM) of the memory array in the pipelined address-able accumulator. A 7-15x speedup and a 2-8x reduction in memory were obtained, with the EMM advantage increasing with the memory size.

# Addresses	# Data Bits	CPU Time (s)			Memory (MB)		
		TLM	EMM	TLM / EMM	TLM	EMM	TLM / EMM
16	16	557	81	6.9	4.2	2.2	1.9
	32	1 095	161	6.8	7.3	3.2	2.3
	64	2 188	315	6.9	13.6	5.2	2.6
	128	4 391	628	7.0	26.3	9.2	2.9
32	16	1 030	100	10.3	8.2	3.0	2.7
	32	2 048	195	10.5	15.3	4.7	3.3
	64	4 102	388	10.6	29.5	8.2	3.6
	128	8 278	781	10.6	57.7	15.2	3.8
64	16	1 992	144	13.8	16.0	4.5	3.6
	32	3 999	283	14.1	30.7	7.8	3.9
	64	7 924	566	14.0	59.8	8.3	7.2
	128	15 824	1 154	13.7	118.0	15.3	7.7
128	16	3 907	248	15.8	31.6	4.6	6.9
	32	7 923	496	16.0	61.6	7.9	7.8
	64	15 547	1 003	15.5	121.1	14.5	8.4
	128	31 079	2 031	15.3	241.7	27.6	8.8

Table 1. Experimental results.

The asymptotic growth of STE, when used together with the TLM and the EMM, is summarized in Table 2, which also does a comparison with symbolic model check-ing, combined with either a partitioned transition relation [4] or with abstraction func-tions [6].

Criterion	Symbolic Model Checking		STE	
	Partitioned Transition Relation	Abstraction Functions	TLM	EMM
CPU Time w.r.t. # Data Bits	quadratic	linear	linear	linear
CPU Time w.r.t. # Addresses	cubic	linear	linear	sublinear
Memory w.r.t. # Data Bits	linear	---	linear	sublinear
Memory w.r.t. # Addresses	subcubic	---	linear	sublinear

Table 2. Asymptotic growth comparison of symbolic model checking and STE when verifying simple pipelined data paths.

However, it should be pointed out that there is a slight difference in the pipelined data path used for the experiments in [4] and [6], as compared with the one used in this paper. Also, the memory requirements of symbolic model checking combined with abstraction functions were not reported in [6].

Hence, the new method for efficient modeling of memory arrays has proven to be extremely promising. It would enable the symbolic simulation of memory arrays far larger than previously possible.

8. Future Work

We plan to improve the EMM software interface by including mechanisms to monitor the assumptions for correct operation of the model and to guarantee that it would behave as a conservative approximation of the replaced memory array. Furthermore, we will examine the integration of the efficient memory model with the symmetry-based technique for verification of transistor-level memory arrays, proposed by Pandey and Bryant [7], as a step towards hierarchical verification of systems containing large embedded memories.

Furthermore, we plan to extend the approach in order to support verification methodologies based on comparing the effect that two execution sequences have on the state of a memory array, similar to the work by Burch and Dill [5]. In other words, given two sequences of memory operations, we wish to test whether they yield identical behaviors. The assumption is that the two sequences start with matching initial memory states. For each externally visible *Read* operation in the first sequence, its counterpart in the second sequence must return the same value. Also, the final states resulting from the two sequences must match. To implement this, we require both a mechanism for guaranteeing that consistent values are used for the initial contents of the two memories and an algorithm for comparing the contents of two memories.

References

[1]   D. L. Beatty, R. E. Bryant, and C.-J. H. Seger, "Synchronous Circuit Verification by Symbolic Simulation: An Illustration," *Sixth MIT Conference on Advanced Research in VLSI*, 1990, pp. 98-112.

[2]   R. E. Bryant, D. E. Beatty, and C.-J. H. Seger, "Formal Hardware Verification by Symbolic Ternary Trajectory Evaluation," *28th Design Automation Conference*, June, 1991, pp. 297-402.

[3]   J. R. Burch, E. M. Clarke, K. L. McMillan, and D. L. Dill, "Sequential Circuit Verification Using Symbolic Model Checking," *27th Design Automation Conference*, June, 1990, pp. 46-51.

[4]   J. R. Burch, E. M. Clarke, and D. E. Long, "Representing Circuits More Efficiently in Symbolic Model Checking," *28th Design Automation Conference*, June, 1991, pp. 403-407.

[5]   J. R. Burch, and D. L. Dill, "Automated Verification of Pipelined Microprocessor Control," *CAV '94*, D. L. Dill, ed., LNCS 818, Springer-Verlag, June, 1994, pp. 68-80.

[6]   E. M. Clarke, O. Grumberg, and D. E. Long, "Model Checking and Abstraction,"*19th Annual ACM Symposium on Principles of Programming Languages*, 1992, pp. 343-354.

[7]   M. Pandey, and R. E. Bryant, "Exploiting Symmetry When Verifying Transistor-Level Circuits by Symbolic Trajectory Evaluation," *CAV '97*, June, 1997.

[8]   C.-J. H. Seger, and R. E. Bryant, "Formal Verification by Symbolic Evaluation of Partially-Ordered Trajectories," *Formal Methods in System Design*, Vol. 6, No. 2 (March, 1995), pp. 147-190.

Symbolic Model Checking of Infinite State Systems Using Presburger Arithmetic*

Tevfik Bultan, Richard Gerber and William Pugh

Department of Computer Science
University of Maryland, College Park, MD 20742, USA

Abstract. We present a new symbolic model checker which conservatively evaluates safety and liveness properties on infinite-state programs. We use *Presburger formulas* to symbolically encode a program's transition system, as well as its model-checking computations. All fixpoint calculations are executed symbolically, and their convergence is guaranteed by using approximation techniques. We demonstrate the promise of this technology on some well-known infinite-state concurrency problems.

1 Introduction

In recent years, there has been a surge of progress in the area of automated analysis for finite-state systems. Several reasons for this success are: (1) the development of powerful techniques such as *model-checking* (e.g., [5, 7]), which can efficiently verify safety and liveness properties; (2) innovative new data structures that symbolically encode large sets of states in compact formats (e.g., [4, 5]); and (3) new ways of carrying out *compositional* and *local* analysis, to assuage the "state explosion" usually associated with concurrency (e.g., [6, 9, 14]). But when transition systems are not restricted to be finite, most of these techniques are no longer applicable, as they inherently depend on all underlying types being bounded. Also general safety and liveness properties become undecidable for infinite transition systems.

We have developed a symbolic model checker to attack this problem, which symbolically encodes transition relations and sets of states using affine constraints on integer variables, logical connectives and quantifiers (i.e., Presburger formulas). Then, it efficiently manipulates these formulas (via a fast Presburger solver called the Omega library [15, 17]) to derive truth sets of temporal logic formulas and their fixpoint computations. Also, we use conservative approximation techniques in analysis of infinite state programs, which guarantee convergence by allowing false negatives.

In this paper we demonstrate our model checker's effectiveness on some classical infinite-state programs, taken from the concurrency literature [2]. While relatively small, they possess some interesting subtleties, especially in the tricky way their infinite-state variables influence control flow.

---

* This work was supported in part by ONR grant N00014-94-10228, NSF YI CCR-9357850 and a Packard Fellowship.

Other methods have been proposed to deal with infinite-state programs like these, and we note some of them here. In [8] Clarke *et al.* present a conservative model checking technique, by producing a finite abstraction of the program (e.g. via a congruence relation modulo a suitable integer), and then checking the property of interest on the abstraction. In [12] Dingel and Filkorn extend this method using "assumption-commitment" style reasoning and theorem proving. While these techniques require the user to find the appropriate abstractions – and hence are not completely automatable – we see them as being orthogonal to our approach. There may be cases where abstraction methods can vastly reduce the state space without achieving a finite representation. In these cases our model checker can be used on the infinite abstract models.

Our work was influenced by known techniques from abstract interpretation [10, 11]; specifically, we use some approximation methods first developed for that domain. Most reachability properties can be formulated as least fixpoints over sets of a program's states; if the state space is infinite, these fixpoints may not be computable. Abstract interpretation provides a way of approximating these fixpoints via a technique known as "widening" – which can compute a least fixpoint's upper bound in finite time. Since our basic temporal operators require similar computations, we were able to successfully use this method in conjunction with the Omega library.

Finally, our encoding of program states is similar to that used by Alur *et al.* in verifying hybrid systems [1]. A hybrid system is a discrete control automaton, which interacts with continuously-changing, external parameters. Like us, Alur *et al.* used an application of widening to help solve verification queries over linear hybrid automata – in which transition relations are defined in terms of affine constraints over the variables of the system.

The fundamental difference in our work is that we encode sets of integers – as opposed to the real numbers used in hybrid systems – and we can thus use Presburger formulas as our symbolic representation. This enables us to express and prove properties such as "x *is even*," using quantification. In general, satisfiability problems over constraints with integer variables are significantly harder to deal with. For example, checking to see if there exists an integer solution to a set of linear constraints is NP-hard, while the analogous real-valued problem can be solved in polynomial time. Also, we take our fixpoints by storing, at each step, unions of convex regions (with possible stride constraints); Alur *et al.* force intermediate results into a single convex region. While their strategy is one way to control potential state explosion, we have found that in our problem domain, most interesting properties cannot be proved unless multiple convex regions are used at each point.

The paper is organized as follows. First we present the syntax, semantics, and Presburger encodings for concurrent programs and their properties. Then we describe our symbolic model checker, and show how it exploits the Presburger representation. After formally defining *conservative approximations*, we discuss the specific approximation techniques for computing upper and lower bounds of fixpoints. Finally, we conclude with some discussion on our results.

Data Variables: a, b: positive integer
Control Variables: $pc_1 : \{T_1, W_1, C_1\}$, $pc_2 : \{T_2, W_2, C_2\}$
Initial Condition: $a = b = 0 \wedge pc_1 = T_1 \wedge pc_2 = T_2$
Events:

e_{T_1} enabled: $pc_1 = T_1$	e_{T_2} enabled: $pc_2 = T_2$
action: $pc_1' = W_1 \wedge a' = b + 1$	action: $pc_2' = W_2 \wedge b' = a + 1$
e_{W_1} enabled: $pc_1 = W_1 \wedge$	e_{W_2} enabled: $pc_2 = W_2 \wedge$
$(a < b \vee b = 0)$	$(b < a \vee a = 0)$
action: $pc_1' = C_1$	action: $pc_2' = C_2$
e_{C_1} enabled: $pc_1 = C_1$	e_{C_2} enabled: $pc_2 = C_2$
action: $pc_1' = T_1 \wedge a' = 0$	action: $pc_2' = T_2 \wedge b' = 0$

Fig. 1. The bakery algorithm.

2 Representation of Programs and Properties

We use the event-action language from [18] as our syntax for concurrent programs, with a semantics defined in terms of infinite transition systems. A concurrent program $C = (V, I, E)$ is represented by (1) a finite set of data and control variables V; (2) an initial condition I, which specifies the starting states of the program; and (3) a finite set of events E, where each event is considered atomic. The state of a program is determined by the values of its data and control variables. We assume that the domain of each variable is a countable set. Each event is represented with an enabling condition and an action, where the enabling condition constrains the states in which the event can occur, and the action defines a transformation on the variables of the program.

Consider the concurrent program shown in Figure 1, which implements the *bakery algorithm* [2] to achieve mutual exclusion between two processes. Here the control points for each process are denoted T, W, C, which stand for *thinking, waiting* or *in critical section*, respectively. If a variable v is used in an event, then the symbol v' denotes the new value of v after the action. If v is not mentioned in the action of an event, then we assume that its value is not altered by that event.

When a process wants to enter the critical section it first gets a ticket, which will be higher than those of all other processes currently in the critical section or waiting for entry. In the above system, variables a and b hold the ticket values for processes 1 and 2, respectively; a process gets its ticket by simply adding one to the highest outstanding ticket number. Note that variables a and b can increase without bound; i.e., this is not a finite-state program.

Given a program $C = (V, I, E)$ in the above language, we model it as an infinite transition system $M = (S, I, X, L)$, where S is the set of states, I is the set of initial states, $X \subseteq S \times S$ is the transition relation (derived from the set of events E), and $L : S \times SF \rightarrow \{\mathsf{True}, \mathsf{False}\}$ is the valuation function for state formulas over the program's variables. (We define the set of state formulas SF below.) The set of states S is obtained by taking Cartesian product of domains of all program variables; hence each state corresponds to a valuation of all the variables of the program.

Every event $e \in E$ defines a binary relation on the program's states, $X_e \subseteq S \times S$, such that $X_e = \{(s, s') : s \in \textbf{enabled}(e) \land (s, s') \in \textbf{action}(e)\}$ where s and s' denote program's states before and after the execution of event e, respectively. The sets $\textbf{enabled}(e)$ and $\textbf{action}(e)$ respectively denote the enabling condition and action of event e. Hence the global transition relation is $X = \bigcup_{e \in E} X_e$. Note that we use an interleaving model, where each transition represents execution of a single event, i.e., only one event can occur at a time.

Presburger formulas. The bakery algorithm's mutual exclusion requirement asserts that the following property stays invariant over all executions: $\neg (pc_1 = C_1 \land pc_2 = C_2)$. We call this type of assertion a *state formula*. And in general, we define the set of state formulas SF for a program C as all Presburger formulas which range over program's variables. Presburger formulas are generated by the following grammar:

$$f ::= t \leq t \mid (f) \mid f \land f \mid \neg f \mid \exists \textbf{var}\ f \qquad t ::= (t) \mid t + t \mid \textbf{var} \mid \textbf{constant}$$

Here, the terminals **constant** and **var** represent integer constants and variables, respectively. Using this base language, we can easily represent formulas including $<$, $=$, $\lor$, $\forall$, as well as multiplication by a constant. The set of closed formulas defined by the above grammar forms the theory of integers with addition, called *Presburger arithmetic*. An important property of Presburger arithmetic is that validity is decidable.

In general, the worst-case time bound for determining validity in Presburger arithmetic is prohibitive [13]. Yet we have found that the Omega library [15, 17] is quite efficient at solving the problems that arise in our analysis, which typically possess a small number of constraints, and do not contain multiple levels of alternating quantifiers. The Omega library uses extensions of Fourier variable elimination to solve integer programming problems, along with a set of transformation functions and heuristics to help convert real-valued approximations into discrete-valued solutions.

Temporal Properties. We use four CTL-style modal operators as the basis for our temporal logic – the "quantified-next-state" operators ($\exists\bigcirc$ and $\forall\bigcirc$), and "quantified-eventuality" operators ($\exists\Diamond$ and $\forall\Diamond$). Thus, the logic we use to reason about a program is generated over the set $\{f \in SF, \exists\bigcirc, \forall\bigcirc, \exists\Diamond, \forall\Diamond, \land, \lor, \neg\}$. As usual, quantified-invariant operators can easily be represented as $\exists\Box f = \neg\forall\Diamond\neg f$, and $\forall\Box f = \neg\exists\Diamond\neg f$, respectively.

The semantics of a temporal formula is defined on the paths of a program's transition system, $M = (S, I, X, L)$. A path $(s_0, s_1, s_2, \ldots)$ is a (finite or infinite) sequence of states, such that for each successive pair of states $(s_i, s_{i+1}) \in X$. Unlike Clarke *et al.* [7], we do not require the transition relation X to be total. Rather, the semantics is defined using maximal paths [3] (as opposed to infinite paths). A maximal path is one which is either infinite, or it ends with a state that has no successors. The semantics of the temporal operators can then be defined as follows: A state s_0 satisfies $\forall\bigcirc f$ ($\exists\bigcirc f$) if and only if for all (some) maximal paths $(s_0, s_1, s_2, \ldots)$ with length ≥ 2, s_1 satisfies f. A state s_0 satisfies $\forall\Diamond f$ ($\exists\Diamond f$) if and only if for all (some) maximal paths $(s_0, s_1, s_2, \ldots)$ there exists an i such that s_i satisfies f.

In this language, the bakery algorithm's mutual-exclusion property is expressed as $\forall\Box(\neg(pc_1 = C_1 \wedge pc_2 = C_2))$, that is, the two processes never reach the critical section at the same time.

3 Symbolic Analysis

Presburger formulas – and their corresponding set-theoretic interpretations – give us a convenient way to symbolically encode sets of program states. Moreover, we also use this encoding to represent the program's underlying transition relation. For a given event e, if we assume that **enabled**(e) and **action**(e) are both representable as Presburger formulas (which prevents us, for example, from defining multiplication within a single event), then X_e is representable as a Presburger formula. This results in $|E|$ Presburger formulas, which together symbolically encode the transition relation X.

To carry out our analysis, we exploit the natural partitioning induced by valuations of the control variables, and we incrementally analyze the program by considering one class at a time. When applied to the bakery program this yields the following partitioning of the state space: $P = \{S_{(T_1, T_2)}, S_{(T_1, W_2)}, \ldots, S_{(C_1, C_2)}\}$ where, for example,

$$S_{(C_1, T_2)} = \{(pc_1, pc_2, a, b) : pc_1 = C_1 \wedge pc_2 = T_2\}.$$

We can then partition any subset of S as follows: If $Q \subseteq S$, then $P_Q = \{Q_1, Q_2, \ldots, Q_n\}$ is a partitioning of Q, where each $Q_i = Q \cap S_i$ (for all $S_i \in P$). E.g., in the bakery program, the set $Q = \{(pc_1, pc_2, a, b) : a < b\}$ denotes all states in which a is less than b. Using a partitioning via control points, we have $P_Q = \{Q_{(T_1, T_2)}, Q_{(T_1, W_2)}, \ldots, Q_{(C_1, C_2)}\}$ where, for example,

$$Q_{(C_1, C_2)} = \{(pc_1, pc_2, a, b) : pc_1 = C_1 \wedge pc_2 = C_2 \wedge a < b\}$$

which is the set of states where a is less than b and both processes are at the critical section.

After partitioning of the state space, we use the Omega library [15] to help *symbolically* compute the truth sets for the temporal properties at hand. The Omega library includes a large collection of object classes to efficiently manipulate Presburger formulas; to date it has mainly been used in high-performance compilers, specifically for dependence analysis, program transformations, and detecting redundant synchronization [16, 17]. The particular Omega functions we use are shown in Figure 2(A). These functions take symbolic representations of sets or relations as inputs (i.e., a Presburger formula representing a set or a relation), and return the symbolic form of a set or a relation as output.

To symbolically compute the temporal operators, we define a function **pred** : $2^S \rightarrow 2^S$, called the *predecessor function*, which, given a set of states, returns

SYMBOLIC OMEGA OPERATIONS	PROCEDURE CHECK(f)
	CASE
$F \cap G$: symbolic intersection	$f \in SF$: RETURN(f)
$F \cup G$: symbolic union	$f = \neg f_1$: RETURN($S - f_1$)
$F - G$: symbolic difference	$f = f_1 \wedge f_2$: RETURN($f_1 \cap f_2$)
F^{-1} : symbolic inverse of	$f = f_1 \vee f_2$: RETURN($f_1 \cup f_2$)
relation F	$f = \exists \bigcirc f_1$: RETURN($\mathbf{pred}(f_1)$)
$F[G]$: restrict domain of	$f = \forall \bigcirc f_1$: RETURN($S - \mathbf{pred}(S - f_1)$)
relation F to constraint	$f = \exists \diamond f_1$: $Q_0 = f_1$
G and return the range	$Q_{i+1} = Q_i \cup \mathbf{pred}(Q_i)$
of the result	RETURN(Q_n) when $Q_n = Q_{n+1}$
$\mathbf{hull}(F)$: convex hull of F	$f = \forall \diamond f_1$: $Q_0 = f_1$
	$Q_{i+1} = Q_i \cup (\mathbf{pred}(Q_i) - \mathbf{pred}(S - Q_i))$
	RETURN(Q_n) when $Q_n = Q_{n+1}$

Fig. 2. (A) Omega functions, and (B) symbolic model checker.

all the states that can reach this set in one step (i.e. after execution of a single event):

$$\mathbf{pred}(Q) \overset{\text{def}}{=} \{s : s' \in Q \wedge (s, s') \in X\}.$$

Using the Omega operator in Figure 2(A) we have $\mathbf{pred}(Q) = X^{-1}[Q]$. Moreover, we can symbolically compute $\mathbf{pred}$ with respect to our program's partitioning, and maintain a formula for each partition class, as follows:

$$\mathbf{pred}(Q) = \mathbf{pred}(\bigcup_{S_i \in P} (Q \cap S_i)) = \bigcup_{S_i \in P} \mathbf{pred}(Q \cap S_i) = \bigcup_{S_i \in P, e \in E} X_e^{-1}[Q \cap S_i].$$

By performing this computation individually for each partition class, we exploit the fact that many formulas inherently involve only small parts of the program's state space. For example, consider the states where both processes are at the critical section, or $Q = \{(pc_1, pc_2, a, b) : pc_1 = C_1 \wedge pc_2 = C_2\}$. Then we have

$$\mathbf{pred}(Q) = \bigcup_{e \in \{e_{W_1}, e_{W_2}\}} X_e^{-1}[Q \cap S_{(C_1, C_2)}]$$

$$= \{(pc_1, pc_2, a, b) : pc_1 = W_1 \wedge pc_2 = C_2 \wedge (b = 0 \vee a < b)\}$$
$$\cup \{(pc_1, pc_2, a, b) : pc_1 = C_1 \wedge pc_2 = W_2 \wedge (a = 0 \vee b < a)\}.$$

Now, given a symbolic representation for a set f, we can symbolically compute $\exists \bigcirc f$ and $\forall \bigcirc f$ using $\mathbf{pred}$, as follows:

$$\exists \bigcirc f = \mathbf{pred}(f) \qquad \text{and} \qquad \forall \bigcirc f = S - \mathbf{pred}(S - f).$$

As for $\exists \diamond$ and $\forall \diamond$, consider the functionals $\tau_{\exists \diamond f} = \lambda y. \ f \vee \exists \bigcirc y$ and $\tau_{\forall \diamond f} = \lambda y. \ f \vee (\forall \bigcirc y \wedge \exists \bigcirc y)$. The least fixpoints of $\tau_{\exists \diamond f}$ and $\tau_{\forall \diamond f}$ are equal to $\exists \diamond f$ and $\forall \diamond f$, respectively. Using well-known properties from lattice theory, it can be shown that every element in the sequence $\mathsf{False} = \emptyset, \tau_{\exists \diamond f}(\emptyset), \tau_{\exists \diamond f}^2(\emptyset), \tau_{\exists \diamond f}^3(\emptyset), \dots$, is a subset of the least fixpoint of $\tau_{\exists \diamond f}$; similarly, every element in the sequence $\mathsf{False} = \emptyset, \tau_{\forall\Diamond f}(\emptyset), \tau^2_{\forall\Diamond f}(\emptyset), \tau^3_{\forall\Diamond f}(\emptyset), \ldots$, is a subset of the least fixpoint of $\tau_{\forall\Diamond f}$. So when these monotonically increasing sequences reach a fixpoint, we know that it is the least fixpoint.

These methods lead directly to the semi-decision procedure shown in Figure 2(B) (subformulas are computed recursively). Given a program and a temporal logic formula, the model checker will (attempt to) symbolically compute the set of program states that satisfy the input formula – and the procedure will yield an exact answer if it converges.

Bakery Algorithm, Revisited. Recall the mutual exclusion requirement for the bakery algorithm, which is equivalent to: $\neg \exists\Diamond(pc_1 = C_1 \wedge pc_2 = C_2)$. To compute the least fixpoint $\exists\Diamond(pc_1 = C_1 \wedge pc_2 = C_2)$, the model checker initialized the first iterate to $Q_0 = \{(pc_1, pc_2, a, b) : pc_1 = C_1 \wedge pc_2 = C_2\}$. After 4 iterations, the fixpoint computation converged to a set Q (for a total computation time of 2.85 seconds on a Sun SPARCstation 5), where Q is partitioned as follows:

$$
\begin{array}{ll}
Q_{(T_1,T_2)} : pc_1 = T_1 \wedge pc_2 = T_2 \wedge \mathsf{False} & Q_{(T_1,C_2)} : pc_1 = T_1 \wedge pc_2 = C_2 \wedge b = 0 \\
Q_{(T_1,W_2)} : pc_1 = T_1 \wedge pc_2 = W_2 \wedge b = 0 & Q_{(C_1,T_2)} : pc_1 = C_1 \wedge pc_2 = T_2 \wedge a = 0 \\
Q_{(W_1,T_2)} : pc_1 = W_1 \wedge pc_2 = T_2 \wedge a = 0 & Q_{(C_1,C_2)} : pc_1 = C_1 \wedge pc_2 = C_2 \wedge \mathsf{True} \\
Q_{(W_1,C_2)} : pc_1 = W_1 \wedge pc_2 = C_2 \wedge (b = 0 \vee a < b) & \\
Q_{(C_1,W_2)} : pc_1 = C_1 \wedge pc_2 = W_2 \wedge (a = 0 \vee b < a) & \\
Q_{(W_1,W_2)} : pc_1 = W_1 \wedge pc_2 = W_2 \wedge (a = b = 0 \vee a = 0 \wedge 1 \le b \vee b = 0 \wedge 1 \le a) &
\end{array}
$$

Since the top-level formula is $\neg\exists\Diamond(pc_1 = C_1 \wedge pc_2 = C_2)$, the model checker computes $S - Q$. Then it checks if $I \subseteq (S - Q)$ and concludes that all of the initial states satisfy the safety property, hence the property is proved.

The model checker also proved the starvation freedom property, $\forall\Box(pc_1 = W_1 \rightarrow \forall\Diamond(pc_1 = C_1))$, which is equivalent to $\neg\exists\Diamond(pc_1 = W_1 \wedge \neg\forall\Diamond(pc_1 = C_1))$. The inner ($\forall\Diamond$) and outer ($\exists\Diamond$) fixpoint computations converged in 9 and 1 iterations, respectively (with a total computation time of 7.64 seconds).

4 Approximation Techniques

Since we have a Turing-computable language, our exact model-checker in Figure 2(B) may keep iterating forever without reaching a fixpoint. Thus we also need a conservative approximation method, which will always converge. A conservative analyzer is one which never yields a "false positive" (and reports that a property holds when in fact it does not), but it may yield a "false negative," and indicate that a property does not hold when it really does.

Indeed, our exact analyzer diverged when we fed it the so-called *ticket algorithm* [2], along with its related mutual exclusion property (see Figure 3). In particular, note its similarity to the bakery algorithm. The difference is that the value of the next available ticket is stored in the global variable t, while another global variable s holds the highest ticket value served thus far. New tickets are obtained by executing a fetch-and-add on t. A customer can enter the critical section when the last-used ticket s catches up to its local ticket number.

When the exact analyzer went to work on the mutual exclusion property of the ticket algorithm, it attempted to symbolically enumerate ways that both a

```
Data Variables: a, b, t, s: integer
Control Variables: pc₁ : {T₁, W₁, C₁}, pc₂ : {T₂, W₂, C₂}
Initial Condition: t = s ∧ pc₁ = T₁ ∧ pc₂ = T₂
Events:
 e_{T₁} enabled: pc₁ = T₁              e_{T₂} enabled: pc₂ = T₂
       action:  pc₁' = W₁∧                    action:  pc₂' = W₂∧
                a' = t ∧ t' = t + 1                     b' = t ∧ t' = t + 1
 e_{W₁} enabled: pc₁ = W₁ ∧ a ≤ s      e_{W₂} enabled: pc₂ = W₂ ∧ b ≤ s
       action:  pc₁' = C₁                    action:  pc₂' = C₂
 e_{C₁} enabled: pc₁ = C₁              e_{C₂} enabled: pc₂ = C₂
       action:  pc₁' = T₁ ∧ s' = s + 1        action:  pc₂' = T₂ ∧ s' = s + 1
```

Fig. 3. The ticket mutual-exclusion algorithm.

and b could be less than s. Since s and t are unbounded, this method failed to converge.

4.1 What is Conservative?

If we cannot directly compute a property f for a program, the next-best-thing is to generate a lower-bound for f, denoted f^-, such that $f^- \subseteq f$. Then if we determine that $I \subseteq f^-$, we have also achieved our objective – that $I \subseteq f$. However if $I \not\subseteq f^-$, we cannot conclude anything.

Since we seek to carry out our analysis in a recursive manner (as in the exact analyzer in Figure 2(B)), we have to compute an approximation to a formula by first computing approximations for its subformulas. Hence, with a property like $g = \neg h$, we first need to compute an *upper* approximation h^+ for the subformula h, and then let $g^- = S - h^+$.

When analyzing a negation-free formula, the compositionality of an approximation follows directly from the fact that all operators other than "¬" are monotonic. This means that any lower/upper approximation for a formula can be computed using the corresponding lower/upper approximation for its subformulas. As for handling arbitrary levels of negation, we can easily generalize the above mentioned method for outermost negation operators. That is, to approximate a temporal formula f, the following procedure determines which of f's subformulas require an upper bound, and which require a lower bound.

1. Mark the root of the parse tree for formula f with a minus sign ("−") if a lower bound is desired, and with a plus sign ("+") if an upper bound is desired.
2. Using a preorder tree traversal, visit each node in the tree, mark each node with the mark of its parent, unless its parent is a ¬ operator. In that case mark the node with the opposite bound.

4.2 Computing Upper Bounds

When the algorithms in Figure 2(B) attempt to compute fixpoints for $\exists\Diamond$ and $\forall\Diamond$, they may generate sequences of increasing lower bounds which never converge. And from elementary fixpoint theory we know that a least fixpoint exists – but it may simply not be computable. Hence our job is to accelerate the computation, and "leap-frog" over multiple members of the chain – perhaps at the risk of over-shooting the exact least fixpoint. As long as the result is larger than the exact fixpoint, we have an upper approximation.

The way we go about this is as follows. If the exact iteration sequence is $Q_0, Q_1, Q_2, \ldots$, then we find a *majorizing* sequence $\hat{Q}_0, \hat{Q}_1, \hat{Q}_2, \ldots$, such that (1) for each i, $Q_i \subseteq \hat{Q}_i$, and (2) the $\hat{Q}_i$ sequence reaches a fixpoint after finitely many iterates. Thus the fixpoint of the $\hat{Q}_i$'s is an upper approximation to the least fixpoint of the Q_i's.

To generate the $\hat{Q}_i$'s, we currently adopt a method developed by Cousot and Cousot, within the framework of abstract interpretation [10]. That is, we define an operator called widening, or "$\triangledown$", which majorizes the union computation as follows: For any pair of sets P, P', $P \cup P' \subseteq P \triangledown P'$. Using a suitable widening operator, we can redefine the procedures for $\exists \Diamond f$ and $\forall \Diamond f$ from Figure 2(B) as:

$$\begin{array}{l|l}
\hat{Q}_0 = f & \hat{Q}_0 = f \\
\hat{Q}_{i+1} = \hat{Q}_i \triangledown (\hat{Q}_i \cup \mathbf{pred}(\hat{Q}_i)) & \hat{Q}_{i+1} = \hat{Q}_i \triangledown (\hat{Q}_i \cup (\mathbf{pred}(\hat{Q}_i) - \mathbf{pred}(S - \hat{Q}_i))) \\
(\exists \Diamond f)^+ = \hat{Q}_n \text{ when } \hat{Q}_n = \hat{Q}_{n+1} & (\forall \Diamond f)^+ = \hat{Q}_n \text{ when } \hat{Q}_n = \hat{Q}_{n+1}
\end{array}$$

From the monotonicity of the **pred** operator, one can easily show by induction that these sequences do indeed majorize the Q_i's computed in Figure 2(B). And the final iterates are upper bounds for $\exists \Diamond f$ and $\forall \Diamond f$.

Our goal is to find a widening operator which (1) yields a suitable (i.e., reasonably tight) upper bound for union, and (2) forces the $\hat{Q}_i$ sequences to converge. In defining our widening operator, we generalized a technique used by Cousot and Halbwachs in [11]. The idea is to "guess" the direction of growth in the model-checker's Q_i iterates, and to extend the successive iterates in these directions. Cousot and Halbwachs' widening operator $\widehat{\triangledown}$ does this for *convex polyhedra* – i.e., regions formed by a conjunction of affine constraints. If both P and P' are convex, then $P \widehat{\triangledown} P'$ is defined by the constraints in P which are also satisfied by P'. For example,

$$\{(x, y) : x - 1 \leq y \leq x\} \ \widehat{\triangledown} \ \{(x, y) : x - 2 \leq y \leq x\} = \{(x, y) : y \leq x\}$$

Intuitively, if a constraint of P is not satisfied by P' this means that the iterates are increasing in that direction. By removing that constraint we extend the iterates in the direction of growth as much as possible without violating other constraints. Since $P \widehat{\triangledown} P'$ is built by simply removing constraints from P and since we cannot remove infinitely many constraints, the finiteness property is satisfied. *But* because it folds all arguments into a single convex region, a direct application of this method failed to work for us. The reason is that on all of our examples to date, all fixpoint computations were composed of a (potentially large) number of disjuncts, each defining a convex polytope. To accommodate this we generalized $\widehat{\triangledown}$ to handle multiple polyhedra. Assume that we have two Presburger sets Q and R, where $Q \subseteq R$. Then Q and R can be represented as $Q = q_1 \cup q_2 \cup \ldots \cup q_m$ and $R = r_1 \cup r_2 \cup \ldots \cup r_m \cup \ldots \cup r_n$, where all the q_i's and r_i's are convex polytopes, and where $m \leq n$, and for all $1 \leq i \leq m$, $q_i \subseteq r_i$. Then we can define our new widening operator to be

$$Q \triangledown R = \bigcup_{i=1}^{n} p_i \text{ s. t. } \forall i \left[i \leq m \to p_i = q_i \hat{\triangledown} r_i \text{ and } m < i \leq n \to p_i = r_i \right] \quad (\dagger)$$

So, assume that we are computing a $\exists\Diamond$ property, and that $\hat{Q}_i = q_1 \cup q_2 \cup \ldots \cup q_m$ where each of the q_j's is convex. Then $\hat{Q}_{i+1} = \hat{Q}_i \triangledown (\hat{Q}_i \cup \mathbf{pred}(\hat{Q}_i))$, with

$$\hat{Q}_i \cup \mathbf{pred}(\hat{Q}_i) = \left(\bigcup_{j=1}^{m} q_j \right) \bigcup \left(\bigcup_{j=1}^{m} \mathbf{pred}(q_j) \right) = (q_1 \cup \ldots \cup q_m) \bigcup (p_1 \cup \ldots \cup p_l)$$

Here the p_k's $(1 \leq k \leq l)$ represent a convex decomposition of $\bigcup_{j=1}^{m} \mathbf{pred}(q_j)$. To form the necessary r_i's, we use a simple algorithm to merge selected q_j's $(1 \leq j \leq m)$ with p_k's $(1 \leq k \leq l)$ in a pairwise fashion. For each q_j $(1 \leq j \leq m)$ we scan the p_k's $(1 \leq k \leq l)$, looking for polyhedra to merge. This is done by invoking an Omega function to compute the convex hull of $q_j \cup p_k$ – denoted $\mathbf{hull}(q_j \cup p_k)$ – and determining if it is equal to $q_j \cup p_k$. If so, we delete the p_k term and replace q_j with $\mathbf{hull}(q_j \cup p_k)$. We continue this process until a maximum amount of merging is accomplished, after which we have:

$$\hat{Q}_i = q_1 \cup q_2 \cup \ldots \cup q_m \quad \text{and} \quad \hat{Q}_i \cup \mathbf{pred}(\hat{Q}_i) = r_1 \cup r_2 \cup \ldots \cup r_n$$

such that $m \leq n$, and for all $1 \leq j \leq m$, $q_j \subseteq r_j$. Then the conditions for $\triangledown$ in $(\dagger)$ are satisfied, and therefore we can use it as our widening operation.

Note that the r_j decomposition of $\hat{Q}_i \cup \mathbf{pred}(\hat{Q}_i)$ may include too many terms if there is little potential for merging the q_j's with the p_k's. To ensure convergence, we also assign an upper bound to the number of disjoint convex regions we wish to represent. When we reach this bound we force-merge disjoint regions by replacing them with their convex hull – even if that loses precision (which is valid since we are computing upper bounds).

4.3 Computing Lower Bounds

Recall that each iteration of an exact fixpoint computation will yield a lower bound for $\exists\Diamond f$ and $\forall\Diamond f$. So to obtain a lower approximation for the purposes of analysis, we need only stop after a finite number of iterations; in this manner we are guaranteed to have a conservative approximation. Of course the question is: when do we stop?

Our verifier uses the following rules: if it is handling the outermost formula, then after each iteration it checks whether the initial states are included in the current lower bound. If so it stops, since the property is proved. If not it keeps going. Obviously there will be cases where this method fails to converge, and if this happens the tool will not be able to prove or disprove the property. However, the user is able to interact with the analyzer, and periodically monitor its progress; thus the user can optionally "pull the plug" on waiting for a response.

If the fixpoint we are computing is a subformula of another computation, the analyzer sets a (user specified) time limit to stop generating an approximation – after which it is used in the next-higher formula. But if the analyzer is unable to prove or disprove the outermost formula, the user may optionally return and improve the lower bound by continuing the fixpoint sequence.

Approximate Analysis of the Ticket Algorithm. Using the negation labeling algorithm, the mutual exclusion property of the ticket algorithm is rendered as $(\neg(\exists\Diamond(pc_1 = C_1 \wedge pc_2 = C_2)^+)^+)^-$. The temporal operator $\exists\Diamond$ is marked with "+" which means that we need an upper bound for the set of states violating mutual exclusion. The upper bound $\hat{Q}$ is computed using the multi-polyhedra widening technique in 9 iterations (with a CPU time of 7.32 seconds). However, since we are actually computing $\neg\exists\Diamond(pc_1 = C_1 \wedge pc_2 = C_2)$, the model checker computes $S - \hat{Q}$, which is a lower approximation for the states which respect mutual exclusion. Then, shows that $I \subseteq (S - \hat{Q})$.

We also wish to prove starvation-freedom. Negation-labeling converts process 1's relevant formula to: $(\neg(\exists\Diamond((pc_1 = W_1)^+ \wedge (\neg(\forall\Diamond(pc_1 = C_1)^-)^-)^+)^+)^+)^-$. Because of the double negation, the inner fixpoint ($\forall\Diamond$) is marked with "−" (i.e., a lower bound), whereas the outer fixpoint ($\exists\Diamond$) is marked with "+." The model checker computes the $\forall\Diamond$ property exactly, in 5 fixpoint iterations; hence the lower bound turns out to be exact. Then it computes an upper bound for the $\exists\Diamond$ property in 7 iterations, by using the widening technique (for a total CPU time of 27.03 seconds). After the lower bound for the whole formula is computed, it reports that all the initial states do indeed satisfy the liveness property.

5   Remarks

We have presented a new symbolic model checker for infinite-state programs, which evaluates safety and liveness properties. We demonstrated our method on two example programs. While they do not contain many lines of code, they exhibit subtle interplay between the infinite-state variables and predicates controlling execution flow. They are the sort of programs usually analyzed in hand proofs.

There is much work remaining. While our multiple-polyhedra widening approximation helped solve one of the problems in this paper, it can often be rather coarse. In general it sacrifices precision for finite termination. We are currently developing more precise methods for reachability properties using transitive closure computation techniques for Presburger formulas [16]. As we acquire more experience with both types of approximations, we hope to determine which techniques work best for different classes of programs, and why.

We also plan to investigate compositional approaches. We currently form our state-partitions over the Cartesian-product of all variable domains. When we scale to large numbers of processes we will obviously need a more compositional approach. To this end, we believe we can use many of the analogous methods developed for finite-state systems.

References

1. R. Alur, C. Courcoubetis, N. Halbwachs, T. A. Henzinger, P. H. Ho, X. Nicollin, A. Olivero, J. Sifakis, S. Yovine. The algorithmic analysis of hybrid systems. *Theoretical Computer Science*, 138(1):3–34, 1995.
2. G. R. Andrews. Concurrent Programming, Principles and Practice. The Benjamin/Cummings Publishing Company, 1991.
3. A. Arnold. Finite Transition Systems: Semantics of Communicating Systems. Prentice Hall, 1994.
4. R. E. Bryant. Symbolic Boolean manipulation with ordered binary-decision diagrams. *ACM Computing Surveys*, 24(3):293–318, 1992.
5. J. R. Burch, E. M. Clarke, K. L. McMillan, D. L. Dill, and L. H. Hwang. Symbolic model checking: 10^{20} states and beyond. In *Proc. 5th Annual IEEE Symp. on Logic in Computer Science*, pages 428–439, 1990.
6. T. Bultan, J. Fischer, and R. Gerber. Compositional verification by model checking for counter-examples. In *Proc. 1996 Int. Symp. on Software Testing and Analysis*, pages 224–238, 1996.
7. E. M. Clarke, E. A. Emerson, and A. P. Sistla. Automatic verification of finite-state concurrent systems using temporal logic specifications. *ACM Transactions on Programming Languages and Systems*, 8(2):244–263, 1986.
8. E. M. Clarke, O. Grumberg, D. E. Long Model checking and abstraction. In *Proc. 18th Annual ACM Symp. on Principles of Programming Languages*, pages 343–354, 1992.
9. E. M. Clarke, D. E. Long, and K. L. McMillan. Compositional model checking. In *Proc. 4th Annual IEEE Symp. on Logic in Computer Science*, pages 464–475, 1989.
10. P. Cousot and R. Cousot. Abstract interpretation: a unified lattice model for static analysis of programs by construction or approximation of fixpoints. In *Proc. 4th Annual ACM Symp. on Principles of Programming Languages*, pages 238–252, 1977.
11. P. Cousot and N. Halbwachs. Automatic discovery of linear restraints among variables of a program. In *Proc. 5th Annual ACM Symp. on Principles of Programming Languages*, pages 84–97, 1978.
12. J. Dingel, and T. Filkorn. Model checking for infinite state systems using data abstraction, assumption-commitment style reasoning and theorem proving. In Proc. 7th Int. Conference on Computer Aided Verification, LNCS 939, pages 54–69, 1995.
13. M. J. Fischer and M. O. Rabin. Super-Exponential Complexity of Presburger Arithmetic. *SIAM-AMS Proc.*, Volume 7, pages 27–41, 1974.
14. P. Godefroid. Partial-order methods for the verification of concurrent systems: An approach to the state-explosion problem. Ph.D. Thesis, Universite De Liege, 1994.
15. W. Kelly, V. Maslov, W. Pugh, E. Rosser, T. Shpeisman and D. Wonnacott. The Omega Library (version 1.00) interface guide. Available at <http://www.cs.umd.edu/projects/omega>.
16. W. Kelly, W. Pugh, E. Rosser and T. Shpeisman. Transitive closure of infinite graphs and its applications. Technical Report CS-TR-3457, UMIACS-TR-95-48, Department of Computer Science, University of Maryland, 1994.
17. W. Pugh. The Omega test: a fast and practical integer programming algorithm for dependence analysis. *Communications of the ACM*, 8:102–104, 1992.
18. A. Udaya Shankar. An introduction to assertional reasoning for concurrent systems. *ACM Computing Surveys*, 25(3):225–262, 1993.

Parametrized Verification of Linear Networks Using Automata as Invariants [*]

A. Prasad Sistla[1]

Electrical Engineering and Computer Science Department, The University of Illinois at Chicago, USA

1 Introduction

Recently there has been much interest in parametrized verification, i.e., verification of a family of systems $\{P_i\}_{i=1}^{\infty}$, where P_i is a system consisting of i number of processes, against a specification given in temporal logic or by an automaton. Such interest is motivated by the fact that many algorithms in practice are designed to work with arbitrary number of processes.

In general, the problem of determining if a family of networks of similar processes satisfies a temporal logic specification is undecidable [AK86]. Nevertheless, automated and semi-automated methods for verification for restricted classes of parametrized systems have been proposed in literature. The works of [SG87, GS92, EN96] present fully automated methods for systems composed of a single control process and an arbitrary number of identical client processes.

One of the semi-automated methods is to show that for certain class of problems (specifically, rings of arbitrary size or client-server problesm) there exists a k such that correctness of families of networks upto size up to k implies the correctness of networks of all sizes; this has bee done in the works of [EN95, GS92].

An alternate method, which we use, is to use induction on the number of processes. Roughly speaking, this method, when applied to a linear network composed of an arbitrary number of processes P works as follows. An inductive invariant I, specified as another process, is obtained. The induction step is shown by establishing that the process $I \odot P \leq P$ where $\odot$ is the composition operator, $\leq$ is an appropriate monotonic pre-order on processes. The basis step is obtained by showing that the system composed of a small number of processes is less than or equal to I in the pre-order. The correctness of the family of systems is established by showing that I itself satisfies the correctness property. All the three steps can be automated if I is a finite state process. The above approach has been taken in [WL89, KM89, BCG89].

Although the above approach of specifying the invariant as another process is elegant, it has the following drawback. It is difficult to specify invariants that involve predicates on global states as well as predicates on communication patterns. To overcome this problem, Abstract Transition Systems (ATS) were

---

[*] This work is partly supported by the NSF grants CCR-9623229, CCR-9212183, CCR-9633536

employed in [CGJ95] to specify the invariant. An abstract transition system consists of abstract states and transitions between the abstract states. An abstract state is specified by a regular expression or automaton that denotes a predicate on the global states of systems with arbitrary number of processes. Thus, ATS uses two different formalisms— the regular expressions to specify properties of global states and the transitions in the ATS to specify computation steps.

In this paper, we propose a unified formalism based on automata on two dimensional strings to specify the inductive invariant. Use of such automata is based on the observation that the computation of a linear network of n processes can be looked as a two dimensional string. One dimension is the time dimension which is infinite and the other is the space dimension consisting of the states of processes at any particular time. An automaton on two dimensional string takes as input the states and transitions of individual processes from the two dimensional string where these inputs are generated by scanning the string from left to right in the space dimension, and bottom to top in the time dimension. The automaton accepts the string by going through a final state infinitely often.

In our approach, the inductive invariant is specified by a finite state automaton A on two dimensional strings. The set of computations accepted by the automaton denotes the inductive invariant. We show how to compose an automaton with a process P to obtain another automaton $A \odot P$. The inductive step is proved by showing that $L(A \odot P)$ is contained in $L(A)$ where $L(A)$ is the set of two dimensional strings accepted A. This method is shown to be sound and complete for verifying correctness of families of linear networks (as well as circular networks) of the form $I \odot P^i \odot E$ (for all $i \geq 0$) where I, E and P are processes. The completeness result we prove is a semantic completeness result. It is for the first time that such a completeness result has been given for induction based proof systems for parametrized networks.

In general checking if $L(A_1) \subseteq L(A_2)$ is an undecidable problem. However, one can show that $L(A_1) \subseteq L(A_2)$ by exhibiting a simulation relation between the states of A_1 and A_2, or by showing that $\mathcal{L}(A_1) \subseteq \mathcal{L}(A_2)$ where $\mathcal{L}(A_i)$ is the set of one dimensional strings accepted by A_i. While automatically checking for the existence of simulation relations can be done efficiently, the problem of checking if $\mathcal{L}(A_1) \subseteq \mathcal{L}(A_2)$ can be done in exponential time using traditional automata theoretic approaches. We illustrate our approach by simple examples.

The above approach is extended for verifying correctness under fairness as well. For this we use generalized Buchi automata [GW91] and define fair composition of such an automaton with a process. The inductive invariants are specified by generalized Buchi automata. We show that this induction based approach for verifying correctness under fairness is sound. However, we do not have a completeness theorem for this case. To the best of our knowledge, all the earlier induction based approaches did not consider fairness.

Our paper is organized as follows. Section 2 defines the automata that we plan to use and the composition of an automata with a process. Section 3 presents the inductive approach for linear and circular networks. It also presents the induction based approach for correctness under fairness. It contains examples illustrating the approach. Section 4 contains concluding remarks.

2 Definitions

Automata. A Buchi automaton on two dimensional strings is defined exactly similar to the way a Buchi automaton on infinite strings is defined. The only difference is that the input alphabet to the two dimensional automaton has a special structure. Each input symbol to the automaton is of the form (u, a, d, u') where u and u' are process states, a is an action symbol which can be an element from $\Delta \cup \{\epsilon, i\tau, c\tau\}$ and d is an indicator denoting if the process is an internal process or a boundary process (if so which). Here u denotes the current local state of the process being scanned by the automaton and u' is the state of the same process in the next global state. If the action symbol a is ϵ then it indicates that the process does not make any transition in the current computational step; if a is $i\tau$ then it indicates that the process makes an internal transition (i.e., no communication) in the current computational step; if a is $c\tau$ then it denotes a synchronized communication with a neighboring process in the current computational step; if a is in Δ then it indicates that the process offers a communication denoted by a to the external world and only boundary processes can offer such communication.

Throughout this section, we assume that S is a set of process states and the states of all the processes are drawn from this set. We also assume that Δ, Δ' are communication alphabets that do not contain the symbols $\epsilon, i\tau, c\tau$, and that they contain complementary action/communication symbols; for an action symbol a, we let $\bar{a}$ denote the complement of a; furthermore, if $b = \bar{a}$ then $\bar{b} = a$.

Formally, an automaton A over Δ, is a 5-tuple $(Q_0, \Sigma, Q, \delta, F)$ where $\Sigma = S \times (\Delta \cup \{i\tau, c\tau, \epsilon\}) \times \{left, right, internal\} \times S$ is the set of input symbols as indicated above, Q is the set of automaton states, Q_0 is the set of initial states, $\delta \subseteq Q \times \Sigma \times Q$ is the next state relation and $F \subseteq Q$ is the set of final states.

Let n be a positive integer. A two-dimensional string σ of width n over an alphabet Δ is an infinite alternating sequence $s_0, a_0, s_1, a_1, ..., s_i, a_i, ...$ where $s_i = (s_{i,0}, s_{i,1}..., s_{i,n-1})$ is an n-tuple of process states and $a_i = (a_{i,0}, a_{i,1}, ..., a_{i,n-1})$ is an n-tuple of process actions where each $a_{i,j} \in \Delta \cup \{\epsilon, i\tau, c\tau\}$ (Note that the representation we used here is a row major representation of a 2-d string; this representation does not cause any loss of information). Each such string denotes a computation in which $s_{i,j}$ denotes the local state of process j in the global state s_i, and $a_{i,j}$ denotes the action taken by process j in the computational step from s_i to s_{i+1}.

A linearization of a 2-d string is obtained by scanning the 2-d string row by row, left to right, bottom to top, and outputting all quadruples of the form (s, a, d, s') where s and s' are the current and next states of the process being scanned, a is the action executed by the process and d is an indicator denoting the position of the process. Formally, a linearization $l(\sigma)$ of a 2-d string $\sigma = s_0, a_0, s_1, a_1, ...s_i, a_i, ...$, as given above, is the infinite sequence $u_{0,0}, u_{0,1}, ..., u_{0,n-1}, ..., u_{i,0}, u_{i,1}, ..., u_{i,j}, ...$ where $u_{i,j} = (s_{i,j}, a_{i,j}, d_{i,j}, s_{i+1,j})$ and for $0 \le i < \infty$, $d_{i,0} = $ *left*, $d_{i,n-1} = $ *right*, and for $0 < j < n-1$, $d_{i,j} = $ *internal*. Here $d_{i,j}$ denotes whether j is the left boundary process, right boundary process or an internal process.

Let $\mathcal{L}(A)$ denote the set of all strings from Σ^ω accepted by the Buchi automaton A when A is considered as an automaton over infinite strings. We say that a 2-d string σ is accepted by the automaton A if $l(\sigma) \in \mathcal{L}(A)$, i.e., the linearization of σ is accepted by the automaton A when A is considered as an automaton on infinite strings. For an automaton A, we let $L(A)$ denote the set of all 2-d strings accepted by A.

Composition of a 2-d string and a Process. Now, we define the composition of a 2-d string with a process. This is needed in order to define a composition of an automaton with a process. A process over an alphabet of actions Δ is a triple (S, R, S_0) where S is a set of states, $R \subseteq S \times (\Delta \cup \{i\tau\}) \times S$ is a set of transitions and S_0 is the set of initial states.

Let σ be a 2-d string of width n over an alphabet Δ and P be a process over the alphabet Δ'. Let $\Delta'' = (\Delta \cup \Delta') - (\Delta \cap \Delta')$. Now, we define the right composition of σ and P, denoted as $\sigma \odot P$, to be a set of 2-d strings of width $n + 1$ over the alphabet Δ'' as follows. Intuitively, a 2-d string δ is in $\sigma \odot P$ if it is obtained by fusing the 2-d string σ with with a computation of P where the fusion is carried out by synchronizing on complementary actions. The formal definition of $\sigma \odot P$ is is given in the full paper [Si97].

Composition of an Automaton with a Process. Let A be an automaton over Δ and $P = (S, R, S_0)$ be a process over Δ'. We define an automaton $A \odot P$ over (S, Δ''), where $\Delta'' = \Delta \cup \Delta' - \Delta \cap \Delta'$ as follows. We call $A \odot P$ to be the right composition of A with P. As we will show later $L(A \odot P)$ will be equal to the union of $\sigma \odot P$ where the union is taken over all $\sigma \in L(A)$.

Intuitively, $A \odot P$ works as follows. When it runs on a two dimensional string, as it goes from left to right, it behaves like A until it reaches the right end, at the right end it will model possible synchronization of action with P and move one more position to the right and possibly simulate a transition of P, after this it will move to the left of the next top row and repeat this process. It knows that it is at the right end if it gets an input symbol of the form $(t, a, right, t')$ where *right* denotes the right end.

Formally, $A \odot P = (Q_0', \Sigma', Q', \delta', F')$ and $\Sigma' = S \times \Delta'' \times \{left, right, internal\} \times S$ where Δ'' is as given above. Each state in Q' is a 5-tuple of the form $(q, s, flag1, flag2, flag3, a)$ where q, s are the states of A and P respectively, $flag1, flag2, flag3$ are binary flags and a is an action symbol. Here $flag1 = 1$ indicates that the next computational step will be caused by a transition of P which is either an internal transition or a transition offering an action in $(\Delta' - \Delta)$. If $flag1 = 1$ then all first n processes in the computational step will not change states and only process P which is the $(n + 1)st$ process will make the above type of transition. $flag2 = 1$ indicates that the automaton has scanned the first n states in the current row; this implies that the next state scanned will be that of the right most process which is process P. When *flag3*= 1 at that time *flag2* will also have value 1; this case indicates that the right most process, i.e., process P, should make a transition offering action a; in this case $a \in \Delta \cap \Delta'$ and this occurs when synchronization on complementary action occurs between P and the nth process. The formal and complete definition of the $A \odot P$ can be found in [Si97].

Theorem 1. *A 2-d string δ of width $(n+1)$ over the alphabet Δ'' is accepted by the automaton $A \odot P$ iff there exists a 2-d string σ of width n over Δ such that $\delta \in \sigma \odot P$, i.e., $L(A \odot P) = \bigcup_{\sigma \in L(A)} \sigma \odot P$.*

We define similarly left composition $P \odot \sigma$ of a process P with a 2-d string σ, and the left composition $P \odot A$ of a process P with an automaton A. We also define left-right composition of a process P with a 2-d string σ and also with a process P, denoted by $P \otimes \sigma$ and $P \otimes A$ respectively. In this case both P and σ and also A should be on the same action alphabet. $P \otimes \sigma$ forces every action of P to be synchronized with a complementary action in σ and vice versa; thus, the resulting set of 2-d strings do not offer any communication to the external world. $P \otimes A$ is defined similarly. The input alphabet of the resulting automaton $P \otimes A$ has only input symbols of the form (s, a, d, s') where $a \in \{\epsilon, i\tau, c\tau\}$ and $d = internal$. The automata $P \odot A$ and $P \otimes A$ satisfy similar properties as given by Theorem 1.

3 Verification of Linear Networks Using Induction

We consider linear networks of processes in which adjacent processes communicate using CCS/CSP type of actions. We assume that the communication actions of processes are drawn from a set Δ which consists of actions of the from a? and a! which are called complemented pair of actions. Communication occurs when two adjacent processes execute complementary actions. In this section, we show how we can verify the correctness of such linear networks and circular networks using automata as invariants. Let Δ be an action alphabet.

3.1 Linear Networks

In a linear network, each process can communicate only with its left and right neighbors. To model this, we assume that the actions a process uses are of the form *left.a* and *right.a* where $a \in \Delta$. Let $\Delta' = \{left.a, right.a : a \in \Delta\}$.

Let $P_0, P_1, ..., P_{n-1}$ be a set of processes with action symbols taken from Δ'. We define the linear composition $P_0 \odot P_1 \odot ... \odot P_{n-1}$, called a *linear chain*, by using CCS composition operator as follows. For each i, such that $0 \le i < (n-1)$, we rename all actions of the form *right.a* in P_i to a_i, and for each i such that $0 < i \le n - 1$, we rename all actions of the form *left.a* in P_i to a_{i-1}. Note that actions of the form *left.a* in P_0 and actions of the form *right.a* in P_{n-1} are not renamed. Let the resulting processes be $P_0', P_1', ..., P_{n-1}'$ (Note that the $\overline{a_i}$ is the complement of a_i). Now we define the linear chain $P_0 \odot P_1 \odot ... P_{n-1}$ to be same as $P_0' \circ P_1' ... \circ P_{n-1}'$ where $\circ$ is the traditional CCS/CSP composition operator.

The set of infinite computations of the chain of processes, denoted as $\mathcal{C}(P_0 \odot$ $... \odot P_{n-1})$ is the set of 2-d strings $\sigma = u_0, a_0, u_1, a_1, ...u_i, a_i, ...$ of width n over the alphabet Δ' satisfying the following properties: for each j, $u_{0,j}$ is an initial state of process P_j' and for each $i \geq 0$, the computational step (u_i, a_i, u_{i+1}) either involves an internal transition of process j, for some $0 \leq j < n$, and in this case $a_{i,j}$ is $i\tau$, or it involves synchronized communication involving two adjacent processes j and $j+1$ and in this case $a_{i,j}$ and $a_{i,j+1}$ are both $c\tau$. If a process j is not involved in the computational step (u_i, a_i, u_{i+1}) then $a_{i,j}$ is ϵ and $u_{i+1,j} = u_{i,j}$.

Let P, I and E be a processes over the alphabet Δ' such that all the actions in I are of the form $right.a$ and all the actions in E are of the form $left.a$ where $a \in \Delta$, i.e., I and E do not offer communication to the left and right respectively. Consider a computation of a linear chain of the form $I \odot P^i \odot E$ for some $i > 0$, where P^i denotes the composition $P \odot ... \odot P$ taken i times. All the action symbols appearing in such a computation are from the set $\{\epsilon, i\tau, c\tau\}$. This is due to the fact that the left most process I does not offer any communication to the left, and E does offer any communication to the right. Let ϕ be an automaton over the alphabet $\{\epsilon, i\tau, c\tau\}$. We say that the linear chain $I \odot P^i \odot E$ satisfies the property specified by ϕ if $\mathcal{C}(I \odot P^i \odot E) \subseteq L(\phi)$.

Let $\mathcal{F}_i$ be be the linear chain $I \odot P^{c+i} \odot E$. Now, consider the family of linear chains $\mathcal{F}_i$ for $i = 0, 1....$ For an automaton $\mathcal{A}$ over the alphabet Δ', let $\mathcal{A}[a/right.a]$ denote the automaton obtained by renaming all actions of the form $right.a$ to a in $\mathcal{A}$. Similarly, $\mathcal{A}[a/left.a]$ and $\mathcal{A}[a/left.a][a/right.a]$ are defined. In the last case, both type of actions $left.a$ and $right.a$ are renamed to a. For a process P, we let $P[a/left.a]$, $P[a/right.a]$ and $P[a/left.a][a/right.a]$ denote processes obtained by similar renaming. Let $\Delta'' = \{right.a : a \in \Delta\}$. The following theorem presents a method for verification of the correctness of a family of linear networks.

Theorem 2 (Soundness and Completeness Theorem). *For $i = 0, 1...$, let $\mathcal{F}_i = I \odot P^{c+i} \odot E$ be a family of linear networks and ϕ be an automaton over $\{\epsilon, i\tau, c\tau\}$. Then, $\forall i \geq 0$, $\mathcal{F}_i$ satisfies the specification given by ϕ iff there exists a finite state automaton $\mathcal{A}$ over Δ'' satisfying the following properties.*

1. $\mathcal{C}(I \odot P^c) \subseteq L(\mathcal{A})$;
2. $L(\mathcal{A}[a/right.a] \odot P[a/left.a]) \subseteq L(\mathcal{A})$;
3. $L(\mathcal{A}[a/right.a] \odot E[a/left.a]) \subseteq L(\phi)$;

Soundness part of the above theorem, given by the "if" part, is shown by proving that, $\forall i \geq 0$, $L(\mathcal{A})$ contains all the computations of $I \odot P^{c+i}$; this follows from part 1 of the theorem and the property of the composition operator of an automaton with a process. The completeness, specified by the "only if" part, is shown by obtaining an automaton $\mathcal{A}$ with the property that the set of 2-d strings accepted by $\mathcal{A}$ is exactly the computations of a linear network of the form $I \odot P^{c+i}$; the automaton $\mathcal{A}$ moves on the 2-d string and ensures that the string is according to the transitions of the individual processes.

In the above theorem $\mathcal{A}$ is the automaton that specifies the inductive invariant, step (1) is the basis of the induction, step (2) is the induction step, and step (3) is the step that checks the correctness with respect to ϕ.

3.2 Linear Networks with Fairness

In this subsection, we present an induction based method for verification of correctness under fairness. The fairness that we consider here is the classical weak fairness; roughly speaking, a computation is said to be weakly fair if every process is infinitely often disabled or infinitely often executed.

The set of fair computations of a linear chain $P_0 \odot ... \odot P_{n-1}$, denoted by $\mathcal{FC}(P_0 \odot ... \odot P_{n-1})$, is defined to be the set of computations that satisfy the fairness requirements for all the processes excepting the boundary process P_{n-1} (the boundary process P_{n-1} is open and its fairness will be taken into consideration when we compose the chain with another process on the right side).

In order to specify invariants, we use generalized Buchi automata [GW91] on 2-d strings. A generalized Buchi automata is almost same as a Buchi automata defined earlier excepting that the acceptance condition is a collection of subsets of states; formally, a generalized Buchi automata $\mathcal{A}$ is a 5-tuple $(Q_0, \Sigma, Q, \delta, F)$ where F is a collection $\{F_1, ..., F_k\}$ of subsets of Q; Q_0, Σ, Q, δ are defined as before. An input string in Σ^{∞} is accepted by $\mathcal{A}$ if there exists a run of $\mathcal{A}$ on the input such that for each $i = 1, ..., k$ some state in F_i appears infinitely often in the run. The languages $\mathcal{L}(A)$ and $L(A)$ are defined as before.

Now we define the fair right composition of a generalized Buchi automaton $\mathcal{A}$ and a process P, denoted as $\mathcal{A} \odot_f P$ as follows. The construction of the automaton $\mathcal{A} \odot_f P$ is similar to $\mathcal{A} \odot P$ excepting that it uses an additional flag to capture the fairness condition on the previous right most process; note that after the composition the new right most process will be P. If F and F', respectively, are the acceptance conditions in $\mathcal{A}$ and $\mathcal{A} \odot P$ then the number of subsets in F' is one more than that in F; the additional subset in F' captures the weak fairness requirement on the previous right most process, and the remaining subsets of F' correspond with those of F. Details of the construction of $A \odot_f P$ will be given in the full paper.

Let I, P and E be processes as defined in the previous subsection and ϕ be a generalized Buchi automaton over the alphabet $\{\epsilon, i\tau, c\tau\}$. As usual we say that the the linear chain $I \odot P^i \odot E$ satifies ϕ under fairness if all fair computations of the chain are accepted by ϕ. Now, we have the following soundness theorem for verifying correctness under fairness.

Theorem 3 (Soundness Theorem). *Let $\mathcal{F}_i = I \odot P^{c+i} \odot E$, for $i = 0, 1...$, be a family of linear networks and ϕ be an automaton over $\{\epsilon, i\tau, c\tau\}$. Then, $\forall i \geq 0$, $\mathcal{F}_i$ satisfies the specification given by ϕ under fairness if there exists a finite state generalized Buchi automaton $\mathcal{A}$ over Δ'' satisfying the following properties.*

1. $\mathcal{FC}(I \odot P^c) \subseteq L(\mathcal{A})$;

2. $L(\mathcal{A}[a/right.a] \odot_f P[a/left.a]) \subseteq L(\mathcal{A})$;

3. $L(\mathcal{A}[a/right.a] \odot_f E[a/left.a]) \subseteq L(\phi)$;

3.3 Circular Networks

Now, we discuss how to verify families of circular networks of processes. Let Δ and Δ' be as defined above. Let $P_0, ..., P_{n-1}$ be processes over the alphabet Δ'. For each i, $0 \leq i < n$, let P_i'' denote the process where actions of the form $left.a$, $right.a$ are renamed to $a_{(i-1) \bmod n}$ and a_i respectively. Note that, we are also renaming $left.a$ in P_0 and $right.a$ in P_{n-1}. We define a circular network, denoted $P_0 \oplus P_1 \oplus ...P_{n-1}$, to be the composition of the CCS processes $P_0'', ..., P_{n-1}''$, i.e., $P_0'' \circ P_1'' \circ ... \circ P_{n-1}''$. The set of computations of such a circular network, denoted $\mathcal{C}(P_0 \oplus ... \oplus P_{n-1})$, is defined as a set of 2-d strings over the alphabet $\{\epsilon, i\tau, c\tau\}$ as before.

Let I,E and P be processes over Δ'. We define $\mathcal{G}_i$ to be the circular network $I \oplus P^{c+i} \oplus E$ where P^i denotes the expressions $P \oplus ... \oplus P$ containing $c+i$ number of Ps. The following theorem tells us how to use induction for verification of families of circular networks. As before we define what it means for a circular network to satisfy a specification given by an automaton.

Theorem 4 (Soundness and Completeness). *Let* $\mathcal{G}_i = I \oplus P^{c+i} \oplus E$, *for* $i = 0, 1...$, *denote a family of circular networks. Let* ϕ *be an automaton over* $\{\epsilon, i\tau, c\tau\}$. *Then,* $\forall i \geq 0$ $\mathcal{G}_i$ *satisfies the specification* ϕ *iff there exists a finite state automaton* $\mathcal{A}$ *over* Δ' *satisfying the following properties.*

1. $\mathcal{C}(I \odot P^c) \subseteq L(\mathcal{A})$;

2. $L((\mathcal{A}[a/right.a]) \odot P[a/left.a]) \subseteq L(\mathcal{A})$;

3. $L(\mathcal{A}[a/right.a][a'/left.a] \otimes E[a/left.a,][a'/right.a]) \subseteq L(\phi)$;

It is to be noted that, unlike in Theorem 2, the automaton $\mathcal{A}$ in the above theorem is over Δ'. Also, we use the $\otimes$ operator in step 3. We can prove a soundness theorem, similar to Theorem 3, for correctness under fairness for circular networks as well.

Now we discuss how to automate the different steps in the above two theorems. All the three steps require checking language containment of automata on 2-d strings. Step 1 can be done by obtaining the automaton corresponding to $I \odot P^c$ and then checking language containment. In steps 2 and 3, we need to compute the composition of an automata with a process, and this can be done using the method given in the previous section. The complexity of this algorithm is proportional to the product of the sizes of the automaton and the process.

3.4 Language Containment Problem

The language containment problem for generalized 2-d Buchi automata (and even for 2-d Buchi automata) is undecidable. However, the following lemma gives us a sufficient condition for language containment that is decidable. It states that, for automata A_1 and A_2, if the set of one-dimensional strings accepted by A_1 is contained in the set accepted by A_2 then $L(A_1) \subseteq L(A_2)$.

Lemma 5. *Let A_1 and A_2 be generalized Buchi automata on Δ. If $\mathcal{L}(A_1) \subseteq \mathcal{L}(A_2)$ then $L(A_1) \subseteq L(A_2)$.*

The condition $\mathcal{L}(A_1) \subseteq \mathcal{L}(A_2)$ can be checked by complementing A_1 using the methods of [SVW85]. However this will have exponential complexity. Now, we give another condition that is easily checkable. This method uses simulation relations.

Let $A_1 = (Q_0, \Sigma, Q, \delta, F)$ and $A_2 = (Q'_0, \Sigma, Q', \delta', F')$ be generalized 2-d Buchi automata. (Note that F and F' are collections of subsets of states). A simulation relation $R \subseteq Q_1 \times Q_2$ is a binary relation satisfying the following properties.

- For every $q \in Q_0$ there exists a $q' \in Q'$ such that $(q, q') \in R$.
- If $(q, x, r) \in \delta$ then for every q' such that $(q, q') \in R$ there exists an $r' \in Q'$ such that $(q', x, r') \in R$.
- There exists a on-to function f from F to F' such that the following property is satisfied:
  For every subset $C \in F$ and for every $q \in C$ and every $q' \in Q'$, if $q \in C$ and $(q, q') \in R$ then $q' \in f(C)$.

The lemma given below follows from known results.

Lemma 6. *If there exists a simulation relation between A_1 and A_2 then $L(A_1) \subseteq L(A_2)$.*

Checking if there exists a simulation relation can be done efficiently for the case when the automata are Bcuhi automata.

Examples. We first consider a simple token passing algorithm for circular networks considered in [CG87]. Here we have circular network of identical processes that communicate by passing a token around in the anti-clockwise direction. The diagram denoting such a process is given in figure 1. A process P is initially in the state N and receives a token from the left by executing the action $left.t$? and enters the critical region C (here, left and right are defined with respect to a person facing the center of the circle). In state C, it executes an internal transition and stays in the same state, or it executes the action $right.t$! and goes to state N. Let I be the same process as P excepting that its initial state is C, and E be same as P. Let ϕ be the automaton on 2-d strings, given in figure 2, that states that exactly one process is in state C at any time.

To verify this property for all circular networks of the type $I \oplus P^{i+1} \oplus E$ for all $i \geq 0$, we use the invariant automaton given in figure 3. The transitions of this automaton are oblivious to the last component in each input symbol (i.e., the component denoting the next state of a process); for this reason each input symbol is given as a triple; a value * in an input symbol should be taken as a wild card; a value of l or r or i appearing as the last component indicates the automaton is scanning the left most, right most and internal processes respectively. States a and g denote the occurrence of a sequence of global states in

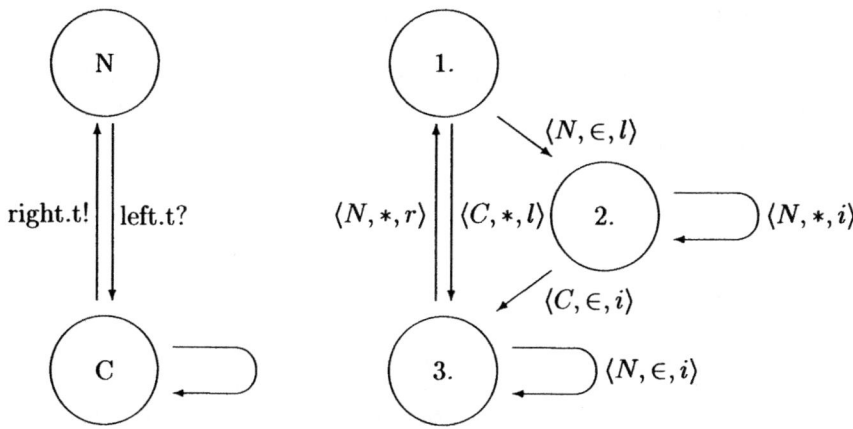

Fig. 1. Process P **Fig. 2.** Automaton Φ

which the left most process has the token and is in the critical section. (State f denotes the situation where a global state has more than one token; this is an error state). States e, c and d denote a sequence of global states in which an inner process has the token and is in critical section. States b and h denote a sequence of global states in which the right most process is in critical section. The transition from h to i occurs when the right most process gives the token to the external world. The transition from i to j denotes the case where the left most process gets the token from the external world.

It can be shown that the above invariant automaton satisfies all the three conditions given in Theorem 4. This can be shown by exhibiting simulation relations.

Now, we show how the same invariant automaton, given in figure 3, can be changed to verify the liveness property that process I enters the critical section infinitely often. The change to the invariant automaton is the addition of the following acceptance condition F which makes it in to a generalized Buchi automaton. F consists of two sets F_1 and F_2. F_1 consists of all states other than a and g, F_2 consists of all states other than c, d, e.

We can also prove the safety and liveness properties of the more complex token ring example considered in [CGJ95]. Details are left out due to lack of space.

4 Conclusions

In this paper we proposed a formalism based on automata on two dimensional strings for specifying inductive invariants for proving correctness of families of linear and circular networks. We proved our inductive approach to be sound and complete (semantical completeness). We have illustrated our approach by simple examples.

We have also given the inductive approach for verification of parametrized systems under fairness. In this case, we use generalized Buchi automata (or

Streett automata) as inductive invariants. For this case, we have proved the soundness theorem.

As part of future work, it will be interesting to automate the different parts of the induction based approach and apply them to real practical examples. It will also be interesting to extend our approach to networks defined by context free grammars [SG89]. Further more, it will also be interesting to investigate logic based approaches for specification of the invariants.

References

[AK86]   K. R. Apt and D. Kozen: Limits to Automatic Program Verification. Information Processing Letters, 22.6 (1986), 307-309.

[BCG89]   M. Browne, E. M. Clarke and O. Grumberg: Reasoning About Networks with Many Identical Finite State Processes. Inf. and Computation, 81(1):13-31, Apr. 1989.

[CGJ95]   E. M. Clarke, O. Grumberg and S. Jha: Verifying Parametrized Networks Using Abstraction and Regular Languages. CONCUR 95.

[CG87]   E. M. Clarke, and O. Grumberg: Avoiding the State Explosion Problem in Temporal Logic Modelchecking Problem. In Proceedings of ACM Symposium on Principles of Distributed Computing 1987.

[EN95]   E. A. Emerson and K. S. Namjoshi: Reasoning About Rings, Proceedings of 22nd POPL conferece, Jan 1995.

[EN96]   E. A. Emerson and K. S. Namjoshi: Automatic Verification of Parametrized Synchronous Systems. Proceeding of the International Conference on Computer Aide Verification 1996.

[GS92]   S. M. German and A. P. Sistla: Reasoning About Systems with many Processes. JACM, July 1992, Vol 39, No. 3, pp 675-735.

[GW91]   P. Godefroid and P. Wolper: Using Partial Approach to Modelchecking. Proc 6th IEEE Symposium on Logic in Computer Science, pp 406-415, Amsterdam, July 1991.

[KM89]   R. P. Kurshan and K. McMillan: A Structural Induction Theorem for Processes. ACM Sym. on Principles of Distributed Computing, Aug. 1989.

[SG89]   Z. Shtadler and O. Grumberg: Network Grammars, Communication Behaviors and Automatic Verififcation. Proc. of International Workshop on Automatic Verification Methods for Finite State Systems, June 1989.

[Si97]   A. P. Sistla: Parametrized Verification of Linear Networks Using Automata as Invariants. Technical report, University of Illinois at Chicago 1997.

[SVW85]   A. P. Sistla, M. Vardi and P. Wolper: The Complementation Problem for Buchi Automata and Applications to Temporal Logics. Proceedings Of The 12th International Colloquium On Automata, Languages And Programming, Greece, August 1985; The journal version of the paper appeared in Theoretical Computer Science, 49, No 2,3 1987, pp 217-237.

[SG87]   A. P. Sistla and S. M. German: Reasoning About many Processes. LICS 87.

[WL89]   P. Wolper and V. Lovinfosse: Verifying Properties of Large Sets of Processes with Network Invariants. Proc. 1989 Intl Wokshop on Automatic Verification Methods for Finite State Systems 1989.

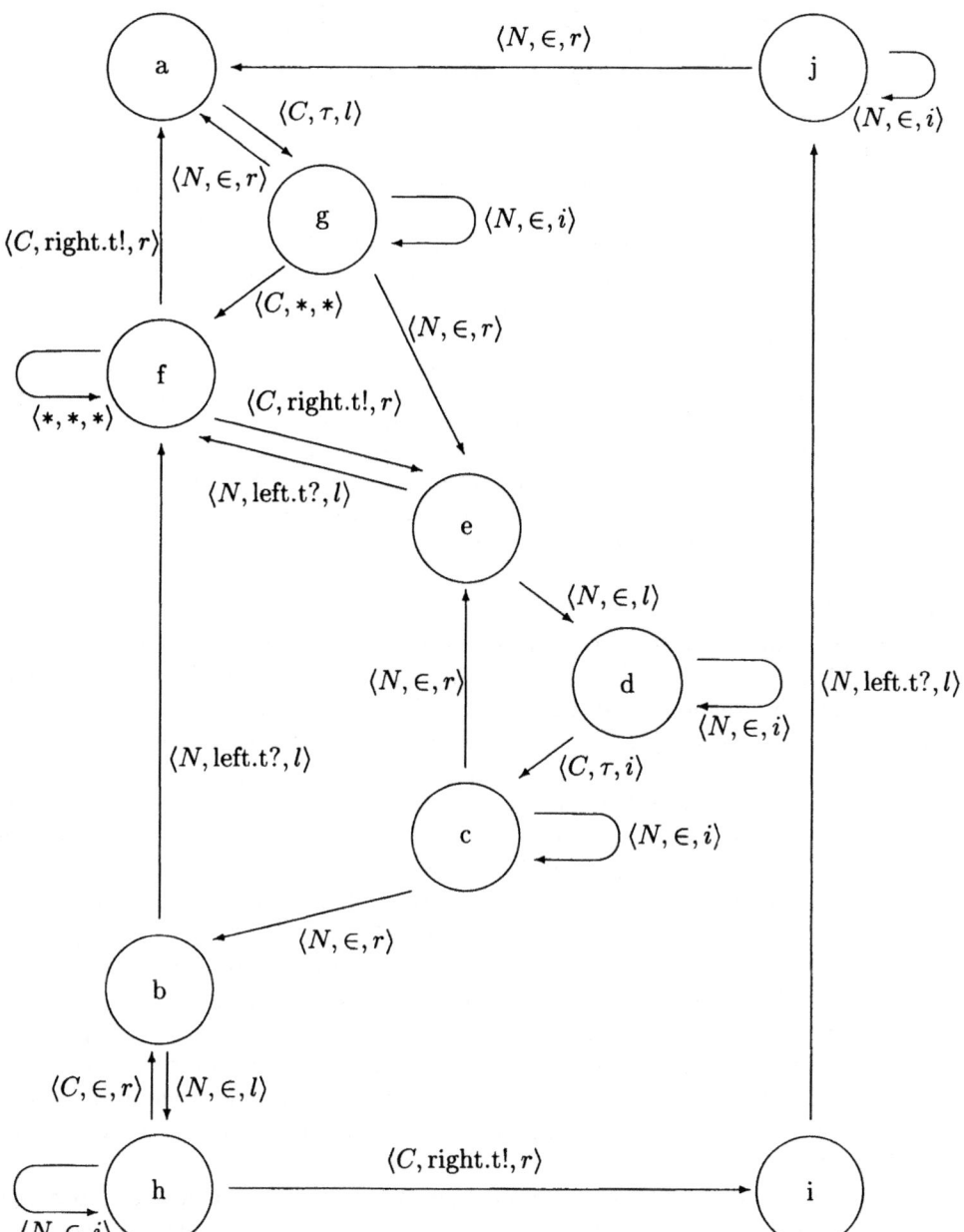

Fig. 3. The invariant automaton A

Symbolic Model Checking with Rich Assertional Languages*

Y. Kesten**   O. Maler***   M. Marcus†   A. Pnueli†   E. Shahar†

Abstract. The paper shows that, by an appropriate choice of a rich assertional language, it is possible to extend the utility of symbolic model checking beyond the realm of BDD-represented finite-state systems into the domain of infinite-state systems, leading to a powerful technique for uniform verification of unbounded (parameterized) process networks.

The main contributions of the paper are a formulation of a general framework for symbolic model checking of infinite-state systems, a demonstration that many individual examples of uniformly verified parameterized designs that appear in the literature are special cases of our general approach, verifying the correctness of the Futurebus+ design for all single-bus configurations, extending the technique to tree architectures, and establishing that the presented method is a precise dual to the top-down invariant generation method used in deductive verification.

1 Introduction

The problem of uniform verification of parameterized systems is one of the most thoroughly researched problems in computer-aided verification. The problem seems particularly elusive for systems that consist of regularly connected finite-state processes (a process network). Such a system can be verified for any given configuration, but this does not provide a conclusive evidence for the question of *uniform verification*, i.e., showing that the system is correct for *all* possible configurations.

We have had a recent experience with the Futurebus+ system, which has been verified for many configurations in [CGH+93] . Using the TLV system [PS96], we were able to analyze additional (and larger) configurations and detected a bug that escaped the previous verification efforts. Having corrected the bug, all of the configurations we have been able to check, verified correctly. However, the question of whether the Futurebus+ protocol in its last version contains another lurking bug, which makes its appearance only in a configuration much larger than anyone was able to check, still remains unresolved. One of our main motivations in the research reported in this paper is to develop a method by which uniform verification of parameterized designs such as the Futurebus+ can be algorithmically performed.

Many methods have been proposed for the uniform verification of parameterized systems. These include explicit induction ([EN95], [SG92]), network invariants, which can be viewed as implicit induction ([KM89], [WL89], [HLR92],

---

* This research was supported in part by a gift from Intel, and an *Infrastructure* grant from the Israeli Ministry of Science and the Arts.
** Future Cad Technology, Intel, Israel. E-mail: ykesten@iil.intel.com
*** Verimag, Centre Equation, 2, av. de Vignate, 38610 Gières, France.
   E-mail: Oded.Maler@imag.fr
† Weizmann Institute of Science, Rehovot, Israel.
   E-mail: {monica, amir, elad}@wisdom.weizmann.ac.il

[LHR97]), methods that can be viewed as abstraction and approximation of network invariants ([BCG86], [SG89], [CGJ95]), and other methods which can be viewed as based on abstraction ([ID96], [EN96]).

In this methodologically simplistic paper, we go back to basics and claim that, with an appropriate choice of an expressive but decidable assertional language, the good old paradigm of symbolic model checking is adequate for uniform verification of parameterized systems. The paper demonstrates this claim by studying in detail symbolic model checking with the assertional languages of regular sets and tree regular sets. For the case of regular sets of strings, we show that many of the examples previously verified using specialized representations or additional theories, such as the examples considered in [CGJ95], [ID96], and [EN96], can be solved by this single and simple approach. The use of regular assertional tree languages is new (except for a brief mention in [HJJ+96]) and its application to a uniform verification of the Futurebus+ system will be a very convincing evidence to the power of the approach advocated here.

One of the inspirations to the work reported here was [CGJ95] (and its predecessor [SG89]), where regular languages was the main instrument used at the end. However, we strongly felt that, with some restrictions, the same verification capabilities can be obtained without the elaborate theory developed in [CGJ95]. In particular, we felt that there exists a redundancy between the *network grammar* used in [CGJ95] just to define the network topology and structure and the additional means for representing the dynamic behavior by another regular language. In our approach, we use a *single* regular language to describe both the topology and the local states of the participating processes. However, we cannot handle as general network topologies as are considered in [CGJ95], and must restrict ourselves to either array or tree topologies. The general principle is still applicable to other topologies but it requires the development of a different assertional language for each family of topologies.

By adopting the idea that a set of possible configurations of an unbounded array of processes can be represented as a set of strings over the process alphabet, we can go further and view the transitions of the system as *rewrite rules* applied to these strings. Hence the model-checking problem for networks can be reduced to the problem of calculating predecessors of a language via a rewriting system consisting of a finite set of *length-preserving* rules[5]. In [BM96], a technique for calculating the reachable states of an alternating push-down process (i.e. an automaton with one unbounded variable, a push-down stack) was presented and used in order to model-check such processes against μ-calculus formulae. This technique (inspired by the construction given in [BO93], pages 91-93) is based on representing a regular set L of stack configurations by an automaton A and then calculating the set of predecessors of L via a rewrite rule by modifying A. In the case of push-down processes the algorithm is guaranteed to converge, but experience shows that it converges in many other cases.

In this paper we generalize this idea in few directions. First, by using finite-state transducers we extend the technique to treat a more general class of rewrite

---

[5] If we ignore process creation and annihilation.

rules. We transfer the concept from theory to practice by implementing it into a working system and applying it successfully to several examples including all single-bus configurations of the Futurebus+. Secondly, we treat processes arranged in a tree architecture. To this end we define sets of process configurations as regular tree languages, employ bottom-up tree automata to represent them, and use tree transducers in order to define predecessors.

The implementation owes much to the MONA system and its underlying principles [HJJ+96]. Similar to MONA, we adopt an S1S-inspired language for the user interface with the system, which is then translated into finite automata represented with BDD-labeled edges. However, unlike some of the applications to verification reported in [HJJ+96] and [BK95], which are essentially deductive in nature, we use similar tools for symbolic model checking. A similar implementation for trees is in the making, with the intended goal of verifying the Futurebus+ for all multiple-bus configurations.

2 Symbolic Model Checking

In Fig. 1 we present the well-known symbolic model checking procedure for showing that the invariance property $\Box\, g$ (**AG** g in CTL) is satisfied by system P, where g is an assertion (state formula). This procedure was already formulated in the early 80's (see [CE81], [QS82], [CES86]). It became practical and widely usable only with implementations based on *ordered binary decision diagrams* (OBDDs) [Bry86], such as [BCM+92] and [McM93]. Procedure SYMB-MC attempts to compute an assertion characterizing all the states from which a $\neg g$-state can be reached by a finite number of P-steps. If the search loop terminates at iteration i, then φ_i provides such an assertion. By checking that none of the "bad" states characterized by φ_i are allowed as initial states of P, we verify that there is no $\neg g$-state reachable from a P-initial state, so g is an invariant of system P.

> **Procedure** SYMB-MC(g: assertion);
>   **assertion:** $\varphi_0, \varphi_1, \ldots$;
>
>   **Let** $\varphi_0 := \neg g$;
>   **For** $i = 0, 1, \ldots$ **repeat**
>   **Let** $\varphi_{i+1} := \varphi_i \vee pred_P(\varphi_i)$;
>   **until** $\varphi_{i+1} = \varphi_i$;
>
>   Check that $\varphi_i \wedge init_P = \mathrm{F}$
> **end procedure**

Fig. 1. A procedure for symbolic model checking.

The procedure uses the assertion $init_P$ as a characterization of all the P-initial states, and the predicate transformer $pred_P$. For an assertion φ, $pred_P(\varphi)$ is an assertion characterizing all states that have a φ-state as a P-successor.

As recommended by the *rich-language symbolic model checking* (RSMC) methodology expounded in this paper, in order to verify that assertion g is an invariant of the (possibly infinite-state) system P, one chooses an assertional language $\mathcal{L}$ and uses it to apply the SYMB-MC procedure. To be applicable, the language $\mathcal{L}$ should satisfy the following minimal requirements:

- The property g and the assertion $init_P$ should be expressible in $\mathcal{L}$.

- The language $\mathcal{L}$ should be effectively closed under the boolean operations of negation and disjunction, and possess an algorithm for deciding equivalence of two assertions.
- There should exist an algorithm for constructing the predicate transformer $pred_p : \mathcal{L} \mapsto \mathcal{L}$ for every system P.

We refer to a language satisfying these three requirements as a language *adequate for symbolic model checking*. Note that identifying an adequate assertional language only guarantees that Procedure SYMB-MC is applicable. It is still only a semi-algorithm which, when terminating, provides either proof of correctness or a counter example, but may fail to terminate. In fact, due to the theoretical results of [AK86], the invariance checking problem for parameterized systems is in general undecidable, and the best we can hope for in the general case is a semi-algorithm.

In the remaining sections, we will consider several useful adequate assertional languages and illustrate their application to parameterized systems of interest.

3 Regular Languages are Adequate

In this section we demonstrate the use of the class of regular languages as adequate assertional languages. As a running example, we will use program MUX of Fig. 2 that implements mutual exclusion by synchronous communication.

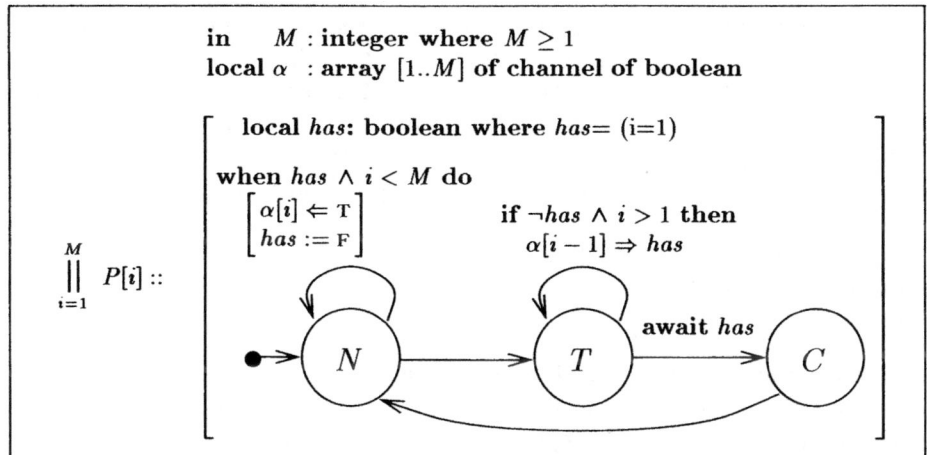

Fig. 2. Parameterized Program MUX.

The body of the program is a variable-size parallel composition of processes $P[1], \ldots, P[M]$. Each process $P[i]$ has two local state variables: a local boolean variable *has* and a control variable π ranging over the set of locations $\{N, T, C\}$ (the noncritical section, the trying section, and the critical section, respectively). Process $P[i]$ sends the boolean value T on channel $\alpha[i]$ to its right neighbor (if $i < M$) and reads into variable *has* a boolean value from its left neighbor on channel $\alpha[i-1]$ (if $i > 1$). As seen in the program, process $P[i]$ can enter its critical section only if $P[i].has = $ T.

A *local state* of process $P[i]$ is a valuation of the local state variables. For example, $\langle \pi : C, has : \text{T} \rangle$ is a local state in which $P[i]$ is in its critical section while its variable *has* has the value T. We abbreviate $\langle \pi : C, has : \text{T} \rangle$ to $\langle C, \text{T} \rangle$, listing just the values assigned to the variables.

A *global state* (also called a *configuration*) of system MUX, is a sequence of local states. Note that every configuration of system MUX can be viewed as a word over the finite alphabet

$$\Sigma_{\text{MUX}}: \quad \{\langle N, \text{F}\rangle, \ \langle T, \text{F}\rangle, \ \langle C, \text{F}\rangle, \ \langle N, \text{T}\rangle, \ \langle T, \text{T}\rangle, \ \langle C, \text{T}\rangle\}.$$

Consequently, we can view a set of configurations of program MUX as a language over the alphabet Σ_{MUX}. Examining procedure SYMB-MC, we identify two languages and one language transformer which need to be syntactically characterized. We will consider each of these in turn.

3.1 Expressing the Initial Condition $init_P$ and the Desired Invariant g

Our general recommendation is to use as an assertional language for a *process array system* P, such as program MUX, the language of regular expressions over the alphabet Σ_P. A regular expression over Σ_P defines a language which characterizes a set of global states. For example, the initial condition for program MUX can be expressed by the regular expression

$$init_{\text{MUX}}: \quad \langle N, \text{T}\rangle(\langle N, \text{F}\rangle)^*.$$

While we propose to use regular expressions in the user interface with the RSMC support system, the internal representation of the data structure "assertion" used in procedure SYMB-MC, is that of a finite-state automaton (FSA) over Σ_P. We consider such an automaton to be given by $A: \langle \Sigma_P, Q, q_0, \delta, F\rangle$, where Σ_P is the input alphabet, Q is the set of *automaton states*, $q_0 \in Q$ is the *initial automaton state*, $\delta: Q \times \Sigma_P \mapsto 2^Q$ is the *transition function*, and $F \subseteq Q$ is the set of *accepting states*.

Next, we consider the desired property g. For the case of program MUX, the required property is that of *mutual exclusion* requiring that at most one process reside in its critical section at any given instance. This property can be expressed by the regular expression

$$g: \quad [x \neq C]^+ \ + \ [x \neq C]^*[x = C][x \neq C]^*,$$

where we use the abbreviations $[x = C] = \langle C, \text{T}\rangle + \langle C, \text{F}\rangle$ and $[x \neq C] = \Sigma_{\text{MUX}} - [x = C]$.

3.2 Expressing the $pred_P$ Transformer

To express the $pred_P$ transformer, we first attempt to describe the change in configurations as a result of a single program step. Consider our running example, program MUX. The (parameterized) fair transition system [MP95] corresponding to this program has two kinds of transitions. There are transitions that affect only a single process and represent internal movements and variable changes within this process. The other kind is the transition that involves two contiguous processes, i.e., $P[i]$ and $P[i+1]$ for some $i \in \{1, M-1\}$. This transition corresponds to the synchronous communication in which process $P[i]$ sends the boolean value T, which process $P[i+1]$ receives and stores into *has*.

We can summarize the transformation effected by the various transitions by the following list of *rewrite rules*:

$$U: \quad \left\{ \begin{array}{lll} \langle N, \text{F}\rangle \rightarrow \langle T, \text{F}\rangle & , & \langle C, \text{F}\rangle \rightarrow \langle N, \text{F}\rangle & , & \langle T, \text{T}\rangle \rightarrow \langle C, \text{T}\rangle \\ \langle N, \text{T}\rangle \rightarrow \langle T, \text{T}\rangle & , & \langle C, \text{T}\rangle \rightarrow \langle N, \text{T}\rangle & & \end{array} \right\}$$

$$M: \quad \left\{ \langle N, \text{T}\rangle \langle T, \text{F}\rangle \rightarrow \langle N, \text{F}\rangle \langle T, \text{T}\rangle \right\}$$

where U (the unary rewrites) represents changes that affect only a single process, while M is a binary rewrite rule representing a joint transition of two contiguous processes. For example, applying the rewrite rule $\langle N, \text{T} \rangle \langle T, \text{F} \rangle \rightarrow \langle N, \text{F} \rangle \langle T, \text{T} \rangle$ to the configuration $\langle N, \text{T} \rangle \langle T, \text{F} \rangle \langle N, \text{F} \rangle$ yields the successor configuration $\langle N, \text{F} \rangle \langle T, \text{T} \rangle \langle N, \text{F} \rangle$, representing the result of passing a token from $P[1]$ to $P[2]$.

A precise characterization of the transformation caused by each of these rewrite rules can be provided by a *finite-state transducer* (FST) $T \colon \langle \Sigma_P \times \Sigma_P, Q, q_0, \delta, F \rangle$, which is an FSA over the alphabet

$$\Sigma_P \times \Sigma_P = \{ [a, b] \mid a, b \in \Sigma_P \}.$$

Let $u = a_1 \cdots a_k$ and $v = b_1 \cdots b_k$ be two Σ_P-words of equal length. We define their *cross product* $u \times v$ to be the $\Sigma_P \times \Sigma'_P$-word $([a_1, b_1] \cdots [a_k, b_k])$. We say that word v is a *transduction* of word u by the FST T if the cross word $u \times v$ is accepted by T.

Consider the FST T_2 presented in Fig. 3. The label *id* appearing in the transducer stands for the set $\{ (a, a) \mid a \in \Sigma_{\text{MUX}} \}$, representing the identity transformation. The transducer T_2 represents the rewrite rule $\langle N, \text{T} \rangle \langle T, \text{F} \rangle \rightarrow \langle N, \text{F} \rangle \langle T, \text{T} \rangle$. For example, the configuration $v = \langle N, \text{F} \rangle \langle T, \text{T} \rangle \langle N, \text{F} \rangle$ is a T_2-transduction of the configuration $u = \langle N, \text{T} \rangle \langle T, \text{F} \rangle \langle N, \text{F} \rangle$, because the joint word

$$u \times v = ([\langle N, \text{T} \rangle, \langle N, \text{F} \rangle] [\langle T, \text{F} \rangle, \langle T, \text{T} \rangle] [\langle N, \text{F} \rangle, \langle N, \text{F} \rangle])$$

is accepted by T_2.

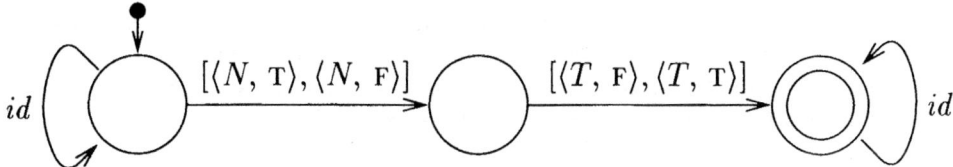

Fig. 3. Transducer T_2 representing a two-state rewrite.

In a similar way, we can construct a transducer corresponding to each of the remaining rewrite rules, expressing the effect of a single transition in program MUX. Since the class of regular languages is closed under union, it is possible to construct a *single* transducer T_{MUX} such that the configuration v is a T_{MUX}-transduction of a configuration u iff v can be obtained from u by a single step of program MUX. We refer to T_{MUX} as the *step transducer* for program MUX.

Given a transducer $T = \langle \Sigma \times \Sigma, R, r_0, \delta_T, F_T \rangle$ and an FSA $A = \langle \Sigma, Q, Q_0, \delta_A, F_A \rangle$, we define their *composition* to be the automaton

$$T \circ A = \langle \Sigma, R \times Q, [r_0, q_0], \delta, F_T \times F_A \rangle,$$

where $[r_2, q_2] \in \delta([r_1, q_1], a)$ iff there exists a $b \in \Sigma$ such that $r_2 \in \delta_T(r_1, [a, b])$ and $q_2 \in \delta_A(q_1, b)$.

It is possible to establish the following claim:

Claim 1 *The language accepted by the composition $T \circ A$ consists of all words having a T-transduction which is accepted by A.*

Going back to the use of FSAs as an assertional language, we observe that if A is an automaton characterizing a set of states of system P and T_P is the step transducer for P, then the precondition transformer $pred_P$ required in procedure SYMB-MC is given by $pred_P(A) = T_P \circ A$.

3.3 Applicability of FSAs as Assertional Languages

We can summarize the previous discussions by the following claim:

Claim 2 *If P is a system with an encoding of its global states into words over an alphabet Σ_P, such that*

- *the initial condition $init_P$ and the goal assertion g can be represented by Σ_P-automata, and*
- *the global transition relation of P can be represented by a step transducer $\mathcal{T}_P$,*

then procedure SYMB-MC *can be applied to the verification of $P \models \Box g$, using* FSA*'s as the assertional language.*

Claim 2 does not guarantee that the application of SYMB-MC will terminate.

We have constructed an implementation of a system that accepts as inputs the automata representing $init_P$ and g and the step transducer $\mathcal{T}_P$, and checks whether g is a P-invariant, although it may fail to terminate. We managed to verify program MUX and other simple programs including versions of MUX with either synchronous or asynchronous communication where the processes are arranged in a ring rather than an array. Finally, two of the four safety specifications which were verified in [CGH+93] and [PS96] were checked for a single-bus version of the Futurebus+ protocol and were found to be correct.

The representation of automata in our implementation uses OBDD-encoded assertions over the local state variables instead of explicit enumeration of the local states which allow a transition from one automaton state to another. Thus, our transition function has the type δ: $Q \times local\_assertions \mapsto 2^Q$, where a local assertion is an assertion over the local state variables.

4 Tree Languages

In this section, we extend the method of regular expressions over strings to deal with regular tree languages (see [TW68], [GS70], [D70]). This will enable us to handle process networks organized in a tree topology. Since process trees may have different out-degrees for different nodes, we have to generalize the notion of tree automata to deal with varying arity.[6]

4.1 Bottom-Up Tree Automata

We define a *tree structure* S to be a finite subset of $\mathbb{N}^*$ (i.e. a finite set of sequences of natural numbers) satisfying:

- S contains the empty sequence Λ.
- If S contains the sequence $(\alpha_1, \ldots, \alpha_k)$, then it also contains the (possibly empty) sequence $(\alpha_1, \ldots, \alpha_{k-1})$ and the sequences $(\alpha_1, \ldots, \alpha_{k-1}, r)$, for every r, $0 \leq r < \alpha_k$.

We refer to the elements of S as the *nodes* of the tree structure S. Obviously, S represents a node by specifying the path that has to be followed from the root in order to get to the node. Thus, in a tree structure, Λ represents the root, and

---

[6] An extension of tree automata to arbitrary arity was made in [KG96] but in a top-down infinite context.

$(1, 0)$ represents the node which is the first child of the second child of the root. A node $\bar{\alpha} \in S$ is a leaf, if it is not a prefix of any other member of S.

Let A be an arbitrary alphabet, i.e. a finite set of symbols. An A-*tree* T: $\langle S, \lambda \rangle$ consists of a tree structure S and a *labeling function* $\lambda: S \mapsto A$, mapping each node of the tree to an A label. We will often refer to nodes in the tree as $n \in T$ and to their labels as $\lambda(n)$.

A (*variable-arity*) *bottom-up tree automaton* (BTA) B: $\langle \Sigma, Q, \Delta, F \rangle$ where Σ, Q and $F \subseteq Q$ are the standard finite *alphabet*, set of *states*, and set of *accepting states*, while

$$\Delta: Q^* \times \Sigma \mapsto 2^Q$$

is a regular *transition function*, i.e. for every $a \in \Sigma$ and $\tilde{Q} \subseteq Q$, the set of words $\{w \in Q^* \mid \Delta(w, a) = \tilde{Q}\}$ is regular. In our presentations of BTAs, we write Δ as a finite number of entries of the form $\Delta(E_i, \Sigma_i) = Q_i$, where E_i is a regular expression over Q, $\Sigma_i \subseteq \Sigma$, and $Q_i \subseteq Q$ indicating that for $q \in Q$, $w \in Q^*$, and $a \in \Sigma$, $q \in \Delta(w, a)$ iff $q \in \Delta(E_i, a)$ for some E_i such that $w \in L(E_i)$.

The way a BTA operates when applied to a Σ-tree T is that it proceeds from the leaves towards the root, annotating the tree nodes with automaton states. A single annotation step can be applied to the tree node $n \in T$ only when all of its children have been already annotated. Assume that the children of n have been annotated with $q_1, \ldots, q_k$. Then, n can be annotated by $q \in Q$ if $q \in \Delta(q_1 \cdots q_k, \lambda(n))$.

More formally, a *run* of the BTA B over the tree $T = \langle S, \lambda \rangle$ is a mapping $r: S \mapsto Q$ satisfying:

For each $n \in S$ with children $n_1, \ldots, n_k$, $r(n) \in \Delta(r(n_1) \cdots r(n_k), \lambda(n))$.

A BTA is *deterministic* if $|\Delta(w, a)| = 1$, for every $w \in Q^*$ and $a \in \Sigma$.

Example: Let us define a BTA B which recognizes all variable-arity trees, labeled by $\Sigma = \{a, b\}$, with the requirement that precisely one node is labeled by b. For the components of B, we choose as follows: $\Sigma : \{a, b\}$, $\quad Q : \{q_0, q_1, q_2\}$, $\quad F : \{q_1\}$,

Δ : Defined as follows:

$$\Delta(q_0^*, a) = \qquad\qquad\qquad\qquad\qquad\qquad\qquad \{q_0\}$$
$$\Delta(q_0^*, b) = \qquad\qquad \Delta(q_0^* q_1 q_0^*, a) = \qquad\qquad \{q_1\}$$
$$\Delta(Q^* q_1 Q^* q_1 Q^*, \{a, b\}) = \Delta(Q^* q_2 Q^*, \{a, b\}) = \Delta(q_0^* q_1 q_0^*, b) = \{q_2\}$$

The BTA B is obviously deterministic. Given an $\{a, b\}$-tree T, automaton B will annotate by q_0 all the nodes n such that the subtree rooted at n is only labeled by a. Nodes rooting a subtree such that precisely one node in the subtree is labeled by b will be annotated by q_1. All other nodes are annotated by q_2. The tree T is accepted by B iff its root is annotated by q_1.

The transition function Δ determines the annotation of a node n, based on the annotation of its children and the Σ-character labeling n. According to the table, n will be annotated by q_0 if all its children are annotated by q_0 and n's label is a. This also takes care of the a-labeled leaves, since the empty word belongs to the language q_0^*. Node n will be annotated by q_1 if either all children are annotated by q_0 and n is labeled by b, or all children are annotated by q_0 except for one child which is annotated by q_1 and n is labeled by a. In all other cases, n will be annotated by q_2 which implies that at least two b's have been detected in the tree. ∎

A tree T is said to be *accepted* by the BTA B if there exists a run r of B over T such that $r(\Lambda) \in F$. We denote by $L(B)$ the set of trees accepted by B. The BTAs B_1 and B_2 are said to be *equivalent* if $L(B_1) = L(B_2)$. By applying the standard subset construction, we can establish the following claim:

Claim 3

1. *Every BTA is equivalent to a deterministic BTA.*
2. *The class of tree languages recognizable by a BTA is closed under the boolean operations of complementation and union.*

4.2 Configurations of a Process Tree as a Tree Language

As a running example, consider program PERCOLATE of Fig. 4. The assertion $leaf(\alpha, S)$ holds for tree address $\alpha \in S$ iff α is a leaf of S.

$$\left\|_{\alpha \in S} P[\alpha] :: \begin{array}{c} \textbf{in } S : \textbf{tree structure} \\ \left[\textbf{local } val : \{0,1,u\} \textbf{ where } leaf(\alpha,S) \leftrightarrow val \in \{0,1\} \right. \\ \left[\begin{array}{l} M := \{m | \alpha \cdot m \in S\} \\ \textbf{repeat} \\ \quad \textbf{if } \forall m \in M : P[\alpha \cdot m].val \neq u \\ \quad \quad \textbf{then } val := \bigvee_{m \in M} P[\alpha \cdot m].val \\ \textbf{until } val \neq u \end{array} \right] \end{array} \right.$$

Fig. 4. Process tree program PERCOLATE.

Program PERCOLATE consists of a tree of processes, each having its local variable val, which ranges over the set of values $\{0,1,u\}$. The value u should be interpreted as "undefined yet", which implies that it will eventually change to either 0 or 1. Initially, all the leaf processes in the tree have $val \in \{0,1\}$ and all other processes have $val = u$. The purpose of program PERCOLATE is to percolate to the root of the tree a value 1 if at least one of the leaves has value 1, and a value of 0, if all leaves have value 0. If $P[\alpha]$ does not yet have a defined value but all its childrens' values are defined then $P[\alpha]$ sets its value to the disjunction of the values of its children. Consequently, we can represent a configuration of program PERCOLATE as a tree over the alphabet $\Sigma_{\text{PERCOLATE}} : \{0,1,u\}$.

The specification of program PERCOLATE can be given by the formula

$$g: \quad P[\Lambda].val \neq u \rightarrow \left(P[\Lambda].val = \bigvee_{leaf(\alpha,S)} P[\alpha].val \right).$$

This formula states that if the root has a defined value then its value equals the disjunction of all val values at the leaves. It is not difficult to construct a BTA which will accept precisely the trees that have the property specified by g. In a similar way, it is straightforward to construct a BTA which will accept the initial configurations of the program.

To complete the demonstration that the assertional language of BTA's is adequate for symbolic model checking of program PERCOLATE, we should specify a tree transducer that will represent the state transformations due to execution of statements within the individual processes.

Let $T_1 = \langle S, \lambda_1 \rangle$ and $T_2 = \langle S, \lambda_2 \rangle$ be two Σ-trees over the same tree structure S. These can be viewed as two different labeling of the same underlying tree. We define the *cross product* of T_1 and T_2 as the $\Sigma \times \Sigma$ tree $T_1 \times T_2 = \langle S, \lambda_\times \rangle$, where, for each $\alpha \in S$, $\lambda_\times(\alpha) = [\lambda_1(\alpha), \lambda_2(\alpha)]$.

A *tree transducer* (over Σ) is simply a BTA over the product alphabet Σ^2. For trees T_1 and T_2 as described above, we say that T_2 is a T-transduction of T_1 if the tree $T_1 \times T_2$ is accepted by T.

Example: A tree transducer that represents the single transition (parameterized by the process address α) of program PERCOLATE is defined as follows:

$$\Sigma \colon \Sigma_{\text{PERCOLATE}} \times \Sigma_{\text{PERCOLATE}} \qquad Q \colon \underbrace{\{q_0, q_1, q_u,}_{Q_n} q_d\} \qquad F \colon \{q_d\}$$

Δ : Defined as follows:

$$\Delta(Q_n^*, [0,0]) = \{q_0\} \qquad \Delta(Q_n^*, [1,1]) = \{q_1\} \qquad \Delta(Q_n^*, [u,u]) = \{q_u\}$$
$$\Delta(q_0^*, [u,0]) = \Delta((q_0 + q_1)^* q_1 (q_0 + q_1)^*, [u,1]) = \Delta(Q_n^* q_d Q_n^*, id) = \{q_d\}$$

The transducer uses four states. Annotation of node α by the automaton states $Q_n \colon \{q_0, q_1, q_u\}$ reflects the value of $P[\alpha].val$ and also implies that in the subtree rooted at α, all the Σ^2 labels are the identity id. Annotation of α by q_d such that no descendant of α is annotated by q_d identifies the only allowed node in the tree structure which is labeled by a Σ^2-character different from id. The rules for such annotations are given by the second line in the definition of Δ. This line allows a change of value from u to 0 if all the children of α are annotated by q_0. It allows a change of value from u to 1 if at least one of the descendants is annotated by 1 and all the rest are annotated by 0 or 1.

Once the first (lowest) node is annotated by q_d, this annotation propagates from each node to its parent, provided none of the siblings is annotated by q_d. This guarantees that only one process in the tree changes its value from u to 0 or 1. ⏝

Given a tree transducer $T = \langle \Sigma \times \Sigma, R, \delta_T, F_T \rangle$ and a BTA $A = \langle \Sigma, Q, \delta_A, F_A \rangle$, we define their *composition* to be the BTA

$$T \circ A = \langle \Sigma, R \times Q, \delta, F_T \times F_A \rangle,$$

where, for every $r \in R$, $q \in Q$, $v \in R^*$, and $w \in Q^*$,

$$[r, q] \in \delta(v \times w, a) \quad \text{iff} \quad \exists b \in \Sigma \text{ such that } r \in \delta_T(v, [a,b]) \text{ and } q \in \delta_A(w, b).$$

Claim 4 *The tree language accepted by the composition $T \circ A$ consists of all trees having a T-transduction which is accepted by A.*

Going back to the use of BTAS as an assertional language, we observe that if A is a BTA characterizing a set of configurations of system P and T_P is the step tree transducer for P, then the precondition transformer $pred_P$ required in procedure SYMB-MC is given by $pred_P(A) = T_P \circ A$.

5 Symbolic Model Checking is Dual to Invariant Generation

An important component in all the modern support systems for deductive verification, such as STeP [MAB+94] and PVS [SOR93], consists of algorithms and heuristics for the automatic generation of invariants. Several of these techniques have been presented in [MP95] and efficiently implemented as reported in [BBM95] and [BLS96]. Perhaps the most powerful and widely applicable is the technique called *top-down invariant generation*. As described in [MP95] and [BBM95], the method starts with a goal assertion g, whose invariance we wish to prove, and applies a series of strengthening steps, until we obtain a stronger assertion ψ which implies g and is *inductive*. Using our notation, the strengthening procedure can be described as in Fig. 5. The predicate transformer $pred_P^\vee$ appearing in the procedure is dual to the $pred_P$ transformer used in procedure SYMB-MC of Fig. 1. It can be defined either by the duality relation $pred_P^\vee(\psi) = \neg pred_P(\neg\psi)$, or by saying that a state s satisfies $pred_P^\vee(\psi)$ iff *all*[7] P-successors of s satisfy ψ.

> **Procedure** STRENGTHEN(g: **assertion**);
>   **assertion:** $\psi_0, \psi_1, \dots$;
>   Let $\psi_0 := g$;
>   **For** $i = 0, 1, \dots$ **repeat**
>   Let $\psi_{i+1} := \psi_i \wedge pred_P^\vee(\psi_i)$;
>   **until** $\psi_{i+1} = \psi_i$;
>
>   Check that $init_P \rightarrow \psi_i$
> **end procedure**

Fig. 5. A procedure for top-down invariant generation.

Procedure STRENGTHEN is a perfect dual of procedure SYMB-MC. One of the procedures terminates iff the other does and, when they terminate, they terminate after precisely the same number of steps. Furthermore, for every $i = 0, 1, \dots$, reached in the application of these procedures, $\psi_i = \neg\varphi_i$, and one of them reports success (implying that g is a P-invariant) iff the other does.

So presenting the considered procedure as symbolic model checking or as part of the deductive set of tools is a matter of taste. The successful verification cases reported in [BBM95] and [BLS96] will work equally well in the approach of symbolic model checking suggested here. Symmetrically, it shows that the two assertional languages of regular languages and regular tree languages analyzed here can be imported into the invariant generation methodology with equal success.

References

[AK86]   K. R. Apt and D. Kozen. Limits for automatic program verification of finite-state concurrent systems. *Information Processing Letters*, 22(6), 1986.

[BBM95] N. Bjørner, I.A. Browne, and Z. Manna. Automatic generation of invariants and intermediate assertions. In *LNCS 976*, 1995.

[BO93]   R.V. Book and F. Otto. *String-Rewriting Systems*, Springer, 1993.

[BM96]   A. Bouajjani and O. Maler, Reachability Analysis of Push-down Automata. *Workshop on Infinite-state Systems*, Pisa, 1996.

[BCG86] M.C. Browne, E.M. Clarke, and O. Grumberg. Reasoning about networks with many finite state processes. In *PODC'86*.

[BCM+92] J.R. Burch, E.M. Clarke, et al. Symbolic model checking: 10^{20} states and beyond. *Information and Computation*, 98(2):142–170, 1992.

[BK95]   D.A. Basin and N. Klarlund. Hardware verification using 2nd-order logic. In P. Wolper, editor, *CAV'95, LNCS 939*, 1995.

---

[7] In comparison, s satisfies $pred_P(\psi)$ iff *some* P-successor of s satisfies ψ.

[BLS96]   S. Bensalem, Y. Lakhnech, and H. Saidi. Powerful techniques for the auto-
           matic generation of invariants. *CAV'96*, 1996.
[Bry86]   R.E. Bryant. Graph-based algorithms for Boolean function manipulation.
           IEEE Transactions on Computers, C-35(12):1035–1044, 1986.
[CE81]   E.M. Clarke and E.A. Emerson. Synthesis of synchronization skeletons for
           branching time temporal logic. *Logics of Programs, LNCS 131*, 1981.
[CES86]   E.M. Clarke, et al. Automatic verification of finite state concurrent systems
           using temporal logic specifications. *ACM Trans. Prog. Lang. Sys.*, 1986.
[CGH+93]   E.M. Clarke, O. Grumberg, et al. Verification of the futurebus+ cache co-
           herence protocol. *Proceedings of the Eleventh International Symposium on
           Computer Hardware Description Languages and their Applications.* 1993.
[CGJ95]   E.M. Clarke, O. Grumberg, and S. Jha. Verifying parameterized networks
           using abstraction and regular languages. In *CONCUR'95*, 1995.
[D70]   J. Doner. Tree Acceptors and some of their applications, *JCSS* 4, 1970.
[EN95]   E. A. Emerson, K. S. Namjoshi. Reasoning about rings. *POPL'95*, 1995.
[EN96]   E.A. Emerson and K.S. Namjoshi. Automatic verification of parameterized
           synchronous systems. In R. Alur and T. Henzinger, editors, *CAV'96*, 1996.
[GS70]   F. Gecseg and M. Steinby. *Tree Automata* Akademiai Kiado, 1984.
[HLR92]   N. Halbwachs, F. Lagnier, et al. An experience in proving regular networks
           of processes by modular model checking. *Acta Informatica*, 29(6/7), 1992.
[HJJ+96]   J.G. Henriksen, J. Jensen, et al. Mona: Monadic second-order logic in prac-
           tice. In *TACAS '95, LNCS 1019*, 1996.
[ID96]   C.N. Ip and D. Dill. Verifying systems with replicated components in Murφ.
           In R. Alur and T. Henzinger, editors, *CAV'96*, 1996.
[KG96]   O. Kupferman and O. Grumberg. Branching Time Temporal Logic and Amor-
           phous Tree Automata. *Information and Computation* 125, 1996.
[KM89]   R.P. Kurshan and K. McMillan. A structural induction theorem for pro-
           cesses. In P. Rudnicki, editor, *PODC'89*, Edmonton, AB, Canada, 1989.
[LHR97]   D. Lesens, N. Halbwachs, and P. Raymond. Automatic verification of pa-
           rameterized linear networks of processes. In *POPL'97*, Paris, 1997.
[MAB+94]   Z. Manna, A. Anuchitanukul, et al. STeP: The Stanford Temporal Prover.
           Technical Report STAN-CS-TR-94-1518, Stanford University, 1994.
[McM93]   K.L McMillan. *Symbolic Model Checking.* 1993.
[MP95]   Z. Manna and A. Pnueli. *Temporal Verification of Reactive Systems: Safety.*
           Springer-Verlag, New York, 1995.
[PS96]   A. Pnueli and E. Shahar. A platform for combining deductive with algorith-
           mic verification. In R. Alur and T. Henzinger, editors, *CAV'96*, 1996.
[QS82]   J.P. Queille and J. Sifakis. Specification and verification of concurrent sys-
           tems in *cesar*. *International Symposium on Programming,LNCS 137*, 1982.
[SG89]   Z. Shtadler and O. Grumberg. Network grammars, communication behaviors
           and automatic verification. In *LNCS 407*, 1989.
[SG92]   A.P. Sistla and S.M. German. Reasoning about systems with many processes.
           J. ACM, 39:675–735, 1992.
[SOR93]   N. Shankar, S. Owre, and J.M. Rushby. The PVS proof checker: A reference
           manual (draft). Technical report, SRI International, Menlo Park, CA, 1993.
[TW68]   J.W. Thatcher, J.B. Wright. Generalized finite automata with application to
           a decision procedure in second order logic. *Math. Sys. Theory* 2, 1968.
[WL89]   P. Wolper and V. Lovinfosse. Verifying properties of large sets of processes
           with network invariants. In *LNCS 407*, 1989.

The Invariant Checker: Automated Deductive Verification of Reactive Systems

Hassen Saïdi

VERIMAG[1]

saidi@imag.fr

http://www.imag.fr/VERIMAG/PEOPLE/Hassen.Saidi/Invariant-Checker.html

1 Design Philosophy

The Invariant Checker [GS96,Saï96] is a tool for the verification of invariance properties of reactive systems using theorem-proving techniques and tools. The system is designed as a front-end for the Pvs [OSR93a] theorem prover. The Invariant Checker can be seen as an extension of the Pvs verification system to handle the notion of transition systems and invariants as well as the usual mathematical objects. These extensions appear at two different levels: the Pvs specification language is extended by the notion of a system, that is a program given as a transition system or a parallel composition of transition systems. The Pvs prover is also extended with a proof rule (cf. [MP95]) dedicated to invariance properties. To check whether a predicate P is an *inductive* invariant of a system S, it is sufficient to check the validity of a set of first order formulas called verification conditions (VCs) (cf. [GS96]), expressing the fact that each transition of the program preserves P. This proof rule also provides a strengthening method for P: if some of the generated VCs are not provable, P is replaced by $P \land \widetilde{pre}(P)$ in a model checking like manner. This method can be completely automatized, but convergence is not guaranteed.

This kind of invariant verification makes a different use of theorem proving than the "classical" one where the program semantics is encoded in the prover's specification language. In this "classical" approach the proof process is complicated by the encoding of semantics and the rewriting of semantics definitions, while the most important and difficult part of the verification process is the reasoning about the program variables and their values. Also, it requires too much user intervention. The objective of our tool is to provide more automatization using a set of features. The architecture of the tool is presented in Figure 1.

2 Features

Syntax: Programs can be described in a Simple Programming Language (SPL), close to the one used in [MP95], where program variables can be of any type definable in Pvs, and can be assigned by any Pvs expression of compatible type. Also, it is possible to import any defined Pvs theory. Programs described in SPL are translated automatically to guarded commands with explicit control.

---

[1] Centre Equation, 2, Avenue de la Vignate, 38610 Grenoble-Gières, Tel: (+33) 4.76.63.48.44, Fax: (+33) 4.76.63.48.50

437

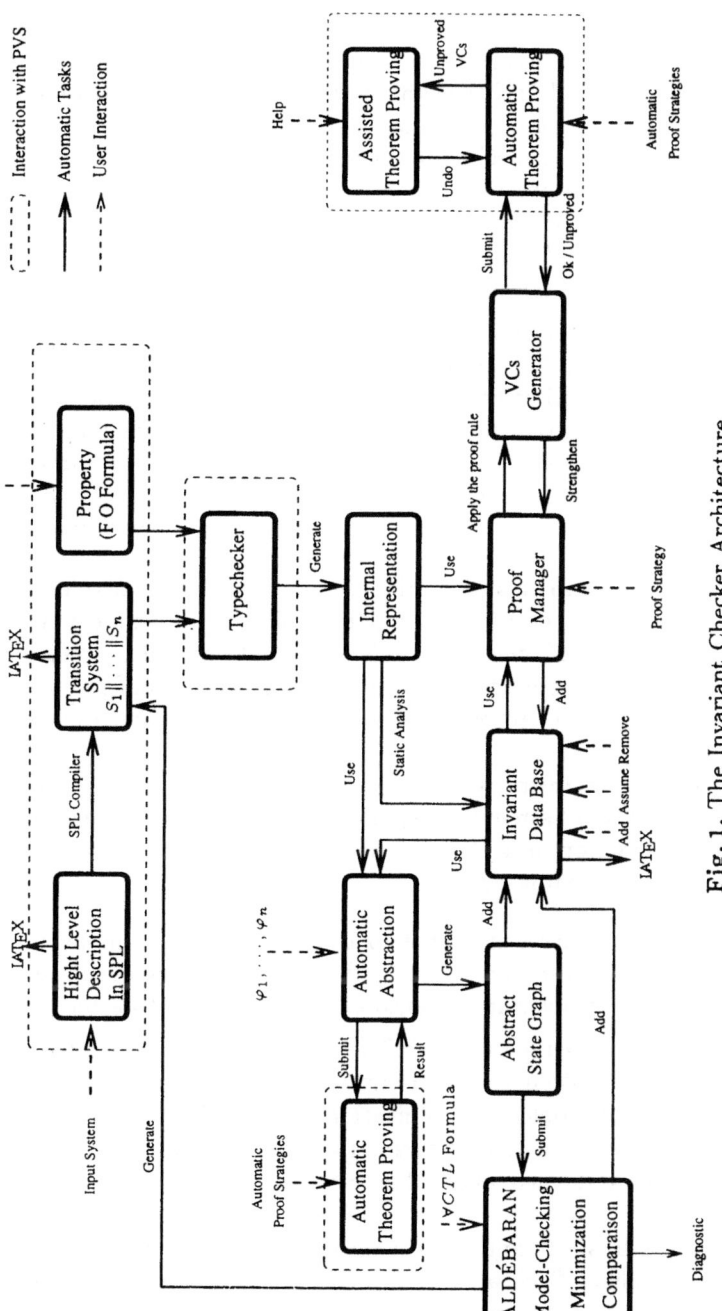

Fig. 1. The Invariant Checker Architecture

Typechecking: Typechecking a program consists in checking that every guarded command is well typed according to a typing context, that is each guard is a boolean expression, and each variable is assigned by an expression of a compatible type. This typing context consists of all variable declarations and the imported PVS **theory**. Typechecking a specification leads to the generation of type correctness conditions (TCCs) which have to be proved as *invariants* and not as valid formulas. If all generated TCCs are proved, this guarantees "absence of run-time errors", such as division by zero or the application of the tail function to the empty list.

Proof session: A proof session starts with typechecking the program and the property to be verified. The program is translated into an internal representation which is used by all components of the tool. One can apply static analysis methods in order to extract inductive invariants using the techniques described in [BLS96]. The generated invariants are stored in the invariant data base. In order to prove that the considered property is an inductive invariant of the program, the user can apply the proof rule using two different modes:

- Interactive mode: In this mode the user invokes the proof rule which generates a set of VCs. Each VC is submitted to the prover, where a proof strategy is applied. If some of the generated VCs are not provable, the user can either try to prove them interactively or he can apply the proof rule again. In this case, the invariant is automatically strengthened, and a fresh set of VCs is generated.
- Automatic mode: In this mode the user indicates to the proof manager the maximal number of strengthening step. The proof rule is then applied without user interaction until this maximal number is reached, or until an inductive invariant is computed.

In both modes, the user can decide to use the invariants in the data base in order to weaken the generated VCs. In this case, for every generated VC, a set of relevant generated invariants is automatically selected to achieve the proof.

Automatic discharging of VCs: The generated VCs are submitted to the PVS prover, where automatic proof strategies combining automatic induction, automatic rewriting, boolean simplification using BDDs and decision procedures are applied. The user can defined such strategies, by combining pre-defined PVS strategies and user defined ones. Non provable assertions are considered non valid.

Invariant data base: It contains the invariants generated using the techniques described in [BLS96]. Each already proved invariant is automatically added to the data base. Also, the user can always enrich the data base. Therefore, with each invariant is associated a status which changes during a proof session. The status has three possible values:

- *assumed:* these are user defined invariants for which no proof is required. They play the role of axioms, and can therefore lead to inconsistent proofs.
- *unproved.*

– *proved*: a proof is associated with such an invariant. It consists of the applied proof strategy and the invariants used during the proof. In order to maintain a coherent data base, if some invariant is removed, all the already proved invariants depending on it, become *unproved*.

Automatic abstraction: Recently, we added a new feature, which consists of the use of abstraction techniques [GS97]. Given a set of predicates $\varphi_1, ..., \varphi_\ell$ on the variables of a program, an abstract state graph (where states are valuations of $\varphi_1, ..., \varphi_\ell$) is constructed in an automatic way using user defined proof strategy. An abstract state graph can be used in many ways:

– It defines an invariant of the program.
– Any verification technique for finite state systems can be applied. We have interfaced our tool with ALDÉBARAN [FGK+96], which allows:
  • minimization of the abstract state graph modulo bisimulation.
  • evaluation of any temporal logic formula without existential quantification over paths.
– The abstract state graph (or its minimization w.r.t to strong bisimulation) can be used as a global control graph from which stronger invariants can be generated and added to the invariant data base.

User interface: Pvs has emacs as user interface. We found convenient to use the same user interface for our prototype. All the functions of the tool can be invoked by emacs commands.

3 Experiments

Using our tool we verified various classical mutual exclusion algorithms , a read and write buffer using complex data types [GS96]. The use of abstraction techniques allow us to prove in a fully automatic way parameterized versions of an alternating bit and a bounded retransmission protocol [GS97].

References

[BLS96]   S. Bensalem, Y. Lakhnech, and H. Saïdi. *Powerful Techniques for the Automatic Generation of Invariants*. In *Conference on Computer Aided Verification CAV'96*, LNCS 1102, July 1996.

[FGK+96] J.-C. Fernandez, H. Garavel, A. Kerbrat, R. Mateescu, L. Mounier and M. Sighireanu. CADP (Cæsar/Aldébaran Development Package): A protocol validation and verification toolbox. In *CAV' 1996*. LNCS 1102, 1996.

[GS96]   S. Graf and H. Saïdi. Verifying invariants using theorem proving. In *Conference on Computer Aided Verification CAV'96*, LNCS 1102, July 1996.

[GS97]   S. Graf and H. Saïdi. Construction of abstract state graphs with PVS. In this volume.

[MP95]   Z. Manna and A. Pnueli. *Temporal Verification of Reactive Systems: Safety*. Springer-Verlag, New York, 1995.

[OSR93a] S. Owre, N. Shankar, and J. M. Rushby. *A Tutorial on Specification and Verification Using PVS*. Computer Science Laboratory, SRI International, February 1993.

[Saï96]   H. Saïdi. *A Tool for Proving Invariance Properties of Concurrent Systems Automatically*. In TACAS'96, LNCS 1056, Springer-Verlag.

The PEP Tool

Bernd Grahlmann

Institut für Informatik, Universität Hildesheim,
bernd@informatik.uni-hildesheim.de

Abstract The **PEP** tool embeds sophisticated programming and verification components in a user-friendly graphical interface. The basic idea is that the programming component allows the user to design concurrent algorithms in an imperative language, and that the **PEP** system then generates Petri nets from such programs in order to use Petri net theory for simulation and verification purposes. A key feature is flexibility; its modular design eases the task of adding new interfaces to other verification packages, such as 'INA', 'PROD' or 'SMV'.

PEP has been implemented on Solaris 2.x, Sun OS 4.1.x and Linux. Ftp-able versions are available via http://www.informatik.uni-hildesheim.de/~pep.

Keywords: Binary decision diagrams, B(PN)^2, Model checking, **PEP**, Petri nets, Simulation, Stubborn sets, Temporal logic, Tool.

1 System overview

The **PEP**[1] tool is a **P**rogramming **E**nvironment based on **P**etri Nets [5]. The main phases of the development of parallel systems (modelling, simulation, analysis and verification) are supported. From an abstract point of view the tool consists of the following three components (see Fig. 1):

1. The editing and simulation component contains editors and simulators for parallel systems from which Petri nets can be generated automatically using the different compilers integrated in this component.
2. The formula component offers the possibility to enter formulae which can either refer to a parallel program or a net. Furthermore, program formulae can be transformed into net formulae [14].
3. The verification component consisted of a model checker [11,15] based on the finite prefix of the branching process [20,10]. Interfaces to other verification packages, like 'INA' [21], 'PROD' [24] or 'SMV' [8], have been added recently in order to offer as many different verification methods as possible and to support stronger logics.

2 Editing and simulation component

The editing and simulation component of the **PEP** system has grown continuously. Corresponding to the main intention of the tool – i.e. to use Petri net theory in order to provide program verification – a program editor and a net editor have been the starting point.

With the first version of **PEP** it was possible to edit parallel algorithms expressed in B(PN)^2, an imperative / predicative programming language. B(PN)^2

---

[1] PEP is a joint project between the 'Universität Hildesheim' and the 'Humboldt-Universität zu Berlin' which is financed by the DFG (German Research Foundation). Furthermore, the work has been partially supported by the projects CALIBAN (ESPRIT) and EXPRESS (HCM)

is called **Basic Petri Net Programming** Notation because it has a compositional semantics in terms of Petri nets [2]. In addition to sequential composition, nondeterministic choice and iteration, parallel composition is available. Parallel processes can share common memory (asynchronous communication) or use (synchronous) channel communication or both.

Originally, the compilation of these programs into Petri boxes, a special class of 1-safe low-level (LL) Petri nets [2], via terms of a process algebra called PBC (**Petri Box Calculus**) [2], which is an extension / modification of CCS, was supported. Later on, an alternative net semantics of $B(PN)^2$ programs was given by means of M-nets, a special class of high-level (HL) Petri nets [3]. The implementation of a procedure concept [12,18,19] extends $B(PN)^2$ to a complete programming language.

Furthermore, a new input interface was added. Parallel finite automata (PFA) with $B(PN)^2$ actions as arc annotations can be edited and compiled into $B(PN)^2$ programs [13].

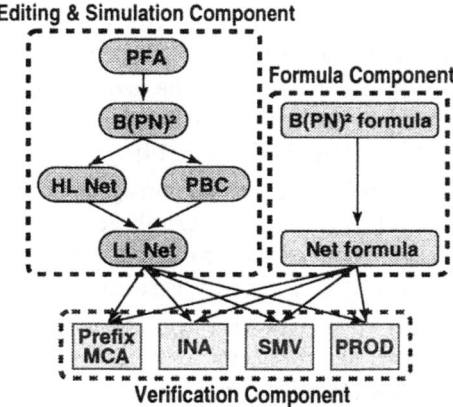

Figure1. The different components of the **PEP** system.

Thus the editing and simulation component of **PEP** presently contains:

1. Editors for PFA, $B(PN)^2$ programs, PBC terms, HL nets and LL nets.
2. Simulators for $B(PN)^2$ programs, HL nets and LL nets.
3. Compilers as follows: PFA $\Rightarrow$ $B(PN)^2$, $B(PN)^2$ $\Rightarrow$ PBC, PBC $\Rightarrow$ LL net, $B(PN)^2$ $\Rightarrow$ HL net and HL net $\Rightarrow$ LL net.

3 Verification component

One of the most important aims during the development of the **PEP** tool was to provide verification in addition to simulation and analysis of standard properties. Therefore, the implementation of a model checking algorithm, in order to allow temporal logic formulae to be checked, was envisaged and carried out. Due to the well-known state explosion problem, efficiency was strongly required.

First a very efficient model checking algorithm for a restricted class of low-level Petri nets was implemented [22], which avoids any state space generation taking the net directly as input. Unfortunately, the class of nets the model checker can handle is too restricted for the **PEP** approach.

Therefore, another model checking algorithm [11,15] was implemented. State graph generation is avoided. The finite prefix of a branching process (an optimised version of the McMillan unfolding [20,10]) of the low-level Petri net is taken as input for this partial order based method. A drawback, which had to be accepted, was that efficiency was gained on the cost of the expressiveness of the supported logic, S_4, a propositional logic on place names, augmented with $\square$ for 'always' (AG in CTL) and $\diamondsuit$ for 'possibly at some future point' (EF in CTL).

It is widely accepted, that no verification method exists (at least not yet) which is superior to all other methods [9,16]. Thus we decided to provide interfaces to other verification packages, so far to INA, PROD and SMV.

There have been three reasons for selecting the SMV [8] package: it offers CTL (Computational Tree Logic) model checking; it uses BDDs (Binary Decision Diagrams) [7] to encode the transition relation; and it is known to be good and easy to integrate. We tested different ways to encode low-level nets using the SMV formalism [25]. Encoding the transition relation directly seems to be the most promising solution. Place invariants, which may be provided by the net generators, tend to speed up the verification. Furthermore, we spent some efforts to improve the way results are reported to the user. S/he can for example choose to animate the firing sequences in the net and/or program editor (as for other analysis method included in the **PEP** tool [14]).

The PROD package [24] has similar advantages: it offers linear time temporal model checking including CTL; state graph generation can be improved by stubborn set reduction [23] as well as symmetrical reduction methods; the user can additionally profit from the on-the-fly verification method.

INA [21] was integrated in a more complete way. Apart from state graph based methods – stubborn set reduction as well as symmetrical reduction are provided on demand – INA includes the most complete available set of Petri net analysis methods. Among others, many elementary properties, e.g. structural properties and different invariants, can be computed.

Even though not every feature of the three packages is available, **PEP** can also be considered to be a comfortable graphical interface to these originally textual tools, in addition to being a stand-alone tool.

4 Conclusion and future work

We briefly presented some of the main features of the **PEP** tool. For a more detailed overview of the **PEP** system we refer the reader to [1,5] and the various papers which are available at http://www.informatik.uni-hildesheim.de/~pep.

Our experiences have prompted us to consider the following future aims:

- A model checker for high-level Petri nets should be developed and implemented in order to avoid the unfolding into low-level Petri nets.
- The integration of the verification packages will be enhanced and interfaces to other verification packages (such as SPIN [17]) will be provided.

Acknowledgement: A lot of people (theoreticians and implementors) contributed to the development of the **PEP** system. Thanks!

References

1. E. Best. Partial Order Verification with PEP. *Proc. of POMIV'96, Princeton.*
2. E. Best, R. Devillers and J. G. Hall. The Box Calculus: a New Causal Algebra with Multi-Label Communication. *Advances in Petri Nets 92,* Springer *LNCS 609.*
3. E. Best, H. Fleischhack, W. Frączak, R. P. Hopkins, H. Klaudel, and E. Pelz. An M-Net Semantics of B(PN)^2. *Proc. of STRICT'95,* Springer.
4. E. Best, H. Fleischhack, W. Frączak, R. P. Hopkins, H. Klaudel, and E. Pelz. A Class of Composable High Level Petri Nets. *Proc. of ATPN'95.*
5. E. Best and B. Grahlmann. *PEP: Documentation and User Guide.* Universität Hildesheim. Available together with the tool via:
   http://www.informatik.uni-hildesheim.de/~pep/HomePage.html.
6. E. Best and R. P. Hopkins. B(PN)^2 – a Basic Petri Net Programming Notation. *Proc. of PARLE,* Springer *LNCS 694.*
7. R. E. Bryant. Graph-based algorithms for boolean function manipulation. *IEEE Transactions on Computers,* C-35(8), 1986.
8. E. Clarke and K. McMillan and S. Campos and V. Hartonas-Garmhausen. Symbolic Model Checking. *Proc. of CAV'96,* New Brunswick, Springer *LNCS 1102.*
9. J. C. Corbett. Evaluating Deadlock Detection Methods for Concurrent Software. *Technical report,* University of Hawaii at Manoa, 1995.
10. J. Esparza, S. Römer, and W. Vogler. An Improvement of McMillan's Unfolding Algorithm. *Proc. of TACAS'96,* Springer *LNCS 1055.*
11. J. Esparza. *Model Checking Using Net Unfoldings,* 151–195. Number 23 in Science of Computer Programming. ELSEVIER, 1994.
12. H. Fleischhack and B. Grahlmann. *A Petri Net Semantics for B(PN)^2 with Procedures. Proc. of PDSE'97,* Boston.
13. B. Grahlmann, M. Moeller, and U. Anhalt. A New Interface for the PEP Tool – Parallel Finite Automata. *Proc. of 2. AWPN'95.*
14. B. Grahlmann. The Reference Component of PEP. *Proc. of TACAS'97, Enschede.* Springer *LNCS 1217.*
15. B. Graves. Identification of Specific Processes Contained in McMillan's Finite Unfolding. Submitted.
16. M. Heiner and P. Deussen. Petri Net Based Design and Analysis of Reactive Systems. *Proc. of WODES'96, Edinburgh.*
17. G. Holzmann and D. Peled. The State of SPIN. *Proc. of CAV'96, New Brunswick.*
18. L. Jenner. A Low-Level Net Semantics for B(PN)^2 with Procedures. In E. Best and H. Fleischhack, editors. *PEP: Programming Environment Based on Petri Nets.* Hildesheimer Informatik-Berichte 14/95. 1995.
19. J. Lilius and E. Pelz. An M-Net Semantics for B(PN)^2 with Procedures. *Proc. of ISCIS-XI'96.*
20. K. McMillan. A Technique of a State Space Search Based on Unfolding. *Formal Methods in System Design 6(1),* 1996.
21. P. H. Starke. *INA: Integrated Net Analyzer.* Handbuch, 1992.
22. T. Thielke. Implementierung eines effizienten Modelchecking-Algorithmus. *Petri-Netze im Einsatz für Entwurf und Entwicklung von Informationssystemen,* 1993.
23. A. Valmari. Stubborn Sets for Reduced State Space Generation. In *APN'90,* Springer *LNCS 483.*
24. K. Varpaaniemi and J. Halme and K. Hiekkanen and T. Pyssysalo. PROD Reference Manual. *Technical Report B 13, University of Helsinki,* 1995.
25. G. Wimmel. A BDD-based Model Checker for the PEP Tool. *Technical Report, University of Newcastle upon Tyne,* 1997.

TermiLog:
A System for Checking Termination of Queries to Logic Programs *

N. Lindenstrauss, Y. Sagiv, A. Serebrenik
Dept. of Computer Science
Hebrew University
Jerusalem, Israel
Email: {naomil,sagiv,alicser}@cs.huji.ac.il

Abstract. *TermiLog* is a system implemented in SICStus Prolog for automatically checking termination of queries to logic programs. Given a program and query, the system either answers that the query terminates or that it cannot prove termination. The system can handle automatically 82% of the 120 programs we tested it on.

1 Introduction

TermiLog is a system, implemented in SICStus Prolog [SICS95], for automatic termination analysis of logic programs. The system accepts as input a Prolog program and a query, and returns as the answer either that the query terminates or that it cannot prove termination. In contrast to some other systems the program does not have to satisfy any condition in order to be analyzed by *TermiLog* (e.g., in the system of [Plu90], the program has to be well-moded). Most predefined predicates of Prolog may appear in the program and are handled directly or by suitable transformations.

The type of termination analyzed by the system is the termination of computing all the answers to the given query, using Prolog's computation rule. As pointed out in [O'K90], this is the relevant notion of termination for Prolog, because even when one is interested only in a single answer, it is still important to know that the computation of all answers terminates, due to the possibility of backtracking.

We have applied *TermiLog* to 120 programs, taken from the literature on termination and some benchmarks. 82% of these programs were analyzed correctly by *TermiLog*, completely automatically. The largest program that was analyzed is the 57-clause credit-evaluation expert system from [StSh86].

---

* This research was supported in part by grants from the Israel Science Foundation

2 Overview of the system

Termination is proved by using well-founded orderings on terms. Formally, we define a *norm* for each term as follows:

$$\|f(T_1, \ldots T_n)\| = c + \sum_{i=1}^{n} a_i \|T_i\|$$

where c and $a_1, \ldots, a_n$ are non-negative integers that depend only on f/n. The norm of a variable X is denoted by X itself. In general, the norm is a linear expression. To be used in a termination proof, however, the norm of the term must be an integer (such a term will be called *instantiated enough*). Note that the norm of a non-ground term may be an integer, since some of the a_i may be zero. Our definition of norm includes, as special cases, the term-size norm [VanG91] and the list-size norm [UV88].

The system consists of three main parts — see [LiSa96, LiSa97] for details. The first does the *instantiation analysis* — that is, it determines which argument positions of predicates are instantiated enough and which are not. The instantiation analysis is done by means of a bottom-up abstract interpretation similar to groundness analysis (cf. [Cous92]).

The second part is inference of constraints among argument sizes. The types of constraints are the *monotonicity* and *equality constraints* of [BrSa89], but the inference is done in a more accurate way. Since inferred constraints are not always needed to show termination, the system provides the option of restricting the constraint inference just to some parts of the given program.

The constraint inference also tells us whether a constraint is recursive or non-recursive. Non-recursive constraints can often be "factored out" from the termination analysis by automatic unfolding. This suggests a completely automatic way of handling, for example, the *mergesort* program, that previously was shown to terminate only by first applying some ad hoc transformation.

The third part consists of constructing the *query-mapping pairs* and applying the test of [Sag91], which was originally intended for Datalog programs and is here extended to general logic programs.

3 Benchmarks

This section sums up the results of applying our system to 120 programs taken from papers on termination [DSD94, Plu90, AP94, Ver92], the benchmark collection of [BGH94], and some other sources. *TermiLog* has analyzed correctly 82% of them. The results are given in the following table—explanations follow. The detailed results may be found in the tables in [LiSaExp].

The *TermiLog* system has analyzed correctly all the examples from the survey of [DSD94] on termination, including the mutually recursive *bool*. It is worth noting that mutual recursion does not require any special consideration in our system, while in earlier work [Plu90, VanG91] special transformations were needed to eliminate mutual recursion.

Source	Number of Programs	Handled Correctly Automatically
[DSD94]	7	7 (100%)
[Plu90]	17	16 (94%)
[AP94]	19	17 (89%)
[BGH94]	24	11 (46%)
[Ver92]	32	26 (81%)
Other	21	21(100%)
Total	120	98 (82%)

TermiLog can handle all the examples of [Plu90] that Plümer's own system can handle, except for the program *perm*. *TermiLog* can also handle the program *mult*, which Plümer's system cannot handle. The program *perm* would be handled by our system once linear equalities among argument sizes are added.

The paper of [AP94] does not deal with automatic termination analysis, but develops a theoretical basis for studying termination of logic programs as well as Prolog programs. Our system can handle all the examples of [AP94], except for program *perm* of [Plu90] and the map-coloring program of [StSh86].

The benchmark collection of [BGH94] has more complex programs than those usually found in the literature on termination. Out of the 24 programs in that collection, our system could handle 11 (46%) programs. Some programs of that benchmark could not be handled because the algorithms we use are not powerful enough to show their termination, while others were too big and caused memory problems.

The examples from [Ver92] are handled automaticallly except for six, three of the latter being programs in which termination depends on the differentiation between *constants* (cf. [Llo87]), which is not made in our abstraction (cf. [LiSa96]).

The *TermiLog* system has analyzed correctly 21 further examples, including
* Four programming examples from the SICStus manual [SICS95].
* Ackermann's function (from [StSh86]).
* Greatest common divisor.
* Huffman codes computation.
* Quicksort using difference lists (from [StSh86]).
* 8 queens.
* Rewriting system for normalizing expressions with an associative operator.
* A game program from [AP93].
* The Yale shooting problem from [AB91].
* The credit-evaluation expert system from [StSh86] (this 57-clause program is the biggest among all those analyzed).

It should be emphasized that all the experimental results reported in this section were obtained by using only the basic algorithms implemented in the system, and *without* any additional program transformations or other ad hoc features intended to increase the power of the system.

An example session with *TermiLog* is given in [LSS97].

References

[AB91]   K. R. Apt and M. Bezem. Acyclic Programs. *New Generation Computing*, 9:335-363, 1991.

[AP93]   K. R. Apt and D. Pedreschi. Reasoning about Termination of Pure Prolog Programs. *Information and Computation*, 106:109-157, 1993.

[AP94]   K. R. Apt and D. Pedreschi. Modular Termination Proofs for Logic and Pure Prolog Programs. In *Advances in Logic Programming Theory*, 183-229. Oxford University Press, 1994.

[BrSa89] A. Brodsky and Y. Sagiv. Inference of monotonicity constraints in Datalog programs. *Proceedings of the Eighth ACM SIGACT-SIGART-SIGMOD Symposium on Principles of Database Systems*, 1989, 190-199.

[BGH94]   F. Bueno, M. García de la Banda and M. Hermenegildo. Effectiveness of Global Analysis in Strict Independence-Based Automatic Program Parallelization. *International Symposium on Logic Programming*, 320-336. MIT Press, 1994.

[Cous92] P. Cousot and R. Cousot. Abstract interpretation and application to logic programs. *J. Logic Programming*, 13:103-179, 1992.

[DSD94]   D. De Schreye and S. Decorte. Termination of Logic Programs: the Never-Ending Story. *J. Logic Programming*, 19/20:199-260, 1994.

[LiSa96] N. Lindenstrauss and Y. Sagiv. Checking Termination of Queries to Logic Programs. http://www.cs.huji.ac.il/~naomil/

[LiSa97] N. Lindenstrauss and Y. Sagiv. Automatic Termination Analysis of Logic Programs. ICLP'97. MIT Press, 1997.

[LiSaExp] N. Lindenstrauss and Y. Sagiv. Automatic Termination Analysis of Logic Programs (with Detailed Experimental Results). http://www.cs.huji.ac.il/~naomil/

[LSS97]   N. Lindenstrauss ,Y. Sagiv and A. Serebrenik. An Example Session with *TermiLog*. http://www.cs.huji.ac.il/~naomil/

[Llo87]   J. W. Lloyd. *Foundations of Logic Programming*. Springer Verlag, second edition, 1987.

[O'K90]   R. A. O'Keefe. *The Craft of Prolog*. MIT Press, 1990.

[Plu90]   L. Plümer. *Termination Proofs for Logic Programs*. Springer Verlag, LNAI 446, 1990.

[Sag91]   Y. Sagiv. A termination test for logic programs. In *International Logic Programming Symposium*. MIT Press, 1991.

[SICS95] *SICStus Prolog User's Manual*. Release 3. Swedish Institute of Computer Science, 1995.

[StSh86] L. Sterling and E. Shapiro. *The Art of Prolog*. MIT Press, 1986.

[UV88]   J. D. Ullman and A. Van Gelder. Efficient tests for top-down termination of logical rules. JACM 35:2(1988), 345-373.

[VanG91] A. Van Gelder. Deriving constraints among argument sizes in logic programs. *Annals of Mathematics and Artificial Intelligence*, 3:361–392, 1991.

[Ver92]   C. Verschaetse. Static Termination Analysis for Definite Horn Clause Programs. Ph.D. Thesis, K.U. Leuven, 1992.

MOSEL: A Sound and Efficient Tool for M2L(Str)

Peter Kelb, Tiziana Margaria, Michael Mendler, Claudia Gsottberger

Dept. of Comp. Science, Universität Passau, Innstr. 33, D-94032 Passau (Germany)
{kelb,tiziana,mendler,gsottber}@fmi.uni-passau.de

1 Introduction

MOSEL [6] is a new system for the analysis and verification in Monadic Second-Order Logic (M2L) based on model construction. The aim is to offer a system-level environment supporting several theories of the logic. MOSEL is a toolset, which, in its complete realization, will include a flexible set of decision procedures for several theories of the logic (e.g., finite and infinite strings, and trees) complemented by a variety of support components to provide input format translations, visualization, and interfaces to other logics and other analysis, verification, and synthesis tools. The presentation will concern the important concepts from the toolbuilders' perspective: *design principles, implementation, efficiency* and *application domains.*

2 Design Principles

The soundness of the implementation and the efficiency of its use are due to the following four main principles underlying our design of MOSEL:

1. Definition of a formal semantics for a minimal subset of the logic. Having started with a M2L(Str) implementation for finite strings the semantics is defined in terms of finite-state automata.

2. Layered approach to the logic. We introduce a hierarchy of logic layers, with increasingly powerful constructs, related by either direct embedding or more elaborate encodings as shown in Fig. 1.

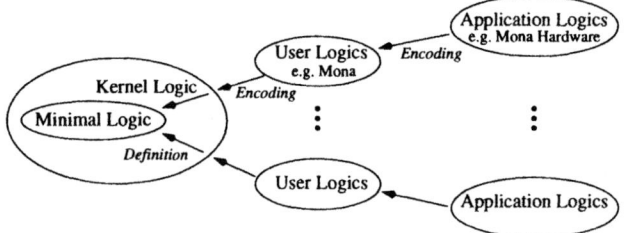

Fig. 1. Layered Logics in MOSEL

The *minimal logic* contains the minimal set of primitives for which the semantics is formally defined. This set constitutes the reference language for proofs involving semantics, which is very economic e.g. in proofs by structural induction on the constructs of the language. While this is the ideal language for developing the theory, it is not adequate for practical use.

The *kernel logic* extends the minimal logic by additional (derived) constructs and coincides with the set of constructs actually implemented as primitives in the semantic decision procedure. The design of this extension is guided by considerations of efficiency of the computations required in the decision procedure.

A set of generic *user logics* correspond to an application-independent layer. They extend the kernel logic by derived operators which do not have a direct implementation, but are comfortable for generic applications. User logics may be rather different from the kernel logic and need not be a simple syntactic extension (e.g. the translation of Mona's [5] input syntax into the kernel logic).

A number of *application-specific logics*, each containing additional admissible predicates and constructs tailored to specific application domains. Here we have direct experience in the domain of verification and synthesis of hardware, where we deal with families of parametric sequential circuits [7].

Due to the principle of implementing outer layers of the logic through successive encodings and definitional extensions to the unique minimal logic, and by making these explicit, the semantic coherence of richer logics with the minimal logic is ensured [6].

Additional advantages of this principle are that the implemented set of primitives is transparent too, and that it is immediately clear which constructs are expensive, due to their (easily computable) definition in terms of kernel logic constructs.

3. Modular design. While other tools, like e.g. Mona, are available only as a single large component, MOSEL is a collection of modules which can be combined or exchanged at need. MOSEL supports flexible adaptation and extension to new input or output formalisms, as well as the interchange of some of its internal components (e.g., users may exchange the BDD package used in the decision procedure, or the automata minimization and determinization algorithms). The aim is that the best-fitting incarnation of the tool may be put together at need, on an application-driven basis, from the collection of existing components.

4. Integratability in a heterogeneous analysis and verification environment. The MOSEL toolset is available within METAFrame®[1], a system-level programming environment. It is thus not just a mere stand-alone tool, but its decision procedure as well as each single component (compilers, interfacing and visualization components) are also available for use in more complex, even heterogeneous METAFrame synthesized tools.

3 Implementation

The current implementation of the MOSEL toolset is written in C/C++ and features three groups of components: *decision procedures*, *translators* between different logics, and graphical *visualization* modules.

Semantic Decision Procedures. The computational kernel constructs for a given formula of the input logic the minimal finite-state automaton characterizing its semantics. The decision procedure is independent to some degree from

---

[1] METAFrame® is a registered trademark.

the chosen input syntax since it works directly on an object-oriented abstract syntax tree.

Logic Translations. A series of interfacing modules translate each of the several logics into the abstract syntax trees accepted by the actual compiler.

Graphical Visualization. Several alternative graphic tools can be used to display the automata generated within MOSEL. As in **Mona**, it is possible to use the daVinci [3] tool to show the structure of the automata as well as the concrete BDD encoding of the edge labels. Moreover, the bidirectional link of MOSEL's automata to METAFrame's ffgraphs library makes it possible to read and generate automata, not only for display but also to be fed into other algorithms and tools of the METAFrame environment.

Automata Representation. The generated automata are deterministic and complete in order to perform an efficient implementation of *negation.* Since the size of the edge labels' alphabet is exponential in the number of second-order variables, an explicit enumeration of the letters is excluded. Rather, edge labels are represented by Boolean functions characterizing the transitions, which are in turn implemented via BDD techniques [1]. MOSEL uses a *hybrid representation* of the automata: graphs with edges encoded as boolean functions and implemented via BDDs. This is widely sufficient if the complexity of the automata is mainly due to complex edge labels, as in our application, rather than to intricate sequential structure.

Automata Minimization Algorithm. One of the main nontrivial operations on automata is *minimization.* In MOSEL this is realized via a modification of the well-known Hopcroft algorithm [4], working on sets of labels instead of single labels.

4 Efficiency

Already 30 years ago Alonzo Church proposed monadic second-order logic on strings as an appropriate specification formalism for reasoning about sequences of bitvectors [2]. This logic is among the most succinct decidable logics known to capture finite state systems. It is decidable, however, only in non-elementary time: the worst-case complexity is a stack of exponentials of height proportional to the size of the formula, a good reason for it having been considered impractical for a long time. Recently this logic celebrates a certain renaissance: despite the worst-case computational 'intractability' of this logic, relevant practical problems are usually far better behaved and can be solved automatically in reasonable time.

The intrinsic complexity of the logic demands careful implementation. Our implementation reflects the effort for efficiency in two ways. On the one side a kernel logic as an extension of the minimal logic is used. This logic directly supports many precomputed predicates which are frequently used in applications, in order to cut down the computation time. On the other side BDD techniques are used to handle complex edge labels of the finite automata.

5 Application Domains

The monadic second-order logic over finite strings conveniently combines two important features in a single formalism: It is both an abstract specification language and an effective programming language.

Fields of application have been the specification, verification, and synthesis, in a fully automatic manner, of relevant classes of parametric systems. In particular, the logic can be used profitably as a description language for model-based analysis of software as well as of hardware systems [7] and is therefore a good candidate formalism for hardware/software codesign. Some examples of distributed systems have been addressed too [5]. Every specification can be translated into an equivalent finite-state automaton, and thus is decidable and executable.

6 Status and Future Work

At the moment we have implemented in MOSEL a semantic decision procedure for monadic second-order logic over finite strings and a set of interface modules. Decision procedures for other variants of the logic as well as further support components are planned to follow at need. Nevertheless, the design principles and the overall system concept of MOSEL are valid in general.

Future work will follow three main threads. As an alternative to the **Mona** user logic we plan to implement a typed predicate logic with facilities for user-specific extensions. At the application layer we are working on the embedding of standard HDL languages, like BLIFF. Finally, future extensions of MOSEL will support other semantic theories e.g. like finite trees or finite sets.

References

1. R.E. Bryant: *"Graph-based algorithms for boolean function manipulation,"* IEEE Trans. Computing, vol. C-35(8), August 1986, pp. 677-691.
2. A. Church: *"Logic, arithmetic and automata,"* Proc. Int. Congr. Math., Almqvist and Wiksells, Uppsala 1963, pp. 23-35.
3. daVinci: the tool is available via ftp at site `ftp://ftp.uni-bremen.de/pub/graphics/daVinci`
4. J. Hopcroft: *"An n log n algorithm for minimizing states in a finite automaton,"* Proc. Int. Symp. on Theory of Machines and Computations, Technion, Haifa (IL), Aug. 1971, pp.189-196.
5. J. Henriksen, J. Jensen, M. Jørgensen N. Klarlund, R. Paige, T. Rauhe, A. Sandholm: *"Mona: Monadic second-order logic in practice,"* Proc. of TACAS'95, Aarhus (DK), May 1995, LNCS 1019, Springer Verlag, pp. 89-110.
6. P. Kelb, T. Margaria, M. Mendler, C. Gsottberger: *"MOSEL: A Flexible Toolset for Monadic Second-Order Logic,"* TACAS'97, Enschede (NL), April 1997, LNCS 1217, Springer Verlag, pp. 183-202.
7. T. Margaria: "Fully Automatic Verification and Error Detection for Parameterized Iterative Sequential Circuits", Proc. TACAS'96, Passau (D), March 1996, LNCS 1055, Springer Verlag, pp. 258-277.

The Verus Tool: A Quantitative Approach to the Formal Verification of Real-Time Systems[1]

Sérgio Campos, Edmund Clarke and Marius Minea
Carnegie Mellon University
campos@cs.cmu.edu, emc@cs.cmu.edu and marius@cs.cmu.edu

1 Introduction

The task of checking if a computer system satisfies its timing specifications is extremely important. These systems are often used in critical applications where failure to meet a deadline can have serious or even fatal consequences. This work describes *Verus*, an efficient tool for performing this verification task. Using our tool, the system being verified is specified in the Verus language and then compiled into a state-transition graph. A symbolic model checker allows the verification of untimed properties expressed in CTL [8]. Time bounded properties can be verified using RTCTL model checking [7]. Moreover, algorithms derived from symbolic model checking are used to compute *quantitative* information about the model [1]. The information produced allows the user to check the temporal correctness of the model: schedulability of the tasks of the system can be determined by computing their response time; reaction times to events and several other parameters of the system can also be analyzed by this method. This information provides insight into the behavior of the system and in many cases it can help identify inefficiencies and suggest optimizations to the design. The same algorithms can then be used to analyze the performance of the modified design. The evaluation of how the optimizations affect the design can be done *before* the actual implementation, significantly reducing development costs. Another advantage of our approach is that the Verus language has been especially designed to allow a straightforward description of the temporal characteristics of programs. This makes modeling real-time systems in Verus a simpler task.

Verus uses a discrete notion of time. A Verus program is modelled by a finite state-transition graph where each transition corresponds to one time unit. The simplicity of this representation makes it amenable to a symbolic implementation using BDDs. The tool is very efficient, as attested by the systems verified. One example has 15 concurrent processes and counterexamples that have thousands of states have been produced in seconds. Perhaps even more indicative of the usefulness of the method are the types of systems verified. We have applied this method to the verification of several real systems, such as an aircraft controller [4], a robotics controller [5] and a distributed heterogeneous real-time system [3]. All examples verified are either actual systems or use components and protocols employed in current industrial products.

---

1. This research was sponsored in part by the National Science Foundation under grant no. CCR-9217549, by the Semiconductor Research Corporation under contract 95-DJ-294 and by the Defense Advanced Research Projects Agency, Information Science and Technology Office, under title "Research on Parallel Computing", ARPA order no. 7330, issued by DARPA/CMO under Contract MDA972-90-C-0035.

2   The Verus Language

The main goal of the Verus language is to allow engineers and designers to describe real-time systems easily and efficiently. It is an imperative language with a syntax resembling that of C. The data types allowed in Verus are fixed-width integer and boolean. Nondeterminism is supported, which allows partial specifications to be described. Language constructs have been kept simple in order to make the compilation into a state-transition graph as efficient as possible. Smaller representations can then be generated, which is critical for the verification and permits larger examples to be handled. Details about the Verus language can be found in [1].

Overview

A fragment of a simple real-time program is used to give an overview of the language. This program implements a solution for the producer-consumer problem by bounding the time delays of its processes. No synchronization is needed if the time delays of producer and consumer are defined properly. The code for the `producer` is shown below. Variable p is an index to the data buffer. After initializing index p and variable `produce`, the `producer` enters a nonterminating loop in which items are produced at a certain rate. Line 7 introduces a time delay of 3 units, after which an item will be produced. Line 8 marks production by asserting `produce`. In line 9 the index p is updated. Line 10 ensures that the event `produce` is observed. It is needed because the state of a Verus program can only be observed at `wait` statements.

```
1   producer(p)
2   {
3     boolean produce;
4     p = 0;
5     produce = false;
6     while(!stop) {
7       wait(3);
8       produce = true;
9       p = p + 1;
10      wait(1);
11      produce = false;
12    };
13  }
```

Figure 1. Producer code

In Verus time passes only on `wait` statements, lines 4, 5 and 6 execute in time zero. This feature allows a more accurate control of time, and eliminates the possibility of implicit delays influencing verification results. It also generates smaller models, since contiguous statements are collapsed into one transition.

The `main` function (not shown for brevity, as well as the consumer code) completes the program by instantiating all processes. Process instantiation in Verus follows a synchronous model, all processes execute in lockstep. Asynchronous behavior can be modeled by using *stuttering*, which introduces nondeterministic transitions. This technique is described in [1].

Other Features

Verus has many other features not shown in this program. For example, nondeterminism is implemented using the `select` statement. To illustrate how `select` works, let's assume that the `producer` is not required to actually produce an item after 3 time units, but may instead leave the value of p unchanged. This can be modelled in Verus by changing line 9 to p = `select{p, p+1}`;

The timing characteristics of the system can be easily modeled using the periodic and deadline statements. For example, the code below specifies that S1 must execute once every 100 time units. Also, it must finish execution in less than 100 units, otherwise an exception will be raised: `periodic(0, 100, 100) { S1; }`;

The first parameter of `periodic` is the *start time*, which specifies how many time units the code will idle before starting its execution for the first time. The second parameter is the *period*, that is, how often the code will execute. The third parameter defines a *deadline*. If execution does not finish before the deadline an exception will be raised. Execution may take longer than the sum of the waits because of synchronization. The `deadline` statement is similar, but it does not specify a period. Exception handling as well as the periodic and deadline statements are explained in [1].

3 The Verification Algorithms

CTL and RTCTL Model Checking

Verus allows the verification of untimed properties expressed as CTL formulas [8] as well as of timed properties expressed as RTCTL formulas [7]. RTCTL extends CTL by allowing bounds on all CTL operators to be specified [7]. Many important properties of real-time systems can be verified using both CTL and RTCTL model checking. For example, we have used RTCTL to show the existence of priority inversion in a real-time system [2]. In this example, we have modeled a simple real-time system in which processes communicate in a non-regular pattern. The bounded until operator allows us to determine the existence of priority inversion, and to check that the solution implemented, priority inheritance, avoids the problem.

Quantitative Algorithms

Most verification algorithms assume that timing constraints are given explicitly. Typically, the designer provides a constraint on response time and the verifier automatically determines if it is satisfied or not. However, these techniques do not provide any information about how much a system deviates from its expected performance, although this information can be very useful in fine-tuning the system behavior.

Verus implements algorithms that determine the minimum and maximum length of all paths leading from a set of starting states to a set of final states. It also has algorithms that calculate the minimum and the maximum number of times a specified condition can hold on a path from a set of starting states to a set of final states. Our algorithms provide insight into *how well* a system works, rather than just determining whether it works at all. They enable a designer to determine the timing characteristics of a complex system given the timing parameters of its components. This information is especially useful in the early phases of system design, when it can be used to establish how changes in a parameter affect the global system behavior.

Several types of information can be produced by this method. Response time to events is computed by making the set of starting states correspond to the event, and the set of final states correspond to the response. Schedulability analysis can be done by computing the response time of each process in the system, and comparing it to the process deadline. Performance can be determined in a similar way.

Selective Quantitative Analysis and Interval Model Checking
The algorithms described above compute the minimum and maximum time delays along *every* possible execution sequence of a real-time system. In many situations, however, we may be interested in computing time delays that relate only to execution sequences that satisfy a given property. We propose a method for specifying and verifying properties such as these. The user specifies a property that must be satisfied in all paths traversed. This property is expressed using *linear-time temporal logic* (LTL) [6]. Special model checking techniques [6] are used to ensure that only paths satisfying the formula are considered by the algorithms.

4 Conclusions

This work describes Verus, a new tool to be used in the formal verification of real-time systems. In Verus the designer specifies the system to be verified in a C-like language, and uses temporal logic model checking and quantitative timing analysis to verify its correctness. The information produced by our tool can help in verifying a real-time system in many ways. It not only assists in determining its correctness, but also provides insight into the behavior of the system. This allows for a better understanding of the system and in some cases it even suggests optimizations to the design.

We have used this tool to analyze several real-time systems of industrial complexity, such as an aircraft controller, a robotics controller and a distributed heterogeneous system. In all cases we have been able to determine the temporal correctness of the system. In several instances the results produced suggested modifications to the design that resulted in more efficient systems.

5 References

1. S. V. Campos. *A quantitative approach to the formal verification of real-time systems.* Ph.D. thesis, SCS, Carnegie Mellon University, 1996.
2. S. V. Campos. The priority inversion problem and real-time symbolic model checking. Technical Report CMU-CS-93-125, Carnegie Mellon University, 1993.
3. S. V. Campos and O. Grumberg. Selective quantitative analysis and interval model checking: verifying different facets of a system. *Computer Aided Verification,* 1996.
4. S. Campos, E. Clarke, W. Marrero, M. Minea, and H. Hiraishi. Computing quantitative characteristics of finite-state real-time systems. *IEEE Real-Time Systems Symposium,* 1994.
5. S. Campos, E. Clarke, W. Marrero and M. Minea. Verus: a tool for quantitative analysis of finite-state real-time systems. *Languages,Compilers and Tools for Real-Time Systems,* 1995
6. E. Clarke, O. Grumberg, and H. Hamaguchi. Another look at LTL model checking. *Computer-Aided Verification,* LNCS vol. 818. Springer-Verlag, 1994.
7. E. A. Emerson, A. K. Mok, A. P. Sistla, and J. Srinivasan. Quantitative temporal reasoning. *Computer-Aided Verification,* 1990.
8. K. L. McMillan. *Symbolic model checking - an approach to the state explosion problem.* Ph.D. thesis, SCS, Carnegie Mellon University, 1992.

UPPAAL*: Status & Developments

Kim G Larsen[1] *Paul Pettersson*[2] *Wang Yi*[2]

[1] Department of Computer Science and Mathematics, Aalborg University, Denmark.
[2] Department of Computer Systems, Uppsala University, Sweden.

1 Introduction

UPPAAL[3] is a tool box for validation (via graphical simulation) and verification (via automatic model-checking) of real-time systems, based on constraint solving and on-the-fly techniques. It consists of three main parts: a description language, a simulator and a model-checker. It is appropriate for systems that can be modelled as networks of timed automata [3, 2], i.e. a collection of non-deterministic processes with finite control structure and real-valued clocks, communicating through channels and shared variables. The description language of UPPAAL is a non-deterministic guarded command language with data types (currently, only `integer` and `clock`, with restricted forms of operations implemented). The semantics of the language is given in terms of labelled transition systems in the tradition of timed process algebras. The simulator enables examination of *possible* dynamic executions in early design stages and thus provides an inexpensive mean of fault detection prior to verification by the model-checker which covers the exhaustive dynamic behaviour.

The two main design criteria for UPPAAL have been *efficiency* and *ease of usage*. An important key to the efficiency of the current model-checking engine of UPPAAL is the application of *on-the-fly* verification combined with a *symbolic* technique reducing the verification problem to that of solving simple *constraint systems* [3, 2]. In contrast to the previous version of UPPAAL which was based on backwards reachability analysis, the current version implements forwards on-the-fly reachability analysis. In addition, it offers both breadth-first and depth-first search of the state-space of a system description. Another important key to efficiency is the restriction to model checking of simple invariant and reachability properties. Other properties such as bounded liveness properties may be checked by reasoning about the system in the context of a testing automata or the decorated system with debugging information. In order to facilitate debugging, UPPAAL automatically generates a *diagnostic trace* that explains why a property is (or is not) satisfied by a system description. Our current research results promises even more efficient verification engines in near future (see Section 3).

To ease the usage of UPPAAL particular effort has been made in developing graphical *user interfaces*. Thus, system descriptions may be defined graphically using an

---

* UPPAAL is developed in collaboration between the Department of Computer Systems at Uppsala University (UPP), Sweden and BRICS (Basic Research in Computer Science, Centre of the Danish National Research Foundation) at Aalborg University (AAL), Denmark. The people involved with the development are Wang Yi (UPP), Kim G. Larsen (AAL), Paul Pettersson (UPP), Johan Bengtsson (UPP), Fredrik Larsson (UPP), Kåre J. Kristoffersen (AAL), Palle Christensen (AAL), Jesper Gravgaard (AAL), Per S. Jensen (AAL), and Thomas M. Sørensen (AAL).

[3] Installation and documentation available at http://www.docs.uu.se/docs/rtmv/uppaal/.

AUTOGRAPH-based interface which is automatically transformed into textual format[4]. Also (certain) multi-rate timed automata are transformable into timed automata.

2 From Verification to Validation

The main novelty in the new UPPAAL version is the addition of a *graphical simulator*, which enables visualisation and recording of possible dynamic behaviours of a system descriptions in terms of sequences of symbolic states of the system. Reports from a number of UPPAAL users indicate that the addition of the simulator significantly enhances the tool box as it allows for inexpensive fault detection in the very early modelling stages. The simulator enables the user to perform *informal validations* and thus to obtain a better understanding of the dynamic (mis)behaviour of a system complementing the existing *formal verification* engine of UPPAAL. In particular, the diagnostic traces generated by the verifier in case of an erroneous system may be graphically visualised using the simulator. During a simulation the following information is presented to the user:

- The current symbolic state. It consists of the *discrete location vector* visualised by highlighted location markings directly in the graphical description and the *constraints on the clocks and data variables* displayed in a separate window.
- The possible next transitions. They are displayed and may be selected; simultaneously the corresponding edges are highlighted in the graphical description of the timed automata.
- The trace that leads to the current symbolic state. It is displayed and may be saved, reexamined, replayed and reset from any intermediate point. In particular diagnostic traces generated by the verifier may be loaded for examination.

The simulator may run either in an interactive mode, where the user selects transitions, or in an automatic mode, where the simulator itself randomly selects transitions. During a simulation various parts of the information may be hidden, e.g. the constraints over clocks and integer variables in the current state. Also, display of the generated trace may be omitted.

3 New Developments

The basic model employed by UPPAAL is that of networks of timed automata extended with data variables. To meet requirements arising from various case studies this basic model has been extended to include features such as *Committed Locations* and *Urgent Channels*.

Various techniques for optimising the space- and time-performance of the reachability engine of UPPAAL has been developed and experimentally examined. The following techniques has already been added to the current UPPAAL version:

Re-Use. This idea is extremely simple, but yields nevertheless significant improvements in time-consumption. Whenever a system is analysed with respect to *several* reachability properties the computed portion of the reachable (symbolic) state-space is re-used, hence avoiding time-consuming recomputations.

---

[4] Of course systems may also be defined using the textual notation directly.

Control Structure Analysis. During a standard reachability analysis all new encountered symbolic states are normally stored in a global data structure (called the Passed list) in order to ensure termination. However, this is not needed if a predecessor of the new symbolic state is already presented in the Passed list. In fact, to ensure termination, it suffice to save only one state for each dynamic loop. An improved on-the-fly reachability algorihtm based on this stragety has been implemented and demonstrates significant space-savings (see Table 1).

The following techniques have been experimentally examined and show high potentials:

Compact Data Structures for Constraints. In the present implementation of UPPAAL the constraint part of a symbolic state is represented using the well known Difference Bounded Matrices (DBM) allowing for efficient emptiness and inclusion checks as well as efficient transformations of the constraints according to the dynamic behaviour of the timed system. The DBM representation gives an explicit bound for the difference between each pair of clocks (and each individual clock), hence using space corresponding to $(n+1) \times (n+1)$ integers. However, in practice it often turns out that most of these bounds are redundant. Recently, we have developed an $\mathcal{O}(n^3)$ algorithm that given a DBM constructs a canonical and minimal set of constraints representing the same solution set[5]. Thus, when saving a symbolic state in the Passed list, we use the (often substantially smaller) canonical reduction of the constraint system. Experimental results demonstrates truly significant space-savings (see statistics in Table 1) and the technique will in short time be part of the official UPPAAL distribution.

Compositional Verification. In a number of papers (e.g. [2]) we have developed the theoretical basis for a compositional verification method which allows components of a network of timed automata to be gradually moved from the system description into the specified property, thus avoiding global state-space considerations. Recently, a prototype implementation in C++ has been made giving experimental evidence of the potential of the technique [1]. Using only 172.3 seconds and 32MB main memory the tool automatically verifies Fischer's protocol with 50 processes.

Table 1 compares the Control Structure Reduction (CSR), the Compact Data Structures for Constraints technique (CDSC), and their combination (CDSC & CSR) with the performance of the standard reachability algorithm of UPPAAL (Standard). Space is measured in number of clock constraints and time is measured in seconds. The improvement of space-performance observed is remarkable.

4 Applications

Since its first release in 1995, UPPAAL has been applied in a number of case-studies by users from both academic and industrial sites. They can be roughly divided in two classes: real-time controllers and communication protocols.

Real-Time Controllers: The representative example in this category is the design and analysis of a gear-box controller for vehicles using UPPAAL by Mecel AB[6]. Other known

---

[5] Given a weighted, directed graph with n vertices, the algorithm constructs in time $\mathcal{O}(n^3)$ a reduced graph with the minimal number of edges having the same shortest path closure as the original graph.

[6] Mecel AB is a Swedish company developing control systems for vehicle industries.

	Standard		CDSC		CSR		CDSC & CSR	
	space	time	space	time	space	time	space	time
Audio	828	0.73	219	0.60	774	0.61	206	0.63
Audio w. Coll.	1 902 816	1 839.21	443 221	1 376.09	886 284	1 343.41	205 734	1 104.76
Box Sorter	625	0.40	139	0.36	150	0.41	32	0.41
Fischer 2	225	0.41	44	0.35	99	0.37	16	0.35
Fischer 3	3 376	0.71	621	0.68	1 376	0.70	237	0.64
Fischer 4	56 825	11.58	9 352	9.95	22 400	9.56	3 528	8.94
Fischer 5	1 082 916	789.15	158 875	651.61	419 112	650.00	59 715	605.23
M. Plant	96 084	14.36	27 042	18.03	51 048	16.44	14 968	16.85
Train Gate	432	0.46	130	0.39	384	0.40	114	0.42

Table 1. Performance Statistics.

examples are the steam generator, the train gate controller, the manufacturing plant, and the mine-pump controller.

Real-Time Communication Protocols: UPPAAL has been mainly applied to model and verify protocols where correct timing is critical, including the bounded retransmission protocol, the collision avoidance protocol, and the audio-control protocol designed by Philips.

In terms of complexity, Philips audio-control protocol with bus-collision is the most comprehensive case-study so far where UPPAAL has been applied. The protocol was developed by Philips to exchange information between components in one of their high-end audio sets. The version of the protocol with *bus-collision handling* was verified using the previous version of UPPAAL installed on a SGI ONYX machine. The main correctness property consumed 7.5 hours and 527.4 MB of memory. Using the current version of the UPPAAL verifier the same property may be verified in 15.49 minutes and 31 MB of memory on a Sun Sparc 4.

References

1. Kåre J. Kristoffersen, Francois Larroussinie, Kim G. Larsen, Paul Pettersson, and Wang Yi. A compositional proof of a real-time mutual exclusion protocol. In *Proc. of the 7th International Joint Conference on the Theory and Practice of Software Development*, April 1997.
2. Kim G. Larsen, Paul Pettersson, and Wang Yi. Model-Checking for Real-Time Systems. In *Proc. of Fundamentals of Computation Theory*, volume 965 of *Lecture Notes in Computer Science*, pages 62–88, August 1995.
3. Wang Yi, Paul Pettersson, and Mats Daniels. Automatic Verification of Real-Time Communicating Systems By Constraint-Solving. In *Proc. of the 7th International Conference on Formal Description Techniques*, 1994.

HyTech: **A Model Checker for Hybrid Systems**[*]

Thomas A. Henzinger[**]   Pei-Hsin Ho[***]   Howard Wong-Toi[†]

Abstract. A hybrid system consists of a collection of digital programs
that interact with each other and with an analog environment. Examples
of hybrid systems include medical equipment, manufacturing controllers,
automotive controllers, and robots. The formal analysis of the mixed
digital-analog nature of these systems requires a model that incorporates
the discrete behavior of computer programs with the continuous behavior of environment variables, such as temperature and pressure. *Hybrid
automata* capture both types of behavior by combining finite automata
with differential inclusions (*i.e.* differential inequalities). HyTech is a
symbolic model checker for *linear hybrid automata*, an expressive, yet
automatically analyzable, subclass of hybrid automata. A key feature of
HyTech is its ability to perform parametric analysis, *i.e.* to determine
the values of design parameters for which a linear hybrid automaton
satisfies a temporal requirement.

From finite to hybrid automata. Model checking [11, 39], and in particular symbolic model checking [10] (*i.e.* the manipulation of state sets rather than individual
states), has been proven an effective technique for the automatic analysis of complex
finite-state systems. The first extensions of discrete models toward mixed discrete-
continuous behavior considered real-numbered time [15]. One such model is the *timed
automaton*—a finite automaton augmented with a finite number of real-valued clocks,
i.e. continuous variables whose rate of change is always 1 [3]. Symbolic model checking for timed automata involves the computation of fixpoints over state sets that are
represented by a restricted class of linear constraints, namely, boolean combinations of
inequalities of the form $x \leq k$ and $x - y \leq k$, for clocks x and y and constants k [31].
Although the state space of a timed automaton is infinite, the fixpoint computation
is guaranteed to terminate. *Hybrid automata* are extensions of timed automata that
allow continuous variables with more general dynamics than clocks [2, 38, 1].

In contrast to most other formalisms for hybrid systems [18, 8, 5], where the proposed analysis methods are deductive, research on hybrid automata has focused on
(semi)algorithmic state-space analysis. This has led to the definition of *linear hybrid
automata*, for which the dynamics of the continuous variables are defined by linear dif-
ferential inclusions of the form $\mathbf{A}\mathbf{x} \leq \mathbf{b}$, for a constant matrix $\mathbf{A}$, a vector $\mathbf{x}$ of variables,
and a constant vector $\mathbf{b}$.[1] For linear hybrid automata, the successor states of a state
set defined by linear constraints are computable, and themselves linearly definable [4].
Thus, symbolic model checking for timed automata can be extended to linear hybrid automata, provided that state sets are represented by boolean combinations of arbitrary
linear inequalities. The price to pay for the increased generality is the loss of guaranteed termination. The theory of hybrid automata—in particular, decidability results
for subclasses of linear hybrid automata—is presented in [30, 21, 20, 28, 22, 29, 36].

---

[*] This research was supported in part by the ONR YIP award N00014-95-1-0520, by the NSF
CAREER award CCR-9501708, by the NSF grant CCR-9504469, by the AFOSR contract F49620-
93-1-0056, by the ARO MURI grant DAAH-04-96-1-0341, by the ARPA grant NAG2-892, and by
the SRC contract 95-DC-324.036.

[**] EECS Department, University of California, Berkeley; tah@eecs.berkeley.edu.

[***] Strategic CAD Labs, Intel Corporation, Hillsboro, Oregon; pho@ichips.intel.com.

[†] Cadence Berkeley Labs, Berkeley, California; howard@cadence.com.

[1] This definition of linearity differs from the definition commonly used in systems theory.

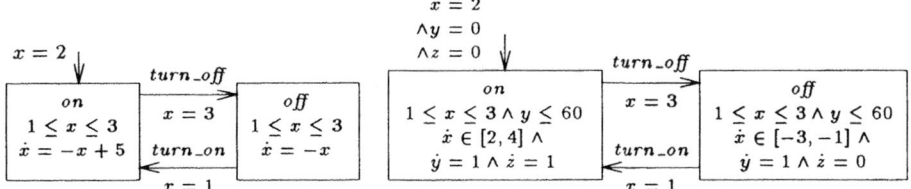

Fig. 1. Thermostat automaton

A simple example. A hybrid automaton is a nondeterministic finite transition graph whose nodes are labeled with differential inclusions. The hybrid automaton to the left in Figure 1 models a simple thermostat. The temperature x is initially 2 degrees, and rising at the rate of $-x+5$ degrees per minute. When the temperature reaches 3 degrees, the heater is turned off, and the temperature then falls at the rate of $-x$ degrees per minute. While the automaton control resides in a given node, the behavior of the continuous variables satisfies the node's differential inclusions. Nodes are also labeled with invariant conditions on the values of the variables. For example, the invariant of the node *on* is $1 \leq x \leq 3$, implying that the automaton control must leave the node before the temperature exceeds 3. Transitions between nodes may be guarded by constraints on the variables (*e.g.* the guard on the transition labeled *turn_off* is $x = 3$), and may incorporate reassignment of the variables, such as resetting a clock to 0. Shared event labels allow transitions in one hybrid automaton to be synchronized with transitions in another (this does not occur in the example).

For algorithmic analysis, we restrict our model to linear hybrid automata, described above. This formalism does not allow general differential inclusions, but is still quite expressive. For example, the model captures stopwatches (variables whose rates may be either 0 or 1), skewed clocks (variables whose rates are constant, possibly different from 1), and variables whose rates have constant bounds, such as clocks whose rates drift within some interval $[1 - \epsilon, 1 + \epsilon]$. Nonlinear hybrid automata may be analyzed either by translating them into linear hybrid automata where possible, or by conservatively approximating them with linear hybrid automata [23, 32].

For example, in order to analyze the proportion of time that the thermostat is on, we use the linear hybrid automaton to the right in Figure 1, which is derived from the original nonlinear hybrid automaton as follows. First, we overapproximate the nonlinear behavior of the temperature by placing lower and upper bounds on its rate within each node (*e.g.* in node *on*, the invariant $1 \leq x \leq 3$ implies that the rate $-x + 5$ is bounded within the interval $[2, 4]$). Next, we introduce a clock y that measures the elapsed time, and a stopwatch z that measures the accumulated time spent in node *on*. We wish to check that the thermostat is on for less than $\frac{2}{3}$ of the first hour of operation. To ensure termination of the computation, we add the conjunct $y \leq 60$ to the invariants. HyTech then fully automatically verifies that no state satisfying $y = 60 \wedge z \geq \frac{2}{3}y$ is reachable from the initial state.

The tool. Early versions of HyTech were built using Mathematica [24, 34]. Building on the observation that a linear constraint over n variables can be represented by the union of n-dimensional polyhedra, the current, more efficient, generation of HyTech [27, 26] manipulates linear constraints via calls to a library for polyhedral operations [19]. A HyTech input file consists of two parts: a textual description of a collection of hybrid automata, and a sequence of analysis commands. The component automata are composed into a product representing the entire system. The analysis language provides access to a variety of operations for polyhedral manipulation within a flexible framework for writing state-space exploration programs. For added convenience, there are built-in macros for reachability analysis, temporal operators, abstract interpretation [25], error-trace generation, and parametric analysis [13, 6].

In parametric analysis, the system is described using *design parameters*—symbolic constants with unknown, fixed values. Standard reachability analysis followed by existential quantification can be used to determine necessary and sufficient constraints on the parameters under which system violations cannot occur. Thus, rather than merely verifying (or falsifying) systems, HYTECH can be used to extract quantitative information, further aiding the design process. Common uses for parametric analysis include determining minimum and maximum bounds on variables, and finding cutoff points for the placement of sensors or the values of timers. For example, to compute an upper bound on the time the thermostat is on during the first hour of operation, we introduce a parameter α and use HYTECH to determine the values of α for which there is a reachable state satisfying $y = 60 \wedge z \geq \alpha$. HYTECH returns the constraint $\alpha \leq 36$, implying that the thermostat is on for no more than 36 minutes during the first hour.

Applications. HYTECH has been used in a number of case studies—primarily control-based applications—including a distributed robot controller [24], a robot system in manufacturing [24], the Philips audio control protocol [35], an active structure controller [26], a generalized railroad controller [26], a nonlinear temperature controller [23], a predator-prey ecology [32], an aircraft landing-gear system [37], a steam-boiler controller [33], and an automotive controller [40]. Corbett [12] has verified robot controllers written in a subset of ADA by automatically translating them into linear hybrid automata for analysis with HYTECH. We are currently experimenting with the modeling and analysis of timed circuits.

Availability. HYTECH has been ported to the following platforms: DEC workstations running Ultrix and Digital Unix, HP workstations running HP-UX, Sun workstations running SunOS and Solaris, and x86 PCs running Linux. HYTECH's home page http://www.eecs.berkeley.edu/~tah/HyTech includes the source code, executables, an online demo, a user guide, a graphical front end (courtesy of members of the UPPAAL project [9]), numerous examples, online versions of papers, and pointers to additional literature. Requests may also be sent to hytech@eecs.berkeley.edu.

Related tools. POLKA analyzes linear hybrid systems with an emphasis on abstract-interpretation strategies [19]. SHIFT provides a simulation environment for generalized hybrid automata, but does not perform state-space analysis [16]. Symbolic model checkers for the more restrictive timed-automaton model include KRONOS [14], timed COSPAN [7], UPPAAL [9], and VERITI [17].

References.

1. R. Alur, C. Courcoubetis, N. Halbwachs, T.A. Henzinger, P.-H. Ho, X. Nicollin, A. Olivero, J. Sifakis, and S. Yovine. The algorithmic analysis of hybrid systems. *Theoretical Computer Science*, 138:3–34, 1995.
2. R. Alur, C. Courcoubetis, T.A. Henzinger, and P.-H. Ho. Hybrid automata: an algorithmic approach to the specification and verification of hybrid systems. In *Hybrid Systems I*, LNCS 736, pp. 209–229. Springer, 1993.
3. R. Alur and D.L. Dill. A theory of timed automata. *Theoretical Computer Science*, 126:183–235, 1994.
4. R. Alur, T.A. Henzinger, and P.-H. Ho. Automatic symbolic verification of embedded systems. *IEEE Trans. Software Engineering*, 22:181–201, 1996.
5. R. Alur, T.A. Henzinger, and E.D. Sontag, eds. *Hybrid Systems III: Verification and Control*. LNCS 1066. Springer, 1996.
6. R. Alur, T.A. Henzinger, and M.Y. Vardi. Parametric real-time reasoning. In *Proc. 25th ACM Symp. Theory of Computing*, pp. 592–601, 1993.
7. R. Alur and R.P. Kurshan. Timing analysis in Cospan. In *Hybrid Systems III*, LNCS 1066, pp. 220–231. Springer, 1996.
8. P. Antsaklis, A. Nerode, W. Kohn, and S. Sastry, eds. *Hybrid Systems II*. LNCS 999. Springer, 1995.

9. J. Bengtsson, K.G. Larsen, F. Larsson, P. Pettersson, and W. Yi. UppAal: a tool-suite for automatic verification of real-time systems. In *Hybrid Systems III*, LNCS 1066, pp. 232–243. Springer, 1996.
10. J.R. Burch, E.M. Clarke, K.L. McMillan, D.L. Dill, and L.J. Hwang. Symbolic model checking: 10^{20} states and beyond. *Information and Computation*, 98:142–170, 1992.
11. E.M. Clarke and E.A. Emerson. Design and synthesis of synchronization skeletons using branching-time temporal logic. In *Logic of Programs*, LNCS 131. Springer, 1981.
12. J. C. Corbett. Timing analysis of Ada tasking programs. *IEEE Trans. Software Engineering*, 22:461–483, 1996.
13. P. Cousot and N. Halbwachs. Automatic discovery of linear restraints among variables of a program. In *Proc. 5th ACM Symp. Principles of Programming Languages*, pp. 84–97, 1978.
14. C. Daws, A. Olivero, S. Tripakis, and S. Yovine. The tool Kronos. In *Hybrid Systems III*, LNCS 1066, pp. 208–219. Springer, 1996.
15. J.W. de Bakker, K. Huizing, W.-P. de Roever, and G. Rozenberg, eds. *Real Time: Theory in Practice*. LNCS 600. Springer, 1992.
16. A. Deshpande, A. Göllü, and L. Semenzato. The Shift programming language and runtime system for dynamic networks of hybrid automata. PATH report, http://www-path. eecs.berkeley.edu/shift/doc/ieeshift.ps.gz, 1996.
17. D.L. Dill and H. Wong-Toi. Verification of real-time systems by successive over- and underapproximation. In *Computer-aided Verification*, LNCS 939, pp. 409–422. Springer, 1995.
18. R.L. Grossman, A. Nerode, A.P. Ravn, and H. Rischel, eds. *Hybrid Systems I*. LNCS 736. Springer, 1993.
19. N. Halbwachs, P. Raymond, and Y.-E. Proy. Verification of linear hybrid systems by means of convex approximation. In *Static Analysis Symp.*, LNCS 864, pp. 223–237. Springer, 1994.
20. M.R. Henzinger, T.A. Henzinger, and P.W. Kopke. Computing simulations on finite and infinite graphs. In *Proc. 36rd IEEE Symp. Foundations of Computer Science*, pp. 453–462, 1995.
21. T.A. Henzinger. Hybrid automata with finite bisimulations. In *ICALP: Automata, Languages, and Programming*, LNCS 944, pp. 324–335. Springer, 1995.
22. T.A. Henzinger. The theory of hybrid automata. In *Proc. 11th IEEE Symp. Logic in Computer Science*, pp. 278–292, 1996.
23. T.A. Henzinger and P.-H. Ho. Algorithmic analysis of nonlinear hybrid systems. In *Computer-aided Verification*, LNCS 939, pp. 225–238. Springer, 1995.
24. T.A. Henzinger and P.-H. Ho. HyTech: The Cornell Hybrid Technology Tool. In *Hybrid Systems II*, LNCS 999, pp. 265–293. Springer, 1995.
25. T.A. Henzinger and P.-H. Ho. A note on abstract-interpretation strategies for hybrid automata. In *Hybrid Systems II*, LNCS 999, pp. 252–264. Springer, 1995.
26. T.A. Henzinger, P.-H. Ho, and H. Wong-Toi. HyTech: the next generation. In *Proc. 16th IEEE Real-time Systems Symp.*, pp. 56–65, 1995.
27. T.A. Henzinger, P.-H. Ho, and H. Wong-Toi. A user guide to HyTech. In *Tools and Algorithms for the Construction and Analysis of Systems*, LNCS 1019, pp. 41–71. Springer, 1995.
28. T.A. Henzinger and P.W. Kopke. State equivalences for rectangular hybrid automata. In *Concurrency Theory*, LNCS 1119, pp. 530–545. Springer, 1996.
29. T.A. Henzinger and P.W. Kopke. Discrete-time control for rectangular hybrid automata. In *ICALP: Automata, Languages, and Programming*, LNCS. Springer, 1997.
30. T.A. Henzinger, P.W. Kopke, A. Puri, and P. Varaiya. What's decidable about hybrid automata? In *Proc. 27th ACM Symp. Theory of Computing*, pp. 373–382, 1995.
31. T.A. Henzinger, X. Nicollin, J. Sifakis, and S. Yovine. Symbolic model checking for real-time systems. *Information and Computation*, 111:193–244, 1994.
32. T.A. Henzinger and H. Wong-Toi. Linear phase-portrait approximations for nonlinear hybrid systems. In *Hybrid Systems III*, LNCS 1066, pp. 377–388. Springer, 1996.
33. T.A. Henzinger and H. Wong-Toi. Using HyTech to synthesize control parameters for a steam boiler. In *Formal Methods for Industrial Applications: Specifying and Programming the Steam Boiler Control*, LNCS 1165, pp. 265–282. Springer, 1996.
34. P.-H. Ho. *Automatic Analysis of Hybrid Systems*. PhD thesis, Cornell Univ., 1995.
35. P.-H. Ho and H. Wong-Toi. Automated analysis of an audio control protocol. In *Computer-aided Verification*, LNCS 939, pp. 381–394. Springer, 1995.
36. P.W. Kopke. *The Theory of Rectangular Hybrid Automata*. PhD thesis, Cornell Univ., 1996.
37. S. Nadjm-Tehrani and J.-E. Strömberg. Proving dynamic properties in an aerospace application. In *Proc. 16th IEEE Real-time Systems Symp.*, pp. 2–10, 1995.
38. X. Nicollin, A. Olivero, J. Sifakis, and S. Yovine. An approach to the description and analysis of hybrid systems. In *Hybrid Systems I*, LNCS 736, pp. 149–178. Springer, 1993.
39. J. Queille and J. Sifakis. Specification and verification of concurrent systems in Cesar. In *Symp. on Programming*, LNCS 137, pp. 337–351. Springer, 1981.
40. T. Stauner, O. Müller, and M. Fuchs. Using HyTech to verify an automotive control system. In *Hybrid and Real-Time Systems*, LNCS 1201, pp. 139–153. Springer, 1997.

SMC: A Symmetry based Model Checker for Verification of Liveness Properties[*]

A. P. Sistla[1] and L. Miliades[1] and V. Gyuris[2]

[1] Electrical Engineering and Computer Science Department, The University of
Illinois at Chicago, USA
[2] Mathematics, Statistics and Computer Science Department, The University of
Illinois at Chicago, USA

Introduction

In this paper, we describe SMC (Symmetry based Model checker) for verification
of liveness properties. This system is based on the symmetry based state space
reduction techniques presented in [ES93, ES95]. The input to the system consists of a concurrent program given as a set of processes specified as transition
systems. It also takes as input a Buchi automaton on infinite strings that accepts
all the incorrect computations, i.e., the automaton accepts the complement of
the correctness property. The system checks if there exists a fair computation of
the program that is accepted by the automaton, i.e., if there exists an incorrect
computation. If such a computation exists it outputs a "YES" answer, otherwise it terminates with a "NO" answer indicating that the program satisfies the
correctness property.

The model checker explores the global state space to check for the existence of
incorrect computations. It exploits symmetry to reduce the size of the state space
that is to be explored. The symmetry existing in the concurrent program induces
an equivalence relation on the global states of the system. The model checker
constructs an Annotated Quotient Structure (AQS) the captures the behavior of
the concurrent program. In the AQS, all equivalent states are represented by a
single representative state. Each AQS edge denotes an edge in the original state
graph between two states belonging to the corresponding equivalence classes.
The edges are labeled with permutations denoting how process indices need to
be permuted in order to get the states in the original state graph as one traverses
along the edge.

The model checker involves the following steps. First, it parses the input and
constructs the AQS. Then it starts computing the product of the AQS and the
automaton using depth first search. During the construction the program checks
if the already constructed part contains a strongly connected subgraph that has
a final automaton state in it and is fair with respect to all the processes. To do it
in an on-the-fly manner, a partition is maintained for each vertex on stack. The
partition indicates that which processes are found to be fair at that state using

---

[*] This work is partly supported by the NSF grants CCR-9623229, CCR-9212183, CCR-
9633536

the information collected up till that time. When the depth first search explores a new edge or node, the corresponding partitions are updated. This method permits early termination. It also reduces the amount of memory as we do not need to store the entire product graph with the edges in the main memory.

In the implemented system some other sophisticated reduction methods are used as well. Those methods utilize, in addition to the symmetry between states, the symmetry of a single state. Details of the algorithms and the theoretical background are in [GS97].

Input Language

The model checker assumes that the input program has the following architecture: processes are divided into modules; all processes in a module are identical upto renaming, that is, any permutation mapping processes in a module to processes in the same module is a symmetry of the system. Processes communicate through shared variables. A shared variable between two processes is speificed by the name together with the indices of the processes. If a process in a module C has a shared variable with another process in module D, then every process in C has such a shared variable with every process in D.

The input concurrent program is specified by an initialization part followed by the specification of a generic process in each module. The initialization part declares all the modules and variables with their initial values. The name of a variable is composed of an identifier and a list of module identifiers. Consider the following example.

```
Module server        = 2;
Module client        = 3;
reqst[server, client] = 0;
```

The above example declares two modules called **server** and **client** having two and three processes, repsectively. It also declares a set of variables reqst$[s,c]$, for each $0 \le s \le 1$ and $0 \le c \le 2$. Variable reqst$[s,c]$ is shared between server s and client c.

The initialization part is followed by a sequence of generic process specifications, one corresponding to each module. The body of a generic process specification is a set of transition schemas. Each transition schema is given by a condition part and an action part. The condition part is boolean expression while the action part is set of assignments. The following is an example transition schema in the server module.
busy$[s]$ = 0 and reqst$[s,c]$ = 1 $\rightarrow$ busy$[s]$=1, reply$[s,c]$ = 1.
For each $s = 0, 1$, the above transition schema represents three transitions in the server process s corresponding to each client process c.

The automata specification language consists of a declaration part and a list of automata transitions. The declaration part specifies the initial and final states. An automata transition is of the form condition $\rightarrow$ state1 : state2.

466

Construction of AQS

The AQS generator uses the internal structures generated by the compiler to construct the AQS. It maintains a queue of states that are generated but that have not been explored. Here exploration of a state involves simply generating all the successors of the state. The queue is initialized to contain the initial global state. The following procedure is repeated until the queue is empty. The first entry from the queue is dequeued into a state s. Each transition of each of the processes is executed in the state s. Suppose s' is the resulting state after execution of such a transition. Then the AQS generator invokes a function that checks if there exists a state that is equivalent to s' that has already been generated. If such a state t exists, then a pointer to t together with a permutation π is returned. In this case, the AQS generator simply introduces an edge from s to t and labels the edge with π. If no such state exists then s' is inserted as a new state and is enqueued in the queue.

Hashing. In order to search for the existence of an equivalent state efficiently, a hash table is employed. Whenever we need to search for a state equivalent to s', we compute an index i. This entry in the hash table points to a linked list of states that are hashed to the same location. This linked list is searched. For each state t on the list, it is checked if t is equivalent to s' under some permutation π which is a symmetry of the system. If such a π exists then a pointer to t together with π are returned.

Choosing an appropriate hash function is quite critical here. Firstly, the hash function has to be consistent with the symmetry, that is, all equivalent states should be hashed to the same location. On the other hand, it is desired that inequivalent states should be hashed to different locations. Satisfying both of these conditions is quite difficult. For example, we can use multiplication hash function where we multiply the non-zero values of all the variables in a state to obtain a number x and use $x \bmod b$ as an index where b is the hash table size. This function is consistent with symmetry.

Checking equivalence of states. Checking equivalence of states even for the above model of processes is a hard problem, as it is equivalent to the graph isomorphism problem. Our equivalence checking algorithm is an approximation algorithm. It runs in quadratic time. Whenever it indicates that two given states are equivalent then they are equivalent; however, the algorithm may err reporting that two states are not equivalent in some case when they actually are. But this error yields that the two equivalent states are stored as distinct ones instead of storing only one of them. In this way the compressed AQS will not be optimal, it will contain redundancies. This will effect the speed of the computation but certainly not the final outcome. So the one sided error in the performance of the equivalence test algorithm will not pose a danger to the algorithm.

Our algorithm partitions the set of processes in both states according to the signature of the processes. The signature of a process consists of the unordered set of values of the variables that contain the given process as an index. Then it incrementally refines the partitions using the signatures based on the previous version of the partition. This method is called *the naive refinement process*. When a fixpoint is reached, the processes in the corresponding classes of the two partitions are randomly paired. Finally a test concludes the algorithm to check if the permutation resulted by the pairing is indeed a valid equivalence.

Exploration of the Product Graph

The product of the AQS and the automaton is explored using the traditional recursive depth-first search algorithm. During this exploration, successors of a product node are generated on-the-fly as and when required. Since we only perform a single depth-first search, the successors of a given node are generated only once. Each state of the product graph is of the form (s, q, i) where s is a state of AQS, q is an automaton state and i is the process that is being tracked. This algorithm uses a seperate stack to maintain nodes in partially generated strongly connected components in the product graph.

In order to detect if a product node has already been visited/generated, we organize all the generated product nodes in to a hash table; this facilitates fast search. With each node, we also maintain a partition vector which is used for detecting fairness condition. The final states of the product graph are taken to be those of the form (s, q, i) where q is a final state of the automaton. As a last step of the exploration of a product state, we check if the already explored part of the product graph contains a fair strongly connected subgraph with a final automaton state. Note that only reachable product states are generated by this method.

Examples

Up to this point, we have used our system for simple examples such as the resource controller example and the Ethernet Protocol. We were able to check the correctness of various liveness and safety properties of this example for systems with as many as 150 processes; such systems can not be handled with a naive model checker that explores all the states. We are currently working on using it on some other real world protocols.

References

[ES93]   Emerson, E. A., Sistla, A. P.: Symmetry and Model Checking. 5th International Conference on Computer Aided Verification (CAV93), Crete, Greece, June 1993

[ES95]   Emerson, E. A., Sistla, A. P.: Utilizing Symmetry when Model Checking under Fairness Assumptions: An Automata-theoretic Approach. CAV95, Leige, Belgium, July 1995

[GS97]   Gyuris, V., Sistla, A. P.: On-the-Fly Model Checking under Fairness that Exploits Symmetry. CAV97, Haifa, Izrael, June 1997

µcke – Efficient µ-Calculus Model Checking

Armin Biere[1]

armin@ira.uka.de, Institut für Logik, Komplexität und Deduktionssysteme,
Universität Karlsruhe, Am Fasanengarten 5, D-76128 Karlsruhe, Germany

Abstract. In this paper we present an overview of the verification tool µcke. It is an implementation of a BDD-based µ-calculus model checker and uses several optimization techniques that are lifted from special purpose model checkers to the µ-calculus. This gives the user more expressibility without loosing efficiency.

Introduction

In [5] µ-calculus model checking with BDDs has been proposed as a general framework for various verification problems like model checking of LTL and CTL or testing for bisimulation equivalence and language containment. With a µ-calculus model checker all these verification tasks could be handled with one tool. Also some applications of symbolic model checking [16] need the µ-calculus as a specification language. On the other hand the most successful applications of model checking [7,2,15,10] all used a model checker with a less expressive specification language than the µ-calculus. The reason for this restriction was that for special purpose specification languages *optimized* model checkers can easily be build [5].

For example the SMV system of McMillan [14] uses fixed allocations of BDD variables for µ-calculus variables (ordering of BDD variables) for current and next state variables and specialized algorithms (collapse) for the computation of the set of states reachable in one step from a given set of states.

Other optimizations [4,14] that avoid the construction of the global transition relation (incremental transition relation generation, partitioning, MBFS) or speed up the computation (forward analysis, frontier set simplification) were only presented for state space analysis or CTL model checking.

In [3] we have shown that all these optimizations can be lifted to the µ-calculus. Especially an automatic allocation algorithm for BDD variables is given. It operates on allocation constraints to generate an allocation that respects the heuristic that all substitutions needed for the evaluation of a µ-calculus term should be fast (fast substitutions do not change the structure of a BDD but only change the variable markings). This is a generalization of the annotation mechanism of [11].

We also presented the $compose\ ite_\exists$ algorithm that is a generalization of the BDD algorithm collapse of the SMV system and of the prelmg-Operator of [8]. It performs a substitution, the calculation of "if·then·else" and a quantification in one pass and thus avoids the unnecessary construction of intermediate results.

For the evaluation of these methods we implemented the µ-calculus model checker µcke. The main goal was to construct a µ-calculus model checker that is as efficient as

[1] sup. by DFG GRK 209/2-96 "Graduiertenkolleg Beherrschbarkeit Komplexer Systeme"

special purpose model checkers like the SMV system and also easy to use. In addition it should be more expressive and more flexible.

Although we found some properties that are more naturally described with the μ-calculus than f. e. with CTL, the μ-calculus is in general not very comprehensible and should not be used as an interface for an engineer that is involved in the design of a system to be verified. A *front end* that translates the formal specification produced by the engineer into the μ-calculus should be used instead. This front end must be changed for different optimizations and different application domains. To ease these adaptions the input language of μcke is similar to C (C++), a widespread used programming language.

Another point is that for special purpose model checkers there exist algorithms for the generation of counter examples if the verification fails. Here we used the method of [13] for the construction of counter examples for the whole μ-calculus.

The author is aware of three further implementations of μ-calculus model checkers [11,12,18] based on decision diagrams. The first and third implementation do not use automatic allocation algorithms and the user has to provide the allocation himself. The system of Janssen [12] (used in [17]) uses dynamic variable reordering [19] instead. We used this approach in a first prototype of μcke too and we were not able to achieve an equally high performance as the SMV system. The reason for the problems with this approach is that the BDD variables allocated for μ-calculus variables bounded by quantifiers may also be reordered by dynamic reordering. So there is no way to enforce fast substitutions. Some simple verification problems like the calculation of the set of reachable states of an *n*-bit counter and a simple arbiter suggested that μcke is 6 to 9 times faster than [12].

μcke

In this section we give an example of the input language of the μcke model checker and show how the optimization of forward analysis can be formulated in the μ-calculus. The example is a version of the alternating bit protocol [6,1] with an explicit description of the channels between sender and receiver. The control state of the sender is an enumeration type and is the first part of the total state of the sender. It also has an alternating bit and needs a place to store the data for retransmission if the first transmission failed.

```
class StateOfSender {
   ControlStateOfSender state; bool ab; Data data; };
```

The states of the channels and the receiver are defined in the same way. The global state of the system consists of the states of the sender, the receiver and the states of the two channels and of a running variable used to model the interleaving semantic:

```
class State {
   Running running; S2RChannel s2r; R2SChannel r2s;
   StateOfSender sender; StateOfReceiver receiver; };
```

Now we define the transition relation of the Sender and the global transition relation with a syntax similar to the definition of a function in C without curly parentheses enclosing the body:

```
bool TransSender(State s, State t)
  s.running = sender & CoStabSender(s,t) & (
    case
      s.sender.state = get :
        t.sender.state = send & t.sender.ab = s.sender.ab &
        t.sender.data = s.sender.data &
        t.s2r.in = s.s2r.in & t.r2s.out = s.r2s.out;
      s.sender.state = send :
        . . .
  );
bool Trans(State s, State t) TransSender(s,t) | . . . ;
```

One (weak) property we want to verify is that it is always possible that the control state of the sender will eventually be get – or AGEF sender.state = get as CTL formula. Translated to the μ-calculus using the optimization of forward analysis (the -f option of SMV) this results in the definition of four recursive predicates:

```
mu bool Reachable(State s)
  Start(s) | (exists State t. Trans(t,s) & Reachable(t));
mu bool EF_sender_state_get(State s)
  Reachable(s) & (s.sender.state = get |
  (exists State t. Trans(s,t) & EF_sender_state_get(t)));
nu bool AG_EF_sender_state_get(State s)
  Reachable(s) & (EF_sender_state_get(s) &
  (forall State t. Trans(s,t) -> AG_EF_sender_state_get(t)));
forall State s. Start(s) -> AG_EF_sender_state_get(s);
```

The model checker μcke now evaluates this last line and answers with true or false. If the user wants to have a counter example or a witness for the formula he must request this separately. Other optimizations mentioned in the introduction can be handled the same way as equivalence preserving term rewriting rules.

Performance

We translated our formulation of the alternating bit protocol into the input language of the SMV system and verified the property AGAF sender.state = get under fair execution of all four processes and fair channels. The performance under forward analysis of the SMV system and μcke with the same algorithm (μcke) and with simplifying the transition relation with the "restrict" operator of [8] (μcke restrict) is shown in the following table (on a Pentium 120). Also a comparison of the performance of μcke for the scheduler of Milner with [11] on the same machine (Sun 4/75) can be found.

#bits	SMV		μcke		μcke restrict	
	MB	sec	MB	sec	MB	sec
4	9.1	13.3	3.3	9.6	2.9	3.0
5	9.4	36	4.0	42	3.4	7.2
6	10.0	77	5.6	112	4.6	16.2
7	11.3	202	8.8	289	6.0	49.2
8	14.4	696	17	807	12.5	122.3

#	[11]	μcke	μcke restrict
	sec	sec	sec
12	145	21.7	17.2
14	233	31.2	22.6
16	348	39.1	29.4
18	569	54.7	38.1
20	850	67.6	46.5

Conclusion

The μcke model checker shows that a μ-calculus model checker can be as efficient as special purpose model checkers. Currently we investigate how to handle functions with other range types than boolean. Also we look for a way to include unions and inheritance into our type system. See http://iseran.ira.uka.de/~armin for more information about μcke or contact the author.

References

1. K. Bartlett, R. Scantlebury, and P. Wilkinson. A note on reliable full-duplex transmissions over half-duplex lines. *Communications of the ACM*, 5(2):260–261, 1969.
2. I. Beer, S. Ben-David, D. Geist, R. Gewirtzman, and M. Yoeli. Methodology and system for practical formal verification of reactive hardware. In Dill [9], pages 182–193.
3. A. Biere. *Efficient μ-Calculus Model Checking with Binary Decision Diagrams*. PhD thesis, Fakultät für Informatik, Universität Karlsruhe, Germany, Jan. 1997. In German. To appear.
4. J. R. Burch, E. M. Clarke, D. E. Long, K. L. McMillan, and D. L. Dill. Symbolic model checking for sequential circuit verification. *IEEE Transactions on Computer-Aided Design of Integrated Circuits and Systems*, 13(4):401–424, Apr. 1994.
5. J. R. Burch, E. M. Clarke, and K. L. McMillan. Symbolic model checking: 10^{20} states and beyond. *Information and Computation*, 98:142–170, 1992.
6. E. M. Clarke, E. A. Emerson, and A. P. Sistla. Automatic verification of finite-state concurrent systems using temporal logic specifications. *ACM Transactions on Programming Languages and Systems*, 8(2):244 – 263, April 1986.
7. E. M. Clarke, O. Grumberg, H. Hiraishi, S. Jah, D. E. Long, K. L. McMillan, and L. A. Ness. Verification of the futurebus+ cache coherence protocol. *Formal Methods in System Design*, 6:217–232, 1995.
8. O. Coudert and J. C. Madre. A unified framework for the formal verification of sequential circuits. In *IEEE Intl. Conference on Computer-Aided Design*, pages 126–129, 1990.
9. D. L. Dill, editor. *Computer Aided Verification, 6th International Conference, CAV'94*, volume 818 of *LNCS*. Springer-Verlag, June 1994.
10. Á. T. Eiríksson and K. L. McMillan. Using formal verification/analysis methods on the critical path in system design: A case study. In Wolper [20], pages 367–380.
11. R. Enders, T. Filkorn, and D. Taubner. Generating BDDs for symbolic model checking. *Distributed Computing*, 6:155–164, 1993.
12. G. Janssen. ROBDD software. Technical report, Department of Electrical Engineering, Eindhoven University of Technology, Oct. 1993.
13. A. Kick. *Generation of Counterexamples and Witnesses for Model Checking*. PhD thesis, Fakultät für Informatik, Universität Karlsruhe, Germany, July 1996.
14. K. L. McMillan. *Symbolic Model Checking*. Kluwer, 1993.
15. V. G. Naik and A. P. Sistla. Modeling and verification of a real life protocol using symbolic model checking. In Dill [9], pages 194–206.
16. J. Philipps and P. Scholz. Formal verification of statecharts with instantaneous chain reactions. In *TACAS'97*, 1997.
17. S. Rajan, N. Shankar, and M. K. Srivas. An integration of model checking with automated proof checking. In Wolper [20], pages 84–97.
18. A. Rauzy. Toupie = μ-calculus + constraints. In Wolper [20], pages 114–126.
19. R. Rudell. Dynamic variable ordering for ordered binary decision diagrams. In *IEEE Intl. Conference on Computer-Aided Design*, pages 42–47, 1993.
20. P. Wolper, editor. *Computer Aided Verification, 7th International Conference, CAV'95*, volume 939 of *LNCS*. Springer-Verlag, July 1995.

prod 3.2
An Advanced Tool for Efficient Reachability Analysis

Kimmo Varpaaniemi, Keijo Heljanko and Johan Lilius
{Kimmo.Varpaaniemi,Keijo.Heljanko,Johan.Lilius}@hut.fi

Helsinki University of Technology, Digital Systems Laboratory

Abstract. prod is a reachability analyzer for Predicate/Transition Nets. The tool incorporates several advanced reduced reachability graph generation methods. The tool also includes a CTL model checker and supports on-the-fly verification of LTL formulas. prod is being used in industrial projects at the Digital Systems Laboratory.

1   Intro

Reachability analysis is a powerful formal way to analyze concurrent and distributed systems such as telecommunication protocols. However reachability analysis suffers from the *state-explosion problem*: the state space of the system can be far too large with respect to the time and other resources needed to inspect all states in the space.

Fortunately, errors can be detected in a variety of cases without inspecting all reachable states of the system. The *stubborn set method* [11],[10] is one of the methods that try to relieve the state space explosion. On the other hand in *on-the-fly verification of a property* the property is verified during state space generation, in contrast to the traditional approach where properties are verified after state space generation.

The Pr/T-net reachability analysis tool **prod** [13], developed at the Digital Systems Laboratory at Helsinki University of Technology, implements among other methods the two above mentioned methods for efficient reachability analysis.

The aim of this article is to give a brief overview of the basic features of the tool and shortly describe some of its applications.

2   The reachability analyzer prod

prod is a command-line driven tool, ie. the user interacts with the tool from a Unix-shell. Currently no graphical user-interface exists. The tool consists of 5 components:

1. the control program **prod**, a make-like program that is used to execute the other components of the tool,
2. the reachability graph generator generator **prpp**, a program that reads a net description given in the Net Description Language, and generates a C-program that when compiled and run generates the reachability graph,
3. the query program **probe**, a tool for navigating the reachability graph,
4. a tool for calculating strongly connected components (**strong**), and
5. an interface to ARA, **araprod**, which will not be discussed further in this article.

Given a file **net.net** with a net description the command **prod net.init** executes **prpp** on the net-file **net.net**. **prpp** generates a C-file **net.c** together with some other data-files, that are then compiled and linked by the native C-compiler to an executable **net**. The program **net** is the reachability graph generator proper. The executable **net** takes a number of options, of which we shall describe the ones relating to reduced reachability graph generation.

prod supports the following reduced reachability graph generation methods:

- The *stubborn sets method* [11] is based on the idea that for the verification of certain properties of the net it is unnecessary to generate all possible interleavings of independent transitions. In **prod** the calculation of the stubborn set can be done with two main algorithms:
  1. The incremental algorithm (option -**s**), selects one enabled transition and then looks for other transitions to include so that the stubbornness property is retained.
  2. The deletion algorithm (option -**d**) starts with the set of all transitions deletes one transitions from it and the looks for other transitions to delete so that the stubbornness property is retained.
- The *CFFD preserving stubborn sets method* (option -**C**) is a version of stubborn set that preserve all chaos-free traces, failures and divergences of the net [10].
- *Sleep sets* (option -**S**) are an alternative method that also utilizes the independence of transitions to reduce the reachability graph. Sometimes sleep sets used in conjunction with stubborn sets can increase the reduction.
- *Symmetries* (option -**e**) are equivalence classes of markings. The calculation of symmetries can be very time-consuming, but it is well known that symmetries together with stubborn set can reduce the reachability graph radically.

On-the-fly verification of a property means that the property is verified during state space generation, in contrary to the traditional approach where properties are verified after state space generation. On-the-fly verification of *linear time temporal properties* [2],[12] with the aid of the CFFD preserving stubborn set method has been implemented in prod.

prod 3.2 also contains a branching time temporal logic CTL model checker, which is implemented as a part of the probe reachability graph navigator tool. It has a new global CTL model checking algorithm [3], which contains a counterexamples and witnesses facility.

3 Applications of prod

prod is and has been used in several academic and industrial projects at the Digital system laboratory. During the last year prod has been downloaded to over 200 sites worldwide.

- *The analysis of the FSR:* The Frame Synchronized Ring (FSR) is a high speed parallel data bus designed for high-throughput applications like ATM-switches. The Medium Access Control Algorithm of the FSR was analyzed for deadlock freeness for arbitary number of nodes, fairness and maximal waiting times [5], [6], [7].
- *The Emma project:* The Emma (Extendible Multi-Method Analyzer) project [4] has developed a dynamic analyzer for TNSDL programs (TeleNokia SDL), which supports the detection of some errors related to parallelism and the investigation of their causes. The Emma analyzer is designed on top of Nokia's TNSDL translator and prod. The user of Emma is working only on the level of TNSDL.
- *Teaching:* prod has been used successfully as a teaching aid in a course on Parallel and Distributed systems. The students do a verification project in groups of 2 or 3. The course is taken by approximately 100 students yearly.
- *Other applications:* Several other substantial models have been built and analyzed with prod including the TCAP/TSL-protocol, a video on demand system [8], [9], an authentication protocol [1], and a specification of a simple telephone exchange (YXA).

4 Availability

prod is available over the Internet. The sources to the tool and a bibliography with relevant literature about prod, and other Petri net research done at the Digital systems laboratory can be found at
http://topos.hut.fi/~petrinet/.

References

1. Tuomas Aura. Modelling the Needham-Schröder authentication protocol with high level Petri nets. Technical Report B14, Helsinki University of Technology, Digital Systems Laboratory, Espoo, Finland, September 1995.
2. C. Courcoubetis, M.Y. Vardi, P. Wolper, and M. Yannakakis. Memory efficient algorithms for the verification of temporal properties. *Formal Methods in System Design*, 1(2/3):275-288, 1992.
3. K. Heljanko. Model Checking the Branching Time Temporal Logic CTL. Research Report A45, Helsinki University of Technology, Digital Systems Laboratory, Espoo, Finland, 1997.
4. N. Husberg. SDL Modelling with High Level Petri Nets. In *Proceedings of the Fifth International Workshop on Concurency, Specification & Programming (CSP), Berlin, Germany, September 25-27, 1996*, pages 85-96, Berlin, 1996. Humboldt-University Berlin.
5. Tino Pyssysalo. Proving Properties of a New High Speed Data Bus with Predicate/Transition Nets. *Microprocessing and Microprogramming*, 40:791-794, 1994.
6. Tino Pyssysalo. The Modeling and Analysis of the Frame Synchronized Ring Using the Predicate/Transition Net Formalism. In *Proceedings of COST 247 Meeting, Berlin, Germany, February 9-10, 1995*, page 6, Berlin, 1995. Humboldt-University Berlin.
7. Tino Pyssysalo. An Induction Theorem for Ring Protocols of Processes Described with Predicate/Transition Nets. Research Report A37, Digital Systems Laboratory, Helsinki University of Technology, 1996.
8. Tino Pyssysalo and Leo Ojala. Modelling of a "Video on Demand" System Using Pr/T-Net Formalism—a Case Study. In *Proceedings of the Third International Workshop on Concurency, Specification & Programming (CSP), Berlin, Germany, October 12-14, 1994*, page 8, Berlin, 1994. Humboldt-University Berlin.
9. Tino Pyssysalo and Leo Ojala. Causal Modeling of a Video on Demand System Using Predicate/Transition Net Formalism. In *Proceedings of the 22nd Euromicro Conference, Prague, Czech Republik, September 2-5, 1996*, page 6, Los Alamitos, California, 1996. The Institute of Electrical and Electronics Engineers (IEEE) Computer Society Press.
10. A. Valmari. Alleviating state explosion during verification of behavioral equivalence. Report A-1992-3, University of Helsinki, Department of Computer Science, 1992.
11. A. Valmari. A stubborn attack on state explosion. *Formal Methods in System Design*, 1(4):297-322, 1992.
12. M.Y. Vardi and P. Wolper. An automata-theoretic approach to automatic program verification. In *Proceedings of LICS'86*, pages 332-344. IEEE Computer Society Press, 1986.
13. Kimmo Varpaaniemi, Jaakko Halme, Kari Hiekkanen, and Tino Pyssysalo. PROD reference manual. Technical Report B13, Helsinki University of Technology, Digital Systems Laboratory, Espoo, Finland, August 1995.

VeriSoft: A Tool for the Automatic Analysis of Concurrent Reactive Software

Patrice Godefroid

Bell Laboratories
Lucent Technologies
1000 E. Warrenville Road
Naperville, IL 60566, U.S.A.
god@bell-labs.com
http://www.bell-labs.com/~god

Abstract. VeriSoft is a tool for systematically exploring the state spaces of systems composed of several concurrent processes executing arbitrary code written in full-fledged programming languages such as C or C++. It can automatically detect coordination problems between concurrent processes. Specifically, VeriSoft searches the state space of the system for deadlocks, livelocks, divergences, and violations of user-specified assertions. An interactive graphical simulator/debugger is also available for following the execution of all the processes of the concurrent system.

1 Introduction

State-space exploration techniques are increasingly being used for analyzing the correctness of *concurrent reactive systems*. These techniques consist of exploring a directed graph, called the *state space*, representing the combined behavior of all concurrent components in a system. In the case of software systems, existing state-space exploration tools can compute automatically a state space from an abstract description of such a system, specified in a *modeling language*. Examples of such tools are CAESAR [FGM+92], COSPAN [HK90], CWB [CPS93], MURPHI [DDHY92], SMV [McM93], SPIN [Hol91], and VFSMvalid [FHS95], among others. In many cases, analyses of complex concurrent systems using state-space exploration techniques were able to reveal quite subtle design errors (for instance, see [Rud92, CGH+93, BG96]).

VeriSoft extends the previous results by being able to directly analyze the implementation of a concurrent reactive software system, rather than a hand-written model of it. Specifically, VeriSoft is a tool for systematically exploring the state spaces of systems composed of several concurrent processes executing arbitrary code written in full-fledged programming languages such as C or C++. It can automatically detect coordination problems between concurrent processes. An interactive graphical simulator/debugger is also available for following the execution of all the processes of the system.

In the next section, we define the state space of a concurrent system composed of processes executing arbitrary code. Then, we present the properties that can be checked with VeriSoft. We conclude with a brief presentation of the tool itself.

2 Concurrent Systems and Dynamic Semantics

We consider a concurrent system composed of a finite set $\mathcal{P}$ of *processes* and a finite set of *communication objects*. Each process $P_i \in \mathcal{P}$ executes a sequence of *operations*, that is described in a sequential program written in a programming language such as C or C++ for instance. Such programs are deterministic: every execution of the program on the same data performs the same sequence of operations. We assume that processes communicate with each other by performing operations on communication objects. Examples of communication objects are shared variables, semaphores, and FIFO buffers. At any time, at most one operation can be performed on a given communication object (operations on a same communication object are mutually exclusive). Operations on communication objects are called *visible operations*, while other operations are by default called *invisible*. The execution of an operation is said to be *blocking* if it cannot be completed. We assume that only executions of visible operations may be blocking.

The concurrent system is said to be in a *global state* when the next operation to be executed by every process in the system is a visible operation. We assume that every process in the system always eventually attempts to execute a visible operation. This implies that initially, after the creation of all the processes of the system, the system may reach a first and unique global state s_0, called the *initial global state* of the system. We define a *transition* as a visible operation followed by a finite sequence of invisible operations performed by a single process. A transition whose visible operation is blocking in a global state s is said to be *disabled* in s. Otherwise, the transition is said to be *enabled* in s. A transition t that is enabled in a global state s can be *executed* from s. Once the execution of t from s is completed, the system reaches a global state s', called the *successor* of s by t. The *state space* of the concurrent system is composed of the global states that are reachable from the initial global state s_0, and of the transitions that are possible between these.

All operations on objects are deterministic, except one special operation "VS_toss", which is used to express a valuable feature of modeling languages, not found in programming languages: *nondeterminism*. Indeed, we consider here closed concurrent systems, where the environment of one process is formed by the other processes in the system. This implies that, in the case of a single "open" reactive system, the environment in which this system operates has to be represented, possibly using other processes. In practice, a complete representation of such an environment may not be available, or may be very complex. It is then convenient to use a simplified representation (software stub) for the environment to simulate its observable behavior. Another reason for providing a specific representation of the environment is to test the system under specific external constraints (test driver). The operation VS_toss takes as argument a positive integer n, and returns an integer in $[0, n]$. The operation is visible and nondeterministic: the execution of a transition starting with VS_toss(n) may yield up to $n + 1$ different successor states, corresponding to different values returned by VS_toss.

3 Properties

In [God97], it is shown that *deadlocks* and *assertion violations* can be detected by exploring only the global states of a concurrent system as defined in the previous section. Deadlocks are states where the execution of the next operation of every process in the system is blocking. Assertions can be specified by the user with the special operation "VS_assert". This operation can be inserted in the code of any process, and is considered visible. It takes as its argument a boolean expression that can test and compare the value of variables and data structures local to the process. When "VS_assert(expression)" is executed, the expression is evaluated. If the expression evaluates to false, the assertion is said to be *violated*.

In addition to deadlocks and assertion violations, VeriSoft also checks for *divergences* and *livelocks*. A "divergence" occurs when a process does not attempt to execute any visible operation for more than a given (user-specified) amount of time, while a "livelock" occurs when a process has no enabled transition during a sequence of more than a given (user-specified) number of successive global states. Note that these definitions of divergence and livelock differ from the standard definitions for these notions, which correspond to *liveness* properties, i.e., properties that can only be violated by *infinite* sequences of operations or transitions [Lam77, MP92]. In contrast, our notions of divergence and livelock can be violated by *finite* sequences of operations or transitions, and therefore are actually *safety* properties. (See [God97] for details.)

4 Systematic State-Space Exploration using VeriSoft

VeriSoft is a tool for systematically exploring the state spaces of concurrent systems as defined in Section 2. In a nutshell, every process of the concurrent system to be analyzed is mapped to a UNIX process. The execution of the system processes is controlled by an external process, called the *scheduler*. This process observes the visible operations performed by processes inside the system, and can suspend their execution. By resuming the execution of (the next visible operation of) one selected system process in a global state, the scheduler can explore one transition between two global states in the state space of the concurrent system. By reinitializing the system, the scheduler can explore alternative paths in the state space.

The scheduler also contains an implementation of a new search algorithm, introduced in [God97], that makes it possible to systematically and efficiently explore the state spaces of such systems without storing any intermediate states in memory. This algorithm is built upon existing state-space pruning techniques known as partial-order methods [God96]. For finite acyclic state spaces, this algorithm is guaranteed to terminate and can be used for detecting deadlocks and assertion violations without incurring the risk of any incompleteness in the verification results. In practice, VeriSoft can be used for systematically and efficiently testing the correctness of any concurrent system, whether its state space is acyclic or not.

VeriSoft searches the state spaces of concurrent systems for errors of the types listed in Section 3. When an error is detected, a scenario leading to the error state is exhibited to the user. An interactive graphical simulator/debugger is also available for replaying scenarios and following their executions at the instruction or procedure/fonction level. Values ot variables of each process can be examined interactively. In manual-simulation mode, the user can also explore any path in the state space of the system with the same set of debugging tools.

VeriSoft has been tested on various examples of concurrent reactive C programs to demonstrate the practicability of our approach. As an example, VeriSoft successfully discovered a previously unknown error in a concurrent 2500-line C program controlling robots operating in an unpredictable environment. These encouraging experimental results bode well for the applicability of VeriSoft to the analysis of actual software products. Several such applications are currently being investigated in cooperation with switching-software development and testing organizations in Lucent Technologies. Additional information on VeriSoft is (and will be) available at http://www.bell-labs.com/~god.

References

[BG96] B. Boigelot and P. Godefroid. Model checking in practice: An analysis of the AC-CESS.bus protocol using SPIN. In *Proceedings of Formal Methods Europe'96*, volume 1051 of *Lecture Notes in Computer Science*, pages 465–478, Oxford, March 1996. Springer-Verlag.

[CGH+93] E. M. Clarke, O. Grumberg, H. Hiraishi, S. Jha, D. E. Long, K. L. McMillan, and L. A. Ness. Verification of the Futurebus+ cache coherence protocol. In *Proceedings of the Eleventh International Symposium on Computer Hardware Description Languages and Their Apllications*. North-Holland, 1993.

[CPS93] R. Cleaveland, J. Parrow, and B. Steffen. The concurrency workbench: A semantics based tool for the verification of concurrent systems. *ACM Transactions on Programming Languages and Systems*, 1(15):36–72, 1993.

[DDHY92] D. L. Dill, A. J. Drexler, A. J. Hu, and C. H. Yang. Protocol verification as a hardware design aid. In *1992 IEEE International Conference on Computer Design: VLSI in Computers and Processors*, pages 522–525, Cambridge, MA, October 1992. IEEE Computer Society.

[FGM+92] J.C. Fernandez, H. Garavel, L. Mounier, A. Rasse, C. Rodriguez, and J. Sifakis. A toolbox for the verification of LOTOS programs. In *Proc. of the 14th International Conference on Software Engineering ICSE'14*, Melbourne, Australia, May 1992. ACM.

[FHS95] A. R. Flora-Holmquist and M. Staskauskas. Formal validation of virtual finite state machines. In *Proc. Workshop on Industrial-Strength Formal Specification Techniques (WIFT'95)*, pages 122–129, Boca Raton, April 1995.

[God96] Patrice Godefroid. *Partial-Order Methods for the Verification of Concurrent Systems – An Approach to the State-Explosion Problem*, volume 1032 of *Lecture Notes in Computer Science*. Springer-Verlag, January 1996.

[God97] P. Godefroid. Model Checking for Programming Languages using VeriSoft. In *Proceedings of the 24th ACM Symposium on Principles of Programming Languages*, pages 174–186, Paris, January 1997.

[HK90] Z. Har'El and R. P. Kurshan. Software for analytical development of communication protocols. *AT&T Technical Journal*, 1990.

[Hol91] G. J. Holzmann. *Design and Validation of Computer Protocols*. Prentice Hall, 1991.

[Lam77] L. Lamport. Proving the correctness of multiprocess programs. *IEEE Transactions on Software Engineering*, SE-3(2):125–143, 1977.

[McM93] K. L. McMillan. *Symbolic Model Checking*. Kluwer Academic Publishers, 1993.

[MP92] Z. Manna and A. Pnueli. *The Temporal Logic of Reactive and Concurrent Systems: Specification*. Springer-Verlag, 1992.

[Rud92] H. Rudin. Protocol development success stories: Part I. In *Proc. 12th IFIP WG 6.1 International Symposium on Protocol Specification, Testing, and Verification*, Lake Buena Vista, Florida, June 1992. North-Holland.

RuleBase: Model Checking at IBM

I. Beer, S. Ben-David, C. Eisner, D. Geist, L. Gluhovsky, T. Heyman,
A. Landver, P. Paanah, Y. Rodeh, G. Ronin, Y. Wolfsthal

IBM Haifa Research Laboratory, Haifa, Israel
contact: beer@vnet.ibm.com

Abstract. RuleBase is a symbolic model checking tool, developed by the IBM Haifa Research Laboratory. It is the result of four years of experience in practical formal verification of hardware which, we believe, has been a key factor in bringing the tool to its current level of maturity. Our experience shows that after a short training period, designers can operate the tool independently and achieve impressive results. We present the tool and summarize our development and usage experience, focusing on some work done during 1996.

1 Introduction

RuleBase is a symbolic model checking tool, developed by the IBM Haifa Research Laboratory with the intent of bridging the formal verification usability gap. It is the result of four years of experience in practical formal verification of hardware and now offers usability, capacity and robustness features that make it an industrial-strength formal verification tool. In this note we present the tool, including several unique features, and summarize our usage experience.

RuleBase uses an enhanced version of SMV [12] as its verification engine, employing CTL model checking [5]. Much of the RuleBase development effort has been put into various techniques to address the state-explosion problem, thereby increasing the capacity of the core SMV engine and enabling verification of industrial designs. In its current state, RuleBase can verify design partitions consisting of up to 300 latches of control logic after reduction. This capacity, coupled with automatic reduction as a pre-processing phase, supports the verification of relatively large models. In pre-reduction terms, the largest unit verified by RuleBase has a few thousands of state-variables of control logic.

To make RuleBase an industrial tool, significant development effort has been made in several areas: First, since the temporal logic CTL is not an easy language for specification by non-experts, RuleBase has its own language - Sugar - built on top of CTL, which makes specification easier. Second, RuleBase supports standard, commonly used hardware description languages such as VHDL and Verilog, and operates within various design environments (e.g. Synopsys and Compass). Third, debugging tools are provided to aid in the analysis of verification results. Fourth, RuleBase is highly automated in every aspect of the verification process, particularly in HDL translation and design size reduction. Finally, RuleBase features a graphical user interface for interactive control of the verification process.

Environment models are written in the RuleBase language, a dialect of SMV which supports multiple environments (for instance, a read-only environment, a write-only environment and a read-write environment). Environment management is a key issue in the RuleBase methodology, facilitating enhanced capacity and usability of the tool.

2 Prime Features of RuleBase

2.1 Withstanding Size Problems

Symbolic model checking, introduced in [12], addresses the state explosion problem by using BDDs. While this has been a major advance and made model checking a useful tool for real hardware designs, the size problem is far from being solved. Much effort has been put into RuleBase in order to withstand the state explosion problem. Some of the methods are described below:

Automatic, Per-Formula Reduction. Usually, a formula is influenced by only part of the design, while other parts are irrelevant to its truth or falsity. For example, if the formula verifies a property of one design output, only this output and its input cone of logic are necessary. RuleBase identifies and removes unnecessary parts.

Efficient BDD Algorithms. RuleBase employs a variety of techniques and algorithms for handling BDD size problems. It uses variations of the dynamic reordering algorithm described in [14]. Additionally, RuleBase employs techniques of keeping the transition relation partitioned, as presented in [4] and [10]. Also, it combines BFS and DFS to maintain small BDD sizes during reachability analysis, following [13].

Checking Safety Formulas On-The-Fly. Formulas belonging to a subset of the CTL logic can be verified while traversing the reachable state space, without the need for the full model-checking algorithm. Several works [6, 11] used this method for formulas of the form $AG(p)$, where p is a Boolean formula containing no temporal operators. RuleBase can check several safety formulas at a time, producing counter-examples to those formulas which fail without building the full transition relation, and continuing to check the rest.

2.2 Sugar - RuleBase Specification Language

RuleBase provides a specification language - Sugar - for hardware designers who are not CTL [5] experts, which allows them to read and write specifications easily. Sugar is built on top of CTL and includes a few additional language constructs. Some of the Sugar constructs are described below.

Within. Experience shows that many design behaviors are repetitive, where a basic transaction occurs again and again, and properties are interesting only within the boundaries of a single transaction. The *within* operator addresses this issue. Its syntax is *"within(start, end)(Sugar-formula)"*, where *start* and *end* are Boolean expressions. The meaning is "check the Sugar formula only in time intervals beginning with *start* and ending with *end*". For example, *"AG within(start, end)(AG (request -> AF acknowledge))"* means: "in all time intervals delimited by *start* and *end*, a request must be followed by an acknowledge".

Next-Event. The operator *"next_event(p)(q)"* has the following meaning: the next time that p occurs, q will occur. For example, *"AG((request & requester=high_priority)*

-> *next_event(grant)(granted=high_priority))"* means: "if there is a request from a high-priority device, then the next time there is a grant, the higher priority device is the one granted". Similarly *"next_event(p)[n](q)"* means that *q* must occur the *nth* time that *p* occurs. For example: *"AG(request -> next_event(data)[4](last_data))"* means: "*last_data* should be asserted together with the fourth data after a request". The CTL equivalent of this formula is: *"AG (request -> !E[!data U (data & EX E[!data U (data & EX E[!data U (data & EX E[!data U (data & !last_data)])])]))".*

Strong and Weak Operators. Most Sugar operators have two forms: *strong* and *weak*. The strong form requires an event to happen eventually (liveness property), while the weak form only states that a bad event cannot happen (safety property). An operator becomes strong by appending a '!' to its name. For example, *"next-event!(p)[3](q)"* (strong version) states that *p* must happen three times and then *q* must hold, while *"next-event(p)[3](q)"* (weak version) states that if *p* happens three times then *q* must hold.

2.3 Debugging Aids

RuleBase has various tools to support the analysis of the model at hand as well as the results of the verification process. Some of these tools are described below.

Timing Diagrams. RuleBase presents counter-examples and witnesses (see below) as timing diagrams, making the debugging process similar to the one employed in traditional simulation-based verification.

Witness and Vacuity. When a formula passes successfully, RuleBase tries to produce a witness: an execution trace that demonstrates a non-vacuous path on which the formula holds. Analyzing a witness may help to discover unexpected behaviors resulting from wrong environment modeling or wrongly-formulated rules [3]. Also, the inability to produce a witness serves to indicate that the formula has passed vacuously.

Reduction Analyzer. RuleBase provides a detailed description and explanation of the reduction process, which users can call upon to explore, debug and control the elimination of state variables. This is specifically useful when experimenting with alternate reductions, of which the full effect is not clear to the user.

3 Experience

RuleBase has been used in various verification projects throughout its development. The following is a partial list of the units which were formally verified using RuleBase.

PCI bus bridges, including PCI-to-ISA, PCI-to-VESA and PCI-to-PCI bridges [1]. For each bridge, several dozens of PCI rules were written and verified. These included the full PCI specification as well as many implementation-level rules (e.g. performance). The formal verification of these units has revealed nearly 200 bugs, including several deadlocks. Three of the chips were fully functional at first silicon realization; the other two were fully functional at second silicon realization. A summary of using RuleBase in the verification of these designs can be found in [1].

An on-line L2-cache for a PowerPC processor. In this unit, formal verification has focused on three key blocks, namely the Processor Interface Unit, the System Interface

Unit and the Cache Control Unit. Near 70 bugs were detected by RuleBase in this unit, which is a significant fraction of the design bugs found altogether with simulation.

Two cache coherency protocols. A 3-level directory-based MESI cache coherence protocol [9] and a distributed shared-memory MESI cache coherence protocol linking a number of tightly-coupled multi-processors [7] were modelled and verified. The formal verification effort revealed subtle specification bugs and omissions which would almost certainly not have been found using simulation.

Bus interface and cache control logic of a AS400 processor. In a very recent project, IBM design engineers have found 65 bugs in the bus interface unit and cache control logic of an AS/400 processor, making a significant impact on the verification of this processor. Further information on this project is found in [8].

References

1. I. Beer, S. Ben-David, C. Eisner, Y. Engel, R. Gewirtzman, and A. Landver, "Establishing PCI Compliance using Formal Verification: a Case Study", Intl. Phoenix Conf. on Comp. and Comm. 1995.
2. I. Beer, S. Ben-David, C. Eisner and A. Landver, "RuleBase: An Industry-Oriented Formal Verification Tool", Proceedings of the Design Automation Conference, DAC'96.
3. I. Beer, S. Ben-David, C. Eisner and Y. Rodeh, "Efficient Detection of Vacuity in ACTL Formulas", this issue.
4. J. Burch, E. Clark and D. Long, "Representing Circuits More Efficiently in Symbolic Model Checking", DAC'91, pp. 403-407.
5. E. Clarke and E.A. Emerson, "Design and Synthesis of Synchronization Skeletons using Branching Time Temporal Logic", in proc. Workshop on Logics of Programs, LNCS 131, pp. 52-71, 1981.
6. A. Eiriksson and K. McMillan, "Using Formal Verification/Analysis Methods on the Critical Path in System Design: A Case Study", CAV'95, LNCS 939, pp.367-380.
7. C. Eisner, "CC/NUMA Formal Verification Project - Summary and Report", IBM Internal Memorandum, 1995.
8. C. Eisner, "AS/400 SCU Formal Verification - Interim Report", IBM Internal Memorandum, 1997.
9. C. Eisner, G. Shurek, G. Meil, R. Raghavan, "CCP (Cache Coherence Protocol) Formal Verification Project Distributed Shared Memory Cache Coherence Protocol - Summary and Report", IBM Internal Memorandum, 1994.
10. D. Geist and I. Beer, "Efficient Model Checking by Automated Ordering of Transition Relation Partitions", CAV'94, LNCS 818, pp. 299-310.
11. D. Long, "Model Checking, Abstraction and Compositional Verification", Ph.D. Thesis, CMU, 1993.
12. K. McMillan, "Symbolic Model Checking", Kluwer Academic Publishers, 1993.
13. K. Ravi and F. Somenzi, "High-Density Reachability Analysis", Proceedings of the IEEE/ACM International Conference on Computer-Aided Design (ICCAD95), November 1995, San Jose, pp. 154-158.
14. R. Rudell, "Dynamic Variable Ordering for Ordered Binary Decision Diagrams", ICCAD'93, pp. 42-47.

Author Index

Lecture Notes in Computer Science

For information about Vols. 1–1179

please contact your bookseller or Springer-Verlag

Vol. 1216: J. Dix, L. Moniz Pereira, T.C. Przymusinski (Eds.), Non-Monotonic Extensions of Logic Programming. Proceedings, 1996. XI, 224 pages. 1997. (Subseries LNAI).

Vol. 1217: E. Brinksma (Ed.), Tools and Algorithms for the Construction and Analysis of Systems. Proceedings, 1997. X, 433 pages. 1997.

Vol. 1218: G. Păun, A. Salomaa (Eds.), New Trends in Formal Languages. IX, 465 pages. 1997.

Vol. 1219: K. Rothermel, R. Popescu-Zeletin (Eds.), Mobile Agents. Proceedings, 1997. VIII, 223 pages. 1997.

Vol. 1220: P. Brezany, Input/Output Intensive Massively Parallel Computing. XIV, 288 pages. 1997.

Vol. 1221: G. Weiß (Ed.), Distributed Artificial Intelligence Meets Machine Learning. Proceedings, 1996. X, 294 pages. 1997. (Subseries LNAI).

Vol. 1222: J. Vitek, C. Tschudin (Eds.), Mobile Object Systems. Proceedings, 1996. X, 319 pages. 1997.

Vol. 1223: M. Pelillo, E.R. Hancock (Eds.), Energy Minimization Methods in Computer Vision and Pattern Recognition. Proceedings, 1997. XII, 549 pages. 1997.

Vol. 1224: M. van Someren, G. Widmer (Eds.), Machine Learning: ECML-97. Proceedings, 1997. XI, 361 pages. 1997. (Subseries LNAI).

Vol. 1225: B. Hertzberger, P. Sloot (Eds.), High-Performance Computing and Networking. Proceedings, 1997. XXI, 1066 pages. 1997.

Vol. 1226: B. Reusch (Ed.), Computational Intelligence. Proceedings, 1997. XIII, 609 pages. 1997.

Vol. 1227: D. Galmiche (Ed.), Automated Reasoning with Analytic Tableaux and Related Methods. Proceedings, 1997. XI, 373 pages. 1997. (Subseries LNAI).

Vol. 1228: S.-H. Nienhuys-Cheng, R. de Wolf, Foundations of Inductive Logic Programming. XVII, 404 pages. 1997. (Subseries LNAI).

Vol. 1230: J. Duncan, G. Gindi (Eds.), Information Processing in Medical Imaging. Proceedings, 1997. XVI, 557 pages. 1997.

Vol. 1231: M. Bertran, T. Rus (Eds.), Transformation-Based Reactive Systems Development. Proceedings, 1997. XI, 431 pages. 1997.

Vol. 1232: H. Comon (Ed.), Rewriting Techniques and Applications. Proceedings, 1997. XI, 339 pages. 1997.

Vol. 1233: W. Fumy (Ed.), Advances in Cryptology — EUROCRYPT '97. Proceedings, 1997. XI, 509 pages. 1997.

Vol 1234: S. Adian, A. Nerode (Eds.), Logical Foundations of Computer Science. Proceedings, 1997. IX, 431 pages. 1997.

Vol. 1235: R. Conradi (Ed.), Software Configuration Management. Proceedings, 1997. VIII, 234 pages. 1997.

Vol. 1236: E. Maier, M. Mast, S. LuperFoy (Eds.), Dialogue Processing in Spoken Language Systems. Proceedings, 1996. VIII, 220 pages. 1997. (Subseries LNAI).

Vol. 1238: A. Mullery, M. Besson, M. Campolargo, R. Gobbi, R. Reed (Eds.), Intelligence in Services and Networks: Technology for Cooperative Competition. Proceedings, 1997. XII, 480 pages. 1997.

Vol. 1239: D. Sehr, U. Banerjee, D. Gelernter, A. Nicolau, D. Padua (Eds.), Languages and Compilers for Parallel Computing. Proceedings, 1996. XIII, 612 pages. 1997.

Vol. 1240: J. Mira, R. Moreno-Díaz, J. Cabestany (Eds.), Biological and Artificial Computation: From Neuroscience to Technology. Proceedings, 1997. XXI, 1401 pages. 1997.

Vol. 1241: M. Akşit, S. Matsuoka (Eds.), ECOOP'97 – Object-Oriented Programming. Proceedings, 1997. XI, 531 pages. 1997.

Vol. 1242: S. Fdida, M. Morganti (Eds.), Multimedia Applications, Services and Techniques – ECMAST '97. Proceedings, 1997. XIV, 772 pages. 1997.

Vol. 1243: A. Mazurkiewicz, J. Winkowski (Eds.), CONCUR'97: Concurrency Theory. Proceedings, 1997. VIII, 421 pages. 1997.

Vol. 1244: D. M. Gabbay, R. Kruse, A. Nonnengart, H.J. Ohlbach (Eds.), Qualitative and Quantitative Practical Reasoning. Proceedings, 1997. X, 621 pages. 1997. (Subseries LNAI).

Vol. 1245: M. Calzarossa, R. Marie, B. Plateau, G. Rubino (Eds.), Computer Performance Evaluation. Proceedings, 1997. VIII, 231 pages. 1997.

Vol. 1246: S. Tucker Taft, R. A. Duff (Eds.), Ada 95 Reference Manual. XXII, 526 pages. 1997.

Vol. 1247: J. Barnes (Ed.), Ada 95 Rationale. XVI, 458 pages. 1997.

Vol. 1248: P. Azéma, G. Balbo (Eds.), Application and Theory of Petri Nets 1997. Proceedings, 1997. VIII, 467 pages. 1997.

Vol. 1249: W. McCune (Ed.), Automated Deduction – CADE-14. Proceedings, 1997. XIV, 462 pages. 1997. (Subseries LNAI).

Vol. 1250: A. Olivé, J.A. Pastor (Eds.), Advanced Information Systems Engineering. Proceedings, 1997. XI, 451 pages. 1997.

Vol. 1251: K. Hardy, J. Briggs (Eds.), Reliable Software Technologies – Ada-Europe '97. Proceedings, 1997. VIII, 293 pages. 1997.

Vol. 1252: B. ter Haar Romeny, L. Florack, J. Koenderink, M. Viergever (Eds.), Scale-Space Theory for Computer Vision. Proceedings, 1997. IX, 365 pages. 1997.

Vol. 1253: G. Bilardi, A. Ferreira, R. Lüling, J. Rolim (Eds.), Solving Irregularly Structured Problems in Parallel. Proceedings, 1997. X, 287 pages. 1997.

Vol. 1254: O. Grumberg (Ed.), Computer Aided Verification. Proceedings, 1997. XI, 486 pages. 1997.

Vol. 1255: T. Mora, H. Mattson (Eds.), Applied Algebra, Algebraic Algorithms and Error-Correcting Codes. Proceedings, 1997. X, 353 pages. 1997.

Vol. 1256: P. Degano, R. Gorrieri, A. Marchetti-Spaccamela (Eds.), Automata, Languages and Programming. Proceedings, 1997. XIV, 862 pages. 1997.

Vol. 1258: D. van Dalen, M. Bezem (Eds.), Computer Science Logic. Proceedings, 1996. VIII, 473 pages. 1997.

Vol. 1259: T. Higuchi, I. Masaya, W. Liu (Eds.), Evolvable Systems: From Biology to Hardware. Proceedings, 1996. XI, 484 pages. 1997.

Vol. 1260: D. Raymond, D. Wood, S. Yu (Eds.), Automata Implementation. Proceedings, 1996. VIII, 189 pages. 1997.

GPSR Compliance

The European Union's (EU) General Product Safety Regulation (GPSR) is a set of rules that requires consumer products to be safe and our obligations to ensure this.

If you have any concerns about our products, you can contact us on ProductSafety@springernature.com

In case Publisher is established outside the EU, the EU authorized representative is:

Springer Nature Customer Service Center GmbH
Europaplatz 3
69115 Heidelberg, Germany

Batch number: 09624486

Printed by Printforce, the Netherlands